THE MIND OF THE NEGRO

As Reflected in Letters During the Crisis 1800–1860

EDITED BY
CARTER G. WOODSON

INTRODUCTION TO THE DOVER EDITION BY
BOB BLAISDELL

DOVER PUBLICATIONS, INC.
Mineola, New York

INTRODUCTION TO THE DOVER EDITION

*If a race has no history, if it has no worthwhile tradition, it
becomes a negligible factor in the thought of the world, and
it stands in danger of being exterminated.*
    —Carter G. Woodson, "Negro History Week"[1]

While Carter G. Woodson's title may suggest to us a psychological
or sociological study, what it is, instead, is a book bursting with
public and private letters that, without mediation, directly reveal,
as Woodson repeatedly remarks in his brief notes, "the mind of
the negro." Rather than arguing his own ideas and analyses of the
pre–Civil War American crisis, Woodson (1875–1950), "the father of
black history," presents the little-known letters by black freedmen,
freedwomen, and slaves. He offers up a treasure trove of the
American Colonization Society correspondence on Liberia as well as
the published newspaper letters on abolition by the leading lights of
African American communities in the North. Intent on publishing
these letters for other scholars and the community as soon as
possible, he thrust a wide variety of collections previously published
in his *Journal of Negro History* into this volume.[2]

As the son of slaves and as a Ph.D. in history from Harvard, Woodson
knew through his life and studies that black men and women, when
they weren't simply misrepresented, had been excluded from or
ignored by American history. Woodson needed this book in print so
that it could reach readers in libraries, schools, and middle-class
homes that his journal may not have reached. While *The Mind of the*

---

1 *The Journal of Negro History.* April 1926. Washington, D.C. 239.

2 "By 1925 the *Journal* devoted at least one quarter of its space to the publication
of transcripts of primary source materials and thereby encouraged their use by
scholars who otherwise would not have known about them," writes his biographer.
"Assisted by black scholars ... Woodson collected materials on well-known and
obscure nineteenth century blacks. The speeches, writings, petitions, and letters
documenting their experiences were published in the *Journal*, and in collections
edited and published separately by Woodson through the Associated Publishers,
such as *The Mind of the Negro Reflected in Letters During the Crisis* and *Negro
Orators and Their Orations.* To aid future scholars, Woodson placed the documents
in context by providing appropriate biographical and introductory material."
Jacqueline Goggin. *Carter G. Woodson: A Life in Black History.* Baton Rouge:
Louisiana State University Press. 1993. 78.

Negro was not an original or new piece of scholarship, it aimed at collecting documents of a particular period within an unrestrictive, fascinating theme: "This book is merely a collection of letters which have already appeared serially in *The Journal of Negro History*," Woodson explained in a journal article.[3] "From this point of view, then, it requires no review here. In the 32 pages of the introduction to this collection however, there appear letters which antedate the collection which has been published. . . . it was considered advisable at the last moment to give some mention also as to what they ['the most distinguished Negroes prior to 1800'] were thinking at this time, although the collection itself is concerned with the mind of the Negro as reflected in letters written between 1800 and 1860."[4]

Woodson took great care as editor in the faithful reproduction of the private letters, with all their fitful spelling and punctuation; the letters that conclude this book were written for the most part by slaves and ex-slaves who had been forbidden in the South from learning to read or write or had been educated illegally by, among others, missionaries and literate slaves.[5] Woodson knew that documentary evidence would be the first and most important step in bringing black history into American history, and he refrained from putting himself forward: *facts*, as the proverb goes, *are a stubborn thing*. Woodson knew that eventually those facts would change prominent historians' opinions, and then, more importantly, the opinions of American blacks themselves. Only about two percent of the content of *The Mind of the Negro* is Woodson's commentary, but in the journal and in this book we sense Woodson's pride and pleasure in publishing all the touching, fiery, pathetic, and moving letters; he continually promoted their existence and their need to be read. His passion was not what he had to say about the letters but what the letters said for themselves about "the mind of the negro." For example, through the files and records of back-to-Africa organizations from the 1830s to the early 1850s, Woodson wants us to discover the needs and interests, the

---

3 Review. (The article is unsigned but written by Woodson.) *The Journal of Negro History.* October 1926. 685.

4 In fact, there are letters written as late as August 1865, months after the end of the Civil War. (See pages 536–538.)

5 One of the documents in this book is a research article published in the *New York Tribune* in 1844 by the famed black doctor James McCune Smith, who wrote, "it is well known that the laws of all the slave States, by heavy penalties—in some, *death*, for the second offense—prohibit the teaching of the slaves to read." (Woodson remarks in his first book [1915], *The Education of the Negro Prior to 1861: A History of the Education of the Colored People of the United States from the Beginning of Slavery to the Civil War*: "Quakers and Catholics ... in defiance of the law, persisted in teaching Negroes to read and write.")

concerns and wonderings of ordinary and extraordinary people who were able to articulate in writing their curiosity about or desire to emigrate to Liberia. Charles Deputie of Hollidaysburg, Pennsylvania, wrote in 1852 to the Reverend William McLain in Washington at the American Colonization Society: "thare has bean men hear that has bean to Liberia and Lecterd to the People and gave Such a bad a Count of the place that it is hard to do much a preasant the Say that thare is nether Horse hog Cow nor nothing Can Live thare that the Natives ware no Close and thare is no Houses but the Govement House."

Woodson was ultimately skeptical and disapproving of the American Colonization Society: "In fact, the colonization movement tended to drain off into the jungle the talented tenth of the free Negro population and thus rendered the race much less efficient at emancipation than it would have been had these enlightened members of the group been left undisturbed." As early as 1831, freedmen were doubtful of the ulterior motives of the colonization; "A Colored Philadelphian" wrote to *The Liberator* newspaper: "I would ask some of our pretended white friends, and the members of the American Colonization Society, why they are so interested in our behalf as to want us to go to Africa? . . . Will some of those guardian angels of the people of color tell me how it is that we, who were born in the same city or state with themselves, can live any longer in Africa than they?" The Liberian experience, about which Woodson would write in later books, was not initially successful; in 1858, Alfred V. Thompson testified to his experiences as a colonist: "Our reason for leaving Liberia, after living there for eighteen months, was on account of bad health . . . Out of the company of emigrants that left America for Africa, numbering 225, at the expiration of the 18 months there was not living more than 85 or 100. We lost two children to the undertaking; my wife and myself suffered immensely."

More successful and of less debate within black America were those men and women who had escaped slavery and were making their way to thriving communities in British Canada. Their letters, some of which were written to family members unfortunately left behind, some of which were to former owners, are among the best letters in the collection. Perhaps because the letters say so much, Woodson scarcely explains what the men and women had experienced in their escapes, in their new homes, in their memories of their lives in the South. John Thompson, in an undated letter (probably from the mid-1850s) to his mother, proudly writes from Pennsylvania: "I have imbrace an opportunity of writing you these few lines (hoping) that they may fine you as they Leave me quite well I will now inform you how I am geting

I am now a free man Living By the sweet of my own Brow not serving a nother man & giving him all I Earn But what I make is mine and iff one Plase do not sute me I am at Liberty to Leave and go some where elce & can ashore you I think highly of Freedom and would not exchange it for nothing that is offered me for it." Frederick Douglass is the most accomplished, dynamic and fully represented figure among the featured correspondents. Douglass, Woodson notes, was so fiercely independent he could not maintain alliances with anyone for long, and on disputed matters, he sometimes simply devastated his old friends and made his way alone (a characteristic Woodson shared with Douglass): "Unfortunately, near the outbreak of the Civil War, Douglass differed so widely from some of the anti-slavery workers that not very much of his correspondence was published in their organs."

To help explain Woodson's unframed, unchronological arrangement of the letters, it's useful to remind ourselves that Woodson wasn't only the editor of the *Journal* and chief researcher, he was the Association's publisher, and because he was continually under-funded (he often used his own money for publication costs), he seemed to feel, "If not now, then when?" What if he were too late to instill and preserve cultural pride? The haste, however, came at a price, believes his biographer: "Woodson's uncontainable enthusiasm for his subject and his sense of urgency—he saw that there was so much to be done that he allowed imperfectly executed work for the sake of at least tackling a particular subject—account for the unevenness in his work. In fact he believed that he was laying the scholarly foundation for others to build upon. . . . Often he failed to introduce or conclude chapters in his books; they merely began at the beginning of his story and ended at the end. The manner in which Woodson composed his books also explains, in part, both his prodigious output and his more than occasional expository inelegancy."[6]

Because his primary interest was to bring the material into the light of day rather than wait for more money and the time to get all the material in order, be warned that this museum of fascination that is *The Mind of the Negro* is something of a labyrinth. Within the first part of Section II, we read of various "Antislavery Letters of the Negroes," starting in 1831, ending in 1833, and wandering in between with letters from Upper Canada and London and Pennsylvania, and in the next part we jump back to an arcane political dispute in Canada's Wilberforce Colonization Company in the early 1830s. As if from various folders in his Washington, D.C., office Woodson was

---

6 Jacqueline Goggin. *Carter G. Woodson: A Life in Black History.* Baton Rouge: Louisiana State University Press. 1993. 182.

packing the trunk for quantity rather than for the ease of access or speed of unpacking. He laid in one set of proofs from *The Journal of Negro History* after another into this volume. As the book's table of contents is remarkably skimpy, the last section of this introduction will serve as a guided tour to *The Mind of the Negro*.

> As the son of former slaves, he moved from sharecropper to coal miner to Harvard graduate student to high school teacher to college professor, and, finally, to editor-scholar-administrator, and drew upon the wellsprings of the collective and cultural memories of his family and other African Americans. In doing so, he contributed immeasurably to black historiography and laid the foundation that several generations of scholars have built upon.
>
> —Jacqueline Goggin,
> *Carter G. Woodson: A Life in Black History*[7]

Carter Godwin Woodson is the sole Ph.D. in history whose parents had been American slaves. He was born in New Canton, Virginia, in 1875, to James Henry Woodson and Eliza W. Woodson. His father, a farmer and carpenter, was illiterate, as had been most slaves, and while he never learned to read, Woodson's mother was educated and she enthusiastically taught young Carter. As a teenager Woodson worked on the family farm in Buckingham County and then followed his older brothers to West Virginia, where he worked as a coal miner. But his interest in history, the result of reading and of listening to tales by former slaves and by Civil War veterans, brought him back at age eighteen to Buckingham County, where, making up for lost time, he finished high school in only two years. He continued his education by enrolling at Barea College in Kentucky, from which he graduated in 1903, after taking summer classes at the University of Chicago in 1902. He taught in a school for black miners' children in West Virginia while working on his college degree and then taught at his old high school. In 1903, he left the United States to teach in the Philippines for three years. After returning to visit his family in 1906, he took a world tour, including studying a semester at the University of Paris (which city he regularly visited in the last two decades of his life). When he had earned his master's degree at the University of Chicago in 1908, he went to Harvard. Once he had completed his course work, he moved to Washington, D.C. There he was able to do research on his dissertation, all the while teaching at various schools. In 1912 he earned his Ph.D. from Harvard. While teaching French,

---

7 Ibid. 207.

Spanish, English and history at the all-black academic M Street High School, he finished his first book, *The Education of the Negro Prior to 1861*. The little evidence that exists suggests he was not a delightful teacher; he was stern and impatient. Meanwhile, in 1915, he started the Association for the Study of Negro Life and History as "director of research" and the journal's editor, in which he was able to publish not only his own studies but thousands of pages of primary, documentary research material.

In 1919, he left the high school, where he had become the principal, for Howard University. As a college professor he found himself with less time than when he ran the high school, and in 1922 he left so he could devote his full time to managing the association's book-publishing arm and *The Journal of Negro History*. No one knew black history more comprehensively than Woodson, and he eventually withdrew himself from academic communities lest they interfered with and compromised his interests and plans. He had various assistants over the years, including a short stint by the man who would become America's most prominent black writer, Langston Hughes. In 1925 young Hughes served as Woodson's "personal assistant" and worked on various tedious tasks, including alphabetizing lists of thousands of names of free blacks in the South.[8] Soon after Hughes quit, Woodson hired the brilliant and lively Zora Neale Hurston as an "investigator," who with her anthropological training and keen ear, published an article for the *Journal of Negro History*, "Cudjo's Own Story of the Last African Slaver," in the October 1927 issue.

But mostly Woodson worked alone. "Even as Woodson advanced in years, he would not relinquish any administrative control over the association. Although he had always been obstinate, desiring to take over any activity in which he participated, Woodson became even more difficult to work with as he grew older, perhaps because he perceived himself to be the 'Father of Black History.'"[9] Though domineering in his office domain, he "realized that he could not correct the historical record alone and believed that black scholars had a major responsibility to preserve historical as well as contemporary documentation on the black experience for future generations of

---

8 "Although I realized what a fine contribution Dr. Woodson was making to the Negro people and to America, publishing his histories, his studies, and his *Journal of Negro History*, I personally did not like the work I had to do. Besides, it hurt my eyes. So when I got through the proofs, I decided I didn't care to have 'a position' any longer. I preferred a job, so I went to work at the Wardman Park House as a busboy ..." Langston Hughes. *The Big Sea*. New York: Alfred A. Knopf. 1940.

9 Jacqueline Goggin. *Carter G. Woodson: A Life in Black History*. Baton Rouge: Louisiana State University Press. 1993. 109.

scholars."[10] In Jacqueline Goggin's *Carter G. Woodson: A Life in Black History*, there is no mention of his romantic life; he was apparently a very private and busy man. On the other hand, he showed great appreciation of the private lives of antebellum black Americans. His fire, unlike the fire and unguardedness of his admired nineteenth century subjects, he kept hidden, as if his personal life would distract him from focusing on the big picture of history.

The Association for the Study of Negro Life and History started its publishing company, Associated Publishers, in 1920 and brought out *The Mind of the Negro* in 1926 and several other works. One of Woodson's proudest accomplishments through the association was creating in 1926 a "Negro History Week" every February, in commemoration of Frederick Douglass's and Abraham Lincoln's birthdays. He wrote of his hopes shortly after the first Negro History Week: ". . . just as thorough education in the belief in the inequality of races has brought the world to a cat-and-dog stage of religious and racial strife, so may thorough instruction in the equality of the races bring about a reign of brotherhood through an appreciation of the virtues of all races, creeds and colors. In such a millennium the achievements of the Negro properly set forth will crown him as a factor in early human progress and a maker of modern civilization."[11] In the 1930s Woodson began publishing his studies and historical research about the West Indies and Africa.

When Woodson died in 1950, he had successfully promoted not only the serious academic study of black history but had helped create popular awareness of it and general interest.

> History is what man has thought and felt and attempted
> and accomplished.
> —Carter G. Woodson,
> *The Journal of Negro History*[12]

Woodson's table of contents is more confusing than useful. I offer here a "map" through the vast mostly uncharted collection of letters that will serve as a guide to the highlights and editorial interjections that might otherwise be overlooked.

After this introduction, and preceding the contents, is Woodson's one-page foreword. He informs us that "these letters were reproduced

---

10 Ibid. 67.
11 "Negro History Week." *The Journal of Negro History*. April 1926. 240. (Negro History Week became Black History Month in 1976.)
12 From Woodson's review of James Weldon Johnson's *The Book of American Negro Spirituals* in *The Journal of Negro History*. January 1926. 221–222.

just as they were found in the sources." That is, Woodson believed even wayward spelling provided evidence of intellectual and social history.

Woodson's foreword is less than two pages. His primary point is to remind us of the marvelous value of private correspondence: "Personal letters are especially valuable because of their unconscious element." What this collection provides us, then, is "the opportunity to judge hundreds of Negroes as they really expressed themselves."

The introduction to the 1926 edition abruptly brings us to the extraordinary writings of the slave Jupiter Hammon of New York, who in 1787 encouraged his listeners (the piece, really a speech to be read aloud, is an "address" to fellow New York slaves) to resign themselves to God's will. To his disappointment, considering the liberty white Americans had demanded for themselves from the British, God's will—*for now*—meant continued slavery: "It may seem hard for us, if we think our masters wrong in holding us slaves, to obey in all things, but who of us dare dispute with God! He has commanded us to obey, and we ought to do it cheerfully, and freely." The slave and renown poet Phillis Wheatley's letters then begin after a short note by Woodson. Wheatley's letters are followed by those of the mathematician and astronomer Benjamin Banneker, including an exchange of Banneker's with Thomas Jefferson. Woodson concludes the introduction with a paragraph mentioning the correspondence of other prominent black men.

Section I surveys correspondence related to Liberia, the American republic in Africa that was set up as a colony for freed slaves in 1822; Southern and Northern blacks, most of them freedmen, weigh in on the advantages and disadvantages and hopes and disappointment of emigration. Woodson writes: "The Southern Negroes were easily influenced by the American Colonization Society and were more easily reached because of the interest of certain whites of that section in the deportation of the free Negroes there and of such others as might be liberated by conscience-stricken slaveholders. Wherever the Negroes had enjoyed freedom in the North, they did not easily embrace the idea of expatriating themselves. The Northern Negroes usually took the position that here their fathers fought, bled, and died for the country, here they were born, and here they intended to die. ... [except] during the fifties when the heel of oppression upon the Negro in the North was becoming heavier and heavier. These letters in themselves are more than interesting."

One of the "more than interesting" writers in this section is Burrell W. Mann, "a most pathetic case, typical, however, of thousands of ambitious slaves," whom Woodson introduces and whose letters plead for financial help to emigrate (June 21, 1847 to August 3, 1849). Woodson introduces S. Wesley Jones, a freedman businessman living in Alabama; Jones's letters, dated June 12, 1848 to April 10, 1859. There are various writers through the rest of the section; Woodson introduces J. B. Jordan, a black businessman from New Orleans who queries after various conditions of life and governance in Liberia. In July of 1851 Jordan mentions his family leaving for Liberia by the next ship; Woodson seems to have found no further correspondence. Readers wishing for follow-ups on the fates of the less prominent letter-writers will be disappointed. (Woodson was no doubt disappointed as well by the paucity of biographical information.)

The first section of the book concludes, just as published in *The Journal of Negro History*, without a final assessment or summation by Woodson.

Section II is divided into fourteen subdivisions, each labeled with roman numerals, though inconsistently (e.g. Part XI *immediately precedes* Part IX). Woodson's note discusses abolitionists and colonizationists; his most important point is this: "These antislavery letters of the Negroes are of unusual significance for the reason that although many of these persons herein reported were editors and orators of consequence during the crisis, they failed to keep complete files of their newspapers or to record their orations for the benefit of generations unborn. In these letters, therefore, the investigator will find the only valuable source to determine what the free Negro was actually thinking and feeling during this period." Most of the letters in this section are directed to William Lloyd Garrison, the editor of *The Liberator*, the abolitionist newspaper in Boston.

Part I of Section II contains letters by several antislavery men. Regarding the emigration debate, an anonymous Philadelphian writes: "I have nothing to say against the very laudable efforts of the Society. It has done, and continues to do, much good for our enslaved brethren; and the Colony at Liberia is well adapted to the bettering of their unhappy condition. I am glad to see they have friends, who will aid in moving them to that highly respected country. But we who have a right to free suffrages, have no disposition to emigrate either to Africa or Canada. If left to our own choice, we would much rather stay at home. It is here we have received our birth, and here we wish to remain."

Part II is headed "Controversial Correspondence." We learn of the Wilberforce Colonization Company in Ontario, British Canada. This settlement began in the early 1830s; the letters describe Wilberforce's arrangement and indeed controversies between the board and its agents. Woodson does not escort us through the thorny paths, and we learn nothing of the resolution of the problems. (Frederick Douglass, in Part III, contributes his insights on this conflict.) Woodson does explain, however, another dispute within the abolitionist community: "This letter of H. H. Garnett shows how the fugitive slave, taught to think of his former condition as deplorable and encouraged to struggle for the emancipation of his fellowmen in bondage, often differed from the abolitionist, who, after all, never took kindly to the idea of allowing Negroes to figure conspicuously in devising the ways and means to promote the antislavery cause. The address referred to was so revolutionary and radical, however, that the Negro convention called upon to consider it refused to give it sanction." That is, Henry Highland Garnett spoke his own mind and resented making it subservient to an organization's political strategy: "I was born in slavery, and have escaped, to tell you, and others, what the monster has done, and is still doing. It, therefore, astonished me to think that you should desire to sink me again to the condition of a slave, by forcing me to think just as you do."

"Letters of Slaves to Former Owners," Part III, is one of the most impressive series of pages in the book. Frederick Douglass's extraordinary letter to "his master" Thomas Auld on the ten-year anniversary of his emancipation is a literary and historical masterpiece: "Oh! sir, a slaveholder never appears to me so completely an agent of hell, as when I think of and look upon my dear children." Douglass's eleven-year anniversary letter follows it, as do William Wells Brown's to his former master and the nearly laughable exchange between the Reverend J. W. Loguen and his former mistress, who tells him, now that he is free in Canada, "If you will send me one thousand dollars, and pay for the old mare, I will give up all claim I have to you."

Part IV, "Anonymous Letters and Others," is a grab bag of letters by slaves, freedmen and former slaves who could have been prosecuted for openly questioning the morality of slavery or for declaiming aloud from the Declaration of Independence. Woodson explains: "In the newspapers there often appeared anonymous letters which decidedly differed from such of today. A Negro signing his name to a document attacking an institution protected by the laws of the country was in danger almost anywhere in this country before the Civil War. The failure to sign his name was not always due to a lack of courage but rather to the desire for self-preservation, the first law of nature. Such letters as these, then, are valuable in determining what the Negro was feeling and thinking at that time."

Part V is a collection of seven letters by David Ruggles, the editor of a New York City abolitionist newspaper. "The existence of a jury trial law, recognizing man as a criminal for wearing the complexion he has received from his Creator, or conceding to slavery the right to incarcerate humanity as a chattel personal, is at variance with my notion of equal rights, the Declaration of American Independence, the laws of Nature, and of the living God," writes Ruggles.

Woodson briefly introduces Part VI, "The Testimony of the Freedmen": "A neglected aspect of the study of slavery is the mind of the slaves themselves. As bondmen, they were generally too illiterate to express themselves. Freed and brought North to be educated, however, they often bore intelligent testimony against the institution."

Part VII features the letters of Dr. James McCune Smith, Macon B. Allen and William G. Allen. In 1844, Smith carried out statistical analyses of schools, health, church and population of slaves and freedmen and here presents his studied answer to the argument of slave-owners that black people were better off as slaves than as freedmen in the North: "The evidence is altogether in favor of emancipation."

The "most widely known Negro in the United States prior to the rise of Frederick Douglass," writes Woodson, was Charles Lenox Remond (1810–1873), the son of free blacks in Boston, whose letters (dated July 3, 1838 to June 9, 1845) to William Lloyd Garrison are the focus of Part VIII. Remond wrote several of the letters while on lecture tour in England.

Now the confusing labeling begins: Part XI (that is, *11* in the *9* spot) "William C. Nell," is a collection of letters to and from the "first Negro to take seriously the writing of the history of the Negro race."

Part IX (that is, *9* in the *10* spot) is a series of letters by the fugitive slave William Wells Brown, who became an important lecturer in the North and in Europe. In his letter of January 30, 1845, Brown tells *The Liberator*'s readers: "Our own citizens cannot have the privilege of free locomotion; they cannot go to the South and declare that all men are created equal, and are endowed by their Creator with certain inalienable rights, and apply it to American Slavery, without being thrown into prison, and compelled to drag out years in chains. Their groans should cause every citizen of the North to cry out, NO UNION WITH SLAVEHOLDERS."

Whether Woodson mixed up the Roman numerals or the parts is unclear, but in the confusion Part X disappeared.

Part XII contains Frederick Douglass's correspondence from November 8, 1842 to June 7, 1851. They seem to me the most electrifying and compelling public letters in American history.

While touring and lecturing in Scotland in 1846, Douglas wrote to the famous editor Horace Greeley at *The New York Tribune*, "I am called, by way of reproach, a runaway slave. As if it were a crime—an unpardonable crime—for a man to take his inalienable rights!" There is spark and penetrating sense in every letter.

Woodson introduces the very short Part XIII, "Slavery and the Church" by remarking "The whites and blacks promoting the antislavery cause did not fail to expose the church as the bulwark of slavery." The only letters are one by Samuel R. Ward of Boston and one by Lewis Woodson of Pittsburgh.

Part XIV concerns "Emigration to Central America." Woodson explains: "One of the ways in which the free Negroes expressed their opposition to African colonization was by presenting a counter proposal to the effect that such emigrants should be settled in the tropics of America." One of the most interesting of the letters is by Alfred V. Thompson, who lived for eighteen months in Liberia, before spending a few years in Jamaica and then a couple of years in America's northern cities. He now expresses his interest in the idea of "the colonization of colored people in South America."

To introduce the four letters in Part XV, "The Martyrdom of John Brown." Woodson suggests, quite reasonably, that "There must be some historic value in learning what the Negroes thought of John Brown, the martyr, who died that they might be free."

In his opening remarks on Section III, "Letters Largely Personal or Private," Woodson makes the point that "Most of these letters [spanning 1800 to 1865] differ from others of this series in that they were not written for publication. ... The aim of most of this correspondence is to inform friends of the situation in which the writers found themselves, to thank them for favors, and to implore their assistance in the future." For example, in 1853 John H. Hill writes from Toronto: "My friend I am a free man and feeles alright about that matter. I am doing tolrable well in my line of business, and think I will do better after little. I hope you will never stop any of our Brotheran that makes their Escep from the South but send them on to this Place where they can be free man and woman."

Woodson does not introduce or conclude Section IV, "Miscellaneous Letters." (Sections III and IV appeared as pages 62 to 214 in *The Journal of Negro History*, January 1926.) The miscellany bounces from 1832 to 1856 with many originating from Canada. Notably, Anthony Burns writes impressively to the Baptist Church in Union, Virginia, on his having been excommunicated by the Church: "Thus you have excommunicated me, on the charge of 'disobeying both the laws of God and men, 'in absconding from the service of my master, and refusing to return voluntarily.' I admit that I left my master (so called) and refused to return; but I deny that in this I disobeyed either the law of God or any real law of men. Look at my case. I was stolen and made a slave as soon as I was born. No man had any right to steal me. That manstealer who stole me trampled on my dearest rights. He committed an outrage on the law of God; therefore his manstealing gave him no right in me, and laid me under no obligation to be his slave . . . You charge me that, in escaping, I disobeyed God's law. No, indeed! That law which God wrote on the table of my heart, inspiring the love of freedom, and impelling me to seek it at every hazard, I obeyed, and, by the good hand of my God upon me, I walked out of the house of bondage."

The index is slightly more informative than Woodson's contents pages but full of holes. There are useful headings, for example, such as "California, proposed for colonization," and "Population, Negro."

Although Woodson's aim, it seems, was to get as many pages as he could afford to publish of documentary history between two covers of a book, that this single volume might enter libraries, institutions and homes not having subscriptions to the journal, *The Mind of the Negro* stands as an important work in its own right. Its components gave Woodson's historical imagination plenty of facts to work with, and it now allows our imaginations the same opportunity.

BOB BLAISDELL
New York City, June 2012

FOREWORD

This collection of letters, like some other publications recently brought out by the Association for the Study of Negro Life and History, is the result of the researches into the free Negro prior to the Civil War made possible by the grant which the Editor obtained from the Laura Spelman Rockefeller Memorial in 1921. Almost all of these letters have been published in a series in the *Journal of Negro History*. They are reproduced here in this convenient form to facilitate research.

The letters to the American Colonization Society were copied from their files, whereas most of those to anti-slavery workers and agencies were extracted from books and newspapers. The chief source of the latter was the *Liberator*, published by William Lloyd Garrison in Boston. A score or more of them, however, were taken from the *National Antislavery Standard*, published by various editors in New York City. Copies of some of these same letters may be found in other antislavery publications like the *Philanthropist* and the *Non-Slaveholder;* but antislavery narratives and the like do not contain many of such letters. A considerable number of these letters were taken from the collection of manuscripts of the Association for the Study of Negro Life and History. Others came from collections of the New York Public Library, the New York Historical Society, and the Boston Public Library. The Anti-Slavery Collection of the Boston Public Library, especially that of the correspondence of William Lloyd Garrison, contains many letters written by Negroes. The most important of them appear in this volume.

These letters were reproduced just as they were found in the sources. Practically all of them were photocopied. In the case of those in manuscript form the copies were carefully studied in preparing them for the printer; and in the case of those found in print the photostat copies themselves were sent to the compositor that they might be reproduced in the original form as nearly as possible.

CARTER G. WOODSON

WASHINGTON, D. C.
February 16, 1926.

CONTENTS

Introduction to the Dover Edition iii

Introduction to the 1926 Edition xxiii

I. Letters to the American Colonization Society......1–158

From Abraham Camp................... 2
 " John B. Russwurm............... 3
 " A Negro in Savannah............. 4
 " "A Man of Color"................ 4
 " John Jones..................... 9
 " "A South Carolinian"............ 10
 " James Drew.................... 13
 " Bureell W. Mann................ 15
 " Lewis C. Holbert................ 47
 " George H. Baltimore............. 48
 " Cecelia D. Lyon................. 50
 " Peter B. Bolling................. 51
 " Branch Hughes................. 52
 " John F. Cook................... 53
 " Alfred Evans................... 53
 " Jacob Anderson................. 54
 " Titus Shropshire................ 55
 " Sherry J. Jackson............... 61
 " S. Wesley Jones................. 63
 " James B. Bland................. 74
 " Alphonso M. Sumner............. 75
 " James R. Starkey................ 76
 " Thomas G. Smith................ 81
 " Sion Harris.................... 84
 " H. B. Stewart.................. 84
 " Samuel J. Lewis................ 88
 " W. H. Burham.................. 90
 " Daniel Strother................ 91
 " Peter Butler................... 93
 " Saml. V. Mitchell............... 94
 " Alfred Payne................... 95
 " Mary Higgins................... 95
 " Henri Underwood............... 96
 " E. W. Baker................... 97
 " N. D. Artist................... 97

Contents

From Isaah T. Wilson.................. 106
"   Edwards Smith.................. 107
"   Mary Moore..................... 108
"   Alexander Harris................. 109
"   Maria Fenemur.................. 109
"   C. L. De Lamotta................ 110
"   Elie W. Stokes.................. 115
"   H. Teague...................... 115
"   J. B. Jordan.................... 116
"   W. W. Findlay.................. 122
"   A. H. Dickinson................. 123
"   E. Duglas Taylor................ 123
"   J. Theodore Holly............... 125
"   Benjamin S. Beebe.............. 127
"   James Winn.................... 131
"   Peter H. Clark................. 132
"   Augustus Washington............ 133
"   Hardy Mobley.................. 145
"   John W. West.................. 146
"   Anthony Sherman............... 147
"   Charles Deputie................ 149
"   John Barlon................... 151
"   Charles Moore................. 152
"   "A Negro in Baltimore".......... 152
"   Geo. Sample................... 153
"   Nathaniel Bowen............... 154
"   John W. Jones................. 155
"   Mobile Colored Missionary Society .. 157
"   Terry McHenry Farlan........... 157

II. Letters to Antislavery Workers and Agencies...159–510

From "R" about John B. Russwurm...... 161
"   "C. D. T." a Philadelphian......... 161
"   Nathaniel Paul.................. 163
"   Thomas Cole................... 171
"   James Forten.................. 175
"   Robert Purvis.................175, 195
"   Austin Steward........180, 184, 188, 190
"   Israel Lewis................... 181
"   Lisbon Wine................... 190
"   J. B. Cutler.................. 191

CONTENTS

From H. H. Garnet...................... 194
"   Wm. C. Nell...................201, 328
"   Frederick Douglass.....202, 210, 384, 505
"   William Wells Brown...........213, 349
"   J. W. Loguen..............216, 218, 267
"   "A Man of Color".............220, 225
"   "A Colored Bostonian"............ 222
"   "Leo"........................... 223
"   "A Colored Philadelphian"..224, 227, 229
"   "Hannibal".................... 227
"   "A Colored Lady"................ 230
"   "Euthymus".................... 232
"   "A Colored Gentleman in Maryland" 235
"   Samson Harris Moody............. 236
"   "A Colored Citizen of Brooklyn".... 238
"   "A Colored Baltimorean".......... 238
"   "A Colored American"............ 241
"   J. B. Vashon..................... 244
"   William P. Powell................. 246
"   "W. J. W."...................... 247
"   David Ruggles................... 250
"   James L. Smith.................. 260
"   W. and E. Craft................. 262
"   Francis S. Anderson.............. 266
"   Anthony Burns.................. 268
"   James McCune Smith.............. 270
"   Macon B. Allen.................. 280
"   William G. Allen................. 282
"   "S. R. W.".................... 290
"   M. R. Delany.................292, 502
"   Charles Lenox Remond............ 294
"   William C. Nell.................. 328
"   George T. Downing............... 348
"   Josephine Brown................. 363
"   Samuel R. Ward................. 490
"   Lewis Woodson.................. 493
"   J. T. Holly..................... 495
"   J. M. Whitfield................. 500
"   M. R. Delany................... 502
"   A. V. Thompson................. 502
"   J. D. Harris................... 504

CONTENTS

From "H. O. W." and others............ 508
  "   "F. E. W.".................... 508
  "   "M. S. J. T.".................. 509

III. LETTERS LARGELY PERSONAL OR PRIVATE...........511–624

From Caesar Brown.................... 511
  "   Medard Portellette............... 513
  "   John Miller..................... 516
  "   Mary Stokes..................... 517
  "   J. J. Roberts................... 518
  "   N. H. Elebeck................... 520
  "   William J. Walker............... 522
  "   John Moshell.................... 523
  "   Adam Plummer and relatives....... 523
  "   Wm. Eden....................... 528
  "   Joseph C. Bustill..............529, 560
  "   Otho Taylor..................... 530
  "   N. B. Harris.................... 530
  "   Jacob A. White, Jr.............. 530
  "   "Hope"......................... 532
  "   "Faith"........................ 534
  "   J. C. White.................... 535
  "   Richard Hackley................. 536
  "   Jourdon Anderson................ 537
  "   C. A. Stewart................... 539
  "   H. Amelia Loguen................ 540
  "   Lewis H. Douglas................ 541
  "   Thomas H. Jones................. 545
  "   Peter Van Wagenen............... 552
  "   "Kale"......................... 553
  "   W. H. Gatewood.................. 554
  "   Henry Bibb..................... 554
  "   J. W. C. Pennington............. 556
  "   William Still................... 556
  "   John H. Hill.............558, 563, 579
  "   "Ham & Eggs"................... 559
  "   Sheridan Ford................... 559
  "   "A Fugitive".................... 561
  "   John Thompson................... 561
  "   William Jones................... 562
  "   "N. L. J.".................... 563

Contents

From James M. Mercer................. 563
"   W. H. Gilliam................... 564
"   John Clayton.................... 565
"   Mary D. Armstead............... 565
"   Isaac Forman.................... 566
"   William Brinkly................. 567
"   Emma Brown.................... 568
"   Joseph Robinson................ 568
"   Nat Ambie...................... 569
"   John Scott...................... 569
"   Israel Whitney.................. 570
"   William Cooper................. 570
"   Edmund Turner................. 571
"   Jefferson Pipkins............... 573
"   Jame Masey.................... 573
"   Henry Trusty................... 574
"   C. W. Thompson................ 574
"   Richard Edons.................. 575
"   Manual T. White............... 575
"   J. W. Loguen................... 576
"   Samuel W. Johnson............. 576
"   Elijah Hilton................... 577
"   William Brown................. 578
"   Flarece P. Gault............... 578
"   E. Weems...................... 579
"   W. H. Actkins.................. 592
"   Harriet Elgin.................. 593
"   W. Boural...................... 594
"   David Robinson................. 595
"   Patterson Smith................ 595
"   George W. Freeland............ 596
"   Samuel Green.................. 596
"   John Hall...................... 596
"   Henry Washington.............. 599
"   James H. Forman............... 600
"   Robert Jones................... 601
"   William Donar.................. 601
"   Ellen Saunders................. 602
"   Frances Hilliard............... 603
"   Samuel Miles................... 603
"   Anthony & Albert Brown.......... 604

Contents

From Anthony Brown.................... 605
"   Albert Metter...................... 605
"   John Atkinson..................... 606
"   W. H. Atkinson................... 606
"   "Several Fugitives"................ 607
"   Henry James Morris............... 607
"   Rebecca Jones.................... 608
"   Daniel Robertson................. 608
"   Thomas F. Page.................. 609
"   Caroline Graves.................. 610
"   John Knight...................... 610
"   Lewis Cobb....................... 611
"   Lewis Burrell..................... 612
"   Oscar D. Ball.................... 613
"   John Delaney.................... 614
"   John B. Woods................... 614
"   Edward Lewis.................... 615
"   George Ballard................... 615
"   "Anonymous".................... 616
"   Joseph Ball...................... 617
"   John H. Dade.................... 617
"   Jacob Blockson.................. 618
"   Stepney Brown................... 618
"   Catherine Brice.................. 620
"   J. W. Dungy..................... 621
"   Louisa F. Jones................. 624

IV. Miscellaneous Letters......................625–663

From Lyman A. Spalding.............. 625
"   S. E. Cornish.................... 625
"   A. Steward............... 626, 637, 662
"   N. Paul......................... 628
"   Benj. T. Onderdonk.............. 629
"   Peter Williams.................. 630
"   William C. Nell................. 635
"   David Ruggles.................. 638
"   J. W. C. Pennington............. 642
"   Wm. W. Findlay................. 651
"   Frederick Douglass.............. 653
"   Anthony Burns.................. 659
"   Wm. L. Garrison................ 662

INTRODUCTION TO THE 1926 EDITION

Letters are regarded by historians as excellent historical evidence. Personal letters are especially valuable because of their unconscious element. Many letters supposedly personal or private, however, are intended for publication. As such they are of no more value than the ordinary newspaper materials, the worth of which is determined largely by the extent to which they reflect the sentiment of the people. The letters herein published are of all sorts. Under the classification herein set forth they can be used to advantage in the study of the development of the Negro prior to emancipation.

From the point of view of psychology of the Negro, which must be taken into consideration as an important factor in the study of history, these letters are of still larger value. The mind of a people, the development of the public mind, has become a new factor in historical interpretation. This factor is now being considered not only as important as the social, political, and economic, but also as productive of these forces.

Until within the last half century, moreover, the style a man used in letter writing often served as an index to his cultural development. Even today a man is frequently judged by the sort of letter which he writes. The multiplication of devices of production and reproduction, however, and the increasing number of well-educated workers whom a man in public life can easily employ, now make it impossible to determine from one's correspondence exactly what his mental development is. But these letters herein given were written when modern facilities had not developed beyond that of frequent use of copyists, and practically all of these letters were written by the Negroes themselves. Here, therefore, we have the opportunity to judge hundreds of Negroes as they really expressed themselves.

To appreciate the importance of such letters one needs only to study the correspondence of distinguished men of a century ago. In the absence of the valuable facilities of communication by wire and newspapers such letters carried more of the significant developments which we would expect today from books dealing with topics of concern to intelligent people. That some of the letters of Negroes found their way to such files is an evidence of the mental development of the Negro and the tendency of the most liberal whites to grant them recognition.

Although this work is intended to deal primarily with the correspondence of Negroes between 1800 and 1860, then, it might be well to present here also a few letters of certain outstanding Negroes who were well known prior to that time.

Jupiter Hammon, the first of these known to fame, was a slave of Long Island. He attained some distinction as a writer of verse and a religious worker. It is highly probable that he was a preacher of local standing. Hammon was born about 1720 and died just before or a little after the close of that century. As a writer of verse he seems very devout. He made some impression on his contemporaries, but he does not rise to the level of the contributions of Phillis Wheatley.

The following letter and address to the Negroes of New York will give an idea as to the mind of Jupiter Hammon:

Gentlemen,

I TAKE the liberty to dedicate an Address to my poor brethren to you. If you think it is likely to do good among them, I do not doubt but you will take it under your care. You have discovered so much kindness and good will to those you thought were oppressed, and had no helper, that I am sure you will not despise what I have wrote, if you judge it will be of any service to them. I have nothing to add, but only to wish that "the blessing of many ready to perish, may come upon you."

I am Gentlemen,
Your Servant,
JUPITER HAMMON.

Queen's Village, 24th Sept.
1786.

AN
ADDRESS TO THE NEGROES[1]
OF THE
State of New-York.

WHEN I am writing to you with a design to say something to you for your good, and with a view to promote your happiness, I can with truth and sincerity join with the apostle Paul, when speaking of his own nation the Jews, and say: *"That I have great heaviness and continual sorrow in my heart for my brethren, my kinsmen according to the flesh."* Yes my dear brethren, when I think of you, which is very often, and of the poor, despised and miserable state you are in, as to the things of this world, and when I think of your ignorance and stupidity, and the great wickedness of the most of you, I am pained to the heart. It is at times, almost too much for human nature to bear, and I am obliged to turn my thoughts from the subject or endeavour to still my mind, by considering that it is permitted thus to be, by that God who governs all things, who setteth up one and pulleth down another. While I have been thinking on this subject, I have frequently had great struggles in my own mind, and have been at a loss to know what to do. I have wanted exceedingly to say something to you, to call upon you with

[1] IN the first impression of the following pages, printed in New-York, 1787, by Carrol and Patterson, they say:

TO THE PUBLIC

As this Address is wrote in a better stile than could be expected from a slave, some may be ready to doubt of the genuineness of the production. The Author, as he informs in the title page, is a servant of Mr. Lloyd, and has been remarkable for his fidelity and abstinence from those vices, which he warns his brethren against. The manuscript, wrote in his own hand, is in our possession. We have made no material alterations in it, except in the spelling, which we found needed considerable correction.

THE PRINTERS.

New-York, 20th Feb. 1787.

WE, the Subscribers, having had personal acquaintance with Jupiter Hammon, Author of the Address to the People of Colour in the State of New-York, believe he supported a good moral character; was much respected in his master's family, and among his acquaintance in general; and we have no doubt but the Address alluded to, is a genuine production of his own.

Arnold Fleet,
Samuel Haviland,
Fry Willis.

Oysterbay, 10th of 1st mo. 1806.

1*

the tenderness of a father and friend, and to give you the last, and I may say dying advice, of an old man, who wishes your best good in this world, and in the world to come. But while I have had such desires, a sense of my own ignorance, and unfitness to teach others, has frequently discouraged me from attempting to say any thing to you; yet when I thought of your situation, I could not rest easy.

When I was at Hartford in Connecticut, where I lived during the war, I published several pieces which were well received, not only by those of my own colour, but by a number of the white people, who thought they might do good among their servants. This is one consideration, among others, that emboldens me now to publish what I have written to you. Another is, I think you will be more likely to listen to what is said, when you know it comes from a negro, one of your own nation and colour, and therefore can have no interest in deceiving you, or in saying any thing to you, but what he really thinks is your interest, and duty to comply with. My age, I think, gives me some right to speak to you, and reason to expect you will hearken to my advice. I am now upwards of seventy years old, and cannot expect, though I am well, and able to do almost any kind of business, to live much longer. I have passed the common bounds set for man, and must soon go the way of all the earth. I have had more experience in the world than the most of you, and I have seen a great deal of the vanity and wickedness of it, I have great reason to be thankful that my lot has been so much better than most slaves have had. I suppose I have had more advantages and privileges than most of you, who are slaves, have ever known, and I believe more than many white people have enjoyed, for which I desire to bless God, and pray that he may bless those who have given them to me. I do not, my dear friends, say these things about myself, to make you think that I am wiser or better than others; but that you might hearken, without prejudice, to what I have to say to you on the following particulars.

1st. Respecting obedience to masters.—Now whether it is right, and lawful, in the sight of God, for them to make slaves of us or not. I am certain that while we are slaves, it is our duty to obey our masters, in all their lawful commands, and mind them unless we are bid to do that which we know to be sin, or forbidden in God's word. The apostle Paul says: "Servants be obedient to them that are your masters according to the flesh, with fear and trembling in singleness in your heart as unto Christ: Not with eye service, as men pleasers, but as the servants of Christ doing the will of God from the heart: With good will doing service to the Lord, and not to men: Knowing that whatever thing a man doeth the same shall he receive of the Lord, whether he be bond or free."—Here is a plain command of God for us to obey our masters. It may seem hard for us, if we think our masters wrong in holding us slaves, to obey in all things, but who of us dare dispute with God! He has commanded us to obey, and we ought to do it cheerfully, and freely. This should be done by us, not only because God commands, but because our own peace and comfort depend upon it. As we depend upon our masters, for what we eat and drink and wear, and for all our comfortable things in this world, we cannot be happy, unless we please them. This we cannot do without obeying them freely, without muttering or finding fault. If a servant strives to please his master and studies and takes pains to do it, I believe there are but few masters who would use such a servant cruelly. Good servants frequently make good masters. If your master is really hard, unreasonable and cruel, there is no way so likely for you to convince him of it, as always to obey his commands, and try to serve him, and take care of his interest, and try to promote it all in your power. If you are proud and stubborn and always finding fault, your master will think the fault lies wholly on your side; but if you are humble, and meek, and bear all things patiently, your master may think he is wrong; if he does not, his neighbours will be apt to see it, and will befriend you, and try to alter his conduct. If this does not do, you must cry to him, who has the hearts of all men in his hands, and turneth them as the rivers of waters are turned.

2d. The particular I would mention, is honesty and faithfulness.

You must suffer me now to deal plainly with you, my dear brethren, for I do not mean to flatter, or omit speaking the truth, whether it is for you, or against you. How many of you are there who allow yourselves in stealing from your masters. It is very wicked for you not to take care of your masters goods, but how much worse is it to pilfer and steal from them, whenever you think you shall not be found out. This you must know is very wicked and provoking to God. There are none of you so ignorant, but that you must know that this is wrong. Though you may try to excuse yourselves, by saying that your masters are unjust to you, and though you may try to quiet your consciences in this way, yet if you are honest in owning the truth, you must think it is as wicked, and on some accounts more wicked, to steal from your masters, than from others.

We cannot certainly, have any excuse either for taking any thing that belongs to our masters, without their leave, or for being unfaithful in their business. It is our duty to be faithful, *not with eye service as men pleasers.* We have no right to stay when we are sent on errands, any longer than to do the business we were sent upon. All the time spent idly, is spent wickedly, and is unfaithfulness to our masters. In these things I must say, that I think many of you are guilty. I know that many of you endeavour to excuse yourselves, and say, that you have nothing that you can call your own, and that you are under great temptations to be unfaithful and take from your masters. But this will not do, God will certainly punish you for stealing and for being unfaithful. All that we have to mind is our own duty. If God has put us in bad circumstances, that is not our fault, and he will not punish us for it. If any are wicked in keeping us so, we cannot help it, they must answer to God for it. Nothing will serve as an excuse to us for not doing our duty. The same God will judge both them and us. Pray then my dear friends, fear to offend in this way, but be faithful to God, to your masters, and to your own souls.

The next thing I would mention, and warn you against, is profaneness. This you know is forbidden by God. Christ tells us: "swear not at all," and again it is said, "thou shalt not take the name of the Lord thy God in vain, for the Lord will not hold him guiltless, that taketh his name in vain." Now, though the great God has forbidden it, yet how dreadfully profane are many, and I don't know but I may say the most of you? How common is it to hear you take the terrible and awful name of the great God in vain? —To swear by it, and by Jesus Christ, his Son—How common is it to hear you wish damnation to your companions, and to your own souls—and to sport with the name of Heaven and Hell, as if there were no such places for you to hope for, or to fear. Oh my friends, be warned to forsake this dreadful sin of profaneness. Pray my dear friends, believe and realize, that there is a God—that he is great and terrible beyond what you can think—that he keeps you in life every moment——and that he can send you to that awful Hell, that you laugh at, in an instant, and confine you there forever, and that he will certainly do it, if you do not repent. You certainly do not believe, that there is a God, or that there is a Heaven or Hell, or you would never trifle with them. It would make you shudder, if you heard others do it, if you believe them as much, as you believe any thing you see with your bodily eyes.

I have heard some learned and good men say, that the heathen, and all that worshipped false Gods, never spoke lightly or irreverently of their Gods, they never took their names in vain, or jested with those things which they held sacred. Now why should the true God, who made all things, be treated worse in this respect, than those false Gods, that were made of wood and stone. I believe it is because Satan tempts men to do it. He tried to make them love their false Gods, and to speak well of them, but he wishes to have men think lightly of the true God, to take his holy name in vain, and to scoff at, and make a jest of all things that are really good. You may think that Satan has not power to do so much, and have so great influence on the minds of men: But the scripture says: *"he goeth about like a roaring Lion, seeking whom he may devour —That he is the prince of the power of the air—and that he rules in the hearts of the children of disobedience,——and that wicked men are led captive by him, to do his will."* All those of you who are profane, are serving the Devil. You are doing what he tempts and desires you to do. If you could see him with your bodily eyes, would you like to make an agreement with him, to serve him, and do as he bid you. I believe most of you would be shocked at this; but you may be certain that all of you who allow yourselves in this sin, are as really serving him, and to just as good purpose, as if you met him, and promised to dishonour God, and serve him with all your might. Do you believe this? It is true whether you believe it or not. Some of you excuse yourselves, may plead the example of others, and say that you hear a great many white people, who know more, than such poor ignorant negroes, as you are, and some who are rich and great gentlemen, swear, and talk profanely, and some of you may say this of your masters, and say no more than is true. But all this is not a sufficient excuse for you. You know that murder is wicked. If you saw your master kill a man, do you suppose this would be any excuse for you, if you should commit the same crime? You must know it would not; nor will your hearing him curse and swear, and take the name of God in vain, or any other man, be he ever so great or rich, excuse you. God is greater than all other beings, and him we are bound to obey. To him we must give an account for every idle word that we speak. He will bring us all, rich and poor, white and black, to his judgment seat. If we are found among those who *feared his name* and *trembled at his word,* we shall be called good and faithful servants. Our slavery will be at an end, and though ever so mean, low, and despised in this world, we shall sit with God in his kingdom as Kings and Priests, and rejoice forever, and ever. Do not then my dear friends, take God's holy name in vain, or speak profanely in any way. Let not the example of others lead you into the sin, but reverence and fear that *great and fearful name, the Lord our God.*

I might now caution you against other sins to which you are exposed, but as I meant only to mention those you were exposed to, more than others, by your being slaves, I will conclude what I have to say to you, by advising you to become religious, and to make religion the great business of your lives.

Now I acknowledge that liberty is a great thing, and worth seeking for, if we can get it honestly, and by our good conduct prevail on our masters to set us free. Though for my own part I do not wish to be free: yet I should be glad, if others, especially the young negroes were to be free, for many of us who are grown up slaves, and have always had masters to take care of us, should hardly know how to take care of ourselves; and it may be more for our own comfort to remain as we are. That liberty is a great thing we may know from our own feelings, and we may likewise judge so from the conduct of the white people, in the late war. How much money has been spent, and how many lives have been lost, to defend their liberty. I must say that I have hoped that God would open their eyes, when they were so much engaged for liberty, to think of the state of the poor blacks, and to pity us. He has done it in some measure, and has raised us up many friends, for which we have reason to be thankful, and to hope in his mercy. What may be done further, he only knows, for *known unto God are all his ways from the beginning.* But this my dear brethren is by no means, the greatest thing we have to be concerned about. Getting our liberty in this world, is nothing to having the liberty of the children of God. Now the Bible tells us that we are all by nature, sinners, that we are slaves to sin and satan, and that unless we are converted, or born again, we must be miserable forever. Christ says, except a man be born again, he cannot see the kingdom of God, and all that do not see the kingdom of God, must be in the kingdom of darkness. There are but two places where all go after death, white and black, rich and poor; those places are heaven and hell.—Heaven is a place made for those, who are born again, and who love God, and it is a place where they will be happy forever. Hell is a place made for those who hate God, and are his enemies, and where they will be miserable to all eternity. Now you may think you are not enemies of God, and do not hate him: But if your hearts have not been changed, and you have not become true christians, you certainly are enemies to God, and have been opposed to him ever since you were born. Many of you, I suppose, never think of this, and are almost as ignorant as the beasts that perish. Those of you who can read, I must beg you to read the Bible, and whenever you can get time, study the Bible, and if you can get no other time, spare some of your time from sleep, and learn what the mind and will of God is. But what shall I say to them who cannot read? This lay with great weight on my mind, when I thought of writing to my poor brethren, but I hope that those who can read, will take pity on them, and read what I have to say to them. In hopes of this, I will beg of you to spare no pains in trying to learn to read. If you are once engaged, you may learn. Let all the time you can get, be spent in trying to learn to read. Get those who can read, to learn you, but remember that what you learn for, is to read the bible. It tells you what you must do to please God; it tells you how you may escape misery, and be happy forever. If you see most people neglect the bible, and many that can read, never look into it; let it not harden you and make you think lightly of it, and that it is a book of no worth. All those who are really good, love the bible, and meditate on it day and night. In the bible God has told us every thing it is necessary we should know, in order to be happy here and hereafter. The bible is a revelation of the mind and will of God to men. Therein we may learn what God is. That he made all things by the power of his word; and that he made all things for his own glory, and not for our glory. That he is over all, and above all his creatures, and more above them than we can think or conceive—that they can do nothing without him—that he upholds them all, and will over-rule all things for his own glory. In the bible likewise we are told what man is. That he was at first made holy, in the image of God, that he fell from that state of holiness, and became an enemy to God, and that since the fall, all *the imaginations of the thoughts of his heart, are evil and only evil, and that continually.—That the carnal mind is not subject to the law of God, neither indeed can be.* And that all mankind were under the wrath and curse of God, and must have been for ever miserable, if they had been left to suffer what their sins deserved. It tells us that God to save mankind, sent his Son into this world to die, in the room and stead of sinners, and that God will save from eternal misery, all that believe in his son, and take him for their Saviour, and that all are called upon to repent, and believe in Jesus Christ. It tells us, that those who do repent, and believe, and are friends to Christ, shall have many trials and sufferings in this world, but that they shall be happy forever, after death, and reign with Christ to all eternity. The bible tells us that this world is a place of trial, and that there is no other time or place for us to alter, but in this life. If we are christians when we die, we shall awake to the resurrection of life; if not, we shall awake to the resurrection of damnation. It tells us, we must all live in heaven or hell, be happy or miserable, and that without end. The bible does not tell us but of two places, for all to go to. There is no place for innocent folks, who are not christians. There is no place for ignorant folks, that did not know how to be christians. What I mean is, that there is no place besides heaven and hell. These two places will receive all mankind, for Christ says, there are but two sorts, *he that is not with me is against me, and he that gathereth not with me, scattereth abroad.* The bible likewise tells us, that this world and all things in it shall be burnt up—and that "God has appointed a day in which he will judge the world, and that he will bring every secret thing, whether it be good or bad, into judgment——that which is done in secret shall be declared on the house top." Then every thing that every one has done, through his whole life, is to be told, before the whole world of angels and men. There, Oh how solemn is the thought! You and I must stand, and hear every thing we have thought or done, however secret, however wicked and vile, told before all the men and women that ever have been, or ever will be, and before all the angels, good and bad.

Now my dear friends seeing the bible is the word of God, and every thing in it is true, and it reveals such awful and glorious things, what can be more important than that you should learn to read it; and when you have learned to read, that you should study it day and night. There are some things very encouraging in God's word, for such ignorant creatures as we are: for God hath not chosen the rich of this world. Not many rich, not many noble are called, but God hath chosen the weak things of this world, and things which are not, to confound the things that are: And when the great and the rich refused coming to the gospel feast, the servant was told to go into the highways, and hedges, and compel those poor creatures that he found there, to come in. Now my brethren, it seems to me that there are no people that ought to attend to the hope of happiness in another world, so much as we. Most of us are cut off from comfort and happiness here in this world, and can expect nothing from it. Now seeing this is the case, why should we not take care to be happy after death. Why should we spend our whole lives in sinning against God: And be miserable in this world, and in the world to come. If we do thus, we shall certainly be the greatest fools. We shall be slaves here, and slaves forever. We cannot plead so great temptations to neglect religion as others. Riches and honours which drown the greater part of mankind, (who have the gospel,) in perdition, can be little or no temptation to us.

We live so little time in this world, that it is no matter how wretched and miserable we are, if it prepares us for heaven. What is forty, fifty, or sixty years, when compared to eternity. When thousands and millions of years have rolled away, this eternity will be no nigher coming to an end. Oh how glorious is an eternal life of happiness! and how dreadful, an eternity of misery. Those of us who have had religious masters, and have been taught to read the bible, and have been brought by their example and teaching to a sense of divine things, how happy shall we be to meet them in heaven, where we shall join them in praising God forever. But if any of us have had such masters, and have yet lived and died wicked, how will it add to our misery to think of our folly. If any of us, who have wicked and profane masters should become religious, how will our estates be changed in another world. Oh my friends, let me intreat of you to think on these things, and to live as if you believed them true. If you become christians, you will have reason to bless God forever, that you have been brought into a land where you have heard the gospel, though you have been slaves. If we should ever get to heaven, we shall find nobody to reproach us for being black, or for being slaves. Let me beg of you my dear African brethren, to think very little of your bondage in this life, for your thinking of it will do you no good. If God designs to set us free, he will do it, in his own time, and way; but think of your bondage to sin and satan, and do not rest, until you are delivered from it.

We cannot be happy if we are ever so free or ever so rich, while we are servants of sin, and slaves to satan. We must be miserable here, and to all eternity.

I will conclude what I have to say, with a few words to those negroes who have their liberty. The most of what I have said to those who are slaves, may be of use to you, but you have more advantages, on some accounts, if you will improve your freedom, as you may do, than they. You have more time to read God's holy word, and to take care of the salvation of your souls. Let me beg of you to spend your time in this way, or it will be better for you, if you had always been slaves. If you think seriously of the matter, you must conclude, that if you do not use your freedom, to promote the salvation of your souls, it will not be of any lasting good to you. Besides all this, if you are idle, and take to bad courses, you will hurt those of your brethren who are slaves, and do all in your power to prevent their being free. One great reason that is given by some for not freeing us, I understand is, that we should not know how to take care of ourselves, and should take bad courses. That we should be lazy and idle, and get drunk and steal. Now all those of you, who follow any bad courses, and who do not take care to get an honest living by your labour and industry, are doing more to prevent our being free, than any body else. Let me beg of you then, for the sake of your own good and happiness, in time, and for eternity, and for the sake of your poor brethren, who are still in bondage, "*to lead quiet and peaceable lives in all Godliness and honesty,*" and may God bless you, and bring you to his kingdom, for Christ's sake, Amen.

Phillis Wheatley, known to fame as a writer of verse during the latter part of the eighteenth century, may be judged also by her correspondence. The following letters to her friends may be studied to this end.

Rev'd Sir

I recieved your kind letter last Evening by M^r. Pemberton, by whom also this is to be handed you. I have also rec^d. the Money for the 5 books I sent Obour, & 2/6 more for another. She has wrote me, but the date is 29 April. I am very sorry to hear, that Philip Quaque has very little or no *apparent* Success in his mission. Yet, I wish that what you hear respecting him, may be only a misrepresentation. Let us not be discouraged, but still hope, that God will bring about his great work, tho' Philip may *not* be the instrument in the Divine Hand, to perform this work of wonder, turning the African "*from darkness to light.*" Possibly, if Philip would introduce himself properly to them, (I don't know the reverse) he might be more Successful, and in setting a good example which is more powerfully winning than Instruction. I Observe your

Reference to the Maps of Guinea & Salmon's Gazetteer, and shall consult them. I have rec^d. in some of the last ships from London 300 more copies of my Poems, and wish to dispose of them as soon as Possible. If you know of any being wanted I flatter myself you will be pleas'd to let me know it, which will be adding one more to the many Obligations already confer'd on her, who is, with a due Sense of your kindness,

Your most humble,
And Obedient servant
Phillis Wheatley

Boston
      May 6, 1774.
The revd S. Hopkins [1]

To Arbour Tanner, in Newport. [2]

Boston, May 19th 1772.

Dear Sister,—I rec'd your favour of February 6th for which I give you my sincere thanks. I greatly rejoice with you in that realizing view, and I hope experience, of the saving change which you so emphatically describe. Happy were it for us if we could arrive to that evangelical Repentance, and the true holiness of heart which you mention. Inexpressibly happy should we be could we have a due sense of the beauties and excellence of the crucified Saviour. In his Crucifixion may be seen marvellous displays of Grace and Love, sufficient to draw and invite us to the rich and endless treasures of his mercy; let us rejoice in and adore the wonders of God's infinite Love in bringing us from a land semblant of darkness itself, and where the divine light of revelation (being obscur'd) is as darkness. Here the knowledge of the true God and eternal life are made manifest; but there, profound ignorance overshadows the land. Our observation is true, namely that there was nothing in us to recommend us to God. Many of our fellow creatures are pass'd by, when the bowels of divine love expanded towards us. May this goodness & long suffering of God lead us to unfeign'd repentance.

It gives me very great pleasure to hear of so many of my nation, seeking with eagerness the way of true felicity. O may we all meet at length in that happy mansion. I hope the correspondence between us will continue, (my being much indispos'd this winter past,

---

[1] *Chamberlain Collection*, Boston Public Library. A.6.20.

[2] These letters to Arbour Tanner may be found in the *Massachusetts Historical Society Proceedings for 1863–1864.*

was the reason of my not answering yours before now) which correspondence I hope may have the happy effect of improving our mutual friendship. Till we meet in the regions of consummate blessedness, let us endeavor by the assistance of divine grace, to live the life, and we shall die the death of the Righteous. May this be our happy case, and of those who are travelling to the region of Felicity is the earnest request of your affectionate

Friend & humble servant

PHILLIS WHEATLEY.

To ARBOUR TANNER, IN NEWPORT.   TO THE CARE OF MR. PEASE'S SERVANT, RHODE ISLAND.

BOSTON, July 19th, 1772.

My Dear Friend,—I rec'd your kind epistle a few days ago; much disappointed to hear that you had not rec'd my answer to your first letter. I have been in a very poor state of health all the past winter and spring, and now reside in the country for the benefit of its more wholesome air. I came to town this morning to spend the Sabbath with my master and mistress. Let me be interested in your prayers that God would please to bless to me the means us'd for my recovery, if agreeable to his holy will. While my outward man languishes under weakness and pa(in), may the inward be refresh'd and strengthen'd more abundantly by him who declar'd from heaven that his strength was made perfect in weakness! May he correct our vitiated taste, that the meditation of him may be delightful to us. No longer to be so excessively charm'd with fleeting vanities: but pressing forward to the fix'd mark for the prize. How happy that man who is prepar'd for that night wherein no man can work! Let us be mindful of our high calling, continually on our guard, lest our treacherous hearts should give the adversary an advantage over us. O! who can think without horror of the snares of the Devil. Let us, by frequent meditation on the eternal Judgment, prepare for it. May the Lord bless to us these thoughts, and teach us by his Spirit to live to him alone, and when we leave this world may we be his. That this may be our happy case, is the sincere desire of, your affectionate friend, & humble serv't,

PHILLIS WHEATLEY.

I sent the letter to Mr. Whitwell's who said he wou'd forward it.

To Obour Tanner, in New Port.

BOSTON, Oct. 30, 1773.

Dear Obour,—I rec'd your most kind epistles of Augt 27th, & Oct. 13th, by a young man of your acquaintance, for which I am oblig'd to you. I hear of your welfare with pleasure; but this acquaints you that I am at present indispos'd by a cold, & since my arrival have been visited by the asthma.

Your observations on our dependence on the Deity, & your hopes that my wants will be supply'd from his fulness which is in Christ Jesus, is truly worthy of your self. I can't say but my voyage to England has conduced to the recovery (in a great measure) of my health. The friends I found there among the nobility and gentry, their benevolent conduct towards me, the unexpected and unmerited civility and complaisance with which I was treated by all, fills me with astonishment. I can scarcely realize it. This I humbly hope has the happy effect of lessening me in my own esteem. Your reflections on the sufferings of the Son of God, & the inestimable price of our immortal souls, plainly demonstrates the sensations of a soul united to Jesus. What you observe of Esau is true of all mankind, who, (left to themselves) would sell their heavenly birth rights for a few moments of sensual pleasure, whose wages at last (dreadful wages!) is eternal condemnation. Dear Obour, let us not sell our birthright for a thousand worlds, which indeed would be as dust upon the balance. The God of the seas and dry land, has graciously brought me home in safety. Join with me in thanks to him for so great a mercy, & that it may excite me to praise him with cheerfulness, to persevere in Grace & Faith, & in the knowledge of our Creator and Redeemer,—that my heart may be fill'd with gratitude. I should have been pleas'd greatly to see Miss West, as I imagine she knew you. I have been very busy ever since my arrival, or should have now wrote a more particular account of my voyage, but must submit that satisfaction to some other opportunity. I am Dear friend,

Most affectionately ever yours,

PHILLIS WHEATLEY.

My mistress has been very sick above 14 weeks, & confined to her bed the whole time, but is I hope somewhat better now.

The young man by whom this is handed you seems to me to be a very clever man, knows you very well, & is very complaisant and agreeable.   P. W.

I enclose Proposals for my book, and beg you'd use your interest to get subscriptions, as it is for my benefit.

To Miss Obour Tanner, Newport.

BOSTON, March 21, 1774.

Dear Obour,—I rec'd your obliging letter enclos'd in your Revd Pastor's & handed me by his son. I have lately met with a great trial in the death of my mistress; let us imagine the loss of a parent, sister or brother, the tenderness of all these were united in her. I was a poor little outcast & a stranger when she took me in: not only into her house, but I presently became a sharer in her most tender affections. I was treated by her more like her child than her servant; no opportunity was left unimproved of giving me the best of advice; but in terms how tender! how engaging! This I hope ever to keep in remembrance. Her exemplary life was a greater monitor than all her precepts and instruction; thus we may observe of how much greater force example is than instruction. To alleviate our sorrows we had the satisfaction to see her depart in inexpressible raptures, earnest longings, & impatient thirstings for the upper courts of the Lord. Do, my dear friend, remember me & this family in your closet, that this afflicting dispensation may be sanctify'd to us. I am very sorry to hear that you are indispos'd, but hope this will find you in better health. I have been unwell the greater part of the winter, but am much better as the spring approaches. Pray excuse my not writing to you so long before, for I have been so busy lately that I could not find leisure. I shall send the 5 books you wrote for, the first convenient opportunity; if you want more, they shall be ready for you. I am very affectionately your friend,

PHILLIS WHEATLEY.

To Miss Obour Tanner, New Port, Rhode Island, fvd by Mr. Pemberton.

Dear Obour,—I rec'd last evening your kind & friendly letter and am not a little animated thereby. I hope ever to follow your good advices and be resigned to the afflicting hand of a seemingly frowning Providence. I have rec'd the money you sent for the 5 books & 2–6 more for another, which I now send & wish safe to hand. Your tenderness for my welfare demands my gratitude. Assist me, dear Obour! to praise our great benefactor, for the innumerable benefits continually pour'd upon me, that while he strikes one comfort dead he raises up another. But O that I could dwell on & delight in him alone above every other object! While the world hangs loose about us we shall not be a painful anxiety in giving up to God that which he first gave to us. Your letter came by Mr. Pemberton who brings you the book you write for. I shall wait upon Mr. Whitwell with your letter and am

Dear sister, ever affectionately, your

Phillis Wheatley.

I have rec'd by some of the last ships 300 more of my Poems. Boston, May 6, 1774.

Miss Obour Tanner, Worcester.

Boston May 29th '78.

Dear Obour,—I am exceedingly glad to hear from you by Mrs. Tanner, and wish you had timely notice of her departure, so as to have wrote me; next to that is the pleasure of hearing that you are well. The vast variety of scenes that have pass'd before us these 3 years past, will to a reasonable mind serve to convince us of the uncertain duration of all things temporal, and the proper result of such a consideration is an ardent desire of, & preparation for, a state and enjoyments which are more suitable to the immortal mind. You will do me a great favour if you'll write me by every opportunity. Direct your letters under cover to Mr. John Peters in Queen Street. I have but half an hour's notice; and must apologize for this hasty scrawl. I am most affectionately, My dear Obour, your sincere friend

Phillis Wheatley.

Miss Obour Tanner, Worcester, favd by Cymberland.

Boston May 10, 1779.

Dr. Obour,—By this opportunity I have the pleasure to inform you that I am well and hope you are so; tho' I have been silent, I have not been unmindful of you, but a variety of hindrances was the cause of my not writing to you. But in time to come I hope our correspondence will revive—and revive in better times— pray write me soon, for I long to hear from you—you may depend on constant replies—I wish you much happiness, and am

Dr. Obour, your friend & sister

Phillis Peters.

Neither Jupiter Hammon nor Phillis Wheatley, however, had undergone as much mental development as another prominent Negro of the eighteenth century, known as Benjamin

Banneker, the mathematician and astronomer. Some of his important letters are here offered in evidence.

LETTER OF BENJAMIN BANNEKER TO GEORGE ELLICOTT [3]

"*Sir*,—I received your letter at the hand of Bell but found nothing strange to me in the Letter Concerning the number of Eclipses, tho according to authors the Edge of the penumbra only touches the Suns Limb in that Eclips, that I left out of the Number —which happens April 14th day, at 37 minutes past 7 o'clock in the morning, and is the first we shall have; but since you wrote to me, I drew in the Equations of the Node which will cause a small Solar Defet, but as I did not intend to publish, I was not so very peticular as I should have been, but was more intent upon the true method of projecting a Solar Eclips—It is an easy matter for us when a Diagram is laid down before us, to draw one in resemblance of it, but it is a hard matter for young Tyroes in Astronomy, when only the Elements for the projection is laid down before him to draw his Diagram with any degree of certainty.

"Says the Learned LEADBETTER, the projection, I shall here describe, is that mentioned by Mr. Flamstead. When the sun is in Cancer, Leo, Virgo, Libra, Scorpio or, Sagitary, the Axes of the Globe must lie to the right hand of the Axes of the Ecliptic, but when the sun is in Capricorn, Aquarius, Pisces, Aries, Taurus, or Gemini, then to the left.

"Says the wise author FERGUSON, when the sun is in Capercorn, Aquarius, Pisces, Aries, Taurus, and Gemini, the Northern half of the Earths Axes lies to the right hand of the Axes of the Ecliptic and to the left hand, whilst the Sun is on the other six signs.

"Now Mr. Ellicott, two such learned gentlemen as the above mentioned, one in direct opposition to the other, stagnates young beginners, but I hope the stagnation will not be of long duration, for this I observe that Leadbetter counts the time on the path of Vertex 1.2.3. &c. from the right to the left hand or from the consequent to the antecedent,—But Ferguson on the path of Vertex counts the time 1.2.3. &c. from the left to the right hand, according to the order of numbers, so that that is regular, shall compensate for irregularity. Now sir if I can overcome this difficulty I doubt not being able to calculate a Common Almanac.—Sir no more

"But remain your faithful friend,

"B. BANNEKER.

"Mr. GEORGE ELLICOTT, Oct 13th, 1789."

[3] Martha E. Tyson's *Banneker, the Afric-American Astronomer*, 28–30.

MARYLAND BALTIMORE COUNTY NEAR ELLICOTS
LOWER MILL May the 6th—1790

Sir

I have at the request of several Gentlemen, calculated an Ephemeris for the year 1791 which I presented unto Mr. Hayes printer in Baltimore, and he received it in a very polite manner, and told me, that he would gladly print the same, provided the calculations came anyways near the truth, but to satisfy himself in that, he would send it to Philadelphia to be inspected by you, and at the reception of an answer he should know how to proceed—and now Sr:, I beg that you will not be too severe upon me, but as favourable in giving your approbation as the nature of the case will permit, knowing well the difficulty that attends long calculations, and especially with young beginners in Astronomy, but this I know that the greater and most useful part of my Ephemeris is so near the truth, that it needs but little correction, and as to that part that may be somewhat deficient, I hope that you will be kind enough to view with an eye of pity, as the Calculations was made more for the sake of gratifying the curiosity of the public, than for any view of profit, as I suppose it to be the first attempt of the kind that ever was made in America by a person of my complexion—

I find by my calculation there will be four Eclipses for the ensuing year, but I have not yet settled their appearances, but am waiting for an answer from your Honour to Mr. Hayes in Baltimore; —So no more at present, but am Sr.

Your very humble and most obedient Servt:

B BANNEKER

To Andrew Ellicott [4]

"August 26th, 1797.

"Dear Female Friend:—

"I have thought of you every day since I saw you last, and of my promise in respect of composing some verses for your amusement, but I am very much indisposed, and have been ever since that time. I have a constant pain in my head, a palpitation in my flesh, and I may say I am attended with a complication of disorders, at this present writing, so that I cannot with any pleasure or delight, gratify your curiosity in that particular, at this present time, yet I say my will is good to oblige you, if I had it in my power, because you gave me good advice, and edifying

[4] This letter was taken from the collection of manuscripts of the New York Historical Society.

language, in that piece of poetry which you was pleased to present unto me, and I can but love and thank you for the same; and if ever it should be in my power to be serviceable to you, in any measure, your reasonable requests, shall be armed with the obedience of,

Your sincere friend and well-wisher,

BENJAMIN BANNEKER."

"MRS. SUSANNA MASON."

"N. B. The above is mean writing, done with trembling hands.

B. B." [5]

Thomas Jefferson, one of the advanced thinkers of his day, showed by a letter to Banneker the impression which this scientific American had made. Banneker had written him the following:

MARYLAND, BALTIMORE COUNTY,

NEAR ELLICOTTS' LOWER MILLS, August 19th, 1791.

THOMAS JEFFERSON, *Secretary of State.*

Sir:—I am fully sensible of the greatness of that freedom, which I take with you on the present occasion, a liberty which seemed to me scarcely allowable, when I reflected on that distinguished and dignified station in which you stand, and the almost general prejudice and prepossession which is so prevalent in the world against those of my complexion.

I suppose it is a truth too well attested to you, to need a proof here, that we are a race of beings who have long laboured under the abuse and censure of the world, that we have long been considered rather as brutish than human, and scarcely capable of mental endowments.

Sir, I hope I may safely admit, in consequence of that report which hath reached me, that you are a man far less inflexible in sentiments of this nature than many others, that you are measureably friendly and well disposed towards us, and that you are ready and willing to lend your aid and assistance to our relief, from those many distressed and numerous calamities, to which we are reduced.

Now, sir, if this is founded in truth, I apprehend you will readily embrace every opportunity to eradicate that train of absurd and false ideas and opinions, which so generally prevails with respect to us, and that your sentimemts are concurrent with mine, which are that one universal father hath given being to us all, and that he hath

---

[5] Martha E. Tyson's *Banneker, the Afric-American Astronomer*, 58–59.

not only made us all of one flesh, but that he hath also without partiality afforded us all the same sensations, and endued us all with the same faculties, and that however variable we may be in society or religion, however diversified in situation or colour, we are all of the same family, and stand in the same relation to him.

Sir, if these are sentiments of which you are fully persuaded, I hope you cannot but acknowledge, that it is the indispensable duty of those who maintain for themselves the rights of human nature, and who profess the obligations of christianity, to extend their power and influence to the relief of every part of the human race, from whatever burthen or oppression they may unjustly labour under, and this I apprehend a full conviction of the truth and obligation of these principles should lead all to.

Sir, I have long been convinced, that if your love for yourselves and for those inestimable laws, which preserve to you the rights of human nature, was founded on sincerity, you could not but be solicitous that every individual of whatever rank or distinction, might with you equally enjoy the blessings thereof, neither could you rest satisfied, short of the most active diffusion of your exertions, in order, to their promotion from any state of degradation, to which the unjustifiable cruelty and barbarism of men may have reduced them.

Sir, I freely and cheerfully acknowledge that I am of the African race, and in that colour which is natural to them of the deepest dye, and it is under a sense of the most profound gratitude to the supreme ruler of the Universe, that I now confess to you, that I am not under that state of tyrannical thraldom, and inhuman captivity, to which too many of my brethren are doomed, but that I have abundantly tasted of the fruition of those blessings, which proceed from that free and unequalled liberty, with which you are favored, and which, I hope you will willingly allow, you have received from the immediate hand of that being, from whom proceedeth every good and perfect gift.

Sir, suffer me to recall to your mind that time in which the arms and tyranny of the British crown were exerted with every powerful effort in order to reduce you to a state of servitude; look back, I entreat you, on the variety of dangers to which you were exposed; reflect on that time in which every human aid appeared unavailable, and in which even hope and fortitude wore the aspect of inability to the conflict, and you cannot but be led to a serious and grateful sense of your miraculous and providential preservation; you cannot but acknowledge, that the present freedom and tranquility which you enjoy, you have mercifully received, and that is the peculiar blessing of heaven.

This, sir, was a time in which you clearly saw into the injustice of a state of slavery, and in which you had just apprehension of the horrors of its condition, it was now, sir, that your abhorrence thereof was so excited, that you publicly held forth this true and invaluable doctrine, which is worthy to be recorded and remembered in all succeeding ages. "We hold these truths to be self-evident, that all men are created equal, and that they are endowed by their creator with certain inalienable rights, that among these are life, liberty and the pursuit of happiness."

Here, sir, was a time in which your tender feelings for yourselves had engaged you thus to declare, you were then impressed with proper ideas of the great valuation of liberty, and the free possession of those blessings to which you were entitled by nature; but, sir, how pitiable is it to reflect that although you were so fully convinced of the benevolence of the Father of mankind, and of his equal and impartial distribution of those rights and privileges which he had conferred upon them, that you should at the same time counteract his mercies, in detaining by fraud and violence so numerous a part of my brethren, under groaning captivity and cruel oppression, that you should at the same time be found guilty of that most criminal act, which you professedly detested in others with respect to yourselves.

Sir, I suppose that your knowledge of the situation of my brethren, is too extensive to need recital here; neither shall I presume to prescribe methods by which they may be relieved, otherwise than by recommending to you and all others, to wean yourselves from those narrow prejudices which you have imbibed with respect to them, and as Job proposed to his friends, "put your souls in their souls stead", thus shall your hearts be enlarged with kindness and benevolence towards them, and thus shall you need neither the direction of myself nor others, in what manner to proceed herein.

And now, sir, although my sympathy and affection for my brethren hath cause my enlargement thus far, I ardently hope that your candour and generosity, will plead with you in my behalf, when I make known to you, that it was not orginally my design; but that having taken up my pen, in order to direct to you as a present, a copy of an almanac, which I have calculated for the succeeding year, I was unexpectedly and unavoidably led thereto.

This calculation, sir, is the production of my arduous study in this my advanced stage of life; for having long had unbounded desires to become acquainted with the secrets of nature, I have had to gratify my curiosity herein through my own assiduous application to astronomical study, in which I need not to recount to you the many difficulties and disadvantages which I have had to encounter.

And although I had almost declined to make my calculation for the ensuing year, in consequence of that time which I had allotted therefor, being taken up at the Federal Territory, by the request of Mr. Andrew Ellicott, yet finding myself under several engagements to printers of this State, to whom I had communicated my design, on my return to my place of residence, I industriously applied myself thereto, which I hope I have accomplished with correctness and accuracy, a copy of which I have taken the liberty to direct to you, and which I humbly request you will favorably receive, and although you may have the opportunity of perusing it after its publication, yet I chose to send it to you in manuscript previous thereto, that thereby you might not only have an earlier inspection; but that you might also view it in my own hand-writing.

And now, sir, I shall conclude and subscribe myself, with the most profound respect, your most obedient humble servant,

B. BANNEKER.

THOMAS JEFFERSON, Secretary of State, Philadelphia.

N.B. Any communication to me, may be had by a direction to Mr. Elias Ellicott, merchant, in Baltimore Town.[6]

In reply Jefferson said:

PHILADELPHIA, Aug. 30, 1791.

Sir,—I thank you sincerely for your letter of the 19th instant, and for the Almanac it contained. Nobody wishes more than I do to see such proofs as you exhibit, that nature has given to our black brethren talents equal to those of the other colours of men, and that the appearance of a want of them is owing only to the degraded condition of their existence both in Africa and America. I can add with truth that no one wishes more ardently to see a good system commenced for raising the condition both of their body and mind to what it ought to be, as fast as the imbecility of their present existence, and other circumstances which cannot be neglected, will

[6] Martha E. Tyson's, *Banneker, the Afric-American Astronomer*, 39–45.

admit. I have taken the liberty of sending your Almanac to Monsieur de Condorcet, Secretary of the Academy of Sciences at Paris, and member of the Philanthropic Society; because I considered it a document to which your whole colour had a right for their justification against the doubts which have been entertained of them.

I am, with great esteem, sir, your most obedient servant,

THO. JEFFERSON.

MR. BENJAMIN BANNEKER, near Ellicotts' lower Mills, Baltimore County.[7]

Writing to Condorcet a little later, moreover, he further supports this position as to the impression which Banneker's letter had made.

We have now in the United States a Negro, the son of a black man born in Africa and a black woman born in the United States, who is a very respectable mathematician. I procured him to be employed under one of our chief directors in laying out the new Federal City on the Potomac and in the intervals of his leisure, while on that work, he made an almanac for the next year, which he sent me in his own handwriting, and which I enclose to you. I have seen very elegant solutions of geometrical problems by him. Add to this that he is a very worthy and respectable member of society. He is a free man. I shall be delighted to see these instances of moral eminence so multiplied as to prove that the want of talents observed in them, is merely the effect of their degraded condition, and not proceeding from any difference in the structure of the parts on which intellect depends.[8]

Writing later, to Joel Barlow, however, Jefferson showed that he was insincere. He said:

"Bishop Gregoire wrote to me on the doubts I had expressed five or six and twenty years ago, in the *Notes on Virginia*, as to the grade of understanding of the negroes. His credulity has made him gather up every story he could find of men of color (without distinguishing whether black, or of what degree of mixture), however slight the mention, or light the authority on which they are quoted. The whole do not amount, in point of evidence, to what we know

[7] Ford edition of *Jefferson's Writings*, III, 138.
[8] Ford edition of *Jefferson's Writings*, V, 377.

ourselves of Banneker. We know he had spherical trigonometry enough to make almanacs, but not without the suspicion of aid from Ellicot, who was his neighbor and friend, and never missed an opportunity of puffing him. I have a long letter from Banneker, which shows him to have had a mind of very common stature indeed. As to Bishop Gregoire, I wrote him a very soft answer. It was impossible for doubt to have been more tenderly or hesitantingly expressed than that was in the *Notes on Virginia*, and nothing was or is further from my intentions, than to enlist myself as the champion of a fixed opinion, where I have only expressed a doubt. St. Domingo will, in time, throw light on the question."[9]

Anticipating the most earnest advocates of peace, the promoters of education at public expense, and reformers of legislation, Banneker published to the world in 1793 as an improvement on the Federal Constitution the following peace plan, to which the war-ridden nations of today might well look for the solution of their problems:

"Among the many defects which have been pointed out in the federal constitution by its antifederal enemies, it is much to be lamented that no person has taken notice of its total silence upon the subject of an office of the utmost importance to the welfare of the United States, that is, an office for promoting and preserving perpetual peace in our country.

"It is to be hoped that no objection will be made to the establishment of such an office, while we are engaged in a war with the Indians, for as the War-Office of the United States was established in time of peace, it is equally reasonable that a Peace-Office should be established in time of war.

"The plan of this office is as follows:

"I. Let a Secretary of Peace be appointed to preside in this office, who shall be perfectly free from all the present absurd and vulgar European prejudices upon the subject of government; let him be a genuine republican and a sincere Christian, for the principles of republicanism and Christianity are no less friendly to universal and perpetual peace, than they are to universal and equal liberty.

"II. Let a power be given to this Secretary to establish and maintain free schools in every city, village and township of the

[9] *Ibid.*, IX, 261.

United States; and let him be made responsible for the talents, principles, and morals of all his school-masters. Let the youth of our country be carefully instructed in reading, writing and arithmetic, and in the doctrines of a religion of some kind; the Christian religion should be preferred to all others; for it belongs to this religion exclusively to teach us not only to cultivate peace with all men, but to forgive, nay more—to love our very enemies. It belongs to it further to teach us that the Supreme Being alone possesses a power to take away human life, and that we rebel against his laws, whenever we undertake to execute death in any way whatever upon any of his creatures.

"III. Let every family in the United States be furnished at the public expense, by the Secretary of this office, with a copy of an American edition of the Bible. This measure has become the more necessary in our country, since the banishment of the Bible, as a school-book, from most of the schools in the United States. Unless the price of this book be paid for by the public, there is reason to fear that in a few years it will be met with only in courts of justice or in magistrate's offices; and should the absurd mode of establishing truth by kissing this sacred book fall into disuse, it may probably, in the course of the next generation, be seen only as a curiosity on a shelf in Mr. Peale's museum.

"IV. Let the following sentences be inscribed in letters of gold over the door of every home in the United States:
The Son of Man Came into the World, Not To Destroy Men's Lives, But To Save Them.

"V. To inspire a veneration for human life, and an horror at the shedding of human blood, let all those laws be repealed which authorize juries, judges, sheriffs, or hangmen to assume the resentments of individuals, and to commit murder in cold blood in any case whatever. Until this reformation in our code of penal jurisprudence takes place, it will be in vain to attempt to introduce universal and perpetual peace in our country.

"VI. To subdue that passion for war, which education, added to human depravity, have made universal, a familiarity with the instruments of death, as well as all military shews, should be carefully avoided. For which reasons, militia laws should everywhere be repealed and military dresses and military titles should be laid aside: reviews tend to lessen the horrors of a battle by connecting them with the charms of order; militia laws generate idleness and vice, and thereby produce the wars they are said to prevent; military dresses facinate the minds of young men, and lead them from serious and useful professions; were there no uniforms, there would probably be no armies; lastly military titles feed vanity, and keep up ideas in the mind which lessen a sense of the folly and miseries of war.

"In the seventh and last place, let a large room, adjoining the federal hall, be appointed for transacting the business and preserving all the records of this office. Over the door of this room let there be a sign, on which the figures of a lamb, a dove, and an olive-branch should be painted, together with the following inscriptions in letters of gold:

Peace on Earth—Good-Will To Man.

Ah! Why Should Men Forget That They Are Brethren? Within this apartment let there be a collection of plough-shares and pruning-hooks made out of swords and spears; and on each of the walls of the apartment the following pictures as large as life:

"1. A lion eating straw with an ox, and an adder playing upon the lips of a child.

"2. An Indian boiling his venison in the same pot with a citizen of Kentucky.

"3. Lord Cornwallis and Tippo Saib, under the shade of a sycamore tree in the East-Indies, drinkin Madeira wine out of the same decanter.

"4. A group of French and Austrian soldiers dancing arm in arm, under a bower erected in the neighborhood of Mons.

"5. A St. Domingo planter, a man of color, and a native of Africa, legislating together in the same colonial assembly.

"To complete the entertainment of this delightful apartment, let a group of young ladies, clad in white robes, assemble every day at a certain hour, in a gallery to be erected for the purpose, and sing odes, and hymns, and anthems in praise of the blessings of peace.

"One of these songs should consist of the following beautiful lines of Mr. Pope:

"'Peace o'er the world her olive wand extends,
And white-rob'd innocence from heaven descends;
All crimes shall cease, and ancient frauds shall fail,
Returning justice lifts aloft her scale.'" [10]

[10] P. Lee Phillips, *The Negro, Benjamin Banneker, Astronomer and Mathematician, Plea for Universal Peace*, pp. 116–120 (reprinted from the Records of the Columbia Historical Society, XX, 1917).

The Mind of the Negro

LETTERS TO THE AMERICAN COLONIZATION SOCIETY [1]

The following letters are not all of the correspondence which the American Colonization Society had with Negroes presenting themselves as prospective emigrants to Liberia. Letters of various sorts typical of a large number of like import have been selected. Although these letters show the methods of colonization, the effect of the movement on the Negro, the hopes that it stimulated, and those that it blasted, the purpose of selecting these documents is not primarily to facilitate the study of colonization but to illuminate the study of the free Negro in the United States. Most of these persons who corresponded with the American Colonization Society were free or became free thereafter on the condition that they should emigrate to Liberia. The value here lies in what is said about the social and economic conditions of the free Negro, about whom such a little is known. These communications, then, constitute a valuable source for determining what this group was thinking, feeling, attempting, and accomplishing at that time.

The Negroes herein represented were largely in the South, where as slaves they had only such opportunities as they could snatch from begrudging masters, or when free only such as a hostile environment occasionally permitted them to enjoy. The Southern Negroes were easily influenced by the American Colonization Society and more easily reached because of the interest of certain whites of that section in the deportation of the free Negroes there and of such others

[1] With the exception of a few extracts from the *African Repository*, as footnotes will show, these letters were photocopied and verified from the files of the *Letters of the American Colonization Society*. These appear in bound volumes of four to each calendar year. These manuscripts were turned over to the Library of Congress a few years ago when the American Colonization Society decided practically to cease to function.

1

as might be liberated by conscience-stricken slaveholders.
Wherever the Negroes had enjoyed freedom in the North,
they did not easily embrace the idea of expatriating themselves.   The Northern Negroes usually took the position
that here their fathers fought, bled, and died for the country,
here they were born, and here they intended to die.   Occasionally, however, the American Colonization Society received
letters from prominent Negroes of the North expressing interest in colonization and seeking opportunities to go to
Liberia.   This was especially true during the fifties when the
heel of oppression upon the Negro in the North was becoming
heavier and heavier.   In writing about the particular thing
they had in mind these seekers mentioned other important
facts as to what was going on in most parts of the country.

These letters in themselves are more than interesting.
They give evidence especially of the mental development of
the Negroes in spite of their handicaps.   Most of them are
written in the poor English characteristic of the Negroes of
that time; but the chirography, which unfortunately cannot
be reproduced here, was sometimes very artistic, although the
orthography was too often unintelligible.   Excellent penmanship appears especially in the letters written by S. Wesley
Jones, J. B. Jordan, Benjamin S. Bebee, J. Theodore Holley,
Nathaniel Bowen, and John F. Cook.

FROM ABRAHAM CAMP

This is an extract of a letter from one of the free Negroes
mentioned in the letter of Mr. McIntosh to the American
Colonization Society, and confirms the statement therein given.

LAMOTT, ILLINOIS TERRITORY, July 13th, 1818.

I am a free man of colour, have a family and a large connection
of free people of colour residing on the Wabash, who are all willing to
leave America whenever the way shall be opened.   We love this
country and its liberties, if we could share an equal right in them;
but our freedom is partial, and we have no hope that it ever will be
otherwise here; therefore we had rather be gone, though we should
suffer hunger and nakedness for years.   Your honour may be
assured that nothing shall be lacking on our part in complying with

whatever provision shall be made by the United States, whether it be to go to Africa or some other place; we shall hold ourselves in readiness, praying that God (who made man free in the beginning, and who by his kind providence has broken the yoke from every white American) would inspire the heart of every true son of liberty with zeal and pity, to open the door of freedom for us also.[1]

I am, &c.

ABRAHAM CAMP.

Elias B. Caldwell, Esq.
Secretary of the Colonization Society of the United States.

FROM JOHN B. RUSSWURM

Rev. R. R. Gurley.[1]

Russwurm was the first Negro in the United States to receive a degree from a college. He was graduated at Bowdoin in the class with John P. Hale who served later as United States Senator from Maine. Russwurm was not at first interested in African colonization, but later emigrated to Liberia and became one of the most prominent functionaries there.

NEW YORK, Feb. 26, 1827.

Rev. Sir,

Owing to an absence of many weeks from Boston, your interesting letter of the 25th December, never came to hand until some weeks after its date. Sometime since then, has been occupied in transmitting its contents to distant friends, and awaiting their answers. All whose advice I have consulted on the subject, are of the opinion, that at present, it would not be advisable to accept the liberal offer of your Board of Managers. Many reasons are brought forward, by them, which are not necessary to be here inserted. I can assure you that among the number consulted is Mr. C. Stockbridge of Maine; whose views are considerably altered, since his address to you.

With a high sense, of the liberal offer of your Board of Managers

I remain yours,

Rev. Sir with respect,
JNO. B. RUSSWURM.

[1] Amer. Col. Society. *Colonization Reports*, Vol. I, page 116.
[2] *Letters received, the American Colonization Society*, 1827.

FROM A FREE NEGRO IN SAVANNAH

The following is an extract from a letter from a free man of color in Savannah, highly esteemed for his intelligence and piety, according to the American Colonization Society.

Sept., 1831

"I have always viewed the principle on which the Society was grounded, as one of much policy, though I saw it was aided by a great deal of benevolence. And when viewing my situation, with thousands of my coloured brethren in the U. States, who are in a similar situation, I have often wondered what prevented us from rising and with one voice, saying, we will accept the offer made us at the risk of sacrificing all the comforts that our present situation can afford us. I have often almost come to the conclusion that I would make the sacrifice, and have only been prevented by the unfavourable accounts of the climate. I have always heretofore, viewed it as a matter of temporal interest, but now I view it spiritually. According to the accounts from Liberia, it wants help, and such as I trust I could give, though ever so little. I understand the branches of a Wheelwright, and Blacksmith, and Carpenter, I also have good ideas of Machinery and other branches. I trust also, were I to go there, I would add one to the number of advocates for Religion. I will thank you to inform me what things I should take for the comfort of myself and family. I dont expect to go at the expense of the Society, and therefore hope to be allowed to take something more than those who do not defray their own expenses." [1]

OPINIONS OF A FREE MAN OF COLOR IN CHARLESTON

This letter was published in the *African Repository* in October, 1832, with this comment by the editor:

We have received a communication from a respectable free coloured man, of Charleston, which contains some thoughts which merit the serious consideration of all his brethren. May the noble spirit of devotedness which he manifests to the good of mankind, soon animate ten thousand of his coloured brethren, that they may go forth, not merely to improve their own condition, but to relieve and bless the long afflicted and degraded children

[1] *African Repository*, VII, page 216.

of Africa. We have omitted some sentences in this article, and made some slight corrections; not affecting materially the sense of the writer. His remarks have reference to the three following heads:

I. A Brief Inquiry into the propriety of the Free People of Colour migrating to Liberia, or elsewhere.

II. The objections urged by many of the Coloured People against emigration.

III. The good likely to result to those who may determine to emigrate.

1st. When we reflect upon the laws of Ohio,[1] that expel from her territory our Brethren—when we look to Virginia, to Maryland, to Alabama and to Tennessee, we must candidly confess, that we have much fearful apprehension, in regard to the laws that may be enacted, bearing heavily upon us, even in our own dear Carolina, which generously cherishes all her inhabitants and gives them support and employment, in all of the various and useful branches of mechanism, without regard to colour or condition. There are many callings, in which the coloured people in Carolina have a decided preference; in some cases they have no competitors; how long this favorable state of things will remain, we are not prepared to say—time alone can correctly decide in this matter.[2] This is an era, however, in our affairs, that we cannot shut our eyes to, and it must appear to the philosopher, the christian, and the sagacious politician, a period of deep and anxious solicitude, as regards the future prospects, hopes and interests of a people little known, but as a nuisance—mere laborers in the most menial capacity; at best a people who seldom deserve notice, or the exercise of charitable acts bestowed on them. Their friends and their foes both desire the removal of the free people of colour; although it is a fact not denied but by a very few, that the descendants of Africa, when transplanted in a country favorable to their improvement, and when their advantages are equal to others, seldom fail to answer all of the ends suited to their capacity, and in some instances rise to many of the virtues, to the learning and piety of the most favored nation. Yet, alas! the prevalence of popular prejudice against our colour, (which

[1] He refers here especially to the "Black Laws" of Ohio enacted to prohibit the emigration of free Negroes to that State and to restrict those already there.

[2] The Negro mechanics and artisans in South Carolina almost had a monopoly in their field there before the Civil War. Some said that the free Negroes of Charleston were better off than those of New York City.

is the more surprising, as it is well known that God alone creates different classes of men, that he may be adored and worshipped by all in the spirit of truth, without regard to complexion) has almost invariably stood as a barrier to our advancement in knowledge. Hence some of us appear to be useless,* and when it is considered that we are a large body of people, growing rapidly every day, without that improvement which the present age seems to require, in moral virtue and intellectual attainments; indeed, when we examine our own conduct, and that of our brethren, and compare the advantages we do actually possess, with so many bright examples before us of christianizing and improving the condition of mankind, both far and immediately under our eyes, we cannot but enquire "how can these things be?" My friends, if we will venture to look around us, we will behold the most encouraging proofs of happiness in the emigrants from Europe to this country. You have no call to look farther than our city (Charleston) to witness the most lively encouragements given to emigrants.* Many who arrive here very poor, are soon made rich: (and so it will be with us in Liberia) enterprising, industrious individuals, also families incorporating themselves in the community, enjoying all the blessings peace can confer on society, and soon successfully advancing on the high road to wealth and respectability, whilst we sink daily in the estimation of all.—Our apparently inactive habits may, in a great measure be attributed to this reason—"That we have no opportunity for the cultivation of our minds by education." As a matter of course, generally speaking, we lose all regard for any, but our individual self * * * * * * *—satisfied with every moral privation, with this certain conviction in our hearts, that our children are likely to be much worse situated than we are—as we ourselves are not as well situated in many respects as our parents were. The next enquiry is, what are we to do? I answer honestly and without hesitation, migrate to Liberia, in preference to any other country, under the protecting hand and influence of the Colonization Society. Here comes my second proposition; a consideration of the objections many have to emigrating to a country whose inhabitants are shrouded in deep ignorance—whom long and deep-rooted custom forbids us to have social intercourse with in the various relations of civilized life upon fair and equal terms of husband and wife, and whose complexion is darker than many of ours. But in all this, my friends, there is no reasonable ground of

* Except it may be when we are employed as laborers.
* Without any tax whatever, whilst we pay a heavy one.

objection to your removal to a country more adapted to promote your interests, because a very plain reason presents itself for such removal—and that is, in Liberia you will enjoy moral and political liberty. Besides, the heralds of the cross who first preached salvation to the benighted sons of Africa, were white men, and numbers of ladies also withdrew themselves from the beauties of highly polished circles in Europe to accompany their husbands in spreading the light in dark places. Those who contribute in money to carry on the splendid work of colonization and religion, who sacrifice their health on the shrine of humanity and deprive themselves of all earthly comforts, even stare death in the face, and prefer to die in the attempt, rather than relinquish the spread of virtue and religion amongst this very people you affect to despise—they are white. Who are they at this very period, rearing up an establishment at Liberia, that bids fair under the protecting smiles of Providence, to crush for ever the monster (the slave trade) that has led to captivity, and chains, and perpetual disgrace, our brethren, who, although formed in the image of God, are doomed in most countries, Liberia excepted, to degradation and servitude? They are white men. Surely this is at least one strong reason that should induce you, cheerfully to migrate to a country, where you can possess all of the importance of free citizens; in fact, all your objections dwindle into insignificance, in view of this one fact stated above. Besides, locating in Liberia, does not necessarily compel you to form private alliance in families, that you dislike; on the contrary, there is no country where you could indulge your own opinions in this respect with more freedom, than in that land of equality.—If you do go, and I hope in my heart all of us may speedily go—will we not go with our families and friends; cementing more strongly the bond of our connections, our customs, and our habits. Look for example to the Jews and other ancient people; scattered all over the world; look at our own situation, wherever we are placed: we see no innovation, nothing likely to break in and change the existing face of society.

III. Much good is likely to result to those who are meek and humble, who can see the advantages of liberty and equality, with the courage to embark in an enterprise, under such favorable circumstances. This is the truth, which is useful for all of us to know, and I have endeavored briefly to lay it before you, for your reflection, and if you once bring your minds to serious reflection, your friends will never blush—no—never under any circumstances, on account of dissensions on your part. Surely, my brethren, there are very strong reasons for us to go—yes go—and invoke Jehovah for his favorable protection to you, and to that country which holds out to us, and to our children, forever, protection, in life, liberty, and property—beside every honor of office, within the gift of a free people.   He who holds in the hollow of his hand the destiny of nations, will be with you, and will bless you, with health and vigor, to contribute your personal services of pious example, to improve the country that invites you to possess its soil.   Moreover, you will have the great privilege of sharing in your own government, and finally of becoming a perfectly free and independent people. And where would you go (go you must, sooner or later) to look for this noble privilege—the power of electing your officers or removing them when need requires.   Yes, my brethren, perhaps much depends on your present zeal and activity for success—and if God be with us, and I have a lively hope that he influences and directs you in this matter, before long the emigrants to Liberia, will become a distinguished nation; and who can prophesy and foretell the future destiny of Liberia.   The day, however, may not be far distant, when those who now despise the humble, degraded emigrants to Liberia, will make arrangements with them, to improve navigation, to extend commerce, and perhaps we may soon conduct and carry on our trade with foreign nations in our own bottoms without molestation or fear.   Such, my brethren, are some of the high expectations to be derived from a well established colony in Liberia, and to you Carolinians, all eyes are directed, all hearts are uplifted to God in prayer, to know what course your good sense will induce you to pursue, under existing circumstances.   Your reputation as a body of first-rate mechanics, is well known; distinguished for your industry and good behaviour, you have with you, carpenters, millers, wheel-wrights, ship builders, engineers, cabinet makers, shoe makers, tailors, and a host of others, all calculated at once to make you a great people.   In Liberia you can erect a temple to worship God, in the beauty of holiness; without fear you can set up, and protect your sacred altars, and pour out the orisons of the devout and pious heart before them, in praise and thanksgiving to God.   In Liberia, you can establish Academies and Colleges, to instruct youth in Theology, in Physic, and in Law. You will there know no superiors but virtue, and the laws of your country—no religion but the revealed revelation of God—and recollect all of this is for you yourselves.[1]

A South Carolinian.

[1] *African Repository*, VIII, pages 239–243 (Oct. 1832).

FROM JOHN JONES

The following letter, like that of many others addressed to the American Colonization Society, had no particular bearing on the deportation of Negroes except to express interest in the movement. The aim here is rather to secure the aid of the Colonization Society in supplying the various needs of Negroes so harassed and harried by foes without and within.

PHILADELPHIA, Jany 30th 1839.

Respected Sir, As I believe you to be a gentleman of Enlarged Benevolence, & a Friend to the Colored Race of People, I beg leave to address you, with the hope that you might be interested in our behalf—I Refer you to Rev. R. R. Gurly (he is acquainted with my views) of Washington, Rev. Docr Benj. Kurtis & Rev. John G. Morris of Baltimore—Rev Docr Bachman, Honl James Hamilton Rev Bishop Bowen, Rev. Docr Gadsden of My Native City, Charleston, S.C—Rev Stephen A. Nealey Rev Albert Barns of this City—I write briefily State to you Sir our greviances—I am Pastor of the Evangelical Lutheran Church, St. Paul in this City, Philadelphia. The church was got up through Individual Enterprise—it was dedicated to the worship of Almighty God by Rev Docr P. F. Mayer & other clergymen of this city—it is near two years since I was persuaded by the highest authority in the Lutheran Connection in this City to Convey the church into the hands of white Gents with the promise that if I comply, the debts of the church would be paid. In obedience to this Command, the property of St. Paul church, was regularly conveyed to Martin Beuhler, C. Schrach & Joseph Devors Esquire in Trust, for the Congregation—The Trustees, at the same time gave their written agreement to raise $1300—the amt due by the church—during the Popular Excitement in this City, in May last. The same high authority that required, The church be conveyed to respectable Gentlemen desired, that the organ, which was Erected in the church & which was partly paid for, should be taken down & Returned to the Builder,—hard as this order was—on the renual of the promise, that if I comply—the debts of the Church whould be paid, the organ was Removed immediately—We had a Fair in Progress—that perhaps whould have assited to pay of The demands of The Church—it was advertised in the Public Papers to be Exhibited in May last—But the Burning of The Pennsylvania Hall prevented it—The Lady who

had the management of the affair was persuaded, during the
Excitement to dispose of the article at private sale—She listened to
the persuasion & sold that which Cost much Labor & pain for $30
—Here I received an appointment as Missionary in This City with
an allowance of $100 per year & Received $25 for which I will Ever
feel grateful—But mark what follows—1 The Church was conveyed
Messrs. Beuhler, Shrach and Devors. They gave their written
agreement to raise $1300 as soon as possible to pay the debts—
2 The organ was taken away from us, with the promise that our
debts whould be paid—3 The Trustees persuaded me to give up the
$30—the Fair sold for—and $50—My allowance to Them to pay a
pressing demand of $80 against the Church—Soon after that last
act was done the Trustees cut loose from us—& send us adrift to do
as well as we can—I have called the Creditors together & lay the
whole matter before them—although the Trustees advised them to
sacrifice our Little Lien—They are not disposed to do so and has
given us Time to Look up Friends—to save our Church—$350 is
pressing—will you be so kind Sir as to assist us—if you will purchase
our church or give us 2 or 3 years to pay—or give us a donation to
assist in Extracating a Society of Poor Helpless Colored People you
will do a Last-Benefit to us, were you can an opportunity to inspect
our Conduct & advise us in your philanthropic project our happiness.

Respectfully in Behalf of St Paul Evangelical

Congregation John Jones—Boston 184 Locust Street.

I have seen your benevolent proposal in the public paper. If you
perform such an act as I have proposed, it undoubtedly will give
us confidence in your offers—Besides you you can, inspect our
Conduct—you will have a House open to you for Lectures to us
and we can confidently look up to those who will help us—if you
think John Jones favorably of the plan & act proptly you will not be
disappointed—2 Feby.[1]

FROM A SOUTH CAROLINIAN

WASHINGTON, March 6, 1839.

Respected Sir:—I claim the privilege of a South Carolinian to
address you, and to beg, sir, that you will interest yourself in behalf
of many respectable colored people, natives of South Carolina, who
are digging out a miserable existence in the northern cities; very
few of these are comfortable, and most of them are anxious to

[1] *Letters received by the American Colonization Society*, January to March, 1838, No. 88.

return home, sweet home, to our dear Carolina, but are prevented by the enactment of law.[1] From careful observation and acquired facts, permit me, sir, to state that I believe it is the interest, as well as the dictates of humanity, that the laws be repealed, which prevents the native Carolinians returning to their home, if they desire it. I am free to say, that not one of us, who left Charleston with high expectations to improve our condition, in morals, virtue or useful enterprising pursuits of industry, but have entirely failed in their expectations, in fact, so different is the living at the north from that of the south, (I never had the most distant idea of the depravity, in all its most varied and complicated forms of wickedness, until I settled in New York and Philadelphia—there is no such wickedness in Charleston,) that Carolinians cannot live comfortably at the north, for this very plain reason: The manners, habits, and pursuits of the people are so vastly different. The Carolinian, at home, engaged in pursuing some respectable occupation, sometimes is grieved that he is not sufficiently protected by law—he removes to Philadelphia or New York, for the enjoyment of privileges there, which are denied him at home. But alas, he fails to acquire by removal the reasonable desires of his heart. He does not find happiness in these cold regions, where prejudice against the colored complexion reigns triumphant, no matter what a man professes himself to be, he keeps far off from colored people; most of us are without employment in winter, and in spring and summer, however careful we may be, are entirely too short, with the little business we have, for us to live and provide against the long tedious inclement winters of the north; I do humbly think, sir, that it becomes the duty of every christian, patriot, and philanthropist of South Carolina, especially, at this particular time, when there is no cause whatever to reject us, the repenting prodigals, from the privilege of returning home. I repeat my most solemn conviction, that I believe it is the interest, as well as the dictates of humanity, that all of us who are anxious, be permitted and encouraged to return home. In this matter I speak the language of a South Carolinian, who loves the soil where first he learned to life up his feeble voice in praise to God and his country. Besides, the repeal of the law will disarm the north of a very important and powerful weapon, now wielded against you; this very law which denies to us native born South Carolinians the privilege to return within her borders, and that too, without crime, operates against

[1] Many Negroes who went North from Charleston often returned prior to the time when there was enacted a law preventing them from so doing.

you, can do you no possible good, whilst it inflicts a very serious injury upon us—we are your friends. When any of us stand up in defence of our state, which is often the case, we are calmly asked if the customs and privileges are such as you represent them to be in Carolina, why do you not go back to Charleston and enjoy them, why do you remain with us? If South Carolina repeal the law which bears heavily upon us, without doing good in any one single instance, the world will sing praises to your magnanimity, your own approving conscience will cheer you for the part you might take to effect its repeal, besides the blessings of many honest hearts, who will return to the sweet embraces of long separated friendship.

So far as regards myself, who was deluded away from home by offers of large salary, &c., for missionary services, all the promise has proved to be base imposition and cruel cheat; it is true that I had some privilege to travel, which I improved carefully, looking out for a home and in reviewing the condition of the colored peopl. In this also I have been sadly disappointed; although I have visited almost every city and town, from Charleston, South Carolina, to Portland, Maine, I can find no such home—and no such respectable body of colored people as I left in my native city, Charleston. The law in my adopted city, Philadelphia, when applied to colored people, in opposition to white people, is not as good as in Charleston, unless the former has respectable white witness to sustain him. Property colored people generally transact their business through the agency of white people. They cannot rent a house in a court or square occupied by white people unless it is with the consent of white neighbors—we are shamefully denied the privilege to visit the Museum, &c.—all the advantage that I can see by living in Philadelphia is, that if my family is sick, I can send for a doctor at any time of the night without a ticket.

Respectfully, your ob't serv't,   —————————

P. S.—A good remedy—if you desire a Carolinian to have an 'exalted ardour for his native state,' permit him to live a few years in Philadelphia, New York, or any other northern city, and depend on his daily exertions for his daily bread, and I will warrant, if he is permitted to return to Charleston, the process will make a perfect cure.

N. B.—I do not know the names of the gentlemen who compose the Charleston delegation in the legislature of South Carolina—and if I did, my time would not permit me to address every individual member, unless I had a printed circular, and do not know if it would be advisable for me to do so whilst I am living in the north. Still, sir, I will be glad if you will furnish the names of the whole assembly—please put it on board one of the Philadelphia packets, it will save the postage.[1]

FROM JAMES DREW

CLARKSVILLE, MECKLENBURG CTY. VA.Mar 27th1847.

Dear Sir

after having consulted Mr John Nelson (who is a member of the Colonization Society with who I am very intermit acquainted residing in this neigbourhood) on the subject of emigrating to Liberia, that in consequence of this being the first offer made to him on such an occasion together with his not being well acquainted with the nature of some late alterations that he fealt apprehensive had been made in the rules connected with that institution; he advis that you should be writin to; who would as Agent give every necessary information and instruction concerning the matter, therefore in as much as myself wife & five children, Bery Lewis, wife & two children who is my son in law, also two young men making in all 13, all of whom are free born persons of color, and are desireous to go to liberia, and as we are in rather limited circumstances to affect such an object at this time without assistance, we wish to know what assistance that the society according to their rules are allow, we do not wish to be misunderstood that we want to be hired, to go to liberia, for we are ————— for going so much so that we had rather go within ourselves if able, therefore whatever assistance we may obtain from any source (if any) may be considered in good degree as a loan, if provided providential aid should secure our health & though it may seem strange to some, to find us rather behind hand at this time (securityship has been the cause), notwithstanding from these ressons I flatter myself we have improved, and if we should fortunatly git there and by using industry and good economy prosper (which I hope we shall) I feal assurd that we shall exercise a similar degree of charity to what we have here been accustomd, which has been to subscribe a benevolent cause in nearly all its bearings; notwithstanding I am considerbly advancd in age, I wish to go with my children to a land which seems throug the kind hand of providence to be destind for the colord man, and as I am favord with a tolerable libural education for colord persons

[1] *African Repository*, 15, pp. 178–180.

in this region of country (which you may some what judge from this, and in addition have figurd through Pikes Arithmetic also fealing assurd that I have been together with two others of my family changd from nature to grace) with these advantages if I should git there and enjoy health and strength of mind I trust that I may prove instrumental in doing some good in that noble cause (colonization) Scripture being my guide.

In as much as we would be glad to go in the next on the trip following in the Liberia Packet we ought to of writin before this so waiting for Mr. Nelsons answer after soliciting him on the subject we had to defur until this therfore I hope you will answer this speedily, and please condecend to remember our case at a Throne of Grace. Also in as much as their is som three or four other families that talks much of going and amongst some of which owns considerable property we wish to know the terms of carying property, I have between 20 & 30 African Repositorys of that number their is one of a No. that appears to wanting, Vol. 21 No. 10 if it should still be wanting I will send it [1]

Clarksville Mg. Cty. Aug. 12th 1847

Dear Sir

In answer to yours of the 4th Inst. I can say confidently that about 12 person will meet the packet at Norfolk about the 1st of Septr. (namely) myself 60 years of age. Mary my wife 47, B. Lewis 27, Delila his wife 24, my Son Peyton 21, my daughter Sophia C, 18, my Son Rufus 14, my daughter Evelina 11, my daughter Julia 8 B. Lewis, Son Wm. 7, his daughter Mary 3, John Quinichett about 40, which makes up the 12—(6 males & 6 females;) Smithea and family are rather uncertain, though If he should come, he has 6 in family, himself about 30 years old, his wife Mary Jean about 30 and has 2 Daughters, & 2 Sons. Their are 2 others talks of coming—Willie Carter about 35, and John Cousins about 22 or 3. Their is between 50 and 100 persons around us here, that seems to be very much in faver of migrating to Liberia, if provided we should after fairly investigating the matter give a faverable account,

Yours &C.

James Drew.

Mr. Noah Fletcher—
Colon.Rooms, Washington City, D. C.[2]

[1] *Letters received by the American Colonization Society*, January to March, 1847, No. 248.

[2] *Ibid.*, July to September, 1847, No. 196.

From Bureell W. Mann

The letters of Bureell W. Mann present in detail a most pathetic case, typical, however, of thousands of ambitious slaves who, after having been imbued with the spirit of freedom offered by the prospect of African colonization, struggled hard and too often struggled in vain to reach this "land of promise." He was a slave of John Cosby of Richmond. Yet in spite of his bondage he had picked up some fragments of education, as these letters written by him will show, and he was serving his people as a minister in the Southern Methodist connection. His superiors, however, did not seem to think well of his ambition to go as missionary to Liberia. In addition to the strong presentation of his own case, the letters give valuable facts as to what was going on among the members of both races in Richmond.

Richmond Va June 21st 1847.

Dear Respected Brother I write to in form you—that I am what is here term a private African Slave Minister belonging to Mr. John Cosby of this city and My determination if possible is to go to Liberia let it cost what it may   This resolution I came to for more than 9 months a go and I have made Many Applications to our Methodist Ministers here to send me as a missionary to some vacant field in Africa and they Spurn me away Saying that they could do nothing for me in these respects if I were not a free Man. So I continue asking them up to the 30th of last May at which time they agreed to send Me as a Mission but they did not agree to raise the funds to buy me, if it should be needful.   So now I intend to ask My Master to let me go on free cost to said Liberia and should he deny me then will I beg him to sell me for that purpose and should I do this I wish to have the Good Brothers of Colonization Society to be here to buy me immediately for the purpose mensioned above Dear Sire I wish you to know that the only object I have in view is my God & the Glory of his Son and in these Southern States We African Sons in the church of God are Cut off for our part So that we can not become wise unto Salvation our selves and can not be the instrument in the hand of God in turning Many to Righteousness and the deprivation of church Rights & priviledges here has made me willing and ready to give up this part of the world & any other object for the Sake of Christ and the Glory of his people in

that continant   Dear Sire a potion of our Methodist Ministers of
the South has So repeatedly defeated me in my attempt that I
could not avoid writing to you hoping and praying that God may
help you to undertake My case and advocate My cause if needful
among the Northern Ministers and people   Dear Sire Mr. John
Cosby bought me about 17 years ago and Should he purpose to
sell me to myself or to the Society he will not charge more than
half as much as he then payed for me which would be about $150
for he only give $300 for me 17 years ago   Dear Sire you here
See the object which I have in view and if it is in your power to
come to Richmond now or in a short time you will please do So,
if not, you will please send Some one to this city to see Me and My
Master and if this can not be done I pray you Dear kind friend to
write to me and teach Me what to do or if not Write to Rev. Mr.
Edwards of Centenary church and teach him the facts that is here
written that he may call for me and hear my determination and
rewrite to you on My behalf & do whatever is proper to be done in
this matter.   My name is Bureell W. Mann now belonging to Mr.
John Cosby and now working at the tobacco factory of Mr. Daid
M. Branch on the bassin and attached to the Methodist church,
on union hill, in Richmond, under the charge of Rev. Joseph Carson.
My little Talent & usefulness can be obtained by writing but I
rather you would come your self or Send Some one if possible
I and am a poor christian here and wishing to get Good and do all
the Good I can while I live on the earth but there is a very Small
chants of doing Much Good in these Southern States——I ever
remain your humble Servant, in Christ Jesus, Bureel W. Mann [1]

RICHMOND VA June 27th 1847

Sire

Your letter of the 22d inst is received which gives me
great consolation to know that my case shall come under the inspection of wise & holy men who loves the African Race and are Striving
with a true heart to raise it from degradation & wo Sire I understand
from your letter that Mr. M. lain is now absent from home and I wish
to inform you that I am very thankful to you for this information
as well as puting yourself to the trouble of writing, I hope Sire that
you will continue to write whenever it is needful in these respects
I would Say for your instruction that My Master, in a few days
will leave Richmond to go to the Springs and there remain for Some
3 months and Should Mr. M.lain return home in 10 or 12 days from

[1] *Ibid.*, April to June, 1847, No. 242.

now he will have the opportunity to come, or write to me, or My Master as he may See proper and should he remain absent from home for more than 12 days you will please write me word and Should Master leave our city in a Shorter time I will write you word——Dear Sire it were my intention to write to Rev. George, Lane, & Tippett, of New York for some information as it relates to Missionaries, church Rights, and priviledges. as they are pointed out in the Methodist Discipline and Should I do So I hope they will give me information upon that Subject as well as needful Aid but this I have not done as yet   Answer this as Soon as you can and look for another in Short.

Yours in Christ, and in friendship

Bureell W. W. Mann. to Mr. M.lain & Fletcher [1]

RICHMOND VA. July 12th 1847.

Dear Respected   Secretary of Colonization Society

I now have the opportunity of sending you a letter by hands hoping at the same time that you will not take it amiss   I wish to inform you that I sent you a letter by the mail the 27th of June which were directed Washington City Colonization Room to Mr. Noah Fletcher and as I have not heard of it you will please to let me know that you have got it in the Answer of this letter and I will also inform you that my mind is the same now as it were at first and if any thing, I am more determine now, than I ever were God being my helper, I wish you to know that my Master is yet remaining in our city and has not gone to the Springs and Should you want more information of Me you will please write for it or if not Come to Richmond and you can learn more of Me than I am able to write please take my case and consider it as soon as you can for heaven Sake answer this forthwith

your humble servant in hast

BUREELL W. MANN

P. S.   Should my request Cause Mr. Mclain to come or Send Some person to see about the business mensioned in my first letter you will please write word before you come and let me know where I may see you, if you should Come or Send [2]

B. W. MANN

[1] *Ibid.*, April to June, 1847, No. 267.
[2] *Ibid.*, July to September, 1847, No. 33.

RICHMOND VA August 1st 1847

Dear Respected Brother & writer for the
Colonization Society

I humbly ask permission to write you again and I entreat you & the officers of said Society not to take it amiss but to hear me with love and great tenderness, here I once more offer myself to the Society to be it servant & Slave untill death on the Shores of Africa, here in these States, my way as a minister is So blockated in Religion that I can not become wise unto Salvation myself nor be instrumental in turning many others to Righeousness So this is the first beginning of my Sorrow Grieve & wo, in my first letter I labour to show what steps I intended to take in addressing My Master on the subject and should that plan be deemed improper in the judgment of the boad of Directors I will pospon it and take any other that you and the boad may judge best if you will write me word what to do and what plans to take in such a case Dear Sir I am a man that you know not and perhaps you rather I should get some Gentlemen to write for me and if it is prefered by you or the boad I wish you would write me word and give me information as to who I should get to write for me, if it is desired, by you, or the boad of directors, I know many Gentlemen that would write for me if it is requested but from being deceived by some in the commence-ment of my communication to the Society, that I at this time know not who to trust, however the Rev. Mr. Edwards of Centenary church in this city is one that you know and you can write to him in regard to this matter and if it pleases you & the boad that I should get Mr. Edwards to write what I have to say to the Society you will please do so as soon as you can, I am the same now as I were when I first wrote, if the Society has any use for me in any part of liberia, in any Colony, and will buy me for that purpose I am ready & willing now to go with the Agent of said Society Dear Sir I have receive one answer to my first letter and the writer informed me that you were absent from the city and promise to send me an Answer in your return, expecting you to come in the course of a month The other letters I have not receive any answer from at all The one Sent by hands I wish to hear from if possible and I wish you to answer this one forthwith as I am a little troubled about others being unanswered My Mind is still the same I am still a member of union church under the care of Rev. Joseph Carson Brother John Nettles & Richerson who are of this city & members of Said church I still belong to Mr. John Cosby now working at Mr.

David M. Branchs factory on the bassin near Mr. Dr. Mosbys
factory and has been attending the post office every day as I expect
to do hereafter, when you answer this always write to Bureell W.
Mann, and I shall be sure to get the letters
I am your true and humble servant

BUREELL W. MANN [1]

RICHMOND VA. September 13th 1847

Dear Sir

I deem it proper to write you again, as I has not heard from you, for
more than a month, and do not know whether, the Rev. Mclain, has
returned home.   Dear Sir, in your letter of August 3d, it seems that
you, expect him home, in a week or ten days, and as it has been
more, than a month, Since I receive your letter, I thought that Mr.
Mclain, had return home to the city, and my case were forgotten.
Dear Sir, My Mind is still the same now as it were, when I first
wrote and should the religion of Jesus Christ, in duce, the Colonization Society, to send Me to any one of Africas Vacant fields,
I am willing to go now, or at any time the Agents, of said Society,
May Call for Me, Finally, Dear Sirs, if a Missionary is wanting, for
the African fields, Here am I, Send Me, I will go with your aid,
God being My helper, if Mr. Mclain has gotten home, to washing-
ton, you will please Answer this letter forthwith, and oblige your
Most humble servant
Bureell W. Mann, To Mr. Noah Fletcher.[2]

RICHMOND VA. (Sept. ?) 18th 1847.

Dear Respected Brother

I receive your letter of the 13th inst which give me much satisfaction
of mind So fare, I am very thankful to God and to you for the
information and advice which I find in your letter   Sir I wish you
to know that when I first offered myself as a missionary it were to
the Missionary Society, thinking that they would buy me, for a
mission to liberia, or if not, give me some help, but they refered me,
to the Colonization Society, telling me, that Colonization had
bought Some mission for liberia, and it would buy me also.   I then
wrote to both The methodist missionaries Society & the Colonization, not knowing, at the same time, what it had done for
others, I think however that colonization will help me some, and I
do hope that the Lord may help the methodist Missionary Society

[1] *Ibid.*, July to September, 1847, No. 115.
[2] *Ibid.*, No. 134.

to do the best they can for me in these respects—My mind is now made up, to get my freedom the best way I can, and on the cheapest terms, I were willing to buy and pay for myself at first if I had the money, but I had no money then, and are not got any now and see no way to get any, in my present condition, it appears from reading your letter, that I might find a friend in our city who would lend me the money to buy myself, but if it is So, I judge, that you know them better than I do, for to my knowledge, I know not one I should be very Glad of the chanst, and thankful to God for the offer, you, in your letter, wish to know what wage I were geting and could still get, I must tell you Dear Sir, that I get non at all My Master who hires me out is now geting from 75 to 80 dollars a year for me and about ten years ago he use to get $150 for me a year but now the price is fell to 75 & 80 dollars a year, which I could get if I were a freeman. The man that now hire me, only pays me 75 cents a week for my boad, and I can see no way as yet, to better my case—I have once offere Myself, to my church, and by it tow ministers, the presiding Elder & Station preacher, and nothing has they done to My knowledge, for me, in this case, and if you think it proper, you will please write me word forthwith and I will offer to them the third time, My Master is now gone to the Springs and as soon as he shall return, I shall see him upon this subject and will write you word in Good time. it is my wishes to find out the Superintendent, Agent, of the Methodist Missionary Society I wish to know his name, & what town, or city, he now live, that I May beg a little and, from them, if you know, you will please write me word forthwith, or if not, you will please writ my case, to the above Agent, asking him at the same time, for a little aid, if I knew him and where he now lives, I would now write him myself— you will please answer this as soon as you can, Dear Sir Since I found you I believe that I have found a Friend

Your Most humble Servant in Love to God & all Mankind

BUREELL W. MANN [1]

RICHMOND VA. Sept. 21-1847

My Dear Sir

I write to inform you that if you know of any person or friend, who will buy me and let me work for them, untill, I can pay for myself, you will please get them, to do it, and after it is done, I will try to pay them, by working as Soon as I can. I am determine to do all

[1] *Ibid.*, July to September, 1847, No. 144.

I can Myself, and to get as many persons, as I can to help me, pay, and if it is meedful for me, to get a Note from My Master, certifying the Price, you, will please write me word, immediately, for I am expecting him every day to return from the Springs, to which, he is now gone—I ever Remain

Your humble Servant in the bounds of a peaful Gospel

B. W. MANN

of Richmond, Union Methodist church [1]

RICHMOND VA   Sept 30th 1847

Dear Sir

yours of the 21 inst is receive and I am very thanful to you for your advice & instruction   Dear Sir it appears that the Gentlemen refer to in your letter are not Station in the city of New York, and if they are, they has not Answer, So much as one letter, that I have written to them of late, for Since I recd your last letter I wrote five letters to them and has recd no answer at all   Three to Rev. Dr. Pitman one to Rev. George Lane the other to Rev. Thomas Bond D. D. the other one I has not written to as yet for want of opportunity   your name I have not mensioned in those letters at all, and I do not intend to mension it no where with out consulting you   Dear Sir I expect My Master home the first of October and if you or the Colonization Society has determined to buy me or any other Good friend you will please write me word as soon as you can for my master will want to see them and if it is needful for me to mension the Society or to call your name to My Master, when I Shall See him, you will please write me word also, and if you know any Gentleman in Richmind who will do it, you will please write to them, and let me know in the next letter who they is, yours in hast

BUREELL W. MANN [2]

RICHMOND VA   October 4th 1847

Dear Respected Secretary of Col. Society

I take this opportunity to inform you that My Master is Come and I have seen him upon the great Subject of which I have been writing, to day and he has consented for me to go to liberia and he seem to be very glad to find such a determination in me, when I first inform him, of the fact, he asked me, for what purpose I wanted to go to liberia,   I told him to preach the Gospel to the hethens,   The next question, that he ask me, were, What does you know about preach-

---

[1] *Ibid.*, July to September, 1847, No. 171.
[2] *Ibid.*, No. 174.

ing, I answered him, Sir, I can tell the hethen how to live in this world, and what they must do in order to go to heaven when they died, he then ask who were to send me, I then told him, the Missionary Society, he then said that I might go, and he would give me some thing, to help me likwise, I told him that I had determine to buy myself, and ask him what would he charge me, and he told me, about half of my value. I then ask him how much was that, he then told me not much, he said to me, that as soon as he see you or Some person whom you may send, he will give me up, and there will be no falling out, about the price, Dear Sir, I think that a white preacher who know much about liberia could get me, with out Price is they would See him them selves, and converse with him for he is an unconverted man whose mind is in a State to receive instruction from a preacher in regard to doing Good, again while he were talking he partly, told me that he would Set, all his Servant free and do a Good part by them, this still lead me to believe that I could be bought for, a little money, or non at all, and if you will Come yourself, or, Send any influenal Man, who unstand, African Woes, and can show them to my master, and then to plead with him So as to get me with word, with out any money charge for me, I will afterward, try by the help of God, to pay you, or them in work or in money, as may be requested. Dear Sir, I am a poor man but my religion induces me to believe that one kindness deserves another, I humbly thank the Lord & you for what has been already done, for me, and I pray that God may help you, to remember me always, & bless you & the whole Society evermore, Come Send, or Write, by the next mail, Should you Come or Send, Enquire for me, I still work at Mr. David M. Branch's factory, Ask for Bureell Mann or Bureell W. Mann at Branchs tobacco factory and any person will tell you, Your letter of Sept 13th requested me to let you know when I had seen my Master. This I have now done, please write me word by the next if you possibly can and do not fail I ever Remain your humble Servant in the bounds of a peaceful Gospel

BUREELL W. MANN [1]

RICHMOND VA October 10th 1847

My Dear & much Respected Friend

Your of Oct—4th is recd. and I have to inform you that my master charge me $400 and fifty dollars for myself which is $150 more than he give for me 16 years ago, having before

[1] *Ibid.*, October to December, 1847, No. 9.

told me on the 4th inst that he would take half of my value   Dear
Sir, you request me to write again, Saying that you would then
See what you Can do for me, now dear Sir if you can, and will, buy
me, I will work it out any way you Say, if, I can not pay you other
wise.   It is fully known in Richmond that I am going to liberia
and I am now labouring to get my church & Brethren to do their
ful duty in regard to me and as I has not Call your Name to my
white Brethren you will please write me word what to do & whether
I must Call it or not.   I recd. a letter from New York but I have no
indications as yet, for any aid you will please continue your communication to Bureell W. Mann untill you can instruct me more in
this matter   I partly promise them that I would give them Some
answer about the money this coming Tusday

Your Most humble Servant

BUREELL W. MANN

Write to me as quick as possible [1]

RICHMOND VA   October 17th 1847

My Dear Respected & kind friend

yours of the 8th & of the 13th inst. is Recd. and likwise the Repository and pamphlet, and I have to inform you that I am very
thankful to you, through Christ Jesus for them and the information
there in contain   I find it to be the very knowledge that My heart
Stood in need of and permit me to inform you that your pamphlet
has taken hold upon the hearts of many of my friends who has
read them and they here request me to write to you to send them
Some,   Saying that they will pay you any price for them, in Reason,
or write word to me, where and how, they can get them, and if you
think fit you can send Six pamphlets naming the Price and how you
can receive the money for them,   Dear Sir Since I last wrote I
have been trying to get my church & white Brethren to aid me in
my undertaken but as yet they have taken no action in the matter
More than to See My Master and to know the Price he charge for me
This evening My Pastor told me that the Methodist, South, could
not do any thing for me by way of buying, nor Sending me even
after I am bought   They Seem to Clear themselves of their duty in
these Respects and refers me to the northern Bishops & Missionary
Societies in said Point, and if you know any of the northern Bishops,
or northern Methodist Missionary Societies, you will be So Good and
kind as to teach me where they are, and their Names and the cities
or towns in which they live,   I thought from your advice, & the

[1] *Ibid.*, October to December, 1847, No. 30.

written Rule of the Methodist church, that the northern Bishops, & head men of the Methodist Missionary Society did live in New York, but My Pastor in conversation with me, to day made Some doubts, on my mind, in regard to where they live, and their names, he did not tell me of, after I had ask him, as many as 3 times, Dear Sir, I shall be very thankful to you if you will give me information how to write to Northern Missionary Board, or to its Bishops, and if the New York Missionary Board, is what is truly term, The northern Mission Board, you will please write me word by the next mail from washington, in order that my letter may get there this coming Wednsday, the very day that the Missionary Board is to meet. I mean, get to new york, The letter from Rev. Dr. Pitman Saith, that I with the Requisite recommendation can get employment in liberia, but he did not Say what that employment were, you can get the balence in my next. Your humble Emigrat in Christ Jesus my Lord

BUREELL W. MANN.[1]

RICHMOND VA   October 24th 1847

My Dear Respected Friend

I promise in My last letter to let you hear the balence of what I had to say, and in the first place, I wish to inform you that I has receive one letter only, in which the writer advises me to get Some benevolent persons, to write in Securing my freedom, and that extra efforts Should be use on my part to get the money as well as on the part of my friends, This letter is from Rev. Dr. Pitman of new york, he saith, that by persuing Such a course, Such a thing has been done for missionaries with the understanding, that said missionaries went to liberia, and he give me to understand that my Recommendation would be wanting, and Dear Sir, it is true, that I have never mension any thing about My charecter to you, nor the Rev. C. Pitman, and as I have been backard in So doing, you will please pardon me for my backwardness, and permit me at this time to Say a word or tow, inrelation to my Recommendation, Dear Sir, if you think it is wanting in the least, just write word, and any person can get it in full, and in quick time, and in regard to the extra efforts of which he Speak, I could use them, if I were already purchased and I could become successful perhaps, in geting Some of the money, toward Paying for Myself, but this can not be done yet awhile, Lest I Should give an offence to Some of my owners,

<hr>

[1] *Ibid.*, October to December, 1847, No. 54.

but I wish you to know, that should the Lord open the way for me, soon, I Shall have the opportunity to visit Many of the Sister churches, whom I know, will give me much aid. Mr. Pitman in his letter never said that I should not be sent as a Missionary to liberia, but that the Society would not allow Slaves to be bought with its funds I then wrote to him, to know if it were against the Rules to help a poor Slave preacher to buy himself, for their own purpose and if it were not, againts their Rules, would they aid me to the small sum as a copper a piece, from each member of Said Society, thinking that where as they could not do much, according to Rule, they could in great Mercy do a little, but to My knowledge they has not wrote to me Since Mr. Pitman informed me that the Mission Board in New York would meet on the 20th inst, which cause me in one instant to write, & the conversation that I had last Sunday with the Pastor & church likwise cause me, to write, for quick information from you, but since that time I thought that they were just trying me, to See if I were determine to go to liberia, The people every day is asking for your pamphlet & Repository, or information where they can buy them, again I wish to inform you that it is my purpose now to beg among the churches, and to do it by writing, untill I can have permission to go about myself, and Should I succeed in So doing would it be any harm to tell My friends to leave with you, whatever money they have to give me toward paying for myself & helping me on to liberia. My Dear kind friend permit to tell you that My mind is Made up to go as a missionary to liberia, if there is any way possible and ever Since I receive your first letter I submited my case into your hands, and in the hands, of a Good God (?) with the willingness to go, and do for going, any thing that may be charged me, by those who bought me for the above purpose and since my determination to go I have written to many but have not as yet, found them to be Such a great friend to me as you have been, Oh let your friendship & kindness continue toward me for I am poor & needy And May the Lord bless you in all things and save you in Glory is my prayer for Christ Sake, your very humble Servant, in Christ My Lord.

BUREELL W. MANN

you may answer both at the same time if you think proper [1]

---

[1] *Ibid.*, October to December, 1847, No. 84.

RICHMOND VA. November 9th 1847

My Dear Sir

I now write to know if Mr. Mclain has returned home and if he is, I wish him to know that I received his two last letters and that of the 24th of October made me fear much, but I still live in hopes that you will succeed in advocating my cause, I mean Rev. Mclain, Sir in your letter you Speaks of it being hard to Raise money for Such a purpose Dear Sir I always thought it to be a hard matter with the Southern Methodist to buy or to aid any one in such a case but I never thought it tow hard for the northern Methodist to advance the money or aid any one who has such a purpose in view as I have, therefore if you find it a hard matter with my own denomination both north & South, you will please try other denominations. I will go for any christian denomination who will help you, to get me out of this distress. The Repository is a pamphlet that our people love and they are desirous to take them by the year if it can be done and Likewise the an. Report. I think it is the wish of the color Female aiding Society to become Subscribers for Said Reports & pamphlets if it can be done you will please write me word and if it is pleasing to you, they will Pay their Subscrition to Mr. James C. Crane in advance, at the time appointed—and if any thing can be done in My case, now is the time to do it, if you can possibly. I have nothing now, and cant get chants, to go about in the churches to get the least aid and yet my master Call for his money and I wish you to know that I have got more discouragement from my own church than from any other but none of these things move me. if you See any way for me to go next January you will please Send me word

Yours ever truely

BUREELL W. MANN.[1]

RICHMOND VA November 21-1847

My Dear Respected Sir

I received yours of the 17th inst and from it I apprehend that you have gotten home. and I will inform you that the Cloud at the time, is very great and my way is more blockcated now than ever. I had hoped Some 18 days back that I should be bless to go next January in the Liberian Packet but the thought is gone out of my mind, in a very great degree. first because I have no money myself and seconly, because my present employers will not allow me any

[1] *Ibid.*, October to December, 1847, No. 173.

chants to go among my friends at the churches, to beg a little aid. and during your absence, the Rev. Mr. Ryland saw my master and asked him all about it, & when he, intended to give me up; & he said, as soon as the money is Paid. and ever since I ask my master's consent about going to Liberia. The man who has been hireing me is much closer & harder with me now than ever he were. So that you will perceive that in my present State I can not help myself nor get the opportunity to go & beg others to help me. I have written to the Bethel church in Baltimore for some aid and entreated them to leav it in your care & likewise to the color Methodist church in Washington but I have never Recd any answer & the churches here & in manchester has been expecting me to visit them for some aid. and my church would not give me a note for that purpose and said that they had no time to attend to me. I found Mr. Ryland to be the very friend of which you Speak in your letter of the 8th October he has given me a good advice and promises to help me pay, & use efforts to get others to help me. but not So with my church. & Preacher they want my Service in their church here, and of course they will not give me money, nor instruction to help me away from them to Heathens in Africa. The only Good time I could have to beg for aid in my case is on Sunday and then at the churches and this I ough to commenced tow week ago but this I have not done because it were out of my power. So I remain now in greater distress than when I first began to write to you. as I have put my case in your hands Some time back, and I Suppose that you have done, what you could, in presenting my case to others, & advocating my cause. and therefore as you See no way, for my request and know of none, I think I had better, take in the report, and let the people of Richmond know, that I can not go. Since I made up My Mind to go to Africa, there is about five persons going, or has determined to go, if I went, their names will be sent hereafter. Send me word how many times in a year will the Repository be Sent.

Yours in many tears
Bureel W. Mann

P. S. As you see no way as yet by which the money can be Raised you will please Send me word whether I must have my Clothes made, or to make any peparation for going [1]

[1] *Ibid.*, October to December, 1847, No. 174.

Richmond Va   November 28 1847

Dear Respected Sir

I will again write, Requesting you to excuse the failures which you find commited in my letters from time to time, as I am in great trouble, but I perceive from all your letters, that you have understood my intention thus fare.   Dear Sir, I wish to inform you that a woman & tow children are given up to go to Liberia Some 5 or 6 months ago but her mind were in a State of indecision, untill I visited her at which time She determined to go with her tow children her name is Gracy Ann Clark.   They are given up by Mrs. Robison. She Saith that, if I can go, the first of January, that She will go also, Mr. Albert Matthews got one of your pamphlet and it converted him, and he now Saith that he is ready & willing to go at any time. he is a freeman.   Mr. Sterling Ruffin were converted with one of pamphlet and are determine to go to Africa.   Mr. Wm. Brown & family, are owned now, by Mr. Jackson, in this city, your pamphlet has induced him to ask his master the second time, to let him, & family, go to Liberia, and his master I think ask him for your An. Report, intending to give said Brown an answer hereafter.   Mr. Francies G. Taylor in hanover Country Va has 6 Servants, that he wishes to go to liberia, but they are unwilling as yet, and I think they stand in need of Some of your pamphlets and a great many others. one Mr. Colds has gotten a pamphlet & has determine to go & is now gone up the country to get his family as I am inform—Dear Sir, I am still determine to go if I can   Rev. Mr. Ryland in his advice give me to understand that it would be some advanage to me if I were to go as a Colonist, as well as a missionary and Should you write again you will please tell me all you can upon this point—I saw Mr. John G. Mosby the other day & he encouraged me much & lovingly invited me to call & see him, when he had more time I am still willing to work out my freedom—your humble Servant

as true as ever

Bureell W. Mann.

P. S.   if you think fit you can write to Mr. Francies G. Taylor in hanover coutry Va and if you Say So, I will write to those 6 persons that he wishes to go to Liberia

B. W. Mann [1]

[1] *Ibid.*, October to December, 1847, No. 206.

RICHMOND VA November 30th—1847.

Dear Respected Sir

yours of the 24th inst were duly Recd, and I had not the opportunity to answer it then. I will however give you a few lines now and in the first place, I will inform you that from the coming of your last letter, my heart is much encouraged, and I am very thankful to you, though Christ Jesus, for the advice & encouragement lately Sent to me. Dear Sir, it is not as I please about going, but as you wilt, or the loving friends of Africa. I find here that it is pleasing to many of the white people that I should go at the first opportunity but what pleases them may not please you & those that are concerned in My case. So if I can go when you and my helpers think best, I Shall be contented, but My desire is to go next January if possible, first because it is agreeable to my health, Secondly because I expect many of my acquaintences to go, who has become willing to go, from hearing that I were going, but I will inform you and leave it in your power to inform others that I am willing at any time. My friends & helpers Say, and I am now laying By the pool waiting for the moving of the waters. 2 more persons, Since the coming of my last letter, has made up their minds to go   Mr. William Joiner about the age of 21 Declared that he will go when I go   Mr. Barlett Harris Saith the Same, in part. Mr. W. Joiner wants a Small pamphlet, & the people is Sending to me for them, from many quarters, & if you have any to Spare, you can Send them, and as I am requested to make a Speech this Sunday in the Female helping Society, you will please Send me Some of your latest Repositories. My aim is in this, to get as many subscribers as I can & to pour the information of the Repository upon the hearts of our Race here, therefore Send me Some forthwith if you think proper and can spare them and you will please send this week, as I shall have to Show them to the Socity This coming Sunday.

Your obedient, as true as ever

B. W. MANN.[1]

RICHMOND VA December 6th 1847

Dear respected

yours of Dec the first is Recd, & I have to inform you that the Rev. J. B. Taylor is now absent from the city & will not be here, for Some long time. If I could go at all, I prefer to go as Colonist & as a missionary from America. With you I am truely sorry for myself,

[1] *Ibid.*, October to December, 1847, No. 218.

and I must say that I never knew the value of being free before;
for had I been a freeman I would have been in Africa long ago &
would not be troubling the Good citizens of America as I now do.
My case I have labour fully to present to you, judgeing that you
would present it to all the denominations that had mission fields in
Liberia, and if you have done this you have done according to my
first intention & wishes upon the Subject; because it were my
purpose first to offer to the methodist mission Board & Should they
Refuse to take me for their Mission, then to offer to all other
denominations, & Boards, who has mission fields in liberia, and as I
have written to C. Pitman & to that board and they will not take
me, you will please present my case to all other denominations, by
writing, those who have mission fields in Liberia & are in need of a
labourer to Send into those fields you may tell any of them my
distress and that I am as willing to go for other denomination as I
am to go for my own—Mrs Gracy Ann Clark and her tow children
Seem to be determine to go out in January, So I give the Said Clark
one of the pamphlet lately Sent to me—Mr. Wm. Joyer is quite
young & wish to See you him Self or to Receive Some information
from you Respecting his departure in January he is also already
free and willing to go if he can get a little fund to prepare him for
his out Set and I let him have a pamphlet—Mr. Ruffin wishes to
see you also   his freedom is paid for and he are determine to go & the
question that he asked Seem to be fare ones, but I were unable to
answer them—and in regard to my Self, I must Say that I am cut of
for my part & my hope is loss.   Answer the 30th of november with
this,

Yours in many Sorrows

B. W. MANN [1]

RICHMOND VA   Dec 12th 1847.

Dear Respected

yours of the 3inst is Recd and I wish to inform you that I received 7
of your Repository for which I were very thankful, as I am for all
your acts of kindness to wards me.   I hope Dear Sir that you will
continue to be a friend & helper to the poor & needy.   The Repositories Some of them are now in the hands of persons who expects
to become subscribers.   They will examine them to day and hereafter Send their names.   One Mrs, Lucy Ann Burl has call on me
for information about Liberia, & about going, and I told her that the

---

[1] *Ibid.*, October to December, 1847, No. 236.

colonization Society could not buy her, but that it would pay her expenses out, & Support her Six months, & I give her a Small pamphlet.   Dr. Henry J. Roberts arrive here as your letter Stated & I must say to you that my heart did rejoice at his arrival in this city,   he give me much instruction about Liberia, & about going, he also promise to Speak a good word to Some Gentlemen on my case, from which I took fresh couruage, if my way should be come possible in time, I Shall rejoice to go with him in January   Dear Sir you will please write, if you think proper & tell the northern board that if they will take me for their mission, they please write you word forthwith, and you will please let me know at the first opportunity   am about to make my last offer, to my church

Your obedient Servant
B. W. MANN [1]

RICHMOND   VA Dec. 19 1847

Sir

I take the opportunity to give you a few lines, beging you not to take it amiss.   as it appears to me, that Mr. Mclain, has been absent from home the last tow weeks I wish you would be So kind as to let me know by writing me a few lines.   My Dear Sir, if he is still absent from your city you will please write me word but if he is home you will please ask him to let me know it by Answering Some letters already Sent and as Soon as I can know that he is in Washington I will let him hear from my poor condition   no more to say at present

Your obedient Servant
BUREELL W. MANN [2]

RICHMOND VA Dec 26th 1847   Yours Dec 23 is Recd

My Dear Respected Sir

humbly ask the liberty, of writting once more.   Sir I hope you will have patient with me and continue to advocate my cause, for I will assure you and every other friend that loves Africa, that my mind is the same about going now as ever it were & I know nothing in Va that can change my mind or turn my attention from going   If I can, and as you can not find any Missionary Societies willing to purchase my freedom, I will inform you, that if you can get any person or persons to advance the money for me now, I will pay them the

[1] *Ibid.*, October to December, 1847, No. 260.

[2] *Ibid*, 1847, No. 300.

money again as soon as I am well settle in Liberia.   Sir, I in making the effort to go, has gotten into great difficulty and I know not what the end may be, very probably, my master may Sell me to Some trader,   If I do not get Settle in the above mensioned way and from now until new yearsday is all the chants I have as fare as I know yet a while therefore if you can find any one who will advance the money for me, you will please write me word forthwith and I will let master know and will get out of this difficul before his Selling time comes on.   and as my Master has promised to aid me, (after Society had bought me).   I think, with his aid, I can get ready by the 15 of Jan.   The Rev. J. B. Taylor has returned home and I think that you can do great Good by writting to him in my case, you can tell him much about me & how long I have been striving to go, and you may tell him tow, that I am more willing to go under the Directions of the Southern Baptist Mission board, than under the Southern Methodist.   Should you write him by the next mail, he will get your leter the Same day that I expects to see him.   I have seen him once Since he come but he had no opportunity, to converse with me.   My Dear Kind Sir you will do the best you can, If you please in getting Some one to advance the money, and to do so as soon as possible because I have got into Distress in puting forth efforts to go to the poor color man home Your very humble & obedient Servant

B. W. MANN.[1]

RICHMOND   VA Dec 28th 1847

My Dear Respected Sir

Please Bear with me a little longer   I wish to inform you, that if you know of any one who would advance the money to pay for my freedom now, that I will Repay them again before I go out to Liberia, this I will endevour to do by my extra efforts & the aid of the Colored Baptist Church, they Seem to be very desireous to Send me as their missionary and willing to Raise a Subscription Paper & to Subscribe to it   My Dear Respected Sir, whenever you meet with Africas lovers you may beg them for me, to do this, and they Shall not be disappointed in no Shape or form.   The Rev. J. B. Taylor has talk with me the Second time, he Spoke very highly of Liberia to me and after a while he dismised me, by Saying, he believed, that I would be of great Service in Liberia, and my Dear Sir, I have got a full Satisfaction of Liberia and of it priviledges &

---

[1] *Ibid.*, October to December, 1847, No. 323.

Prospects, from Reading your Pamphlets and Repositories, I must Say I know tow much about Liberia, to be deprived of going there, while I am willing to do all I can to go. My Dear Respected, you will please remember me in prayers to God & answer my tow last in friday evening mail, Good news or bad news

Yours ever truely

B. W. MANN.

P. S.

it is the expectation of the Baptist Brethren to get me in to their colony and as a colored people, they Say that they will help me to Repay any one who will advance the money now and get me out of the present difficul—B.W.[1]

RICHMOND VA   Jan 1, 1848

My Dear Respected Friend

yours of Dec 30th is Recd and I am glad that it is as well with me as you find it Recorded in this letter. I wish you to know that the matter between me & my master, Stands now in the Same way as it did, when I first addressed him upon the Subject of going to Liberia. When he Spoke of parting with us all, Some of his Servants had freted him, but in regard to my case, I now find no change in his mind. he has hired me out on conditions & the others of his Servants as useal, and I do truely believe that he will do what he Said at first & comply with the promise he first made to me, which promise when fulfilled will nearly pay any gentlemen who will now advance the money to pay for my freedom, and Dear Sir, I do truely tell you that I see other way by which I could get money for these purposes, but not in my present condition. In my State I can not So much as Get the money that my master has promise me. again Dr. H. J. Roberts told me while he was sure that a missionary is wanting in the Baptist Colonies here the Baptist members is after me continually to join them that may be sent to the Baptist Colonies in Liberia. Dear Sir, their every days Cry to me is, Raise your Subscription Paper and we will help you pay for your Self and from one to five dollars, they has pledge them selves to Subscribe. Some promise me 1 dollar Some 2 Some 3 & from that to five and what would it be if all these were white ministers. Should I get one of this State & get 3 Subscription Papers from some disinterested American Minister, I will soon make myself known to all the white ministers & white members in Va as soon as the colored people

[1] *Ibid.*, October to December, 1847, No. 334.

who has promise to help me, but I have ask my own church to give me Subscription paper and they would not. If any other Minister do it, before my freedom is pay for, they will become offended therefore I can not expect, to get along in my undertaken till my freedom is pay for, and as you speak of uncertainty in your letter, and the probability of Sickness & death. I will here inform you that I am as healthy in Va as any other man I know, and if you, or any other Gentleman, will advance the money now I will be that Gentlemans Property on the American Shores till the debt is paid. Dear Sir, I know that African Baptist church of Richmond wants Missionaries and while Some are willing to help me pay, others will aid me, only by beging, not by paying money. but I will inform you that if you, or any other Gentleman advance the money for me, & they get me into their colony they will have to help me pay them, who now advances the money for me. I do not think I can be going the next vessel. Answer this as soon as you can—Your humble Servant

B. W. Mann [1]

Richmond Va　Jan 5th 1848

My Dear Sir

yours of the 3 inst is Recd and I understand from yours of Dec 23, that the vessel will Sail about the 15th of Jan, at which time I do not expect to go, unless it is done in an extra manner, unknown to me at present. therefore I have prepared My Mind to go, in the Summer, if I can. My Dear Sir, if you have done all you can, to get Some friend to advance the money for me, and they would not, I now ask you to advance it for me, if you please, and I will Repay you again, time enough, to be ready, to Start in the first Summer Voyage to Liberia. Sir I Should be Glad if Africas friends in Richmond, knewed my determination, about going to Liberia as well as you do. and I judge Sir that you know all the names of them that has Emigranted to Liberia, and I do not know whether you have ever met with one that has strove to let you know the trouth of their intention more So than I and I now ask you to advance the money for me, because I am the Same in heart as you has found me, in words ever Since you first began to write. I think Sir, that my intention is fully pointed out in every letter that I have written to you. I have been trying here to get Some friend to advance the money, and they refuse, before I could fully express my

<hr>

[1] *Ibid.*, January to March, 1848, No. 2.

self to them on the subject, but I do hope, Dear Sir, that you will patiently hear all that I have to say now, & hereafter upon this subject. My Dear Sir, I wish you to advance the money for me, as soon as you can and I will tell you, if you know not, how you can do, in order to be sure, that you will get it again. Sir if you will do it, I will come to washington and there remain under your inspection untill you is Repaid or if not, I will remain under the inspection of any Gentleman or Minister in this city that you may prefer. Dear Sir, Mr. John G. Mosby, the Rev. Mr. Ryland, & Rev. Taylor, are Gentlemen of this city in whose hands I am willing to be place, untill the money is Raise to Repay you. and if I do not comply with what I here promise, I am willing for you, or those in whose hands I may be placed, to sell me again, to any Citizen in Richmond, or Washington. These Gentlemen has seen my face in the flesh but they do not know my mind Relating to Liberia as you do. the Rev. Ryland & Taylor is interested in my case Mr Ryland has promise to give me some money & to be my Agent, to See me righted, if I could get any one to advance the money. in my last conversation with the Rev. Taylor he Seem to be So much interested, that he promise me, that he would See 2 other ministers upon the same subject, and it is not tow late to write to Mr. Taylor now, in regard to my case and Should you do it you will please let me know and I will go to see him again,   forgive me if you please & bear with me patiently

Your most obedient
B. W. MANN

Servant of John Cosby   Richmond Va for 1848
you will please teach me your ways & I will walk there in B. W.[1]

RICHMOND VA Jan 23-1848

My Dear Respected Sir

yours of the 8th inst were duly Recd and this is the best opportunity I have had to answer it. I find in your last, that you are astonished at My imaginations, & Petition. Dear Sir I do not think that you are made of money, & did not know that you did not have the money, and I thought as I had no money My self and were asking others in America to advance it, that I had a right to ask you—See your advice in Sept 10th 1847 your own letter tells me, to use efforts to get Some friend, if possible to advance the money, and having tryed many persons who did not know as much about it as you, then thought it proper to ask you to do it. and if my actions are wrong

[1] *Ibid.*, January to March, 1848, No. 20.

in these respects, you will please pardon them, and hereafter, teach
me how to think & ask—It is a hard matter to hire my self now—
My Master would think, that emigranting as a missionary to Africa
Were all a Sham, and it would cause him to think wrong of me in
other respects. This is the late advice of Rev. Taylor. It may be
that, I could not Raise the money as you think by the next vessel,
and should I not do it, I do not think that it would take me nine
months to Raise it, by extra efforts as well, as by working you will
please continue to advocate my cause & do the best you can for me
Answer this Soon—Your humble Servant   B. W. MANN.[1]

RICHMOND VA   Jan   27th 1848
My Dear Sir

yours from Baltimore is Recd, of the 14th inst. & I have to
inform you that I have sent a letter to washington for you dated
23rd Jan, if you has received it, you may answer that one with this.
With pleasure, I will make known your request to my friends, to the
concern & unconcerned and as the Liberian Packet has not arrive
you will please write me word when the chartered vessel shall start,
& I will inform any person from this Port, that they are to be at the
place of embarkation, tow days before the vessel Sails. If Dr.
Henry J. Roberts is there, or is to Start in this vessel you will please
tell him to write me, if he can, a week before he takes his departure
or if others of the Liberian Citizens be there, you may tell them my
case & tell them to write to me.

Yours very truely in many tears

B. W. MANN.[2]

RICHMOND VA   February 12th 1848
My Dear Sir, I Sent you a letter the 23 of January, from which,
I have received no answer. I received yours of the 24th of Jan.
which cause me to think that you were in Baltimore but from being
not certain that you were there, I Sent a letter to Mr. James Hall of
Baltimore for you & I never got any answer from that one, So I
judge it to be a bussy time with you then, and I thought proper to
forebear, writting untill now, if you has gotten those letters you will
please answer them with this one and let me hear the prospects of
the last vessel of Emigrants to Africa and whether The Liberian
Packer has arrive. My Philanthropist & Religion is the Same, for

[1] *Ibid.*, January to March, 1848, No. 112.
[2] *Ibid.*, No. 134.

My fellow men in Liberia and I am at a loss to know how I shall go to them. I hope Dear Sir, that you are not weary in advocating my Cause. if you See, or hear of any thing that are of advantage to me you will please take an active part in My case, or if not write me word forthwith. This year, I live with Mr. H. Dickison. Should you have any hasty intelligents for me you can write in care of Mr. H. Dickison for me, or you may continue to write in the useal way This may be done when you are in any other City or Town, or have any thing to inform me of quick. I remain your humble

Servant true & Study-

B. W. MANN-[1]

RICHMOND VA   March 20th 1848

My Dear Respected-

yours of Feb 17th is Recd from which I learn that the Vessel has Sailed from Baltimore to Africa with 44 Emigrants, and the only thing that pain me, was that I were not one in that number. yet not withstanding, all Sickness is not unto death. I hope that my time will come ere long,—Dear Sir, as I can not find any friends in America, who will advance the money, for the purpose above mension, It came into my mind, of late, to write to the Liberian Government, to inform Said Government, that if they will Redeem me from this Slavery, that I will go as a Colonist, and I will Repay the Government the Same money again, and work at my Trade there every day, and in the missionary field of Sundays. but I judges it proper to get your advice upon the Subject. you will please give me all the information you can in regard to this point and if it be in your power you will please answer this by returning mail, or in Some Short time.

I Still remain the Same, B. W. MANN.[2]

RICHMOND VA   March 28th 1848

My Dear Respected

yours of the 22 inst is Recd. & I will inform you, that if you think it will do Good, I will write to J. J. Roberts and Send the letter to you, fold in brown paper after which you can Direct it & Send it, by the Liberian Packet to the above mensioned person—I shall not Seal it, that you May have an opportunity to read it if, you like—You Stated, that you expect to be here Some

[1] *Ibid.*, January to March, 1848, No. 195.
[2] *Ibid.*, No. 335.

time in April, at which time you hoped to See me.   I am Glad to
hear that you are coming & hope to see me.   But I am very Sorry,
that I have no good, tiddings, to tell you, in regard to my case—I
live on the Cary Street number 14 Street, leading to Mayos Bridge,
at Mr. Hiram, B. Dickisons Tobacco, Factory.—When you arrive
in Richmond you can find me at the above mensiond Place, or if it is
more Suitable to you to Send for me after you arrive here, you will
please send for me, or write in the office as useal.—a week ago I
wrote to Dr. Pitman, but I got no answer.   I Seem to be forgotten
by our mission Board.   you may look for the letter to J. J. Roberts
—Your humble Servant

Slave of John Cosby

B. W. MANN [1]

RICHMOND VA   May 2nd 1848

My Dear Respected Sir,

The letter that I intended for J. J. Roberts, I have already Sent to
you, folded in Brown paper as I before Said, and as it were Directed
to you, by the Post Master, I have feared that he made Some
mistake, that you have not gotten it.   therefore if you have gotten
it I shall be much please to know whether you have sent it out by
the Packet, and I Should be much please to know the prospects of
the Packet which were to Sail the 11 of April and Should you
continue your notion about coming to Richmond you please let me
know in the P. office a fews days before hand.   I long to see you,
My heart would Rejoice Much.—in yours of March 22 you Speak of
coming to Richmond which in duced to look for you every Morning
in P. office, for a month, and I am Still looking for you,   Try &
make my case known any where you think proper and let the friends
know that my Resolution is Greater now than ever about going to
Liberia.   you will please if possible let me from the Missionary
fields in Liberia.   Your humble Servant in great haste.

B. W. MANN—[2]

RICHMOND   VA May 27th 1848

Dear Sir.

I am sorry I have to trouble you on this occasion.   I hope however
you will pardon me for being So officious.   Sir I wish to ascertain
whether The Rev. W. Mclain is at home, at this time, or, you will
please let me know, in what city or town he is, so that I can write

---

[1] *Ibid.*, January to March, 1848, No. 378.
[2] *Ibid.*, April to June, 1848, No. 126.

to him., It has been more than tow months Since he wrote to me,
& I have been looking for him ever Since the last of March, I had
thougt that if he were not Sick, he were paying visit to other city,
or towns.   Please answer this by the next mail.

Yours humble Servant.

B. W. MANN.[1]

RICHMOND VA 10th 1848

Dear Respected

it is very important with me at this time to know the Resident of
Rev. J. Tracy.   Where are his office?   In what State is he located,
when he, is Said to be at home?   for if Boston were his Stationed
place I think he would have gotten the letter that I Sent, and as he
has given me no answer, as yet, I thought that he were there on a
visit.   Again in looking over an old African Repository I find him
to be a Minister, and the Secretary of the Massachusetts Colonization Society.   This lead me to think that Boston were not his
Stationed place.   Had I known this before I wrote, I should have
Addressed the whole of the above Society.   It is very important
for me to know if President Roberts continue his visit in Boston,
and what cities or towns he will hereafter visit & when he leaves you
will please let me know as much of these points as you can & as
Soon as you can.   I am Still an object of pity

Yours most truly,

B. W. MANN.[2]

RICHMOND VA   August 4th 1848

My Dear respected Friend.

yours of the 24th of July is receive and I will in form you That as yet,
I have received no answer from the Rev. J. Tracy.   I hope how-
ever he will write me as soon as he can, yet at the same time I am
not weary in waiting on the Lord.   I am her requsted, by certain
Persons to ask you a few questions in regard to emigrating from
America to Liberia   First the enquire wishes to know, will the
American Colonization Society take a person who goes from a Slave
State, to a free One, and Colonize, That person, or persons to
Liberia?   Secondly Will they treat emigrants of this discription as
well as they do others?   Thirdly Do any other Colonization Society
own Packets, like the Liberian Packet?   And forthly can Such

[1] *Ibid.*, April to June, 1848, No. 211.
[2] *Ibid.*, July to September, 1848, No. 41.

persons go to Liberia? Dear Sir, if all these questions can be answered in the affirmitive you will please answer them in your next to me. and Should you See any way for me, you will please let me know as quick as you can, as it will be, great Advantage to the Colonization Society. hereafter you will hear from your last years Pamphlets & Repossitory.   Yours in Great haste
                                                    B. W. MANN.[1]

RICHMOND VA   Aug 13th 1848
      My Dear respected Sir

your two last is Received. and I am very thanful to you for the information of the first, by informing me in Due time of Mr. Payne visit to this city & of the Second which informed me of the arriv of the Liberian Packet and of the time it will again Sail. My Dear Sir I must Say That in regard to the Rev Paynes visit here, That Great good has been done, and I judge that Lord were with him Because he brought what we believe to be the True & good Report of the Place Secondly he made a short Speech in the African baptist church, at which time he pull down many untrue Reports, which had been publish about Liberia, thirdly, he in the evening, preach to the colored congregation of Trinity church and aided in administing, the Lords Supper. These actions here done by a Liberian Minister, has Created great excitement here and has left them in a wonder. I having to preach in Manchester church, Could not be there to hear him, at this time, but these things were told me by christians Brethren who were there. In regard to my case I must Say that I am Still over whemed in deep waters and know not what to do, and it does Seem, to me that Mr Tracy of Boston has forgotten me or he has not answer my letters.—as I were disappointed by the Rain, you will please tell Mr Payne farewell.
                          Your humble Servant B. W. MANN [2]

RICHMOND Sept. 15th 1848
      My Dear Sir.

                          you will please bear with me a little longer.
I thought it proper not to write in your bussey time but to wait untill after the Sailing of Packet when you might have more time to hear my case

---

[1] *Ibid.*, July to September, 1848, No. 142.
[2] *Ibid.*, No. 173.

I Some time back promise to let you hear the Effect of the African Repository, this I can do in part, only as it relate to me & my family   It has prepare My mind fully for going as a colonist and my whole family is also willing to go if possible

My Dear Sir

   I have not heard from the Rev Tracy up to this moment & if it is possible you will please write to him of my case & get him to do the best he can in my case and as he has never answered one letter from me it has led me to think That if he ever thought of me in pass times, he has forgot me now.   I Should be Glad to hear how many Emigrants has been Sent out this year & when the next vessel will Sail for Liberia.   I will esteem it a great favor on your part if you can get any one to advance the money.   Write me as Soon as you can, if you please.

B. W. MANN.[1]

RICHMOND VA Sept 26th 1848

My Dear respected Friend.

I humbly thank God, That I have it in my power to inform you That I has Received a letter from the Rev. Mr Tracy, in which I find no Small Consolation.   It was written Aug 17th and as it had My Masters Name on the outside, It were taken out of the office & preserve by Some person untill My Master returned from the Springs.   he arrived here on the 23 Sept & having Read the letter "he gave it to me on the 25th, and I forthwith Sent it to My Pastor & Church, and next Tusday night it is to be examined before that Body.   although My Master Read the letter, he had nothing to Say againts it.   Should you know of any one wishing to write to me you will please tell them not to put my master name on the out side, but, Mr B. W. Mann or Mr. Bureell W. Mann, will suit.

  My Dear Sir I must say That Mr Tracy s letter has cheerd my spirit much, and has cause me to see as I never saw before, & I humbly thank God for his goodness to me in these Respects & all others, of his, servants for their aid in my Case, and in regard to you, and Mr Tracy, I must say That I feel myself under ten thousand obligations to you both for the active part you have already taken in My case.   I hope Dear Sir That each of you will Continue to do So untill I am fully Restored to the home of my forefathers.—as soon as I get the decission of our church Relative to Mr Tracy s

[1] *Ibid.*, 1848, No. 285.

letter I will write you. yours of the 25th inst is Recd. which lead
me to say That you need not Send my last to Mr Tracy in Boston,
if you have not done it, for I wrote him on the 25th inst & I judge
that he is Satisfied So fare inregard to the one letter, he wrote
me first

I do truly think Dear Sir, That the Lord is now about to trouble
the Waters,   May God Grant it I pray.   Should you wish to know
any of me, or my family, just write forthwith, or if not wait untill
I write again as I intend to let you hear from our church.   Yours in
great hase.

B. W. MANN.[1]

RICHMOND VA.   January 2nd 1849
Rev Sir.

It Seemeth proper that I Should inform you of
my present State, and the expectations of the Methodist in this
place, and also a misunderStanding Relative to the Price that my
master charge for me, from first to last.

Sir, the chains of Slavery Do hold me up to the
present moment and I can not help Myself now But I do hope that
I shall be able hereafter to Repay any Body of men who may be the
least dispose to join the Boston Methodist, in raising the a mount of
money.   Sir, the methodist people here are waiting to hear whether
Dr. Pitman wants me for a missionary in Liberia, and to write to
them all needful information.   They, the above mensioned people
has been expecting a letter from Nr. Pitman for more than nine
weeks and if Dr. Pitman do not show them by writting that I am
much needed in Liberia, as a missionary and manifest his desire
to Send me as Such, That I can never go.   Oh! My Dear kind Sir, if
you have time, and have reason to think that you can do any Good
by way of writeing to him, you will please do me this, one more
kindness.   Sir, Great is the difficulties that I have had to contend
with Since I offered My Self to Missionary Board,   The Scattering
of my children to the four winds of heaven, and the Selling of My
beloved Wife! together with other heart breaking Circumstances!
are all discouraging, and Serious in their tendency.   But in the
words of one of old, None of these things moves me.   I do not
Weep to stay in any part of America, But to go home to my forefathers Land!   The trumph of God, I trust will bring my Wife &
children together at the day of judgment at which time Sinful

[1] *Ibid.*, July to September, 1848, No. 324.

parting will be done a way. The misunderStanding aluded above, is That in 1847. The Rev. Mr. Courtney Seem to have misunderstood the Price that my master charge for me, that whereas he said it were 4.50. dollars. It is only 400 dollars. Should any friends, to your knowledge, be desireous to know the fact in this Matter, Let them write to my master Saying, That they has heard that he charge $400 and beg him to write them word, But do not mension the $4.50. Because he told me & others, that he charged $400. about 3 weeks a go.

yours most truely
in Great hase
B. W. Mann.[1]

Richmond Va May 12th 1849

My Dear Sir

       yours of March 27th were duly receive from which I learned That Mr. M.Lain were expected to be home at Washington. your letter expected him the first or Second week in May, and I thought it best not to write untill now and I write now, to know if he has return home, if he has, you will please Show him the last Three letters that I Sent to him or you may show him this letter and if the above Mension letters are misplace any way, you or him will please write me word

       My Dear Sir, I am very thankful to you for your kindness and also to Mr M.Lain I do feel myself in debt to Mr. M.Lain for his past kindness to me, in advocating Cause I hope he continue in So doing, untill I am restored to the land of my forefathers.

Yours Most truly
B. W. Mann.[2]

Richmond Va Jany 28th 1849

Rev And Dear Sir

yours of the 6 inst is Recd. and I have to inform you That the church here has lately gotten a letter from Dr. Pitman Relative to my case, in which there were a very little Good done, if any. he did not so much as manifest to our church, the least desire to Send me out as a missionary nor as a colonized Preacher. his letter only Suited those in this city that did not wish to aid in this matter. As I

---

[1] *Ibid.*, January to March, 1849, No. 21.
[2] *Ibid.*, No. 172.

learn from our Secretary, that it will cause our church to with draw its efforts in Aiding me   In this city the question now is   What is the use of trying to raise the money When the missionary Board will not Receive you as a missionary nor as a colonized Preacher? Mr. Pitman has three Recommendations from our Secretary & Preachers.   Should you or any other friend wish to See them you will be So kind as to write to Dr. Pitman for them or if not, let me know and I will write for them.   Great is my trials now on the right hand and on the left.   My family are now Sold to the traders and gone; But this does not go So hard with me as the Being deprive of going and Preaching the Gospel to the down trodden Sons & Daughters of Africa   Great is my zeal for their souls and Great is my philanthropy for that Country at large.

Sir if I can get any person, or persons to Stand for me a few months, or to Lend you the money, So that you might Pay for me, It is my purpose to pay all for myself, That you can not borry   Some may be dispose to give a little for the Gospel Sake.   others may be dispose to lend you Some for Africas Sake and Should this be So you will please Write how much each person may lend you for the purpose That I may know how to make applications, to other quarters, to get help.   now I do not expect any thing from the colonization Society nor do I expect any thing from the missionary Society   But I do expect that the lovers of God, and of Africa, will give you a little and lend you the balence. No one from these quarters is to know any thing about my paying a cent, and if I do have to pay all It must go in the name of the Boston methodist and of others who may Join to help if this can be done, It is my purpose to come to Washington where you is and to remain there untill I Repay to you as much as you may now have to borry. I Say that the Boston methodist is to bear the name of doing it Because they first promised by letter to help and not only So, my master has Seen the letters which they Sent   Sir, my mind is made up to work & pay you for all your trouble!   Please oblige me if you can, and if there is the least hope for poor me, Write Soon, yours.

B. W. MANN.

P. S.   This letter contain my new resolutions and efforts to go to Liberia.

in my above remarks I Spoke of moving to wahington as Soon as the money are raise and paid for me.

by this, I shall quickly gat the money That my master has promised to give me and my determination is to appropriate it in paying

those that lends you the money now.   I have other reasons for
wishing to move to Washington, of which I will hereafter Speak if
it be needful

Please bear with me, & help me, untill I can help my self
and then I will repay you and all that now lend you.[1]

RICHMOND VA Feb. 14th 1849.

Rev And Dear Sir

yours of the first inst is receive from which I learn that nothing can
be done in my case at present   My Dear Sir if you think that there
is the least hope of borrying the money in days to come,   There is
some hope of my going as mission to Liberia or if by your influence,
A agent could be Sent out to beg and use extra efforts to Raise the
money.   I do Say that there is some hope in my case   Not with out.
Sir my face you never has seen; But I tell you that non in America
knows as much of my purpose and determination as you do!   and
you may take my word for it.   That if any of the above mensioned
Steps are taken and the money raised and left into your hands, to
pay for me I will as Soon as it is done commence to Repay what
ever may be required by you or those friends who may be kind
enough to lend you, for the purpose.   My condition requires me to
remain in one Spot, working for my master and since he promised
to let me go for $400. he has got $150. and I know very well That
if you can not Succeed in non of the above mension cases, I need
not hope ever to go. for I will be hire out always and my master
will get the money.   Now while this is lawful here It does not suit
in my case; for if I could have borried the money at first, and paid
for myself, I could by this time have paid, by my trade, $150. and
by next Christmas 250 dollars.   Not including extra aid, nor the
money that is promised me by my master himself.   My kind Sir,
If any friend can trust you for the money, I am willing to remain in
your hands, as there property untill I pay the money again,   This
is my Second reason for wishing to live in your city a while.   As you
has never Seen my Recommendations from my church you please
write to Mr Pitman for all three of them or if not, you will please
get Mr Tracy to write for them and Send them to you, for I think
the other missionary Boards will wish to See them besides Mr
Pitman s.   The influence of Colonization here is So great at present
that I as a Slave can not talk as much now about going to Liberia
as I has done in pass days,   you will please answer this as soon as

[1] *Ibid.*, January to March, 1849, No. 262.

you can   After which I will let you hear from many of the free
people   I remain truely your,
                                            B. W. MANN.[1]

RICHMOND VA March 4th 1849.

Rev And Dear Sir

I promise in my last to give you some remarks relative to colonization in this place among the colored people and this I should
have done before now if it had not been for the want of time and a
qualification to write.

Sir, as a true friend of Liberia
and of the cause of colonization, I do Say, That the excitment among
the color people relative to Liberia, are greater now than, it ever
were before, and that many from this place has determine to
emigrant to Liberia and many are Still making up their minds to be
settle in Liberia.   This seem to be the State of things among many
of the free color people,—and in regard to the Slaves, I can not tell
how many they are who are desireous to go.

On last Sunday evening in the
African baptist church,—a missionary, for Liberia preach for the
color people, after which J. B. Taylor made a few remarks which
seem to bring about new determinations in the hearts of many upon
Subject.   May the Lord bless the colonization Cause ever more and
induce all to return to their own lands that have it in their power to
do so.   I wrote in my last requesting you to get Mr Tracy to write
to Dr Pitman for the three Recommendations of mine which he has
receive from the methodist church South relative to me, if you or
Mr Tracy has gotten them, you will please let me know when you
answer my other and you will please give me an Answer as Soon
as you can

I remain your humble servant
                                            B. W. MANN [2]

RICHMOND VA. March 22nd 1849.

My Dear Sir

I have written twice to Mr. Mclain, and have receive no Answer,
and this cause me to think, that he are absent from your city,
you will please write me word of what town or city he is in at present,
or when he will return home.

[1] *Ibid.*, January to March, 1849, No. 354.
[2] *Ibid.*, No. 423.

You can Say to him that I am not out of patients, in waiting for an answer from him, and that my heart is Still fix to go, if I can to Liberia.

Your most obedient Servant
B. W. Mann.[1]

Richmond Va August 3rd 1849

My Dear Sir,

you will please let me know whether Mr Mclain has return home from his long voyage if he has, you will please Show him this letter and give him to understand that I Sent Some letters while he were absent from home, and know of him, whether anything can be done in My case, and Begg him to write me word and if he are not there you will please give me a Small answer yourself informing me where he is.

your most humble Servant
B. W. Mann [2]

From Lewis C. Holbert

Philadelphia, Sept. 7 # 47.

My Dear Sir

As I did expect to go this fall to Liberia for to see for my self but my famely was so much aganst it I could not leave and all my feriends so much opposed to it but for my peart I am rady to go this moment for I am convinsed of the place and of it value the coloured race and by ouer industery it may be in time as richly covered with citys farms and commerse as the grate United States of Amarica which 300 years ago was an wilderness but I hope I shall See the lande for my self for I discier long to go I hope you will write and let me know the latest news of Liberia I suppose the packet left on the first of the month May kind Heaven fill her sales and waft her across the brode Atlantic and land them all in health to injoy the free soile of ouer forfeathers. Rev. Sir I hope your in good health write soon direct to the Columbia House Chesnut street Philadelphia.

Rev. W. MClain. I remain your O.b. Sr..

Lewis C. Holbert.[3]

[1] Ibid., April to June, 1849, No. 137.
[2] Ibid., July to September, 1849, No. 142.
[3] Ibid., July to September, 1847, No. 108.

PHILADELPHIA   Oct. 2nd 1847. (?)

My Dear Sir

       I received yours dated Sep 11th and was glad to hear that some of my colored feriends had seen that this land is not thear country of Liberty & freedom but that land which ouer forefeathers lived I hope I shall be able to go the next sail of the Packet I wish to go not that I do exspect to become rich and set at ease but it is the love of liberty and freedom and by us who are free and bornd free as it regards slaves leave this land to astablish a free goverment of ouer own I think therre is nothing could be more dissiarble to us people of colour as for my peart to know it is a grate blessing to us people of colour and I hope the time will soon come when all of my colour will see as I see but the main object of my writing to you at this time is that thear was a gentlemen called at the Columbia house the other day and wished me to call at the Colonization Rooms but as I was ingaged I could not talk to him much he toald me whare theay was but I could not find them I think he said his name was Mr. Cressen but I hope you will write and let me know where and what street thear in. I am yours Lewis C. Holbert.

REV. W. MCLAIN.[1]

FROM GEO. H. BALTIMORE

Messrs. Editors:—In reading the notice of a call in your paper for a National Convention of colored people to be held in the city of Troy, October 6th, I can adopt all its suggestions, excepting one, that is as follows: to recommend immigration and colonization, not to Africa, Asia, or Europe.   This I consider a fling at the American Colonization, and even to stagger the minds of those of our people, who are desirous of going to their fatherland.

    The Colonization Society, with all its faults, has done too much good in the eyes of the world in planting the colony of Liberia; and the few colonists have affected too much good in the minds of the immediately surrounding native tribes, in abolishing the slave trade, for us, the free people of color at this day, to say aught against them.   We should bear in mind this very Liberia has been so prosperous, that it is now on the eve of taking a stand among the independent nations of the earth.   Already England and France are making propositions to them for the purpose of trade, and American naval officers stationed on the western coast of Africa,

[1] *Ibid.*, October to December, 1847, No. 8.

are appealing to the government of the United States, not to be beackward in doing the same.   If I do not choose to immigrate, or share in the glory and honor of the Liberians, in building their villages and cities, constructing their canals, raising their ships, and above all, the suppression of that evil, the slave trade, which has been upon our race for so many centuries, not only on the American continent, but in Africa, I will at least be silent.   These are the reasons why I do not attach my name to the call, though I shall attend the Convention.[1]

GEO. H. BALTIMORE.

Whitehall, Sept. 21, 1847

MITCHELL VILLAGE   August 22, 1848

Rev an Dear Sir.

    I received yours of June the 22.   In answer to the information I required an should have answered. and i also intended, to have seen you an veiwd Capital of Capitals of the U. S. before this time.   I am rather woman like around my little ones, and i suppose rather to much so, when they are sick for my own good.   I feel thanfull to say by the blessing of heavens it is about well an I have not been well myself so i have been busiing myself an collectting facts, for a little historical work that i am trying to write.   I wish to inform you that i was in Troy my native City the later part of May.   I visited the Rev Mr Stele the Methodist personage an we converst on the cause of colonization.   I told him That i would speak in his session room: he said he would rather give me an invitation to lay the subject, before the coming conference wich would meet in a few days.   The above mentioned sickness prevented; I read the Repository an i find them extremely interesting especially the July and August number.

Yours for the oppress an colonization

GEO. H. BALTIMORE

Rev Wm McClain.
Washington City.[2]

Aug. 26, 1848

Sir some times when a single word is left out it spoil the whole face of a letter.   In my letter to you of the 22 or 23. I did not thank you

---

[1] *The African Repository*, XXIII, 374.

[2] *Letters (received by the American Colonization Society*, July to September, 1848, No. 207.

for the required information. you will now please accept my
sincere thanks.

Yours &c. GEO. H. BALTIMORE.[1]

Rev. Wm Mc Clain
          Washington City (Errata.)

FROM CECELIA D. LYON

BALTIMORE January 16, 1848

Dear Sir & friend

this will inform you that I am In Baltimore.   I arrived
here yesterday   I Came the land rout expecting to finde the vessel
redy.   But as I have been disappointed I am Compeled to throw
myself on the Society for the time I shall remain here.   I left home
with bearly money enough to pay my expenses for I made up mi
mind not to let any thing prevent me from going to Liberia with
My Children although I have nothing to begin with yet I trust the
lord will provide for those that put there trust in him.   I expected
to have got eight or nine hundred dollars that is in the hands of a
gentleman but I am compele to leeve it and prehaps I may never
get it.   this would have enable me to Commence some little bisiness
in My new home, but so it is a colord person cant get there right in
the Countrey that I am from.   I am now at the House with other
emigrant, where I finde the Land Lady very kind—But the House
is crowded and I cannot have a room so as to make myself and
Children Comfortable.   I am sorry I did not Come to washington
I am very anxious to see you sir the one that has been so kind
I moste truly desire to see to get your advice and to returned you
thanks for your kind attention to my letters &c.   In Savannah the
people appears quite anxious to go to Liberia.   before I left three
famelyes Came to me and pledg there worde that they would Come
out on April and many, speak, favorable of the Coloneys.   I
received a letter from my Father and all so the Constitution and
other papers which I endevourd to shew to as meny as I could and
I think it will have a good affect

Your humble and obedient Servant
CECELIA D. LYON

P. S.

There is a man by the name of Clay a Preacher that will go on
with us   I expect him daly [2]

C D

[1] *Ibid.*, July to September, 1848, No. 222.
[2] *Ibid.*, January to March, 1848, No. 76.

FROM PETER B. BOLLING

MOBILE ALABAMA 13th March

MR. W MCLAIN

Dear Sir

I received your kind letter a few days ago wherein you put forth so conspicuously the choice that should be made by those emigrating to Liberia (Namely that of benefiting my fellow man) It is with this and no other that I wish to go and every endeavor will be made by me and mine to do what good we can towards converting a people from Ignorance Superstitution barbarism & Paganism to the true religion & civilization that characterises the United States. Perhaps you have thought me dilatory in answering your letter But with my excuse I think you will not blame me which is that I have been looking out some of my Bretheren who would accompany me with the same feelings I have myself and those you say a man should have imigrating there, and thank God I believe I have found some of the right stripe, at least six who would like to engage in the mighty work and I assure you there are none of thim Lofers loungers dandies or those who wish to cut a swim. But all plain industrous and well meaning men who wish to take their tools of the Various employments they have and go right to work when they get there. But here is one question which I hope you will satisfy me in regard to when you answer this (namely) What is the best articles to take with us, for I have been informed and I think not wrongfully that there are some things would be more bineficial than money, and if employed as it, the natives would assist us in building &c when we get there & you will greatly oblige me by letting me know what is most needful & answer this as soon as practicable and oblige Your humble Servant

PETER B. BOLLING [1]

MOBILE Dec 1 st 1848

Dear Sir

Your favor of the 6th Nov has been received—Much to my regret I shall not be able to leave by the next vessel as I have not been able to dispose of my place with out making a greater sacrifice than I wish to submit to—I being the leader of the movement in this city my friends are not willing to go without me of which there some twelve or fifteen who are anxious to go—

[1] *Ibid.*, July to September, 1848, No. 2.

It would have afforded me much pleasure to have met with my
old friend Pres. Roberts as we were raised together from children—
Please let me know how or where we are to pay our subscriptions to
the Af. Repository as I & several of my friends wish to subscribe
for it—

I shall be pleased to hear from you
occasionally by letter

Your Obt Servt.

PETER B. BOLLING

Mr. W. McLain
        Baltimore [1]

FROM BRANCH HUGHES AND E. DUNSTAN

March 27 1848

GRANVILLE COUNTY NORTH CAROLINA—

My Dear Sir

I was very Glad to here that the emigrants all landed well
and the Surviving are doing well and I was very Sorry to here of
The death of Friend Drew for I Think it rather disencouraging To
the feelings of some Tho some of us are yet in spirit of liberia   Tho
myself nor none of my acquaintance are ready for this voyage.
I can only Say that myself and some others are trying to make
Ready for the first of Jan if there will be an opportunity   Myself
and Mr. Drews friends were expecting letters by the packet   we
hope to get them by the next opportunity   I close by Saying I
hope you will forward to us all necessary information   yours with
respect until Death

BRANCH HUGHES

P. S.   Please to say to us what are The Fraight of a family of 8 or 10
persons from baltimore To liberia and if there is any danger in
caring infants and oblige   Your humble Servant

—E. DUNSTAN [2]

[1] *Ibid.*, October to December, 1848, No. 228.
[2] *Ibid.*, April to June, 1848, No. 7.

From John F. Cook

April 9, '48

Rev. Wm Mc Lain.
        Present.

Dear Sir:

        Your note together with Mr. Ball's came duly to hand.
I regret to say that I cannot now determine positively whether it
will be in my power to witness the departure of the Packet for
Liberia, I told Mr. B—— I would if I could make it convenient.
I can only say at this time the same to you.   If I can make any
arrangement with reference to my School, &c. I shall endeavor to
be in Balt. on the occasion named, do not depend however on me for
an address, as I feel my incompetency, but would rather be a looker
on—only.   But if present will not hesitate to wish them a safe
passage &c.   My thanks for your considerations.

                        I am very respectfully
                            Yours, &c.
                        John F. Cook.

Washington April 9th, 1848.
Sabbath P. M.[1]

From Alfred Evans

Mobile Alabama May the 16 1848

My Dear Sir   I Now take this opportunity of writing to you inorder
to inform you that I have made up my mind to go to liberia and I
want to emigrant with the company that first gose to liberia and I
wish to get your advice So I may know what plan to fall a upon
and my dear Sir I am a free colored man of mobile alabama and
therefor I have very little money to carry me to liberia and wish
to have the Society aid to carry me there and Mr. rev. W mclain
as you is the agents of the Society and I be glad for you to let me
know by this letter as you can for I am ready now to by the first
opportunity and please to tell me by the letter you Will Send to me
in mobile and I have a Wife and Child   my Wife name is patiences
Evans   my Childs name is francis Evans   and only three in my
family that is myself making the three and please to give me the
understanding of the place in liberia and the State of things in that
land and how a man is to get a long there and direct your letter in
the care of mr. Jacob Anderson in mobile and I thinke that the

[1] *Ibid.*, April to June, 1848, No. 53.

is many more in mobile that Wants to go to liberia now and this
is all I have to write now

Alfred Evans your [1]

From Jacob Anderson

Mobil　May the 20th 1848

Mr. Wm Mc lain *Sir*　I has bin Requested by a family of free
pepeal Nam Alford Evens wife　And 1 child　he has consiederable
esteat that he his sold And turning to mona that tha may be Rady
the fust opportunuty that may be a fordid　to Emigrant to liberia
pleas Receiv these fue lings from a frind　And pleas give me such
direction is you may think Best And it will be thankfully Recd
I Remember you good laber of love & that the Blessing of god may
be with you　　your Respectful

Jacob Anderson [2]

Mobil　Oct the 29 1848

To the Revd Wm Mc lain

Dear Sear I tak this oppertunity By the Request of my friens to
inform you that one of my intellajent frinds namley Jack Georg (?)
is ingage ing Bying himself in order to go to liberia　his master
charge him six hundred doller And he his now th $300 doller Ready
to pay And untell he can git Som frind to helph him he cannot get
a long well　Dear Sear is you wil Be So Kind is to Advance $300
doller on the sam princable that you did with Edmon I can pay
the mona Back ing one year　my Case is Before you　Be pleas to
give it Such a investagaesion is you ing your Judgment may think
proper　But you instructsion from you will Be gladly Received
I hav Sen Edmon D Taylor And famelay　All well　he Say that By
the 20th of december he will complet the payment of six hundred
doller And the Ballanc of the mona he can get　And mak payment
in ful So that he may sav the insouren　Dear Sear the mona deu
you from me for the Repository Be ing no Eagunt Ana infearmasion
on the subject Will Be comply　I Want the liberia hearel you Will
pleas Send me som informasion on the subject　And I Will send
the mona

I Re mann
you Respectful
Jacob Anderson [3]

[1] *Ibid.*, July to September, 1849, No. 4.
[2] *Ibid.*, April to June, 1848, No. 276.
[3] *Ibid.*, October to December, 1848, No. 97.

MOBILL Febuary the 16 1849

THE REV AND *dear Sier*

I tak the oppertunaty to send you the names of sum new sub sbribir for the Repository

Directsion

1 Peter Bolling to H C peabody
4 Mary F leaving
4 Thomas Robinson
4 John Bryent   the care of Thomas leaving 3
4 John Center   to Thomis S King
4 Louis Bowen
4 Willam Simpson   the car of Edmon D. Taylor 2
4 Peter Williams   to Miller Fre
4 William Johnson to the care of Jacob Anderson
4 Garet Butler to H N Gold

I will send the Ballenc of the money ing Appril   you will pleas exsept $5

JACOB ANDERSON
to the Rev W mc lain [1]

MOBIL Sept the 10 1849

TO THE REV W MCLAIN *Sear*   I hav Subscrib for the liberia hearil When you pas though last winter And hav not Recev my paper you Will pleas Send them

I Allso pad a Subscribsion For the Repository for *Mr Guilford Ward* that has not bain Rece   you Will pleas correct this cas

You Respectfull

JACOB ANDERSON [2]

FROM TITUS SHROPSHIRE

These letters of Titus Shropshire show that his case was somewhat like that of Bureell W. Mann. He finally obtained his freedom but had some difficulty thereafter in establishing the right of his family thereto. They were liberated by the will of an owner whose name the slaves bore. The heirs, however, endeavored to prove that the manumission was illegal for the reason that the owner had only a life interest in the slaves, but the highest court in Missouri

---

[1] *Ibid.*, January to March, 1849, No. 275.
[2] *Ibid.*, July to September, 1849, No. 268.

decided in favor of the slaves.   Many such bondmen whom
their kind masters sought to transplant to Liberia lost their
freedom in the entangling law suits instituted by malevolent
relatives and ill-designing persons.

May the 21, 1848

Dear Sir

You will please not to stope the African repository on me as I am
a poor Slave but a cording to will Expects to Goe to Liberia before
long and would like to know all a bout it   you would be please If
you have on hand the April & may numbers to Send them to me
If you cant Send gratuitous I will Try to rease the money before the
year is out and Send your paper is a Grate light to me

TITUS SHROPSHIRE   Tippecanoe
W Mclain [1]   mo

August 24, 1848

Dear Sir

your Letter Come to hand July 18 Which give mi grèate Satisfaction
to know that you would send the reposotory to mi   you send mi a
pamphlet for Which I thank you very much   I would be glad that
you would Send me Sum of your Africas Summarys and the Liberia
herald if you please   I think as you do I will be glad when the Time
Come for me to go to Liberia but I will leave that matter with God
I loock at the Colonization Society as the greatist thing a mung man
kind and the mend the greatist of mend for thay must be Good men
any thing from you would be greate with me

to William M Clain
TITUS SHROPSHIR

Sum of your numbers of the Liberia herald [2]

LANCASTER Mo. October 7 1848

Dear Sir

by this you will see that your letter has bin rec but I must Truble
you agine   You will please Sind all my papers to Lancaster. the
Letter that you receved from me Last from Cherry Grove was
handed to a Gentleman and he mail It at the rong post office.
the Repository for Sept has not bin rec as yet.   I would be Glad
If you please to Send the September nomber   If it will not Truble

[1] *Ibid.*, April to June, 1848, No. 193.
[2] *Ibid.*, July to September, 1848, No. 216.

you to much as I Like to See Every thing from Liberia   Lancaster
Mo

I am Yours Titus Shropshire.

William McLain

> the September number.   I have no dough but it bin mist lade
> for you have any by you please Send one of that number [1]

March the 30 1849.

Rev Mr McLain *Dear Sir*

three mounth has pass a way and I have not received the African
Repository   I hope you have not Stope It   You will please Send the
January and *february* and *March* Nos.   If you have them by you
and them Liberia papers that you promus me   If the Packet have
Return from Liberia you writen in your last letter to me that when
the Packet Return, you would Send me Sum   I hope you have
Not for Got me

Titus Shropshire

lancaster

Mo.

Rev. W. Mclain [2]

Chrry Grove October 14th 1849   Mo

Mr McLain   *Dear Sir*

I Take this oppertunity of write you a few Linds to let you know
that the old Lady is dead and Left us all for Liberia but her children
is about to Bring suit for the family and we may not get of Before
nixt fall but we want to be of as soon as posserble thire Lawyers
Tells thim that thay can Brake the will but our Lawyers says thay
cant Brake the will   I hope I will not be from my calling as preacher
of the gospel of the lord Jesus Christ upon the soil of Africa   we are
all in the hands of a administrator   Know Sir any thing from you
on that subject will be great   with us that is on the subJect of
Liberia

I sill an yours

Titus Shropshire

Mr MCLain

Washingont [3]

[1] *Ibid.*, October to December, 1848, No. 20.
[2] *Ibid.*, January to March, 1849, No. 460.
[3] *Ibid.*, October to December, 1849, No. 37.

LANCASTER SCHUYLER Co Mo   April th14, 1850

MR McLAIN   *Dear Sir*

I Take my pen in hand to in form you that there have ben no suit
as yet Brough a Gine us and I think Will not be the Adminerstator
says he will wind up the business as soon as he can and Let us be of
we want to be of About Dec or Jan or feb nix we have Tow
Children to try to Take with us to Liberia if our frinds will help
us to git them and five at home with us and we hope to git you and
the Colonization Society to help us to get them the friends in this
country say thay will help us all thay can will you please to send
the *March nomber of the repository* as i see agrate meney Letters
has come to your office & to you will you be so Good as to send me
som of your *Liberia papers* the *herald* & the Summary and Ill pay
the postage if any

                        I am your in Tuth
                        TITUS SHROPSHIRE.

To William McLain
Washington City.[1]

                November the 12 1850

        Rev Dear Sir

I receved your faver of may and the papers that you sent me   you
wish to know the names of the famaly   my wife is name Ellin C
She 37 years old my oldes Daugher Charlotte J 17 years old   John
W 15 years Ruben Monrovia is 14 years old   Randolp R is 12 years
old   Mary Jane is 10 years old Wilson Oing is 7 years old Josephine
is — years old Thomas Buchanan is 6 months old   myself 40
years old

                TITUS SHROPSHIRE

you Will please When you are don Reading some of your Liberia
herald send me som of them
we Will leve for Liberia as soon as the Admin winds up the Estate
you Will please Take Notice that To of the Children we have To
Try to by as soon as we see how all things Workes

                TITUS SHORPSHERE

William McLain [2]

    [1] *Ibid.*, April to June, 1850, No. 56.
    [2] *Ibid.*, October to December, 1850, No. 135.

LANCASTER SCHUYLAR Co Mo July 6th 1851
deare Sirs

I Take this liberty
to Writ you a few Lind to let you Know that sence I Rote you in
January last that the heirs of the Late Mrs Shropshire have Brought
suit agine our Administrator but the attorneys in the case say the
is No danger at all the Trail Come of in the September Court of our
County

Dear Sirs the Repository of May and June have never come to
hand I thought mabe you had Stope it if So please Sent it on for
I would Rether pay $200 for it and to have you stop it
please send the to Back nombers

TITUS SHROPSHIRE to
Rev W Mclain and
J W Lugenbeel [1]

LANCASTER SCHUYLER COUNTY Co Mo January 4 1852
Dear Sir

I Take my pen in hand to inform you a little abut our Suit. the
case have not come of yet as we had no court last fall but I am
Requsted to Say to you by Mr Caywood our administrator that
he thinkes the Suit will be at a End in the Spring and the Blacks
reddy for Liberia in the fall as for the Repository the administrator
Say he will pay me som money between now and Spring. I will
Send it to you you must not be oneazy I will pay you

TITUS SHROPSHIRE
W McLain [2]

LANCASTER SCHUYLER Co Mo Nov 22th 1852.

MR McLAIN *Dear Sir*

I Take my penn in hand to write you a few lines to let you know
that we sill Expect to Go to Liberia our souit come on the september aparte of the case was Trid James S Green our lawyer
says that he will Gain the hold case in the Spring he Gaind my
freedom and he says he will Gain the other parte of the famley in
April nixt you will please send Repository tell April Court by
that time we can tell you all about it will you send me one copy
of Dr lugenbeels sketches of liberia you will please send me the
little Book by mail call the histry of the new Republic and I will
send you the money and oblige   yours Titus Shropshire [3]

[1] *Ibid.*, July to September, 1851, No. 28.
[2] *Ibid.*, January to March, 1852, No. 31.
[3] *Ibid.*, October to December, 1852, No. 268.

LANCASTER SCHUYLER COUNTY Nov 15th 1853
MR McLAIN *Dear Sir*

I Take this oppertunity to say to you that my wife and children lost there suit at the november Term of the Court on the groundes of the late Mrs Shropshire having only a life time Estate in the woman Sir I am free my Self but my famley is Left in Slavry and I still hope to go to liberia yet if I can git my famley will not the friends of houmanity do som thing for the woman and Childrien to helpe them to git to liberia as we all want to go our friends in this County say that if the friends of Colonization a broad will help pay for the famley and let them go to liberia thay will do all thay can to raise I will write to the Rev Mr Showmate and git him to do Business for us and write to you and all the friends of the Course you will write to Richard Caywood a lawyer in this County and he will State the case to you in it Tru light Sir I do think if the Methodist Church a few years ago could raise twenty tow hundred dollars to by tow Girles that the friends of the course can raise a nuft to send a family to Liberia you will please write as soon as you git this

I Am yours TITUS SHROPSHIRE
W McLain [1]

LANCASTER MISSOURI August 25 1855
REV WILLIAM McLAIN
Dear Sir

I write you a few Lines to let you know that I will send you the money for the Repository in october and I want to send som money then for to pay for one of Capten footes Book I will say to you that the case of my wife and childrien has been Trid in the lower Courte and Taken up to the supreme Court I Think then that we will Be Able to Be of to Libria it will Be Trid in october

I am your in Truth
TITUS SHROPSHIRE [2]

LANCASTER SCHUYLER COUNTY Mo January 11th. 1857
MR MCLAIN Sir

I Take my pen in hand to say to you that the Supreme Court givt thier opinion in the case of my family the Court decided them all free by the will we Expect to trie to git of to liberia in the fall

[1] *Ibid.*, October to December, 1853, No. 248.
[2] *Ibid.*, July to September, 1855, No. 255.

the court decided the 23 day of December   you will please say to mr Gurley to sill send me the Repository and I will soon send him the money   I am yours Titus Shropshire

TITUS SHROPSHIRE [1]

LANCASTER SCHUYLER Co Mo January the 9 1859

MR R R GURLEY

Dear Sir   I want you to still send me the Repository and write me how much I owe on the Repository as I have for got what I do owe on it   I Think we will be Thiough with our law suit nixt spring and in the fall be Ready for Liberia   I would have sent you the money in Advance but I have had to pay lawyers fees in a greate meney casus but I will send you the money soon   If you have any liberia papers you will please send me A nomber som Times the Liberia Advocate or the lone stear or the hearld

Your frind TITUS SHROPSHIRE [2]

FROM SHERRY J. JACKSON

June the 12th 1848   REV. W. MC LAIN *Sir*

Having recd. your letter with pleasure and it our determination to go on to Libera we are making preperation fast as possible that at the appointed time that which we have not done must go undone.   I have recd a letter frome my sister a teacheress in New York who will and is agoing on with us which will make 7 in number. I sent early   be shure and give or reserve us a birth. Sir   you mention of our bretheren the Slavey to beshure we feal for them and at our family altar morning and night we remember them not only them but we pray for those who hold them in bondige that God may in mercy soften the hearts of their masters, in reading the repository it stated that a number of slaves were liberated and that One or a white man had to claim them as his own in order to get them safely on abord the vessel   it appears that there is danger for those that are free to reach the vessel   however I lay the thing before you   we are not able to pay our fair but this we will promis you or the Society   if we get their and over with the fever or I should say live through it you shall receive yearly as far as I am able money to aid in the cause of the Col Society   my Father is welthy but will not give me one cent because I go but our minds are established and cannot be removed.   It has ben said that in

---

[1] *Ibid.*, January to March, 1857, No. 57.

[2] *Ibid.*, January to March, 1859, No. 22.

this Town Colchester that there could not befound 3 abolitioners but I tell you Sir since I recd your letter and they see my determination they all protest against the colonizeation all appeard to be abolitioners even our Rev. T——A seams to draw back all tho he first surgest it this is my mind Concerning the colored people these that are able worth propity they love this friendly country stand in fear, of slavery dread to cross the Atlantic immagine there is some sketch in it hate to leave their homes and the abolition is no help to Aid them on and they will not go till a few more frome the free states go I have a Brother 1 and sisters that are able or quite welthy but Will not go till they have heard from me there is more than 50 which have requested me to write the particentars of the plase back to them

    I put my trust in Him who is able to save both soul and Boddy this from your most humble servent   SHERRY J. JACKSON

        Colchester Conn

           O Sir we should be verry happy to hear from you soon.[1]

COLCHESTER   Feb the 5th 1849

           Rev Sir yours is recd. The reverend Mr Ely while at our residence gave us this advise that we had better go the coming fall than this winter for going from this extencive cold winter in so warm a climat saith he we shall not do so well this is my advise saith he keep your children in School and be reddy by next fall and we will assist you I asked some question to which he gave answer to our satisfaction we concluded to follow his advice we shall be on hand then in season our bosoms burn to be landid on the shores of Africa Mrs. Jackson is quit impatient we supposed Mr Ely has inform your honaor of us or I should have written before let this not be a disappointment to you the time will soon be here we by kind Providence help we shall not fail one article at the time to be shure we shall make a grate sacrifice by going away but we cannot help it it is impossible to give you the number this time for seeing my family is all agoing there is several of our most respectted young peopll that intend to go with us there has sinse I recd your leter a accomplished teacher reddy to go with us two as mishionary so you will see that good may be don by our delay we should be glad to hear soon from you

    [1] *Ibid.*, April to June, 1848, No. 253.

to know if you are discourage in writing to us and wating for us
your most humble servent

SHERRY J. JACKSON

(N. B. I shall have 2 fine boys 3 girls
to go)

Pleas to mention to the Pres. Mr Ely that his uncle James Ely died
in a short time after he left.

To revd W. MC Lain
Washington Citty.[1]

FROM S. WESLEY JONES

The letters of S. Wesley Jones, of Tuscaloosa, Alabama,
not only give valuable information as to the progress of the
colonization movement in that quarter but illuminate the
general situation in that state.   He was a Christian of fundamental education and a business man owning considerable
property.   He hoped to emigrate to Liberia as soon as he
could close up his business, and while waiting to do so he
aided the movement by speaking to the people in that city
and by lecturing to others in cities and towns near by.   What
he had to say about things in general is valuable evidence as
to the conditions which there obtained.

TUSKALOOSA, ALA.,
June 12th, 1848.

Rev. and Dear Sir:—After a long silence, I again take up my
pen to communicate to you some facts in relation to the subject
that lay nearest my heart, save that of the Christian religion, that
of African colonization.   You no doubt think me a dull and unworthy correspondent, and very justly too, for I ought to have
written you months since, and I am quite ashamed of myself for
not doing so.   Pardon me, kind sir, for the past, and I promise you
to do better for the future.   Your very kind favor of the 27th
February, was duly received; likewise, the different numbers of the
Repository you was so pleased to send me, i. e. the January, February, March, and April numbers.   The May and June numbers I
have not received, and am indeed puzzled in mind as to the reason
why, unless it is my unfaithfulness in corresponding; and should

[1] *Ibid.*, January to March, 1849, No. 216.

this be the fact, I have not a word of complaint to utter, for I do assure you, sir, I feel myself under undying obligations to you for the care that I have received at your hands, to say nothing of the flattering and kind manner in which you regarded and noticed my letter; and if you have been induced to stop sending me the Repository because of my failing to write you, please pardon my past negligence, and send me the May and June numbers, together with the subsequent numbers. I have used some efforts to make the numbers of the Repository that I have received, useful, so far as lay in my power to do so. I have read and caused to be read, to the superstitious and prejudiced of our people, every opportunity, and I am proud to say, with some success. I have not failed in but a single instance, of removing old prejudices; and I still think, with patience in one hand, and perseverance on the other, I may succeed, even in that instance. I have traveled some the past winter, and have met with a great many free persons, and have never failed to bring the subject before them when an opportunity offered; and though I have met with the enemy in his stronghold, I have never failed to completely rout him by and with the aid of your valuable Repository. There are many in the State that are willing to go to Liberia, and all they wait for, is to see certain ones of their friends make the move. I candidly believe if I were ready at this time to go, I could easily raise a company of an hundred or more; but when I would reason with any upon the subject, they bring this to their relief: That I am willing they should go, but am not willing to go myself. Sir, my intention fully is to go to Liberia if it should please the Lord to spare my life. I have a ten years' business to try to settle up in this country, before I can leave for Africa's shores. If I can succeed only tolerably in collecting what is due me in this country, I shall be able to go to Liberia independent of aid from your benevolent society; but if I can't collect my dues, I shall be poor and dependent. So you percieve, sir, that it only requires a move to be made by some one in whom the people have confidence, to put the whole column in motion. My word for it, whenever there is a start made in Alabama, the whole body of free people will join in a solid phalanx. I intend making a tour through North Alabama, and perhaps I may extend my trip into Tennessee, as I have some business in that part of the country; also some relations, that I desire to confer with concerning Liberia. Should I go, sir, you shall hear from me at Huntsville. I will write you from that place, informing you of the results of my labors in that quarter. Fail not to send me the Repository, and write me upon what grounds it was discontinued, and if you are tired sending it gratis, write me and inform me as to the subscription price, and the money shall be punctually paid, for I would not be without it under no consideration. I will write you again upon the reception of your answer to this.

Believe me, sir, with considerations of the highest regard and esteem,

Your obedient servant,
S. WESLY JONES.

Rev. Wm. McLain,
    Washington City, D. C.[1]

TUSKALOOSA ALA May 2nd 1849.

Revd Sir

after a long Silence (of which I am ashamed) I again Take up my pen to write you a line to acknowledge your many Kindnesses to me wards. your letter was Duly Received and appreciated you mentioned in your letter that you was sorry that I could not get off to Liberia sooner than Ten years my dear Friend your Simpathising Heart could never (under the afflicting Despensations of Providence though they were to deprive you of Mother Father Sister Brother wife & children) be as Heavy as my Poor Heart would be if I thought that had to spend Ten years more in this Country you misunderstood that part of my letter it was a Ten years Business I had To Try to Settle up that had been Transacted not to be transacted. I have been making Some Efforts to collect what is due me here that I may be able to get off next spring if I should live but I have succeeded very poorly as yet but let me tell you Friend Mclain without an alteration in my mind Make or Brake I Start for the land of Promis (to the collord man) next spring. Please accept my Thanks for the valuable Paper you Sent me Pubd. in Philadelphia allso your valuable Repository which have come Regularly to hand since I wrote you last. I have given them to different persons to whom I Thought they would be Beneficial you Requested me in your letter to write you who in this community you could sind the Repository to that would take it. I have not ventured to make any enquiries among the white citizens in Regard to the matter from the fact that this is a very difficult part of the country in Such things and it would not do for one like me To talk to them about Such Things with a very few Exceptions.

[1] *African Repository*, XXIV, 268–269.

However I will venture to Suggest to you a few names among our white citizens who I think you might with Propiety Send your Repository to

Hon. H. W. Collier chief Justice Supreme Court of alabama Rev Mr. Furguson Pastor M. E. church in this city Revr Saml K. Jennings Alexc Glascock J. P. Turner Geo Purcell Jno Percell Revd N. H. Cobbs. Revd Mr. Peek Revd. Mr. White all of whom I have conversed with upon the subject of colonization Except Mr. White and found them to be strong Friends of the cause there are Some collord Persons allso who would be glad to have you Send it to them I will mention the names of Soln. Pertect Edward Berry whose Post office is in this city Martin Grear at Romulus Tuska County ala.

I contemplate writing you again Soon as if there are any others that I can find out or Think of I will write you in my next the Trip that I had in contemplation when I wrote you last have never been Performed yet in consequence of Sickness Both of my Self and family and my Business Engagements. I am compelled however to make that Tour before I leave this country But I dont expect to be able to make it untill I get Ready to leave my letters which you Published caused some Excitement hereabouts a Gentleman in this city had the good conscience to Say to others that I was Seeking an agency at your hands and stated that I had writen you a letter to that Effect and that he had Seen the letter and Said that I Stated to you in my letter that I had Travelled over Ten States and had Spent all the money I had & if you did not Furnish me with means that I could go no Farther and many other Such things that he thought would injure me and the cause of coln. this man is our Post master he is my worst Enemy I Believe in the world and from no other cause than that he owns a man of the Same Prefession as myself and the United Efforts of he and his man cant get my Business from me I had no thought of you Publishing the letters or I Should Requested you not to have done So not that I cared for any ones knowing the True contents of my letters only I knew they would be Exagerated and that to my Injury and allso the cause of colinization for of all the States of this Great Republic colinization has less friends in alabama than in any other I have just today Red the April number of the Repository and among the list of Passengers per the Barque Laura Discover some with whom I am Personally well acquainted my Soul was made glad to see alabama Breaking the Ice and my Thoughts Ran with lightning Speed across the Great Atlantic to their future home and contemplating them under their own vine and figg Tree in the full Enjoyment of all the Blessings of True freedom and Equality. I wish you would Send me the last annual Report and any other Documents you may be in possession of that you can spare which you think would be of any advantage to me. I think I can safely Say that I will leave this Country for liberia in the spring of 1850, there are several others will move when I do. Please write me and give me by letter all that you think will be Interesting I have to Request you not to Publish my letters for the time to come at least untill further Instructions

Revd Wm. Mclain

Respectfully yours.

S WESLEY JONES.[1]

TUSKALOOSA Aug 4th 1849

Revd & dear Sir

your last favor Came duly to hand & its contents appreciated I have delayed answering untill now for the Purpose of collecting Some information in Regard to the Persons who are likely to Emigrate from the imediate vicinity of this Place that I might inform you of thier intention condition &c. there is Some 25 in this vicinity of Tuskaloosa with whom I have conversed on the Subject of Emegrating to Liberea that manifest much anxiety to leave here as Soon as posible & I am Sorry to Say that there is as many more who listen to the well invented Tales of the Enemies of Coln. and Refuse to Emegrate untill Some one have gone to liberia who they Personally know & write or come back and given them information. well Sir when that is done I doubt very much whether it will have the Effect to Remove their foolish Prejudices or not there is Such an amount of Ignorance among our People i.e. Some of them that they are Easily gutted (?) by the whites who are disposed to do it the People who want to go from this Region are all free People and nearly all of them free born they are however Poor there Being a very few of them able to Pay thier Passage or any Part of it there is Some few that will be able Perhaps to pay there Entire Expences you will See as to that however when I Send the list on I wrote you in my last to Send me a copy of the last anual Report of the A. C. Society you Sayed nothing of it in your letter and I concluded you had overlooked that Part of my letter or forgoten it I Renew the Request in this letter if it is to be abtained please

[1] *Letters received by the American Colonization Society*, April to June, 1849, No. 100.

Send it to me as Soon as you can   you need not fear to Send me any document that you think would be Serviceable   there is Some information allso I wish to obtain from you Both for myself & for my friends who wish to go to Liberia.   do the Society pay the Expenses of those who are unable to pay from the place of their Residence to the Place of Embarkation and are they allowed to carry their Beds and Bed Clothes   these Questions are frequently asked me and I am not able to give satisfactory information   please write me on these Subjects as Soon as Posible   I have information from North Alabama that there are Several in that Section of the State who design going out next Spring   I Expect a letter from there Soon and I Shall Know all about it and in my next I will give you what additional information I may be able to collect   you need not Entertain any fears as to what you write me doing harm   write freely upon any Subject for your letters comes Safely and no one See them but my Self   I will allso write to the Eastern Part of this State today to Some friends and old acquaintances of mine who told me when I Saw them last that when I Started they would certainly go too of which I will inform you in my next

Yours Respectfully
S. Wesly Jones

P. S.   I am certain to go next
Spring if life & health last
I wish you allso to inform me what
is the charge for childrens Passage
of twelve years & under

S. W. J.[1]

Tuscaloosa, Ala.

I am proud to be able to inform you that colonization is growing in favor rapidly in this State, among both black and white.[2]

I see in the public journals a proposition laid before Congress by a gentleman from this State by the name of Bryan, for the building of four large steamers of the first class, to ply between Liberia and the ports of the United States, for the purpose of carrying the mails and passengers.   I have heard much talk upon this subject.   It is one that is received with as much favor in Alabama, as any that has come before the National Legislature for many years.   All classes speak of it in the highest terms, and seem to be very anxious

---

[1] *Ibid.*, July to September, 1849, No. 143.

[2] This letter was probably from S. Wesley Jones also.   At times it was not expedient for him to sign his name.

that it be carried out. If it is carried out, I candidly believe that in ten years from the date of the first trip, there will not be a free man of color left in the southern or slave-holding States. The most obstinate among us give way, and agree that they will willingly go if this project is carried out. The great length of the voyage, and the time it takes a sailing craft to perform it, deter very many, and the expense of the trip keeps many others away from the Ethiopian Republic; all of which would be obviated, if these steamers were in operation. My sincere prayer to Almighty God is, that they may be speedily put on the line, and that every free man in these United States may avail himself of the great advantage of getting to his fatherland.

It is gratifying to me in the highest degree to see colonization taking such strong hold upon the hearts of the people of this great Republic, and upon that class that is able to give the cause that aid which is so much needed—I mean pecuniary assistance: the rich merchant, the wealthy farmer, the large slaveholder, are all joining their hearts and hands to the cause, and raising their voices in its praise and defence, all over the land. And I think it would be well for the friends of colonization to set apart some day for the purpose of returning our sincere, devout and humble thanks to the Disposer of the hearts of men, for his goodness towards us, and offer up our prayers and supplications for the continuation of the same.[1]

TUSKALOOSA, ALABAMA,
Dec. 29, 1851.

Rev. and Dear Sir: Colonization is rapidly growing in favor in this State. Ere this, doubtless you have heard of the formation of a State Colonization Society in Alabama, having for its object the colonizing her free people of color on the west coast of Africa, or in other words, sending them to Liberia. And I doubt not that the day is not distant when there will be an uprising of the free people of color—not only in Alabama—not only in the much persecuted South, where it is said by the fanatics that we are sorely oppresst, and inhumanly treated, but in the liberal and philanthropic North. We are treated about as well here, at least those who behave themselves, and conduct themselves as they should, as the same class of persons in the North. You ask the question, are you ever going to Liberia? My answer is, yes, without hesitation. I heartily thank you and the society which you represent for your kind and

[1] *African Repository*, XXVI, 276–277.

liberal offer of a free passage, and six months support. I regret exceedingly that I shall not be able to avail myself of the offer tendered at so early a day as the 10th January, but trust you will keep the privilege open a few months at least; and I think myself and several others will accept the proffered boon. We would most certainly go now, if we had our little matters closed, but those of us who want to go to Liberia are men who have been striving to do something for ourselves, and consequently have more or less business to close up. I think, however, that we will be able to leave here in a few months. There will be a handsome company from Alabama, I think, about next spring or fall. I have been informed by a correspondent at Huntsville, in the north end of this State, that there is several about there that have in part made up their minds to go, and they only want a little encouragement to settle them fully in favor of Liberia. The day is coming, and I trust is not far distant, when every free person of color in this country will esteem it a privilege to be sent to Liberia.

I am rejoiced to see that the free people in the great North is coming to their right minds at last. I was much pleased with the letter of Mr. Washington, of Hartford, on the subject of the condition of the colored people in this country. I trust there will be found ere long many Washingtons in the field laboring in behalf of Colonization. I was also pleased to see an account of a meeting of the colored people of New York, not long since, to take into consideration the expediency of emigrating to Liberia. I trust that these meetings will be gotten up in every State in the Union. Let the free colored people of every State meet in convention in their respective States, and exchange opinions, and make their views known to each other, and if needs be, hold a grand convention of all the States at such time and place as they may think proper; and let those State conventions send delegates to Liberia, or if they should think proper to have a general convention, let that convention send delegates. There is upwards of two thousand free colored people in Alabama; and if each of these would contribute but twenty-five cents a piece, we could have a fund sufficient to send two delegates to Liberia. Now, it does seem to me, if we, as a people, do feel any interest in our own welfare and that of our children, we will have no objection to inquiring into a matter of so much moment to us, at so small a cost.

I trust my brethren will think of this matter, and arouse themselves, and let national pride be kindled up in their hearts, and go to

and make us a great nation of our own, build our own cities and
towns, make our own laws, collect our own revenues, command
our own vessels, army and navy, elect our own governors and law
makers, have our own schools and colleges, our own lawyers and
doctors, in a word, cease to be "hewers of wood and drawers of
water," and be men.

Believe me, yours, and Colonization's devoted friend,[1]

Rev. W. McLain.   S. W. JONES.

HUNTSVILLE ALA April 18th, 1852

Revd and dear Sir

your favor of the 27th ult came to hand via
Tuskaloosa on the 15th inst. I Rd the Report alluded to in your
letter and found much Interesting matter in it. I have been careful
to have it Read by Every free Cold. Person of my acquaintance and
those who could not Read themselves to Read it to them Especially
the Report of the Maryland delegates. Thier Report Seem to give
Entire Satisfaction to the people so far as they have heard it   indeed
it is so Encourageing that many of them are fully made up and are
making preperations to Leave this country at an Earlier day than
befor anticipated by them. I am still more than Ever Encouraged
to believe that we will have a large and Inteligent company from
Alabama in the fall or spring at farthest. I have been in this place
two weeks to day. I have visited nearly all the free families here
and made it convenient to talk with them about Emigrating to
Liberia and I am gratified to inform you that Every one of them
with whom I have conversed seem to be alive on the subject and
many of them Express a determination to go to that country and
that as soon as they can Posibly get away   there are many interesting People in this part of the state and if we could get them to
Liberia they would indeed be valuable to themselves, to Society
and to thier country

there is a Gentleman here with whom I am staying by the name of
John Robinson who is a valuable man in any community   he has an
Interesting family of five children and wife a son in law who by the
by is an Inteligent and valuable man and four grand children the
ofsprings of this son in law and four other grand-children which
ar the offsprings of one of his sons, making a family of seventeen
besides several orphans, under his charge left by a free woman who
died here some time since   his children can all Read and write and

[1] *African Repository*, XXVIII, 148-149.

are very inteligent. *Robinson desire me to say to you that he is together with his family candidates for Liberia he wishes you to send him the African Repository during his stay here and Requests you will be carefull to direct to John Robinson Levy stable Keeper,* as there are several Gentleman here by the same name and if not directed as above he would in all Probability never get it. I visited yesterday a family fifteen miles from this place named Sampson I Read to them the Report of Messers Janifer & fuller which seemed to gratify them much Sampson wife has a Brother in Liberia who is a member of the Legislature his name is M. H. Smith the whole family seemed anxious to Emigrate and they say they are going and no mistake there are many others in and about Huntsville who Express much anxiety on the Subject and I think I have never seen a people among whom an agent of your society might Effect so much good as this people. I have leave here for Tuskaloosa on the 19th I hope I shall be in time to meet Mr Pease if I should meet him there I shall take pleasure in complying with your Request when I get home I will write you more fully

Your devoted friend
S. Wesly Jones

Revd Wm McLain [1]

Tuskaloosa Ala Nov 7th/56
My dear sir

your favor of the 29th ult have been Red the contents was cheering to the Persons Interested. they Express a Great deal of Gratitude for your and the societys Kindness in Extending to them a free Passage and Six Months support in Liberia and will avail themselves of the oportunity and desire me to say to you that they will be in the City of Baltimore In time for your vessel to sail on the 1st Decr next. I would be Gratified could I obtain Names Enough to fill up the Blank form Sent in your letter there is Several Persons here in the same condition as those for whom I applied In my last letter I.E. as Regards the Law, having bought thier time: some of them have made money and have somthing ahead. they will be compelled under the Existing law to leave this state. they have entertained erronious opinions in Regard to Liberia. Ignorant and designing Persons having misrepresented the country the Coln Society and Every Person connected with the Coln. Interest but

---

[1] *Letters received by the American Colonization Society,* April to June, 1852, No. 96.

the spell Is begining to Break and they are now thinking of making Liberia thier future home.

I have not left a Stone unturned to convince them of what I honestly believe to be their true Interest I.E. that Liberia is the country Emphattically the Country for the Colored Race and the only Country upon this Green Earth where they may or can Enjoy Social and Political Liberty which is the dearest of Earthly Blessings

You doubtless think that I am Slow In making up my mind about going to Liberia but such is not the Case for my mind have been for years Settled upon the Question but thier are hindering causes in the way that Prevents my Going for the Present. and they are of a character that is wholly beyond my control. I had fondly hoped they would have been Removed long ago but such Is not the case & I must Patiently bide the time when they will be Removed. In the mean time I have lost none of the zeal manifested years gone by In favor of the Coln Cause & Liberia but feel deeper Interest and a more abiding Fidelity than Ever In both. With the deepest Gratitude for Past favors, and the most ardent desire for the Prosperity of your Self the Coln Society and Liberia I am my dear Sir

Most Respectfully
your obt Humble Servt

Revd Wm Mclain   S. WESLEY JONES
Washington Cty [1]

TUSKALOSSA ALA April 10th/59

My dear Sir

your letter came to hand several days since and I have been waiting for a hearing from Frank Owen after Reading to him your letter. I wrote to you at his urgent Request and after the Society so kindly a Second time complying with his Request I am Pained to say he declines going to Liberia

the cause of Refusul (he says) being that his wife have been Tampered with by some designing Person or Persons, who have got her to believe that to go to Liberia is to die of Starvation or be Eaten by the Natives, and Rather than subject herself to Either of these Evils, She will Remain a Slave in Alabama   I have seen her   She will listen to nothing or any Persons save her deceptive advisers

I much Regret that I troubled you or the Society with the Case

[1] *Ibid.*, October to December, 1856, No. 176.

trusting what I have said will be satisfactory in the Premis
I Remain My dear sir

your obliged Humble Servt
S WESLY JONES

Revd Wm MLain
    Washington City
        D.C.[1]

FROM JAMES M. BLAND

CHARLESTON So ca   July 3 1848

Rev Sir

    I trust that you will not take it to be a liberty in my ad-
dressing you not having been known to you before but your position
with respect to the Collonization Society have induced me to make
bold to entreat your kind offices in my behalf, I have a Son at
present residing in Philadelphia, Allen M. Bland is his name, you
may perhaps have seen him as he has visited Washington city;
during his childhood he received the best Instruction attainable in
this City which enables me to say that he received a very fair
Education as his Tutor was a graduate of the Charleston College
and bestowed uppon him much attention and from his displaying
much faculty for acquisition and very rapid progress for one of
his years. I was induced after his school course were completed
to consent to Sending him north in the view of his having Superior
oppertunities to improve his mind and be placed in a sphere of
usefullness, but these hopes are not realized and he is without any
Steady calling in Philadelphia, therefore Sir my object in addressing you is to entreat you to endeavour to induce President
Roberts to take him into his Service in Some capacity and take him
along with him to Liberia as his being now but on the verge of
manhood the Recommendation and concern in his behalf of Pres.
Roberts would not doubt conduce much to his welfare, Refferences
of his character may be had from Rev. Daniel Paine Philadelphia,
by complying Rev Sir with the above entreaty you will do an
invaluablé Service to an anxious Father and Mother and place them
under the highest obligations of gratitude to you, please should
you Succeed Address him at Philadelphia and myself at this city
                and permit me to Subscribe myself your most
Obt Servt

JAMES M BLAND

his Residence is no 157 South Sixth St
        Philadelphia.[2]

[1] *Ibid.*, April to June, 1859, No. 34.
[2] *Ibid.*, July to September, 1848, No. 26.

FROM ALPHONSO M. SUMNER

WASHINGTON, July 6, 1848.

Rev. Mr. McLain.—Sir, having determined to visit Liberia, Cape Palmas and some other parts of Africa, if found practicable, for the purpose of collecting such tangible and incontestible evidence as shall enable me to work effectually in the advocacy of truth in opposition to the prejudices of my brethren entertained so generally against emigrating to Africa, I have been advised by a number of the distinguished clergymen and gentlemen of Philadelphia to come to this city to solicit aid.   I have been for many years familiar with the views and feelings of the colored people in the free States, and have recently made myself acquainted with the sentiments of the free colored people of the southern States.

The more intelligent among them in both sections are greatly divided—a respectable minority at least are strongly inclined to emigrate beyond the limits of the United States, believing (as I do) that unrestricted freedom, political, and social elevation cannot be attained here.   I am strongly inclined to the opinion, that at the present time at least, Liberia and colonization present the only tangible prospect. The question therefore with them is, can we emigrate there with a reasonable prospect of living.   It being under the tropical sun, you will say, sir, I doubt not, that they have abundance of proof.   But I would respectfully reply, that we have had the most exaggerated statements upon both sides, and been forced into opposite extremes; many have gone in search of an El Dorado—came back disappointed, and represented the colony as a "Grave yard."   While others still maintain that there is no place on earth so blessed.

Unfortunately, every thing is attributed to interested colonists or persons favorable to banishing the free colored people from the United States, that slavery may be made more permanent.   I unhesitatingly confess that the latter is the opinion entertained by the humble writer for many years, an opinion formed from hearing the speeches of eminent agents; and the only legitimate one deducible from what I was in the habit of hearing, urged as reasons for supporting the scheme where I resided.

But I have been led to examine the subject in connection with that of emigrating to Canada and the West Indies, and have come to the conclusion above indicated.   I believe also, that the success of colonization promises the only reasonable hope of civilization and Christianizing the natives; and that the abolition of the slave trade cannot be hoped for upon any other ground, while a market exists in any country.

I have thought proper to be thus particular, sir, in order to inform you precisely what I aim at, as I am seeking to obtain your approbation and patronage. My design is, to go to Africa as soon as practicable, and remain there a sufficient time to obtain whatever information shall be deemed attainable and necessary; and then return to the United States for the purpose of disseminating the useful information. I have for some time published a small weekly paper at Cincinnati, Ohio, devoted to the elevation of colored people, which will be used as the channel of communication, should I live to return.

In addition to the letters I have, I would respectfully refer to the fact, that I have the confidence of a number of distinguished friends of humanity, as will be seen from my subscription paper, among whom are the Rev. J. B. Durbin, D.D., Rev. J. Parker, D.D., Rev. A. Potter, D.D., Rev. J. W. McDowell, D. D., Rev. J. H. Kennard, Rev. T. L. Janeway, Rev. R. B. Dales, D. D., Rev. E. W. Gilbert, D. D., Hon J. Jones, Messrs. P. T. Jones, J. Hazelhurst, R. B. Davidson, W. Wurts, esq., and Drs. John Bell and S. P. Gebbard, M. D., of Philadelphia. Also, Messrs. R. and W. Lennmons and S. Sands, Rev. T. B. Sargent, J. A. Collins, and Rev. Mr. Morgan, of Baltimore.

The gentlemen whom I have consulted, advise me to call upon you, sir, believing that should I be able to secure your confidence and approbation, I might succeed in obtaining considerable aid in this city.

In the hope of meeting with your approval and patronage, I remain your humble servant,

ALPHONSO M. SUMNER.[1]

FROM JAMES R. STARKEY

NEWBERN, N.C.

July 12th, 1848.

Rev. and Kind Sir:—Your favor of the 23d June was very thankfully received, and with regret I learn that the constitution of the Colonization Society forbids the use of its funds for such a purpose as mine and therefore cannot advance the money I need. But I feel extremely thankful to find in you, sir, a friend who will try and borrow it for me: should the effort succeed, I assure you,

---

[1] *African Repository*, Vol. XXIV, 243–244.

sir, it shall not be abused. My master is at present in the western part of the State and will not return until November, when I hope a final arrangement will be made.

I have authority from the Rev. William N. Hawks, of this place, to refer you to him for my character, &c., and if you will drop him a line it will be forthwith attended to. I did not give all my real name in my first letter for fear of detection and punishment, not knowing how it would take under the laws of this State, but since I have consulted the Rev. Mr. Hawks, he assures me that there is not the slightest danger in the world in such a correspondence as this. My real name is James Rial Starkey. I am a barber, and follow that business, and were my wages stopped I could in a very short time refund it back. I am sorry to say that I do not belong to any church, but I flatter myself that I am not the vilest sinner. I am a regular attendant of the Episcopalian Church. Mr. Hawks will be glad to hear from you, sir. You exhort me not to be too much encouraged, but wait with patience: but, sir, I must feel encouraged as long as there is a glimmer of hope of me ever seeing the country I long to make my home.

Respectfully, your humble servant,
James R. Starkey.

To the Rev. Wm. McLain.[1]

New Bern NC   Nov 21st 1848

Rev and Dear Sir

I trust you will not construe the reception of this letter as any act of impatience on my part with regard to my case for I assure you Sir I am thankful and content to await my fortune whatever it may be and hope for the best.

I would simply call your attention to the fact that I have some what of a limited time to arrange my business with my master he gives me to the first of January to see what I can do for myself. any intelligence between this and then you may be pleased to communicate will be indeed very thankfully received. I See in the Repository of october my letter published and with some success God grant the remainder may be raised and should I ever be so fortunate as to reach Africa s suny clime where I shall raise my voice in unison with those gone before me "The Love of Liberty Brought me Here" then I hope to be able to remember my friends

[1] *African Repository*, Vol. XXIV, 304–305.

and particular those who remembered me, Respectfully your Humble Servant

JAMES R. STARKY [1]

NEW BERN N. C. Feb. 26th 1849.

Rev and Dear Sir

your very obliging favor of the 6th inst. was received by Mr Hawks, and he directs me to Say to you Sir, that my prospects has again brightened a little since I write to Mr. Pinney. my value being reduced $150, and I have every reason to believe that I will be able to rais by the end of the present year through my own exertion aided by a few friends here, a sufficient amount ($200) to meet the sum that you has been so kind and instrumental in raising for me. should I succeed (which at present appearances I believe I can) it will be that much money paid and *not* borrowed. So therefore I will be able at once to enter uppon the payment of your $450.- will you be good enough kind Sir to inform us through Mr. H. whether or not you can induce those benevolent and noble hearted gentlemen who has contributed so largely to my aid, to stay the amount for that length of time (12 months) or in other words, whether the loan can be affected at that time.

Sir I am not at all insensible of the fact, that I have been exceedingly troublesome to you for the last nine months. but for which I hope Sir, the interestedness of the case to myself *personally* will plead my apology. accept then kind Sir, my sincere thanks for the noble part you has taken in my behalf. you will ever live in my memory whilst on earth I stay, and Sir, as I am unable to reward you, I trust that *he* who rules the destiny of all things will reward you for me.

By answering the above inquiry you will greatly oblige your very humble Servant

JAS R. STARKY.

P. S. I called on the Rev Mr Brown the agent for this State when he was here a few weeks since, and conversed with him freely upon Liberia and its future prospects, of which he spoke very encouragingly, and he promised to do all he can for me on his route—

J. R. S.

To the Rev Wm M Lain.
Washington City
D. C.[2]

[1] *Letters received by the American Colonization Society*, October to December, 1848, No. 188.
[2] *Ibid.*, January to March, 1849, No. 319.

New Bern   May 6th 1849.

Rev and Dear Sir

Yours of the 6th March is recd. and by it I am informed that you were then on the eve of leaving the city of washington and would necessarily be abscence some two months. at the end of which time you desire me to drop you a line of information—that time being now about to expire   I sincerely hope these few lines will meet you and your safe arrival in the district in the injoyment of good health.

Sir I regret that my last was not sufficiently intelligible to be understood.   "I inform you Sir that my *Master* is willing to wait for the present price which he asks for me, till the end of the present year and by that time I *will* be able to raise the *balance* necessary to meet your $450   should you be able to secure that amount for me."—Sir I was much grieved on ascertaining that the arrangements you had made for me were all put to flight in consequence of the price being raised but I do hope those arrangements will once more come together.

if they do, I certainly intend to avail myself (honestly) of their benefits.—I am truly sorry to trouble you so much Sir and that too with a subject intirely of no importance to you.   but I trust my motive will be duly appreciated and therefore excuse me.

Should you be fortunate enough to again raise the $450 I think I shall be able to have the *remainder here* in time to meet it.

Be kind enough to let us hear from you Sir through Mr H: and accept my sincere thanks for your unwearied attention to my interest.—

Very Respectfully

To Rev. Wm McLain   Jas. R. Starky.

Washington City D.C.[1]

P. S. if you heave any numbers of Liberia newspapers that is of no service to you, I like to see a number Sir if you can conveniently enclose one to my address.

J.R.S.

New Berne Aug 17th/49

Rev and Dear Sir

I trust you will pardon me for again interrupting you   I know I have been more trouble to you now then I shall ever

[1] *Ibid.*, April to June, 1849, No. 112.

be able to repay, But I sincerely hope it wont be very long before my troubles shall *cease*. Your letter in answer to my last, was received with the two newspapers, for which I am greately obliged to you. they have been read by a great meny persons both white and colored

My object in writing you now Sir, are simply to inform you of the fact, that we shall be ready to receive any thing you can do for me by the first of September should it be convenient with you, as our arrangements are all made and ready. But if you should not be ready Sir, and if there is any *probability* of any thing being done for me at any other *time*, I can *gladly* await its forthcoming.—

Be good enough kind Sir to let us hear from you, either through Mr Hawks or Mr Stratton.

If I can make it convenient when the agent of your Society passes here again, I will subcribe to the Liberia Hearld, as I like it much

Respectfully your humble Servant
JAS R. STARKY

to Rev Wm Mclain
    Washington City
       D C [1]

NEW BERN N. C. June 23 1850

REV MR MCLAIN, *Sir*

I understand that the Libria Packet will sail in a few days for Monrovia. if so you will greatly oblige me by forwarding the enclosed letter to Andrew H. Dickinson—

Allow me to avail myself of this occasion to return you my heart-felt thanks for past favors. Tho your efforts and those of others, has as yet proved unsuccessful, yet I cannot forget the gratitude I owe you and thim for the zeal manifested in my behalf. Sir, the way yet looks dark and dim before me. yet I hope ere long to discover a ray of light that will continue to brighten until its beams are sufficient to light my path-way to the suny shores of Liberia. Should you yet see any way to relieve me, I assure you sir, that intelligence of the same will be most thankfully received.—

I see in the last Repository the publication of a little Book called *The New Republic* will you be so good as to *send me a copy* to the care of Rev Mr Stratton or Rev Mr Hawks, and tell

[1] *Ibid.*, July to September, 1849, No. 188.

us the price as it is not stated in the Repository and I will send it you, also a Liberia Newspaper and oblige your
humble Servant

JAS. R. STARKY [1]

FROM THOMAS G. SMITH

CHARLESTON So. CA June 30 1848

Rev. Sir

I am directed by Resolution of the Liberia Association Institution constituted by a number of Free Colored male Inhabitants of this City and its Suburbs and intending to Emigrate to Liberia as you will perceive, to solicit your kindness in perusing the enclosed Communication to President Roberts and if you perceive nothing exceptionable therein to Seal and forward it to him, and should you or he at any time desire to Communicate to us any thing thereto relating or of the Republic of Liberia, I think that a letter directed to the undersigned and envelloped and addressed to Mr. S. Howe will be certain to reach its destination and the postage will be defrayed by me.

Hoping Rev. Sir that you are in the enjoyment of good health I Subscribe myself most Respectfully your   Obt Servt.

THOMAS G. SMITH
Pres. Liberian Association

P. S.   I have given the names of myself wife and two male children to Mr. S. Howe as intended Emigrants by the next trip of the Liberian Packet as per notice in the Repository   TGS [2]

CHARLESTON So CA July 13th 1848

Rev Sir

I have received yours of 7th Ult. and it afforded me much Satisfaction to learn of your approval of our Communication to President Roberts and your anticipation of his Responding thereto, with respect to the publication of the said Correspondence in the Repository I can See no harm to arise therefrom as I feel comfident that Pres. Robts. will communicate nothing unbecoming for Publication   all that I would like is for the names of the Committee to be excepted as we are all disposed to avoid unnescessary notabillity and I do not deem that the mention of the names would be Essential to the form of Publication.

[1] *Ibid.*, April to June, 1850, No. 324.
[2] *Ibid.*, No. 297.

I am quite glad to learn of the voyage of the Packet and will inform the Friends that I know to be a going out in her to make ready.

And trusting Rev. Sir that you are in the Enjoyment of good Health

> I Subscribe myself with great Respect
> Your Obt. Servt
>
> THOMAS G. SMITH
> Pres. Liberia Association [1]

CHARLESTON SO CA   August 11th 1848

Rev Sir   I intrude uppon your known Spirit of Kindness by addressing you a few lines feeling assured that if you cannot comply therewith you will not conceive my Sugestions as offensive, we have received the glad tidings of the Safe arrival of the Packet I have received a very encouraging letter from F. P. David whom you will remember as being one of the Howards Emigrants, from this City, he speaks highly of monrovia his Kind reception, its churches Buildings &c, now Sir my object is to State that in consequence of the very favorable auspices of all things connected with your great and Humane work that there exists quite a Sensation on the Subject in these Parishes and I feel confident that unless Something unfavourable Should turn up that Charleston will become a regular annual Contributor of Emigrants for Liberia, now when it seems that Folks are apprehensive about the danger of the Affrican Voyage prior to the Autumnal Equinox Therefore Rev Sir I think that if it would harm no Interest it would be bestowing uppon us a great boom to delay the departure of the Packet untill the latter of September when it will be Safe and convenient for all parties; Trusting in the Kindness of your disposition towards your change and knowing that whatever your conclusion may be it will be Such as the circumstances of the case require, and Trusting that you continue in the Enjoyment of good Health I Subscribe myself with great Respect

> Your Obt Servt
>
> THOMAS G. SMITH. [2]

[1] *Ibid.*, July to September, 1848, No. 58.
[2] *Ibid.*, No. 160.

CHARLESTON So ca Nov 16th 1848

Rev Sir, I trust that these few lines will meet you in good health, My object in communicating the Same is to bring myself to your remembrance having had some former correspondence with you which you will no doubt recollect, having been unavoidably detained from Emigrating with the late Expidition, I am a Candidate for the January trip from Baltimore, mine together with another family, they moving pretty much by my advice, Viz J Ballantine and his, to endeavour to Secure a passage as above is the cheif object of writing as we have made all our arrangements &c and trust that Providence will bless the Society with the means to continue the good work,

I Subscribe myself with much Respect   your Obt Servt

THOMAS G. SMITH

N.B. we have reported to Mr Howe [1]

CHARLESTON So ca. Febry. 8th 1849.

Rev.Sir

I hope that these few lines will find you in the enjoyment of good health, eer you receive which, we will have Sailed from this City for Baltimore to take the Liberia voyage in the Packet, we will leave in the Schooner Monteray expecting to Sail on tomorrow the 9 Inst,   Three familys consisting of Eleven persons (including children) forms our party,   I have been advised by a correspondent in Liberia to apply to Mr. E Cresson of Philadelphia with respect to a School Located at Factory Island Liberia in which there is a vacancy of a tutor,   Rev Sir you will do me a favor by acquiring the particulars concerning the Same and inform me thereof when I meet you in the City of Baltimore,   I felt much Interest upon learning of your late visit to New Orleans and was gratified to learn of your being enabled to defer the Expedition and thus escape from your Eminent Liability to danger.   The late accounts from the Emigrants to Liberia I regard as being decidedly favorable.

In haste, With great Respect I Subscribe myself   your Obt Servt.

T. G. SMITH.

REV W McLAIN [2]

[1] *Ibid.*, October to December, 1848, No. 169.
[2] *Ibid.*, January to March, 1849, No. 231.

From Sion Harris

Baltimore. Aug 3 1848

Rev. Mr. Mclelan

Sir I received your letter this morning in answer
to the one that the Dr. wrote   he thinks you did not understand
the drift of his letter from your answer   But he will answer it
himself as he wrote it.   I did not wish you to think hard I only
wanted to know whether I would be any service to you or whether
you would want me planely or not as I could not git here any sooner
I am here and if I can be any service I am willing & if not I only
thought I would try to get home   do not think that I wish to tuch
or hurt your feelings in the least   I did not I believe you are a man
of your word if not I would have been in Africa   But I am here
willing to do what I can if any thing Just what you think is the
best I am willing to do   I am in a land amungs Strangers   I look
to you & what you say   I will try to do as far as right   I only
wanted to know what you would do & what you could do that was
all   Dr. Hall will answer that letter   I send this to let you know
that I did not mean any harm if you had no work for me I ment to
go home in the packet   this is not Liberia no more   My love to
Mary Moore   Say to here Mrs Harris is well the Dr. will write to
you what that letter ment   he says he will write tomorrow   then
your mind will be settled and you can let me know what I may lie
apon in that answer then my mind will be at ease I know It takes
time for all things

yours Sion　Harris [1]

From H. B. Stewart

Savannah 17th Guly 1848

Dear Sir   I Reciev your leter dated the 23 Gune Together with
the packedge come Safe to hand and and I will a Shure you I was
more thin glad to have such a complement pade to me in this part
of the world for it was a Sorse of gate Satisfaction to Reciev Such
a masterly pease of work as that more Esspesily Be cause it came
from one of the fabel Sons of Africo   I must Repeat it   it is in my
humble (?) Gugment it is as good an adress as Eny I ever Read
I a Lude to President Roberts inagural addres and more So Because
the foundation of his ReMarks is a humble Relience upond the
aide of the almity for on lest he is at the heade of all our affares all

---

[1] *Ibid.*, July to September, 1848, No. 138.

of our ledguslative (annacments) will only End in confusion   iam
?   also made them glade in Reading that Part of the address
witch asshure to the peopel that in a leter from you (Mr mclain)
the Bord of directors had no intention of with drawing thear aide
from the paple of liberia Be cause they have declare themselves as
free and independente But Reather to in crease thear efford for in
my Gudgment if the american Colonization was to with draw their
aide thousands of the free collour people in this country will have to
Remain and Sufer for they have not the monie to Emigrat to liberia
for it is to that Society and that Society a lone ande in the Blessing
of God. the mass of free people in this country Seeks for delivernce
fr the present Bondege an degredation they ear labering ounder and
if Liberia Ever Became a great nation She will Ever owe her origin
to american colonization Society may heavin Smile apound the
Benefeshens of man kind——Dear Sir I have converse with a
number of Respectuble free men of color and thear united Sentiment
is sind ous a vesel in April or may   may is peferabell Eny how
Sind ous in the Spring   Some of them I doubt nothing in Saying
that theay will Be yousfoull Citizin to that young Republeck   Som
of them Ear men of worth among them Ear mecinist, talors Enge-
niers masians Black smiths, farmers and ministers &c and now as
thear will be call apound the Society the Behalf of the people of the
South I am Requested to say to you in this leter will you in shure
ous a vesel at that month above   if it lay in your power   Sind ous
notice in due time So that thear will be no dificulty in thear making
Sutable arangements   a disapointment in a vesel coming will be
the ocasion of much disipount to ous all no more——as information
is heard to get at in this place you will obledge me very much by
Sinding me the African Repository commencin from Guly on   I
leave this place and Eny Papers that may come from Africa on and
Sind me word how you will get your mony—Pardin me for digressing
from my main subject   pleas Sind if you have it in your power the
Eage of Presdnt Roberts and the State that gave him his Birth and
his color all of witch you will a Blidge me much no more   But
Remie yours the Frind of Africa direte yours as her to for

H. B. STEWART [1]

SAVANNAH   August 20th 1848

Dear Sir   I Receive your leter dated the the 27 Guly and was glad to
hear from you and mad it nown to my frinds the contents that it

[1] *Ibid.*, July to September, 1848, No. 69.

contaned witch give a Generl Satisfaction　thanking you allso for
your Kind atention in fording on to me the Reposortory a work
witch Evry colored man in the younited State aught to poseste for
By it the Reader coms in perseson of all the leading princeble that
Actuaed the A m can Col ni sation Society it point him to a land
of liberty and fredom whear he can Be yousfull in in Evry spear of
life　In Redding that work he coms in persion of all the that is
going on in that country　it meet the abgecteter in Evry point he
may attemp to lerin him Self—you will aso confer a faver on me
if you Ever Recev the African papers to Sind them to me if you
have them to Spare I have Send Some leters to your care to Be
bound on to liberia by the first opertunity you hav　hear after you
will a Blidge me By sinding my leters to me throw the Post ofices
my name only to it　I am aso Very hapy to See that all our frind
a Rive Safe to Monrovia making a passeg in 55 days　no more
Right me Soon as you can

H. B. STEWART [1]

SAVANNAH OCTO 23 1848

TO THE REV W MCLAIN

Dear Sir　I Right you a few lines on on the last of August in forming
you that I Had Sent 4 leters to you to Be forwid to liberia By the
packet that weher weher to Saile for that place in Sept. from
Baltomor—and not nowing weather I was doing Right or not I
Requisted you to let me now　I had never Reecd and ancr from
you you will con fer a faver on me By leting me now—I have Gust
Reecd Sevrl from Sinow all of wich wehr of great Satisfaction thear
and from Mr. Gor Simpson he Rights that Sinow is for the most
Preferred place　he is my farther in low　his accounts is much
relied on hear and will mak a very faverable im preshion hear
the minds of the pople Ear very much Sturd upt hear a failear of
a vesil will greatly disapoint ous I hope that god will bless the cause
an open the hearts of the people the thear will Be now lack of mens
No more　But Resp. yours

H. B. STEWART.

Di Rect my leter to me By maile [2]

[1] *Ibid.*, July to September, 1848, No. 202.
[2] *Ibid.*, October to December, 1848, No. 86.

SAVNNAH   January 11th 1849.
Revd & Dear Sir

Yours of the 20th Oct last was thankfully Reced. in 9 or 10 days after date and was very glad to See that you have Sent my leters that I have Sent to your care for Africa   I have also Sent som others throu your Kindness in informing me of an opetunity of Sinding leters to Liberia on the 15 Nov. for witch kindness I Shall never for get you—   Sir in takeing upt my pen to Right you I hardly now what to Say   having So much to Say I hardly now whear to Begin   But the moust that interrest me now is my new contemplated home and what is the prosspect of things in Regard to EmBarCation   I my Self apehend now Difcullty from former leters that I have got from you   But as the time is drawing near the Emigrant Ear geting warmer in thear inquiring for in for mation our Agent hear if & agent cant tell ous Eny thing mor then thear will Be a vesel   the minds of the people the Same, as lumber is Scarce in that country please Say to me what will Be the fratedg per thousand Board & lumber from this place   You will o Blidg me By Righting me as Soon as you can

> H. B. STEWART

Rev. W. MClain
Washington City.[1]

SAVANNAH 17th fbry 1849.
Rev. And

Dear Sir   yours of the 26th Ganry last came Safe to Hand,   I have inqired into the Qubek post & I find it will Be to ous very Dear Boards,   At that price it will cost 25 dollar on the frate i.e. *loade*. I think if you posoble could lore your frate to half that price & Sind ous a larger vesel that a large Quantity of lumber wold be taking ought   in ancer to your ReQuest we will let you now in due time how much frate of lumber will be takein from hear as near as posoble through Rev Thoms. Bening Eagent.   I wold take the liberty in Saying to you that we had a very large society Appointed By the agent on the first of the mounth   Evry indecation of a large number in & a Round this vicinity for liberia and of the Emagrant the greater part will Be, children   I have Recd leters from my Relation in Linoe Greanvill   all well and Ear much please with thear a dopted country & Ear doing well   have partly gorn throu the Accomating fever   No more at preasant But Shall Ever hould you in greatful Rememberence for the meny favors you have Shewn me in Righting to me from tim to tim,   my febuary number of the Reposatory has not as yet Ben Recd   pease send them to me, I think we have at least 150 for Linoe.   yours truly in hast

H. B. STEWART.[1]

FROM SAMUEL J. LEWIS

PETERSBURG VA   September 24, 1848

REV MR MACLAIN

Dear Sir I take my pen in hand to communicate to you though a Strange   Sir my mind has become Excite on the Subject of Colonization and from all that I have learnt on that Subject   my mind is fully made up for to imigrate to Liberia   I am a free man but has no family.   I am also a member of the Baptist denomination and being aroused in my mind on the Subject of Colonization was advised by some friends to address you on the Subject being the general agent.   I do hope that you will answer this immediately and give me all the nessesary information on the subject thats required for one wishing to Emigrant to that Country.   you will Excuse my boldness of writing as well as disconnecting Sentences. So far as my arrangments is concern I can bi in readiness for the next vessel that Sails to liberia   I wait an immediate answer from you

Your Obedient Servant

SAMUEL J. LEWIS.

To the Rev. Mr. William Maclain
Washington, City D. C.[2]

P. S. I was informed that you were the proper person for me to make my communication to   I have not the means to convey my self to Africa and therefore if I go it must be at the Expence of the Colony   I am no trade man   I may only be Considered a labourour but believing as I do that Liberia is infatically the only home of the Colored man I will risk my lot there as many has done before me taking the promise of the Almighty for my Support.   I judge from my incoherent manner of writing you that you will well understand all that I wish to communicate to you on the present ocasion therefore I hope in your answer to this that you will give me all the instruction that I need upon the Subject of Colonization and by So

[1] *Ibid.*, January to March, 1849, No. 286.
[2] *Ibid.*, July to September, 1848, No. 320.

doing you will confer a favour on me.   May it please your honour to answer immediately and you will Oblige your Servant

Samuel J. Lewis
To the Rev. Mr. William Maclain

Petersburg Va   Nov 15, 1848

Dear Mr. Mc Lain I now imbrace the Present oppotunity of wrighting you a few lines hoppen you are well   Sir will you Give me the right time of Sail of the Ship the Reason I want to now is because I want to be in time and whare   shall I or we take our Leave how Shall I geat to Baltimore   what will it cost me from Petersburg to Baltimore   Sir Sence I Received your letter a good number of persons have made up their minds to Settle in Liberia

as to my Part and Sheir By the as Sistance of my and your god I will go depending upon my and your god   Severl of my Native People are in favour of imegranting them Selves to that fare and distant land whar a Great meney people finds fault of who neaver yet has been there   please Sir Send me word how much will it Cost from Petersburg Va to Baltimore and Presisely what day of the month She will take hir the Partur and Brother Watkins Jones wishes to have Sum conversasion with you By a letter   Sir you Can only Say in my letter there is one in the office for Watkins Jones I would Say more But I will Cume to a Close By Saying I am your Obt Servent

Samuel J. Lewis Esq.
Petersburg Virginia

Please Excuse my mistakes if you please.

S.J. L. Esq.[1]

Petersburg January 15th 1849.

Revd Mr. Mc lain   I imbrace the Present oppotunity of writeing you a few lines hopin you at this time will Receave them with Pleasure   dear Sir I have been very on well for the last 2 or 3 weeks and I am quite on well at this time Present So I would ask you to Excuse me in this Ship and also I have not any money at all So I Put my Self with a gentleman to See if I could geat Some few dollars a head in the cose of time and also Sir I have coated a woman and She have Promused me if I would waite un tell next year She would go to Africa with me   Dear Mr. Mc Laine   I wish you would

[1] *Ibid.*, October to December, 1848, No. 162.

Perpose my time in leaveing for africa   dear Sir I do not wish to
draw back at all & I hope you do not think So these are my Reasions
for So Sayin I am with out money and wishes to geat marred be
fore I leaves and also Severl Persons Says if I waite untill the in
Suing year they will go to Africa if God Pares them   dear Sir I
wish you would look over this and considder my Case   Sir if you
please and also you may Send me and answer as Soon as this Cums
to hand

       Nothing more at Present   But remain yours

            Samuel James Lewis, Esq.
                Petersburg
                Virginia.[1]

From W. H. Burnham

           Lanesville Oct 17/48

Rev Mr. McClain

         Sir

                from the fact of your being the Agent of the
American Colonization Society has induced me to address you for
the purpose of obtaining such facts in reference to the republic of
Liberia, &c as I have every reason to suppose you are in possession
of here.   I must say that I am about to make preperations to
visit that country for the purpose of satisfying my self in reference
to its facilities &c And I am thinking of going there.   I have thought
it would not be bad policy to take with me some $1000 to $3,000
Dolls. worth of goods in the event of my doing so it would be
necessary for me to obtain facts in relation to the kind of goods that
would be best adapted to to that country—What freights would be
from Balt. N. York or Norfolk & at what time will a vessell leave
either of these ports for the coast of liberia—Sir by giving me this
information & any other that you may think benificial would place
the humble writer of this who is a colored Man under many obligations to you.

             Yours very Respectfully
               W. H. Burnham

P. S.   What has become of Alphonso M. Sumner   Did he leave for
liberia

                         W.H.B.[2]

---

[1] *Ibid.*, January to March, 1849, No. 78.
[2] *Ibid.*, October to December, 1848, No. 63.

From Daniel Strother

Carlyle Cinton Ill. Oct the, 18 1848

Mr Mc Claine Sir   after complyments I Wold wish to in form you that I am geting verry Impatianet A Bout going to liberia   I have been Reddy since Early last Spring and looking every day for orders to go. But have not Recived them yet. your letter in the Spring And all so Mr Christ in formed me that I Should go Enny how By the first Days in Oct and now I See in the papers that That Experdishion is gon and we are her yet. Sir if you pleas in form me By A few lines where I May Depend on goin if ther is now chance for me to go   I want to for I am not Dooing no good   I cant compose myself til I now wether I am to go or not

No more   But Re manes

yours trully   Daniel Strother [1]

Carlyle Ill 1848
Nov 27

Dear Sir

I received your letter dated the 6th Nov. and am afraid the time is too short   it would be almost impossible for me to get off,   Now Sir if you thought a vessel would sail in the Spring I would rather go then   my family is not very well and the whether is very cold, still if not, I will endeavour to get off if you will write immediately after receiving this for you may rely on me going you wish to know how many and names and ages

Rebecca my wife aged 37

Children $\begin{cases} \text{Martha.......D} & 15 \\ \text{James Madison..D} & 13 \\ \text{Louisa........D} & 10 \\ \text{Frances Helen...D} & 5 \end{cases}$ and Myself Danial Aged 37

Please to be certain to write word if a vessel will sail in the Spring also I want to know if Mr. Criss will bear the expences or not as he offered to do so when he was here   I am not very particular how it is but if the is the rule I wished to know before I leave also whether I am to go when I am ready or whether the Agent will be on to see us off

Yours Respectfully

Danial Strother [2]

---

[1] *Ibid.*, October to December, 1848, No. 74.
[2] *Ibid.*, No. 211.

January the 21, 1849.
CARLYLE ILLINOIS

Dear Sir
        your favor marked December the 6 1848 has come to
hand but two late for me to be in New orleans at the time it was to
Start for liberia an I want you to write to me when there wil be A
vesel Sail from washington or baltimore   your letter came one the
24 of December   I want you to write   I want you to let me know
in time So   be there   I want to go whether I take my famly or not
there is Some four or five here that wants to go to liberia   thare is
a good many more here that would go if anny one would go from
here and Come back   See what the prospect was in that country—
                                                DANIEL STRAUTHER.[1]
McLain

CARLYLE ILLINOIS Nov 12th 1850

My Dear Sir yours of the 30th oct is before me with the pamphlets
and form of appely for which I give you my thanks and her with
Enclose the foorm with Such information as you Require and Say
to you that you may Depend on our going.   We wish to Repoir (?)
to New Orleans as it is Much more Convenient for us and will wait
your order for that Purpose and wish you to Write to me in Due
time in order that we may be there at the time.   I wish to know
what time the vesel will be there and how Long it will lay there and
at what time we meust be there as we do not wish to be Desappointed
and whither there is any Danger in going to New Orleans as we are
unaquainted with the mater and are Some times told that Colored
People will often meet with Difficulties in get on to the vesel.
Pleas give us Such information as will Enable us to get Safe to the
vesel and we will be very thankfull to you for it   Please to Send
me the amount that ti will cost for our passag.   I wish you to be as
Liberal as Posible   we can Pay our Passage and Perhaps have one
Hundred and fifty Dollars Left.   there is a company of twentyfve
making up that wishes us to wait for them but I will Do just as you
Say   I have been Some time waiting and anxuious to be off if I
Should not be able to Collect all that is Due me can I have it
Sent me
We can Pay and are willing to Do so for our fare when called for
as to good Morall Character you can have any amount of Recom-
mendation if Needful while I Remain yours with Respect
                                                DANIEL STROTHER
Mr. W. McLain [2]

[1] *Ibid.*, January to March, 1849, No. 127.
[2] *Ibid.*, October to December, 1850, No. 136.

ILLINOISE CLINTEAN COUNTY CARLYE

desemder 1 the yar 1850 Dar fend
McCain i reciv you the 27 of novmber and giv me gerdt satfaction
to hear that you Reddey to teak me off   i want to steat as qick as
i Can   i Choug rethe joy in that vessel then too in new orlens
vessel   mi family want to steat varry Bad But a perse that i Cant
git rieddey as sune as you say the vessel will Sale   you would Say
tell i coud get thar   ief you will wait tell git thar i will Cum   i want
you to rit to me as qick the letter Cum or Cend it to   I Chal dow
what you say as Best   i want you to B as easey as you Can   i
excpet to pay mi fare miself   i will Cum to Baltimore ef you will
Say tell i git thar   if not i goy to obleans   i though you wold let
me goy Like the Rest   tha say that you Let them goy at 20 dealers
Let it Cost what it may i int en to goy   Rit to me as qick as posable
an If you Can wait i Chal Cum and If not i Chal goy to Newaleans
Ser McClain

DANILL STROTHER

i rot it qick got the the letter in gert hurry
excus mi hand rit ing for ant no good hand for hadant a Chanc to
git no person to dough it for me   i am Corlictin mi money i expect
to mat git all i want to git to Senit to you or to Cend it to me
no more at present [1]

FROM PETER BUTLER

PETERSBURG VIRGINIA November the 17 1848

Rev and Dear Sir   I have maid up my mind and
wish to in form you that I wish to Go to Liberia So as I may teach
Sinners the way of Salvation and also Educate my children and
ingoy the Right of a man   I have tride a great meny placeis in
these united state and I find that none of them is the home for the
Culerd man and So I am bin Looking in my mind for a home and
I find that Liberia is the onley place of injoyment for the Culerd
man and their fore I wish to in form you that I the Said Peter
Butler wish to be and Emigrant for that Land of my auntsestors
as I wish to do them all the Good in this World   I can and So I
Wish to know if you can take me as a Emigrant in the nex ship
or know   I hope you Will answer this and also Send me the nonbers
of this year Emigrants and also the Report of the Country and if I
cant not Go in January Send me Word When I Can Go and I

[1] *Ibid.*, October to December, 1850, No. 214.

Would Like to Keep up a corospondance with you about Liberia. I Wish to Go verry much and and corry all of my familey which we ar four in family

no more   but Remaind your umble Servant

PETER BUTLER   To Rev Mr. Wm McLain [1]

PETERSBURG VIRGINIA   Jany. 20 1849.

Dear & Rev. Mr. William McLain I urdress you with a Letter Nov. Last Wishing to imagrant to Liberia I was anshous to go and had maid up my mind to Sail for that part of the globe but Sence that time my familey is 3 in nomber & myself make 4 and I must say to you that my wife is not willing to traviel that diston in her preasant situation the time that the ship Will sail is the time that she will be confind in chile birth namely a bot the last of Feby or the first of March & So you can See that she is not fit to traveal in hir preasent situation for she is under apperhenchtion that hir Life would deturming upon the voige in hir case and so you Can See that it would seam hard for me to leave my wife and chidren in Virginia and seat of to go that diston from them to ingoy my Self & they sufring hear be hind I hope you will look at this in the asspect that it bare on my mind   see the corse I Love my Wife and children So well that I would not Like to part with them in no way, but Death no more   When she Recover and is able to preform the jurney I will Rite you word and then We will go to Liberia   no more but Remaind your &———

PETER BUTLER.

I thought when I Roat to you that the ship would sail the firs Decm. but you Roat me word that you Coul not tell whether I could go or Know and So I have not maid any priperation my self as yett.[2]

FROM SAML. V. MITCHELL

Nov 19 1848
CHARLESTON SO CA.

Reverend and Dear Sire.

I have taken up my pen to trouble you with a few items of instruction i and my family have put down our names to emigrate for Liberia in the Spring but i have seen in one

[1] *Ibid.*, October to December, 1848, No. 174.
[2] *Ibid.*, January to March, 1849, No. 124.

of the northern papers that the emigration from Savannah is uncertain and if it is not so Dear Sir do tell me if the vessel will be large enough to carry any freight or not being my old Mother and children are going along i would like to carry a few pieces of furniture as freight i have seen the rates of freightage in one of the repository if not from Savannah if you please sir inform me if you know of any going from any other port in the spring i would go in January but being I have and old Mother that is feeble i would not like to carry her north for it would be too cold for her being i was so sure of going in the spring i have made some arrangement already i wants to go to Sinoe being i am related to Richard Murray i am in a situation and i have give notice that i am going i have a small piece of ground and have made arraingment even for to sell it you will oblige me Sir by answering as correct as possible you can direct it to

Saml V Mitchell

in the care of G. & H. Cameron [1]

From Watkins Jones

Petersburg Va Nov 21, 1848

Dear Sir your letter came safe to hand to day which I was pleased to receive Sir I am the man of which the Rev. W. B. Rowzie made mention of in connexion with George Hargrave some 4 or 5 weeks ago I take the present opportunity of informing you that I am a miller by trade and would be glad to know from you whether or not such a trade would be profitable to me in Liberia or not would wish you to inform me whether or not the Society would aid one in getting some tools provided they are not able of themselves to get tools. I am prepared for the voyage with the Exception of the above mentioned articles I shall be pleased to hear from you as soon as convenient your Obedient Servant Watkins Jones [2]

From Alfred Payne and Mary Higgins

Nashville Ten Nov 23 1848

William Forkner

Dear Sir I write you these few lines to let you that I am very sorry that you have went off and leave me and my mother in distress I my-self is a slave man and to lend a free

---

[1] *Ibid.*, October to December, 1848, No. 180.
[2] *Ibid.*, No. 206.

man of color $100,00 out of kindness and to be fooled out of it is hard   Flem Higgins Says that he owes you nothing and what he gives me it is for himself not for you and says he never made no contract to pay it for you   As a man and as a gentleman I Appeal to your honour to leave it where I can Secure it.   If you dont I will have to lose it   Please send me an answer and let me know what you will do for us   Mr Higgins says he thought you wanted him to make you a present of that much

I believe Sir yet that you will send it to me   If you is going to let us have it please write to Mr Peter Lowery   Mr. Forkner if you dont send it to us we will never get a cent.

I am Respectfully

ALFRED PAYNE

MARY HIGGINS

Remember William the burden all fell on me for letting you have it If it had not been for me you the money would have been in his pocket or where he could get it if he wanted it   I hope the lord will open your heart and send that money back   the citizens of Nashville what has got hold of it say you will not let us have it   I hope you will deceive them   I have got confidence in you until death

MARY HIGGINS

I have been abused by Higgins very bad and he says we would not lent it to him   he wont make it good.

M.H.[1]

FROM HENRI UNDERWOOD

BOWLING GREEN KY   November the 23

Revant and honored Sir

I have oppertunaity of writing to you afew lines to you consurning the money which I borrow from you August last an which I promist to pay it over to Mr underwood for you but i have fail to it one the account of my travling So mutch   I have not the meanes to spir at the presant time   I will have to begging that you will indulge me little longer   I have not Seen Mr Cowin yit my travels has been the gain of meany Free pursom at tention for that country I wish to viset Nashville as i can mak it convenat   I will Sir Send you the money by Mr underwood Nt Sprnge to which I hope will Suit you at

Yous humble Survant   HENRI UNDERWOOD

My love to you and family [2]

---

[1] *Ibid.*, October to December, 1848, No. 194.

[2] *Ibid.*, No. 197.

From E. W. Baker and A. J. Crane

Richmond Dec 7th 1848

My Dear Sir

I am Truly Thankfull for Information you have given me Through my friend Mr. A. J. Crane about Liberia and The Time of going Thire. I have fully made up my mind to go but would rather leave in spring or fall as I have others to take along with me, and since I have determined on going, menney of my frinds will go with me If they can be accommodated in your letter to Mr. Crane you promise to write please do and how menny can be accommodated

Yours Truly

E. W. Baker.

Rev. Wm. McLain
Washington City

Rev. Mr. M Lain:

Above you will find a letter from Edlow Baker: It is his own & I have preferred to leave it as it is: He is the same person whom I wrote you about a few weeks Since: He would be an acquisition to any one of the Colonies = He is a very good *physician* for a colored man. He was in Dr Clark's office 31 years: is of good character & quite intelligent: You will do me a favor to give him the information he seeks:

Very Respf

A. Judson Crane [1]

From N. D. Artist

The letters of N. D. Artist show unusual activity of the man. He wrote frequently but found it advisable to sign his name *Hatim Tai*. He was interested not only in going to Liberia himself, but he wanted to take with him a hundred or more others to establish a Missouri colony there. He desired therefore to know the climate and the economic possibilities of the country. While some of his questions seem absurd, he shows nevertheless that he had some ideas worthwhile.

[1] *Ibid.*, October to December, 1848, No. 248.

January 1st 1849.

ST. LOUIS MISSOURI

TO THE REV. W McCLAIN.

My Dear Sir

A stranger begs leave to address you and hopes his object will be appology for his boldness—May he be alowed to say that he is a reader of the Liberian Advocate and have been Since the publication of its first number—The writer does not deam it necessary to State further that he is a general observer of Liberia and the Doings of the Colonization Society. But only desiring of your Honour a small favour by way of a little information respecting that Country.

The writer asks you to be pleased to do him the Kindness and inform him whither there has been established a "Colony" in any part of Western Africa, by the name of "Missouri or St. Louis or whether or not there has been any potion of the Territory of Liberia Set apart for a Colony from this State. If there has or have not you will oblige (Hatim Tai) one who has the intrest of the whole African people at heart—

Yours Truly

(Hatim Tai) This is all way my assumed Signature) My real name is N. D. Artist.[1]

May 1st 1849.

SAINT LOUIS MO.

MR. WM. McCLAIN

Dear Sir,

I have just sent to your care 1 letter and some Books and 2 Newspapers for Mr. John H. Paxton in Monrovia Liberia Western Africa — The person whom I got to mail them—I am not certin whether he thought of setting down the name of ("*Monrovia*") If after they come to hand—and you find any mistake in the directions you will Oblige me by forwording them with the proper direction.

If it is not to much trouble you will please Send me a few lines in answer to this and tell me when or by what vessel my package will go— Also I desire to Know from you—when the different Liberian Packets are to go from the United States this year. You will be so Kind Sir, as to send a few lines with my package of Books Papers &c. telling Mr. Paxton that they are from Hatim Tai.

[1] *Ibid.*, January to March, 1849, No. 2.

I am anxious Sir to have your Advice on a very important subject— in About 3 weeks you may expect me to trouble you Again— on the Subject here Alluded to— at which time I will lay all before you   I think something of subscribing for your paper the Repository— if you can spear them send me a few back numbers— Your letter of the 26th January has been thankfully received— and I should have ecknowledged it before this but I have been waiting for an Opportunity to send a package to you care for persons of respectability living in Liberia

Yours Most Truly
N. D. Artist.[1]

Saint Louis Mo   June 29th 1849.

Mr. McClain,
>Sir

I mailed to your care a letter and some books for "Mr. John H. Paxton" a distinguished citizen of the "Liberian Republic"—And I also wrote to you (all post-paid) requesting an answer, and asking Mr. Paxton's papers to be forwarded to him in Liberia,   I have waited in surspence—to here from the letter and pamphlets.   But up to this time I have looked in vain.   I think it was about the 28th of April that I mailed those papers to your care— And not having heard or received any word from them Since that time— will venture to write to you again on the subject.   By reading the "African Reposetory, and Colonial Journal"—of the sixth instant I observe with pleasure the Sailing of the Bark Huma from Savannah Ga   May 14th 1849   But tutching my letters and papers to the Hon. John H. Paxton, I desire to add that I have a great and laudable object in view.   And it is my earnest desire to correspond —and communicate with intelegent Colord and White persons; in the United States   And likewise, I must and will find a Channel though which I can Send letters—books & papers—As well as correspond with citizens living in Liberia   Then Sir, it was for this object that I troubled you with my letters—It is for that reason that I now write to you—In conclusion I will be under many obligations to you—if you will inform me whether you received my favors or not— And if you will condescend to indulge a correspondence with me apportaning to matters connected with the people of the Liberian Republic—you will much oblige

Yours with high Estimation.
N. D. Artist.

To Mr. Wm. MClain   Box No. 27
>Washington D. C.[1]

[1] *Ibid.*, April to June, 1849, No. 99.
[1] *Ibid.*, No. 272.

SAINT LOUIS July 18th 1849

Dear Sir

  Your letter of the 7th Instant is receivd. Please except my heartiest thanks for the kind favor. I notice in your letter and by the National Intelligencer the arival of the Liberia Packet at Baltimore 3 July. I was much pleased with Mr J. N. Lewis' published letter and the hansome and pleasant manner in which he speaks of the flourishing condition of his own Liberia. I long to be there. For a long time I have believed that Liberia is the country for me and all those of my cast who are not content with the mock freedom for the colord man in the United States and who have not lost all love for liberty and mental elevation. My Dear Sir. I must still beg you to indulge me from time to time with my letters And if I should tax your *distinguished attention* to much I hope you will pardon me. There is however an important subject which I desire to call your attention to and which I have up to this time withheld because I thought I would become better acquanted before I dared venture to far with you. I desire to inform you Sir that I am trying to raise a company of one hundred men and ther families for the purpose emigrating to Liberia and then settling a "Colony" to be known as "Missouri". I have published several articles on the Subject, and I would add that I am greatly incouraged in the undertaking by persons here of the most respectable and highest standing I beg to say one word more asregards the plan of emigration and then close—But first I would say to you that I wish you would Please Send me the "Repository", for six months and please Send me The National Intelligencer of the 7th July, and the money for six months subscription of your paper shall be forworded in my next letter. Health—Money—and friends—are the things most necessary for the accomplishment of a Missouri Colony in Liberia and I would say that if we had a potion of Territory Set apart for the above purpose one of the great difficulties would be over— However, I shall hope that you will speadly lay the matter before the propper authorities of the Liberian Government, November 1850 is the time proposed to Start with the "Colony" and allow me to say that the matter can be accomplished the frends of the Caus will ack promptly— Yours with high esteem—*N. D. Artist.*[1]

[1] *Ibid.*, July to September, 1849, No. 69.

St Louis Jany 10th 1850

MR. McCLAIN

     Sir.

Having this day Recd an interesting letter from Mr. Nugent Hicks of Liberia and it being the only one come to hand from that country I am at a loss to know why I did not get answers to the two letters which was sent out to Mrss. John N. Lewis and Jno. H. Paxton, I wrote to them both respecting the establishment of a *Missouri Colony* in some part of *Liberia* If in deed those gentlemen have failed to answer my letters or have not sent the things which I snt to them for I shall be greatly disappointed—You will please send me a few lines in answer to this and let me Know what things —Books, papers or letters have come in the Packeet for me— If you have any things for me let me me know how I shall get them.

                              Yours Truly

                              N. D. ARTIST [1]

St. Louis, Feby 1st 1850

MR. NOAH FLETCHER.

     Very Dear Sir,

Yours of the 21st has been thankfully recived But your letter does not give the information that I had hoped to get from Mr McLain. Your are a totial Stranger to me and I must beg you to pardon me for my freedom of expression—And as I am in Some way like a boat that has lost her way in a fog—I shall therefore go on and explain to you my meaning—perhaps it may be in your power to assist me by information. Since Writing my letter of 10th Jany to Mr McLain, I have recived 13 Liberian Newspapers, a Coppy of Liberian National Flag, 3 letters, 1 from Gen Jno. N. Lewis 1 from Newgent M. Hicks, and the other, with all the rest of the things mentioned, are from Mr. John H. Paxton, Now, Singular as it may appear thease things letters and etc Ware Sent to my address In care of Rev Wm McLain Washington City—Since Sitting down to write I think I have discovered why Mr McLain did not See the things that was Sent to his care for me—

On examing the letters I find that all have ben taken from the Ship by the Agent or some good friend of mine and Mailed from the City of Baltimore Md to me in StLouis—And me Seeing Mr McLain name attached to the envellope of each Article thought he forwored them to me—

    [1] *Ibid.*, January to March, 1850, No. 53.

I will get you if your please Mr Fletcher *send to Baltimore
and enquire of the Custom house Officer or proper Agent for Such
things—whither any Books—Coffee—or heavy materials came in the
last Liberian Packet.*   Also please send me word who the gentleman
was that forworded those favors already came   I sent to Liberia
9 months ago for the National Flag—The Federal Constitution of
Liberia—some Liberia Coffee—Newspapers etc   *Mr Paxton informed me in his letter* that all the above things was sent to me by
the Packet

(We) The free Colored citizens of St. Louis are to hold a Grand
Mass Liberian Meeting on the 11th inst in the Centenary (White)
M.E. Church—and I am in a great hurry to here from you—Please
answer by Telegraph as Soon as this comes to hand and I will pay
all cost

I will send you the last Number of Liberia Advocate   It contains
an Article from (my) Hatim Tai's pen—

             I shall tellegraph to you at 12 o,clock on
Monday the 11th if this does not reach you nor I dont here from
you before

Yours in hast
N. D. ARTIST

Mr Noah Fletcher
     Washington City D C [1]

ST LOUIS Nov. 8th 1850

DR J. W. LUGENBEEL.   *Sir.*

You will please excuse a Stranger for addressing you a few lines.
I hope my object will plead an appology for me.   I have recived
lately some articles from Liberia—14 different kinds African Wood,
and 4 kinds of native Iron.   Thease with other things wiru (?)
send to mi by Mr. John H. Paxton, of Liberia.   The wood and
Iron, have been examined by hundreds, all with few exception have
believed the truth of their being *Native African Products.*   My
object however is to learn from you one important truth, and that
is, does this Iron grow, or is it to be found in pure State in Liberia
or any part of Western Africa.   The fact of pure Iron growing in
the soil of Liberia or any part of Western Africa was disputid by
one of professor McDowells students a few nights ago. and he and
another gentleman pronounced my assertions about the purity of
the Iron a mere fabrication.   A falshood got up by Mr Paxton and
others, for the purpose of deception and spectulation.

[1] *Ibid.*, January to March, 1850, No. 287.

I hope you'l give me your experience in regard to the Iron and relieve me from my difficulty Please inform me if there is not to be found among the citizens—and emigrants from this country to Liberia an equal, or general average of Black—Mulatto,—and Quadroon—persons, and do they not have generally as good health in Liberia—after acclimation (?) as they have in the United States. I ask thease queston because is an impresson in the minds of the colord people here that Yellow—Mullatto—nor Quadroon—person can not posibly have health in Liberia.

Please answer as soon as convinent

Your Most obedent, and humble Servent

N. D. ARTIST

Dr. J. W. Lugenbeel

Late Colonial Physician and U. S. Agent in Liberia [1]

StLouis October 5th 1851

REV. WILLIAM McLAIN. *Sir,*

This letter is to gain information from you respecting any expedition Ship or Packet, that may be Sent by the Am. Col. Society this winter from New Orleans for Liberia Western Africa. The time has come for me to commence getting readey to go. I expect to commence the 1st November closeing up my affairs and would like to take Ship at N Orleans about the 20th Januay if this would Suit the convenience of the Society. I am very Sick at this time, hardly able to Sit up and write this letter. I commenced one to you two weeks ago and was not able to finish on accont Severe illness. I have been confind to my room ever Since, so you must really excuse this letter. Your exlent journal all ways comes to me contaning useful information about Libiria and African Colonization &c. Since I have been taking that Journal, I have got information about Liberia that I could not have got from any other Sourse. It is my intention to Lecture on Liberia in Galena Illis and St Louis before I Start. My friends here and in that town have promis to raise all the mony that I will need—Therefore I am expected and have promised them that I would go and live in Liberia as a Sort of public correspondent. It must be well Known to you how deep the prejudice of the most of our free colord people is against any thing that the Colonization Society has any thing to do with or any controle over. This being the case, I believe I can do more good by going out biassed or free from private obligations. My doctrin is that our people must emigrate from from this land of oppression, if they would better thir condition. Canida, Jamaca, Mexico, and Liberia, are all better places for us than the United States. Indeed there seams to be at this time a general disposition on the part of Some of leading man to encourage emigration to Canida. They have alredy purchased Some thousans of acres of land for the purpose.

A Mr. Anderson from Jamaca Seames to be holding out very flattering inducements to encourage emigration thinkin If things are as this gintlemen has presented them to be in a late Newyork paper, I cant see mut what his enterprize may after a while employ the serious attention of many of our most inteligent and enterprising men of color. Of all the places, I prefer Liberia for many reasons Some of which If I had the time and Stringth I would tell. I believe that the man of color must go Seak and obtain a home a peace of earth that he can call his own. he must till that peace of earth with his own hands and water it with the sweat of his brow. he must plant the tree of liberty, and buld a temple, Sarced to Religion and Justic. Than Shall the forest blosom like a rose. Ethieopea shall stretch out her hand to God. please Send me your Bill gainst me up to Jany 1st 1852. I will thak you for any thing that would give me further information respecting emigration to Liberia for the Cost of any pamphlets please put in my Bill

I am very anxious that you would answer this letter as Soon as it comes to hand, as I Shall wate for your answer before I Start to Galena And it is very important that I should get positive word when a Ship will Sail for Liberia. I receved last Octr. from Mr. Paxton one letter and 16 Newspapers. he informed me that he also sent 14 different kinds of native wood and 4 kind of native Iron all from Liberia. I wrote to Mr. Hall, at Baltimore twist, but nevr got any answer. I will get you to inquire into it for me— I have never Seen the Constitution of Liberia. If it is in your power Send me one,

yours,
N. D. ARTIST [1]

ST. LOUIS 7th Nov 1851

MR WILLIAM MCLANE

      Sir, yours of the 14th October, has been thankfully receved, and I take thie first opportunity to answer it.

---

[1] *Ibid.*, October to December, 1851, No. 21.

As regards any other persons going to Liberia from StLouis I confess I am not able to say. At the time of holding the Liberia Mass Meetings by a number of the colord friends of Liberia here there was a desided inclination on the part of several families to go this fall. But Sense the passage by the Congress of the U. S. of the "fugertive Slave Law" and the no less stringent and oppressive "free negro Law" lately enacted by the States of Illinois, Indiana and Iowa, many of them are vext at ther heard and still hearder fate and declare they will either go to Jamaica or the Canadais, in prefrence to emigrating to the Republic of Liberia. There is truly an indifference generaly manifest among the colord people here about going to Liberia, that was not to be seen before the passage of those bad Laws. As oppression, and injustice, never softens the human heart, but must tend to harass allienate the affections from the greate object in view. I can not conceive the good, or benefit the colonization cause expect to derive from the enactment of those Free negro and Mulatto Laws. I have often regreted the folly of those diceptive friends of the African race, and candidly believe that their efforts to force the colord people to Liberia by the passage of those wost than "Cuban" or Russian Laws, and must only tend to drive them to the British dominions, and must prove a fas (?) to the true Colonizationist as will as an envoy (?) to Liberia. I will add no more on This Subject and will close by thanking you for your Kindess towards me in giving me your Journal and sending the Constitution of Liberia free. Since last wrote you I have found my 14 different Kinds of African wood and 4 kinds of native Iron, Sent by Mr Paxton I shall try to be ready for the vessel in time.

Yours most truly, N. D. ARTIST.[1]

Changed Nov 5'52

BURLIGTON IOWA, Oct, 26th 1852.

REV. MCLANE *Sir,*

I expect to remove back to *St.Louis* about the 10th November. and in consequence *you will please sind my number* of your Journal to *that city.* Two months ago I came to this place and went in buisness with a very good man, but unfortunately like many others, has contracted the habit of intemperance, which makes it necessy for us to disolve— I have just receved the October No. and I can truly say that I am more and more pleased with the liberal Spirit of some of the articles which have lately appeard in

[1] *Ibid.,* October to December, 1851, No. 163.

the Repostory more perticularly the one on Educating the colord
people—The one or at least the doctrine it promulgates is in my
opion, the only practical method by which the strong cords of
ignorance and predgudice can be removed from the Colord mans
mind in regard to his emigration to Liberia   I took hold of the
Liberia cause with cautious hands—for a long time looked with
distrust and suspission upon all the acts and proseedings of all Colonization organizations and now thank God much of the dark colord
of pridgudice against the cause has intirely left my mind.   Light
is what we want, Eluminate the Soul, and mind, with true princiles
of Religion and mental light and the Africans Civilization and
endependence is complete.   I shall speak of your Articles on Education more at length in my letter to Mr. Paxton.

Yours truly   N. D. ARTIST.[1]

FROM ISAAH T. WILSON

NORFOLK VA. Jany. 20/49

MR. W. MCLAIN

Dear Sir

I have taking the liberty of Writing to you to inform of My presant
Efords to giet to Liberia. as I am now Trying to Raise a sufishon
a mount of mony to pay for myself—after my asnwer to yours of
the 28th Dec 1846—Mr A. Jarris to who I then Belong giev me an
offer to purchas myself which I exseptted for the purpis of going to
Liberia and after I had paid him $150 Dollers he told me that he
could not hold me. and he sold me to Mr James Gordon Jr a commission murchant in Norfolk. after that I felt as if my oppertunity
of going to Liberia was over as Mr. Gordon valured me So hily as
also did Every person that I have ever Lived with.   on the a count
of my industry honstry and intellignce.   Which is the cause of it,
Beaning So hard for Me to giet of from them— But Beaning So
prest in my mine which I Beleav is from god that I should go to
Liberia and Spend and Be Spent in that field to Preaching the
gospel to those milans who are in heathon Darkness   thearfore I
was ConStrand to ask my master the Liberty to Try purchase
myself which after Sume time he consented and giev me a certificate
to that efect Saying if I can Raise Six hundred Dollers that I am
at Liberty to purchas myself.   Which I am Try to Do and after I
had got a certificate from the Church and from Mr Harris and from
Mr Jas. R. Wilson and had Commenc to Corlec. he told me that

---

[1] *Ibid.*, October to December, 1852, No. 114.

if I could Raise the Six hundred Dollers By the time the Packit Sald
that he Would take all plesur in fiting me up   But if not I muse giev
it out all to gather thearfore I now Write and ask you pleas to
Releav Me as the time is So Short and I am not at Liberty to go out
of this place to Corlec any and I have got but a very little at presant
Not more thin 100 one hundred Dollers   there will a corlecsion
takeing up in the methodist E. Church of which I am member on
Sunday the 4th inst and I intend to call on all the Collerd Churches
in this City and in the County if I Should have time   But I will
not have time Exsept I am Releaved By sum person at once.   By
paying the mony before the time Errive for the packit to Sale
Dear Sir I ask you Will pleas advance me the Sum of five hundred
Dollers that I my Be Releast and I will comtinuer to Corlec in
Evry city until I giet to your or go corcordin to your Derecsion and
By So doing I may Be able to get it Before the Packit Sales and
if I Should not Susead in time for her this Trip I Would Be Redy
for her when She Return on for the first oppertunity Before She
come—Dear Sir do all you can for me—You Washed to know how
much Education I had   I answered you that I had a Common
Education   I yet cirtify the Same Such as to Read Write and
cypher. it is very True that it is Consitterd to BE very good
Education By all that know me and I can Say that I have not
Seeing any person of Culler in this place have En Education Equel
to Mine— I Will also Send you the certificate from Messr Gordon.
Mr. Harris and Mr. Wilson   if you Would like to See them.   Pleas
answer this as Sune as posibil and Let me know What you can Do
for Me.   I Do not Desier to Leav for Liberia Before I had Returned
the Mony to you agan But that you Would help me at once to giet
Clare So that theare Will be a Sertinta A Bout My goin which I
Beleav Will Be Don if I can Be Releavd—Pleas answer me at once
if you can

Your umbol Servant in hart.
ISAAH T. WILSON.[1]

FROM EDWARDS SMITH

Respected   CHARLESTON   Febuary 27th 1849.
        Sirs   to the Colonization Society

Sirs I take this apertunity of wrighting thease few lines to your
praize worthy Society as it is the only source to which I can appeal,
Sirs you will please excuse the liberty which I have taken, as I am

---

[1] *Ibid.*, January to March, 1849, No. 123.

so situated and knewing that your society Is for the purpose of addin those that are un able to assist them selves, that are desireous to go to Africa I am one of those that wants to go there and have no means to assist my self in going there and stands grately In need of help.   If it is in the power of the society which I have no doubt that there Is to releave me and I am willing from my heart to return the amount   If God be my helper that is to purchase me and I am perfectly wiling to return it back if God be my helper that all that I can say but hope for the beter,   the iner paper is a specement of my trade,   I now leaves it to your's entire aprobations and now awaite your candid decisions up on the mater

I am your Obediant servant
EDWARDS SMITH [1]

FROM MARY MOORE

NASHVILLE TENN   Feb 28th 1849.

Dear Sir I drop you a few lines to let you know that I am well at present hopeing this few lines may find you the Same   my Respects to you and your family   I am Still in Nashvill   I have one of my Sisters with me   I am verry anxious to Get home and I am verry Short of money   Mr Toms Says that my Sister will have to pay her own passage to Liberia   I do not think that is wright   I paid her passage from Fayettsville to New Orleans and back to Nashville and that is curtailed my money.   So I will not be able to take her with me without She can have a free passage to Liberia   I had a free passage when I went out,   I am verry anxious to take her with me   I know it is better for her to go to that country,   I have a little money and I wish to buy a few things to take with me and I will not have money to pay my passage and buy the articles that I wish to buy. and I want you to rite to me whether you can fix it So That I can get home, before I pay my passage   I will pay it when I get home, I have about a hundred dollars with me,   rite me whether you will be in new Orleans when the next vessel Starts, and when do you think we will get off,   no more at presant.

I remain yours &c   answer this in hast
MARY MOORE

A Citizen of Liberia [2]

[1] *Ibid.*, January to March, 1849, No. 322.
[2] *Ibid.*, No. 327.

FROM ALEXANDER HARRIS

SAVANNAH March 11, 1849

REV. WM M LAIN

Dear Sir

Some of my Relatives, who left this place in May last for Liberia, left Some of their furniture in my care, such as chairs, Bedsteads &c. They have written to me to Send them if possible, as they are in great want of many comforts which they cannot procure in Liberia—Mrs Marshall, their former owner, who Emancipated them, is also desirous to contribute, to their comforts, by Sending them something, to assist them if the Vessel will take freight *free of charge.*

Mrs Marshall says she will send them Two Thousand feet of Boards, to Build Cabins, ½ doz chairs, and probably some other articles of furniture, provided the Vessel will take it *free of charge,* but she is not willing to incur the expense of freight, I spoke to Mr Benning—the Agent here, and he told me, he did not think they could go without the freight being paid—Please write as soon as possible & let me Know on what condition the Vessel will Carry freight, I have taken the priviledge of writing you on the Subject, hoping that you would be able to do something in behalf of our friends in Liberia—

Very Respectfully
Your obdt Servt.
ALEXANDER HARRIS

Please direct
To the care of
N. B. & H. Weed.
Savannah
Geo [1]

FROM MARIAH FENEMUR

PITTSFIEND MASS TTS.   March 19th 1849.

REVD. MR. WILLIAM MCLANE

Dear Sir

This comes to inquire wither Mr. Henry J. Roberts of Liberia Monrovia West Africa, have Sent, to your care, for, me a Box containing one or more Gaires of Preserves,

[1] *Ibid.,* January to March, 1849, No. 402.

I received a letter from Him in the month of January Stating, that he had Sent a Box, as discribed a bove,   If he has not Sent anything to your care for me, you will please to answer this, and If He has, Dear Sir, you will confer, a lasting favour on me to forward It Immediately,   and Oblige yours,

Address

MARIAH FENEMUR
Pittsfield
Mass. tts

MARIAH FENEMUR
Pittsfield
Mass. tts

To
Revd. Wm. McLane
    Washington City
       D. C.[1]

FROM C. L. DELAMOTTA

Journal page 252

SAVANNAH July 7 1849

MR. REV. W. McLAIN

Deare Sir

as I wish to get one of the *Constitution of the Republic of Liberia* and *a map* I dont know wot the price is but I Send here *50 cents* and if it is more you will be plese to let me know and I will give it to the Aghant or I will Send it, and I Send here *$2* for tow person that wish to Subscribe for the monthly Repository Namly *Abraham Bourk* and *Garson Frashar* and I wish you will Send them as Sune as you can for thare is anshus to Se them and i wish you will be plese to let me know when thare is a opetuety to write to Liberia and you will dou me a faver and Send me oll the infermation you can and I will try to get all the Subscribes I can

Repos. etc sent July 12, '49

I remain your humel Sirvent

C. L. DELAMOTTA [2]

Sent Jany   No. 1848, which contains all that i wanted
July 20, 1849, N.F.

[1] *Ibid.*, January to March, 1849, No. 508.
[2] *Ibid.*, No. 24.

SAVANNAH July 16th 1849

Dear Sir

I Receve your letter with the Annual Report of 1848, witch contans the Constitution and tow maps witch I sent for but the Constitution is not Such a one as I have Sene for that which I have Sene a yeare ago it did imbrase the hold transaction of the Selabration of the Republic when the flag wos deliverd that wos wot I wonted to See they is Som Gentelmons that is very anktious to See it and, Dear Sir, I hav not Receve my July Nomber and for wot Reson I wold lick to know I have thre others that wish to subscribe for the African Repository but thay wos not Reddy with the monny Now but will be abourt the las of this weake, and I will Sen for I will use my influince among them

Respectfully yourse,
C. L. DeLamotta [1]

SAVANNAH August 29th 1849

Mr W. McLain

Deare Sir. I have tow mor Subscriber for the African Repository I take the opertunity to write you a fue lins, hoping thay may find you Sir in good helth. I Sir having a grat intres in the Republic of Liberia I hold my Self as a man of coller to give enny infermation about Liberia or the Society and I wod badg you to Send me enny extry infermation that may not be in the Repository and I Shall use it for the good of the Society and I wold badg you to Send me one of the Liberia Herald. and Do let me know for Sirton wether thare will be a nother vessle go from her nex year or not for my goin depends on the nex vessel. I Send you hear *$1.50* for the Subscribers for the Repository 50 cents for *Mr A. C. Coller* Six month and when that is out dont Send mo more for he expect to go away in that time. $1 for *Mr Daniel Virdare* for one year

no more at present but Remaine your obedent Servent

C. L. DeLamotta [2]

---

[1] *Ibid.*, July to September, 1849, No. 60.
[2] *Ibid.*, No. 135.

SAVANNAH Sep 16th 1849

MR. McLAIN *Deare Sir*

           I recev your letter of the third in witch you Stat that you had Recev mine of the 29 Aug and it incloce $1.50 for Repository for *D. C. Virdare* and *A. C. Coller* and thay have not receve them. and I allso Bedgs you to Send me one of the Liberia Herial. and I hav not Receve it and I am very Sorey that thay have not receve the Reposy. and by youre'Requst I hav trid to find out wether thay will be Enny obgection of Sending an a nother Vesell from this place nex yar not with Standing wot has ben Sed Sence the departher of the Huma. I ask fore or five Gentilmen about this and Som Says that thay dont think thay will be much obgection, and if thay Shuld be eny more pepil that wonts to go that if the Society wod petition to the Councill that it wold be granted on Som turmes or other. I intended to go and See the Mayor and ask him about this as I am well acquanted with him and I know that he wold talk with me on the Subject but I cold not yet mak it convented and as I am interested about the Subscribers not Receving the Rep.y I thort I wold writ and I heare with Send you the procedings of the Council on the Subgect as I dont know wether you hav Send it or not and you Says you Shuld like to know wether thare is enny heare that will like to go. I know of fifty or Sixty that is makin peperation to go next yar expecten that a vesill will go from heare and I cold name them if it wos wonten and as I hold myself allways reddy to giv enny infermation that may be ask concuring the Society or the Republic it has oftin bin ask me wether a vessill will go nex yar or nor and I tel them that I wold writ to you and find out

yours with respect
C. L. DeLaMOTTA [1]

SAVANNAH Nov 19 1850

Reven and Deare Sir

           I take this opertunety to writ you a fue linds for a litel infermation as I am often ask and bedgs to inquire from you. Dear Sir I had the plesur of receving a letter from my wife in Liberia informing me of hur good healt and hur injoying of hur fredom in a free land which afords me much plesur and all that She neds to mak hur hapy in this world is the present of hur affection hursban which is my wish but the condition that I am plast hendurs So I must wate on the provdance of God trusten that he will provid

[1] *Ibid.*, July to September, 1849, No. 285.

the inquiring is when will the packet Sale and ware from and whend will we have a Agant in Gorga and when will a vesel go from Savannha   Deare Sir I will be thankful for these infermation and all others that you may have

Deare Sir I wold lik to Send a box of Sope to my wife and I wish to ask you a faver if I Send the mony if you will get it and Send it for me

thar is a grat complant making janruly by the Subcriber of the Repository that it is allway So late in the month before thay are receve for the last fore or five months thare is never receve befor the 19 or the 20 and this monts we just Receve them this moring I wish that you wold See to this if you plese for thay will be anxous to See the next months expecting to here Som thing new and incuring (incurging?)

I Remaing your true freand to the Colonization Society

C. L. DeLamotta

to the Rev W. McLain
        Washing City [1]

Savannah December 10 1850

Reven and deare Sir

I wonts to ask you to do a faver for me which will be one inded   my wife Sent to ask me to Send her a box of Sope by the first opertunety and Deare Sir you will oblidg me if you wil get it and Ship it in the Packet for me   I heare Send you $3 plese to git the Serprior famley Sope mad by C. W. Smith and Send it to Greanvill Sino Couty for Mrs Martha, A, De Lamotta dow dont lete the vesel leve it and plese to writ and let me know if Send it and if thare is eny difrance I will Surtenly Send the balance

I remane your humbl Survent

C. L. De Lamotta [2]

Savannah Dec 30th 1850

Reven and Dearer Sir

I wrot you a letter on the 10 of this month and I inclose in it $3 and bedg you to get Som washing Soap and Send to my wife Martha A. DeLamotta Grenvill Sino Couty and to

[1] *Ibid.*, October to December, 1850, No. 162.
[2] *Ibid.*, No. 248.

Send it by the packet and I have not hard from you if it was recev
Deare Sir you wod oblidg me if you wod writ and let me know
about it

I heare inclose *50 cent* to Subcribe for 6 months African Repository for *A. C. Coller only for Six month*
Sir Severel pursen from Charleston and Agusta have ben to me for
infermation about emegranten to Liberia in Aprel and I give them
all the infermation that I Receve

I am your humbel Sirvent

C. L. DeLaMotta

Rev W McLain
                Washington
                City [1]

SAVANNAH October 14 1851

Rev and Deare Sir

I Set don to write you a fue linds in hast hoping it
may find you in beter helth than when I wrote you last   I wrote
you in June last in be half of tow Society one in witch I wos Presedent
of one Sending $10 for mishinary in Liberia in which letter the
perticlers wos wrot   I recev a letter in ancer from J. W. Lugenbeel
that the mony did not go at that time   will you be plese to writ me
the perticlars about it now that it may give sattisfaction to those
that is interested about it   Deare Sir I beg you to excuse this but
compose and wrot letter as it is don in hast as I jest receve my
repository and I see that a vesel will sale from Baltimor the 25 of
this month I Sene that I had now time to Spare I wrote Dr. Hall
a month a go perticler to know when thay wold be an opertunety
to writ and I got now information   Deare Sir in the last nomber of
letters receve I receve a fue from my wife and freands   my wife sed
that she hat Som thing to Send to me but She did not know how to
Send it that I mit be surten to recev it   So She wonts me to make
an arangement with Som one in Baltimor to recev it and foured it
to me   Sir I which to ask for infermation if it cant be Sent to Dr.
Hall, care for me and when he recev it to writ me word and I will
Send the mony to pay the frate and instruct him Ship it to T. J.
Walsh Savannah Gor for me   Dear Sir I am truley Sory to be so
tegest and onuneform with you on this Subject but having meny
thing to Say I pend them as they com to mine

[1] *Ibid.*, October to December, 1850, No. 320.

Deare Sir you wold oblidg me by given me all the instruction and infermation that you may have as quick as posebel

I remaine yours truley
C. L. DeLaMotta

to the
Rev W McLain
Washington City [1]

A Letter from Elie W. Stokes

Providence July 9, 1849

My Dear Sir

You will doubtless ere this have received my late communication, which I hope you will find satisfactory relative to the point at issue, which should have been my last. concerning present business, had I not have received a notice from you this morning apprizing me of the determination of the Packet for liberia to sail on the first of August please therefore be informed that I have this day packed my Books, which will be put on board of a Baltimore packet to morrow morning, which will sail for that port on Saturday next the Proprieters having assured me that the Packet will arrive in full time for the liberia Packet, etc I hope to set out from this city for Baltimore, on friday next and may reach there in four or five days, in order to be in time to purchase some articles necessarily needed in my future home, —please attend to my wishes noted in my last.

yours very Respectfully
Elie W. Stokes [2]

From H. Teage

Baltimore July 27, 1849

Rev. Mr. McLain

I just returned from N.Y. via Philadelphia. I reached this place this morning 4 OClock. I am sorry to tell you that I have been wholly unsuccessful in collecting a cent of money either on my own or the Government's account. Some to whom I addressed circulars, answered—expressing willingness but regret that circumstances prevented them from doing any thing at present.

[1] *Ibid.*, October to December, 1851, No. 65.
[2] *Ibid.*, July to September, 1849, No. 31.

The consequences is I am in an awkward predicament. I had I
supposed just enough money to pay my expenses, but I have had
to pay higher for every thing than I expected. I am now wholly
out of money even to pay my board here. I have therefore to
request that the Society will loan me One Hundred dollars for which
I will give an order on the Government or my own note. Now my
dear Sirs I trust I will not be disappointed. If the Society cannot
or will not that you will do just as I would were we in Liberia in
like curcumstances—I would let you have it—Please let me hear
from you at once

Yours Respectfully
H. TEAGE [1]

FROM J. B. JORDAN

This gentleman, as his letters will show, was a well-
prepared man like so many others who desired to go to Liberia.
Having equipped himself for business or government service
he desired assurance of economic possibilities and employment
in the higher pursuits of labor. Many other Negroes in this
country had undergone such training and those of their
number who went to Africa not only saw themselves too often
disappointed but went heartbroken to untimely graves. In
fact, the colonization movement tended to drain off into the
jungle the talented tenth of the free Negro population and
thus rendered the race much less efficient at emancipation
than it would have been had these enlightened members of
the group been left undisturbed.

NEW ORLEANS August 1st 1849

REV WM McLAIN
Secretary Am Colsn Society,
Washington D.C.

Dear Sir

A Servant man waiting on Genl Downs,
Senator from this State, named Richard W. Barrington, Subscribed
while in Washington in January last for me to the "African Repository", and left directions, as he informed me, to have it sent to
me at this place, to care Wm M Beal

[1] *Ibid.*, July to September, 1849, No. 113.

Many months having elapsed without my having received the first publication from your office, I am afraid Some mistake has been made, and therefore plead that fear as my excuse for this interruption to you.

I should be pleased to learn if you have any works relating to the Climate, Soil, products and natural resources of Liberia. If Such be for Sale, and the price at which they are held. I am anxious to acquire all the information respecting a country So advantageous for me to dwell in, and in which I could realise the value of my own abilities without being charged with presumption. I should too be pleased to know when the "Liberia Packet" is expected to depart again, and the price of a passage, as Several of my friends here *who can go* desire to meet her.

Please address me as above

Very Respectfully
J B JORDAN [1]

NEW ALEANS Augt 25th 1850

REV WM McLAIN
Washington, *Dear Sir*

I have been in receipt of your favor of the 31st July for some time, and delayed writing for so long with a hope that the African Steamers Bill would pass the House of Representatives—intending if it did to ask at what time the vessel would be put afloat, and further to know if it is at all likely that an Agent for the Steamers would be wanted at Monrovia, having an idea of offering my Services to the Company after awhile if things look favorable for the enterprise.

I have read an reread your letter, and am more pleased each time with the course you have pursued in the disposition of the open letter I sent to Mr C J Roye, through you and I now beg you to destroy the same, and to accept my thanks for the interest you have taken in my welfare. Some mistakge has been made by me however with regard to————————and I think in the name, in mistaking Roye for Roitz or Royce. Though disappointed in the man, I shall not slacken in my effort to obtain a promise of a Salary before I go to Liberia, either as Clerk, Agent or Supercargo—.

You will add to the many favors conferred upon me by giving me your views as to my immigration to Liberia with remarks about the wants of the country in a commercial sense, and as to what

[1] *Ibid.*, July to September, 1849, No. 134.

business is more profitable, upon the operation of a capital of one thousand Dollars—. I may be induced to go out very soon, probably by the vessel to leave here in the Spring with about fiften hundred Dollars—if I have any reliable information about trade, and the articles generally imported there.

I should be pleased to know the result of the shipments of the Chesapeake & Liberia Trading Company. I have been told that the profit on Shipments usually amounts to 100 per cent. If Dr Hall can give me any information upon this subject, I shall be greatly obliged to him & to you for it—.

Several men of property, ie., 2 to $3000, desire to go out to Liberia—Some are anxious to purchase a Saw Mill to be put up there—and have asked my opinion Will you allow me to ask yours, as I cannot answer them.

Are there any Consuls in Liberia— Is there any probability of the U.S. Government recognising the Independence of Liberia— If yes, when? Do you think any increase in Commerce between the two Countries would ensue immediately thereupon?

I understand that the Agent of the Amn. Government at Monrovia receives about Two Thousand Dollars per annum for his Agency, which post gives him many advantages. Do you know anything of it—. If a vacancy were to occur would it be worth the effort on my part to make application for the office—. Would any foreign influence be likely to carry of the Palm? I have strong claims upon Mr Conrad and Mr Crittenden, and through Judge Chinn of this State and Mr John Bell of Tennessee, might enlist Mr Clay's interest.

I have noticed of late several large consignments from Africa (Siera Leone I think) at New York, to Soule Whitney & Co and D H L M'Cracken Esq. I thought it might be that some of these gentlemen are engaged in the Liberia trade.

By reading and forwarding the enclosed letter to Mr Saml Quarles at Salem Mass. you will see my present aim. If you can further my object at all, I shall be glad to come under additional obligations to you. If I can get any business at all from this Country, I shall leave the United States in the ensuing year for Liberia, if not I shall them in the absence of a better offer to go to that Country, leave for South America, Mexico or California. If you know of any parties in this Country whose interest or philanthropy has interested them in the African trade to whom I might write as I do to Mr Quarles, you will confer a favor by opening a correspondence with them for me.

Having, as I believe I have, done everything that tends to show my desire to emigrate to Liberia, I shall close this long letter with the expression of a hope that you will at all times bear me in mind and will omit no occasion consistent with your obligations, if you have any, to your friends here and elsewhere, to press my pretensions as a business man, wherever promptitude, industry, perseverance, and integrity can be available—

With great recpect

J B Jordan [1]

New Orleans Octr 1st 1850

Dr J W Lugenbeel

Dear Sir

I have the pleasure to acknowledge the receipt of your Esteemed favor of the 9th ultimo in response to mine of the 25th of August to Rev Wm McLain. I thank you for your Courtesy, and am pleased that you have written me, as it has opened the way for correspondence, that will I trust be no less pleasant to you than to myself.

For the last nine years, I have been extolling the advantages of emigration to Liberia. At first I was laughed at and rudely treated by those colored people who profiting by the good times many years ago, made money and investied it in property here. About five years ago the dislike to Colonization seems to have passed away. Some few would talk of it whilst others in their timidity would only listen. Now there are few persons who hesitate to speak of Colonization and of their intention or desire to emigrate to Liberia in a few years. Several men of property from this City and Mobile are preparing to go, and some three or four men of family, good workmen, possing means and of intelligence, I will go out in the next vessel from this Port.

It is but very recently that I have become possessed of my own freedom. For want of a knowledge of mechanics or Agricultural pursuits, I am forced to rely for years to come upon my present avocation of Accountant for an income or support. Twelve months hence I shall be in an easy position, and unless some accident befall me, shall have about $1300 in cash. That sum I should like to invest in such goods in this country, as would be most likely to yield a profit, or shipment to Liberia. Your remarks about the value of a Saw Mill in Liberia have caused me to reflect very much—

[1] *Ibid.*, July to September, 1850, No. 202.

and I am now inclined to purchase a mill—and as my means are inadequate to pay for such a steam Saw Mill, as I would desire, the idea has suggested itself to me to write to you to know—

1st   What kind of buildings—stand best the wear and tear of the African climate?

2nd   Do not the white Ants attack wooden buildings, so much as to make them objectionable to persons whose means will allow them to build brick or Rock & Brick houses?

3rd   What kind of Building Timber is there in Liberia—What is the size of the trees in diameter or circumference, and what is the length—? Is Timber abundant?

4th   Where would you advise a location for a Steam Saw Mill—?

5th   Is it difficult to procure horses or oxen to work in a Horse Power Mill? What is the general cost of either, and how far in point of strength endurance and use are they compared with those animals in this country?

6th   Does not the cost maintenance and risk attendant upon the climate and the Insects make it objectionable to reply upon Horse power in starting a saw Mill?

7th   Is there any scarcity of good wood for fuel to run a Steam Mill?

8th   What think you of Sugar? Can it be raised in Liberia to advantage with the Aid of steam and the proper apparatus under the management of a man of industry skill and practice? There is such a man who has some $2000, who has promised to join me in anything I may propose that is safe as a business in Liberia, and I have thought the engine for a Saw Mill might easily be transferred to a Sugar House if desired, and as the cost of an engine would not be short of $1,250, I have thought it worthy of attention to know if there is any prospect of its being subservient to some business other than that of a Saw Mill. A Saw Mill and Sugar Mill could be worked alternately by one Steam Engine. And if Sugar can be easily raised I see nothing objectionable to our embarking the business and as I shall write him at once on the receipt of your answer to this, I shall be obliged to you if you give me a prompt answer, with all the information and advice you have been enabled to arrive at and to give by your long residence in that country. I apprehend no difficulty in procuring seed cane, and will be pleased to have you confirm this opinion, with remarks as to its quality and the possibility of importing seed cane from the West Indies, which I presume to be far superior to that in Liberia.

If your response should be so far encouraging as to induce my friend to enlist in the enterprise with me, I shall engage a Steam Saw Mill of about 10 horse power of Mr Page, the Machinist of Baltimore, to be shipped from that Port, and as I shall very probably sail from that port in Such case, I shall take pleasure in calling upon you, while there in the ensuing Summer, to make acknowledgements for your kindness, and for my feelings towards you for your efforts to ameliorate the condition of my race.

Tendering my best regards to you & to Mr McLain, I am

Very Respy

J B JORDAN [1]

Please send me a copy of the
present Liberian Tariff

NEW ORLEANS April 18th 1851

REVD WM MCLAIN
Washington, D. C.

Dear Sir

I have not had the pleasure of hearing from you of late, although I had no right to anticipate a letter, as there was nothing left unsaid when we were corresponding so briskly, to justify the expectation.

My feelings have undergone no change since I last addressed you, upon emigration to Liberia. Although not decided as to the time of my departure, I now think I will go in the next expedition sailing from here. I will therefore be pleased to learn when that will be, and also what freight you will charge me on goods—boxes—barrels both wet and dry, and light goods by measurement, from here, as I may arrange to put about 200 barrels &c aboard, which would require a vessel with two decks, thereby giving one entire deck to the emigrants which would be more agreeable to them. If the rate of freight be low I may go far beyond the quantity named here, as some friends of mine desire to make up a consignment for me.

I should be pleased to receive the earliest advice of the departure of the Expedition hence when decided upon, and in the mean time will thank you to Send me a copy of the Liberian Tariff, with a list of articles suitable to the trade.

[1] *Ibid.*, October to December, 1850, No. 6.

My Repositories come irregularly—please Send the numbers for Jany—feby—May—June & August 1849—and febry 1851—none of which were received. In haste—

Very Respy.

J. B. JORDAN.[1]

NEW ORLEANS July 24th 1851

REVD WM MCLAIN

Dear Sir

I am induced to write you, at present, to request you to send me the June & July issue of the "African Repository", which I have not received. My papers and letters are always placed in the box of my employer Mr Gwathmey, and as I have inquired at the general delivery for them without finding them I think they must have miscarried altogether.

I should like to have the missing numbers, which I never received, of the Repository named in my last respects, as I desire to have the three last volumes bound.

You will please take note that my mother, stepfather, Sister, brother & Son will leave here in the next vessel, for Liberia. My Sister is 15 and the boys 9 & 7 years old

With much respect

I am

J B JORDAN

Pray don't forget the
Liberean Tariff promised me [2]

FROM W. W. FINDLAY

COVINGTON Sep 11 1849

MR MCLANE

Dear Sir I wish to now from you the time that a vesile will Sale forom New Arlenes So that I ma be ready if possible to at that time I am very poor and have got a large famaly So I Should like to now as soon as possible I am not able to Say how meny tha will be that will go but I am a frade tha wont be many that will go pleas to let me now as Soon as you can and by So doing you will oblige your homble Servant

W. W. FINDLAY [3]

---

[1] *Ibid.*, April to June, 1851, No. 76.
[2] *Ibid.*, July to September, 1851, No. 119.
[3] *Ibid.*, July to September, 1849, No. 273.

FROM A. H. DICKEISON

NEWBERN, 24th Nov. 1849.

Rev. and dear Sir:

Will you be pleased to accept of my unfeigned thanks for what you have done for me in using your influence in procuring the freedom of myself and family? I beg you return my unbounded thanks to Revd. Mr Pinney, Agent of the N. York Colonization Society for what he has done for my humble self and to the Editors of the Journal of Commerce. Indeed, I find him, like yourself, indefatigable in exertions and untyring in labors of benevolence. May the smiles of Heaven ever rest upon you and yours.

To speak of my kind and liberal benefactors, I am at a loss for words to express the deep gratitude of my heart.

I have cause highly to appreciate and ever to remember the kindness always manifested towards my by my affectionate master. May his last days be his best days.

In Newbern, I have Spent many years. Of her beneficent citizens I take pleasure to acknowledge the reception of unmerited attention. May kind Providence ever protect them

Yours most humbly

Rev. W. McLain [1]   A H DICKINSON

FROM E. DUGLAS TAYLOR

Aug 3, 50

Rev and deer Sir i have fer sum time past want to know if you have receved infermation that i will leve this winter fer liberia three of us in family. one A Chile three years old. we wants a passage and we want to know when the time of Starting will take plase and all So i wants to know what i must Expect from the Society after hard toiling to rech this end. plese give mee Sum directio of this in point hole matter of leveing. this Cuntra and a riveing in liberia, we are all well and in high Spirits for liberia we are Saveing Seeds to take out with us. plese recommen mee to sum frend that you are acquaned with as a regular house Carpenter

i expect to be ordaine befor i leve for liberia i am one that loves our lord jesus Christ and are striven to get to heven by the hlp of god. remember mee in your prays and i all So will remember you in pray. to the lord have you a map of liberia. i wish mush to get

---

[1] *Ibid.*, October to December, 1849, No. 188.

one. if you have any to Sell plese Send mee one to the Care of
mr. nall. i will pay him the mony. i am Striven to get my passage
paid here if it Can and if i fail i mus ask it of you
i have three in family. one Child three yeas 11 months old. thair
is much inquire about what room will be aloud to ech one with
his bagige.

they ask all So if they take freight out. will you Charge them
lightly for thair freight plese excuse this wrieting i never had eny
lerning. no mre at present.
I Remain yours O Bediant Suvent

E duglas tayler. mobile. alabama
August the 3—1850 [1]

MOBILE Aug 22 1850

Dear Sir
I recieved yours of the 12 with much plesure and happy to
find that you received my letter and now take an opportunity you
a few lines more the No that we expect to leve Mobile are 11
Jack Garrne that is now geting fix as fast as he can he move over
to Mobile a few days ago from New Orleans where he is now liveing
to get his business orringe in order to get of in Jan next. he came
over to see his white friends how said they would assis him. his
white friends Prommus to met demans at the Close of the years
that he may Go
I am now wating to see Dr Hammiton how are now out of the City
to see what Can be done concerning making up that Nomber or
nere but I Can give you no more information un tel I see the Doc.
about that afar auntil I write again We belve that the Col. take in
the in the state alabama the free people of color is fabibile to Col
and I think sir ef you Address Mr Hammiton
on that subjict sum thing Can be done
Please address him sumthing for surculation and I think sir it
will be the meins of stating a Col Society in the City of Mobile
I have return you My thanks for ? of of a free pasage I am
at prasant al despose which unable me to do any thing with a bone
feln on my finger I thank you sir for the information you give me
about frat I have not as yet received the maps that you sent me
but Expects It you said in your letter that Expect to Cind but the
washes to leve the family in Monrovia and Go out and see for thim

self. We are happy to say that Coole (Creole?) of Mobile are seeking information about the Col Society

I now remain your ob servant

E. Duglas Taylor

To Mr W Mclain [1]

From J. Theodore Holly

Burlington Vt Aug. 8th 1850

Rev. Sir

Yours of the 31st ult. is answer to mine under date of June 25th ult. is at hand. As you conjectured I was somewhat surprised at not receiving an answer before, but I finally supposed that your attention to the National agitation at Washington indisposed you to Reply immediately. However the receipt of your letter dispells all conjectures, and brings me to my subject.

On further reflection I have concluded to forego the desire to introduce at present those new experiments in Liberia; for I am forced to acknowledge the truth of the homely adage, that, "the child must crawl before it walks", and that it is sufficient for the present to introduce these, the sure, and well attested means of civilization, as the Soil whereon future improvements may be nourished.

My mind had already centred upon the point, which your advice indicated and I have been thinking about further qualifying myself to discharge the high mission of a teacher in my fatherland.

I have made the acquaintance of the Rev I. Converse Sec. of the O.S.C.S. since I mailed my first letter to you,—a most amiable gentleman, who has very kindly offered to assist me further in my Classical Reading, which I have been prosecuting alone, since I received some elementary lessons from a private teacher about two years ago. If I prosecute a thorough Classical and Scientific education by devot ng my spare hours to private study, and relying upon the incidental instruction of such private teachers as I may come across, my progress must necessarily be slow in arriving at a completion; but I hope to make a solid acquirement ultimately, and consecrate it to the service of Liberia.

I am a Shoemaker by trade, and follow it for a livelihood, and contribute mutually with my brother to sustain a home for our Mother, Sister and ourselves. I learned my trade in Washington City with my Father (the late James Holly) who was well Known

[1] Ibid., July to September, 1850, No. 195.

in that city as an industrious Mechanic up to 1844, when re removed northward with his family to be releived of *some* of the disabilities free Colored men labor under in the South. He used to boast of having made the the pair of *Jefferson-Shoes* that President Madison wore on the day of his inauguration in 1809.

I would be willing to work at my trade in Liberia if the hereditary predisposition of my constitution to consumption and general debility did not admonish me that I must soon quit the seat, as a necessary precaution to preserve my health. But notwithstanding I should calculate to work at it in Liberia to supply my own demand at least, and to do more if necessity or interest required it.

Two other colored young men here, have embraced the desire to improve their education and emigrate to Liberia. I have succeeded in creating quite a spirit of inquiry in relation to Colonization amongst my associates here, since I wrote to you, by debating the following question with my brother, before several meetings, viz: "Can the colored people of the U. S. best elevate their condition by remaining in this country, or by emigrating to Liberia?" He supported the first proposition from earnest conviction, and in like manner I advocated the latter.

I am very grateful to you, for your kind offer to furnish me gratuitously with the Nos. of the Repository hereafter; I will receive them with pleasure as a great favor. I shall also be very glad to receive counsel from you, and from your proffered kindness, I shall feel at liberty to solicit your advice at any time. I have received the July & August Nos. of the Af. Rep. but the No. of the Liba Her. you informed me you had sent, I have not yet received. I expect it has been misplaced, or detained at the Washington P.O. because it was transient paper not sent from the office of its publication, I am as thankful as though I had received it, and feel deeply compensated for its loss by the Repositories you sent for which I am under many obligations to you.

Respectfully Yr. Mst. Obt. Servt.

J. THEO. HOLLY

Rev W. McLain
Washington City D.C.[1]

[1] *Ibid.*, July to September, 1850, No. 163.

Burlington Vt. Sept. 3rd 1850.

Rev Sir:

Yours of the 29th ult. is at hand. I have Received two copies of the Naval Committee's Report of the H of R. for which I am very thankful to you.

One copy I have given to a friend to Read and circulate, and I shall do the same with the other.

I am glad that you have Reason to be sanguine of the favorable action of Congress in Relation to the project.

As you informed me that if knew of any of my friends who would be benefitted by Reading the Repository, you would send it to them *Gratis;* I have accordingly spoke to several, and the following names persons (of this town) expressed a desire and thankfulness to Receive it: *James Taylore,*[1] *Augustus C. Jackson,*[2] and *Andrew J. Dolby.*[3] Those individuals admit that they do not understand the principles of Colonizationists, nor know anything of the Real condition and prospects of Liberia; but are desirous to be Rightly informed on these points: I therefore propose them for your proffered Gratuity; they will be willing to Read and circulate it amongst their friends.

I wish it was in my power to devote myself entirely to Study, for my anxiety to enter in the contemplated field of my labors is great; but I must be content with the decree of circumstances.

Perhaps to fit and prepare myself through toil and privation for such a mission will furnish my life with a prouder event than if accomplished under easier circumstances. "The love of liberty" shall make me persevere.

Respectfully Yr Mst Obt. Sevt J. Theo. Holly
Rev. Wm McLain Washington, D.C.[1]

From Benjamin S. Bebee

This writer was a student preparing himself for the serious task of the uplift of his people in Africa. As a student he seems to have made much progress. His first letters to the Colonization Society do not show as good a command of the English language as he exhibited in his correspondence some time later. He pursued a course somewhat like that of our high schools of today, but apparently took up higher branches

---

[1] *Ibid.,* July to September, 1850, No. 224.

before he mastered the fundamentals. Some of his news as to the future prospect of the Negro in the light of his status at that time are at least interesting.

SPRINGFIELD MASS August 1850
    REV. W. MCLAIN

        Friend of the colored people of America. I, bing of that race, for whose wellfare you have labored so diligent and successful, write you this epistle praying you that you would lend me some of your generous assistence, that I may be able to educate myself, moral and menatally, to employ it to the further advancement of my race, in whom have been most strikingly verified, the prediction of the Patriarch Noah. From no point do I think I could do it more effectual, than in that colony for whose interest you have labored so steadfast and ardently, The colony of Liberia; from that, and I think that point alone, will the African be able to show to the whole world, that he can be a man; how mch is comprehende in the word man. But upon this subject I cannot dwel. I know that if you take the subject of my being fitted by you or your Society for Liberia in hand some doubts will rest upon your minds whether I do this for the sake of obtaining my education and then deceive you in your hopes. God forbid that I should barter away my soul by such base purjury. It is my desire to go to liberia to labor there for my people The African. please let me know what you can do for me I am 16 years of age reside in Springfield Massachusetts

BENJAMEN S. BEBEE,

Springfield August 1850
    Please excuse a bad pen,

N B, I thought I would let you know what branches I have been studying; I have nearly finished Geography, Arithmetic, Grammar & History of the United States. Instead of studying Arithmetic and Grammar, I shall study Algebra and Latin but whether I shall finish these studies God only knows for I am a poor young man [1]

WASHINGTON Oct 30th 1850

    REV MR MCLAIN

Dear Sir;

I received your letter, together with the pamphlets which you sent. I feel much obliged to you for answering my letter, you being the

---

[1] *Ibid.*, July to September, 1850, No. 191.

first person of note with whom I have had the honer to corespond. You requested I believe in your last letter, to know what I expected to be; if I had my own choice I would be a professor mathematic; mathematics is my favorit sudy; I think it tends more to the strengthning of the mind than eny one sudy I am acquainted with. With regard to Liberia whos situation geographical, political and moral your pamphlets gave so accurate an account; I think I should go out there provided I could carry on my studies there after having habituated my self, to the change of climate to be sure I should expect to work some of the time. Yes I repeat that I should like to go out, even if I could not presue my studies before before a year shall have elapsed after being out there. But if I went out I should have to be sent out by one of your societies, am a poor yong man.

BENJ S. BEBEE

Springfield Oct 30th 1850 [1]

SPRINGFIELD May 21st 1851

REV MR McLAIN.

Dear Sir: I would again introduce my-self to you, as as the colored young man who had the honer of corresponding with you, 8, or 9 months ago. I have read a number of pamphlets, relative to the Colony of Liberia. I look upon the Colonization of Liberias as one of the noblest enterprises of the age in which we live. Commenced with the spirit of the gosepe and sustained and supported by men, who have devoted them-selves to this noble enterprise, it cannot ultimaly fail of accomplishing the great design, of causing the glorious light of the gospel, to shine upon Africa's benighted tribes. How nobe and patriotic is the sprit of a nation who, rather than suffer oppression, will continue to resist until either victorious, or byond the reach of a tyrant's power; bur nobler still is that spirit, that is animated by the spirit of the gospel, and having a soul burning with pity and love for his afflicted brethren, will surmount every obstacle, braving even death itself ot render his assistance. In vain may the fanatic abolitionist seek to destroy your power of doing good or scatter the seed of discord among you. I confidently believe that your society is highly favored of God, and if God be for your who can be against you? As an African, I feel solicitous for the continual progress of my people in the broad road of civalization; and I would devote my unworthy talents to its advancement and prosperity.

[1] Ibid., October to December, 1850, No. 92.

In Africa, there are great mines of information unexplored; the geological formation is but partialy understood, the interior of this vast continent has never been explored by many, pestilence and death meets the traveler before he has begun his researches. It remains for the naitive alone to bring to light the hidden knowledge of ages.

But I must close here.

Yours With Respect,
BENJMIN S. BEBEE [1]

AMHERST July 30 1852

REV. MC MCLAIN

   Dear Sir it affords me relaxation and pleasure To turn my mind from study to the contemplation of the present promising condition of the Liberian Republic which under your fostering care aided by Divine Providence has arisen to its present position showing by a practical demonstration the capabilities of the African race under favorable circumstances for self government. The future destiny of the African race is no longer wraped in the cloud of obscurity. The son of prosperity shines clearly upon it revealing the rich blessings of social happiness of moral and intellectual advancement. Greatful hearts will thank you for the many sacrifices you have made and for your patient perseverance under every trial that beset your path in your attemps to build up the poor fainting Affrican. A feeling of gratitude and exultation runs through my breast as I contemplate the future destiny of my oppressed brethren. Yes upon my on native shores a republic of my countrymen is rising founded upon those high and holy pincipals that grentee to man those inestimable privileges which belong to every virtuous man. Though I may not live to behold the great blessings that are in store for my people yet I wish that those who suceed me upon the stage of action may see and rightly appreciate them. May they wipe out the remembrance of the degradation of their fathers by the cultivation every good quality which will elevate them among the nations of the of the earth. I would be in favor of African Colonization because it is for the interest of my people The white man is there superiors in intellect and civalization and in their present position it is imposible that they should overtake him or successfully compete with him. A mutual fear and prejudice exists between the two race endendering that spirit of antagonism

¹ *Ibid.*, April to June, 1851, No. 191.

which must ultimately turminate in the entire exterpation of the weaker race. If I could cause my voice to be heard from the Atlantic's raging billows to the calm bosom of the pacific I would warn (them) my people of the disasterous fate that awaits them and their posterity. They must be absorbed and that to at no very distant period thay must be lost in the great flood of emigation that is yearly pouring into this country.

Hen fuge crudeles terras fuge litus avarun

I have sir read the speeches of The Hon Merssr Stanton Webster and Rev Philip Slaughter in the March pamphlet of 1852. The resolution and the speech offered in suport of that resolution by Mr Stanton is the most able document in point of clear logical argument that I ever read. You of course do not expect that I shall attemp to say that the Hon D. Webster made a great speech for we don't expect any thing else from such a gigantic mind. Before closing this letter I would ofer a scanty tribut of respect to the great immortal name of Henry Clay. That noble generous spirit whose bosome beat with the sentiments of the purest patriotism for his country and christian philanthropy for the whole family of suffering humanity and to whom your society is much indebted for its present prosperous condition will ever be remember in the hearts of his country and when Liberia shall shine forth in her moral and intellectual glory we shall delight to remember the name of so illustrious a man who has don so much for her prosperity. Well may a nation mourn and exhibit the emblems of sorrow for one of her bright suns has left this stage of existence to shine with incresed splendor in a better world. Let us remember and practice his transcendent virtues Let us like him spend our lives usefully and when we shall at last lie down to slepp withe the innumerable dead that through the deep caverns of the earth the sweet insence of gratitude may be offerd upon the alters of our memory.

Yours Respectfully
BENJ S BEBEE
Amherst J 30 52 [1]

FROM JAMES WINN

LYNCHBURG VA Sept 6th 1850

Dear Sir I take this oppertunity to write to you in regard to Liberia, as I wish to do thare this fall (you will excuse my bad spelling as it is the best that I can do)

[1] *Ibid.*, July to September, 1850, No. 128.

Sir I wish to know If the Colonization Society will send me and my family to Liberia free of expence on my side that is ef I can git my wife to make up her mind in time   we are very poor and wold not be able to defray anything towords our expences   my Self and Famely are very bright mulattois and are told by some of our wite friends that it would be imposible for us to stain the African fever, Sire I have two young children

I have seen all them books and maps an informtion about going to Liberia and I destribeted them among the free people and done geat good, but Sire a little a little while and thay recieved letters here from Liberia informing us that a geat many of the people that went threw Lynchburg from Lexington on way to Liberia was dead and some twlve or feeftee others had fell with this African fever and that laid them all cold?

the fever the fever the acclamating fever is all that my wife, and the free people of color in this plase is fread off.   P.S. we herd the death several other lately John henry and famley.

Nothing more at present but Remain
your umble servent
JAMES WINN

P. S.   we informed that one third of the emergrants died with the acclamating fever soon after thay gits to Liberia.   thar is a grat meny here wants to go to Liberia this fall as well as my self, you wold obidge my wife and a great many of the free people here for some information about the fever as thay contemtats going to Liberia

JAMES WINN [1]

FROM PETER H. CLARK

Sept 17 1850

MR McLAIN
          Sir   Having in connection with a couple of my friends resolved to emigrate to the Republic of Liberia.   We have thought it best to apply to you for information on the subject as from your position you would naturally be able to afford all the information necessary.   We would like to know at what time at what place we would be able to embark   I at present know of no chance. this year excepting the vessel which Governor McDonogh will dispatch from N. Orleans of this we are not certain whether we can obtain a passage   We think of taking a course in Book-keeping and pen-

[1] *Ibid.*, July to September, 1850, No. 237.

manship before we go, would there be any chance for us to obtain situations as book-keepers, if so what salary.   The chance for a school teacher, what amount of clothing it would be advisable to carry out with us, the price of boarding, clothing, what prices flour, pork, and other articles of western produce will command in the Liberia market.   The quality of the clothing, and in fact all the information you may have at your command that would be useful to us as emigrants   My two companions Messers L. W. Minor and Wm R Carey are both students at Oberlin College one in the Senior and the other in the junior years years.   As for myself I have but a common school education.   My address is Peter H Clark, Court St Cincinnati.   If you can find time amid your pressing duties to answer my queries you will confer a great favour

Respectfully Yours PETER H CLARK

Cincinnati Sept 17th 1850 [1]

FROM AUGUSTUS WASHINGTON

HARTFORD, July 3, 1851

As the infant Republic of Liberia is now attracting the attention of the enlightened nations, and the press of both England and America, I may hope that a communication in regard to that country, and the Afric-Americans in this, may not be deemed a subject instrusive nor foreign to the public interest.   And I am encouraged by the just and liberal course you have taken in favor of the proposed line of steamers to the Western Coast of Africa, and also the boldness with which you have lately urged the propriety and interest of some of the colored people emigrating from our crowded cities to less populous parts of this country, as the great West, or to Africa, or any other place where they may secure an equality of rights and liberty, with a mind unfettered and space to rise.   Besides, as your paper is generally read by the progressive and more liberal portion of white Americans and some of the most intelligent of the colored, I may also hope to be confirmed in my present sentiments and measures, or driven to new and better convictions.   I do not wish to be thought extravagant, when I affirm what I believe to be true, that I have seen no act in your public career as an editor, statesman and philanthropist, more noble and praiseworthy than that of turning your pen and influence to African colonization and civilization, after finding that you could not secure for the black man in America those inalienable

---

[1] *Ibid.*, July to September, 1850, No. 275.

rights to which he, with other oppressed nations, is entitled, and for which you have heretofore labored. Though the colored people may not appreciate your kind efforts, and those of many other good and true men who pursue your course, we trust you will not on account of present opposition be weary in well-doing. Though dark the day, and fearful as is the tide oppression is rolling over us, we are certain that it is but the presage of a more glorious morrow. We do not despair. We thank God that notwithstanding all the powerful combinations to crush us to the earth, as long as the Bible with its religion endures, there will ever be a large number of the American people whose prayers, sympathies and influence will defend us here, and assist and encourage our brethren who have sought, or may in future seek liberty on a foreign shore. If these no other reward awaits, the time is not distant when they shall receive at least the thanks and benedictions of a grateful people, "redeemed, regenerated, and disenthralled by the genius of universal emancipation." Ever since the annexation of Texas, and the success and triumph of American arms on the plains of Mexico, I have been looking in vain for some home for Afric-Americans more congenial for their feelings and prejudice than Liberia. The Canadas, the West Indies, Mexico, British Guiana, and other parts of South America, have all been brought under review. And yet I have been unable to get rid of a conviction long since entertained and often expressed, that if the colored people of this country ever find a home on earth for the development of their manhood and intellect, it will first be in Liberia or some other part of Africa. A continent larger than North America is lying waste for want of the hand of science and industry. A land whose bowels are filled with mineral and agricultural wealth, and on whose bosom reposes in exuberance and wild extravagance all the fruits and productions of a tropical clime. The providence of God will not permit a land so rich in all the elements of wealth and greatness to remain much longer without civilized inhabitants. Every one who has traced the history of missions in Africa, and watched the progress of that little Republic of Afric-Americans on the western coast, must be convinced that the colored men are more peculiarly adapted, and must eventually be the means of civilizing, redeeming, and saving that continent, if ever it is done at all. Encouraged and supported by American benevolence and philanthropy, I know no people better suited to this great work—none whose duty more it is. Our servile and degraded condition in this country, the history of the past, and the light that is pouring in upon me from every source, fully convinces me that this is our true, our highest and happiest destiny, and the sooner we commence this glorious work, the sooner will "light spring up in darkness, and the wilderness and the solitary place be glad, and the desert rejoice and blossom as the rose."

I am aware that nothing except the Fugitive Slave Law can be more startling to the free colored citizens of the Northern States, than the fact that any man among them, whom they have regarded as intelligent and sound in faith, should declare his convictions and influence in favor of African Colonization. But the novelty of the thing does not prove it false, nor that he who dare reject a bad education and break loose from long-established prejudices, may not have the most conclusive reasons for such a course.

I am aware, too, of the solemn responsibility of my present position. It must result in some good or great evil. I maintain that, clinging to long-cherished prejudices, and fostering hopes that can never be realized, the leaders of the colored people in this country have failed to discharge a great and important duty to their race. Seeing this, though a mere private business man, with a trembling pen, I come forward alone, joining with friend and foe in moving the wheel of a great enterprise, which, though unpopular with those it designs to benefit, must result eventually in the redemption and enfranchisement of the African race.

With the conviction of a purpose so noble, and an end so beneficent, I cannot notice the misrepresentations, slander, and anathemas, which I must, for a while, endure, even from those whose approbation and good will I would gladly retain. It was no difficult task to have seen, that unless they could force emancipation, and then the perfect, social, and political equality of the races, human nature, human pride and passions, would not allow the Americans to acknowledge the equality and inalienable rights of those who had been their slaves. One or the other must be dominant. For this reason: seven years ago, while a student, I advocated the plan of a separate State for colored Americans—not as a choice, but as a necessity, believing it would be better for our manhood and intellect to be freemen by ourselves, than political slaves with our oppoessors. I enlisted at once the aid of a few colored young men, of superior talent and ability; and we were earnestly taking measures to negotiate for a tract of land in Mexico, when the war and its consequences blasted our hopes, and drove us from our purpose. About five years ago I told my excellent friend, George

L. Seymour, of Liberia, (who, after a residence of some years there, had returned to this city to take out his family,) that I knew only one way to develop the faculties of our people in this country, and that by their entire separation from oppression and it influences; and that if I was compelled to abandon my plan of a separate State in America, I would devote my voice, my pen, my heart, and soul, to the cause of Liberia. I have since written to him that he has my heart in Africa now, and in two or three years, if we live, I will shake hands with him on the banks of the St. John.

Ever since a lad of fifteen, it has been my constant study to learn how I might best contribute to elevate the social and political position of the oppressed and unfortunate people with whom I am identified; and while I have endeavored, in my humble way, to plead the cause of three millions of my enslaved countrymen, I have, at the same time, thought it no inconsistency to plead also for the hundred and fifty millions of the native sons of Africa. But every word uttered in her behalf subjects us to the imputation of being a Colonizationist, and covers us with the odium our people attach to such a name; as if something unjust and wicked was naturally associated with the term, when in fact that odium, if such I may call it for the sake of argument, can exist only with those who have forgotten the history of Plymouth Rock and Jamestown, or who are determined not to know the truth, in spite of facts and the evidence of the most enlightened reason. What is Colonization? For the benefit of those who treat it with contempt, and think that no good can come out of it, I may merely remark that the thirteen original States, previous to the Declaration of Independence, were called the Colonies of Great Britain, the inhabitants colonists. The companies and individuals in England that assisted in planting these colonies were called Colonizationists. These colonists came from the land of their birth, and forsook their homes, their firesides, their former altars, and the graves of their fathers, to seek civil and religious liberty among the wild beasts and Indians on a foreign, bleak, and desolate shore. Oppressed at home, they emigrated to Holland, and after remaining there twelve years, returned to England, and found not the hope of rest until they came to America. That very persecution and oppression of the mother country planted in America the purest civil and religious institutions the world had ever seen. And now this powerful Republic, by her oppression and injustice to one class of this people, will plant in Africa a religion and morality more pure, and liberty more universal, than it has yet been the lot of my people to enjoy. I never have been of that class who repudiate everything American. While I shall never make any compromise with slavery, nor feel indifferent to its blighting, witherin effects on the human intellect and human happiness, I cannot be so blind as not to see and believe that, in spite of all its corrupting influences on national character, there is yet piety, virtue, philanthropy, and disinterested benevolence among the American people; and when, by the progress of free thought and the full development of her free institutions, our country shall have removed from her national escutcheon that plague-spot of the nation, she will do more than all others in sending the light of liberty and everlasting love into every portion of the habitable globe. In our enthusiasm and devotion to any great benevolent cause, we are generally unwilling to make the best use of men as we find them, until we have wasted our energies in accomplishing nothing, or a calmer reflection convinces us of our error. It is well for those to whom this reflection comes not too late. We have been an unfortunate people. For 400 years the avarice, fraud, and oppression of Europeans and their descendants have been preying upon the children of Africa and her descendants in America. Says my eloquent correspondent, in writing upon this subject: "I know this was the soil on which I was born; but I have nothing to glorify this as my country. I have no pride of ancestry to point back to. Our forefathers did not come here as did the Pilgrim fathers, in search of a place where they could enjoy civil and religious liberty. No; they were cowardly enough to allow themselves to be brought manacled and fettered as slaves, rather than die on their native shores resisting their oppressors." In the language of Dr. Todd: "If the marks of humanity are not blotted out from this race of miserable men, it is not because oppression has not been sufficiently legalized, and avarice been allowed to pursue its victims till the grave became a sweet asylum."

During the past thirty years, two influential and respectable associations have arisen in our behalf, each claiming to be the most benevolent, and each seemingly opposed to the intentions and purposes of the other.

The American Colonization Society, on the one hand, proposed to benefit us by the indirect means of planting a colony on the western coast of Africa, as an asylum for the free colored people and manumitted slaves of the United States; and by this means also to send the blessings of civilization and religion to the benighted

sons of that continent. The principal obstacle in the way of their
success has been, that the free colored people, as a body, everywhere, have denounced the whole scheme as wicked and mischievous,
and resolved not to leave this country; while those who have gone
to that colony, from a state of slavery, as the condition of freedom,
have been least able to contribute to the knowledge and greatness
of a new country, and impart civilization and the arts and sciences
to its heathen inhabitants. This Society was one of the few that are
popular in their very beginning. But that which made it most
popular with the American public furnished the cause of the
opposition of the colored people. They erected a platform so
broad, that the worst enemies of the race could stand upon it with
the same grace, and undistinguished from the honest and true
philanthropist. It could at the same time appeal for support to
the piety and benevolence of the North, and to the prejudices and
sordid interest of the South. I state this simply as a fact, not for
the purpose of finding fault. It is always easier to show one plan
faulty than to produce a better one.

Notwithstanding the different and adverse motives that have
prompted the friends of Colonization, they certainly have labored
perseveringly and unitedly for the accomplishment of one great
purpose. And in spite of all our former distrust, we must give them
the credit at least of producing as yet the only great practical
scheme for the amelioration of the condition of the free colored
man and the manumitted slave. They did not profess nor promise
to do more. Instead of engaging in clamorous agitations about
principles and measures, they turned what men and means they
had to the best purpose, and engaged industriously in founding
and nurturing a colony for the free colored people, where they have
an opportunity of demonstrating their equality with the white race,
by seizing upon, combining, and developing all the elements of
national greatness by which they are surrounded. Thus far the
end is good; we need not stop now to scan their motives.

The Abolitionists, on the other hand, proposed by moral means
the immediate emancipation of the slave, and the elevation of the
free colored people in the land of their birth. And this they did at
a time which tried men's souls. Theirs were a platform on which
none dare stand who were not willing to endure scorn, reproach,
disgrace, lynch law, and even death for the sake of oppressed
Americans. At first, interest, reputation, office nor profit, but the
reverse, were the reward of an Abolitionist. Now that Anti-

Slavery has become popular with many of the American people, it assumes another name, and is converted into political capital. Even Free-Soilism was not so much designed to make room for our liberties, as to preserve unimpaired the liberites of the whites. The Abolitionists have not yet accomplished any thing which we can see to be so definite and practical. Yet they have divested themselves of personal prejudices, aroused the nation to a sense of its injustice and wrongs toward the colored people, encouraged them in improving and obtaining education here, broken down many arbitrary and proscriptive usages in their treatment, and convinced this nation and England that they are a people capable of moral, social, and political elevation, and entitled to equal rights with any other community. Both of these benevolent societies might perhaps have accomplished more good, if they had wasted less ammunition in firing at each other. While one has formally declared a moral and intellectual inferiority of our race, with an incapacity ever to enjoy the rights and prerogatives of freemen in the land of our birth, the other has declared that hatred to the race and love of slavery were the only motives that prompted the Colonizationists to action. In taking a liberal and more comprehensive view of the whole matter, we believe that whatever may have been the faults, inconsistencies and seeming opposition of either, both have been instrumental in doing much good in their own way; and under the guidance of an allwise Providence, the labors, devotion and sacrifices of both will work together for good, and tend toward a grander and more sublime result than either association at present contemplates.

For our own part, under the existing state of things, we cannot see why any hostility should exist between those who are true Abolitionists and that class of Colonizationists who are such from just and benevolent motives. Nor can we see a reason why a man of pure and enlarged philanthropy may not be in favor of both, unless his devotion to one should cause him to neglect the other. Extremes in any case are always wrong. It is rare to find that all the members of any association, untrammelled by interest, act solely from high moral principle and disinterested benevolence. The history of the world, civil, sacred and profane, shows that some men have, in all ages, espoused popular and benevolent causes, more or less influenced by prejudice or selfishness. Human nature, with its imperfections, remains the same.

Ever since the adoption of the Constitution, the government and people of this country, as a body, have pursued but one policy toward our race. In every contest between the great political parties we have been the losers. But this result it is reasonable to expect in a Republic whose Constitution guarantees protection alike to our peculiar and our free institutions—thus securing the rights and liberties of one class at the expense of the liberties of another. Besides this, Texas and all the States that have since come into the Union, have surrounded us with political embarrassments. Every State that has lately revised or altered her Constitution, has been more liberal in extending rights to the white and less so to the colored man. In view of these facts, I assume as a fixed principle that it is impossible for us to develope our moral and intellectual capacities as a distinct people, under our present social and political disabilities; and, judging by the past and present state of things, there is no reason to hope that we can do it in this country in future.

Let us look a moment at some of the consequences of this social and political distinction on the entire mass. They are shut out from all the offices of profit and honor, and from the most honorable and lucrative pursuits of industry, and confined as a class to the most menial and servile positions in society. And, what is worse than all, they are so educated from infancy, and become so accustomed to this degraded condition, that many of them seem to love it.

They are excluded in most of the States from all participation in the government; taxed without their consent, and compelled to submit to unrighteous laws, strong as the nation that enacts them, and cruel as the grave.

They are also excluded from every branch of mechanical industry; the work-shop, the factory, the counting-room, and every avenue to wealth and respectability, is closed aginst them.

Colleges and academies slowly open their doors to them, when they possess no means to avail themselves of their advantages, and when their social condition has so degraded and demoralized them as to destroy all motive or desire to do so.

They are by necessity constant consumers, while they produce comparatively nothing, nor derive profit from the production of others. Shut out from all these advantages, and trained to fill the lowest condition in society, their teachers and ministers as a class educate them only for the situation to which the American people have assigned them. And hence too many of them aspire no higher than the gratification of their passions and appetites, and cling with deadly tenacity to a country that hates them and offers them nothing but chains, degradation and slavery.

Since things are so, it is impossible for them while in this country to prove to the world the moral and intellectual equality of the African and their descendants. Before such an experiment can be fairly tested, our colored youth from childhood must be admitted to a full participation in all the privileges of our schools, academies and colleges, and to all the immunities and rights of citizenship, free from every distinction on account of color, and the degrading influences that ignorance, prejudice and slavery have heretofore thrown around them.

The same inducments as to white Americans should engage them in agriculture, commerce, manufactures, the mechanic arts, and all the pursuits of civilized and enlightened communities. Every man of common intelligence knows this has not been done; knows, too, it cannot be done, for the first time, in the United States. In the face of these facts, we are compelled to admit that the Afric-Americans, in their present state, cannot compete with the superior energy and cultivated intellect of long-civilized and Christian Saxons.

And, hence, we are driven to the conclusion that the friendly and mutual separation of the two races is not only necessary to the peace, happiness and prosperity of both, but indispensable to the preservation of the one and the glory of the other. While we would thus promote the interests of two great contients, and build up another powerful Republic, as an asylum for the oppressed, we would, at the same time, gratify national prejudices. We should be the last to admit that the colored man here, by nature and birth, is inferior in intellect, but by education and circumstances he may be. We could name many moral and intelligent colored young men in New York, Philadelphia, and Boston, whose talents and genius far excel our own, and those of a majority of the hundreds of Saxon students with whom we have at different times been associated; men who, if liberally educated, would operate like leaven on our whole people, waken responses in the unexplored regions of Africa, and pour new light on the republic of letters; but who, for the want of means and an unchained intellect, will probably live and die "unknown, unhonored and unsung."

> "Full many a gem of purest ray serene,
> The dark unfathomed caves of ocean bear;
> Full many a flower is born to blush unseen,
> And waste its sweetness on the desert air."

This may appear ridiculous to those who know the colored man only as a domestic slave in the South or a political cypher in the North. But the generations living sixty years hence will regard him in a very different light. Before that time shall have arrived, American Christians, as an expiation for the past, have a great duty to discharge to a prostrate nation, pleading in silent agony to God,

> "With tears more eloquent than learned tongue
> Or lyre of purest note."

We too have a great work to perform. To the Anglo and Afric-American is committed the redemption and salvation of a numerous people, for ages sunk in the lowest depth of superstition and barbarism. Who but educated and pious colored men are to lead on the van of the "sacramental host of God's elect" to conquer by love, and bring Africa, with her tractless regions, under the dominion of our Savior; to baptize her sons at the font of science and religion, and teach them to chant the praises of liberty and God, until

> "One song employs all nations; and all cry,
> 'Worthy the Lamb, for he was slain for us!'
> The dwellers in the vales and on the rocks
> Shout to each other, and the mountain tops
> From distant mountains catch the flying joy,
> Till, nation after nation taught the strain,
> Earth rolls the rapturous hosanna round."

Whatever may have been the objections to Colonization in former times, I call upon colored people of this country to investigate the subject now under its present auspices. When I consider the kind of treatment they have received from their professed friends in America, I do not blame them in the past for exclaiming, "God deliver us from our friends, and we will take care of our enemies." I can never forget the round of applause that range through an audience when a talented colored man of New York, in an earnest harangue against Colonization, said: "Mr. President, the Colonizationists want us to go to Liberia if we will; if we won't go there, we may go to hell." It seemed to indicate that they felt there was too much truth in the remark. Their principal objection has been, that men who professed the greatest love for them in Africa, did the most to exclude them here from the means of education, improvement, and every respectable pursuit of industry. And their personal treatment was such as colored men only are made to feel, but none can describe. When the temperance men treated the inebriate as an outcast—a wretch debased and lost—they accomplished nothing, but repelled him from their kind influences; now, when they recognise him as a man and a brother, their efforts are crowned with great success. In keeping with other reforms, I think that colonizationists have become more liberal and kind than formerly. Whether this be true or not, if I can dispose of a single objection, I shall be confident that Afric-Americans are to be benefited more by the cause they advocate and sustain, than by any other practical scheme philanthropy has yet devised. I should have been glad if this Society, consistent with its leading purpose, had done something for the improvement and education of colored youth. And this would have been a great auxiliary to their main object. They have thought that, if they encouraged their education here, they would not go to Africa. This is a mistake! If they would aid and encourage them in obtaining such education as white men receive, they could not keep them in this country. They would entirely unfit them for the debased position they must here occupy. Give me but educated intellect to operate upon, and I can send Liberia more useful men in three months, than I can in five years' labor with society as I find it. I speak only from my own experience, when I say that, during a life of constant struggle and effort, I never have received any sympathy or encouragement in obtaining an education, nor in aspirations to usefulness, from any of the advocates of Colonization, except my noble friend, J. C. Potts, Esq., of Trenton, N. J. Yet from some little acquaintance with many others, I believe they are good and true friends, ready to do any thing for colored Americans that they would for white men in similar circumstances. I have never doubted the good motives and true benevolence of such gentlemen as Benjamin Coates, Theodore Frelinghuysen, A. G. Phelps, J. B. Pinney, John McDonogh, and a host of others, whose sentiments and efforts in our behalf I know only by reading. But slavery and its consequent degradation, together with our social position, have kept us farther apart than if separated by the waters of the Atlantic. However good the men and worthy their cause, it cannot flourish without the co-operation of Afric-Americans here. Our brethren across the Atlantic have been struggling thirty years, and in tears and joy have laid the foundations of a free Republic with civil and religious institutions. They now call on us to assist in sustaining them and participate in their blessings; to aid them to civilize its inhabitants and extend the rising glory of the Lone Star of Africa. We should examine their cause, and if it is just, we should no longer withhold our aid; and especially when, in benefiting them, we must benefit ourselves. If, by my feeble efforts, I shall ever be able to do any thing that shall tell in future blessings on that injured country, it will be very much owing to the sympathy and encouragement received, in the course of my education, from S. H. Cox, D. D., of 1844, and Lewis Tappan, Esq., that unchanging and unflinching advocate of the slave.

But we have never been pledged to any men or set of measures. We must mark out an independent course, and become the architects of our own fortunes, when neither Colonizationists nor Abolitionists have the power or the will to admit us to any honorable or profitable means of subsistence in this country. I only regret that I come to the aid of Africa at a time when I possess less ability to speak or write in her behalf than I did five years since. Strange as it may appear, whatever may be a colored man's natural capacity and literary attainments, I believe that, as soon as he leaves the academic halls to mingle in the only society he can find in the United States, unless he be a minister or lecturer, he must and will retrograde. And for the same reason, just in proportion as he increases in knowledge, will he become the more miserable.

"If ignorance is bliss, 'tis folly to be wise."

He who would not rather live anywhere on earth in freedom than in this country in social and political degradation, has not attained half the dignity of his manhood. I hope our Government will justly recognise the independence of Liberia, establish that line of steamers, and thus give Africa a reinforcement of ten thousand men per annum instead of four hundred.

Pardon my prolixity. The subject and the occasion have compelled me to write more than I expected to. In attempting to be just to three classes, I expect to please none. While the press and our whole country is vexed and agitated on subjects pertaining to us, if I can do nothing more than provoke an inquiry among Afric-Americans, I shall have the satisfaction of hoping, at least, that I have contributed something to the interest and happiness of the citizens of the United States and the people of Africa.

Augustus Washington [1]

[1] *African Repository*, XXVII, 259–265.

FROM HARDY MOBLEY

GEORGIA RICHMOND COUNTY

AUGUSTA August 12/51

REV MR W MCLAIN

    Dear Sir I Take this opportunity to address My Self in a letter to you Concerning of a Society Whitch the Coloured Methodist in this place desire to have for the purpose of Raising funds for the Support of the African Mission Whitch they Wish to Call the African Methodist Auxiliary the Methodist in this place Never have had a Society of this Kind. the Coloured Baptist of this place have a Society whitch they Call the Walker African Missionary Society Whitch Some of the Methodist Colod of this place are Members of. it have been Said that this Mony all Goes to the use of the Baptist all to Gather and None to the Methodist there & (?) as We Suppose that you Know Whether this Report be true or Not, I ask you for information Whitch you Will pleas Give in answer to this letter

         Yours mosrefuley and obeent

Servant and Clerk of Colod Methodist Church Augusta

        HARDY MOBLEY [1]

AUGUSTA Octr 8 1851

REV. W. MCLAIN

    Dear Sir I Take this opportunity To Address My Self to you in a Letter hoping you Will answer to My Inquire With all Candour Sir Will the Colonization Society pay or pay part for a preacher and his family and Send him With his family to africa to preach to the people of that Land Sir there is one of this place that Would Like to go to that Counry for that purpose he is a Methodist preacher age forty years having a Wife and Six Small Children Sir If you Wish name and Character it Can be Given in My next Letter Sir you will pleas answer this Letter forth With nothing more Sir until I hear from you

        Respectfully your &C

        HARDY MOBLEY [2]

---

[1] *Letters received by the American Colonization Society*, July to September, 1851, No. 185.

[2] *Ibid.*, July to September, 1851, No. 30.

AUGUSTA Oct 21 1851

MR MCLAIN

  Dear Sir I recid your Letter of the 14 inst With Some
other documents Whitch afford me Great Conciliation a bout
africa Sir What you Wish to Know a bout persons Going to africa
I Can not answer now. Sir I Was Speaking to a White Gentleman
a bout our transacting Letter &c. and he advise me to Sto et as the
Counry is in a Confusetion a bout things of this Sort there for you
will please Send nothing more until I Write you again I am very
Happy to learn that you Would pay a preachers pasage to liberia
also his family it May be next Spring be for I Write again as tims
is as they is Sir I do not Wish to do any thing against the rules of
the Counry in Whitch I Live nothing more at Present
  I remain yours truly
       HARDY MOBLEY [1]

AUGUSTA GA Jany 15 1852

REV W. MCLAIN

  Dear Sir I Write to inform you that I Saw Mr Hall
Whom you Give me an introduction to and heard him Speak of
Liberia in it blest Condition also I Saw the Rev I. Morris Pease
When he vitited our City and had a talk With him Concerning
that Counry it afforded me Great Consolation indeed Sir also
he Consolated us a bout the Society which we have to aid the the
Methodist Mission in Liberia Sir I am a Subscriber to the Africa
Repository last year also this year also Henry Saxton Both years
he is Sir very actve a bout this work I think you would do Well
to have him as an agent for the Repository in this City he have
Got Some new Subscribers this year Say A. Grimage, L. Wood,
J Harris, R. Kent and R Dent
yours truly in Lord
       HARDY MOBLY [2]

FROM JOHN W. WEST

September the 3d 1851 rutlant Dane county Wisconcin to Mr.
maclain at Washington sittty Dear Frend I agane rite to inform
you that I am Well and hope that When you recd this letter that
you may be injoying good Helth Sir I have bin Doing som better
business this somer I made som better Wages then formly in this

---

[1] *Ibid.*, July to October, 1851, No. 39.
[2] *Ibid.*, January to March, 1852, No. 86.

Western country I have a grate cropp for a small man but grane
is selling very low heare oats 10 to 12 cents Wheete 30 to 45 cents
corn 15 to 20 cents Drigoods and grocereys very hi in Deed one
100 Per cent hiar then new york Priseis Wee have a fine country
heare We Wont rale roads hear and then Sir We shall have the
grateist state in the united younited states I am a living in a good
country the best People I ever saw thay allow my children to go
to the Publick Schools I am intreeted Well With thise People but
I am not satisfide I Wont to go over to liberia ef I can go this fall
from millwaukey to new york Sir I allways understood that your
sociaty Wold Pay the Way of everry collerd Person from the
younited states to liberia I Did not no that Wee had to go 1 or
2,000 miles to git to Washington or to baltimore before we cold
start to liberia ef that be the case I Dont neede youre Pamplitts
rite sir ef I cannot be takeand in at shicagg or—millwaukey I
Dont no that ever I shall go over to liberia for I am With good
nabours but sir I am redy in mind to go ef I can betakand an from
millwauky Wisconcin you will Plesd to rite me and let me no
somthing about your Paying my Way from milwaukey ef I go I
Want to go this fall ef I Dont start this fall I must git me a track
of congres land settle not far from foort Wenebago I must no my
Dependences soon I have had one Pamplit this yeare and that is
all I have hade I shall be gladd for yo to send me the nuse every
month yours and John W West

JOHN W. WEST [1]

FROM ANTONY SHERMAN

Journal p. 100
SAVANNAH September 23 1851

MR MCLAINE

Dear Sir I hope you will excuse me for the liberty I have taken to
write you these few lines but Sir I feel so anxcious to hear from Mr
Pease that I conclude it would be the best to write you as I know
not where to direct to him. during his Stay here I went to See
him & I had a conversation with him an I told him how anxcious
I was to emmagrate to africa with my family an he told me he would
try an See what he can do for me after he return home Soon after
Mr John Anderson receive a letter from him to know if my Owners
would Sell me and wish to know what they would take for me. My
Mistress consent to Sell me no other way but to Satisfy me an her

[1] *Ibid.*, July to September, 1851, No. 260.

price to oblige me she say she would let Me go for five hundred 50 dollars wich I know if nothing happens to prevent that I could verry well return it in 2 years time. I have 50 dollars towards it & I could borrow 50 more wich a hundred towards it would be a great help to cut of the intrust of the money an I would be More than thankful to you an Mr Pease Sir if you would do all you can for Me wherin I am paying My wages wich would be stop. My Mistress has ask me several times if I herd from Mr Pease an do Dear Sir pleas give me answer as soon as convenient to you. I was truly Sorry to here of your illness for I was quite disappointed by you not being able to come but I hope this time Sir that your health is quite restoured. I send you Sir *2 dollar* for the Repository wich I beleave Sir will settle us at presnsant I have lent the Repository the 3 las months ones out a great deal wich I beleave Sir for lending them I have gaine Several warm friends to Africa I shall try and do all I can in lending them. Sir I will thank you kindly to answer this as it is convenient to you

I am your humble Servant
ANTONY SHERMAN [1]

SAVANNAH March 25 1853

    Reved Dear Sir

yours of 12 came to hand on the 2d and I shall let all my friends Know and it has done a great deal of good among many who appear anxcious to know if the emmagrants where come in the Ship, you want to know if any of the folks has backout I can Say now Sir firmly No Sir Many that was wondering about the vessel bringing emmagrants Says now they will positivly go in june the 4 you Spoke of that Barlon and Currier Sent you I am certain they will go Now but I have been trying My best to git the 200 hundred and it is hard work Now Sir they are a great Many who wants to go but Say they Cannot go before the fall and that time I know you can get the Number you Mention or more than I have Never Seen Such a Stir about Liberia as Now that I am certain you will be call on for another vessel, for there is a great many who is trying to purchase themselves and cannot remaine after they have finish payed please Sir dont forgot what I ask you about the log Cabin if it is convenient as My family is large and I have Another one added to My family one Rachel Hover her Master has given her her freedom to go to her Husband who lives in Sinou County and her

[1] *Ibid.*, July to September, 1851, No. 352.

Master name is Mr John Hover. we are dayly looking for the Rev Mr Gurly we all will be happy to See him I wish you would Send me some More of the Sketch of Liberia and the information I would be glad to give to Some who wants to See some of them in My Saying a vessel Chatter in this place I ment just what you wrote one coming empty we are delighted to have you mention about Such a lovly vessel I only wish when Mr Gurly comes he may get the Number

I am your humble Servant
ANTHONY SHERMAN [1]

FROM HENRY SAXTON

AUGUSTA Feby 10 the 1852

REV. W. MCLAIN

Sir I Write to acknowledg the Recept of five Repositorys one for *Lairay Wood* one for *Alexander Greimage* one for *James Harris* one for *Rodrick Dent* also one for *Robert Kent* When I Expected one for Bro: *H. Mobly* and one for My Self *Henry Saxton* as Bro Mobly and My Self Both are old Subscribers to the Repository Sir you Will pleas Send one for *Hardy Mobly* and one for *Henry Saxton* my Self also I have Some more new Subscribers Say *Samuel Drayton Edward Purdy Benjamin Lampkins all making Ten Names which you Will please Send to Me in the Care of J. F. Turpin Esq* as I wish to Keep up My Carespondence betwen Me and you by Mr. J. F. Turpin Whin he have Sent Six dollars and have recd nery one Sir I did not intend any of them direced to Me But did not think to Mention it in My other letter
Sir the Nombers for the five first names Both last month and this have Come So you Will pleas Send last months and this for the five last Names all to the Care of J F Turpin as he have Sent the monney for them all you Will pleas Continue accoring to this in Struction for this year your truly

Henry Saxton
per H Mobley [2]

FROM CHS. DEPUTIE

HOLLIDAYSBURG July 5th 1852

Dear Sir your favour was Receivd and thare is but one of the boys in this place the other is in Pittsburg

---

[1] *Ibid.*, January to March, 1853, No. 503.
[2] *Ibid.*, January to March, 1852, No. 200.

this one has not made up his mind altogather what he will do thare is many annameys to the Colonization Caus hear the have went so far as to Say that I am trying to a Sist his master in getting him and have taken much abuse by the Colord People but I Consider that I have only don my Duty to the Boys and the Cause any thing that I can do will be don and Should he make up his mind to go to Liberia I will inform you the have bean trying to get him to go to Canady thare has bean men hear that has bean to Liberia and Lecterd to the People and gave Such a bad a Count of the place that it is hard to do much a preasant the Say that thare is nether Horse hog Cow nor nothing Can Live thare that the Natives ware no Close and thare is no Houses but the Govement House Evary thing that had a tendency to bare on the minds of the Enamys of the Place was Said, but for my own part I Still feel willing to go if I Can make the Arangement in getting the means to go with. I know that the Society is imposed upon and for the Sake of my friends is (?) wish to go and are Prepard to Recommend my Self from the Best men in this Country I was brought up by the Famly of the Hon. Dr Joseph Henderson of Mifflin Co well known by Hon James Irvin has known me from my youth Rev Mr Linn is also maried in the Henderson Famly knowing that the all have a deep interest in the Cause makes me more desire to go and Rebut those Slanders, I have written to Mr Coppinger in Phila. but have not Receivd an answer

pleas drop a Lin in the Corse of the preasant month what you think would be sufficient to take me out and Bring me Back all the assistance I Expect to get will be from my White Friends I had to get a friend to atend to hunting the Boys up as it was un Safe for me to do any thing the Excitement was so great among the Colord People but Still I am not discoraged in the least but intend to do all I Can for the Cause

Mr W. M. Lain

yours truly

CHS. DEPUTIE [1]

HOLLIDAYSBURG Aug 15th 1852

Dear Friend

yours of the 9 July was Received with pleasur you Say that you will give me a Free passage that is to go and Return for My Famly and Report to my Frineds I am getting Reddy as fast as I Can the Friends will asist me as I must provide for my

[1] *Ibid.*, July to September, 1852, No. 21.

Famly So that the may not want in my abcence Should I be Sucksesfull I want to provide my Self well as I will have the best accomdation that any man Should be proud of

Should the Law be in my favour it would put me in posession of five hundred Dollars which would be me a Start but I must waite the Result of the Law. I will not Set any time to Return Should the Society have Sumething to do teaching or any thing I would Remain Sume time and at the Same time prepair for my Famly pleas Say what I mus take a Long if it is nessesary to take Bedding Mr Williams from Johnstown is well known to me and is a Gentleman

I intend visiting Huntingdon Bellefonte and Jamestown before I go in order to See the People of Collar

Enter my Name on your List for Nov 1st the Lord willing I will be on pleas Say what nomber of Persons will go out all the opposition that I have met with makes me more Stronger in the Cause

With Respect I Remain yours in Cause of God and Liberty

Mr W McLain   CHS. DEPUTIE [1]

pleas Answer

FROM JOHN BARLON

SAVNH   Jan 11th 1853

MR MCLAIN

        Sir I send you seven numbers of the repository which you enquired of & if you should want any other number that I have I shall be happy to send them on at any time

I am requested by those that are Desirous of emigrating to enquire of your Particularly what time there will be a vessel here for Africa there are many here & in the up country & in a few day we will have a full list They think they could be ready in May I wish you to write me that I may write to the up country for myself I wish to know in time that I may have an opportunity to dispose of my little Property in time and also that I may get you to Purchase such goods for me in Baltimore as I would want Please to answer this and accept my

Best respects

JOHN BARLON [2]

[1] *Ibid.*, July to September, 1852, No. 187.
[2] *Ibid.*, January to March, 1853, No. 77.

FROM CHARLES MOORE

Jan 14, 1853

Rev and Dear Sir: i trust you will not be one to disdane this note that i now hand you. pirhaps you will tirme it imprudent though i wish to oppining request request you to relate to the cesiety if you please to do so being you are ingaged in that greate bisness and are indeverin to do all you Can in the cause i am thankful to god that he has blest me with the oppirtunity of making my first effirt to lurn whither the friends of the cause will ade me in my strong zeld or no   this has been a birden on on my mind evir sence i was A boy of foreteen years old in hearing my mothir tell a Bought hir grandfathir being kidnaped and brought from His mothir country   i studded a bought him and thought how His country had ben berefed of him and at lenth a suddent thought struck my mind that by the helpe of god That i might be planted som time in his room so i am Now intermingild with the beggirs though i dont Wish tha cesiety to firnish me with money have none—Tiru (?) because i beleve that in a few years in libery according to infermithion that i can rase money to repay Back in full and sir whither tha can be money raseed or no   please sir send me a lettir and let me know A bought the hole mattir and i will then let you in My nex   the hole of my vues. so sir. i will close

Mr Wm Mcclain   Shooting creeke po——
your sirvant Etc   N Carolina chirokee
            County   CHARLES MOORE
        Sirvant of John Moore [1]

FROM A NEGRO IN BALTIMORE

BALTIMORE,
January 19, 1853.

TO THE SECRETARY OF THE A. C. S.

Sir: I percieve that this Society is progressing very rapidly, and that many are being sent to that country to which every colored man looks forward, as being his or his children's future home; and I think from observation, that there should be more active measures taken in this country to instruct my people in the mechanical arts, that when they arrive in the land of promise, they may be able to impart every useful pursuit to the rising generations. If these things are rightly conducted, I feel satisfied

[1] *Ibid.*, January to March, 1853, No. 410.

that my people may yet be redeemed. I hope that the day is not far distant when we may claim a name among the nations of the earth.

Which request I hope will be kindly received as coming from one of the down-trodden of the African race.

Yours very respectfully,

L. W.[1]

From Geo. Sample

Journal p. 254

Fred'g March 3rd 1853

Mr McLain

Rev Sir—enclosed you will find *one year's Subscription for* the *African Repository.*
Address   Henry Frazar, Fred'g. Va.
Your humble Servant

Geo, Sample.

P.S.

African Colonization is gaining ground down this way very rapidly. The colored people is beginning to think, and to See for themselves that Liberia is the only home for them. Notwithstanding, Some of the Sable Gentlemen about here are very much opposed to African Colonization, and I am very to See that some of them are opposed to emigrating to Liberia, as I would not like to See the Republic of Liberia disgraced by Such a trivial Set of people as those who are opposed to African Colonization.

Some of our most intelligent, and enterprising people of color, about here are very much in favor of emigrating to Liberia. I would write you more, but the bearer of this will leave in a few minutes for Washington, so I will have to close.

The Rev. Mr McLain, will plase to Send a few of the pamplets containing Messrs Fuller & Janifer report of Liberia, or anything pertaining to Liberia, will be thankfully received. C. H. Brook. the bearer of this will bring anything you are pleased to Send.

Your Obedient humble

Servant

Geo, Sample [2]

---

[1] *African Repository,* Vol. XXIX, p. 99.

[2] *Letters received by the American Colonization Society,* January to March, 1853, No. 385.

FROM NATHANIEL BOWEN
Letter from a young colored man in New York

ROME N.Y. Aprile 26th 1853

Dear Sir:

I take a favourable opportunity to write few lines, to ask a favour which I hope you will grant me, and that is, to favour me with the African Repository within the last few years. I have taken the opportunity offered me to read the accounts of the doings of Liberia. I have always given the subject of colonization but little consideration till within the last two years. I have been a listener to the arguments of men who I thought were more competent judges of the subject than myself; but I now perceive that it has been a blind prejudice that has caused the colored people to be blinded to their best interesets. In this place, where I now live, I find that the people are much opposed to colonization, but the family with whom I am a part does hold sentiments favourable to colonization, that is to a certain extent; and I feel confident that they will think, in a little while, as I do, that colonization is the only means and the only thing calculated to raise us from our present debased condition. A great many has talked of emigrating to Canada, but I think if they had the welfare of their children in view, as they say they have, they would emigrate to Africa. I am quite young myself, yet I think I can do more good for myself and others in Liberia than I can by living in a country where I am not acknowledged as a citizen, for we possess only partial freedom this side of the broad Atlantic. My Uncle, with whom I now live has a family of small children that has showed great aptness to learn and I think Liberia the best place for them and my self also. And think with the aid of the Repository, I can convince them of their error, for when I get to talking to them on the subject, they pay very strict attention to what I have to say, and will admit that it is the best for us all. Now I hope you will not fail to let me have any thing by which I can gain information on the subject. You may be somewhat acquainted with the family with whom I am connected; Anthony Bowen, who has been a messenger at the Patent Office for quite a number of years, is my uncle. I think I have heard him speak of you before I left Washington. I have been away from home some four or five years, and have travelled over the Northern States pretty well, and have found but a slight difference; if any thing, the prejudice is greater in the north than it is in the south. I hope you will pardon my boldness but I feel to be speaking the candid truth. I must now bring my letter to a close. I hope you will excuse blunders and mistakes, for it is from the pen of a laborer that works hard for his living. With much respect, I am, Dear Sir,

Your humble and obedient Servant

Nathaniel Bowen,

Rome Oneida County

N Y

I shall try and send you the money for the Repository by the first of May or shortly after please do what is in your persude the folk in Washington to do what is in their power   encourage them

N B [1]

FROM JOHN W. JONES

May, 24the 1853. SHELBY COUNTY OHIO

JOHN W. JONES, TO THE REV. W. MCLAIN. *Dear Sir*, Some good frind a few years past sent me the African repository but it discontinued, in the year, 1850 June I rote to Mr D. Crista to have it sent to me and write to me and I would send him the money I got no anser from him. Last winter I herd that ther was some pamples in the post office for me, and I went and got two numbers, befour January 1853. And they have come monthly ever since. I wated for a letter from Mr D. Crista to know if he had paid for the year, I got no letter from him, so I throught he had not paid for them. I now Sir send you two dollars, on the State bank of Ohio. I ented (?) for the post master to put it in and back this letter to you. And you can rite to me when to send you some more money. I wish for you to write my name, Dr J. W. Jones, it is the name I am known by. I am indian doctor, or botinast

Dear Sir I have ben takinge some notice of the American Colonization Society ever since its formation, and think it riseinge and importance, and one of the greatest blessings for the colored people in the united States of America, if they did but think so but the most of them have and are blinded to their best intrust to the present day. By lislinge to a socitey of people, that is not their true frinds, but it is dyinge away very fast. Our people is very ignent abought Liberia and the goodness of the county, So I make a great allowance for them. For a very few of them can read or take

[1] *Ibid.*, April to June, 1853, No. 175.

news papers or the repository, to inform them selves. Very few
of them are aware that the goverment is amakinge, any priperation
to send them to Liberia, for they are astonuous, to hear that the
different states are pasinge sich strenous laws as to prohibit them
from going into any of the free states and settle.   I do believe that
the two races of people cannot ?dell to greather much longer, apon
one soil, agreable to the bible.   For the gosple must be prached to
all, the nations of the earth befour the end of time.   And who is
bether calculated to bear the glad tidings of the gosple to Africa
then the colored people of the united states of Ameraca, With their
own concent.   All they want I think is infermation on the subject
and let each state tell them planly to make a priperation for moving
some where out of this country

May 24, 1853

Dear Sir   I will now give you some infermation, abought
my self and family.   I am a colored man with one fourth of african
blood, and my wife is a bout the same.   I move from the state of
tenesee, in the year 1824. to the City of Cincinnati and live there
ten years and move one hundred milds north in mercer county
fuour years, since then I move to Shlaby county wher I now reside
at present   we have six children four sons and two daughters   my
children lives most of them in Cincinnati and are opose to goinge to
liberia and I am sorry for it.   I have ben in the notion of going to
Liberia for afew years past but I have ben in debt so I could not go.
If I, could sell my little farm and pay my debts, my children will
come and see me this Summer if they can, and we will try to come
on soum understading, abought it.   Please send me the pamphlet
containing abought going to Liberia and a few of the Liberia news
papers if you can.   If I can sell my land and git some of my children
to go with with me I want to do some time next year or the year,
after.   If the Lord is willen.   Please to anser this letter, as soon
as you can.   I am a doinge great deale of good and have done,
with the pamphlets.

DR. J. W. JONES

Please to excuse my orthographey [1]

[1] *Ibid.*, April to June, 1853, No. 312.

FROM THE MEMBERS OF THE MOBILE COLORED MISSIONARY SOCIETY

MOBILE Sept 11th/54

To the
  Rev W McLain

Dear Sir

some time last spring, We the undersign, Members of the Mobile Colored Missionary Society, forwarded through *Dr W T Hamilton* Seventy five, 75 Dollars to be appropirate to the cause of Mission on Coast of *Africa* for which we have no receipt. will you take the Trouble to acknowledge the above *amt* to Mr D. Chandler of this city. by So doing you will much encorarg the Members of the Society

S. A. TURNER	F. H. SMITH,
PHILLIP WILSON	ELIJIAH VAUGHON
JAMES SOMERVILLE	GODFREY TAYLOR
SIMON ASHE	DAVID WILSON
A SAXON	AND 100 OTHERS

Members of the Goverment Street church Missionary Society [1]

FROM TERRY McHENRY FARLAN

Journal p. 202

Petersburg va Aug 19th 1856

Dear Sir

Seeing that my time has expired for the Respository for 1. year, I here enclose to you one dollar to continue my subscription, & Sir I would say to you that I have a burning desire to go to Africa, to preach the word of God to the native, & yet I am a Slave, but my trust is in the Lord upon this matter, but I would like to get some advice from you, on this subject, my master is plenty able to let me go, & not to feel any want therefrom, for he do worth thousands of dollars, his name is Robt B. Bolling he used to take great delight in the Colonization Cause at one time, but I dont know how it is now, & I never have said anything to him about going to Africa for I have often felt that I want a entercessor in this matter, for I can assure you Sir that I am willing to do anything

---

[1] *Ibid.*, July to September, 1854, No. 326.

for the advancement of Christ Kingdom upon Earth, 'tis true that my chance is slender in accumulating any money, placed as I am, I have a wife & one child belonging to Some one else, I am about 26 years old & if I were a free man as some I see here, I would take the next ship that goes, to Africa, & go there   My dear I would not like to worry your patience in Reading my long story, for this is not half I could say of my feelings about going to Africa, if I never reach that Shore.   please to send me a copy of information & sketches, of Liberia   I shall look for an anser soon

your most humble and obedt Servt

Terry McHenry Farler

to Rev Wm McLain   Washington City D.C.

this is my own hand writing for I had to study very hard to get to this height in writing, not having much instruction given to me. T McH Fr.[1]

[1] *Ibid.*, July to September, 1856, No. 200.

To expect the abolitionists to tell the truth about slavery is now considered by historians as most preposterous. Abolitionists are generally branded as unusually excited persons abandoning themselves to their emotions, while portraying the slave as a persecuted saint and his owner as the devil incarnate. On the other hand, the colonizationists boasting of the most "respectable" membership, doing and saying every thing possible to deport the free Negro to safeguard the institution of slavery, are regarded as persons disposed to tell the truth about the situation at that time.

To a candid thinker, however, there cannot seem to be any more truth in the declarations of the colonizationists who were trying to carry out one program than there was in those of the abolitionists who endeavored to solve the problem of Negro uplift in a different way. The protagonists of both sides said and did those things which espoused the particular cause in which they were interested. They belonged to the same race, lived in the same country, and had developed under the same influences. That one group should be especially truthful and the other the contrary is a conclusion which can be supported only by bias and prejudice.

It has been said, moreover, that the contributions of Negroes to the abolition organs were revised by the editors in keeping with the thought that they desired to weave into the productions of the Negro writers. As a matter of fact, however, the evidence is to the effect that communications addressed by Negroes to newspapers underwent less change in the case of the abolitionists than in that of the colonizationists. Most of those addressed to the latter usually came from Negroes of the South once held as slaves or expecting to be freed in the near future. Having had little opportunity for education, they could not easily express themselves. They, therefore, often called upon white friends to write letters for them and when they submitted their own, the editors of colonization organs often published them with notes to the effect that the language had been changed to improve the style of the letters.

In the case of the abolitionists this was generally unnecessary for the reason that Negroes exercising such freedom of speech as to express themselves on the issues of the day usually lived in the North where they had better facilities of education. The Negro spokesmen through abolition agencies, moreover, were very often learned men who had undergone sufficient mental development to compare favorably with reformers thus functioning among the whites. There was, therefore, little necessity for a change in the letters of Negroes addressed to antislavery men and agencies.

These antislavery letters of the Negroes are of unusual significance for the reason that although many of these persons herein reported were editors and orators of consequence during the crisis, they failed to keep complete files of their newspapers or to record their orations for the benefit of generations unborn. In these letters, therefore, the investigator will find the only valuable source to determine what the free Negro was actually thinking and feeling during this period.

I. John B. Russwurm, Nathaniel Paul, James Forten, Robert Purvis, and Others

The following letters do not show a charitable disposition toward John B. Russwurm, who had at one time been popular as the editor of *Freedom's Journal,* published in New York during the 'thirties. At first, he refused to connect himself with the colonizationists, but finding their later proposals more flattering, he joined their ranks, going to Liberia where he served as an editor and public functionary. In advocating rather strongly the cause of colonization, he incurred the displeasure of some of his former friends, as these letters show.

To the Editor of the Liberator.

SIR—Notwithstanding the many preposterous arguments of colonizationists, and their wild and incoherent freaks, in support of their imaginary scheme of civilizing Africa, by draining the people of color from this their original and only home; notwithstanding the many hyperbolical accounts, which they so assiduously and conscientiously circulate about that pestiferous clime;— I never felt so indignant at any of their manœuvres (for every step they take to facilitate their plans, tends but to expose their inconsistency) as at a piece of composition which appeared in the twelfth number of the 'Liberia Herald,' written by its editor John B. Russworm. This John B. Russworm is known, I presume, to every one of us; his ingratitude is but too deeply stamped on the minds of many, who have been requited in a manner, which neither time nor space will ever obliterate. After he subverted the pledge he made to his colored brethren, he left, to our satisfaction, his country—suffused with shame—and branded with the stigma of disgrace—to dwell in that land for which the temptor MONEY caused him to avow his preferment. He has resided there more than a year, publishing doubtless to the satisfaction of his supporters, their many glorious schemes, and eulogizing to the very skies the prosperity of his goodly LIBERIA. Not contented with lauding the retreat in which and about which he may flame with impunity, he has the audacity to reprove those with whom he played the traitor. Out of much he said, let this suffice as an example:

'Before God, we know of no other home for the man of color, of republican principles, than Africa. Has he no ambition? Is he dead to everything noble? Is he contented with his condition? Let him remain in America.'

To this we reply, that before God, we know of no surer burial place than Africa, for men of any color; that we will never envy John B. Russworm his ambition; and that we will pray God, that his notions of nobleness may never enter our hearts, and that we will not be contented with our condition, but will make it better in this our native home.   R.[1]

Philadelphia, April 8th, 1831.

To the Editor of the Liberator.

SIR—I have read from the U. S. Gazette of Philadelphia, a paragraph published by Mr Russwurm at Liberia, which I pre-

[1] *Liberator*, April 16, 1831.

sume was intended for the perusal of the colored people of this country—viz:

'It is with much pleasure that we have witnessed the daily spread of the cause of colonization. Our brethren of color are beginning to view it in a more favorable light. And though a few of them, misled themselves, have endeavored to mislead the more ignorant to Canada, how have they succeeded? Do not the resolutions of Upper Canada speak volumes? Are they not viewed as intruders? Will not the arbitrary laws, or rather prejudices, which have been raised in Ohio, be planted and matured in Canada? It requires no prophetic eye to foresee, that to them and their posterity there is no abiding place on the other side of the Atlantic. Canada will hardly afford them a temporary shelter, against the bleak winds of winter. Before God, we know no other home for the man of color, of republican principles, than Africa.'

Read for yourselves, my colored brethren, the language of Mr Russwurm, and then you will be able to judge of the change which this world's goods are calculated to make in the principles of man.

When Mr Russwurm was employed in the editorial department of the Freedom's Journal, and paid for services which were not rendered, he was as much opposed to the colonizing of the free people of color in Africa as I am; but when his patrons failed to support the Journal, he, not being able to live without other subscribers, converted the people's paper to the use of the Colonization Society, by which change he worked himself into their employ; and you now have evidence of his faithful performance to his worthy employers.

I have nothing to say against the very laudable efforts [?] of the Society. It has done, and continues to do, much good [?] for our enslaved brethren; and the Colony at Liberia is well adapted to the bettering of their unhappy condition. I am glad to see they have friends, who will aid in moving them to that highly respected country. But we who have a right to free suffrages, have no disposition to emigrate either to Africa or Canada. If left to our choice, we would much rather stay at home. It is here we have received our birth, and here we wish to remain.

Mr Russwurm tells us, he knows no other home for us than Africa. If he were in Philadelphia, and would make this assertion to me, I would tell him it was a palpable falsehood, and would prove it by his former editorial documents. I would ask whether Mr R. would have gone to Africa even on a visit, had he been in flourishing circumstances? I answer, no. I am too sensible of this fact, that he would as reluctantly fall a victim to the lion, the tiger, the serpent, or the climate, as any one of us: it was real necessity that drove him to seek in Africa an abiding home, as he terms it; and as his usefulness is entirely lost to the people, I sincerely pray that he may have the honor to live and also die there.

C. D. T. a Philadelphian.[2]

The following ideas from the Rev. Nathaniel Paul become more interesting when we think of him as one of the first to join the antislavery ranks. He was denouncing slavery years before Garrison, Phillips, and Sumner appeared upon the scene.

It will doubtless be gratifying to the numerous friends of this highly respectable individual in this country, as well as to his colored brethren in Upper Canada, to be apprised of his welfare and success in England. Mr Paul sailed from New-York on the 31st of December, as the agent and representative of the colonists in Wilberforce to the British Court, for the purpose of procuring the protection and patronage of the Crown, and exciting the sympathies of the people of England in behalf of the colonists. We have received a letter from him, dated London, July 3d, a portion of which we have extracted below. Mr Paul informs us that the apostate Quaker Elliot Cresson, the agent of the Colonization Society, was making rapid progress in deceiving the English philanthropists, until Mr P. clogged his chariot wheels. 'He had represented the Society,' says Mr P. 'as engaged merely *to break down slavery;* but I have boldly contradicted his statement, and shown to the people that its obvious tendency is to promote and perpetuate that odious system.' It is fortunate for the cause of truth and benevolence that Mr Paul happens to be in England at this time; and we sincerely hope that he will spare no efforts to expose the base imposition which Cresson is palming upon the generous-hearted Britons. Let them but fairly understand the principles and operations of the Colonization Society, and he will no longer dare to solicit their charities in its behalf. Cresson's assertion, that the Society is engaged to overthrow slavery, is a gross misrepresentation. The Society, through a thousand responsible organs, has protested *ab origine* that its object is not the emancipation of the slaves, but the expulsion of the free people of color. It is not hostile to

[2] *Liberator,* April 30, 1831.

slavery in any sense of the term, but gives it protection and nour-
ishment. Mr Paul's account of the enthusiasm which pervades
the minds of the British people on the subject of abolition is indeed
most cheering.

LONDON, July 3d, 1832.

MY DEAR FRIEND GARRISON—It is with pleasure that I improve
this opportunity in writing you a few lines from this far distant
country. I know that it is a matter of satisfaction to you to hear
of any thing that is of importance in relation to the interest of the
colored people, in whose cause you have been and still are so
ardently engaged. Allow me then to say, sir, that the people of
this country are alive to the cause of abolition. The zeal of many,
who are members of the Anti-Slavery Society, is without a parallel,
except in the apostles and martyrs of the cross of Christ. What
would you think, sir, of seeing a petition *a half a mile long,* and
containing more than ONE HUNDRED AND FIFTY THOU-
SAND NAMES, sent to the Congress of the United States? Surely
you would think that, ere long, slavery must be abolished in this
country. Shame on your republicans! No such sight has ever
been seen in America. But, thank God! we have seen it here.
This was but one petition. Several others have been sent, and
more than THREE HUNDRED THOUSAND NAMES have gone
to the House of Commons, praying that this accursed system may
be abolished. Indeed, the recent outrages committed in Jamaica
will have a powerful tendency to hasten on the glorious event.

It may be probably interesting to you to hear how I am getting
along, in regard to the object for which I came to this country. I
would therefore say that, at the time I came, it was a time of peculiar oppression in this city. The Cholera had just broken out,
and this, in connexion with the political state of the kingdom,
threw every thing into such a state of agitation, that it was impossible for me to prosecute my business with any degree of success. But things are now more settled than when I arrived. The
Reform Bill having passed, and received the royal sanction, the
political peace of the kingdom is restored, and the Cholera, although it has not entirely subsided, nevertheless it is not so fatal
or general as it hitherto has been. I feel, therefore, in hopes that
I shall be able to prosecute the object of my mission with greater
success. I will only say, that I have not met with a single objection to the object, but with much encouragement from ministers

and gentlemen of the first standing, such as Wilberforce, Clarkson, &c.

* * * * * *

God bless you!

NATH'L PAUL.[8]

Bristol, (England,) April 10, 1833.

MY DEAR FRIEND GARRISON:

Having an opportunity of sending to America, I improve it in writing you a few lines. I have much to say, and I hardly know what to say first; but I will begin with that subject which, next to the salvation of the soul, I know lies nearest your heart—viz. the liberation of the helpless slave, and the elevation of the people of color from that state of degradation that they have so long been in.

Let me say, then, sir, that the voice of this nation is loud and incessant against the system of slavery. Its death warrant is sealed, so far as it relates to the British West Indies. The advocates of slavery are trembling, for the signs of the times proclaim that the end of their oppression draweth near. The tune of the planters is changed. They formerly threatened, but they now begin to supplicate pity for themselves and their children. But how shall those who have felt no pity for others, think of exciting pity for themselves? Their entreaties come too late. The course of the people is determined, and by the help of God they will continue it until slavery shall cease. And let it rejoice your heart, sir, that no half way measures are to be taken. Tired of that delusive song of gradual emancipation, they have resolved to be satisfied with nothing short of total, absolute, and immediate emancipation. A bill will be introduced by his Majesty's government in a few days to this effect; and as soon as this is done, the tables in both Houses of Parliament will groan beneath the weight of the Petitions that will be sent in. Men, women and children stand ready, with pen in hand, to act their part when called for. As well might the slaveholders try to stop the sun in his course, as to think of impeding the cause of liberty. The cause is God's and must prevail. And I believe that those bright luminaries, CLARKSON and WILBERFORCE will yet live to witness its triumph.

Your 'Thoughts on Colonization' are the thoughts of the people here. I only regret that your book had not come sooner. Cresson

[8] *Liberator,* August 25, 1832.

is now somewhere, I believe, in this country; but the people have their eyes open, and I have met with but one gentleman who did not regret that they ever countenanced his cause. Extracts from your book are published in several of the most respectable periodical publications. It has done much good.

I have been engaged, for several months past, in travelling through the country and delivering lectures upon the system of slavery as it exists in the United States, the condition of the free people of color in that country, and the importance of promoting the cause of education and religion generally among the colored people. My lectures have been numerously attended by from two to three thousand people, the Halls and Chapels have been over-flown, and hundreds have not been able to obtain admittance. I have not failed to give Uncle Sam due credit for his 2,000,000 slaves; nor to expose the cruel prejudices of the Americans to our colored race; nor to fairly exhibit the hypocrisy of the Colonization Society, to the astonishment of the people here. And is this, say they, republican liberty? God deliver us from it.

And now, to contrast the difference in the treatment that a colored man receives in this country, with that which he receives in America, my soul is filled with sorrow and indignation. I could weep over the land of my nativity! ' I would ask those hypocritical pretenders to humanity and religion, who are continually crying out, 'What shall we do with our black and colored people?' Why do ye not do them justice? What! are you better than Englishmen? Admit them to equal rights with yourselves; this is all that they ask; this is all that is needful to be done. What hinders you from doing this? Is it any thing but the pride of your hearts? Here, if I go to church, I am not pointed to the 'negro seat' in the gallery; but any gentleman opens his pew door for my reception. If I wish for a passage in a stage, the only question that is asked me is, 'Which do you choose, sir, an inside or an outside seat?' If I stop at a public inn, no one would ever think here of setting a separate table for me; I am conducted to the same table with other gentlemen. The only difference that I have ever discovered is this, I am generally taken for a stranger, and they therefore seem anxious to pay me the greater respect.

I have had the pleasure of breakfasting twice with the venerable WILBERFORCE, and have now a letter in my pocket that I received from him, a few weeks since, which I would not take pounds for.

Once I have been in the company of the patriotic CLARKSON. I must say I viewed them both as Angels of liberty. God bless and reward them.

In regard to the object that brought me to this country, I would say, that, considering the peculiar state of the country, I have been quite as successful as I could expect. The object has met with the most decided approbation from all classes of people. I do not hold out the delusive idea that the whole of the colored people are going to Canada; but have invariably said, that in spite of all that will ever remove there, or to any other part of the world they will continue to increase in America. It is only to open the door for all such as choose to go, or that prefer Canada to the United States.

When I shall return, I cannot at present say; but I think that it will not be under several months.

Farewell, in the name of the Lord. Let us trust and persevere to the end.

NATHANIEL PAUL.[*]

LONDON, (Eng.) August 29, 1833.

TO ANDREW T. JUDSON, ESQ.

Of the Town of Canterbury, State of Connecticut.

SIR—Through the medium of the American newspapers, I have seen your name, and the names of your worthy coadjutors, and have read your noble and praiseworthy deeds, in regard to the establishment of a school in your town, conducted by one Miss Prudence Crandall, for the instruction of young ladies of color! And believing that acts so patriotic, so republican, so Christian-like in their nature, as yours, against the unpardonable attempts of this fanatical woman, should not be confined to one nation or continent, but that the WORLD should know them, and learn and profit thereby;—I have thought proper to do all in my power to spread your fame, that your works may be known at least throughout this country. Nor will you marvel at my magnanimity when I inform you that I am, myself, a native of New-England, and consequently *proud* of whatever may emanate from her sons, calculated to exalt them in the eyes of the world.

And as I have been for some months past and still am engaged in travelling and delivering lectures upon the state of slavery as it

[*] *Liberator,* June 22, 1833.

exists in the United States, and the condition of the free people of color there, it will afford me an excellent opportunity of making this whole affair known; nor shall I fail to improve it. Yes, sir, Britons shall know that there are men in America, and whole towns of them, too, who are not so destitute of true heroism but that they can assail a helpless woman, surround her house by night, break her windows, and drag her to prison, for the treasonable act of teaching females of color to read!!!

Already is the State of Connecticut indebted to me for my gratuitous services since I have been in this country, in her behalf; especially the city of *New-Haven*, and its worthy Mayor. Their magnanimous conduct in regard to the establishment of a college for colored youth in that place, I have spread from 'Dan to Beersheba;'—and Dennis Kimberly may rest assured that the name of Benedict Arnold does not stand higher in the estimation of the American people than *his* does in England! It is my intention, sir, to give you an equal elevation.

I shall make no charge for the service I may render you. Nevertheless, if you think I am truly deserving, and ought to have a compensation, whatever you may feel it your duty to give, you will please to hand it over to the Treasurer of the 'American Colonization Society,' of which, I understand, you are a member and an advocate.

Respectfully yours,
NATHANIEL PAUL,[5]
Representative of the Wilberforce Settlement, Upper Canada.

13, *Scarsdale Terrace, Kensington, near London, 22d Jan.,* 1834.

My Dear friend Garrison:

Your letter of Nov. 5th I received a few days ago. I was engaged at that time in writing an answer to a *new philippic* of that devoted friend of Elliott Cresson and the Colonization Society, Dr. Hodgkin. I had got about half through the work when I ascertained that Capt. Stuart and the Rev. John Scoble had anticipated me—therefore, of course, I gave it up. Dr. Hodgkin seems to be almost the only friend that Cresson has left. I think, however, that *he* will soon be glad to keep quiet, after the castigation he has received from the above named gentlemen.

<hr>

5 *Liberator*, Nov. 23, 1833.

I am happy to hear of your safe arrival at the scene of your former labors; nor was I surprised or disappointed that the colonization and slaveholding persecutors should have assailed you in the manner that they have done. Pitiful creatures! Will they never be satisfied or tired of their brutal and fiend-like atrocities? Have they not already sunk themselves low enough in the estimation of all liberal and enlightened men? I pity them from my soul! and pray God to give them repentance ere they die; for, if there be a corner in hell where the anger of a righteous God burns the most fierce, that place must be theirs.

And so they throw out their threats against me! and I, too, may expect to be marked a victim of satanic fury on my return to my native country!! If they have not drunk sufficiently of the blood of my fathers and brethren to quench their insatiable thirst, they are welcome to mine! They may take my life, if they wish to take it; but, let not the base tyrants insult me with their threats, supposing that they can thereby prevent me from pursuing my work, or hinder my exposing their conduct to the censure of the British public.

The pledge that I gave to ANDREW T. JUDSON and his worthy coadjutors, in the letter addressed to him a few months since, I have steadily kept in view; and, so far as I have gone, I have most sacredly redeemed.

I must tell you of a meeting I held in the city of Norwich, but a few weeks since. The meeting was convened, under the sanction of the Mayor, in a spacious room known by the name of S. Andrew's Hall. At the hour appointed, the hall, which will contain from three to four thousand people, was literally filled. Dr. ASH, a leading and highly respectable member of the Society of Friends, was called to the chair, who opened the meeting with a short and appropriate speech, and introduced me to the audience. I then rose and spoke for an hour and a half. I was followed by W. B. Youngman, Esq., the Rev. John Scoble, the Rev. Mr. Alexander, and Capt. G. Pilkington. I wish that that whited wall, Judge Daggett, Dennis Kimberly, Andrew T. Judson, and the rest of the persecutors of Miss Prudence Crandall, and of the colored people, had been near by, to have their names and their conduct exposed, and to have witnessed the utter contempt and indignation which a recital of their deeds elicited from the meeting; they would ever after have sought to hide their 'diminished heads' in some obscure corner of the earth, remote from human observation.

It is, however, almost beyond endurance, to hear these men talk of your having slandered your country while in England. To slander America, with regard to her treatment of her slaves and free colored people, would be tantamount to slandering his satanic majesty, by calling him wicked! Her nakedness is already discovered, and her shame cannot be hid! If she would wish to redeem her character as a nation, it must be by other means than by that of *tarring and feathering abolitionists.* She must effect it by driving such men as Daggett from the bench, and Judson from office, and consign their associates in wickedness to that oblivion which their conduct has merited, by abandoning their Colonization crusade, and annihilating slavery, and their cruel prejudice against the colored people. She may then raise her flag of liberty, and spread it out unstained and uncontaminated, for the world to look upon and admire.

My dear brother, I am aware you need no stimulus from me in pursuing your noble and philanthropic career. Still, justice to you demands the assurance from my pen, that you *do indeed* possess the confidence, the esteem, and share in the prayers of the abolitionists, and friends of religion, humanity and liberty, in England. Miss CRANDALL also shares the admiration and sympathy of the friends of religion; and is, and will be supported by the prayers of the christians in Britain, while they heartily bid her God-speed in her heroic and praise-worthy undertaking.

Pray be particular in forwarding the Liberator. I have only obtained four since you left, and for those I paid *half a crown a piece.* I am getting on pretty well in my business. Tell my friends to be patient—I shall return as soon as I can get through with my mission, but cannot at present specify any probable time.

I have received from my friends in New-York, a few copies of the excellent Eulogy on the Life and Character of the late Wm. Wilberforce, Esq. pronounced by Mr. Benjamin F. Hughes. It is a splendid production.

My wife joins me in love to you, to my dear sister and children, and to all the friends who hold me in affectionate remembrance.

Farewell, dear brother—fear not! God is on your side, and victory is sure.

Most affectionately yours,
NATHANIEL PAUL.[6]

[6] *Liberator*, April 12, 1834.

THOMAS COLE

The first of these letters from Thomas Cole gives information about the Negro in general and the second mentions his interest in politics.

NEWPORT, R. I., Aug. 7, 1840.

BRO. JOHNSON:

Presuming that some of my friends would like to hear from me occasionally during my absence from the city, I take the liberty to request the insertion of a few words in the Liberator.

Saturday afternoon, Aug. 1, I took the cars at Boston for Providence, and arrived at the latter place in less than two and a half hours.   The accommodations upon this route for persons of color are tolerably good—much better than they formerly were. The proprietors have appropriated seats for colored people in the first class of cars.   The accommodations, in themselves, are good enough—for the seats are as well cushioned as any in the whole train; but my objection lies against the exclusive principle which prevails—the principle which colonizes us without our consent, as if we were not fit to ride in company with others on terms of equality.   This is not as it should be.   The day is coming, I trust, when these paltry distinctions will be done away.   The wrongs which we as a people suffer, are enough to make even the angels bow their heads and weep.   We are hunted and despised, and like the Son of Man, have not where to lay our heads.   Our condition reminds me of the exiled Israelites, who sat and wept on the banks of their lovely streams.   The iron heel of oppression is crushing the hearts of many colored Americans to the earth.   Our spirits, however, can never be subdued, if we are only united and true to our interests.   Our souls, like the mountain's crest, will yet tower high above surrounding difficulties.

The first of August, the anniversary of British emancipation, was observed in Providence in a very appropriate manner.   An address was delivered at Masonic Hall by James Richardson, Jr., a young man of fine talents.   I had the pleasure of hearing part of his discourse.   He depicted the horrors of American slavery in glowing colors.   I hope his address will be published, for it would prove one of the choicest specimens of anti-slavery literature.   An address was also delivered by a young man of color in one of the churches of the colored people.   Of this address, also, I heard only a part; but what I did hear was deeply interesting.

August 2d, I left Providence for Newport at 8 o'clock, A. M. This is one of the most beautiful places in the whole Union. It has a noble harbor studded with beautiful islands and lined with shipping. A whale ship arrived on Wednesday last, which brought 2,500 bbls. of oil—a cargo valued at $80,000. What is called the old town of Newport is situated on a gentle acclivity sloping down to the water in the form of a semi-circle. The population is 8000. The colored inhabitants number about 350 or 400. They have a very neat little church, where the great body of them worship. A few, however, have seceded and set up worship by themselves. The people of both sexes to whom I have been introduced are very intelligent and affable, and display a becoming taste in their dress.

On Sunday I had the pleasure of listening to two sermons from Rev. Peter Williams of New York. He preached in the church where the colored people mostly worship. He, as well as myself, is staying at the house of friend Remond, the father of C. L. Remond, now in England. Friend Remond has a very pleasant location, and an interesting family.

Your readers are doubtless aware that Newport was settled in 1639 by William Coddington, a Quaker, and seventeen others. Mr. Coddington was afterwards governor. It has been the scene of many a bloody war. The British held possession of the island during three years of the Revolution. The remains of *old* forts and entrenchments are yet to be seen. Fort Adams has been seventeen years in building, and will not be completed in less than five more. It is a stupendous work. There are several places here of fashionable resort—among them a 'Purgatory,' a 'Paradise,' and the 'Spouting Rock.' Many strangers resort here to spend the summer in a quiet and healthy retreat.

Excuse me for spinning out such a 'long yarn,' and allow me to subscribe myself.

Yours, in behalf of the oppressed,

THOMAS COLE.[7]

BOSTON, November, 1840.

DEAR SIR:—Knowing the deep interest you have always manifested in whatever relates to the welfare of the colored man, I take the liberty to communicate a few thoughts.

[7] *Liberator*, Aug. 21, 1840.

Since President Van Buren has met his Waterloo defeat, I have been led to contemplate the political aspect of society.

What is a political life? I think it may be regarded as a good school for the development of the intellectual faculties, but not for the cultivation of moral sensibility. I speak of course of political life, as it now exists, and has existed.

I can conceive of a state of society, so elevated and so moral, as to render politics a school for the exercise and attainment of moral and Christian virtues. But such is not the state of society now.

Political parties of the present day give no encouragement to the cause of emancipation, morality and religion; political honesty at the present day, is an anomaly. In separating the church from the state, politicians have separated the state from heaven.

Political parties, as they now exist, are undoubtedly hostile to the interest of the slaves and the nominally free. Our present rulers have been great sinners. Van Buren was an original sinner. I rejoice that he is soon to be released from the cares of office, and return to Kinderhook, for his servility to the slaveholding interest of the South.

Consider the temptations to which a political man is exposed. You will not wonder that his moral delicacy is blinded, and should be assailed. Office is generally the gift of party, for some party services rendered. Is it not so? Is not a politician, then, under an implied obligation to consult the wishes of his party?

We, as a people, I apprehend, have erred greatly in the advocacy of our rights to freedom and equality. How many of the privileges that we now enjoy, would have been secured to us without the aid of the friends of freedom? Our rights are secured by constitutional law. We have yet a host of friends who have not 'bowed the knee to Baal'—men who are worthy the name—whose characters and principles show the elevated stand they are taking to attain for us 'liberty and equality.' Let our watchword be, liberty and equality, as it is our birth-right. I do not despair of triumph as our cause is founded upon the rock of eternal truth.

We must take a more comprehensive view of our condition, and every thing that relates to our highest and best good. We must study politics for ourselves, and place ourselves in a condition where our influence will be felt wherever we have the right to exercise the political franchise. Then, and then only, will equal justice be meted out to us. What have we and the friends of liberty to expect from the party who are soon to go into power, and legislate in the councils of this nation? Absolutely nothing. The policy of the South is the maintenance, at all hazards, of the institution of slavery. A metallic currency has been their only rallying cry! No vested rights, is the motto of those whose principal property is nothing but vested rights in slaves. Where has slavery its sanction, except from the decrees of the statute book?

Do the whig party, as such, possess more moral courage than the democrats, which will lead them to act conscientiously in defiance of a corrupt public sentiment, or of their constituents? I do not say that individuals among them may not possess this moral courage of thought and action: I only ask, is it not more probable that, as a party, they will oppose all measures for our enfranchisement and elevation, which are unpopular with the majority, rather than incur odium and loss of station, by supporting them? 'And where is the man,' says an eminent writer, 'who, for his own advancement, will not willingly injure the whole human race?' I firmly believe, that the majority of politicians would sacrifice their principles rather than their popularity.

Ever yours, for the suffering slave,

THOMAS COLE.[8]

JAMES FORTEN AND ROBERT PURVIS

James Forten, one of the most influential men of his time, and probably the most distinguished Negro to develop in Philadelphia prior to the Civil War, was the moving spirit of the convention movement among Negroes, beginning with the first meeting in Philadelphia in 1830. He was not sufficiently young and energetic to take a leading part in the intense abolition agitation of the 'thirties, but this comment and letter show that he was giving the cause his moral support.

Among the colored citizens of the republic, there is not one who is held in higher estimation than the venerable JAMES FORTEN, of Philadelphia; not merely because, by his industry, skill and prudence, he has risen to affluence, but mainly on account of his gentlemanly qualities, shining virtues, and intellectual and moral char-

8 *Liberator*, Dec. 18, 1840.

acteristics. He suffered many hardships in the revolutionary war, and was captured by the British while endeavoring to save his country from a foreign yoke. Ungrateful country! The following letter from his pen, written by himself almost in *copper-plate* style, illustrates the spirit of this noble man:

PHILADELPHIA, Aug. 31, 1841.

Mr. WM. LLOYD GARRISON:

ESTEEMED FRIEND,—I am very happy to have the opportunity, which the visit of a young lady, a friend of my family, to Boston, presents, to forward the enclosed, my subscription to the Liberator. It gives me great pleasure, in reading it from week to week, to hear of the successful progress of our cause; and I never lay down the Liberator without feeling my faith in its final, and I trust speedy triumph, renewed and invigorated. I regret to say that my health is not improved since I saw you in the Spring; for, although I have been occasionally relieved, yet the complaint is not renewed, and I am at present suffering from a more than usually severe attack of it. Although unable to participate actively in anti-slavery labors, my interest in it is undiminished, and as ardent as ever. That you may long be spared to carry on the warfare against all oppression, is the sincere and heartfelt wish of

Your true friend,

JAMES FORTEN.[9]

Robert Purvis, the distinguished coworker of James Forten in Philadelphia, much younger than the latter, lived to see abolition enjoy some of the fruits of its labor. This letter shows his attitude toward the movement and what he was doing to promote the cause.

LONDON, July 13, 1834.

MY DEAR GARRISON:

This pleasure I expected to have had soon after my arrival in this country; but such were the demonstrations of friendship which I received from my friends here, that I could never find the time to send you an epistle; and even at this moment, I am forced to write hastily and briefly.

You must know, my dear friend, that I am regarded in this country as 'Abolition property'—and you must also know, that

[9] *Liberator*, Sept. 17, 1841.

there is a very '*particular* price' set upon such property, especially too, when the coloring of the building happens to fall below the inconstant and wavering shade of white, to the more substantial black or brown.

Our dear friend GEORGE THOMPSON has not yet left this country, but will embark on the 24th inst. You and all our friends may expect him in August.

The Abolition friends, in this country, hear with astonishment and indignation the *slanderous* assertion, that the departed WILBERFORCE affixed his signature to the Protest against the American Colonization Society when his mind was enfeebled by disease. 'No,' say they, 'WILBERFORCE was in the full possession of his mental faculties.' In fact, notwithstanding the artifices of a *certain one,* [Elliott Cresson,] he had mistrusted both Society and Agent long before he signed the Protest.

I had, at the House of Commons, an introduction to the Hon. DANIEL O'CONNELL. On my being presented to the Irish Patriot as an *American Gentleman,* he declined taking my hand; but when he understood that I was not only identified with the Abolitionists, but with the proscribed and oppressed colored class in the United States, he grasped my hand, and warmly shaking it, remarked— '*Sir, I will never take the hand of an American, nor should any honest man in this country do so, without first knowing his principles in reference to American Slavery, and its ally, the American Colonization Society.*' In reply I remarked, that it was asserted in America, that he had caused his name to be stricken off the Protest against the American Colonization Society. Mark his answer! 'He who asserted that, Sir, asserted a *lie,* to the full extent and meaning of the term. I have heard,' he continued, 'that much was made of what I said, in relation to the Americans—their Slavery, and their Colonization; but'—(turning to my friend, Rev. Mr. Scoble, to whom I was indebted for an introduction,) 'I shall express myself more fully and decidedly, in relation to these matters. Get you up a meeting for that purpose, and I will subscribe £5, or more, to defray the expenses.' Such, verbatim, was the language of that fearless advocate for universal freedom. Now, will Cresson dare again to say, that DANIEL O'CONNELL erased his name from the British Protest?

Yours, most truly,
ROBERT PURVIS.[9a]

[9a] *Liberator,* Aug. 23, 1834.

PHILADELPHIA, Nov. 8th, 1841.

MR. GEO. L. CLARKE:

Dear Sir—Circumstances prevented, until this time, the acknowledgment of your letter, over date of 28th ult. I regret that I shall be unable to be with you at the approaching anniversary, of the Rhode Island State Anti-Slavery Society, but hope that those now threatened with political disfranchisement, as well as the true friends of man and liberty, will use their best and mightiest efforts, to disappoint those pseudo republicans, whose vile proscriptive propositions, in regard to the "colored people," will blacken their names with the deepest infamy.

How cowardly, mean, and despicable the movers of this unrighteous proposition must appear, in the eyes of an enlightened world! Nay, the pettiest despot at the South, spurns the venality of such "dough-faces;" for it is but the vassal spirit of the North, adapting itself to the dirtiest work, which the great charnel-house of slavery *can* afford, for those base spirits who seem to "live, move, and have their being," upon southern patronage and generosity.

There is a wickedness and meanness in the contemplated measure, that at once excites my indignation and pity—indignation, at the impudent and sacrilegious invasion upon human rights; pity, for the miserable creatures who are either catering to the South, or, under the influence of "Yankee" prejudice against *caste*, more virulent and fiendish than any where else felt or known.

But I hope the result of this matter will be to show that the inhabitants of your State have been properly and rightfully influenced, conformable to the spirit of its great and good founder; and that nothing was done incompatible with freedom, sound policy, the rights of man, and the laws of God.

Yours, for God and liberty,

ROBERT PURVIS,

270 Lombard-street.[9b]

MANLY PROTEST AGAINST WRONG.

The *Liberator* of December 16, 1853 said:

The following manly Protest (which we find in a late number of the *Pennsylvania Freeman*) is made by one of the most intelligent, estimable and gentlemanly colored citizens of Pennsylvania, the latchet of whose shoes not one of the thousands of those who

[9b] *National Anti-Slavery Standard*, Dec. 2, 1841.

assume to look down with scorn upon the colored race are worthy
to unloose.

BYBERRY, Pa., Nov. 5th, 1853.

FRIEND BURLEIGH: Amid the animating and encouraging signs
of the times, occurrences there are which seem to dash our hopes,
and drive us into the very darkness of despair. The recent outrage upon Misses Remond and Wood, and my son, at the Franklin
Exhibition—Alderman Mitchell's decision in the case, when, too,
he had, previously to the suit being brought before him, properly
characterized it as most brutal and infamous—the continued high-
handed exclusion of my children from the Public School in this
Township, against law, justice and decency, perplexes and excites a
spirit of belligerancy, at war with the peace of my soul and body.
It seemed impossible to bear any longer this robbery of my rights
and property, by those miserable serviles to the slave power, the
Directors of the Public Schools for this Township, and feeling it
impossible, I wrote the following letter to the collector of taxes,
which you may publish in the *Freeman,* should you deem proper.

Yours, very truly,

ROBERT PURVIS.[9c]

———

BYBERRY, Nov. 4th, 1853.

MR. JOS. J. BUTCHER—*Dear Sir:* You called yesterday for the
tax upon my property in this Township, which I shall pay, excepting the 'School Tax.' I object to the payment of this tax, on the
ground that my rights as a citizen, and my feelings as a man and
a parent, have been grossly outraged in depriving me, in violation
of law and justice, of the benefits of the school system which this
tax was designed to sustain. I am perfectly aware that all that
makes up the character and worth of the citizens of this township
look upon the proscription and exclusion of my children from the
Public School as illegal, and an unjustifiable usurpation of my
right. I have borne this outrage ever since the innovation upon
the usual practice of admitting *all* the children of the Township
into the Public Schools, and at considerable expense, have been
obliged to obtain the services of private teachers to instruct my
children, while my school tax is greater, with a single exception,
than that of any other citizen of the township. It is true, (and
the outrage is made but the more glaring and insulting,) I was in-

9c *Liberator,* Sept. 16, 1853.

formed by a *pious Quaker* director, with a sanctifying grace, imparting, doubtless, an unctuous glow to his *saintly* prejudices, that a school in the village of Mechanicsville was appropriated for '*thine.*' The miserable shanty, with all its appurtenances, on the very line of the township, to which this *benighted* follower of George Fox alluded, is, as you know, the most flimsy and ridiculous sham which any tool of a skin-hating aristocracy could have resorted to, to cover or protect his servility. To submit by voluntary payment of the demand is too great an outrage upon nature, and, with a spirit, thank God, unshackled by this, or any other wanton and cowardly act, I shall resist this tax, which, before the unjust exclusion, had always afforded me the highest gratification in paying. With no other than the best feeling towards yourself, I am forced to this unpleasant position, in vindication of my rights and personal dignity against an encroachment upon them as contemptibly mean as it is infamously despotic.

Yours, very respectfully,

ROBERT PURVIS.[9d]

II.   CONTROVERSIAL CORRESPONDENCE

The following letters show how difficult it was not only for the white abolitionists to work in harmony but even for the Negro leaders to do so. Whether with reason or without, the one often did much to destroy the other. The most striking case here is taken from Canada. At first things seemed to be going along nicely.

COLONY IN UPPER CANADA.

The Rev. Nathaniel Paul, agent of the Wilberforce settlement in Canada, and formerly pastor of the African Baptist Church in this city, arrived here on Wednesday, the 10th Aug. bringing with him letters of instruction and other credentials, authorizing him to visit Great Britain, to solicit such aid as may be conducive to the prosperity and future welfare of that infant settlement. Mr. Paul's papers were signed by his Excellency the Lieut. Governor. The information received from the above gentleman was truly gratifying, and it is to be hoped that the friends to that and every other good cause, will assist him in his philanthropic exertions, so

[9d] *Liberator*, Dec. 16, 1853.

requisite to the immediate prosecution of his mission abroad. The
state of affairs in the settlement may be seen from the communication in this number from the above place. Editors friendly to the
above-mentioned settlement, will please give the communication an
insertion in their papers.—*Albany African Sentinel.*

WILBERFORCE SETTLEMENT, U. C.

Mr Editor—It will no doubt be gratifying to our friends who
in different parts of the state of New-York and elsewhere, have
taken an interest in our welfare, and have aided us in effecting
this infant settlement, to hear from us, to know how we are getting
along; we therefore beg the favor of communicating to them,
through the medium of your very useful paper, a short account of
our affairs: Through the blessing of God, we have all enjoyed our
usual degree of health. We have erected for our accommodations
comfortable log buildings, and have a portion of our land in a
state of cultivation; our crops at present continue to smile upon
the labor of our hands; we shall raise the present year nearly
enough to supply the present number of settlers. The people are
industrious, and well pleased with their present location; and it is
believed that none of them could be hired to go back to the states.
Two religious societies have been organized, one of the Baptist,
under the pastoral care of Elder Nathaniel Paul, and the other of
the Methodist, under the care of Elder Enos Adams; and we are
happy to add, that the utmost degree of harmony exists between
the two churches. A sabbath school, under the superintendence
of Mr Austin Steward, late of Rochester, is in successful operation;
and a day school for the instruction of the children, is taught by
a daughter of Elder Benjamin Paul, late of the city of New-York;
and in addition to which, a temperance society has been formed,
consisting of about thirty in number; and the voice of the people
is decidedly against ardent spirits ever being introduced as an
article of merchandise among us. There are, however, a number
of families who have emigrated from the states, whose pecuniary
circumstances will not admit of their coming at present to join us,
but are compelled to take lands in the neighboring settlements upon
shares, and hundreds more in the states are longing to join us, but
on account of their limited means are not able to carry their designs into effect. We feel grateful for past favors, but will not the
eye of the Philanthropist be turned toward their condition, and

his hand opened to supply their wants, that they may thereby be enabled to join their brethren, to help forward one of the most noble enterprises that ever was started, to elevate the too long degraded African, this side the Atlantic?

The annual election of the board of Managers, whose duty it is to appoint agents, and to take the oversight of the general concerns of the settlement, took place July 11th, when the following persons were duly elected:—Austin Steward, Benjamin Paul, Enos Adams, William Bell, Philip Harris, Abraham Dangerfield, Simon Wyatt. The newly elected board, considering the limited means of the colored people generally, and the absolute necessity of pecuniary aid, and in order to carry so desirable an object into effect, and to secure its permanent character, have re-appointed Mr Israel Lewis their agent to obtain collections in the states, and the Rev. Nathaniel Paul, late of Albany, whose standing as a minister of the gospel, and whose devotedness to the cause of his colored brethren, are too well known to need any recommendation from us, to embark for England, for the same purpose. He will probably sail as soon as the necessary means shall be obtained to defray the expense of his voyage—and should a kind Providence smile upon the exertions of our agents, we have no doubt but in the course of a few years, that this settlement will present to the public such a state of things as will cheer the heart of every well wisher of the African race, and put to silence the clamor of their violent enemies.

By order and in behalf of the Board.

AUSTIN STEWARD, Chairman.[10]

BENJAMIN PAUL, Secretary.

Cazenovia, Jan. 26, 1833.

TO THE PUBLIC.

I have just seen an article in the Rochester Anti-Masonic Inquirer of the 22d inst. signed by Austin Steward, and others, of the Wilberforce Colony, declaring themselves to be the Board of Managers of the legitimate affairs of that colony. This is not the first article that has been published by that undiscerning band of wicked men. I would have said something to confute the wickedness of that party before now; but knowing that a controversy

------

[10] *Liberator*, Sept. 7, 1831.

among ourselves would go to retard our progress, I have heretofore refrained from saying any thing in public print, in a party
way. But in justice to the Wilberforce Colony, which I had the
honor to plant, I will make a few remarks on the causes which have
induced Austin Steward and his unprincipled band to pursue the
course that he has. To be sure, it is painful for me to state acts of
the kind about my own color; but necessity compels me to do so.

One year after I had planted the Wilberforce Colony, and commenced travelling for the purpose of getting aid for the Colony, I
went to Rochester where this Austin Steward lived. He was
recommended to me as a man of color supporting a fair character.
I induced him to go to Wilberforce, and there got him in as one of
the Board of Managers—took him into my house to live with me
until he could get a home, knowing that he supported a good name
where he came from. Some time in the course of the season, I lost
a twenty dollar note of hand out of my house, which I found some
the article which appeared in the Rochester paper, it is stated that
I have refused to submit monies collected by me, to him and others
to distribute. This I do not deny, having the right to do so,
guaranteed to me by the original board of managers. I feel myself quite responsible for all my acts, so far as they relate to that
Colony. I will add by saying, there is no man of color living in the
Wilberforce Colony by the name of *Sharpe*, which the article seemed
to say was an agent for the Colony. Nor neither do I recognize
any board of managers but the one I belong to. I would say more;
but knowing that all we say, not tending to unite, is so much wrong
in most instances. There is one thing that gives me some satisfaction; that is, discerning men know that in all great undertakings like this, those engaged in them must be more or less persecuted; more especially when they stand in the midst of an ignorant
people, coming from different sections of the country, under different views, and with different habits. A tight rein is the best to
manage the affairs of such a people, under such circumstances.

ISRAEL LEWIS,
President and Agent of
Wilberforce Colonization Company.

SCHENECTADY, Feb. 11th, 1833.

FRIEND GARRISON:—In reading your paper of the 9th inst. I
was much surprised to find that you had copied an article in your

useful paper, touching that which, to me, is dearer than life, my public and moral character—sent forth from a few disaffected and ungenerous men of our colony. When any thing and every thing which may be fabricated against me, and all who are connected with efforts tending to the meliorating the condition of my injured brethren, is published by those who are not professedly engaged in pleading the cause of the colored man, I am not at all astonished. But knowing that you must be aware of the difficulties connected with founding, sustaining and managing a settlement like that of Wilberforce, and that great diversity of views must be expected—knowing that you profess to be, and, as I hope, are our friend—I was shocked and grieved to find that you had so prematurely given publicity to the article to which I have alluded, *without first having examined the facts in the case.* It appears to me that you could not have forgotten that more than six months since, I resigned that agency, which I prosecuted in connection with the Board of Managers, who then had the oversight of our affairs. If I mistake not, you published it in your paper, on the 11th of July last, on the day of General Election by a majority of the settlers, the former course of proceeding and Board of Managers were voted down, and a new organization was formed, known by the name of the 'Wilberforce Colonization Company,' and also a new Board of Managers were appointed, with whom I am connected, and for whom I now act as Agent. A small minority were dissatisfied, as might be expected; and among other means employed by them to counteract our influence, they have brought me before the public as a base impostor, unworthy of confidence. As you have unhappily contributed the influence of the Liberator in spreading these slanderous reports, particularly among my colored brethren, I hope you will do me the justice to copy from the Republican Monitor, of Cazenovia, certain articles touching this subject. The above named paper I send to you.

Yours respectfully,

ISRAEL LEWIS.

The Monitor also publishes the following Certificate:

Wilberforce, Nov. 10, 1832.

'This certifies to all whom it may concern—that I have known the bearer hereof, Mr Israel Lewis, for about one year, and from the best information that I can obtain, he is the founder of this colony—and may the good Lord prosper him in all his undertakings.   BENJAMIN PAUL,

11 *Liberator,* Feb. 23, 1833.   Pastor of the First Baptist Church.11

WILBERFORCE, March 12, 1833.

MESSRS GARRISON AND KNAPP—I saw in your Journal of the
Times a communication to the public, signed by one Israel Lewis,
and first published by the Republican Monitor of Cazenovia. Were
the true character of that Israel Lewis well known by all who may
chance to read his false representations, I should never have taken
up the pen to answer them, much less have troubled you with these
few lines—you who are advocating the most holy cause that falls
to the lot of man. I say your excellent paper may be more profit-
ably employed in pleading the cause of thousands who cannot, who
dare not speak for themselves. But the very cause which you are
advocating requires me to answer those base falsehoods. It is a
duty that I owe my numerous friends—it is a duty I owe the friends
of this Colony—and last, but not least, it is a duty I owe my family
and myself.

Some time in the spring of 1830, I received several communications from Mr James C. Brown and others, relative to a settlement
for colored people in Canada. I resolved to visit the place of the
contemplated settlement. While I was preparing for the journey,
who should arrive in Rochester but Israel Lewis. He introduced
himself to me as Agent for the colored people in Ohio. I always
being willing to accommodate my colored friends, took this Lewis
to my house, and treated him with the urbanity of a colored man.
He then made known to me his want of money, and by my influence
he got up a subscription both among the white and colored friends,
which amounted to something like $100. While we were preparing
to start to Canada, Messrs Hickman and Ross arrived, bound for
the same place. We made the necessary preparation, and started
for Canada. We arrived at London, about twelve miles from the
Huron tract. We fell in with Mr James C. Brown and Mr Stephen
Dutton. Said Brown was the President of the Ohio Board. The
greatest diffiulty arose between Brown and Lewis—Brown could not
get Lewis to account for monies that he had received, and L. borrowed a pistol and declared that he would shoot Brown, but we persuaded him from doing so. We all met on the ground that is now
called Wilberforce. We organized a meeting and proceeded to
business; and among other things, the question came up, what the
name of the Settlement should be. I being sensible of the great
exertions that Mr Wilberforce had made in behalf of our colored
brethren, moved the Settlement be called after him, and it was car-

ried without a dissenting voice. I then returned home to arrange my business, and prepare to move to Wilberforce. During this year, there came on a number of emigrants from the city of Boston, which are the bone and sinew of the Settlement. In May, 1831, I set out for Wilberforce; and on my arrival, I found things in the most unsettled state—the inhabitants, I believe, to a man, were opposed to Lewis. I had made a partial bargain for a house with a Mr Charles Jackson, which was about two miles from where Lewis then lived. Lewis entreated me to go and live in his house. I took a lease of it at one dollar per week, but did not live in it more than a year; for I found that I had got into bad company, and I was glad to get away as soon as I could. When I first took the house, I took Lewis and a woman that I then supposed to be his wife, to board with me. The house that Lewis had possession of, is built on lands owned by Mr Wm. Bell, for Lewis does not own one foot of land in the Colony, to my knowledge. As I have above stated, the settlers were arrayed against Lewis, with the Rev. Nathaniel Paul at their head, trying to get a settlement with Lewis, but they could not. He could not or would not exhibit a fair account. If books were shown, some of the leaves would be missing. Common report says of his subscription books, he burnt them, for fear we would know the amount of money collected. What to do in this dilemma, we knew not. We had come to this place to build an asylum for our oppressed brethren; and should what money Lewis had collected defeat the grand object? I folded my arms and surveyed North America from the gulf of St. Lawrence to the gulf of Mexico. I saw no resting place for the *black man,* where he could have all the *political* and *religious liberty* that rational intelligent creatures are entitled to. Prejudice, insatiable prejudice, had sunk deep into the hearts of the American people. I saw the operations of the American Colonization Society—it was taking off a few hundred of my oppressed countrymen, and transplanting them on the inhospitable shores of Africa! where before the earth had performed her annual circuit, they would be consigned to an untimely grave. I turned my mind from the heart-sickening scene again to the affairs of Wilberforce, resolving to overlook the imperfections of the past as respects Israel Lewis, and see if we could not show a settlement worthy of the liberal patronage that it had received from the state of New-York. Lewis at the same time promised that he would do the best that he could for the Colony.

About this time there appeared a publication in the papers, cautioning the public against the impositions of Lewis, from the Ohio Board who had appointed him, and a notice of his removal. Frederick Storer, a man who belongs to the much respected Society of Friends, had been looking on and saw that the ways of Lewis were perverse and wicked. He, F. Storer, gave publicity to the above publication. L. then commenced a suit againt F. S. for defamation, and he, L. agreed to discontinue the suit before I would consent to his appointment. The conduct of L. towards Friend F. S. must be mortifying to *every colored man.*

I then went to work establishing schools—one Sunday school— one day school—one temperance society. L. after his appointment went to the States and borrowed of our friends $700, expressly as Agent, and for the immediate use of the Colony. When he returned home, did he pay over the money as he was in duty bound to do? No, not one dollar did he pay over to the Board. I then made known to L. my disapprobation of the course he was pursuing, and told him if he adhered to it, I must oppose him as Agent.

Here is the commencement of the difficulty between L. and myself in Oct. 1831.

When L. was about starting to the States, a man by the name of Cole held a note of hand against L. for twenty dollars, which he told L. must be paid, or he would stop him. L. came to me with said Cole, and requested me to take up said note, and he would pay me the money for the same. That satisfied said Cole. L. went off to the States on the 13th day of Oct. I paid Mr. Cole the twenty dollars for the note, and took it into my possession as my property, of course, and kept it until May last. Some time in March, 1832, when our much respected friend, B. Lundy, visited our settlement, the people called a general meeting of the inhabitants in order to pay their respects to that truly philanthropic individual. After the meeting was organized, they reviewed the conduct of L——, passed resolutions against him, declared his agency of no benefit to the Colony, and directed the Board of Managers to discharge him. L. returned home in a great rage, and declared that he would cut the throats of the Board of Managers. Mr. B. Paul took me aside and told me that I had better let the Board of Managers go down, and assigned as a reason, that L. was so enraged, that he did not know what he, (L.) might be led to do. I answered that I was placed there to guard the public interest, and I should do so, let the consequences be what they might. We tried to get a settlement with L., but to no purpose. L. refused to give up the papers that he received from the Board, and they directed me, as chairman of the Board, to publish him as no longer Agent. Then it was that L. was determined to ruin me, because he knew that I was favorably known, and what I wrote was likely to be believed. He resolved to destroy my character, even if he had to resort to false swearing to do it. He was apprised of my intended journey to Rochester, where his true conduct would be known. As I have before stated, I tried to get a settlement with him before I left home, and I put off my intended journey a week or two longer for that purpose; but to no effect. I at last started for Rochester. I got sixteen miles on my journey, where I had some business to transact for the Colony, such as giving the Rev. James Sharpe, our newly appointed Agent, his credentials. L. was there. As soon as he saw his successor clothed with the necessary power to prosecute the object of his mission, he (L.) made oath that I was indebted to him in the sum of one hundred and sixty dollars, and had me arrested as an absconding debtor, thinking that my short acquaintance would prevent my giving sufficient bail; but in that he was disappointed. I declared the oath that L. took, wherein he swore that I owed him $160, to be a falsehood. It has been since tried by twelve men as Jurors of the country, and I got judgment against him. He (L.) then swore that I owed him $70—$50, for rent and $20 for that note, which, it will be recollected, I got from Mr. Cole. The reason why he sued me for the note was, to make his conduct appear consistent. After he sued me for $160, I then gave the $20 note against L. that I got of Mr. Cole, to A. Talbot, Esq. for collection; and I hold his receipt for the same. Then I went on my intended journey, done my business, and returned to Wilberforce. Ever since my return, L. has been trying to blast my reputation, so that he can go out with his falsehoods and collect money in the name of the poor, and put it in his own pocket. He (L.) found that he had got himself in a trap by false swearing in two instances above named. In order to make things appear in his favor, he went before the Grand Jury, who are bound to hear but one side of the case, and swore that the note was feloniously taken from his house; which I pronounce as base a perjury as ever was committed by any wretch that ever disgraced the walls of a State Prison.

AUSTIN STEWARD.

I certify that I have read the foregoing letter, and believe it to be a fair statement of facts. As far as regards the note obtained from Cole, I feel confident that Mr. Steward came by it in a proper manner. I have taken cognizance of the matter as a Magistrate. I believe Steward to be an honest, well conducted man.   A. TALBOT, *J. P.*

London, 13th March, 1833.

————

WILBERFORCE, March, 1833.

FRIEND GARRISON—We saw in your paper a publication signed by the notorious Israel Lewis, in which he calls the lawfully constituted Board of Managers of this Colony, 'a few disaffected men of the Colony.' Sir, if you knew one half of the baseness of character of that Israel Lewis, you never would have admitted into your paper, which may emphatically be called the guardian of the black man, his libellous publication. In order that you may judge of the correctness of his statement, we shall send herewith the proceedings of a public meeting. It is at all times painful to us as a people, poor and despised as we are, and struggling for existence, to be called upon to record acts of unfaithfulness in those of our own color. But we have no other alternative left; we are compelled to go forward and publish Lewis' conduct to the world; and this we do out of no personal enmity, but as a duty we owe to this infant settlement, and also to our numerous friends every where, and, in so doing, we believe we have taken the only safe and sure path. The inhabitants of Wilberforce are peaceable, industrious and happy, with a few exceptions; and they say by their votes that Israel Lewis should be removed from the Agency of this Colony, and that for good cause.

1. Israel Lewis never has rendered a satisfactory account for the money that he has received to relieve the wants of our poor, but has spent it in the most prodigal manner at the taverns and other public houses.

2. He has run into debt wherever he could, without, in our opinion, any reasonable probability of paying, and thereby brought a reproach upon us as a people.

3. Israel Lewis, who ought to be the guardian and protector of his colored brethren, is the first to cheat them in order that he may live in idleness; and to effect this, he will stop at nothing, no matter how base! how ungenerous! how unrighteous!

Israel Lewis would be glad to make the public believe that he is doing every thing in his power for the benefit of his colored brethren.   Indeed, friend Garrison, to hear Lewis talk about exerting himself for an injured people, reminds us of the Devil chiding sin.

Let us review the ground, and see what this mighty man Lewis has done for his much oppressed colored brethren.   Has he bought any land in Wilberforce?   We answer, no—not one foot.   Has Israel Lewis founded any schools at Wilberforce with the thousands of dollars he has drawn out of a generous public in the States?   We answer, no.   What then has he done of such great importance for the colored people?   We answer, he has collected money and basely squandered it away; and shut the door where good might have been done for our colored friends.

Resolved, That the conduct of Israel Lewis is disgraceful in the extreme, in pretending that there is no Board of Managers at Wilberforce.

Resolved, That we know that all that Lewis has published is so completely void of truth, that it needs no refutation where he is known.

Resolved, That the foregoing, together with these resolutions, be sent on to Messrs Garrison and Knapp, to be inserted in the Liberator.

> AUSTIN STEWARD, *Chairman*,
JOSEPH TAYLOR, *Secretary*.

PHILLIP HARRIS, JNO. WHITEHEAD, WM. BELL, PETER BUTLER, SAMUEL PETERSON.

WILBERFORCE, March 12, 1833.

At a large and respectable meeting of the inhabitants of Wilberforce, to take into consideration certain libellous publications signed by the notorious Israel Lewis and published in the Liberator, Mr Lisbon Wine was called to the chair, and Mr Joseph Murry was appointed Secretary.

Whereas, the recent conduct of Israel Lewis, more especially since his removal from the Agency of this Colony, is ridiculous in the highest degree; and whereas, his scandalous conduct in attacking the character of one of our most respectable fellow-citizens, calls for the animadversion of every honest man—

Resolved, That we must have other testimony than that of Israel Lewis, a man who has been dealing in falsehoods by wholesale ever since he has been known in this country, before we can for a moment believe him even upon his oath.

Resolved, That we highly approve of the course pursued by the Board, in standing for the rights of the settlement. We are satisfied they have not lost sight of the great object for which they came to Wilberforce, viz. the melioration of our colored brethren.

Resolved, That no man, who has the good of our colored brethren at heart, can, after residing at Wilberforce, and reviewing with an impartial eye the conduct of Lewis, give him his support.

Resolved, That we have an unshaken confidence in the fidelity of the Rev. James Sharpe.

Resolved, That the African Canadian Colonization Company is a sheer fabrication, got up to gull the public out of money for individual purposes, by Israel Lewis.

Resolved, That the proceedings of this meeting be signed by the Chairman and Secretary, and sent to Messrs Garrison & Knapp, to be published in the Liberator.

LISBON WINE, Chairman,

JOSEPH MURRY, *Secretary*.

Whereas, a Settlement has recently been formed in the District of London, in the province of Upper Canada, called the Wilberforce Settlement, which Settlement is intended as an asylum for persons of color, who may be enabled to emigrate from the United States of America—

And whereas, the said Settlement now consists of nearly 200 persons who, in the month of July last, elected a Board for the management of its affairs, and the adoption of such measures as might be deemed expedient for the support, maintenance and respectability of the said Settlement—

And whereas, the said Board, having full power so to do, did nominate, constitute and appoint Israel Lewis as Agent to the Settlement, with power and authority to solicit subscriptions and contributions for the said Settlement, from all persons desirous of promoting the cause of universal emancipation—

And whereas, the said Board, having good cause to suppose that the said Israel Lewis hath not faithfully discharged the trust reposed in him by the said Board, have now dismissed him from the Agency aforesaid, and have in his stead appointed the Rev. James

Sharpe to do and perform all duties which by virtue of the appointment aforesaid, did appertain to the office of Agent in the person of the aforesaid Lewis—

Now know all men by these presents, that I, Austin Steward, Chairman of the said Board of Management, having power and authority so to do, do nominate, constitute and appoint the said Rev. James Sharp to fill the office of Agent for the said Settlement, with full power and authority to solicit from the humane and benevolent such contributions as they may feel disposed to make, in order to enable the said Settlement to build a place of worship, erect and endow schools, and relieve the needy and destitute among them. And whatever this my said Agent shall do in the premises, (the settlement having full faith and confidence in him,) shall have the same force and effect in law and equity as if I, as chairman of the said Board, were personally present.

In testimony whereof, I do hereunto set my hand, and affix my seal, at London, in the District of London, and Province of Upper Canada, in presence of the undersigned witnesses.

Signed, sealed and delivered in presence of Edward Allen Talbot and Ross Robertson, at London aforesaid, this twenty-ninth day of May in the year of our Lord one thousand eight hundred and thirty-two.

A. STEWARD.[12]

E. A. TALBOT, *J. P.*
Ross ROBERTSON.
   London District, U. C.

TO THE COLORED CITIZENS OF BOSTON.

Gentlemen and Brethren:

At a public meeting held by you on the 11th of Sept. to express your sentiments relative to the late 'Clerical Appeal,' you authorized your Chairman and Secretary to sign its doings, and to forward a copy to the Liberator, N. E. Spectator, and the Colored American at New York, with a request to have them published. No time was lost, on our part, in conformity to the orders of that meeting; and we state with much satisfaction, that both the Liberator and Spectator gave publicity to those proceedings agreeably to request. But, alas! the *Colored American,* to our great mortifi-

---

[12] *Liberator,* April 13, 1833.

cation, has excluded them from its columns, though it is the professed organ of the colored population of this country, as set forth
in its prospectus. No one could have persuaded you into the belief, that such would have been the conduct of that paper, especially
as it receives, at your hands, such liberal patronage. We leave it
to your own sense of duty and of self-respect to say, how you will
regard this extraordinary procedure. For ourselves, we do not
conceive that the editor of the American has the slightest grounds
for objecting to the insertion of your proceedings; for if he did not
entirely approve of them, he might have accompanied them with his
objections; and, moreover, we deny that any responsibility at-
taches to an editor, where official signatures are appended to a
document. He is as free from blame in that case, as though it were
a mere advertisement.

What has been assigned as a reason for suppressing your doings,
is worse than none; and the editor himself must be conscious of this
fact. But the refusal is serviceable to you, since it has plainly disclosed the policy of that paper. You have now tested it.

The prospectus of the American sets forth, that it would be the
organ, through which the colored man should freely and fearlessly
utter his sentiments—'Its columns will always be the organ of
your wishes and feelings, and the proper medium for laying your
claims before the public.' Thus much for the promise But a few
months have elapsed, and, behold! it is recreant to its pledge. The
editor says, he wishes not to take sides in the little differences upon
the non-essentials of abolitionism among our 'dear friends,' as he
would have it. How doctors disagree! He treats it as a small matter; but the 'clerical five' deemed it of sufficient importance to sever
the cord which bound them and Garrison together.

Again—he refuses to publish the very proceedings upon which
he has commented. How unmanly! He goes further still, and tells
us to withdraw any communication we may have sent to the Liberator. Nay, more—he requests its editor to advise us on these
points; as though Mr. GARRISON would advise us to join those who
are treacherous to our cause! This is adding insult to injury. In
smothering our doings from the public gaze, he shows that a spirit
of jealousy or of fear reigns somewhere. A servile spirit ought to
be despised. By this very policy, do the South shut out abolition
publications from their cities. This is what might be justly termed
'furnishing food for the devil;' a better proof of which we need not,

than the rejoicing of our enemies at the act. Had we been desirous of receiving the instructions suggested by the editor of the American, (and we believe we are yet sane men,) we certainly should have sought it prior to the passage of our resolutions. We desired none but those dictated by our own judgment.

We are mistaken in your character as Bostonians, if you do not regard that paper as being no longer a free organ of the colored man, and frown with disapprobation upon its illiberal treatment. As to William Lloyd Garrison, we of all others know best how to appreciate his labors. Every day brings with it fresh proofs of his exalted worth. Here he first promulgated his principles, from which there has been no deviation. Here his voice of thunder was first lifted up for God and Liberty. We have been at his side in the dark hour of trial. We have seen his patience tested, and witnessed his manly fortitude and untiring zeal. We feel that his and our interests are one—that we must rise or fall together. His sufferings, which have been many, are yet fresh in our recollections; and to forsake him when our friendship is most needed, is an insult to our understandings to demand it. But, thanks be to God, brethren, he has all your confidence, and the best affections of your hearts; and no human efforts can wrest them from him. In his honesty, courage and fidelity, do you glory, and in his presence your hearts leap for joy. And now, in conclusion—may the God upon whom he relies for support and success render both you and him mutually prosperous and happy, is the prayer of [13]

Your obt. fellow serv'ts.

J. B. CUTLER, *Chairman.*

J. T. Hilton, *Sec'y.*[13a]

This letter of H. H. Garnett shows how the fugitive slave, taught to think of his former condition as deplorable and encouraged to struggle for the emancipation of his fellowmen in bondage, often differed from the abolitionist,

[13] The newspaper here under criticism was owned and edited by Negroes. In January, 1837, it appeared as the *Weekly Advocate,* the second newspaper in the United States edited by a Negro, *Freedom's Journal* being the first. On March 4, 1837, the name of the *Weekly Advocate* was changed to the *Colored American.* Mr. Phillip A. Bell was the proprietor, and Charles Bennett Ray was the editor. It was against these gentlemen that this complaint was lodged.

[13a] *Liberator,* Oct. 6, 1837.

who, after all, never took kindly to the idea of allowing Negroes to figure conspicuously in devising the ways and means to promote the antislavery cause. The address referred to was so revolutionary and radical, however, that the Negro convention called upon to consider it refused to give it sanction.

To Mrs. Maria W. Chapman.

NOVEMBER 17th, 1843.

RESPECTED MADAM:

Some time ago you wrote an article in the Liberator, condemnatory of the National Convention of colored people, which was held in the city of Buffalo, in the month of August last. I should have sent a reply, ere this time, had I not been engaged so much in the cause of freedom, since the appearance of your article. I must confess that I was exceedingly amazed to find that I was doomed to share so much of your severity, to call it nothing else. And, up to this moment, I have not been able to understand the motives which led you to attack my character as you have in the paper referred to. I am a stranger to you, comparatively, and whatever of my public life has come to your notice, you have seen nothing impeachable. I was born in slavery, and have escaped, to tell you, and others, what the monster has done, and is still doing. It, therefore, astonished me to think that you should desire to sink me again to the condition of a *slave*, by forcing me to think just as you do. My crime is, that I have dared to think, and act, contrary to your opinion. I am a Liberty party man—you are opposed to that party —far be it from me to attempt to injure your character because you cannot pronounce my shibboleth. While you think as you do, we must differ. If it has come to this, that I must think and act as you do, because you are an abolitionist, or be exterminated by your thunder, then I do not hesitate to say that your abolitionism is abject slavery. Were I a slave of the Hon. George McDuffie, or John C. Calhoun, I would not be required to do anything more than to think and act as I might be commanded. I will not be the slave of any person or party. I am a Liberty party man from choice. No man ever asked me to join that party; I was the first colored man that ever attached his name to that party, and you may rely upon my word, when I tell you I mean 'to stand.'

You likewise adopt all that E. M. Marsh, of Buffalo, has said of the Convention and myself. I shall not attempt to say anything more than this, in regard to him. My friend, Mr. March, is a man of a very unstable mind. He is one thing to-day, and another thing to-morrow. He was once a Liberty man, but he is now a no-church and no-government man. I never saw such an unfair statement penned by a man calling himself a Christian. Every thing that he has written, is either false, or exaggerated. I have no more to say of him—I leave him alone in his glory. But I am sorry that you have echoed his false allegations. I am sorry that all the old organization journals have likewise echoed that libellous report.

But the address to the slaves you seem to doom to the most fiery trials. And yet, madam, you have not seen that address—you have merely *heard* of it; nevertheless, you criticised it very severely. You speak, at length, of myself, the author of the paper. You say that I 'have received bad counsel.' You are not the only person who has told your humble servant that his humble productions have been produced by the '*counsel*' of some anglo-saxon. I have expected no more from ignorant slaveholders and their apologists, but I really looked for better things from Mrs. Maria W. Chapman, an anti-slavery poetess, and editor *pro tem.* of the Boston Liberator. I can think on the subject of human rights without 'counsel,' either from the men of the West, or the women of the East. My address was read to but two persons, previous to its presentation at Buffalo. One was a colored brother, who did not give me a single word of counsel, and the other was my wife; and if she did counsel me, it is no matter, for 'we twain are one flesh.' In a few days I hope to publish the address, then you can judge how much treason there is in it. In the mean time, be assured that there is one black American who dares to speak boldly on the subject of universal liberty.   I am, very respectfully,

Your servant,
HENRY HIGHLAND GARNET.

25, Liberty-street, Troy, N. Y.[14]

FROM ROBERT PURVIS, ESQ.

BYBERRY, Philadelphia Co.,
August 22, 1853.

DEAR FRIEND GARRISON—I see by 'Frederick Douglass's Paper' of the 12th instant, that I am most maliciously referred to by its

---

[14] *Liberator,* Dec. 3, 1843.

editor. Now you were present at the meeting in Boston where I made a few remarks, by way of explanation of something our friend Remond had said, in which I made no allusion whatever to Douglass, as you can testify; nor did I, as you can bear witness, exhibit any 'gall' in relation to the 'National Council.' Whatever opinion I expressed,—and the right to express an opinion I presume is still left me,—was properly and becomingly done, as I supposed, without offending any one present or absent from the meeting. I beg you would say so much for me through your paper. As touching the matter of the '*blood-stained riches*' to which this shameless ingrate and base slanderer alludes, I have but to say, that my father (from whom I inherited my property) was never a slaveholder—that he made his money as a merchant, by honest mercantile pursuits—and was known while living as a friend and benefactor of the free and enslaved colored man, (as there are now living witnesses to testify.) My own early detestation of slavery was owing, doubtless, to the seeds implanted in my bosom by my revered parent, by furnishing me with Dr. Torrey's Portraiture of Slavery, and the work entitled 'Sandford and Merton.' But why pursue this matter? A life's consistent hatred of slavery in every form, a willingness, to the best of my ability, to do and suffer with my oppressed brethren, to maintain a reputation 'unspotted before the world,' and thereby live down the calumnies of the enemies of our race, is, in the fury and violence of this meanly ambitious man and foulmouthed slanderer, of no account. To gratify his ire, and serve his bitter and malignant spirit, I am pronounced as being 'practically an enemy of the colored people.'

Yours, ever and truly,

ROBERT PURVIS.[15]

The Liberator said on Dec. 16, 1853:

'Either he must
Confess himself wondrous malicious,
Or be accused of folly.'—CORIOLANUS.

In his paper of the 9th instant, FREDERICK DOUGLASS occupies twelve columns in reply to sundry brief articles in the *Pennsylvania Freeman, Anti-Slavery Standard, Bugle,* and *Liberator,* respecting his feelings and attitude towards his old friends and associates

15 *Liberator,* Sept. 16, 1853.

in the cause of emancipation. Such portions of it as relate to the other journals referred to, we leave them to dispose of as they may think proper. We quote all that is personal to us, in addition to a considerable portion of Mr. D's exordium; and from this sample, our readers can easily infer what the remainder must be.

The history of the Anti-Slavery struggle has been marked by instances of defection, alienation, apostacy, on the part of some of its most efficient supporters for a given time; but by none more signal, venomous, or extraordinary, than the present. Mr. DOUGLASS now stands self-unmasked, his features flushed with passion, his air scornful and defiant, his language bitter as wormwood, his pen dipped in poison; as thoroughly changed in his spirit as was ever 'arch-angel ruined,' and as artful and unscrupulous a schismatic as has yet appeared in the abolition ranks.

Having long endeavored, by extreme forbearance, to avoid any collision with him; having omitted in many cases to make even a passing reference to what we deemed unworthy of his position; having criticised, with brevity and moderation, some very objectionable articles from his pen, only because we could not be true to our convictions of duty, if we suppressed the expression of our surprise and sorrow; and having no feelings of personal animosity to gratify; we have no intention to make a protracted rejoinder in the present case, but shall submit the whole matter, in a very few words, to the impartial judgment of all who take any interest in the controversy.

It is difficult to believe that the author of the article of 'enormous' length and character, now under consideration, is the FREDERICK DOUGLASS once so manly, generous, and faithful. The transformation—or, rather, the revelation—is the most astounding and severely painful event in our experience; and 'the end is not yet.' He now assumes an attitude which is eliciting the warmest encomiums from the most malignant enemies of the Anti-Slavery movement, and which is undisguisedly hostile to his old companion in arms. No marvel, therefore, that he can speak of the 'Garrisonians' with as much flippancy as any of our pro-slavery contemners; or that he can aver, '*Word*-wise, these Garrisonians are my best friends—*deed*-wise, I have no more vigilant enemies'; or that he is able to say of the 'REFUGE OF OPPRESSION,' that, 'of late, it has become about the best part of Mr. Garrison's paper, and about which nobody cares a single straw;' or that he can utter the

monstrous untruth, that 'a fierce and bitter warfare' is waged
against him, 'under the generalship of William Lloyd Garrison,'
with a view to destroy *his anti-slavery usefulness!!*

The untruthfulness of Mr. D. is matched only by his adroitness
in striving to excite popular sympathy, as though he were a poor
innocent lamb, about to be torn in pieces by a pack of famished
wolves! Though he is the aggressor, he affects to have made no
effort even in self-defence, and whiningly says—'I shall be silent
no longer (!) The impunity allowed to my adversaries, by my
silence, like all other submission to wrong, has failed to soften the
heart of the wrong-doers (!) They have waxed more arrogant as
I have waxed humble' (!) 'Gerrit Smith is an independent nation. Alas! I am but a rebel. While those against whom I have
rebelled would treat with Mr. Smith, they would hang me.' Again
—'I had reason to know that prejudice against color—yes, prejudice against my race, would be invoked, as it has been invoked,
on the side of my adversaries (!)—and in all the likelihoods of the
case, the question between me and my old friends would be decided
in this case as between white and black—in favor of the former,
and against the latter—the white man to rise, as an injured benefactor, and the black man to fall, as a miserable ingrate' (!)
Again—'The spectacle of a rich (!) and powerful (!) organization,
largely provided with the appliances of moral warfare, is now seen
marshalling its forces, its presses, and its speakers, for the moral
extermination of one humble, solitary individual (!!!)—for the
purpose of silencing, and putting to open shame, *a fugitive slave,*
(!) simply because that fugitive slave has dared to differ from
that Society, or from the leading individuals in it, as to the manner
in which he shall exercise his powers for the promotion of the anti-
slavery cause, and the elevation of the free people of color in the
United States (!!) Again—'The hatchet of fratricidal war is uplifted; nay, it is now flung at the head of its appointed victim, with
the combined force of three strong arms, and with the deadly aim
of three good marksmen' (!!!) And this is his estimate of the
American Anti-Slavery Society, its presses, and its speakers! Now,
as a specimen of low cunning and malignant defamation, we have
never seen this surpassed. It is too palpable to need a single word
in reply, and we should be lost to all self-respect to treat it as
worthy of serious consideration.

Mr. Douglass sneers at the regret expressed by us, and others,

at the necessity of noticing his hostile assaults, and scoffingly says
—'They have had to overcome mountains of reluctance in getting
at me; and it is amazing, considering the ruggedness of these mountains, that they ever succeeded in crossing their Alpine heights!'
If this does not indicate either that we have never, in his opinion,
been his true friends, or that, ever selfish and untrue himself, he
is incapable of experiencing the pang of misplaced confidence and
disappointed friendship, we know not how to interpret language.
In either case, it places him in a most unenviable position.

Jaundiced in vision, and inflamed with passion, he affects to
regard us as the 'disparager' (!) of the colored race, and artfully
endeavors to excite their jealousy and opposition by utterly perverting the meaning of our language. We said, that 'the Anti-
Slavery cause, both religiously and politically, has transcended the
ability of the sufferers from American slavery and prejudice, *as a
class*, to keep pace with it, or to perceive what are its demands, or
to understand the philosophy of its operations'—meaning by this,
that the cause requires religious and political sacrifices, which, 'as
a class,' they do not yet see, or, seeing, are not yet prepared to
make, even though they are the victims to be delivered—and also
meaning that what was at first supposed to be local, is now seen to
have a world-wide bearing, and must be advocated upon world-
wide principles, irrespective of complexional differences. There
is nothing really or intentionally invidious in a statement like this:
and yet, how does Mr. Douglass treat it? 'The colored man,' he
says, 'ought to feel profoundly grateful for this magnificent compliment to their high moral worth and breadth of comprehension,
so generously bestowed by William Lloyd Garrison! Who will
doubt, hereafter, the *natural* inferiority of the negro, when the
great champion of the negroes' rights *thus broadly concedes all that
is claimed respecting the negro's inferiority by the bitterest de-
spisers of the negro race'!!!* Now, if this were blundering stupidity, it might readily be pardoned; but it is unmitigated baseness,
and therefore inexcusable.

Again we said—'It does not follow, that, because a man is or
has been a slave, or because he is identified with a class meted out
and trodden under foot, therefore he will be the truest to the cause
of human freedom'—a truism which nothing can make plainer.
Yet Mr. Douglass presumes upon the color of his skin to vindicate
his superior fidelity to that cause, and to screen himself from

criticism and rebuke! This trick cannot succeed. Of the colored people he says—'What is theory to others, is practice to them. Every day and hour is crowded with lessons to them on the subject, to which the whites, as a class, are strangers.' Very true—but what then? Does it indicate the same regard for universal justice, for those who are oppressed to desire to gain their freedom, as it does for others, not of their complexion, and not involved in their suffering, to encounter deadly perils and make liberal sacrifices in seeking their liberation? The former may be animated by motives limited to a narrow selfishness; the latter must be actuated by feelings of disinterested benevolence and world-wide philanthropy. Once, Mr. Douglass would have promptly recognized this distinction; now, beneath the blackness of his skin he is attempting to hide the blackness of his treachery.

How low he has fallen is further indicated by his despicable insinuation—'Even Charles L. Remond, who was scarcely recognized as one of the 'tried' and 'true,' *when poor, has, since making himself well off by marriage,* rapidly risen in Boston favor'! Is not this at once the acme of absurdity, the extreme of falsehood, and the lowest depth of moral debasement? When Frederick Douglass was 'poor,' and in utter obscurity, and not as now every where visible, was *he* a stranger to 'Boston favor,' and was nothing done to raise him up to respectability and influence? But this is to hint that he is destitute of grateful emotions—and gratitude is something about which he does not like to be reminded.

So, too, when he speaks of the faithful, intelligent and worthy WILLIAM C. NELL as 'a hanger-on' and 'a pitiful tool'—and of OLIVER JOHNSON as 'not caring two straws about Christ's precepts' in regard to peace, whom he (Douglass) would be the first to assassinate, if he believed it right to kill his enemies, as he has not 'a more malignant enemy than Mr. Johnson is giving proof of being' —he reveals a state of mind as frightful as it is deplorable.

Referring to the Rev. Dr. Campbell, of the *British Banner*, he says, 'There is not a man in England, whose friendship I more highly prize, or of whose commendation I ought to be more proud'; and his *Banner* he places at the head of all other journals for its 'moral courage, true manliness, high independence, steadfast adherence to the right, and to the cause of progress'—the last attributes to be attributed to that venomous, Ishmaelitish and really proslavery sheet. There is not a more unfair disputant or a more unscrupulous defamer at the head of the press, than this same dogmatical, quarrelsome, and double-dealing Dr. Campbell. The American Anti-Slavery Society and *The Liberator* have not a more malignant and outrageous assailant abroad than himself; and if he were in this country, we have no more doubt that he would be found on the side of pro-slavery conservatism, and a holder of slaves if a resident of the South, than we have of the position of Franklin Pierce. The fact that Mr. Douglass deems it an honor to be complimented by such a man, is another melancholy proof of the loss of his integrity to the Anti-Slavery cause.

A word in regard to our allusion to a bad adviser in Mr. D's printing-office, whom we accused of exerting a pernicious influence upon his mind and judgment, and 'causing much unhappiness in his own household.' That last allusion was not meant unkindly, nor intended to imply any thing immoral; but, though it is strictly true, and we could bring a score of unimpeachable witnesses in Rochester to prove it, we regret it was made, as it had no relevancy. Our only object in referring to that nameless 'adviser' was, to indicate to such inquirers as our Chicago correspondent, that there had been secret causes at work to alienate Mr. Douglass from his old associates, and we felt bound to throw out the intimation as a clue to much that would be otherwise inexplicable to those not familiar with the facts in the case. Mr. D. says—'I am profoundly grateful for the eminent services of that "adviser," in *opening my eyes* (!) to many things connected with my anti-slavery relations, to which I had before been partially blind.' That tells the whole story, and is all we care to extort. In what condition his vision now is—and whether in slumbering in the lap of a prejudiced, sectarian Delilah, he has not at last enabled the pro-slavery Philistines to ascertain the secret of his strength, cut off his locks, and rejoice over his downfall—we leave our readers and the uncompromising friends of the Anti-Slavery cause to judge.

REPLY OF MR. WM. C. NELL.

The last number of '*Frederick Douglass's Paper*' contains some editorial references to myself.

1st. 'Mr. Nell, (who) goes *grumbling* about in private that he ought to have been successor in the anti-slavery office in Boston to Henry W. Williams, and complained that he, a colored man, was pushed out of employment to make way for Mr. Wallcut,' &c. &c.

To be brief. This version of the matter is a false one, as my friends can bear testimony.

As to his second charge, that the printed copy of my speech at the Boston meeting 'was essentially different from that made on the occasion,' it would be an easy matter to prove it to be also false; but though much remains unsaid, I shall content myself with this denial.

These wrongs should be righted where perpetrated, in the columns of 'Frederick Douglass's Paper;' but as its Editor has ignored all candor and magnanimity towards me, the prospect of any change in that respect is a hopeless one.

What I *have* said and done, touching this controversy, has been prompted solely by that fidelity which I have cherished for the anti-slavery cause since its advent in Boston in 1831; and as a looker-on, when not a participant, from that time to the present. I have borne allegiance to PRINCIPLES, rather than to MEN; and whether good or ill betide me, I shall not shrink from any responsibility which the position legitimately demands of me.

WILLIAM C. NELL.

Boston, December 12th, 1853.

III. LETTERS OF SLAVES TO FORMER OWNERS

Closely connected with what the fugitives thought of their former condition should be presented the thought of the fugitives years thereafter in writing to their former masters.

FREDERICK DOUGLASS TO HIS MASTER.

THOMAS AULD:

SIR—The long and intimate, though by no means friendly relation which unhappily subsisted between you and myself, leads me to hope that you will easily account for the great liberty which I now take in addressing you in this open and public manner. The same fact may possibly remove any disagreeable surprise which you may experience on again finding your name coupled with mine, in any other way than in an advertisement, accurately describing my person, and offering a large sum for my arrest. In thus dragging you again before the public, I am aware that I shall subject myself to no inconsiderable amount of censure. I shall probably be charged with an unwarrantable, if not a wanton and reckless disregard of the rights and proprieties of private life. There are those North as well as South who entertain a much higher respect for rights which are merely conventional, than they do for rights which are personal and essential. Not a few there are in our country, who, while they have no scruples against robbing the laborer of the hard earned results of his patient industry, will be shocked by the extremely indelicate manner of bringing your name before the public. Believing this to be the case, and wishing to meet every reasonable or plausible objection to my conduct, I will frankly state the ground upon which I justify myself in this instance, as well as on former occasions when I have thought proper to mention your name in public. All will agree that a man guilty of theft, robbery, or murder, has forfeited the right to concealment and private life; that the community have a right to subject such persons to the most complete exposure. However much they may desire retirement, and aim to conceal themselves and their movements from the popular gaze, the public have a right to ferret them out, and bring their conduct before the proper tribunals of the country for investigation. Sir, you will undoubtedly make the proper application of these generally admitted principles, and will easily see the light in which you are regarded by me, I will not therefore manifest ill temper, by calling you hard names. I know you to be a man of some intelligence, and can readily determine the precise estimate which I entertain of your character. I may therefore indulge in language which may seem to others indirect and ambiguous, and yet be quite well understood by yourself.

I have selected this day on which to address you, because it is the anniversary of my emancipation; and knowing of no better why, I am led to this as the best mode of celebrating that truly important event. Just ten years ago this beautiful September morning, yon bright sun beheld me a slave—a poor, degraded chattel—trembling at the sound of your voice, lamenting that I was a man, and wishing myself a brute. The hopes which I had treasured up for weeks of a safe and successful escape from your grasp, were powerfully confronted at this last hour by dark clouds of doubt and fear, making my person shake and my bosom to heave with the heavy contest between hope and fear. I have no words to describe to you the deep agony of soul which I experienced on that never to be forgotten morning—(for I left by daylight.) I was making a leap in the dark. The probabilities, so far as I could by reason

determine them, were stoutly against the undertaking. The preliminaries and precautions I had adopted previously, all worked
badly. I was like one going to war without weapons—ten chances
of defeat to one of victory. One in whom I had confided, and one
who had promised me assistance, appalled by fear at the trial
hour, deserted me, thus leaving the responsibility of success or
failure solely with myself. You, sir, can never know my feelings.
As I look back to them, I can scarcely realize that I have passed
through a scene so trying. Trying however as they were, and
gloomy as was the prospect, thanks be to the Most High, who is ever
the God of the oppressed, at the moment which was to determine
my whole earthly career. His grace was sufficient, my mind was
made up. I embraced the golden opportunity, took the morning
tide at the flood, and a free man, young, active and strong, is the
result.

I have often thought I should like to explain to you the grounds
upon which I have justified myself in running away from you. I
am almost ashamed to do so now, for by this time you may have
discovered them yourself. I will, however, glance at them. When
yet but a child about six years old, I imbibed the determination to
run away. The very first mental effort that I now remember on
my part, was an attempt to solve the mystery, Why am I a slave?
and with this question my youthful mind was troubled for many
days, pressing upon me more heavily at times than others. When
I saw the slave-driver whip a slave woman, cut the blood out of her
neck, and heard her piteous cries, I went away into the corner of
the fence, wept and pondered over the mystery. I had, through
some medium, I know not what, got some idea of God, the Creator
of all mankind, the black and the white, and that he had made the
blacks to serve the whites as slaves. How he could do this and be
good, I could not tell. I was not satisfied with this theory, which
made God responsible for slavery, for it pained me greatly, and I
have wept over it long and often. At one time, your first wife,
Mrs. Lucretia, heard me singing and saw me shedding tears, and
asked of me the matter, but I was afraid to tell her. I was puzzled
with this question, till one night, while sitting in the kitchen, I
heard some of the old slaves talking of their parents having been
stolen from Africa by white men, and were sold here as slaves.
The whole mystery was solved at once. Very soon after this my
aunt Jinny and uncle Noah ran away, and the great noise made

about it by your father-in-law, made me for the first time acquainted with the fact, that there were free States as well as slave States. From that time, I resolved that I would some day run away. The morality of the act, I dispose as follows: I am myself; you are yourself; we are two distinct persons, equal persons. What you are, I am. You are a man, and so am I. God created both, and made us separate beings. I am not by nature bound to you, or you to me. Nature does not make your existence depend upon me, or mine to depend upon yours. I cannot walk upon your legs, or you upon mine. I cannot breathe for you, or you for me; I must breathe for myself, and you for yourself. We are distinct persons, and are each equally provided with faculties necessary to our individual existence. In leaving you, I took nothing but what belonged to me, and in no way lessened your means for obtaining an *honest* living. Your faculties remained yours, and mine became useful to their rightful owner. I therefore see no wrong in any part of the transaction. It is true, I went off secretly, but that was more your fault than mine. Had I let you into the secret, you would have defeated the enterprise entirely; but for this, I should have been really glad to have made you acquainted with my intentions to leave.

You may perhaps want to know how I like my present condition. I am free to say, I greatly prefer it to that which I occupied in Maryland. I am, however, by no means prejudiced against the State as such. Its geography, climate, fertility and products, are such as to make it a very desirable abode for any man; and but for the existence of slavery there, it is not impossible that I might again take up my abode in that State. It is not that I love Maryland less, but freedom more. You will be surprised to learn that people at the North labor under the strange delusion that if the slaves were emancipated at the South, they would flock to the North. So far from this being the case, in that event, you would see many old and familiar faces back again to the South. The fact is, there are few here who would not return to the South in the event of emancipation. We want to live in the land of our birth, and to lay our bones by the side of our fathers'; and nothing short of an intense love of personal freedom keeps us from the South. For the sake of this, most of us would live on a crust of bread and a cup of cold water.

Since I left you, I have had a rich experience. I have occupied

stations which I never dreamed of when a slave. Three out of the
ten years since I left you, I spent as a common laborer on the
wharves of New Bedford, Massachusetts. It was there I earned
my first free dollar. It was mine. I could spend it as I pleased.
I could buy hams or herring with it, without asking any odds of
any body. That was a precious dollar to me. You remember when
I used to make seven or eight, or even nine dollars a week in Baltimore, you would take every cent of it from me every Saturday
night, saying that I belonged to you, and my earnings also. I
never liked this conduct on your part—to say the best, I thought
it a little mean. I would not have served you so. But let that
pass. I was a little awkward about counting money in New England fashion when I first landed in New Bedford. I like to have
betrayed myself several times. I caught myself saying phip, for
fourpence; and at one time a man actually charged me with being
a runaway, whereupon I was silly enough to become one by running away from him, for I was greatly afraid he might adopt
measures to get me again into slavery, a condition I then dreaded
more than death.

I soon, however, learned to count money, as well as to make it,
and got on swimmingly. I married soon after leaving you: in
fact, I was engaged to be married before I left you; and instead of
finding my companion a burden, she was truly a helpmeet. She
went to live at service, and I to work on the wharf, and though we
toiled hard the first winter, we never lived more happily. After
remaining in New Bedford for three years, I met with Wm. Lloyd
Garrison, a person of whom you have *possibly* heard, as he is pretty
generally known among slaveholders. He put it into my head that
I might make myself serviceable to the cause of the slave by devoting a portion of my time to telling my own sorrows, and those
of other slaves which had come under my observation. This was
the commencement of a higher state of existence than any to which
I had ever aspired. I was thrown into society the most pure, enlightened and benevolent that the country affords. Among these
I have never forgotten you, but have invariably made you the topic
of conversation—thus giving you all the notoriety I could do. I
need not tell you that the opinion formed of you in these circles, is
far from being favorable. They have little respect for your honesty, and less for your religion.

But I was going on to relate to you something of my interesting experience. I had not long enjoyed the excellent society to which I have referred, before the light of its excellence exerted a beneficial influence on my mind and heart. Much of my early dislike of white persons was removed, and their manners, habits and customs, so entirely unlike what I had been used to in the kitchen-quarters on the plantations of the South, fairly charmed me, and gave me a strong disrelish for the coarse and degrading customs of my former condition. I therefore made an effort so to improve my mind and deportment, as to be somewhat fitted to the station to which I seemed almost providentially called. The transition from degradation to respectability was indeed great, and to get from one to the other without carrying some marks of one's former condition, is truly a difficult matter. I would not have you think that I am now entirely clear of all plantation peculiarities, but my friends here, while they entertain the strongest dislike to them, regard me with that charity to which my past life somewhat entitles me, so that my condition in this respect is exceedingly pleasant. So far as my domestic affairs are concerned, I can boast of as comfortable a dwelling as your own. I have an industrious and neat companion, and four dear children—the oldest a girl of nine years, and three fine boys, the oldest eight, the next six, and the youngest four years old. The three oldest are now going regularly to school—two can read and write, and the other can spell with tolerable correctness words of two syllables: Dear fellows! they are all in comfortable beds, and are sound asleep, perfectly secure under my own roof. There are no slaveholders here to rend my heart by snatching them from my arms, or blast a mother's dearest hopes by tearing them from her bosom. These dear children are ours—not to work up into rice, sugar and tobacco, but to watch over, regard, and protect, and to rear them up in the nurture and admonition of the gospel— to train them up in the paths of wisdom and virtue, and, as far as we can to make them useful to the world and to themselves. Oh! sir, a slaveholder never appears to me so completely an agent of hell, as when I think of and look upon my dear children. It is then that my feelings rise above my control. I meant to have said more with respect to my own prosperity and happiness, but thoughts and feelings which this recital has quickened unfits me to proceed further in that direction. The grim horrors of slavery rise in all their ghastly terror before me, the wails of millions pierce my heart, and chill my blood. I remember the chain, the gag, the bloody whip, the death-like gloom overshadowing the broken spirit of the fettered bondman, the appalling liability of his being torn away from wife and children, and sold like a beast in the market. Say not that this is a picture of fancy. You well know that I wear stripes on my back inflicted by your direction; and that you, while we were brothers in the same church, caused this right hand, with which I am now penning this letter, to be closely tied to my left, and my person dragged at the pistol's mouth, fifteen miles, from the Bay side to Easton to be sold like a beast in the market, for the alleged crime of intending to escape from your possession. All this and more you remember, and know to be perfectly true, not only of yourself, but of nearly all of the slaveholders around you.

At this moment, you are probably the guilty holder of at least three of my own dear sisters, and my only brother in bondage. These you regard as your property. They are recorded on your ledger, or perhaps have been sold to human flesh mongers, with a view to filling your own ever-hungry purse. Sir, I desire to know how and where these dear sisters are. Have you sold them? or are they still in your possession? What has become of them? are they living or dead? And my dear old grand-mother, whom you turned out like an old horse, to die in the woods—is she still alive? Write and let me know all about them. If my grandmother be still alive, she is of no service to you, for by this time she must be nearly eighty years old—too old to be cared for by one to whom she has ceased to be of service, send her to me at Rochester, or bring her to Philadelphia, and it shall be the crowning happiness of my life to take care of her in her old age. Oh! she was to me a mother, and a father, so far as hard toil for my comfort could make her such. Send me my grandmother! that I may watch over and take care of her in her old age. And my sisters, let me know all about them. I would write to them, and learn all I want to know of them, without disturbing you in any way, but that, through your unrighteous conduct, they have been entirely deprived of the power to read and write. You have kept them in utter ignorance, and have therefore robbed them of the sweet enjoyments of writing or receiving letters from absent friends and relatives. Your wickedness and cruelty committed in this respect on your fellow-creatures, are greater than all the stripes you have laid upon my back, or theirs. It is an outrage upon the soul—a war upon the immortal spirit, and one for which you must give account at the bar of our common Father and Creator.

The responsibility which you have assumed in this regard is

truly awful—and how you could stagger under it these many years is marvellous. Your mind must have become darkened, your heart hardened, your conscience seared and petrified, or you would have long since thrown off the accursed load and sought relief at the hands of a sin-forgiving God.. How, let me ask, would you look upon me, were I some dark night in company with a band of hardened villains, to enter the precincts of your elegant dwelling and seize the person of your own lovely daughter Amanda, and carry her off from your family, friends and all the loved ones of her youth—make her my slave—compel her to work, and I take her wages—place her name on my leger as property—disregard her personal rights—fetter the powers of her immortal soul by denying her the right and privilege of learning to read and write—feed her coarsely—clothe her scantily, and whip her on the naked back occasionally; more and still more horrible, leave her unprotected—a degraded victim to the brutal lust of fiendish overseers, who would pollute, blight, and blast her fair soul—rob her of all dignity—destroy her virtue, and annihilate all in her person the graces that adorn the character of virtuous womanhood? I ask how would you regard me, if such were my conduct? Oh! the vocabulary of the damned would not afford a word sufficiently infernal, to express your idea of my God-provoking wickedness. Yet sir, your treatment of my beloved sisters is in all essential points, precisely like the case I have now supposed. Damning as would be such a deed on my part, it would be no more so than that which you have committed against me and my sisters.

I will now bring this letter to a close, you shall hear from me again unless you let me hear from you. I intend to make use of you as a weapon with which to assail the system of slavery—as a means of concentrating public attention on the system, and deepening their horror of trafficking in the souls and bodies of men. I shall make use of you as a means of exposing the character of the American church and clergy—and as a means of bringing this guilty nation with yourself to repentance. In doing this I entertain no malice towards you personally. There is no roof under which you would be more safe than mine, and there is nothing in my house which you might need for your comfort, which I would not readily grant. Indeed, I should esteem it a privilege, to set you an example as to how mankind ought to treat each other.

I am your fellow man, but not your slave,

FREDERICK DOUGLASS.[16]

TO CAPT. THOMAS AULD, FORMERLY MY MASTER.

No. 4 ALEXANDER ST., ROCHESTER,
September 3d, 1849.

DEAR SIR:—I propose to celebrate this, the 11th anniversary of my escape from your dominion, by addressing to you a friendly epistle on the subject of slavery.

I do this partly with a view to the fulfilment of a promise I made you on this day one year ago, and partly to neutralize certain charges which I then brought against you.

Ungrateful and unjust as you, perhaps, deem me, I should despise myself if I could wilfully malign the character even of a slaveholder; and if, at any time, I have appeared to you guilty of such conduct, you have greatly misapprehended me. I can say, with a clear conscience, in all that I have ever written or spoken respecting yourself, I have tried to remember that, though I am beyond your power and control, I am still accountable to our common Father and Judge,—in the sight of whom I believe that I stand acquitted of all intentional misrepresentation against you. Of course, I said many hard things respecting yourself; but all has been based upon what I knew of you at the time I was a slave in your family. Of the past, therefore, I have nothing to take back; but information concerning you and your household, lately received, makes it unjust and unkind for me to continue the style of remark, in regard to your character, which I primarily adopted. I have been told by a person intimately acquainted with your affairs, and upon whose word I can rely, that you have ceased to be a slaveholder, and have emancipated all your slaves, except my poor old grandmother, who is now too old to sustain herself in freedom; and that you have taken her from the desolate hut in which she formerly lived, into your own kitchen, and are providing for her in a manner becoming a man and a Christian.

This, sir, is good news; it is all the more gratifying to me, since it deprives the pro-slavery public of the North of what they deem a powerful argument against me, and the abolitionists generally. It proves that the agitation of the subject of slavery does not hinder, if it does not help, the emancipation of slaves at the South. I have been frequently told that my course would have an unfavorable influence upon the condition of my friends and relatives in your possession; and the common argument against abolitionists may be stated as follows: Let slaveholders alone, and they will emancipate their slaves; and that agitation only retards the progress of the slave's liberation. It is alleged that the slaveholder is induced to clutch more firmly what is attempted to be wrested from him. To this argument, your case is a plain contradiction. If the effect of anti-slavery were such as is thus alleged, you would have been among the first to have experienced it; for few slaveholders in this land have had a larger share of public exposure and denunciation than yourself; and this, too, from a quarter most calculated to annoy, and to provoke resentment. All this, however, has not prevented you from nobly discharging the high duty you owed alike to God and to the slaves in your possession. I congratulate you warmly, and I rejoice most sincerely, that you have been able, against all the suggestions of self-interest, of pride, and of love of power, to perform this act of pure justice and humanity. It has greatly increased my faith in man, and in the *latent virtue* even of slaveholders. I say *latent virtue*, not because I think slaveholders are worse than all other men, but because, such are the power and influence of education and habit upon even the best constituted minds, that they paralyze and disorder, if not destroy their moral energy; and of all persons in the world, slaveholders are in the most unfavorable position for retaining their power. It would be easy for me to give you the reason of this, but you may be presumed to know it already.

Born and brought up in the presence and under the influence of a system which at once strikes at the very foundation of morals, by denying—if not the existence of God—the equal brotherhood of mankind, by degrading one part of the human family to the condition of brutes, and by reversing all right ideas of justice and of brotherly kindness, it is almost impossible that one so environed can greatly grow in virtuous rectitude.

You, however, sir, have risen superior to these unhallowed influences, and have added another striking proof to those already existing, that the heart of the slaveholder is still within the reach of the truth, and that to him the duty of letting 'the oppressed go free,' is not in vain.

I shall no longer regard you as an enemy to freedom, nor to myself—but shall hail you as a friend to both.—Before doing so, however, I have one reasonable request to make of you, with which you will, I hope, comply. It is thus: That you make your conversion to anti-slavery known to the world, by precept as well as example. A publication of the facts relating to the emancipation of the slaves, with the reasons that have led you to this humane act, would doubt-less prove highly beneficial to the cause of freedom generally—at the same time that it would place yourself in that high estimation of the public mind to which your generous conduct justly entitles you. I think you have no right to put your candle under a bushel. Your case is different in many respects from that of most repentant slaveholders. You have been publicly and peculiarly exposed be-fore the world for being a slaveholder; and, since you have ceased to be such, a just regard for your own standing among men, as well as a desire to promote the happiness of a deeply injured people, re-quires you to make known your sentiments on this important sub-ject. It would be truly an interesting and a glorious spectacle to see *master* and *slave*, hand in hand, laboring together for the over-throw of American slavery. I am sure that such an example would tell with thrilling effect upon the public mind of this section. We have already had the example of slaves and slaveholders side by side battling for freedom; but we yet lack a master working by the side of his former slave on the anti-slavery platform. You have it in your power to supply this deficiency; and if you can bring yourself to do so, you will attain a larger degree of happiness for yourself, and will confer a greater blessing on the cause of freedom, than you have already done by the generous act of emancipating your own slaves. With the example before me, I shall not despair of yet having the pleasure of giving you the right hand of fellowship on the anti-slavery platform.

Before closing the present letter, I wish to set you right about a matter which is, perhaps, of small importance to yourself, but is of considerable consequence to me.

In your letter, written three years ago, to Mr. A. C. C. Thomp-son, of Wilmington, respecting the validity of my narrative, you complained that I failed to mention your intention to emancipate me at the age of 25. The reason of this failure is as follows: You will remember that your promise to emancipate me preceded my first attempt to escape; and that you then told me that you would have emancipated me, had I not made the attempt in question. If you ask me why I distrusted your promise in the first instance, I could give you many reasons; but the one that weighed most with me was the passage of a law in Maryland, throwing obstructions in the way of emancipation; and I had heard you refer to that law as an excuse for continuing your slaves in bondage; and, supposing the obstructions alluded to might prove insuperable barriers to my freedom, I resolved upon flight as the only alternative left me short of a life of slavery. I hope this explanation will be satisfactory. I do not regret what I have done, but rather rejoice in it, as well for your sake as mine. Nevertheless, I wish to be fairly understood, and have, therefore, made the explanation.

I shall here conclude this letter, by again expressing my sincere gratitude at the magnanimous deed with which your name is now associated—and by repeating the ardent hope that you will publicly identify yourself with the holy cause of freedom, to which, since I left your service, I have been most unremittingly devoting myself.

I am, Dear Sir,

Very respectfully yours,

FREDERICK DOUGLASS.[17]

WILLIAM W. BROWN TO HIS MASTER.

To CAPT. ENOCH PRICE, of St. Louis, Mo.:

SIR,—When I left you fifteen years ago, I had not the most remote idea that I should ever correspond with you, either publicly or privately. But as this seems to be an age of progression, and reform the order of the day, I have taken the liberty of addressing you. Since we last parted, the world has made rapid advances in civilization. The principles of human rights have been to some extent discussed, and their blessings secured to a great portion of mankind. The amelioration of the condition of the human family seems to be the great idea of the present age. All Christendom is unsettled, and its ocean of mind is heaving and advancing towards the high mark of Christianity. Almost all the nations of the earth are discussing the rights of man. Not only the civilized, but the semi-civilized are acting under the guidance of the clearer light of the nineteenth century, and the higher motives of the present day.

The subject to which I wish to call your attention is one with which you are intimately connected, namely, Chattel Slavery in the United States. The institution of slavery has been branded as infamous by the good and wise throughout the world. It is regarded as an offence in the sight of God, and opposed to the best interests of man. Whatever in its proper tendency and general effect destroys, abridges, or renders insecure, human welfare, is

[17] *Liberator*, Sept. 14, 1849.

opposed to the spirit and genius of Christianity. There is a proverb, that no man can bind a chain upon the limb of his neighbor,
without inevitable fate fastening the other end around his own
body. This has been signally verified by the slaveholders of
America. While they have been degrading the colored man, by
enslaving him, they have become degraded themselves; in withholding education from the minds of their slaves, they have kept
their own children in comparative ignorance. The immoralities
which have been found to follow in the train of slavery in all countries and all ages, are to be seen in their worst forms in the Slave
States of America. This is attributable to the degree of ignorance
which is deemed necessary to keep the enslaved in their chains. It
is a fact admitted by the American slaveholders themselves, that
their slaves are in a worse state of heathenism than any other
heathen in the civilized world. There is a constant action and reaction—the immoralities of the slave contaminate the master, the
immoralities of the master contaminate the slave. The effects of
the system are evident in the demeanor of the slaveholders. For
example, they are proverbial for their want of courtesy to those
who differ from them in opinion. They are noted for their use of
the 'bowie-knife,' an instrument peculiar to the 'peculiar institution.' Slaveholding parents sending their children to the free
States to be educated, frequently find a difficulty in getting boarding places for them, from the mere fact that they have been found
to spread their vices among the children with whom they have
associated in the free States, to such an extent that parents have
often taken their children out of school on the introduction of the
children of slaveholders. As deep and malignant as is the prejudice in the free States against the colored people, there are those
who would rather have the companionship of colored youths for
their children, than the society of the sons of the most distinguished
slaveholders in the South.

These are the legitimate results of an institution, which sets at
defiance the laws of God and the reason of man. Believe me, sir,
it is from no wish of mine to hurt the feelings of yourself, or those
with whom you are associated, that I give publicity to these facts.
Connected as I am with the slaveholders of America by the blood
that courses through my own veins, if I could I would throw the
mantle of charity over the disgusting institution, and everything
connected with it. But the duty I owe to the slave, to truth, and

to God, demands that I should use my pen and tongue so long as life and health are vouchsafed to me to employ them, or until the last chain shall fall from the limbs of the last slave in America and the world.

Sir, you are a slaveholder, and by the laws of God and of nature, your slaves, like yourself, are entitled to 'life, liberty, and the pursuit of happiness,' and you have no right whatever to deprive them of these inestimable blessings which you claim for yourself. Your slaves have the same right to develope their moral and intellectual faculties that you have; but you are keeping them in a state of ignorance and degradation; and if a single ray of light breaks forth, and penetrates to their souls, it is in despite of your efforts to keep their minds obscured in mental darkness.

You profess to be a Christian, and yet you are one of those who have done more to bring contempt upon Christianity in the United States, by connecting that religion with slavery, than all other causes combined. Were it not for slavery, the United States would be what they have long professed to be, but are not, the 'land of the free, and the home of the brave.' The millions in Europe, who are struggling for political and religious liberty, have looked in vain to the United States for sympathy. The Americans, busily engaged in spreading slavery over new territory, and thereby forging chains for the limbs of unborn millions, are not in the position to sympathise with the oppressed in other countries. America has her Red Republicans, as well as her black slaves; their hands are crimsoned with the blood of their victims. If the atrocities recently practised upon defenceless women in Austria make the blood run cold through the veins of the humane and good throughout the civilized world, the acts committed daily upon the slave women of America should not only cause the blood to chill, but to stop its circulation.

In behalf of your slaves, I ask you, in the name of the God whom you profess to worship, to take the chains from their limbs, and to let them go free. It is a duty that you owe to God, to the slave, and to the world. You are a husband:—I ask you then to treat the wives of your slaves as you would have your own companion dealt with. You are a father:—I ask you, therefore, to treat the children of your slaves as you would have your own legitimate offspring treated. When you take your own child upon your knee, and thank God that no one can snatch it from you, and place it upon the auction block, and sell it to the highest bidder, think of the children that you have sold from their parents. When you look upon your own parents, sisters and brothers, and feel thankful that you are kept in safety together, think of him who now addresses you, and remember how you, with others, tore from him a beloved mother, an affectionate sister, and three dear brothers, and sold them to the slave trader, to be carried to the far South, there to be worked upon a cotton, sugar or rice plantation, where, if still living, they are now wearing the galling chains of slavery. By your professed love of America, I conjure you to use your influence for the abolition of an institution which has done a thousand times more to blacken the character of the American people, and to render the name of their boasted free republic more odious to the ears of the friends of human freedom throughout the world, than all their other faults combined. I will not yield to you in affection for America, but I hate her institution of slavery. I love her, because I am identified with her enslaved millions by every tie that should bind man to his fellow-man. The United States has disfranchised me, and declared that I am not a citizen, but a chattel: her Constitution dooms me to be your slave. But while I feel grieved that I am alienated and driven from my own country, I rejoice that, in this land, I am regarded as a man. I am in England, what I can never be in America, while slavery exists there.

Sir, you may not be pleased with me for speaking to you in so plain a manner; but in this I have only done my duty. See that you do yours!

I am, Sir, with all due respect,
WM. WELLS BROWN.[18]

London, Nov. 23d, 1849.

LETTER TO REV. J. W. LOGUEN, FROM HIS OLD MISTRESS.

The *Liberator* said on April 27, 1860:

The following letter was received a day or two since by Rev. Mr. Loguen, of this city, from his old mistress 'way down in Tennessee.' The old lady is evidently 'hard up,' financially, and attempts to frighten her former servant into the payment of $1,000 as 'hush money.' We imagine she sent to the wrong man, as Mr.

18 *Liberator*, Dec. 14, 1849.

Loguen needs no 'bill of sale' to secure himself from capture in this section of the State. Besides his own stalwart arm, he has hosts of friends who would make this region too hot to hold the man-hunters who would venture on such an errand as the old lady hints at in her somewhat singular epistle. Her lamentations about the old mare are decidedly funny, (we may add womanly,) and all the misfortunes of the family are traced directly to the escape of 'Jarm.' But here is her letter:

> MAURY COUNTY, State of Tennessee,
> Feb. 20, 1860.

To JARM:—I now take my pen to write you a few lines, to let you know how we all are. I am a cripple, but I am still able to get about. The rest of the family are all well. Cherry is as well as common. I write you these lines to let you know the situation we are in,—partly in consequence of your running away and stealing Old Rock, our fine mare. Though we got the mare back, she never was worth much after you took her;—and, as I now stand in need of some funds, I have determined to sell you, and I have had an offer for you, but did not see fit to take it. If you will send me one thousand dollars, and pay for the old mare, I will give up all claim I have to you. Write to me as soon as you get these lines, and let me know if you will accept my proposition. In consequence of your running away, we had to sell Abe and Ann and twelve acres of land; and I want you to send me the money, that I may be able to redeem the land that you was the cause of our selling, and on receipt of the above-named sum of money, I will send you your bill of sale. If you do not comply with my request, I will sell you to some one else, and you may rest assured that the time is not far distant when things will be changed with you. Write to me as soon as you get these lines. Direct your letter to Bigbyville, Maury County, Tennessee. You had better comply with my request.

I understand that you are a preacher. As the Southern people are so bad, you had better come and preach to your old acquaintances. I would like to know if you read your Bible. If so, can you tell what will become of the thief if he does not repent? and, if the blind lead the blind, what will the consequence be? I deem it unnecessary to say much more at present. A word to the wise is sufficient. You know where the liar has his part. You know that we reared you as we reared our own children; that you was never abused, and that shortly before you ran away, when your master asked you if you would like to be sold, you said you would not leave him to go with any body.

                                        SARAH LOGUE.

MR. LOGUEN'S REPLY.

SYRACUSE, (N. Y.) March 28, 1860.

MRS. SARAH LOGUE: Yours of the 20th of February is duly received, and I thank you for it. It is a long time since I heard from my poor old mother, and I am glad to know that she is yet alive, and, as you say, 'as well as common.' What that means, I don't know. I wish you had said more about her.

You are a woman; but, had you a woman's heart, you never could have insulted a brother by telling him you sold his only remaining brother and sister, because he put himself beyond your power to convert him into money.

You sold my brother and sister, Abe and Ann, and twelve acres of land, you say, because I ran away. Now you have the unutterable meanness to ask me to return and be your miserable chattel, or, in lieu thereof, send you $1000 to enable you to redeem the *land*, but not to redeem my poor brother and sister! If I were to send you money, it would be to get my brother and sister, and not that you should get land. You say you are a *cripple*, and doubtless you say it to stir my pity, for you knew I was susceptible in that direction. I do pity you from the bottom of my heart. Nevertheless, I am indignant beyond the power of words to express, that you should be so sunken and cruel as to tear the hearts I love so much all in pieces; that you should be willing to impale and crucify us all, out of compassion for your poor *foot* or *leg*. Wretched woman! Be it known to you that I value my freedom, to say nothing of my mother, brothers and sisters, more than your whole body; more, indeed, than my own life; more than all the lives of all the slaveholders and tyrants under heaven.

You say you have offers to buy me, and that you shall sell me if I do not send you $1000, and in the same breath and almost in the same sentence, you say, 'You know we raised you as we did our own children.' Woman, did you raise your *own children* for the market? Did you raise them for the whipping-post? Did you raise them to be driven off, bound to a coffle in chains? Where are my poor bleeding brothers and sisters? Can you tell? Who was it that sent them off into sugar and cotton fields, to be kicked and cuffed, and whipped, and to groan and die; and where no kin can hear their groans, or attend and sympathize at their dying bed, or follow in their funeral? Wretched woman! Do you say *you* did not do it? Then I reply, your husband did, and *you* approved the deed—and the very letter you sent me shows that your heart approves it all. Shame on you!

But, by the way, where is your husband? You don't speak of him. I infer, therefore, that he is dead; that he has gone to his great account, with all his sins against my poor family upon his head. Poor man! gone to meet the spirits of my poor, outraged and murdered people, in a world where Liberty and Justice are *Masters*.

But you say I am a thief, because I took the old mare along with me. Have you got to learn that I had a better right to the old mare, as you call her, than Mannasseth Logue had to me? Is it a greater sin for me to steal his horse, than it was for him to rob my mother's cradle, and steal me? If he and you infer that I forfeit all my rights to you, shall not I infer that you forfeit all your rights to me? Have you got to learn that human rights are mutual and reciprocal, and if you take my liberty and life, you forfeit your own liberty and life? Before God and high heaven, is there a law for one man which is not a law for every other man?

If you or any other speculator on my body and rights, wish to know how I regard my rights, they need but come here, and lay their hands on me to enslave me. Did you think to terrify me by presenting the alternative to give my money to you, or give my body to slavery? Then let me say to you, that I meet the proposition with unutterable scorn and contempt. The proposition is an outrage and an insult. I will not budge one hair's breadth. I will not breathe a shorter breath, even to save me from your persecutions. I stand among a free people, who, I thank God, sympathize with my rights, and the rights of mankind; and if your emissaries and venders come here to re-enslave me, and escape the unshrinking vigor of my own right arm, I trust my strong and brave friends, in this city and State, will be my rescuers and avengers.

Yours, &c.,　　　　　J. W. LOGUEN.

IV. ANONYMOUS LETTERS AND OTHERS

In the newspaper's there often appeared anonymous letters which decidedly differed from such of today. A Negro signing his name to a document attacking an institution protected by the laws of the country was in danger almost anywhere in this country before the Civil War. The failure to sign his name was not always due to a lack of courage but rather to the desire for self-preservation, the first law of nature. Such letters as these, then, are valuable in determining what the Negro was feeling and thinking at that time.

To the Editor of the Liberator.

ESTEEMED FRIEND—I have perused, with infinite pleasure, the first and second number of the new-born infant, with the above title. How sweetly sounds the name in the ears of every descendant of Africa!

As I am one of that unfortunate people for whom you have volunteered both life and fortune to redeem, if possible, from their present state of degradation to a rank among the rest of mankind; I cannot but feel interested in every thing touching their cause. It was, therefore, with no small sensation of joy, that I beheld this instrument of good, referred to above, established in this metropolis; especially as it is to be particularly devoted to the cause of my depressed race throughout the United States. The word *Liberator*, which character your paper assumes, is a phrase highly distinguished, if I rightly understand its meaning. May it be as influential in the accomplishment of its object, as that mighty spirit which it breathes; and as eminent and popular in its character, as is the illustrious name which it bears. May your appearance in this city prove as fruitful as the coming of Titus into Macedonia.

That heaven has given you ability to perform the work in which you are engaged, is not questioned even by your most bitter opponents. Agreeing with them and all others in this fact, it is not to be supposed that I am attempting to render aid in any of your editorial labors; for I would by no means flatter myself with the capacity, though my will be ever so good. The principle, therefore, by which I have been governed in making these remarks, springs alone and purely from a deep-felt sense of gratitude, and a strong desire of your final success in your undertaking. And should you, through the blessing of God, be successful in this most noble enterprise, my greatest hope, my strongest desire, and sincerest and best wishes will truly be answered. Thus will great good be done to the African race, and more honor to your country than all that which has been acquired by military exploits.

I see, however, before you, a mountain over which you have to travel, steep and dark, and pregnant with deep-rooted prejudice of long duration. I am also happy to see that you have measured out the ground, and estimated the cost, and are going onward clothed in Paul's spirit of perseverance, and carrying along with you the courage of Leonidas, the Grecian hero. May your success be like that of Gideon of old; may there arise a Howard, a Clarkson, and a Sharpe, to give you aid in removing that foul stain, *slavery*, from your country's *Constitution*. And may all this be done without bloodshed. For though I advocate, like yourself, the doctrine of universal emancipation, and am anxious, with the rest of my brethren, for our just rights and the enjoyment of those inestimable blessings which the providence of God has allotted to the human race; yet I am very far from wishing a second St. Domingo warfare in the United States. I wish, therefore, that the spirit of the Egyptians may not long reign in America. But it is my hope that the eyes of this people will shortly be opened to their true interest, by opening the prison doors and letting the oppressed go free.

I do, therefore, sincerely and devoutly hope, that by the force of truth, sound and mild reasoning, many will come up to your assistance in this great work of human rights, of which we are not so ignorant as many have supposed.

Public opinion is a masterly engine; and I hope you will secure it in your present enterprise; for to have both wind and tide to steer against, is a task not easily managed. But to tell you what you already know is no news at all; and as I place great confidence in the sincerity of your intention, I doubt not that you will pursue the best course for the furtherance of the cause which you espouse. I believe your motive to be far more noble and pure than what your enemies have asserted it to be. I believe, also, that your eyes are fastened upon the good of your country, as much so as it is upon liberating the descendants of Africa. And may the wisdom of a holy God direct your pen; and may his grace enable you to move human pride and prejudice before you, as the darkness moves before the rising sun! I invoke the blessings of God upon the new-born infant, as I term it. I implore his holy benediction upon your labor of benevolence, hoping it may flourish before you like the green bay-tree, and be as a handful of corn upon the tops of the mountain, whose fruits shall shake like Lebanon. I invoke his peace to dwell with you forever; and may you be carried along in the current of his Holy Spirit. A MAN OF COLOR.

DEATH OF WALKER.

To the Editor of the Liberator.

SIR—Having been prompted, by the inquiries of the Journal & Tribune, to make some researches respecting the circumstances of the death of Walker, author of a flagitious pamphlet, so called; I have spared no pains to obtain correct information relative thereto. The result has not been very satisfactory to me, and probably will not be to the public.

The most I can learn is, that some one or more, recently from the south, spread a report in this city that a reward of $3000 was offered by southern planters to any one who would take the life of Walker. The report is believed by many of our population, who have no higher source of intelligence, to be true. Many well-informed persons of color there are, however, who have a strong suspicion that Walker came to his end otherwise than by a usual visitation of the Providence of God. Whether their suspicion be groundless or not, is a question—a question, too, under circumstances hard to be answered. In cases of law, presumptive evidence, I believe, is valid. Why not in this case? Were I asked, what is the presumptive evidence? I should answer, Prejudice—Pride—Avarice—Bigotry—in a word, the self-love of a wicked country, which outweigh all civil, moral and religious principles contained therein. If murder and robbery, with their correspondent evils, are practised by the refined part of society, ought it to be thought a wonder that a man, like Walker, should fall a victim to the vengeance of the public? Is it not well known by individuals, that the whole country has set the example for them for centuries, by imbruing their hands in innocent blood? Is it not the language of the country to every individual, 'GO AND DO LIKEWISE'?

A COLORED BOSTONIAN.[19]

19 *Liberator*, Jan. 22, 1831.

To the Editor of the Liberator.

SIR—I have received and read with great satisfaction the first two numbers of the Liberator, with the exception of the notice you have taken of Walker's Appeal, which production I have ever been opposed to (1)—opposed to, in the first place, not because he is a man of color, but because I do not believe that he wrote it; for the matter brought forward in said pamphlet is the result of more reading than could have fallen to the lot of that man, and, at the same time, have left him so vulgar as he has been represented to me. (2)—Besides, sir, he could never have read all the authors quoted in his book, and seen of what true greatness consisted, and then bestowed such unbounded praise upon one whose name the political, the moral, and the religious world will be found equally indifferent about handing to those who may come after us (3)—To say nothing of the excellent criticisms upon the speeches of the most talented men of the age—all of which discover to us a greater degree of education than we have any reason to believe that he possessed.

I am aware, sir, that I differ very widely from many of those with whom I stand intimately connected; for some of them are so infatuated as to believe it an inspired work. Such inspiration is passing strange with me.

We are forbidden, by high authority, to do evil that good may come. Why then cast this firebrand so injudiciously among the stubble? Behold its injurious effects! In many of the southern states, the free people of color enjoyed some privileges and good situations, which not only afforded them the means of support but also of education—so that the rusty mind was daily becoming bright, and its brilliancy beaming forth to the destruction of prejudice. These privileges are now taken away.

I am opposed to the pamphlet, therefore, in the second place, because I believe it to be at the bottom of the recent enactments of severe laws in the southern states, such as are too notorious to be mentioned.

There is no man among us, who is more sensible of his political degradation than I am; but, at the same time, I am unwilling to resort to any dishonorable means of deliverance—such as Walker points out.   LEO.

Philadelphia, Jan. 21, 1831.

---

(1) We know not wherein we differ from 'LEO' in his view of the pamphlet. We have repeatedly expressed our disapprobation

of its general spirit. It contains, however, many valuable truths and seasonable warnings.

(2) We are surprised at this incredulity. Mr Walker was personally unknown to us; but we are assured, by those who intimately knew him, that his Appeal was an exact transcript of his daily conversations; that, within the last four years, he was hurtfully indefatigable in his studies; that he was not 'vulgar,' either in manners or language; and that he was a blameless professor of religion. The historical facts which he has collected were too familiar to have required extraordinary research. Besides, the internal evidence of the pamphlet clearly substantiates its authorship.

(3) We cannot find that there is any other individual extolled than the venerable and worthy bishop Richard Allen of Philadelphia. Surely our correspondent cannot mean to deny *him* the tribute of merit which Mr Walker has bestowed? [20]

To the Editor of the Liberator.

SIR—I have read the several numbers of your excellent paper with much pleasure, and cannot refrain from tendering my sincere thanks to you for the active part that you have taken in behalf of myself and colored brethren of this country.

That we are not treated as freemen, in any part of the United States, is certain. This usage, I should say, is in direct opposition to the Constitution; which positively declares, that all men are born equal, and endowed with certain inalienable rights—among which are life, liberty, and the pursuit of happiness.

I would ask some of our pretended white friends, and the members of the American Colonization Society, why they are so interested in our behalf as to want us to go to Africa? They tell us that it is our home; that they desire to make a people of us, which we can never be here; that they want Africa civilized; and that we are the very persons to do it, as it is almost impossible for any white person to exist there. I deny it. Will some of those guardian angels of the people of color tell me how it is that we, who were born in the same city or state with themselves, can live any longer in Africa than they? I consider it the most absurd assertion that any man of common sense could make, unless it is supposed, as some have already said, that we are void of understanding. If we had been born on that continent, the transportation would be another matter; but as the fact is the reverse, we consider the United States our home, and not Africa as they wish to make us believe;—and if we do emigrate, it will be to a place of our own choice.

I would also mention to the supporters of the Colonization Society, that if they would spend half the time and money that they do, in educating the colored population and giving them lands to cultivate here, and secure to them all the rights and immunities of freemen, instead of sending them to Africa, it would be found, in a short time, that they made as good citizens as the whites. Their traducers would hear of fewer murders, highway robberies, forgeries, &c. &c. being committed, than they do at present among some of the white inhabitants of this country.

If a man of color has children, it is almost impossible for him to get a trade for them, as the journeymen and apprentices generally refuse to work with them, even if the master is willing, which is seldom the case. Even among laborers, there is a distinction. During the late snow storm, thousands of persons were employed in cleaning the gutters, leveling the drifts, &c. Among the whole number, ☞ there was not a man of color to be seen, when hundreds of them were going about the streets with shovels in their hands, looking for work and finding none. I mention this fact merely to show what a great distinction exists, more or less, between the whites and blacks, in all classes—and as much among aliens who have been in this country three or four months, or perhaps a year, as any class of persons that I can mention.

In bringing this subject to a close, I will only say, that I am under the impression that the time is not far distant, when the prophecy which says, ' Ethiopia shall stretch forth her hand unto God,' will be fulfilled.

A Colored Philadelphian.[21]

Philadelphia, Feb. 3, 1831.

To the Editor of the Liberator.

Sir—The total defeat of tyranny and noble triumph of liberty in some of the old countries, awaken in me sensations too strong to be suppressed. My soul is filled with joy to perceive that, instead of man's continuing the protector or ruler of his fellow man, God alone will be the ruler over all. It is a sight pleasant indeed, to

[21] *Liberator,* Feb. 12, 1831.

witness the increasing liberality and wise policy which the whole continent of Europe is manifesting in relation to its governmental affairs. But, sir, my joy is still greater to know, that this mighty reformation has been effected not by deadly weapons, but by strict attention to education and an uplifted eye to the Deity. The heart of man is always rightly directed when his eyes are fixed upon God. Let the mind expand, and methinks the time will ere long arrive when there will not be a man, from the equator to the poles, whose soul will not burst forth in the strains of Homer, and shake the yoke of slavery from his neck as the lion 'shakes the dew-drops from his mane.'

Nothing was ever more true, sir, than the sentiment put forth by Mr Jefferson in the Declaration of Independence, that all men are born free and equal;—and there is no stronger proof of this truth, than to see, wherever an opportunity presents itself, the oppressed grasping the banner of liberty and breathing forth this sentiment in peals of thunder. That the spirit of liberty is born in the breast of every man is an undeniable truth: it is also true that the sensation accompanies him from his cradle to the grave; and though sometimes suppressed by the sword and bayonet, it often bursts forth, like the smoking volcano, striking terror into the heart of the oppressor. May its mighty power shake the pillars of oppression until they crumble like 'the baseless fabric of a vision.'

I glory, sir, in your general call to my brethren in the United States, to awake out of sleep; and as the trumpet is in Zion, so may your voice be in directing them to the vast importance of educating themselves and their children, in the true spirit of the gospel and the golden principles of liberty.

I believe, sir, that the obtainment of our just rights depends more upon this, and devout supplications to God, than upon any other means. I know that God hears the prayers of the righteous; and if our people will devote themselves to piety and the study of useful knowledge, the Lord God will hear and answer their cries when they supplicate his throne.

I earnestly entreat my brethren, then, to look up to Him from whence cometh their salvation; for he is able to save to the uttermost all that will come unto him. Awake and arise, my beloved brethren, nor linger so; but cast your eyes on Europe, and see for yourselves what has been recently accomplished in the march of mind. These things are truly the precious fruits of education.

Awake, then, and let your actions tell the world that you are men—
the workmanship of a mighty God. O Capitien, Sancho, Vassa,
Cugoana! send back your ambitious spirits into the bosoms of your
brethren, that they may sweetly repose under the shadow of your
wisdom, and meditate upon your virtues with great delight.

A MAN OF COLOR.[22]

To COLONIZATIONISTS.

How long, oh! ye boasters of freedom, will ye endeavor to per-
suade us, your derided, degraded fellow countrymen, to the belief
that our interest and happiness are prized in high estimation among
you? Be it known, that we are not all such misguided, deluded
mortals as to be duped by your plans; that we will not suffer ourselves to become so infatuated as to 'hurl reason from her throne,'
and succumb to your glittering, showy, *dissimulating* path to eminence. We spurn with contempt your unrighteous schemes, and
point the finger of derision at your fruitless attempts. You have
commenced them in a day, when liberty, justice and equality are
claimed by almost all, as Nature's rights; for behold! a beam of
science, lucid as the sun, has divinely fallen upon the lightless
intellects of a portion of that ignoble part of your fellow creatures,
who have been so long the victims of your fell injustice and in-
humanity. Would to God that conscience might subdue your malignant prejudices. Tell us not that our condition can never be
bettered in the land of our birth: you know it not. Make but the
attempt in consecrating a portion of your time, talents and money
upon us here, and you would soon find the cause of Afric's injured
race vindicated by her descendants; and the day which now dawns
would be speedily ushered into blazing light, declaring in its efful-
gence the joyful sound of Liberty—Justice—Equality to all mankind.

Philadelphia.   HANNIBAL.[23]

To the Editor of the Liberator.

SIR—It is with additional pleasure that I have perused the 8th
number of your useful and entertaining paper; and I am under the
impression that it will meet with much encouragement in this city,
as it is almost impossible for any persons of color, who feel interested for themselves or posterity, to do otherwise than to subscribe

---

[22] *Liberator,* Feb. 19, 1831.
[23] *Ibid.,* March 12, 1831.

to it, if they can possibly spare the price of subscription. It is a grand engine for us to make known our difficulties, deprivations, &c. that we have to encounter in these United States; and I hope the time is fast approaching, when we shall be able to boast that we have a press (solely to vindicate the cause of the people of color) in every State in the Union. I am heartily glad to hear that our friend and brother (Mr Stewart) is about to publish a paper in Albany, devoted to our cause. May the Lord bless him abundantly in his undertaking; may he thrive in his editorial labors, like a tree planted by the water side; and may he meet with that encouragement, which will enable him to continue it as long as his life shall last.

It is utterly impossible for me to proceed any further, without saying a few words concerning the Colonization Society, the advocates of which are more and more engaged in devising ways to rid the United States of the free people of color. Auxiliaries are forming in almost every city for the *laudable* purpose of raising funds to transport us across the wide Atlantic ocean to Africa, to breathe our last soon after, or perhaps before, we arrive. But I am fully convinced, that it is a matter of no consequence to the persons interested in that Society, and likely to some who are not, what becomes of us after we leave the United States. All they are anxious for is, that we, who have the name of being freemen, (but who, I am sorry to say, are not treated as such,) should leave the country. Why do they not turn their minds to the slaveholders at the south, and solicit them to set their slaves free; and send such home again as have been stolen from Africa; and such as have not, educate and treat them as they ought to be in this free country? But no: it is the free people they want out of the way, and not the slaves; as they are perfectly aware that the latter are kept in fear generally. But the other class, they say, have too much liberty; and if they are not sent off, they will in time overrun the country. But if the whites will give us our rights, establish good schools for our children as well as theirs, give them trades, and encourage them after they have become masters of their business, they will have nothing to fear: they will find us as true to this our country and home, as any class of persons that do or shall hereafter exist in these United States—is the opinion of

A Colored Philadelphian.[24]

Philadelphia, Feb. 28, 1831.

[24] *Liberator,* March 19, 1831.

To the Editor of the Liberator.

SIR—It is with much pleasure that I now make the following remarks, which you are at liberty to publish, if you deem them worthy of an insertion in your excellent paper. It has been some time since I addressed you on any subject whatever; but in perusing the 29th number of your paper, a paragraph attracted my attention, concerning the conduct of the slaves and other colored persons at the late fire in Fayetteville, N. C., which fire, I am under the impression, was a visitation from God, for their cruelty to our brethren which is inflicted upon them with the utmost rigor imaginable.

I was informed by a person from that place, (who was an eyewitness to what I am about to relate,) that in the very town where the fire was, he saw a free man of color, as he was termed, stripped and tied to a whipping post, before a great concourse of brutes in human shape, (with a few exceptions,) and there lacerated by an inhuman overseer till he was covered with blood; to such a degree, indeed, that it would have caused any person, who had not a heart of stone, to weep bitterly at the treatment he received. His crime was merely for passing a joke with one of his white neighbors, in this boasted land of liberty, which is termed by some, an asylum for the inhabitants of all foreign nations; but which, I am sorry to say, is the worst place for colored persons in the known world.

When we take a retrospective view of things, and hear of almost every nation fighting for its liberty, is it to be expected that the African race will continue always in the degraded state they now are? No. The time is fast approaching when the words 'Fight for liberty, or die in the attempt,' will be sounded in every African ear throughout the world; and when he will throw off his fetters, and flock to the banner which will be then floating in the air with the following words inscribed upon it—'Liberty or Death;' and when they will die to a man sooner than be slaves any longer to persons (I am sorry to say) not so good as themselves, merely because their skin is something of a darker hue than their own. O Liberty! sound delightful to every African ear! And when the sound has once struck them, may they seize upon it as a drowning man would to anything that comes within his grasp, and never let go till they get that which they ought to have enjoyed ever since they have been in existence, but which has been torn from them by a set of persons who can be termed nothing less than pirates.

The Colonization Society is still busy in trying to get free persons of color to embark for Africa, (but whom I would recommend to stay at home,) where almost every eight out of ten die by the time they get within sight of that land; and if they should by chance touch the shore, they do not exist but a short time, with very few exceptions. They tell us they want to better our condition. What absurdity! If so, let them do it in America, and not in Africa. But no; their object is to rid this country of us, as they think we are getting too numerous, and that some time or other a collision may take place; but I assure them that if they will treat us as we consider we ought to be treated, they need never fear the least trouble from us. All we want is our rights, and these we will have. I may never live to see that joyful time; but I am fully persuaded that the time will come, when every colored man must and will have his liberty.

In coming to a close, I am aware that if we look forward to the great 'I Am' for help, we shall never be in danger of falling like those who walk upon a line. If we keep our eyes fixed upon one point, we may step forward securely, and nothing shall molest or make us afraid.

A COLORED PHILADELPHIAN.[24a]

Philadelphia, July 28, 1831.

TO THE PEOPLE OF COLOR.

BY A COLORED LADY.

On reading the painful account of the slave ship in the last Liberator, I am induced to write a few lines of encouragement to us as a people. Although it does seem to us, at times, as though we had more hardships and difficulties than we are able to bear,— deprived of almost every blessing and comfort which we see our white friends enjoying,—yet, reflection will show that we have every thing that can be called good in this world to encourage us. For God hath no respect of persons, but doth bless continually, both in temporal and spiritual blessings. God hath made the world, and all things that are in it. The same God that made them, hath made us, and will save all who put their trust in him: therefore let us strive to put our trust in God, for he is able to deliver us from the power of the enemy, and from the bondage that is to come. For if a man doth gain the whole world, and lose his own soul, what

[24a] *Liberator*, Aug. 20, 1831.

doth it profit him? Lay not up for yourselves treasures upon earth, where moth and rust doth corrupt and where thieves do break through and steal; but lay up for yourselves treasures in heaven, where neither moth nor rust doth corrupt, and where thieves do not break through and steal. For the Scripture saith, 'whoso keepeth the law is a wise son.' Although men may bind our bodies, they cannot bind our souls; for the Lord searcheth the heart, and knoweth all our need. Let us raise our hearts to God in prayer, that he would own and bless our souls. He doth delight to own and bless all those who put their trust in him. Better is it to be of a humble spirit with the lowly, than to divide the spoil with the proud; for he that handleth a matter wisely shall find good, and whoso trusteth in the Lord, happy is he; for the Lord is able to deliver us from evil, and from the hands of sinful men. That God who delivered Daniel from the lion's den; who protected the three men in the fiery furnace, and did not suffer so much as a hair of their head to be injured, is still the same.

Better is a little with righteousness, than great revenues without right: for righteous lips are the delight of kings, and they love him that speaketh right. How much better is it to get wisdom than gold, and to get understanding rather than silver! For Wisdom saith, riches and honor are with me, yea, durable riches and righteousness: my fruit is better than fine gold, and my revenue than choice silver; I lead in the way of righteousness, in the midst of the paths of judgment, that I may cause those that love me to inherit sustenance, and I will fill their treasures.

Although the Lord doth comfort us, and deliver us from the cruel hands of the slaveholders, still we do sympathise with those of our friends in a southern clime: therefore let us as the heart of one person be united, and raise our hearts to God in humble prayer that he would send deliverance to the captives, and enlighten the hearts of the slaveholders, that they may see that they are bound as well as those whom they are still holding in bondage; yea, they are bound by Satan's slavish chains. And I do awfully fear, that unless they quickly repent, and turn unto that God who doth have mercy upon all men, they will sin away the day of grace.

Can it be that they will buy and sell those who are as good, by nature, as themselves? Will they sell their souls for gold, which will profit them nothing in a dying hour? Look at the rich man in the gospel, who had much goods laid up for many years, and said

unto his soul, 'Soul, take thine ease; eat, drink, and be merry.'
But the Lord said unto him, 'Thou fool! this night thy soul shall
be required of thee.' Although he had great possessions, it could
not save him from death; but, as we are informed, he died, and was
buried; and in hell he lifted up his eyes, being in torment, and cried
for Lazarus that he would come and dip the tip of his finger in
water, and cool his parched tongue, for he was tormented in the
flame.

It is my prayer to God, daily, that he would enlighten the hearts
of the children of men. Let us, my friends, begin with new en-
gagedness to seek and serve God. Let us raise our hearts to him
continually, that he would bless us as a nation; that he would let
his holy spirit descend and rest upon us, and guide us in the way
of all truth. For the high way of the upright is to depart from
evil. He that keepeth his way preserveth his soul. For if faithful
to God until death, we shall secure that crown of glory which will
never fade away. Let us take the bible for the guide of our life,
and so live that when called to die, we may die in peace, and rest
in the arms of a crucified Redeemer.

Middletown, July 29, 1831.[25]

To the Editor of the Liberator.

SIR—Permit a colored subscriber, and constant reader of your
most valuable paper, to cast his mite into the casket of the Liberator.

ACTS xvii. 25. God hath made of one blood (take notice, 'of
one blood'—not white blood) all nations of men, (black and white,)
for to dwell on all the face of the earth.

Now, it takes all sorts of people to make a world. What, then,
can be more preposterous than for any set of men to institute
schemes for the transplantation of the colored sons of America,
whom the God of nature has designed should fill up the vacancy
intended for them on these happy shores of America? The hue of
the people of color has been explained to denote intended subjec-
tion. I do not think it worth while to engage (nor could I) in a
philosophical speculation, respecting the origin of that variety of
complexions, which now characterises our race; though all de-
scended from the same parents, and parents too, whose color, we
have every reason to believe, was neither white nor black, but a

25 *Liberator*, Aug. 27, 1831.

medium between both; for the first was called Adam, which signifies a red man.   Solomon, whose head was an epitome of the world's wisdom, was a colored man.   Esau was a man of color.   Jethro and other illustrious men were men of color; and if any person wishes to know whether or not it is hateful in the sight of God to despise a man merely on account of his color, let him read the 12th chapter of Numbers.   The first white man, that we have an account of, became white for forging a falsehood.   Not that I would cast a stigma on any of our fairer brethren; no, rather would I have an arm amputated.

It is not an improbable conjecture, that climate and mode of life have produced the diversification of color in the human species. We have an incontrovertible instance of it in the case of the modern Jews.   While it is an indisputable fact, that the Jews have remained a distinct people to the present day, the English Jew is white, the Arminian olive, the Arabian copper, the Portuguese swarthy.   But let color be as it may, I would gladly learn in the book of God or nature, that color is the standard of relative rank in the scale of humanity, and how this scale is graduated.   I know not that the great Author of nature has any where informed us, that the whites have a right to tyrannize over any of the human race; to make the poor people of color their hewers of wood and drawers of water, and beasts of burden.   Why have the whites any more claim upon the African than upon the Indian because he is red, or upon the Asiatic because he has a light or a dark olive complexion?   Why is color in one a mark of superiority, and in another an indenture of servitude?   Why has the American a better right to enslave a man of Africa, than an African to enslave an American?   When the English Jew has a right, on the ground of complexion, to hold his darker brethren in bondage, then, and not till then, will a citizen of these United States have a right, on the ground of justice and equity, to deprive the African brother of liberty.

But it is predicated, that the Africans are inferior in their nature, and therefore the whites are authorized to hold them as their property; yea, some have even asserted that the negro, an opprobrious epithet which they attach to the human race, is a species of monkey.   But this is absurd in the abstract.   In the first place, it is well known that a monkey is ranked among quadrupeds, and has no soul; is destitute of that vital principle which the great

Author of nature places in man; for God breathed into man the breath of life, and he became a living soul. Secondly—neither have they a gizzard or musculous stomach, as we find in a human being. I care not what Buffon and the Naturalists say about the physical organization of colored persons; but this I know, place a white man in like circumstances with a man of color, and we have no very strong reason to believe that his intellect would flash any more light upon the world than the latter.

Suppose the man of color inferior to the white man, is any man or set of men warranted to enslave a man on the ground of his intellectual inferiority? No, no! I say no man has any more right from Scripture or reason to hold a fellow creature in bondage, than I have to go, in the dead hour of night, to the stable of my neighbor and take out his horse. Every descendant of Adam, no matter whether his parents are in servitude or not, is born free and independent. Nature never forged a collar or a chain. O, look at the inconsistency of Americans! One day signing the declaration of independence, and brandishing a slave whip the next. This conduct covers America with shame.

I call upon the ministers of the gospel, of every denomination, to come out plainly and boldly for God, and vindicate the cause of our colored brethren. They can do much. Let not the blood of two millions of the human race rise against you in the day of judgment. Ministers, preach the word; reprove, rebuke, push all principles to their utmost power of activity, on this topic. Care not for the frowns nor the smiles of the world; it is for God; neglect no part of your sacred function; perform faithfully all the duties of which it is composed.

'We hold these truths to be self-evident,' says our boasted Declaration of Independence, 'that all men are born equal; that they are endowed by their Creator with certain inalienable rights; that among these are life, liberty, and the pursuit of happiness;' and either the man of color was forgotten, or he was not recognized as a human being, or he is an exception to the universal rule, or his right is superseded by the paramount right of his master to hold him in servitude, and to work, scourge and sell him like a slave.

EUTHYMUS.

Columbia, Pa., August 11, 1831.[26]

[26] *Liberator*, Aug. 27, 1831.

Extract of a letter from a colored gentleman in Maryland.

"I have just been thinking that if Stephen Girard had left you, your partner, and the weather-beaten veteran, B. Lundy, a few thousands a piece, what an incalculable amount of good you might then be enabled to accomplish; but hod carriers stand a better chance for riches than reformers.   While on this subject, I was led to ponder on the inscrutable ways of Providence, and could not dismiss the subject, satisfactorily, until I read upon the golden page: 'The Lord God is a sun and a shield; the Lord will give grace and glory; *no good thing* will he withhold from them that walk uprightly.

The Liberator, I perceive, continues to thunder and lighten; but I very much fear that it will be proscribed by our Legislature: this seems to be the general sentiment.

The times in regard to us seem peculiarly portentous; but strange as it may appear, we do not, in general, give ourselves any undue uneasiness or concern about the event.   And why should we?   We read, Eccl. v. 8, 'If thou seest the oppression of the poor, and violent perverting of judgment and justice in a province, marvel not at the matter: for he that is higher than the highest regardeth, and there be higher than they.'   We, for the most part, enjoy all that peace of mind and confidence in Divine favor and protection, which a consciousness of innocence never fails to inspire. We know that

> The God that rules on high,
>   That thunders when he please,
> That rides upon the stormy sky
>   And manages the seas,

is our Father, our Protector, our Defender.   He has told us if we fear him and keep his commandments, no weapon formed against us shall ever prosper—that he is a very present help in every time of need—a strong hold in the day of trouble—and finally, that all things shall work together for good to them that love God; 'therefore will we not fear though the earth be removed, and though the mountains be cast into the midst of the sea: though the waters thereof roar and be troubled; though the mountains shake with the swelling thereof.'   Ps. xlvi. 2. 3.   And should our Legislature compel us to remove to Canada, Hayti, or to Mexico, we will sing even on our passage thither:

> There's mercy in every place;
>   And mercy, (encouraging thought,)
> Gives even affliction a grace,
>   And reconciles man to his lot.

But we apprehend little of this.—I was glad to find that the Governor of North Carolina disapproved the enactment of additional sanguinary laws: this is the true, the right policy. I hope his recommendation may have some influence upon our own Legislature. —The memorial from the Friends offered to the Virginia Legislature, is above all praise. The Lord abundantly bless that people for their labors of love; for they have done us much good. We are told that the Legislature received the memorial with 'marked respect'—verily 'the Lord God Omnipotent reigneth.' He is sitting on the whirlwind, and he will direct the storm. I had almost thought that the heart of sympathy had ceased to beat for us,— that the lips of philanthropy were totally sealed.' [27]

TO THE AMERICAN CONVENTION FOR PROMOTING THE ABOLITION OF SLAVERY.

GENTLEMEN—It has been my intention, for some time past, to write on the subject which you propose for an essay, but I have been prevented by other occupations.

The following, I hope, will meet your approbation; not that I hope to receive the premium, but merely for the benefit it may be to the slaves and their masters, as I wish the welfare of the whites of the South.

The only way in which the Slaves ought to be treated, in my opinion, is, in the same manner, and with the like indulgences, as hired servants. They must be civilized and naturalized before they can be made tractable, and be of any real benefit to their owners: otherwise they are like the lion in the wilderness or a tiger broke loose from his cage, which they will copy after, if they have any chance of obtaining revenge for cruelty practised on them.

Now I will ask the learned, what method to pursue? I will myself answer:—First, to abolish the importation of slaves altogether, because there are already sufficient to be of any advantage to the white population, who are even at this moment under continual apprehension of their rising; and if they should, murders innumerable would be committed. Their offspring are increasing,

[27] *Liberator*, Jan. 21, 1832.

which will undoubtedly supply any deficiencies. Secondly, I propose to have them educated in a manner that may make good citizens of them hereafter; and the only way is, to give them a good education, and bring them up in a moral and religious way. They will then look upon their masters as their fathers rather than as tyrants, which they do now. In such case, they will think it as much a crime to commit murder as a white man. Then give them encouragement to believe they will be free men; after such a time of good conduct, well pursued, and to the satisfaction of their owners, they shall be set free.

I never was of opinion that such a vast number should be free at once, especially in the situation their minds and habits are now in, without being immediately hired as free laborers, and instructed in all the useful branches of knowledge; for, otherwise, emancipation would be almost fatal for both parties.

I say free them, and hire them as you would other servants, until they can earn sufficient to benefit themselves and the public likewise; and by proper management and encouragement, in lieu of the lash, I have no doubt but many of them might make valuable citizens.

They are well adapted to the climate, and I believe are naturally industrious, when they are made to know it is for their future benefit and their wives and children's happiness.

What can a man care for the future, if he knows that, let him work ever so hard, he and his family must live and die slaves? His whole mind is given up to revenge and murder, not only the guilty but the innocent, the moment he can find a safe chance.

What I have written is as much for the benefit and safety of the white men of the south as the poor slaves, and I hope they will take this into their consideration.

They (the slaves) are under great obligations to that humane and generous gentleman who offers the premium, as I think it will bring forward a great deal of good sound reasoning before the public, which it may be impossible for those concerned in that inhuman traffic to withstand.

If these few hints, given from the heart, can be of any advantage to either party, I shall think myself well repaid for this essay given in their favor, as I hope.   Gentlemen, sincerely yours,

SAMSON HARRIS MOODY,

Boston, 1832.   *A colored man.*[28]

[28] *Liberator*, March 24, 1832.

MR GARRISON—I find that the Wilberforce settlement has far exceeded the expectations of many, (especially our enemies,) in its rapid growth, within the course of two years. It appears that the extensive emigration from the United States has augmented that settlement to about 2,000 souls, within this short space of time. What a vast difference between this and the colony of Liberia on the western coast of Africa! The Colonization Society has been straining to accomplish in sixteen years, what has been done in about sixteen months, besides the advantage it has had over these patriotic settlers. Hundreds of dollars have been collected and lavished, and continue to be wasted upon that colony, where, before half, or I may say two thirds of its emigrants become naturalized to the climate, they are swept away as with a besom of destruction. Not so with the settlement of Wilberforce. They have the salubrious air of the high latitudes—they prefer going there, because they are not exposed to the danger of the seas, nor the enormous expense of transportation; and, besides, they are received there by the Canadians as brethren and fellow subjects to his Majesty King William IV; whose laws are not so hard to them as the laws of the U. S. made and executed by about ten millions of majesties, called freemen, or free tramplers upon the rights of the red and sable race; to the blush of reason and humanity. About six thousand of us went to Hayti, assisted by that philanthropic people; but we found that a settlement there did not suit our extensive population. Thus you see that the Lord is opening a way for us to pack up and march off, without crossing the seas, to Canada, and I hope soon, to the Texas, or some neighboring province.

A COLORED CITIZEN OF BROOKLYN.[29]

Brooklyn, N. Y.

BALTIMORE, March 7, 1833.

To the Editor of the Liberator.

SIR:—It is known throughout the land that the free people of color cling with unconquerable tenacity to this, their own, their native land; and that nothing can drive them from it but persecution, injustice and cruelty without a parallel in the history of the world. It is known that we have most earnestly remonstrated against the principles and designs, the anti-republican and antichristian doctrines of the American Colonization Society; that we

[29] *Liberator*, April 7, 1832.

are indignant at those designs,—that we do most sincerely depre-
cate the spread of those principles, and the propagation of those
doctrines. Being thus influenced, we cannot but be deeply ag-
grieved when we see ministers of the gospel, occupying dignified
and responsible stations in the church, in their solemn, deliberative
assemblies putting the broad seal of their approbation upon the
principles and doctrines of the American Colonization Society; and
thereby inflicting a deep, perhaps an irreparable injury upon thousands who are wont to look up to them as their spiritual guides.
And what gives additional pungency to our grief is the reflection,
that these gentlemen know our sentiments, but are totally unmindful of them.

The exciting cause of these remarks is the address on Colonization of the Rev. Mr. Hammett (a methodist minister) published in
the Christian Advocate of the 1st of March. This distinguished
personage, after a few preliminary observations, commences with
the usual, monotonous cant of colonizationists:—'The evil which
this Society proposes to remedy, has already spread to a fearful
extent, and is becoming more and more alarming every day.' This
hackneyed proposition may be briefly dismissed in the language of
an influential colonizationist, recently used in the Legislature of
Maryland, on a different subject: 'Do,' says he, 'what is just, and
then you will have nothing to fear.'

Mr. H. proceeds to reiterate the prediction, that 'that class of
the community to whom it [the Col. Society] affords succour,
though nominally free, can, *in fact*, NEVER be so in this country.'
Now as the gentleman would have us implicitly believe the truth
of this prophetic declaration, we would, with all due deference,
desire him to exhibit, for our conviction, the supernatural data
upon which his prediction is predicated. If this reasonable proposition cannot be acceded to, he will permit us to be incredulous as
to his infallibility. The gentleman ought to reflect that as we are
all short-sighted mortals, and '*know not* what *a day* may bring
forth,' we may, at least, be permitted to hope to see better days;
and he must be cruel indeed, who would rob us of this invaluable
boon of Heaven—this soother of all our sorrows—this, our only
solace in the darkest hours of distress. But the Rev. gentleman
denies us even this consolation: he would not have us to be influenced by the scriptural doctrine that 'godliness with *contentment*
is great gain;'—he would hide from our eyes the declaration of

Paul: 'I have learned in whatsoever state I am, therewith to be *content.*' No, he would have us feel that our condition is intolerably grievous—irremediably hopeless.

Hear him: 'A gloom hangs over them, through which they can never *hope* to penetrate.' Now, we would tell this messenger of 'glad tidings' that we perceive the 'gloom,' the creature of pride and prejudice, of which he so forcibly speaks, and that it is not so dark to our vision as to preclude all *hope* of penetrating its apparently impervious mists. What! has it come to this, that we must not, in this christian land, even indulge in *hope?* And is it true that 'the land of the free and the home of the brave' has been converted into tophet, where

'Hope never comes, that comes to all?'

But this is the true policy of colonizationists. They design to make us miserable here, that we may emigrate to Africa *with our own consent.* Their tender mercies are cruel! And have they yet to learn that, so far as Liberia is concerned, we have chosen rather

——————'to bear the ills we have,
Than fly to those we know not of?'

Mr. Hammett continues: 'They groan under a *weight of prejudice,* from which they can never expect to rise. The *consequence* is that intellectual effort is paralyzed, and *morals* among them are *prostrated.*' Here then he concedes that the prostration of our morals is an inevitable consequence of the unholy prejudices of his brethren. And this he perceives and acknowledges, without the moral courage to denounce those prejudices, or the benevolence to attempt a reformation of those morals. Indeed, he seems to think that we are all, in this country, incorrigible sinners by a fatal necessity. To us he cannot preach repentance, nor upon us inculcate any system of ethics, for he pronounces us to be '*a class of beings* (are we human?) who,' he says, 'at home, *among us* can scarcely be *elevated by religion,* or controlled by law.' To the white citizens of the United States he indirectly declares they are under no obligation to regard the injunction of Paul: Honor *all* men;—that they may give to the winds the doctrine of the bible: If ye have *respect to persons,* ye commit sin;—that they may violate with impunity the golden rule of our Lord: 'All things whatsoever ye would that men should do to you, do ye even so to them.' He would paralyze the hand of *private* benevolence,—he would seal up the fountains of *public* justice,—he would have us, if we remain in this country, to be 'wretched, and miserable, and poor, and blind, and naked,' without help and without *hope*. Do you accuse me of misrepresentation? Well, then, he shall speak for himself: 'Find them where you may, whether in Philadelphia, Cincinnati, Richmond, or Charleston—in a free or in a slaveholding State, you find them, with *very few* exceptions, (the Lord pardon him, for he must be ignorant of us) the same degraded, demoralized race. No *individual effort, no system* of legislation, *can*, (moral impossibility) in this country, redeem them from this condition, nor raise them to the level of the white man, nor secure to them the privileges of freemen. *It is utterly vain to expect it.*' Sir, does not the heart of the patriot sink within him at this description of his country's morals? Does not the church of Christ bleed at every pore at the promulgation of such odious doctrines by one of her most gifted but deluded sons? 'I ask you,' with all the earnestness of which I am capable, 'is it not amazing that such' doctrines 'should meet with' approbation 'from any lover of his country—from any lover of freedom?' What, then, are we to think of those religious editors who copy into their papers such injurious sentiments without animadversion? What are we to think of the editors of the *Christian* Advocate, who not only publish Mr. Hammett's address approvingly, but with the ostensible design of diffusing its sentiments far and wide over the land, and especially among the 'nearly six hundred thousand communicants, and' the 'not much short of ten thousand ministers' of the Methodist Episcopal Church, who, Mr. H. tells us, 'unitedly approve the objects of the American Colonization Society?' Does this formidable host *now* imbibe the very exceptionable doctrine of the Rev. gentleman? or is it intended to make the *Christian* Advocate the medium of disseminating those doctrines?—to make this widely extended journal the *Advocate* of the principles and designs of the American Colonization Society? If so, we shall only add for the present, 'O tempora! O mores!'

A COLORED BALTIMOREAN.[30]

My DEAR FRIEND:—If I have ever felt a disposition to sympathize with the persecuted, the deeply injured abolitionists, the firm and uncompromising friends of our despised, neglected, and proscribed race, it is now:—*now*, while their lives and all they hold

[30] *Liberator*, March 23, 1833.

dear in life are at the tender mercies of infuriated mobs:—*now,* while they are threatened with assassination, and ruthlessly assailed in their persons—their houses pillaged, and their property given to the devouring flames:—it is *now,* while some of the professed ministers of Jesus, and the avowed enemies of all righteousness, have made it a common cause to stigmatise the consistent followers of the Savior, as 'visionary enthusiasts,' 'fire brands,' 'incendiary fanatics,' 'blood-thirsty' 'cut-throats,' &c. &c.—it is *now,* while some who occupy high and responsible stations in society, have so far forgotten the age, and the country in which they live, the institutions with which they are surrounded, as to appeal, not to the sober reason of the people, but to their vindictive passions and insane prejudices:—it is *now,* while the unthinking and credulous multitude, listening to the most flagrant misrepresentations, and cruel slanders of our enemies, seem determined to put down by brute force what they cannot do by moral power. And can these men have a reasonable hope of ultimate success? Can they annihilate the eternal truths of the sacred page?—subvert the moral government of God, frustrate his benevolent designs, and arrest forever the onward and majestic march of the Redeemer's kingdom? Can they measure arms with omnipotence? Can they withstand the Lord of Hosts? 'Surely, O God, the wrath of man shall praise thee, and the remainder of wrath shalt thou restrain.'

I perceive with mingled emotions of surprise and contempt, that one of the most implacable of the colonization prints in New York, has guaranteed abolitionists their lives on condition that they repudiate their principles, and ingloriously abandon the cause they have so generously, nay, *conscientiously* espoused. Abolitionists may live, it seems, on condition that they obey man rather than God—on condition that they renounce allegiance to the great King of heaven and earth—on condition that they apostatize from Him who has said to all his consistent disciples: 'Be not afraid of them that kill the body, and after that, have no more that they can do. But I will forewarn you whom ye shall fear: Fear him, which, after he hath killed, hath power to cast into hell; yea, I say unto you, Fear him.' 'For whosoever will save his life shall lose it; and whosoever will lose his life for my sake shall find it.' These gentlemen have yet to learn that abolitionists have counted the cost, and will, by the help of God, abide the issue—that they have the 'moral force of the universe' on their side, and are, consequently, invinci-

ble—that if they should be called to seal the truths they inculcate
with their blood, they will be sustained even in the hour of death
with the consolitory thought that

> 'They never fail, who die in a great cause.
> The block may soak their gore;
> Their heads may sodden in the sun;
> Their limbs be strung to city gates and castle walls;
> But still their spirit walks abroad.'

We pray, however, that abolitionists may be preserved—the
hearts of their enemies turned, and the people convinced that 'the
Lord God omnipotent reigneth.' The principles, sir, which guide
you and your noble coadjutors will be to you a tower of strength
in every situation and circumstance of life. Upon them you may
ever gaze with complacency. They are the emanations of Deity;
and while you cherish them, you shall have the favor and protection
of Him 'who is mighty to save and strong to deliver.' In the
darkest hours of distress, they will embolden you to exclaim,
'Though a host should encamp against me, my heart shall not fear;'
or in the language of the veteran Lundy—'Notwithstanding the
threatening aspect of the times—the portentous appearance of the
gathering storm—my head is bared to its pitiless peltings. My eye
winks not at its fiercest lightnings. The awe-inspiring thunders
may roll around; the electric fire may stream from every cloud;
the demon of the storm may hurl his death-doing bolts;—yet, if I
be not stricken lifeless to the earth, my humble labors shall not
cease.' [31]

To the Editor of The National Anti-Slavery Standard.

THE season is close at hand when the tide of politics must naturally ebb and flow; and the editor of the Philadelphia *North American,* and men of like stripe, think it their duty to begin to beat the
old tattoo of Colonization and Negro-hate, in order to prepare the
public mind for the coming elections. But, if they drive us darkies
all off to Africa, I don't know where they and their party will get
black ponies to ride into power on. But I want you to tell the editor aforesaid for me, that he may as well save his ink and paper,
and give himself no trouble about us darkies, for we are not going
to Africa. We have no more claim on Africa than he has; that
country belongs to the Africans, and not to us. We are Americans;

[31] *Liberator,* Aug. 2, 1834.

this is our country, and we have no claim on any other. There may be many colored adventurers who will go to Africa as there are some now going to California, Australia, Frazer River, and elsewhere, in search of wealth; but the masses will stay here. The Anglo-Saxons planted us here, without our wish or consent, and God has sent the early and latter rains on us, and we have taken root and have grown and multiplied here; and now we have no wish or intention to leave our native soil. Here we were born, and here we intend to die. Tell him there will be millions of our descendants here when he and his present sentiments will be numbered amongst the things that were. There will be multitudes of them here when Gabriel blows the trump for Judgment, for we are destined to spread, with those that planted us here, from sea to sea and from the rivers to the ends of this Continent, and to live in all the States on it, both in the present Union and out of the Union; and we will make a large number of the inhabitants of America when his name and sentiments shall have perished with his body. The problem that perplexes the gentleman is, to know what is to be done with us. I think if he would look over the decision of the Baltimore Convention, which was got up especially for the benefit of free negroes, he might gain some light on the subject; and if really he does want to know, and will only have patience to wait until Colonization hate has died out, as die out it will, and universal Emancipation has come in, as come it will, he will see that the blacks will dispose of and take care of themselves, which they are doing now without his help and in spite of his ado. It would be a waste of time to attempt to refute all the false charges made by the gentleman; they are plain enough to the observation of every reflecting individual. My only object is to inform the editor of the Philadelphia *North American* what we will and what we will not do.

A COLORED AMERICAN.[32]

For the Liberator.

MESSRS GARRISON AND KNAPP—Allow me to express the high satisfaction I feel on seeing the enlargement of the Liberator. It affords matter for very pleasing reflection to observe this, as being an indication that inquiry is *awakening* in reference to the condition and rights of a people who have been long and cruelly oppressed.

[32] *Liberator,* Aug. 27, 1859.

I would fondly hope, that in this land where Liberty is said to dwell, clothed with all her most fascinating enchantments, your noble and untiring efforts in the cause of humanity and natural rights may not be fruitless and unavailing. Why should not this land, which is an asylum for the persecuted of almost all nations, also be a sanctuary of security and repose to the wearied and depressed African? Humanity and justice can assign no sufficient reason.

Permit me, gentlemen, to say that I am impressed with sentiments of deep and lasting gratitude to you, for the able and fearless manner in which you have exposed the wickedness and moral deformity of slavery, as likewise for your views on the character and tendency of the Colonization Society. Your articles upon this subject breathe the spirit and sentiments of every colored man of any intelligence. Why establish a Society for the purpose of inducing the African to forsake this soil which he has enriched with his labor, and watered with his tears; which the violence and rapacity of Europe and America have made his native land? Why plunder him of his liberty, degrade his character, and then entice him into a foreign, and to him a strange land? This is not justice. Is it mercy? You have shewn the scheme to be impracticable and delusive. No man, who takes a sober view of the question, can entertain a doubt. But suppose the Society could attain what it is, and has been attempting, viz. the removal of the free people of color, it would then have done more towards tightening the cords and strengthening the chains of slavery, than ten thousand laws against freedom, sanctioned and enforced by the whip and the gibbet. It is well known that the slave has no chance of being informed of his natural rights, but by his intercourse with those of his color who are free: it therefore becomes highly desirable for those who wish to see oppression firmly established, to remove the free people of color. Thus the free African who permits himself to be allured from his debased countrymen, gives a bond, as far as he is concerned, that his kinsmen who are in bondage shall continue meek and submissive as beasts of burden. Let the free colored man reflect—let him consider deeply, before he puts the seal upon this compact—the seal is the blood of his countrymen.

You will pardon me, gentlemen, for saying so much on this question, as it is one in which I feel the most deep and lively interest. I join with the friends of equality and justice every where, in wishing that your efforts in this great and arduous enterprise may be crowned with success.

Yours, respectfully,

J. B. VASHON.[33]

Pittsburgh, March 16th, 1832.

BOSTON, 7th mo. 10, 1839.

DEAR FRIEND:

Circumstances entirely beyond my control constrained me to forego the pleasant interview that I expected to have had with you on Tuesday evening, previous to my leaving the city: consequently I embrace this opportunity of expressing my regret at the unexpected disappointment. But before leaving the city, allow me, through the medium of this letter, to indulge myself in a few remarks concerning the advancement of the *holy cause of Abolition.*

'When doctors disagree, who shall decide?' says the moralist. And when abolition doctors disagree about prescribing medicine to cure the infectious *disease* of slavery, who shall we look to for a decision? My answer is—to the *patient.* And professing to be one who has been sick *all* his days, and knowing that the *disease* still continues to make sad havoc among my colored countrymen, I venture to decide for myself.

Before examining the disagreement of abolition doctors, allow me to notice the experimental medicine used by the Colonization Society. These doctors proposed to remove such free colored people as were convalescent to a purer air, where the scorching rays of an African sun would make them a healthy nation of *Freemen.* But some how or other, they very imprudently furnished them with 'the cordial for all our fears,' (rum,) which, when mixed with a little gunpowder, and taken in strong doses, soon brought on a *relapse;* and dreadful to relate, many died or—were decently *killed!* Things went on in this way for some years, when a young printer proposed to try a new medicine, (immediatism,) which, when rightly applied, would cure the disease without *bleeding.* So confident was he of the efficacy of his medicine, that he applied some of the same to a slave-trader in Maryland, which threw him into such a fit that with the assistance of twelve jurymen and others, the printer was pronounced a *quack* and thrown into close confinement.

[33] Sometimes the writer dared to sign his name. *Liberator*, March 31, 1832.

But, if I am rightly informed, through the liberality of a *Gotham-ite*, he was soon after released.   Afterwards, he established a *school* in Boston, consisting of eleven or twelve pupils, and astonishing to relate, the whole country is now overrun with schools to the number of 2000, and pupils without number.   Certificates were coming in from all quarters, testifying to the astonishing cures effected by using his *life*-preserving medicine.

But after all, this printer entertained two or three *ultra notions,* viz:—that in the nineteenth century, women were to all intents and purposes—*persons,*—entitled to be respected as such in *all* the relations of life.   That divine government is preferable to human government, &c.   Consequently, 'the staff of accomplishment' must be taken from him and others, and placed in the hands of an electioneering and time-serving clergy.   Now, dear friend, as they are about to administer strange medicine, I, for one, (and I know I speak the sentiments of *all* my colored brethren) will neither touch, taste nor handle the unclean thing; and I warn all true-hearted abolitionists to buy and circulate the genuine medicine to cure the 'infectious disease of slavery,' to be had only at No. 25 Cornhill.   I would like to say more, but time and paper fails me.   Go on in the good cause and heaven will be your reward.

Yours truly,
WILLIAM P. POWELL.[34]

MR. EDITOR:—

Although not complexionally identified with you and your noble coadjutors in the great work of human freedom, yet when, in the gratitude of my heart, I grasp you by the hand, and salute you by the endearing name of brother, I have reason to believe you do not repudiate the affinity.   Perhaps, sir, I cannot employ a leisure hour more advantageously than by a line or two in reference to that most odious and infamous enactment, denominated the Fugitive Slave Bill—a bill so utterly repulsive, so hideous in its every feature, that bare reflection upon it is sufficient to 'freeze our blood, and cause each particular hair to stand on end, like quills upon the fretful porcupine.'

Mr. Editor, every citizen of this Commonwealth is, by the provisions of this bill, imperatively forbidden to obey the express declarations of the word of God.   Should you, sir, remembering them that

are in bonds as bound with them, whisper in the ear of the panting
fugitive, 'Escape for your life! look not behind you!' you are liable
to an enormous fine, and a home in the State Prison is provided for
you, without money and without price, where you can reflect for
six months upon the enormity of obeying the Divine injunction,
'Whatsoever ye would that men should do to you, do ye even so to
them.' Should the poor hound-hunted fugitive, after having endured all the perils and privations incident to a flight from that
land where the demon of Slavery holds his infernal orgies—should
he arrive here, and locate himself on Bunker Hill, at the very base
of the monument which is the boast of America, that monument
dedicated to Freedom, and upon which our fathers, who fought
and bled and died, never dreamed a slave should ever, for one
moment, gaze—should he, in his humble tenement, surrounded
by his wife and little ones, commence his song of praise to God
for having given him the North Star to guide his weary feet,
at that very moment, on that consecrated spot, the merciless slave-
hunter may snatch him from his wife and children,—bone of his
bone and flesh of his flesh,—and carry him back to interminable
bondage. And should you, sir, believing it to be your duty to resist oppression manfully, irrespective of the source whence it emanates, 'with pitying eye behold his helpless grief,' meet him at the
threshold of the poor slave's domicile, and command him to desist
in his work of blood—'hitherto shalt thou come, but no farther'—
then this liberty-loving nation has ordered that *your* liberty be
taken from *you;* and you shall have a punishment inflicted upon
you, sufficient to recall you to a lively sense of your constitutional
obligations, and you be metamorphosed into a good citizen of the
Commonwealth.

All this is done, sir, by a people whose flag of freedom waves in
the broad sunlight of heaven—a people who profess to be the freest
and most enlightened nation under heaven. Well might we, in view
of such gross hypocrisy, such manifest inconsistency, exclaim with
the Savior, 'O generation of vipers, how can you escape the damnation of hell!'

But, perhaps, as slaveholding is attempted to be justified because Paul sent back Onesimus to his master, not as a servant, but
as a *brother beloved,* the late lamented Clay and Webster (*par
nobile fratrum!* 'we ne'er shall look upon their like again') had
their attention directed to that portion of the Scriptures which

speaks of the apostles as *fishers* of men. And with characteristic
reverence for the Word, wishing to emulate the Savior's example,
they thought they would frame a law, which virtually declares to
the sons and daughters of the Pilgrims—'Behold, we make you
hunters of men, women and children!'

But then, we are told, it was all done in a spirit of compromise
—its tenacious supporters *hoped* by its passage to effect a settlement of the slavery question. Why, gentlemen, 'was the hope
drunk wherein you dressed yourselves?' Know you not, O Daniel!
that this great question cannot be settled by compromise? The
word cannot be found in the vocabulary of an honest man's heart,
for the simple reason that it imports a mutual dereliction of principle. If, sir, the institution of slavery is right and just in the
sight of God and man, then, in the name of justice, do all you can
to perpetuate it; if not, if the whole system is inherently iniquitous,
abolish it, and give to the winds your concessions and compromises.
And these men pretend to be the friends of the colored man! We
tell them, once for all, despite our innate inferiority, aside from the
obliquity of our mental vision, our perceptions are sufficiently acute
to discern iniquity, whether shielded by the helmet of senatorial
wisdom, or stalking abroad in the earth in all its native hideousness,
its heart-appalling deformity.

But the Bill has passed, and its passage has elicited the respect
of all persons—but those whose respect is worth having. Its ardent
supporters have won golden opinions from all sorts of people—but
those who have honest hearts in them. How forcibly the passage
occurs to our memory, 'O Capernaum, who wast once exalted unto
heaven, but art now cast down to hell!' *Sic transit gloria mundi!*

Will the people of New England tamely submit to this miserable
indignity? Will they implicitly obey the imperious mandates, the
cruel enactments of bloodthirsty tyrants, or that 'higher law,' in
exact conformity with which all others should be enacted, or sink
into comparative insignificance? I am no prophet, nor the son of
a prophet; yet I venture to predict, that no man will be taken from
Massachusetts. And, although the doctrine of the righteousness of
the law of retaliation may not abide the scrutinizing test of scriptural criticism, yet our charity must be elongated to an almost indefinite tension, our religious organs must be most wonderfully developed, before we shall suffer our liberty to be wrested from us,
without an arduous struggle to retain it. But we believe that more

can be accomplished by the all-controlling power of public sentiment, than by guns, bowie knives or pistols. And we believe public opinion is on our side. Why should it not be so? What have
we, the colored people of this Republic done, that we should be
trampled upon and crushed beneath a weight of proscription almost
sufficient to crush an angel? Why, sir, an all-wise Providence has
seen fit to give us a skin not colored like the white man's. 'The
head and front of our offending hath this extent, no more.' But
Ethiopia shall yet stretch out her arm, unparalyzed, to God. Like
other causes which have for their object the amelioration of the condition of the human race, the cause of human liberty has encountered many oppositions calculated to impede its progress. But it
will ultimately triumph. Our enemies cannot annihilate our aspirations after liberty. Our cause has been stamped by God with the
impress of imperishable vitality. The spirits of liberty and slavery
are even now, with characteristic skill and vigor, marshalling their
respective forces for a mighty contest. And, if 'coming events cast
their shadows before,' if the history of the past be any precedent
for the future, then have the friends of freedom all things to hope
for, and nothing to fear; for just so sure as God rescued the children of Israel from Egyptian bondage, just so sure will he hear our
groans, and come down to deliver us.   W. J. W.[35]
    Boston, October 9th, 1850.

V. David Ruggles

    David Ruggles, as the editor of the *Mirror of Liberty*,
published in New York City, was constantly on the firing
line, fighting side by side with other abolitionists. Unfortunately a complete file of his valuable publication is not
extant. However, from letters written by him from Northampton, to which he went during the early 'forties to regain
his health in the employ of the Association of Education
and Industry, there may be obtained much information as to
his opinions and policies.

                                New Bedford, June 23d, 1841.
To the Editor of the New Bedford Daily Register:—
    Sir,—Permit me to inquire of your readers, what is Highway
Robbery? and if the following outrage is not Robbery, and Assault

[35] *Liberator*, Nov. 1, 1850.

and Battery.   I left New Bedford on Saturday last, the 19th inst.,
on board the Steamboat Telegraph, for Nantucket.   On the passage
thither, when called upon to pay the fare, I stepped forward to the
Captain's office, and inquired the price of the passage.   I learned
that there were two prices; one $2, the other $1 50.   The passenger
who pays the first price is entitled to all the privileges of the Boat.
The one who pays the second price purchases a forward deck privilege.   I concluded to pay $2, which the Capt. repeatedly refused to
take, and insisted on my purchasing the forward deck privilege,
which I did not choose to take, on the grounds, first, no man or
body corporate has a right to decide for another person what he or
she shall purchase; second, no man can justly compel another to
pay for what he does not want.   The Capt. became furious at my
position, commenced an assault and battery upon my person, took
from me by force my private papers.   Finding myself 'a stranger
in a strange place,' shorn of hat and important papers, I was compelled to leave the Island without accomplishing the object of my
visit; on my return passage, Capt. Lot Phinney received $2 fare.   I
state these facts to *caution* the public, who may travel in the Steamboat between New Bedford and Nantucket.

Yours for Equal Rights,
DAVID RUGGLES.[86]

————'Know ye not who would be free,
Themselves must strike the blow!'

COLORED AMERICANS:

   The time is fast approaching, it will soon be at hand, when the
friends of reform, of outraged human nature, should convene at
the important Convention of the American Reform Board of disfranchised commissioners, which is to be held in the city of New-
York on the 8th of September next, where you are expected to
'unite and energize in securing our immediate relief and enfranchisement'—a measure which can never be effected until we adopt
principles and measures conducive to that end.   Know we must our
true condition, our relative position, to the policy or blighting
machinations formed against us.

   You will permit me to inform you of the request of the executive committee of the A. R. B. of disfranchised commissioners, who

[86] *Liberator*, June 9, 1841.

expect you to meet them as members or honorary members of the
Board which has been established to promote a bond of union and
action which is essential to the safety and prosperity of our cause.

Fail not to collect and report to the Convention—

First. The statistics of our people in the place in which you
reside.

Secondly. The number of children in schools, and the state of
education.

Thirdly. The number of mechanics, their different trades, and
how employed.

Fourthly. The number of persons known to be in chain gangs
at the south.

Fifthly. The number of churches, church members, and clergymen, designating their denomination.

Sixthly. The condition of our people generally, in relation to
the 'pursuit of happiness.'

Notwithstanding the unpardonable state of supineness, which
every where exists among us, the age in which we live is pregnant
with events which claim our every attention. Our condition is
every where identical. Rise, brethren, rise! Strike for freedom,
or die slaves! The storm of colonization has come upon our brethren in Maryland, and threatens to visit us throughout this land.
Come up, and help us! In our cause, mere words are nothing—
action is every thing. Buckle on your armor, and appear at the
Convention, remembering that our cause demands of us union and
agitation—agitation and action, from the east to the west, from the
north to the south.

Yours for reform,
DAVID RUGGLES.[37]

NORTHAMPTON, Jan. 23d, 1843.

DEAR GARRISON:

I rejoice to see, by the last Liberator, that you have survived
the severe attack of a blighting fever, and, having buckled on the
armor, have re-entered the conflict against our COMMON FOE—
SLAVERY. I have a strong desire to be with you on duty, in the
field; but the stubborn, though declining affection of the diaphragm
compels me to continue on a furlough. I have sojourned in this
delightful region since last fall, with a community of practical

[37] *Liberator*, Aug. 13, 1841.

Christians—the Northampton Association of Education and Industry, which promises to be a paradise. By the synopsis of the proceedings of the late Latimer Convention, held in this town on the 9th inst., (that appears in your paper on the 20th,) and of which I was a member,—that it may not be inferred by your readers that I voted for the third resolution, and thereby conceded to slavery my own right, and the rights of those with whom I am proscriptively identified, (our complexion being recognised as the presumptive evidence of slavery,) I wish to state that I took exceptions against the first part of it, which is in the following words:

'Resolved, That the recent decision of the Supreme Court of the U. S. in the case of Prigg vs. Pennsylvania, and sustained by the Supreme Court of Massachusetts, by which the ancient and sacred right of trial by jury, and the habeas corpus act, are denied to every person in this Commonwealth, who may be claimed as a slave, thus converting Massachusetts into a hunting ground for southern kidnappers, and exposing every man, woman and child, to the cupidity of southern slave-owners,' &c.

Now, I do not acknowledge that an act or proceedings under a law to question a man's inalienable right to liberty can be 'sacred' or holy. It may be seen, by a reference to the first resolution passed in Convention, which reads thus: 'Resolved, That the right of all men to be free can never be alienated'—that the meeting conscientiously erred by adopting the third resolution.

The 6th resolution adopted, also bears witness against the third.

The existence of a jury trial law, recognizing man as a criminal for wearing the complexion he has received from his Creator, or conceding to slavery the right to incarcerate humanity as a chattel personal, is at variance with my notion of equal rights, the Declaration of American Independence, the laws of Nature, and of the living God.

I cannot see that the 'recent decision in question has destroyed the habeas corpus act, or converted Massachusetts into a hunting ground for southern kidnappers.' This State, in common with the others of this Union, having been what they are now since the existence of the law created by Congress in 1793.

I wish the friends of freedom would, instead of taking issue against Justice Story, or the Supreme Court, for explaining the true bearing of the law, go against its constitutionality.

I apprehend that the 'recent decision' has nullified the existence of unholy and proscriptive jury trial laws against complexion, and has emancipated and rebuked the people of the States wherein they existed, for volunteering their *legal* and *military* support to the odious system of slavery. I think also, that the idea expressed in the resolution, viz: that the 'recent decision has exposed every man woman and child to the cupidity of southern slave-owners,' is unfounded, usage and experience having shown that the law bears exclusively on us, who are disfranchised, and *appointed for destruction.*

I regret that a resolution of a similar import to the third adopted at the Northampton meeting was passed by the friends of liberty at the Concord Latimer Convention, Jan. 2d.

I am aware that the view which I take of the decision of the Supreme Court, and the jury trial laws, is at variance with that of many gentlemen, learned in the legal profession; but, if it is recollected that lawyers are as liable to differ and err in expounding the civil law as clergymen are the moral law, I may be excused for holding such an unpopular opinion against that entertained by the good and the learned of the country.

Yours, truly, for equal liberty,

DAVID RUGGLES.[38]

The pleasant view of our cause, as presented weekly by the Standard, is really refreshing to us up here in the mountains. Among many other things, I have noticed, with deep interest, the "Sixth Annual Report of the Canada Mission," in your paper of the 26th of January, by our friend, Hiram Wilson. I rejoice to learn the success with which the indefatigable labors of himself and his co-workers have been crowned.

The 10th article of the Ashburton treaty is so inimical to the safety of persons emigrating from slavery to Canada, that our friends should be cautious, and not render their reports charts, by which slaveholders may pursue their game with uninterrupted success. I think that article of the treaty has rendered the Canadas, *yea* the whole British province, as much a hunting-ground for American slaveholders, as the law of Congress, of 1793, has rendered several States of this Union. A slave is one in the possession of another, and subject to the will of another; in other words, he is a *chattel.* But if he becomes the subject of his own will, and declares his independence of slavery, by emigrating to Canada, he becomes a *person*, and may be *"charged with robbery, &c.* Under the forms of the laws of the States, he may be pursued and arrested in any part of the British provinces as a criminal, and returned to the United States, under a plain construction of the treaty. Had I not arrived at this conclusion from the words of the 10th article of the treaty referred to, the explanation of Lord Ashburton, represented by Lewis Tappan to have been given to a committee of the American and Foreign Anti-Slavery Society, as published in the Journal of Commerce, and the Standard, would have led me to form such an inference.

DAVID RUGGLES.[39]

NORTHAMPTON, May 1st, 1843.

I regret that you did not state, in your remarks introducing an extract of my letter in the Standard of the 6th ultimo, that I sojourn here as a member of this great and interesting family, called "The Northampton Association of Education and Industry," established to live out the hallowed principle of *"equal brotherhood— the all-embracing law of love—*so emphatically taught by true Christianity."

That no member is considered to be "in the employ of the association;" but that each and every member *employs* himself and herself in promoting the welfare of all, by preparing this family, "by an enlightened and never-ending education, to be peaceful, happy, and active fellow-laborers together," in promoting a higher development of the race.

I shall remain here a few months longer, until I gain sufficient physical and mental strength to re-enter the arena for the redemption of our enslaved and perishing countrymen.

I wish that the fact could be generally known among such of our disfranchised friends as are desirous of securing an education, and a trade, at the same time, for their children, male or female, and who are able to pay the sum of one hundred dollars a year for board, washing, and tuition, while they pursue an English and classical education, with a practical knowledge of agriculture, horticulture, and silk growing or silk manufacturing, carpentering, brick and stone masonry, blacksmithing, cutlery, or tailoring.

I regard the privileges and advantages afforded to the pupils

[39] *National Anti-Slavery Standard*, April 6, 1843.

and members of this association, to be superior to any with which
I am acquainted in this country.   Among the members of this interesting community of practical abolitionists, are our well-known
friends, George W. Benson, and Dr. Erasmus D. Hudson.   The
standard of equality here erected and sustained, ''recognizes no
distinction of rights, or rewards, between the strong and the weak,
the skillful and the unskillful, the man and the woman, the rich
and the poor; but welcoming all to an equal participation in God's
blessed bounty.''   I am truly your friend,

DAVID RUGGLES.[40]

To the Editor of the Albany Northern Star:

ESTEEMED FRIEND MYERS—This letter comes to communicate my
thanks to you, and to the Publishing Committee of the Albany
Northern Star, for the honor conferred on me, by the appointment
of agent for your interesting paper; and to express regret that it
is not in my power to serve you, in the noble cause in which you
are engaged.

Having retreated for health and quiet from the inhospitable
city of New-York, to the delightful and fertile hills of New-England,—where the unwritten music of the fresh mountain breezes,
through the trees and the valleys—of the sonorous peals of thunder
succeeding the warm spring showers—of the rippling hills, and
meandering brooks—of the robin, and the wren, the blue-bird, and
the sparrow, the pe-wit, and the lark, and of other minstrels of the
various feathered tribes, whose mellifluous strains may be heard
from every tree, on either side of the pathway—of the chattering
squirrels leaping from branch to branch among the trees—and of
many other animals, rational and irrational, from the sheep and
the lambs, to the boys and the girls, the men and the women, conspire to a harmony in exciting wonder and admiration, love and
veneration, for the beautiful in Nature, the workmanship of God.
Being here sheltered by friendship, and cherished by love, in this
promising Home for Humanity, until health and sight shall allow
me to re-enter the field of reform, for the regeneration of the race,
the redemption of Humanity, I must be content to remain yet a
little longer in quiet neutrality.   Do me the justice, therefore, to
omit my name from the list of agents, and introduce instead, Stephen Christopher Rush, who is able and willing to serve you.

[40] *National Anti-Slavery Standard,* May 11, 1843.

No friend of a newspaper, devoted to the cause of reform, should allow his name to stand, as agent, without being able to act—every agent of a paper in such a cause, should feel that he incurs a responsibility, which is but a short remove from that of the Editor, or principal, because, he professes to act *instead* thereof, within the limits of his appointment.

I admire the title of your paper, because it is indicative of light and inflexibility—while the North Star of the heavens, shines alone, by its own light, it may add to the refulgence of the 'Northern Star' of Albany, by borrowing light from such bodies, or stars, as may be attracted near your polar region, to form a constellation of correspondents—there are Wm. Whipper, Robert Purvis, Sarah Douglass, R. F. Wake, L. Bodine, J. McCune Smith, Eliza Richardson, John Peterson, Rebecca Fenwick Bell, P. Loveredge, John J. Zuel, Sarah Ennals, W. P. Powell, P. Reason, Thomas Jinnings, Wm. C. Nell, N. A. Borden, Sarah Forten Purvis, Robert Hamilton, J. C. Morell, John T. Hilton, F. Seanlen, J. B. Sanderson, Ezra Johnson, P. C. Howard, Frederick Douglass, and C. L. Remond. Let these differ as they will, in magnitude, each one is as important to the moral and intellectual constellation, as the *inflexibility* of the 'Star' is to the shipwrecked inebriate—who may follow its beacon-light to the haven where he should be.

As my eyes do not now serve me to make *sidereal* observations, I may be allowed to enquire—what of that dark body, or *phenomenon*, which appeared in the North-west, at or near Buffalo, in August last, called a Convention? Did it give any light to the world? or was it a total eclipse? Do, if you can, furnish some philosophical remarks respecting its character.

Seeing the Albany Committee of Vigilance has the reputation of being the most efficient organization in the State of New-York, in the business of aiding the way-worn and weather-beathen refugee from slavery's shambles,

On the track for Liberty! in Queen Victoria's land;

I expect that you take cognizance of the cruel machinations formed by slaveites in other States, to enslave our fellow-countrymen and women, and therefore ask for information, in relation to the case of our unfortunate brother, James D. Lane, late steward of the Empire, under the treacherous Capt. Wm. Powell, who betrayed him, (as I am informed,) to be sacrificed by the slave power of Virginia, for his fidelity to the cause of human rights. Some of the facts appear in the 'National Anti-Slavery Standard' of Jan. 18, 1844, which show that a certain cob-web-making, spider-living lawyer of N. York, who treats men as spiders do the flies—by taking advantage of their ignorance, and *extorting* a fee of '*one hundred dollars*,' to bring a useless suit against said captain, when the spirit of the law, common sense, and the advice of the true friends of humanity, were against the proceedings.

Mr. Lane's case is an important one, and should arrest the attention, and secure the sympathy of every disfranchised inhabitant of the State. Humanity pleads, and Justice *demands* that he be redeemed, and restored to liberty! If there is no other remedy in Mr. L's case, seek it under 'Seward's protective law of 1840,' providing that when a '*free citizen, or inhabitant of the State of New-York shall be wrongfully seized, or imprisoned, or otherwise deprived of rights, in southern States*,' &c. Solicit, nay, *demand* gubernatorial interference in the case. If you are not possessed of all its legal features to proceed thus, correspond with some member of the New-York bar, who has a character for professional ability and honor, and for true humanity. You may rely on Messrs. Hiram Ketchum, Theodore Sedgwick, Alanson Nash, John Jay, and John Hopper, for legal information; or upon that sage veteran and friend of human freedom, Isaac T. Hopper, who has had more experience in such cases, than any other man in America.

If you are not fully possessed of all the particulars in the case, I trust that you will not hesitate to become so, and to make this a common cause, by appealing to the philanthropy of every disfranchised man and woman, causing them to feel, reason, and *agitate*— until victory is secured over *slavery*, in the redemption of our suffering brother, James D. Lane.

When we, a proscribed, outraged, disfranchised and downtrodden people shall *know* our condition, and live in obedience to the laws of our being—ignorance, slavery, and all other evils afflicting us, will be no more—and we shall be free indeed.

Yours truly,

DAVID RUGGLES.[41]

41 *Liberator*, May 24, 1844.

NORTHAMPTON WATER CURE,
Dec. 5, 1848.

FRIEND GARRISON:

As the sympathetic, menacing, and explanatory letter of Seth Marshall, of Painesville, Ohio, in the Liberator of the 1st instant, in regard to the part he took in aiding his friend Wilcox's departure from my establishment, with a knowledge of his intentions to commit fraud, places him in a worse light before the public than did my allusion to him in the article which you copied from the Springfield Republican; and as he complains that I did not do him justice, by stating that Wilcox took the cars to Springfield in company with him, and that one of my neighbors had a small bill against him for horse-hire, a fact which he admits in his letter, together with the circumstances which induced him to become an accessary after the fact in the affair; I can only say, that as my letter to the Republican was written on the day they left, I had not sufficient knowledge of the interest he took in his friend's departure, to award him that justice in the matter which was really due. The unaccountable intimacy which existed between Wilcox and Marshall, when the latter knew that his friend was not what he should be, and the fact that Marshall, through Wilcox, hired the carriage in which they went to the depot; and that when Marshall took leave of us, he drove off to overtake Wilcox on the road near the point where he had concealed his bundle of clothing; and that he was seen by several persons to drive back and forth, near the place, apparently to give Wilcox an opportunity to throw his bundle into the wagon undiscovered; and that the man who returned with the horse and carriage, protested to him that nothing was said to him by Marshall or his friend in regard to the pay, had the effect to excite suspicion, and shake the confidence of those who had heretofore regarded Marshall as a man of true self-respect and integrity. If Marshall was ignorant of Wilcox's intentions to leave in such a manner, until he threw his bundle of clothing into the wagon, why did he not request one of the gentlemen who saw him driving back and forth on the road to afford his friend an opportunity to smuggle his bundle, to ride to the depot with him, and return the horse? Or why did he not return to the establishment, as he was but a few rods off, and invite one of the patients to ride with him? He had ample time to do so. It appears that Marshall's reasons for going on with his friend were, that he was told

by Wilcox that I had 'abused him, and was keeping him to get his
money, and that Dr. Denniston told him that he was well, and
ought to have left long ago'—when he knew that Wilcox had been
discharged from the establishment for unprincipled conduct, and
was only permitted to remain a few weeks longer, after apologising
for his course, and promising to do better. Dr. Denniston may
have advised Wilcox thus; but it is not believed that he would
hazard his reputation by giving such advice. If he did so, and if
all that Marshall represented his friend to have said had been true,
it would seem strange that an honest man should compromise his
honor by aiding another in such a dishonorable transaction, at the
expense of one for whom he has so much sympathy, that it re-
strained him from prosecuting for a libel. Marshall's self-respect
and sympathy for me are evinced in the following extracts from a
letter addressed to a gentleman in the establishment, *two* days
after his arrival at New-York, under date 24th October. In alluding to his departure with Wilcox, he says:—'He had told me that
he should leave soon, but wanted me to say nothing of it, which I
promised him.' 'What was the occasion of his leaving? Did he
owe the Doctor, and take that method of paying it?' Now, was
Marshall ignorant of his friend Wilcox's intention to leave? Had
he no more agency, was he no more responsible for his departure in
that manner than yourself? Judge ye!

Yours, for truth and justice,

D. RUGGLES.[42]

VI. The Testimony of the Freedmen

A neglected aspect of the study of slavery is the mind
of the slaves themselves. As bondmen, they were generally too illiterate to express themselves. Freed and
brought North to be educated, however, they often bore intelligent testimony against the institution. In so doing,
they have given a picture of the institution from a different
point of view.

Mr. Wm. Lloyd Garrison:

Respected Friend—I take the liberty of calling you friend, although I have never had the pleasure of seeing you. But, from

[42] *Liberator*, Dec. 15, 1848.

your ardent zeal in the cause of humanity, I think I may with safety call you 'my friend.' And not only myself, but if the poor slaves, whose lot it is to toil day and night on the cotton, and sugar, and rice plantations, only knew of what you have done, and are still doing and suffering for them, I think they would send up their united praise to God, for having raised up one so faithful to plead their cause: but these things are hid from them, as far as it is possible. But I believe the time will come when these things will be published upon the house-tops. Dear friend, do not think that I am trying to flatter you. No—it is the language of my heart. I am one of those unfortunate beings, who fell among thieves, and have been stripped and wounded; whom the people of this nation, priest and levite alike, have passed by on the other side, and left me without one to bind up my wounds, or to comfort me. Nearly thirty years of my life was I in this condition, at the close of which, God was so good as to open a way whereby I made my escape. The Lord truly took me by the hand, and led me on. He was a wall round about me, and kept me from being molested, until I found myself in Philadelphia, in the bosom of friends, who, as it were, seemed to have been waiting to receive me at my coming. Yes—they were ready to feed and clothe me: after which, by their help, I was then enabled to resume my journey, until I found myself in Dr. Osgood's 'stranger's room' in Springfield. Being assisted by him, I obtained a place of service, where I continued one year; at the close of which, besides paying for my board and clothing, I found myself with the first hundred dollars that I ever could call my own, although I had earned many. This will go to prove to some, that the slaves 'cannot take care of themselves.' In relation to myself, I found it much less difficult to take care of myself, than to take care of myself and my master too. So much for freedom. Freedom, did I say? Not in the full sense of the word—but only partially so.

Think you, sir, that I can feel free, while millions of my countrymen are held in chains and fetters by this professed christian nation; while our soil is wet with blood, caused by 'the whip on woman's shrinking flesh,' and God's own image is bought and sold! Think, sir, that I can feel free, while these, my countrymen, are stripped, and wounded, and left in the cottom fields and the rice swamps, to bleed and to die; and, among them, my own brothers and sisters, who are as dear to me as my heart's blood? No—I cannot feel free. I am still bound with my brethren. I feel the cruel lash, and their chains.

At the close of the first year, being, as a matter of course, almost entirely destitute of education, I thought that I would go to Wilbraham school, knowing of no better place at that time. I did so, and spent one year and six months in said school. Now, sir, this school professes to be based on christian and humane principles; and not only so, but a majority of this school are professed abolitionists; and yet, will you believe me when I have told you, that during the time which I have been in this school, I have been obliged to wait until my aristocratic abolition white skinned brethren had been served, before I could be admitted to the table? And not only so, but I was not permitted even to room in the same house; and yet I had to pay the same as the other students, for my board, room and tuition! Not that I thought myself above eating at the second table; but I was grieved to see the pro-slavery feeling that existed among this professed christian-loving people, 'without partiality or hypocrisy,' —many of them, too, preparing to preach the impartial love of Christ, and hoping to go to heaven. Perhaps they will expect a first table there, and a negro table for negro souls. But I have come to the determination to leave them; and as I wish to continue my studies, I shall seek a place elsewhere. But the abolitionists of this institution, I learn, are anti-Garrison abolitionists. Not that I would condemn all that belong to this party, or even all in this institution; but I think you may judge from the above remarks, whether the majority of this school, notwithstanding all their profession of humanity and philanthropy, have not prejudice deep-rooted in their hearts. For the last two months, I have been trying those of the old stamp—the true friends of Garrison and of the slave; and I must say, that I have found as much difference as there is between a mere nominal profession and a true Christian. I am received as a man and a brother, and am made to forget that I have a colored skin; and am not only admitted to the same table, but in many instances the same bed.

You can dispose of this as you think best.

JAMES L. SMITH.[43]

OCKHAM SCHOOL, near Ripley, }
SURRY, (Eng.) Nov. 29, 1851.}

MY DEAR FRIEND:

I hope you will not think that we have in the least degree forgotten your kindness towards us, though it may seem so by our not

[43] *Liberator*, March 26, 1841.

writing to you before. The reason has not been the want of interest on our part, or [of] the proper valuation of true friends. But merely because we, as you well know, have been deprived of the art of writing, and consequently felt our inability of addressing a letter to you.

But the letter of introduction which you were so kind as to give us, was to such a kind and valued friend, that we trust not to labor under this disadvantage much longer.

Through the aid of Mr. Estlin, and some other kind friends, we have been able to settle at the above school, to get such an education as we hope will enable us to do something for the liberties and the elevation of our enslaved countrymen.

And as writing becomes more easy to us, we will take great pleasure in sending you a few lines from time to time, to let you know how we are getting on. And will be much pleased if you will send us the *Liberator* occasionally, so that we may know what is going on.

We were very sorry that the slaveholders were successful enough to get a slave from Boston, but were much pleased with the difficulty they had in doing so.

We think a few more such cases as the Christiana affair will put a damper upon slave-catchers.

Please to remember us very kindly to Mr. Garrison, Mr. Wallcut, and all other inquiring friends,

And believe us to be,

Yours very truly,

W. & E. CRAFT.[44]

Ockham School, Nov. 10, 1852.

My Dear Mr. May—I know that you and other friends will heartily rejoice to hear that my wife has given birth to our first free born babe, on the 22d of October, and I am more than thankful to say that both he and his dear mother are now doing well. It is true, her sickness was of the severest nature, yet she bore it all firmly, and without a murmur, because she knew that she was not bringing a human being into the world to be brutified, but one whom the blessings of liberty and the pursuits of happiness may ever rest upon;

[44] The thrilling escape of William and Ellen Craft from Macon, Georgia, is very well known. Being an octoroon, she posed as the master of her husband, who drove her in a carriage through the land of slavery into freedom. They then went to England for safety and better opportunities.—*Liberator*, 1851.

for I assure you, my dear friend, nothing can be more consoling to the heart of a fugitive slave, than to look upon his new-born infant, and feel that there are no chains and fetters waiting in readiness to grasp and stunt his physical structure, and no hell-born despotism like American slavery hanging over his head, ready to drop, and crush his intellectual faculties to the dust, should they dare to expand beyond the tyrant's will.

We have heard of the very incorrect article which has been going the rounds of the American papers, that my wife wished to return to the barbarous land of whips and chains! But you know that the statement is entirely false, therefore I deem it unnecessary to say any more on this point.

I have just heard that another great man has passed away from our native country; and, oh! how I wish he had lived so that every slave and every other true lover of liberty might have seriously mourned his loss to society! But can my wife or myself, or any other victim of the Fugitive Slave Law, weep? No! for whenever we hear of a great genius like Daniel Webster being snatched from the world, with the innocent blood of a whole race clinging to his skirts, we can only say, Lord, have mercy upon him!

'Uncle Tom's Cabin' and the 'White Slave' are arousing a very great feeling of indignation in the English mind against America's peculiar institution.

We have received the *Liberator* regularly, and have always looked forward to its arrival with great pleasure, for it is the only American anti-slavery paper we have seen for months, except a few copies of Mr. Douglass's paper, and one copy of the *Standard*. We have also received Mr. Garrison's interesting volume, which he was kind enough to send us, and the *Liberty Bell* from Miss Weston. Do give our sincere thanks to them both, for I assure you we feel highly gratified, as well as honored, by receiving the paper and the books.

Our boy's name is Charles Estlin Phillips, after our kind friend Mr. Estlin of Bristol, and after Mr. Wendell Phillips, the eloquent champion of human liberty.

Ellen joins me in kind remembrances to yourself and other kind friends.

Yours, very truly,
WILLIAM CRAFT.[45]

[45] *Liberator*, Dec. 17, 1852.

The British Anti-Slavery Advocate introduced this letter thus:

In our last number, we mentioned that a strange report has gone the round of the slave States, to the effect that Ellen Craft had grown so tired of liberty, and of the blessings of education in England, and had become so lost to self-respect, that she had deserted her husband, and had placed herself under the protection of an American gentleman in London, on the express condition of his undertaking to restore her to that bondage from which she had so bravely emancipated herself. Of course, we did not believe this absurd calumny. Being personally acquainted with Mrs. Craft, we knew that such a course was simply impossible to one with her keen perceptions of the monstrous injustice and cruelty of slavery. Although her experience has not been by any means of the worst, it has been tremendous. No woman of refined feelings and vigorous understanding, such as she possesses, could wish to return to the Southern Sodom. However, to put the matter beyond doubt, we wrote directly to herself, and here is her answer :—

Ockham School, near Ripley, Surrey,
Oct. 26th, 1852.

DEAR SIR,—I feel very much obliged to you for informing me of the erroneous report which has been so extensively circulated in the American newspapers: 'That I had placed myself in the hands of an American gentleman in London, on condition that he would take me back to the family who held me as a slave in Georgia.' So I write these few lines merely to say that the statement is entirely unfounded, for I have never had the slightest inclination whatever of returning to bondage; and God forbid that I should ever be so false to liberty as to prefer slavery in its stead. In fact, since my escape from slavery, I have got on much better in every respect than I could have possibly anticipated. Though, had it been to the contrary, my feelings in regard to this would have been just the same, for I had much rather starve in England, a free woman, than be a slave for the best man that ever breathed upon the American continent.

                    Yours very truly,

                              ELLEN CRAFT.[45a]

[45a] *Liberator*, Dec. 17, 1852.

LONDON, April 21, 1851.

MY DEAR FRIEND MR. GARRISON:

I hardly know how to begin a letter to you, being as I am such a poor scholar; but I hope you will excuse my poor penmanship. I arrived safe in Liverpool on the 26th of last month, and I thank God for his kind mercy to me whilst crossing the sea; for, indeed, I had a very rough time of it. I was sick all the voyage over. I would have given any thing to have been at my journey's end before I was half way; but, withal, I thank God that I am a free man. I consider myself freer than I ever was before. I can call this, with safety, the land of the free and the brave. (1)

Your kind letter arrived a fortnight ahead of us. I have not language to express my thanks to you; for your letter has carried me far in London and Liverpool; and, likewise, that from Capt. Reese to the Rev. Mr. Burnet. Mr. B. received me very kindly indeed. He took me to two noblemen's houses, to see if he could not get me a situation as waiter, and thinks he shall succeed in it; and he took me to the exhibition. I cannot give you any idea of the things I saw there: they were so many in number, I cannot remember all. And I have seen Buckingham Palace, but have not yet seen her Majesty. She was in town when I went to the Duke of Wellington's house, with a letter for a gentleman there.

I got to London on the 13th of April, and was very kindly received at the depot by one of the Rev. Francis Bishop's friends, of Liverpool. They took us to his house, and got us lodgings for that night; and the next day he took us to the house of a friend of his, and we were kindly congratulated by them also. The Bishop of London could not have been kinder to his own brother than to us.

We had some very fine meetings while we were in Liverpool. My friend that is with me gave a lecture. I could not put confidence in myself to speak in a public meeting. I expect to speak in London tonight, (if God spares me)—but, O! I wish I had words to speak my gratitude to you for your kind letters. But there is One who can reward you better than I can. I have not forgotten to praise his holy name. No—blessed be God, I will praise him while I have breath. Although the slaveholders would not let me have a place in America to rest the soles of my feet, glory to God! I expect one day to have a place of rest, both for soul and body. I know, when I get there, the slaveholders cannot chase me—I shall be free as any white man. Is it not a blessed thing, that the poor black men have got a resting-place some where? I can tell you, my dear friend Mr. Garrison, if we should never meet in the flesh again, I expect to meet you, by the grace of God, in bright glory. Tell the slaveholders to go on, for God is about to take the poor negroes home to rest. Please to tell all the poor runaways to serve the true and living God, for he is able to deliver them safe through all trials and hard crosses. Please remember me to all my friends in Boston; the blessing of God on them is the prayer of their humble servant. Please to remember me to Captain Reese. I thank him kindly for his letter. Mr. Burnet is well, and wishes to be remembered to him. Please to tell Captain Reese that Mr. Jones has left.

Your most obedient servant,
FRANCIS S. ANDERSON.[46]

P. S. Mr. Duval desires his respects to Mr. May, and feels very thankful to him for a kind letter which he received from him, containing letters of introduction, and says he had a very pleasant passage over, not having had a day's sickness; and he desires that if any friends ask after him, that you will be so kind as to give his love to them, and tell them that he is quite as comfortable as can be expected under the circumstances in which, through divine providence, he is placed. And may the Lord bless the labors of the abolitionists!

This letter, together with the comment thereon, shows the aggressive attitude of many fugitive slaves in spite of the non-resistance doctrine of their best friends, the abolitionists.

SYRACUSE, April 28, 1854.

MY DEAR FRIEND—I want you to set me down as a *Liberator* man. Whether you will call me so or not, I am with you in heart. I may not be in hands and head—for my hands will fight a slaveholder—which I suppose THE LIBERATOR or some of its good friends would not do. But I do not say but they are doing more good in their way than I am in mine. I am a fugitive slave, and you know that we have strange notions about many things. But, notwithstanding, I will love THE LIBERATOR and its noble editor, WM. LLOYD GARRISON, because he has been for many years a standing and true friend to my poor people in slavery. His name is now known and loved by them even in the slave pens of the South. So let the name of WM. LLOYD GARRISON be borne on every breeze, until the chain shall be knocked off of the last slave!

I am, yours for liberty,   J. W. LOGUEN.

☞ This tribute from 'a fugitive slave,' in the person of our esteemed friend LOGUEN, is of course very gratifying to us. 'A true friend' to the colored population of this country, whether bond or free, we trust ever to remain. We are not surprised that Mr. LOGUEN, educated as he has been, is unable to accept the doctrine of non-resistance, while hourly in danger of being seized by prowling slave-hunters, and carried back to the South; but he will yet realize the truth, we hope, that it is solely because of war and violence that slavery exists; because the slaveholders and slave-hunters are not non-resistants, that they can hold and hunt slaves; and because there are so few disposed to return good for evil, that injustice and oppression are so universal. The principle which disarms the slave, at the same moment disarms his master also, and therefore renders the enslavement of any human being impossible. But while men claim the right to kill their fellow-men at discretion, to subserve their own interests or protect their own rights, the spirit of usurpation will continue to prevail in the world. Rely upon it, the philosophy of Jesus, in regard to the treatment of enemies, as taught and exemplified by him, is divinely adapted to all exigencies, and effectual to the overthrow of all forms of oppression. In comparison with 'Uncle Tom,' for real moral grandeur of character and the spirit of unconquerable goodness, how low is the plane on which they stand who believe in the war principle! Such are our views—but, 'Let every man be fully persuaded in his own mind,' and true to his own convictions of duty.—*Ed. Lib.*[47]

The case of Anthony Burns is as dramatic as that of any of the efforts at rescuing fugitives in the North. Through the intercession of friends he finally obtained his freedom and, after undergoing some training, became a useful man.

MR. EDITOR: DEAR SIR:—Having seen a piece from a Richmond (Va.) paper, stating that I was in the Massachusetts Penitentiary,

[47] *Liberator,* May 5, 1854.

I avail myself of the opportunity to say that the accusation is a lie without a father. I am not, nor neither have I been, nor do I expect to be in the Penitentiary, unless some one should attempt to deprive me of my liberty, as before—then I would enforce the motto of Patrick Henry, 'Liberty or Death.'

Again; if such had been the case, I should only have fallen back into the midst of such a class of individuals as I was among before my escape from the South—that of liars, cradle-robbers, thieves, murderers, whoremongers and idolaters, such as ought to be in the Penitentiary for the murdered mothers, children, fathers, sisters and brothers of the South.

I now call the attention of the public to the place where I have been residing since my return from the South. I have for two years been prosecuting my studies in Ohio at Oberlin Institute— the light of the world—and since that time at Fairmount Theological Seminary, Cincinnati—striving hard, with the aid of my friends, to store my mind with that knowledge which I have been deprived of by slavery, &c. I have no doubt but that I shall find friends enough, with abundant means, who will aid me in my noble object.

I am now in Maine, making preparations to travel with a panorama, styled the Grand Moving Mirror—scenes of real life, startling and thrilling incidents, degradation and horrors of American slavery—for the purpose of selling my book, a narrative, giving a full account of my life in slavery from childhood, with many other facts connected with the system of slavery. The proceeds are to enable me to complete my studies, at which time friends will have the opportunity of seeing, hearing, reading and knowing for themselves.

I have no doubt but there are some who would be glad if the above report was true. The gentleman who thus informed the public that I am now in the Massachusetts Penitentiary wished to be kicked into notice, and who, like Balaam's ass, would not have spoken if his master had not given him an awful lashing. Whoever he may be, I can assure him that he shall never be kicked into notice by me.

ANTHONY BURNS,[48]
of Boston, Mass.

[48] *Liberator*, Aug. 13, 1858.

VII. DR. JAMES McCUNE SMITH, MACON B. ALLEN AND WILLIAM G. ALLEN

Taking up the question statistically, Dr. James McCune Smith published in the *New York Tribune* the following in the form of letters evoked by a lecture delivered by Dr. Orville Dewey. A graduate of the University of Glasgow, Dr. Smith had not only distinguished himself in his practice in New York City but also in such discussions of the race problem as the following.

FREEDOM AND SLAVERY FOR AFRICANS.

Rev. ORVILLE DEWEY, D. D.:

SIR,—A report of the Lecture delivered by you last night, which you will find in the New-York Tribune of this morning, contains the following sentence:

'Emancipation has taken place here, (in the free States,) yet the blacks are worse off than the slaves of the South—not being so well clothed, fed or so happy.'

Presuming the above to be a correct report of your remarks, I beg to say that, being the son of a slave, owing my liberty to the Emancipation Act of the State of New-York, and having kindred in a southern State, some of them slaveholders, others slaves, I feel proposition which you have announced as above. And I hold myself prepared to prove, either in oral discussion, or in any manner you may choose:

1st. That the free blacks of the free States are *not* worse off than the slaves of the South.

2dly. That they are better fed than the slaves.

3dly. That they are better clothed than the slaves.

In regard to the last clause of the proposition, the term 'happy' will bear various interpretations. If, by that term, you mean, insensibility to degradation, an ignorance of, and therefore carelessness regarding, human responsibility, with a consequent enjoyment of the '*alterum cum belluis commune*,' then you are right in asserting that the slaves are happier than the free blacks; but if you affix to the term 'happy,' a human signification, I will show,

4thly. That the free blacks are happier than the slaves; and

5thly. That the experiment of emancipation in the free States, proves the safety and expediency of emancipation—being the 'angel voice' teaching the South how to act.

In seeking to discuss this matter with you, Rev. sir, I am impelled by the same motives which led you to deliver the lecture of last evening—with this difference, *you* stood up to defend 'American Manners and Morals' from assaults which are seasoned with some variety and originality; *I* am forced to defend a class of our countrymen from stereotyped libels of unmitigated platitude. These libels had their origin in the American Colonization Society, which found them profitable in a pecuniary point of view; they have been industriously retailed by foreigners who may be excused when they *lie* for their bread—but when the same libels are dovetailed into a hollow argument, by the able, the eloquent, the manly Mr. Dewey, it is time they should be met and tried at the bar of public opinion.

They assume a serious form when endorsed by your highly respectable name, and I am forced to 'call you out' to defend your proposition which contains them. So long as they were confined to the interested, I was willing, along with my colored brethren, to live them down; but now, when they are uttered by the disinterested and the candid, it is clear, that they are gaining a credence which will operate fatally against our efforts at improvement, and even against our opportunities to earn our bread. Bereft of the support which slaves receive, and yet partially enslaved—burdened with all the responsibilities of freemen, but denied a large share of the rights of citizenship—our *good name* is all we have left us (under God) in our struggle for sustenance and for advancement. You, sir, have robbed us of our *good name;* and it is fair and manly that you should afford us the opportunity to repair the mischief which might thereby befal us. You have done the act inadvertently, repeating the hearsay of others; but I am mistaken in you, if you will inadvertently trample upon the weak, and then shut your ears against their appeal for justice.

In this matter I have no vindictive feeling to pacify, no insulted pride to avenge, no soaring ambition to gratify—but am governed by a sincere and single desire to make known the facts in regard to the free people of color—facts which will show a steady improvement in their condition since their emancipation—facts which will take away the reproach from that portion of Freedom which has been granted them—facts which will open the eyes of

candid men to the falsehood of the assertions that 'Freedom, in
this Republic, is no boon to the black man,' and 'That there are
difficulties in the way of the South AFTER emancipation.' It is important to those whom you have libelled, that these facts should be
attached to a name sufficiently prominent to attract public attention, hence yours has been selected: and it has been chosen for the
additional reason that you are a man open to conviction, and of
sufficient independence to obey your convictions, come what may.

Let me beg that you will accept this proposal. It comes from
the lowly, and is addressed to the lofty; yet it is from man to man.
Do not let the 'impassable barrier' of a difference in complexion
hinder you from the contest: *Truth* and *Justice* know no complexion, and their followers should emulate their example. Let us
reason together on this subject, and I doubt not that you will find
that the Providence of the Almighty, in regard to the Free Blacks
of these States, is one of the most interesting displays yet opened
to the observation of man.

> Very respectfully, your obedient servant,
> JAMES M'CUNE SMITH.[49]

New York, January 11th, 1844.

FREEDOM AND SLAVERY FOR AFRIC-AMERICANS.

TO THE EDITOR OF THE TRIBUNE:

Figures cannot be charged with fanaticism. Like the everlasting hills, they give cold, silent evidence, unmoved by the clouds
and shadows of whatever present may surround them. Let us see
what they say of the

VITAL STATISTICS

of the slaves of the South, and of the free blacks of the North.
There are one or two preliminary remarks necessary to enable us
to judge of this matter: they relate to what statists call the 'disturbing influences.' It is generally assumed that the rigor of the
northern winter is more destructive to the Afric-American constitution than the milder influence of the southern clime. How much
should be allowed for this, I am at a loss to say: by the late census,
however, the free colored population of the northern and southern
States have nearly an equal per centage above 36 years of age, not
more than 1, 12 per cent. being in favor of the South. But this

49 *Liberator*, Feb. 16, 1844.

small per centage is more than balanced by the facility with which colored men and women turn white at the North. The keen and practised eyes of Southern men can instantly detect the most remote admixture of African blood; and interest and pride urge them to exercise a rigid conservatism. But here at the North, the boundary line is less distinct: the colored white has merely to change his place of abode, cut his old associates, and courtesy will do the rest—he is a white. There is not a path in literature or science in our State, in which I could not point out very distinguished colored men. Of one hundred boys who attended with me in the N. Y. African Free School in 1826–7, I could name six now living—all white.

There is another 'disturbing influence.' You have probably heard of the great Anglo-Saxon race, the Irish people, and the Bersekirs. You have also heard of their indomitable energy, which overwhelms all opposing obstacles and races. During the last thirty years, the Northern States have been the scene of a silent struggle. The combatants have been and are, on the one hand, the great Anglo-Saxon race, the Irish people and the Bersekirs, (I have borrowed the name from Mr. Emerson,) having in their possession the 'arts of war and peace,' their numbers swelled by an immigration of 23,000 per year, which has fallen into rank and file by naturalization and enfranchising laws—on the other hand, are the free blacks, taught to believe themselves naturally inferior, barely admitted to common school instruction, shut out from the temples of higher literature, and taunted with ignorance, barred from the jury bench, and driven from what are called churches, yet branded with impiety. This has been no trifling conflict. The Indian race have perished in a like encounter. It has severely tried the vitality of the free blacks, whilst the slaves of the South have had no such battle to fight in their struggle for bread. This should show the percentage of longevity in favor of the slaves, other things being equal.

The Texan slave-trade, or migration, consisted chiefly of slaves under 36. The voluntary migration to Canada of the runaway slaves (about 10,000) has also consisted, chiefly, of a class of persons under 36 years of age. Both of these disturbing influences would throw the balance of longevity largely in favor of the slaves of the South; for the medium ages being diminished, the extremes should be greater.

Longevity is an admitted test of relative condition. Take two classes of persons, equal in other respects, and place them in like condition, their longevity will be equal: place the same classes of persons in different condition, and that condition which yields less longevity will be the *worse* condition. By the census of 1840, it appears that there are of

FREE COLORED IN THE FREE STATES,

	Males.	Females.
Aged 36 and under 55—16.12 per ct.		15.62 per ct.
" 55 and under 100—6.5 per ct.		7.1 per ct.

SLAVES.

	Males.	Females.
Aged 36 and under 55—11.65 per ct.		11.22 per ct.
" 55 and under 100—4.11 per ct.		4. per ct.

THAT IS TO SAY:

Free colored of 36 and under 100—22.68 per cent.
Slaves   36 and under 100—15.49 per cent.

Difference,   7.19

Here we find that whilst 22.68 per cent. of the free black population of the North live beyond 36 years of age, only 15.49 per cent. of the slaves of the South pass that period of life; showing a difference of 7.19 per cent. in favor of the longevity, i. e. of the *condition* of the free blacks. And as the only difference between these classes of population is, that the one is free and the other enslaved, it follows that slavery has actually destroyed at the very least 7.19 per cent. of the slave population. Had the slaves been in no worse condition than the free blacks of the North, instead of numbering only 2,487,355 in June, 1840, they would have numbered 2,666,440, the difference, 179,085, having been MURDERED by the system of slavery. What mockery it is for men to talk of the kindness of masters in taking care of aged slaves, when Death has relieved them of so large a share of the burden! Have not the Northern States a right, in view of this awful fact, to call upon the South to emancipate her slaves, so that she may 'do no murder?' If a hundred thousand dollars, sunk in the mire of repudiation, is sufficient cause for great and pious men to whine about, what rush of sympathy is sufficiently rapid, what language is intemperate, which pleads for the loss of a hundred thousand human lives, cut off in their prime, and blasted from all usefulness? This is no accidental result of a single census. By reference to Professor Tucker's very able work on the 'Progress of Population,' &c. (press of Hunt's Merch. Mag. N. Y.) it will be seen that in the census of 1820 and 1830, the same per centage of the slave population, only 15 per cent. live beyond the age of 36 years, while the free black population has steadily improved its per centage beyond that period of life from 17 per cent. to 22.68 per cent.

Here, then, is evidence from unprejudiced witnesses, that the free blacks of the North are *not* worse off than the slaves of the South; and that the former have gradually improved in longevity: that is, in the comforts of life, since their emancipation. As a portion of these comforts must be food and clothing, it is a fair inference that they are not worse fed or clothed than are the slaves.

There is corroborative evidence in the annals of this city. Dr. Niles states that in 1824, '5 and '6, the deaths among the free black population of this city was 1 in 18.88. By the City Inspector's Report of 1840, I find that the deaths of the same class were only one in 32.16. Slavery was abolished, or terminated, in New-York in 1827; and a large proportion of those who died in 1825, &c. were slaves recently emancipated. These facts prove, that within fifteen years after it became a free State, a portion of the free black population of New-York have improved the ratio of their mortality 75 per cent.—a fact without parallel in the history of any people.

It is a prevalent opinion, that emancipation has made the free blacks deaf, dumb, blind, idiots, insane, &c. &c. The Southern Literary Messenger has quite a pretty theory on this subject, based upon certain statements, announced as facts in the census of 1840. An editor at Buffalo, and subsequently Dr. Jarvis of Dorchester, Mass., have demolished that theory by proving that the statements announced in the census were not facts. Those statements made Maine a very mad-house, yet they contradict themselves in the following manner. In that State, saith the census of 1840:

TOWNS.	Total col'd inhab.	Col'd insane.
Limerick,	0	4
Lymington,	1	2
Scarboro'	0	6
Poland,	0	2
Dixfield,	0	4
Calais,	0	1
Total,	1	19

To make 19 crazy men out of one man, is pretty fair calculation even for 'down east.' The census is equally incorrect as to the proportion of deaf, dumb, &c. Freedom has not made us mad; it has strengthened our minds by throwing us upon our own resources, and has bound us to American institutions with a tenacity which nothing but death can overcome.

Very gratefully yours,

JAMES M'CUNE SMITH.[50]

New-York, Jan. 29, 1844.

FREEDOM AND SLAVERY FOR AFRIC-AMERICANS.

No. III.

In regard to the intellectual statistics of the slaves, it is well known that the laws of all the slave States, by heavy penalties—in some, *death*, for the second offense—prohibit the teaching of the slaves to read. In Ohio and the northwestern States, there is no such law, nor is there any public provision for the instruction of colored children; yet there are many schools, supported by the people of color, in those States. All the free States, east of Ohio, afford public instruction, alike to white and colored children.

Who are worse off, the slaves, whose children are doomed to brutal ignorance, or the few blacks of the North, the offspring of whom are for the most part permitted to enjoy common school education? The answer depends on the extent to which the parents of the latter, embrace their superior privileges. In our own State, to a population of 50,000, there are twenty-two public schools for colored children. In this city, to a population of about 17,000, there are seven public, and four private schools for colored children, with two exceptions, taught by colored teachers. The average attendance of colored children at the public schools, by the last report, was 1,031 per day. From a document issued by the board of trustees of the public schools, (in March, 1842,) I have carefully made the following statement of the relative standing of the boys in the 8th and 9th classes: Number 1 being best, 2, good, &c. &c.

---

[50] *Liberator*, Feb. 16, 1844.

	White boys.	Colored boys.
Reading	2.18	2.50
Punctuation	2.59	1.75
Spelling	2.31	2.50
Definition	3.03	3.25
Arithmetic	1.87	2.25
Grammar	2.73	2.50
Geography	1.75	2.00
Astronomy	1.66	2.00
Slate writing	2.46	2.00
Paper writing	2.71	3.00
Total average	2.32	2.47

Showing a difference of 15, about 1-7, in favor of the white boys.

The whole number of schools among the free black population of the North, is 66.   There are a large number of colored youth attending white schools; some of them are pursuing the higher branches of education, at Oberlin, Western Theological Seminary, Lafayette College, Dartmouth College, and Oneida Institute. There are, in the free States, sixteen colored literary societies, with libraries varying from 100 to 1,400 volumes; and there are one semi-monthly and three weekly papers, edited by colored men, and devoted to the advancement of the people of color.   There are also one hundred and nineteen benevolent societies.   All these schools, &c. have been established within the last forty years.   Have the free black population made no improvement since the emancipation? If it be true, that we have not yet produced any literature worthy the name, it is because we are waiting for the Anglo-Americans to lead the way.   The next subject is

Religious Statistics.

African churches in the slave States,	24
African churches in the free States,	114

(*United States Gazeteer: History of the African Methodist Episcopal Church, by the Rev. Christopher Rush, New-York*, 1843.)   Including bond and free, the whole colored population of the slave States, is 2,702,920; the colored population of the free States is 170,718.   The African churches in the slave States are, nearly all of them, the property of the free colored population of those States: but, granting them *all* to the slaves, there are in the slave States, one church to 112,620 slaves, in the free States, one church to 1,580 free blacks. Of the colored churches in the free States, 103 have been erected within 43 years. It is true that these churches have not quite so much of the "temple made with hands," as may be seen in some Broadway edifices, yet they are endowed, in one respect at least, with a more Catholic spirit—they are "no respecters of persons."

It may be thought that I underrate the religious advantages of the slaves, because the Methodist and some other churches reckon many thousands slaves in their communion. But these churches grant nothing but *oral instruction* to the slaves, whom they do not teach to read the Bible. And may I not be excused from calling that "Christian fellowship," which expressly denies the common rights of men to those whom they have enrolled as brethren ! Are those churches, wherein bishops, priests, and deacons, ministers, and preachers who

Perfusi sanie vittas atroque veneno,

their hands bound and their utterance choked, whilst in their ministrations before the altar, not of God, but of slavery, they croak the changes upon *"Servants obey your masters?"* Such are the churches in the slave States, with one exception; let it be written upon every Protestant brow, for that one is the Roman Catholic Church—her doors, and her consolations are open alike to black and white, bond and free ! She alone does not make, in the church militant, distinctions, which it were blasphemy to predicate of the Church triumphant.

In view of the schools, churches, and benevolent institutions organized *by her free black population, under the genial smile of emancipation,* may not the North, affectionately, earnestly, and reasonably, call upon the South to follow the example ? This question has additional force when we find that a blessing has followed those of the free States, which have acted justly towards their free black population. New-York, led on by her Murrays, Jays, and Tompkins—Massachusetts, yielding to the common-sense argument of Paul Cuffee, and Rhode Island, urged by a bloodless revolution, have pre-eminently encouraged and fostered their free black population: and these are noble States and prosperous, their sons need be proud of them in either hemisphere or any clime. Pennsylvania, in 1838, cruelly disfranchised her free colored people, and in 1843— she became bankrupt. Men who look deeper than the surface of things will perceive in the former act, a moral obliquity, to which the latter was a necessary sequence.

I now, respectfully, submit the case. Let the public judge whether it be made out. If, to have a right over his own person, be better than to be deprived of that right,—if, to possess his own wife, be better than to hold her at another's will—if, to enjoy common school privileges, be better than the doom of brutal ignorance—if, to sit under his own gospel vine, be better than to listen to alien adjurations to passive obedience—if, to live long in the land, be better than to be cut off in life's early prime—then the free blacks of the North are *not* worse off than the slaves of the South. The evidence is altogether in favor of emancipation.

Much has been said about the free black population of the North, filling the almshouses. Some inquiry enables me to state that most of them to be found in these almshouses, are those who have escaped, maimed, halt, or blind, from the slavery of the South, or remain from the slavery of our now free states. In 1836 the free colored people of Philadelphia, paid into the poor fund of that city, $500 more than was required to support colored paupers living at the public expense. In the city of New-York, the colored population is to the white as 1 to 18.1; of 3,089 persons in the almshouse department on Saturday, January 20, 1844, there were 198 colored persons, about 1 colored to 15.5 white. In the lunatic asylum, December 23, 1843, there were 278 white and 17 colored patients: or 1 colored to 17 white: taking into account the number of whites in private institutions, it would seem that there is less insanity among the colored than the white population.

I cannot conclude without pointing out two sources of the errors which many commit in judging of the free black population. One is, that men, ignorant of our actual condition, and hindered by their prejudices, from inquiring thereinto, gather their opinions of us from specimens visible in the Five Points—they seem satisfied by a single glance at the "deformed leg." Again, men of narrow views and limited information are apt to conceive that society and refinement are confined to the little heaven in which they are privileged to "thunder," regarding all as outcasts—*barbaroi*—who are not embraced within their charmed environ: such men cannot perceive that there is around every intelligent "home," all the elements of refined manners and dignified deportment. They are, thank heaven, a thousand such homes among the free blacks of the free States—

homes, in which the sounds of "my wife," "my child," "my mother," "my father," *"my Bible,"* and their thousand clustering joys, weave the sweet harmonies of content and happiness. We toil hard for these, but we toil willingly, with stout and hopeful hearts. And, if, occasionally, one from "wandering to and fro over the face of the earth," be sent among us, to try us with the affliction of a Parthian warfare, we shall be found at our post, ready and willing to give an account of the faith that is in us—a faith which holds first to the Bible, and secondly, to American institutions, which have made us free, which will free our brethren in bonds, and which will be triumphant in pulling down the strongholds of tyranny throughout our globe.

I sincerely thank you, Mr. Editor, for your kind liberality in publishing these letters without money or price, but with perfect typographical accuracy. With your clear head and sound heart, long may you preside over the Tribune of the people. Very gratefully yours,

JAMES M'CUNE SMITH.[51]

MACON B. ALLEN

Macon B. Allen, a Negro lawyer, got into trouble by refusing to sign a pledge not to sustain the government in its war with Mexico, apparently waged to acquire slave territory. It did not suffice when Allen explained that as a lawyer he had taken the oath to support the Constitution of the United States.

BOSTON, June 1, 1846.

MR. GARRISON:

DEAR SIR:—An incident occurred at the late Anti-Slavery Convention, in Faneuil Hall, on Thursday last, in relation to myself, which I think it proper for me to notice. I should have sought an explanation of it at the time, but the Convention being almost in the act of finally adjourning, and every moment seeming to be required for the despatch of their business, I did not wish to interrupt them.

When papers were being circulated for pledges of persons not to sustain the government in any event, in the present war with Mexico, a gentleman, whom I do not know, came to me, and pressed me to sign one of them. Feeling that I could not sign the paper, and

[51] *New York Tribune,* 1844.

wishing, without touching the merits of the subject, to give him my most prominent reason for declining, I softly told him that I was under oath to support the laws of the country, and must, therefore, be excused. It is generally known, I presume, that a lawyer has to take this oath before he can be admitted to practice.

To my great surprise, a few minutes after this, I heard this gentleman, in answer to some question as to his progress in getting signatures, openly announce, to the *whole house*, that *I* had refused to sign the pledge.

Now, I assume, primarily, that in the fact itself, whether I did, or did not, sign the pledge, there was not, nor could there possibly be, the slightest importance, not equally applicable to the like action on the part of any other person at the Convention. And I charge that the conduct of that gentleman, towards me, was highly indecorous. It was a breach of good manners and conventional usage, and a wanton disregard of one's feelings, which I did not expect would be committed by any one who had any duty assigned him in so respectable a meeting. Why was he thus personal, singling out an individual? Did he wish to hold me up to the public animadversion, upon his partial statement? Did he wish to make it appear that I care not for the condition of the slave? If so, my own conscience acquits me of any such imputation. Though not in the habit of declaring what sentiments I entertain, deeming it of little consequence, I trust that it will not seem presumptuous if I embrace this occasion, thus brought about, to say, that I sympathize as strongly with my brethren in bonds—with whom I am identified in almost every particular—as my nature, not a cold one, enables me to do; and, according to the light that is in me, and my humble ability, am ever ready and willing to do all I can for their melioration. The cause of the colored man, in whatever section of our country, especially, is really my own cause; and it would be monstrous indeed, if I did not so regard it.

I ask my friends who may have been prejudiced against me, by the course of the gentleman, to be assured that there is no cause for such prejudice.

With great respect,

MACON B. ALLEN.[52]

[52] *Liberator*, June 5, 1846.

WILLIAM G. ALLEN

In this letter of William G. Allen, of McGrawville, New York, Horace Mann, known as a friend of the Negro, is adversely criticised on account of his views with respect to the emigration of the blacks to the tropical regions; but he is defended from the attacks of the Negroes in New Bedford, Massachusetts, who, reading his remarks on the native ability of the race, received the impression that he considered the Negro inferior.

FREDERICK DOUGLASS, ESQ.:

DEAR SIR—I regret exceedingly that the colored citizens of New Bedford, Mass., should have taken umbrage at an extract of a letter sent by Horace Mann to the colored Convention in Cincinnati, held in January last. The resolutions recently passed by them (the colored citizens of N. B.) seem to be hasty and ill-advised; and certainly do injustice to a noble man, who has given abundant evidence of sincere love for the oppressed millions of America.

Mr. Mann believes, that as compared with the Caucasian, the African is inferior in intellect, but superior in sentiment and affection. Certainly there is nothing terrible in this, and nothing which by any means can be construed as disparaging to the African race, but rather as exalting it. The heart is king of the head. In that better day when mere calculating intellect (for this is the kind of intellect in which the Caucasian excels the African) shall have only its place—and no more, the African will unquestionably stand at the head of a true civilization. Mr. Mann exalts the African race above *all* the races, not only Caucasian, but Mongolian, and others, in sentiment and affection.

Mr. Mann also believes that independent nations of each race may be greatly improved by the existence of independent nations of other races. I believe so too: while at the same time I believe that all nations are made of one blood, to dwell upon all the face of the earth; and that human beings who are equal in character are equal to one another. It is convenient that this world should be divided into nations, as it is convenient that a community should be divided into families.

Mr. Mann believes further, that there is a band of territory around the earth on each side of the equator, which belongs to the

African race; and that the commotions of the earth have jostled them out of their place, to which they will be restored when the terrible crimes which displaced them shall be succeeded by reason and justice. I believe so too: but differ with Mr. Mann in regarding the colored people of this country as an *African* race, in contradistinction from any other. The colored people of this country are essentially a *mixed* race. Already more than half Anglo-Saxonized, it will not take Henry Clay's two hundred years to make them *wholly* such. At this moment, there sits at my side a young man of two-thirds Anglo-Saxon blood: now, since he is to be designated by either the term African or Anglo-Saxon, what propriety or scientific accuracy is there in calling him an African, since Anglo-Saxon blood predominates? Among the hundreds of colored people whom Mr. Mann has seen at Washington, those who represented in their purity the African color and features, were but a fraction of a fraction, while many, very many of the so-called colored people were as white as himself. It is by no means uncommon for travellers from the North to remark, that in promenading a Southern city, it is frequently a puzzle to tell, so far as complexion is concerned, who is the slave and who is the master. No one can be surprised at these results, who understands the character of slavery.

I repeat, I believe as Mr. Mann does, that when the commotions of the earth are settled, the African race will be restored to the territory of earth on each side of the equators; but by the African race, I do not mean the colored people of this country. So, also, I believe if slavery were abolished to-morrow, there would be an overwhelming tide of emigration to the South, on the part of the colored people of the Northern States, and of Canada; and for the reason that that is the soil on which they were born, and which is congenial to their nature.

Had Mr. Mann come out point blank in favor of Colonization, it would have been well for our New Bedford friends to pass their resolutions; but as he has simply uttered a theory which, considered scientifically, means no wrong, I cannot but regard our friends as acting hastily, and even ungenerously, towards a great and noble man. Whether Horace Mann has outgrown fully the prejudice of color which he learned in his youth, I know not; but this I know, he has a generous nature, and deserves to be approached, not as we approach those whose hearts are little and minds narrow. So far, however, as the action of our New Bedford friends may be regarded as a protest against the Colonization Society, I rejoice at it. The idea of going to Africa is not a horrible one to me; but the idea of being the white man's slave or pet in Africa any more than in America, is to me worse than horrible—it is 'terrible horrible.'

Sincerely yours,

WILLIAM G. ALLEN.

McGrawville, Oct. 25, 1852.[53]

LONDON, Eng., 26 Swinton street,
June 20, 1853.

WM. LLOYD GARRISON, ESQ.:

DEAR SIR,—I cannot resist the temptation to address you a few lines; if for no other purpose, certainly to thank you for the very kind letter which I found at JOSEPH STURGE'S. That letter was an introduction to one of the dearest men (GEORGE THOMPSON) with whom it has ever been my lot to become acquainted. We have visited Mr. Thompson several times, and though I had heard him on the platform, and was filled (as who has not been?) with admiration of his genius and efforts in behalf of the oppressed of both hemispheres, yet it was not until I had enjoyed his home circle that I had a full appreciation of the loftiness of his character, as it is evinced in his child-like simplicity. Mr. Thompson is hardly less eloquent in conversation than in public speaking, and one cannot leave his house, after spending a day or an evening with him, without feeling himself invigorated in mind and heart, and in better love with whatsoever things are beautiful and true.

'Old England' is a wonderful country. There is grandeur in the looks of it. There is poetry, too—the ride from Liverpool to London taking one through a region of country all the way blossoming as the rose. The English people, too—I am in love with them. There is nobility in their hearts and dignity in their bearing. They have also a quiet repose of character, which is certainly a pleasing contrast to the hurly-burly of the American.

That in Englishmen which most favorably impresses the colored man from America is the entire absence of prejudice against color. Here the colored man feels himself among friends, and not among enemies;—among a people who, when they treat him well, do it not in the patronising (and, of course, insulting) spirit, even of hundreds of the American abolitionists, but in a spirit rightly appreciative of the doctrine of human equality. Color claims no precedence over character, here; and, consequently, in parties given by the 'first people' in the kingdom may be seen persons of all colors moving together on terms of perfect social equality. Rev. SAMUEL R. WARD, of Canada, than whom it is hardly possible to be blacker, and who is an honor to the race in intellectual ability, has been in London several weeks, and can amply testify to the fact that his skin, though 'deepest dyed,' has been no barrier to the best society in the kingdom. Mr. Ward and myself were both present, by invitation, a few evenings since, at a party given by the Prussian Ambassador, at his residence in Regent's Park. That which, in an American community, would startle it more than seven thunders could—i. e., the marriage (or even the surmise of it) of two respectable persons, one of whom should be white and the other colored, passes as a *matter of course* in England. In no party, whether public or private, to which we have been, in no walk which we have taken, in no hotel at which we have had occasion to put up, in no public place of amusement, gallery, museum, &c., have we met the cry of 'amalgamation,' either outspoken, or as manifested in a well-bred sneer. This state of things, of course, evinces that prejudice against color is entirely a local feeling, generated by slavery, and which must disappear, not only as colored men rise higher and higher in the light of intelligence and virtue, but as the dominant race in America becomes wiser and more liberalized by the spirit of a true Christianity.

I must not forget to tell you of what pleasant evenings we have spent with Mrs. Follen and Miss Cabot. They were pleasant, because spent in the society of true and noble-hearted women, warm in their sympathies and active in their efforts in behalf of the enslaved millions of America. These noble American women—how long could slavery last, did America count such by the hundreds?

I must not forget to tell you, also, of a pleasant evening with Mr. ESTLIN—hardly a stranger to those who have read THE LIBERATOR, and a blessed good man and warm friend of humanity. Here we met many good friends of the cause from America, some of them quite recently.

Mrs. STOWE has gone to Paris. Her visit to this country has created much sensation. The papers here criticise both the Professor and Mrs. Stowe variously, and one or two, I think, unjustly; especially those that intimate that she is seeking self-glorification.

MRS. Stowe has never suffered martyrdom, and, however much others may honor her, she has too much sense and piety, and is too great-hearted, to covet honors which more properly belong to those who have led on in the fore-front of this battle.

J. MILLER MCKIM, Esq., of Philadelphia, has also gone to Paris. Miss SARAH PUGH leaves, in a few days, in company with Mrs. FOLLEN, for Switzerland. Dr. BAILEY, of the *National Era*, is in the city, and so also is Rev. J. FREEMAN CLARK, formerly of Boston; the latter I have seen.

Our friend WM. WELLS BROWN is as active as ever. There seems to be no end to his enterprise. He has, beyond a doubt, been a most efficient laborer in this country in the great cause of anti-slavery. Mr. FARMER and himself have aided us much in ferreting out notable places and getting a sight of notable people—for which we thank them both.

Rev. S. R. WARD holds a meeting to-night in Freemason's Chapel—the Earl of Shaftsbury in the chair—to consider measures for aiding the fugitives in Canada. Ward will be successful.

I rejoice exceedingly that you had so good a meeting in New York. It may be that slavery and compromise have not quite eaten out the heart of the nation, and that there is yet hope.

What a speech was that of DOUGLASS! A masterly production, and which should gain him immortal honor. Some of the criticisms upon it by the American papers would be villanous, if they were not so ridiculous, and some again are amusing. That was decidedly cool of Thurlow Weed, that 'if'—'if Douglass's great mind were imbued with kindlier sympathies'!! Now, it is all proper enough that all men, in whatever relation of life, should feel kind towards each other; but only think of it—asking, not the man who strikes, but the stricken, to be kinder. Surely, slavery has made bad work with the heart and conscience of the American people. It is the reformer's duty not to be content with *ameliorating*, as Weed would have Douglass do, but only in *rooting out* evil. Radicalism is the only ism that ever blessed the world, or ever will or can. These conservatives are singular folks. They have neither genius nor philosophy. They would have their boy learn to swim by making his motions upon the sand-bank; and neither he that led on the barbaric host against the gates of imperial Rome, nor Luther, ever would be model-men of theirs.

But I must not make you too long a letter. You know all about the Exeter Hall meeting.   Whatever may be its results, I am satisfied of one thing—it is directly to the point to get up a public sentiment against slavery abroad.   Slaveholders must be driven into isolation; and I am very glad to know that they themselves are finding out that the thing is being done.   I have but little sympathy for the feeling which apologises for and explains away their sins, on the plea of converting them to the truth.   A single self-application of the Golden Rule would open the whole subject to them, in its length and breadth, and height and depth.

Now is an excellent time to spread anti-slavery truth among the people of this country.   I shall do what I can (little though, of course, it will be) to help bring about the time when

> 'Worth, not birth, shall rule mankind,
> And be acknowledged stronger.'

Our passage from America to England was a pleasant one, barring the melancholy accident—the loss of four sailors at sea—of which you already know; and our stay of two weeks in Liverpool was rendered more than agreeable by the kindness of our mutual friend, WM. P. POWELL, Esq., formerly of New York.   Mr. STURGE, also, of Birmingham, received us with great kindness and cordiality, and has placed us under many obligations to him for his friendly deportment towards us.

We are in good health, and, you may well imagine, we enjoy life.   There is but one drawback; the light of British liberty has revealed more clearly than ever the inner chambers of the American prison-house of bondage, and disclosed how more than mangled and bleeding are the victims that lie therein.   This makes me sad, but more determined to work on and work ever.

Very faithfully yours,
WM. G. ALLEN.[54]

L. Kossuth, visiting this country to arouse interest in the elevation of his oppressed countrymen, soon found himself face to face with the abolition movement, similar in many respects to the cause which he was promoting.   To espouse abolitionism as the antislavery groups urged him, however, would have doomed his mission to failure.   As he did not respond favorably to the proposal thus to express

[54] *Liberator*, July 22, 1853.

himself, he incurred the displeasure and invited the attacks of the friends of freedom as the letters of S. R. Ward and William G. Allen show.

FREDERICK DOUGLASS, ESQ.—DEAR SIR:—You have seen the address of the colored people of New York city to Kossuth. What a stupendously foolish thing! Not a word of their own wrongs—their sufferings—their enslavement;—no point, no directness, no nothing, except the mere rhetoric. Palaver, the whole of it; and to cap the climax of absurdities, the address winds up with the assurance to the Hungarian, that, on the day of giving, they (the colored people) will be on hand with at least the 'widow's mite,' if no more. Where did mortal man ever read of such folly as this before? Just as though, if the colored people are to invest money for the benefit of the oppressed, justice, consistency, and the commonest self-respect, do not require that such money should be expended in some way for the benefit of the four millions in our own land who are ground to the dust in chains and slavery, and the tens of thousands of others, who, by cruel laws and customs are kept in poverty and degradation.

The men who wrote that address are not fools. No equal number of men in the Union can present a greater amount of native intellect and talent; and in education and accomplishments, some of the members of that committee are by no means inferior to the most favored of their oppressors. How much the more guilty then are they! I cannot let them go gently by. Though no other colored man should speak out, I, for one, will do so; and let it be known that there is at least one of the oppressed in America, whose feelings that address, lacking, as it does, so much of vitality, does not represent, and who can find next to nothing to applaud in so ridiculous a performance.

The address, milk and water as it was, failed to make any impression upon Kossuth; and, as a matter of course, he treated those who presented it with the most withering contempt. *'Gentlemen, the time for addresses is past, and the time for action has come.'* If that isn't 'summary,' I should like to know what is? Poor men! how they must have felt as they sneaked away from his presence!

Kossuth is a man of matchless power of mind. He sets aside all orators, whether of ancient or modern date. He is positively an intellectual wonder. Nevertheless, he has proved himself not only

mortal man, but capable of cherishing views and feelings which
are not in accordance with the laws that lie at the basis of our common humanity, and which bind us together in one bond of general
brotherhood.

Kossuth is not asked to turn anti-slavery lecturer, though this
is what Wright of the Commonwealth charges upon Wm. Lloyd
Garrison. He is not asked to turn aside from the Hungarian cause,
or to divide his energies between the cause of the American slave,
and that of the Hungarian oppressed. Nobody but a fool would
ask that. He is simply asked to do nothing or say nothing while
here, which would imply that he regarded the liberty of the American black man as less sacred than that of the Hungarian white man:
in other words, he is simply asked to see that there does exist among
us such an institution as American Slavery, and to utter to the
Americans, face to face, one burning rebuke by way of its condemnation. Do less than this, he could not, and maintain his integrity;
and doing less than this, it is my prayer at least, that such 'Apostles
of liberty' as he, may be fewer than ever were angels' visits, and a
great deal farther between.

'*My principle*,' says Kossuth, in his card, '*in this respect is,
that every nation has the sovereign right to dispose of its own domestic affairs, without any foreign interference; that I therefore
shall not meddle with any domestic concerns of the United States.*'
Four millions of Africans and their descendants, therefore, may
toil on in a worse slavery than ever the Hungarian knew; and, for
all Kossuth cares, the devil catch them at last. This is benevolence,
surely! Why comes he here to induce us to meddle with the
'domestic concerns' of Austria? If the enslavement of the blacks
to the whites in this country be a 'domestic concern,' then the oppressed condition of the Hungarians to the Austrians is a 'domestic
concern.' And if, being a 'domestic concern,' the enslavement of
the one class be outside of his notice, then why, with equal justice,
should not the oppressed condition of the other class, being a 'domestic concern,' be outside of our notice? O, consistency, thou art
a jewel!—and, besides, I hate hypocrisy.

The plain truth is, Kossuth's disclaimer will get him more
money; but be it known unto him, that money gotten thus will
curse him, and not bless him.

Some men I know at this point read us lectures on 'Common
Sense.' Let them read on. I acknowledge no common sense which
is in contravention of the law of rectitude.

Much better would it have been for the cause of freedom the world over, had Kossuth maintained his integrity. One word from him to this people would have startled this nation into a sense of propriety never felt before; and would have given such an impetus to the cause of freedom as would almost have enabled us to fix the very day when the good time should come. What retards the cause of republican freedom in Europe more than our abominable inconsistencies? Do not tyrants take courage at our position, and laugh us to very scorn? Were we a one with our professions, democracy could not lag in Europe. It would come quickly; and not only so, but be a fact, fixed, firm, immovable.

No good comes of the spirit of compromise, and compromising with right and duty. He who cannot read that fact in this country's history, is quite too stupid to be endured. Do not wise men begin to fear that unless we do something for slavery, soon slavery will do something for us? And is this fear ill-founded? Are they foolish who fear that slavery, in destroying itself, may destroy the nation, and that in a way the equal of which has never yet been written upon any page of human history? But I forbear to say more. May God help the weak; and give wisdom and power to those who are laboring to bring slavery and oppression to the dust, not only in Austria or Hungary, but wherever they may be found.

Faithfully yours,

WM. G. ALLEN.[55]

McGRAWVILLE, N. Y., Dec. 30, 1851.

I was very much pleased with Professor Allen's strictures upon the action of the New York Committee of Thirteen. Kossuth certainly knows little and cares less about the black people of this continent, and it seems to me to be wanting in self-respect for our people to run after such a man. Besides, we must do more for ourselves, before we can expect the self-liberators of the old world to pay much attention to our notices of them. Gentlemen who voted for the slaveholding tool of despotism, Millard Fillmore, and Washington Hunt, who has the hardihood to deny that blacks can live in the same community with whites without becoming extinct—a statement lived down every day in Canada—have yet to learn how to become consistent *voters* in their own cause, ere they can do much to aid other men to become successful *fighters* in theirs. The pro-

[55] *Liberator*, January 9, 1852.

slavery church relations of too many of the Committee of Thirteen
are very much in the way of their doing a great deal for the oppressed, who are much nearer to them than Hungary.

But what are we to hope for, from the great mass of professed
philanthropists who visit the United States from Europe? How
many of them have paid any attention to our cause, while in
Yankeedom? Jenny Lind, you know, proved herself one of the
most heartless misanthropes that ever travelled through slavedom,
and received the blood-stained gold of woman whippers. Fredrieka
Bremer boldly apologised for the slave system to your very face,
in your own parlor. And just so have almost all of those Europeans who have been made lions and lionesses in your *very hospitable* country. Kossuth meddled not with the English method of
treating or mal-treating Ireland, and, with a consistency worthy of
himself, he meddles not with the American method of enslaving
Americans. An aristocrat, the former owner of a princely fortune,
a man of high office, civil and military at home, and the guest of
the aristocracy wherever he goes, (except in Turkey,) he is not expected to show feelings in common with the poor of any country
or color. To thrust ourselves upon the attentions of such a man
and to expect aught from him were positively absurd. Such is my
humble opinion. I shall be much mistaken if the Ex-Governor of
Hungary does not show himself quite capable of leaving the United
States without the utterance of a single syllable against the *Hay-
nauism of America,*—the slavery thereof.

The extravagant notions of Mr. Thomas, I do not wonder at,
knowing, so well as I do, that gentleman's habit of over estimating
every thing that at all strikes him favorable. But I do wonder
how even John Thomas could call Kossuth the greatest man of the
age, or how he could suppose Kossuth to be finishing up the anti-
slavery work of the age; or how Mr. Thomas could reckon upon
any anti-slavery influence especially in New York, as resulting from
the visit of the Great Hungarian. Beside Gerrit Smith Kossuth is
but a child, a pigmy. The noblest ideas of the latter were long
since avowed and insisted on by the former. International rights,
free trade, the application of the fundamental principles of Christianity to our civil and international relations, pray to whom are
these *new ideas,* who has read the writings or heard the words of
the Man of Peterboro'? When Kossuth shall have learned to apply
his principles to social life, and live at home, as Smith does, the

great doctrines of human equality, then he will get even the name of the imitator, or disciple, or coadjutor of the greatest man of the age, but not till then. Still, I repeat, I do not wonder at Mr. Thomas's extravagance in this matter, for it is so like him.

P. S. I agree with Wendell Phillips and yourself, exactly, about Kossuth. Mr. Thomas' whitewashing of the great Magyar, does not, after all, make him anything else than a political adventurer, with axes to grind, regardless of the woes of downtrodden Americans. The despots of Europe will hurl this in his face when he goes back, and most richly does he deserve the bitterest taunts of the worst enemies of liberty in the old world. What a pity it will be that he can reply, 'I had the approval and defence of one of the editors of the only organ of the Liberty Party, the most radical abolition party in the American Union!' Such an apology may very justly bring American Liberty Partyism into disrepute on the other side of the Atlantic. Much the better way, in our judgment, is to hold European and American apostles of liberty as alike hypocritical, unless they can see and feel the force of the application of the doctrine of inalienable human rights to others than those immediately connected with themselves. S. R. W.[56]

Commenting here upon the review of his book, M. R. Delany not only shows his determination to have the rights of a freeman, but having become disgusted with this country, he hints at the necessity for colonization.

PHILADELPHIA, May 14, 1852.

MR. GARRISON:

MY DEAR SIR:—I thank you, most kindly, for the very favorable and generous notice you have taken of my hastily written book. This, to many, may appear singular, that the author of a work should send words of thanks to an editor for his notice of him, but this favor of yours came so opportune, that it seems like a God-send.

The errors and deficiencies, which you are pleased to pass by unnoticed—justly taking my prefatory apology as sufficient—I have corrected, and will so appear in the next issue, shortly to come out. The corrections you make concerning *yourself*, I shall add as a NOTE at the conclusion of the work.

[56] *Liberator*, Feb. 27, 1852.

I thank those editors of Philadelphia and elsewhere, who have favorably noticed this work, and would add, that the ever good, generous Gerrit Smith has sent me a letter of approval of the work in general.

I am not in favor of caste, nor a separation of the brotherhood of mankind, and would as willingly live among white men as black, if I had an *equal possession and enjoyment* of privileges; but shall never be reconciled to live among them, subservient to their will—existing by mere *sufferance,* as we, the colored people, do, in this country. The majority of white men cannot see why colored men cannot be satisfied with their condition in Massachusetts—what they desire more than the *granted* right of citizenship. Blind selfishness on the one hand, and deep prejudice on the other, will not permit them to understand that we desire the *exercise* and *enjoyment* of these rights, as well as the *name* of their possession. If there were any probability of this, I should be willing to remain in the country, fighting and struggling on, the good fight of faith. But I must admit, that I have no hopes in this country—no confidence in the American people—with a *few* excellent exceptions—therefore, I have written as I have done. Heathenism and Liberty, before Christianity and Slavery.

> 'Were I a slave, I would be free,
>   I would not live to live a slave;
>   But boldly *strike* for LIBERTY—
>   For FREEDOM or a *Martyr's* grave.'

Yours for God and Humanity,
M. R. DELANY.[57]

VIII.   CHARLES LENOX REMOND

Charles Lenox Remond, the most widely known Negro in the United States prior to the rise of Frederick Douglass, spent most of his time lecturing to antislavery groups while other prominent Negroes divided their energy between the platform and the pen. Mr. Remond never wrote an extensive sketch of himself and his glory waned so early in the midst of the increasing popularity of Frederick Douglass that no one found it profitable to undertake such a task.

[57] *Liberator,* May 21, 1852.

From his numerous letters, some of which are herewith presented, may be obtained sufficient data to make an estimate of his contribution to the uplift of his race and progress of his country.

WINTHROP, ME., July 3d, 1838.

MY DEAR FRIEND:—I take advantage of the earliest opportunity to inform you, that on the third day after bidding you farewell, I met my friend Mr. Codding, at Brunswick, at which place, on the following Sunday afternoon, I addressed the friends a short time, and was well received.   On Tuesday following, left Brunswick for Alfred, to attend the formation of a County Anti-Slavery Society. There was not much interest taken in the meeting.   On the following evening I was invited to address the meeting and complied.   On the next day, I was invited to go into the country a short distance. I cut loose from Mr. Codding very reluctantly, and commenced lecturing in my feeble way.   Received requests to lecture in four different places on four successive evenings.   I consented, and spoke in each place an hour and a half; and although my audiences were generally dark on the subject of prejudice and slavery, I received on every occasion the most marked attention, and assurances of good feeling for the cause, and wishes for the success of our enterprise. At one place, they resolved at the close of the lecture, to form a society and lend their assistance in the great work.

On Wednesday last I went to Saco, to attend the conference meeting of the Congregational denomination.   The delegation of ministers was very numerous, and much interest was manifested to every great and good, and benevolent undertaking, save the cause of the poor slave in our own beloved but guilty country.   On Thursday evening I was invited to speak on the subject in the Baptist meeting-house.   My audience was almost entirely composed of ministers who were attending the conference, and a good number of interesting and intelligent ladies.   At this place they have determined to do something forthwith for the slave, by forming a male and female society, and contributing to the cause.   On last Sabbath afternoon, I lectured in the meeting-house in Bowdoin.   Nothing special occurred.

I am now at the house of our kind and devoted friend, Rev. David Thurston, and the feeling manifested on every occasion by his wife and daughters in behalf of human liberty is indeed such as may well make glad the hearts of our brethren in bonds. It is of no use for me to attempt to give you any thing like a description of the change which I believe is now taking place on the subject of slavery and the elevation of the nominally free. We have every thing, friend Thomas, to encourage us. Slavery is trembling, prejudice is falling, and I hope will soon be buried—buried beyond resurrection; and we will write over its grave as over Babylon—'Prejudice, the mother of abominations, the liar, the coward, the tyrant, the waster of the poor, the brand of the white man, the bane of the black man, is fallen! is fallen!' Yours truly,

C. LENOX REMOND.[58]

MR. JOHNSON—I have just received an interesting letter from my friend Remond, who is an agent of the American Anti-Slavery Society, and is now lecturing in various places in Maine with good success. The letter is cheering, because it furnishes evidence that prejudice is melting away, and that the cause of abolitionism is moving onward, and its friends rapidly increasing. The principles which abolitionists are promulgating are like the majestic oak, which strikes its roots deep in the earth. They cannot be prostrated by the blasts of sectional jealousy or party violence. Freedom is an inborn principle of our nature, emanating from the great Creator, and extending to all mankind indiscriminately. Slavery is the subversion of this principle.

As Mr. Remond is a colored man, and has been so well received in Maine, I have thought that the publication of his letter might cheer the hearts of those who are struggling to elevate themselves above the prejudices which now press heavily upon them. As a colored man, my own heart has been encouraged by its perusal.

Yours for the oppressed,

Boston, July 7, 1838.
T. COLE.

————

LONDON, June 30th, 1840.

MY DEAR FRIEND RAY:—Faithful to my promise, although in the midst of engagements, I steal a moment, not to fill this sheet, as my time will not admit, but to inform you of my safe arrival and good health at this time; and that this sheet may meet you with your wife, sisters and friends in possession of the same privilege is

[58] *Liberator*, July 20, 1838.

my best wish. In referring to the subject of anti-slavery on this side the Atlantic, permit me to say, as a silent listener, I was much interested in the discussions during the sitting of the British and Foreign Anti-Slavery Society, (not World's Convention, as we had fondly and anxiously anticipated, which facts, with many others, forbid my taking a seat, and participating in its deliberations.) That on my arrival I learned with much sorrow of the rejection of the female delegation, I need not mention. And in few instances through life have I met with greater disappointment, especially in view of the fact, that I was almost entirely indebted to the kind and generous members of the Bangor Female Anti-Slavery Society, the Portland Sewing Circle, and the Newport Young Ladies' Juvenile Anti-Slavery Society, for aid in visiting this country. And I can assure you it was among my most happy reflections to know, that in taking my seat in the World's Convention, I should do so, the honored representative of three female associations, at once most praiseworthy in their object, and efficient in their co-operation. And sure I am, that could the members of these associations have had even a place in the imaginations of those who voted for their exclusion, the decision would have been otherwise, far otherwise. Thanks be to Providence, I have yet to learn, that the emancipation of the American slave, from the sepulchre of American slavery, is not of more importance than the rejection of females from the platform of any Anti-Slavery Society, Convention, or Conference. In the name of heaven, and in the name of the bleeding, dying slave, I ask, if I shall scruple the propriety of female action, of whatever kind or description. I trust not—I hope not—I pray not, until the bastard system is annihilated, and not a vestige remains to remind the future traveller, that such a system ever cursed our country, and made us a hissing and a by-word in the mouth of every subject of every Monarch, King, Queen, Despot, Tyrant, Autocrat and Czar of the civilized and uncivilized world!

My friend, for thirteen years have I thought myself an abolitionist; but I had been in a measure mistaken, until I listened to the scorching rebukes of the fearless O'Connell in Exeter Hall, on the 24th June, when before that vast assemblage, he quoted from American publications, and alluded to the American declaration, and contrasted the theory with the practice; then was I moved to think, and feel, and speak; and from his soul-stirring eloquence and burning sarcasm would every fibre of my heart contract in abominating the worse than Spanish Inquisition system in my own, I almost fear, devoted country. Let it suffice to say, the meeting at Exeter Hall more than compensated me for the sacrifice and suffering I experienced in crossing the Atlantic, under circumstances which I shall make known at some future time. Until the facts are known, let no one envy me in my voyage or undertaking. A few words in relation to slavery's grand handmaid, in the States proclaimed to be non-slaveholding—I mean *prejudice*, that acts the part to slavery of second king at arms, and exercises its authority by assisting in kidnapping the innocent and free at the capital, disfranchises the citizens of Pennsylvania, proscribes the colored man in Rhode Island, abuses and gives him no resting place as a man in New-Hampshire, which murders in Illinois, cries out amalgamation in Maine, mobs him in New York, and stones him in Connecticut. I say this hydra-headed personage, thanks be to God, has but few advocates in this country; if any, I have it to learn; and if you would rouse the honest indignation of the intelligent Englishman, tell him of our school and academy exclusions. If you would enlist the sympathies of the pious, refer him to our negro pews in the house of worship, and when you tell him of the Jim Crow car, the top of the stage coach, the forward deck of the steamboat, as the only place for colored people to occupy, he at once, turning pale, then red, inquires if this is American republicanism, if this is the fruit of our many religious institutions; and as a West Indian remarked to me yesterday, that liberty in my country was, in its best estate, but the grossest licentiousness. I could not—I dare not contradict him, as my presence in England, at this time, proved too much for his argument. More hereafter. I was happy to meet R. Douglass and W. Jeffers, in the city, and especially to find William well situated in business, and his health much improved. I hope to receive a copy of the Colored American soon, and in the mean time I remain, desiring to be remembered most kindly to the several members of your family, and to my many friends in New York.   Most truly yours,

For truth and the oppressed,

C. LENOX REMOND.[61]

To the Rev. C. B. Ray.

P. S. I will not mail this sheet without saying that, notwithstanding the pleasant circumstances with which I am surrounded,

[61] *Liberator*, Oct. 16, 1840.

I long to tread again the country of my birth, again to raise my feeble voice in behalf of the suffering, again to unite with you in razing to the ground, the system which is, and ever has proved too faithfully, the fell destroyer of our race and nation.

Again, yours,   C. L. R.

From the Anti-Slavery Standard.

LIVERPOOL, Aug. 25th, 1840.

MY DEAR FRIEND JACKSON:—On the departure of each of the friends for the United States, your solicitation on the day of our sailing, upon the Battery, in New-York, that I would write you during my stay in England, has not unfrequently reminded me of my obligations; and I regret exceedingly I have not time to give full vent to my feelings (if I may be allowed the expression,) on many topics in which I know you feel an interest, viz: the deliberations of the was-to-be World's Convention, recently held in London, for the overthrow of slavery throughout the world. Magnificent undertaking! most praiseworthy object! philanthropic motive! soul-stirring contemplation! Heaven-pleasing proposition! God-approving cause! But, friend Jackson, how far the action of the British and Foreign Anti-Slavery Conference will tend to the accomplishment of the same, is, to my mind, matter of conjecture. That I was surprised at the whole proceeding, I need not state; that I was disappointed in the character of the meeting, I need not say; that I was pained with the treatment which a part of the delegation of the American A. S. Society received, you may well suppose. Some may think it for the best: I think otherwise; unless the gratification of new organization is the life, sum and substance of the arduous undertaking. Who would have supposed, three years ago, the voice of a rational human being would have been stifled upon the platform of the World's Convention? Who would have supposed that the voice and sentiments of a Clarkson, and Buxton, and Phillips, and Adams, would have been hushed, and circumscribed, and put down, in a Convention similar to the one we have had in contemplation for the last year and upwards? No sane mind. Who would have supposed that the mention of William Lloyd Garrison's name would have been drowned by manifestations of disapprobation in the World's Convention, for the overthrow of slavery throughout God's entire domain? Who would have supposed that

George Thompson, the colored man's unceasing, devoted, and noble advocate, the West India slaves' deliverer, would be coldly looked upon by professing abolitionism? If this is the boon for which such men have labored, I have grossly mistaken the object; but may God *give,* and continue to them, health, and strength, and talent, still to prosecute the work in which they have engaged; and over the head of bigotry, pride, prejudice, party, denomination and politics, this holy cause shall yet be carried. The human work of erecting a tunnel across the Thames, may be stayed; the steamer across the Atlantic may fail the undertaker; Victoria, through man's perfidy, may lose Great Britain's diadem; Martin Van Buren may lose his election, and Daniel Webster may sacrifice northern interests and northern principles to southern policy; but God has commanded, and all nature cries out, undo the heavy burdens, and let the oppressed go free. The law is, 'Thou shalt love the Lord thy God with all thy heart, with all thy strength, and with all thy might, and thy neighbor as thyself.' And who is my neighbor?

'Thy neighbor! 'tis he whom thou
Hast power to aid and bless:
Whose aching heart and burning brow,
This soothing hand may press.
Thy neighbor! Yonder toiling slave,
Fetter'd in thought and limb,
Whose hopes are all beyond the grave,
Go thou and ransom him.
Oh, pass not, pass not heedless by,
Perhaps thou canst redeem
The breaking heart from misery,
Oh, share thy lot with him.'

Such, friend Jackson, is my view of this subject; and when the day shall roll round, that I am not willing to act upon such principles, I shall become unworthy the name of abolitionist, if my feeble efforts deserve the appellation,—and most sincerely do I believe the hour not far distant when many will feel and acknowledge the injustice they have done the pioneer of this cause—the man who, alone and unaided, first dared to grapple with American slavery, and called things by their right names—who desired no applause, and refused all favors which should make a sacrifice of principle the condition—who declared, in the face of heaven and earth, that he would publish the whole truth upon this subject, though every tile upon every house-top should be a devil, and bid him hold his peace; he who was unawed by influence, and unbribed by gain—he who, on no occasion has failed to denounce northern oppression in the character of prejudice, branding the nominally free with infamy and shame, and condemning him to exile and misery; the man whose services and sufferings I would not overrate, but in the name of justice and the bleeding slave, I would claim for him that name to which his eminent and never-to-be-over appreciated services entitle him—the slave's first and firmest friend. But coming generations will do him justice, though those who were once proud to stand by his side during the days of persecution, shall now desert him and the old storm-proof platform of Massachusetts anti-slavery.

I must not omit to mention that portion of the colored people who acknowledge the genuineness of Mr. Garrison's abolitionism, but who would desert him as abolitionists, because he holds to doctrines with which they have no sympathy. Were they true in their first love, and consistent with their first adopted principles, they would adhere to the old platform, though W. L. Garrison turned Infidel or Socialist. No local jealousy should swerve us from our first position, unless that proves to be unsustainable in first principles, and this no one pretends to question. But when I commenced, I did not think of writing a letter, and the clock is now striking 12, P. M., and you will not only excuse me from saying more, but excuse my many imperfections and mistakes, together with the scribbling, as my light is very dim, as you may suppose, and I write with a steel pen, which to me is equal to a tenpenny nail. Remember, those who write, deserve an answer. Thy letter will be anxiously looked for. Please remember me in kindness to those who inquire, and believe me to be, most sincerely, ever

Your attached friend in bonds,

For the suffering and oppressed,

C. LENOX REMOND.[60]

P. S. It was my purpose to have said something respecting the National Standard, and shall do so in my next, and will now say, may the Standard be one which shall make oppressors tremble in view of their conduct, and coming events. May the good and true give it their support. I wish it had a faithful agent in England: and from no consideration allow N. P. Rogers to excuse himself

[60] *Liberator*, Oct. 9, 1840.

from the editorial chair. He is the man, and must be its editor. The paper looks the man, and he can and will sustain it, God helping him. Direct letters and papers 27 New Broad Street, London. Again yours,

C. L. R.

Manchester, England, Aug. 31, 1840.

My very dear friend:

It affords me no small degree of pleasure in forwarding, through the kindness of our mutual friend George Bradburn, Esq. this hurried letter; entertaining the hope that you, together with friends Rogers and Fuller, arrived safe home, to the embrace of anxious and affectionate wives, children, relations and friends; and that, ere this, the American oppressor has been apprised of your return through the columns of the Liberator, National Standard, and last, but not least, Herald of Freedom. Your names have not remained dead letters since your departure from this country, I can assure you; nor will they be, although not enrolled among the members of the *was to be* World's Convention.

For some days after parting with you and friend Rogers, on the Clyde, I was confined with inflammatory fever at the house and truly hospitable home of my dear friend John Murray, Esq. Bowling Bay; since which, I find myself much restored, and hope my health may be adequate to my engagements for a few weeks to come.

The contemplated meeting on British India was held at this place, on Wednesday evening last. The tickets were all disposed of, and hundreds were refused admission for want of room, while the meeting was convened in the Corn Exchange, the most commodious hall in the place. That fearless champion, Daniel O'Connell, M. P. and George Thompson, Esq. the peerless advocate of oppressed humanity, stood forth on the occasion, each in his turn convincing, convicting, overpowering the vast assembly on the subjects of injured, wronged and abused India—as the almost thundering rounds of applause, at times shaking the very rafters of the large building, most clearly demonstrated. My feelings on the occasion beggar description, as the withering sarcasm, burning rebukes, scorching reproofs, astounding statements, and matchless eloquence, fell from the lips of the speakers. Would to heaven every slaveholder of our country had been present to witness with his own eyes, and to hear with his own ears, these as it were first movements in behalf of In-

dia, and in relation to the cotton trade in this the largest manufacturing town in the kingdom.   England is beginning to see and feel
her inconsistency upon this all important question; and when England shall be made acquainted with the entire facts, she will speak
as one man, and in keeping with the language of the writer of a
pamphlet now before me, which extract he will pardon me for quoting, as follows:

'What must be the obduracy of those flinty hearts, what must be the
malignity of those demon spirits, which are inaccessible to all the gentleness,
and patience, and submission, and suffering of the simple-minded and kind-
hearted negro; which cannot be allured to one solitary act of redeeming justice; which cannot be melted into kindness, nor softened into pity, nor attracted
to virtue, nor deterred from crime, by such feelings and sympathies as touch
and move the souls of other men;—not by the recollections of all the past, of
all the atrocious felonies they have so remorselessly committed, of all the
countless benefits they have so ungratefully requited:—not by the contemplation of all the present, of all that should elevate and humanize the spirit of
men, of all the happy gratulations of ransomed thousands breathing forth their
humble gratitude to their divine and human benefactors, and to them, too, their
thankless oppressors, the scourge and curse of their name and race;—nor by
the anticipation of all the future—a future, big with the promise of prosperity
and happiness to their sable brethren, but which, to them, if they heed not its
prophetic admonitions, and madly persist in the unhallowed course, can issue
only in merited and unpitied destruction. Let them take warning from the
tyrant's fate: The horse and rider were thrown into the sea.'

Five years ago, it was said by abolitionists in America, that the
days of the accursed system were numbered; and I may safely say,
in British India also.   Let O'Connell of Ireland, Thompson of England, and Garrison of America, take courage, and be strengthened.
God, truth, and the oppressed, will ere long conquer, prevail and
live.   England will soon learn her duty, and, knowing it, with her
is to perform.   England can and will abolish East India slavery.
England can and will abolish American slavery, the philosophy of
George Mc'Duffie, the computation of Henry Clay, and the com-
mittal of Daniel Webster, to the contrary notwithstanding;—and
let those base men who calumniate the disinterested O'Connell, and
those cowardly ones who pursued and sought the life of the noble
Thompson, know that these are the men destined, God helping them,
to bring about this unlooked for change on this side the Atlantic.
I say, let the American editor, who cast the epithet of *lying scoundrel* upon George Thompson, and he who more recently styles Daniel O'Connell a base and brutal abolitionist, know that were they in

this country, such abuse would be laughed to scorn. Very chivalrous indeed to speak and print these things some thousand miles distant! Shame on the name of such infatuated creatures, who disgrace the ashes of their ancestors, and bring dishonor upon the clods which cover their remains, by endeavoring to defame the men who advocate the principles for which their fathers pledged their *lives,* their *property,* and their sacred *honor.* American editors appear in great trouble, because the English believe human rights to be human rights, and more than skin-deep; because high-minded Englishmen, and Irishmen, and Scotchmen, pity their ignorance, and contemn their impudence, when they appear among them, mad with the colorphobia distemper.

It was my happiness on Wednesday of last week, to dine in Manchester in company with Mr. O'Connell, ——— Brooks, Esq. Boroughreeve, and six or eight gentlemen of high distinction and profession, at the house of my esteemed friend, Daniel Lee, Esq.; when Mr. O'Connell remarked, that, of all things in the United States, the prejudice against the free people of color was the most wicked and absurd. And when it was stated that not even merit of the highest character secured them from insult and proscription, and disfranchisement, two gentlemen at the table involuntarily exclaimed, they could not visit such a country.

As regards old and new organization, as it strikes me in this country, I should be glad to say much; but *'Tempus fuget,'* and I must close; but not without saying that it has been my privilege to enjoy, for the last few days, the society of your much regarded friends and esteemed coadjutors, Miss Elizabeth Pease, (who, with her father, have been in Manchester,) and Mr. George Thompson. You, with friend Rogers and all who have their acquaintance, will admit that the treat must have been no ordinary one. On the evening before last, Miss Pease said she wished to visit our country, that she might enter her protest against American prejudice. The Boston Female Anti-Slavery Society would joyously welcome her among them, and extend to her at least the freedom of Boston antislavery. We speak of you and friend Rogers often, and, notwithstanding the many attempts made to now organize England's entire anti-slavery, there still remain not a few who may be called the Gideonites, storm-beaten and storm-proof, who will not bow the knee to Baal; who will think and speak for themselves; who believe women have hands, and should work; who believe women have hearts, and should feel; who believe women have tongues, and should speak.

Please present my love to the many friends, and believe me to be,

Your very affectionate friend,

In bonds for God, truth, and the oppressed,

C. LENOX REMOND.[59]

EDINBURGH, Sept. 21st, 1840.

MY VERY DEAR FRIEND:

Upon the table before me is the Liberator of the 28th ult. apprising me of your safe arrival home, together with friend Rogers, Fuller, Grosvenor, and Galusha. It afforded me great pleasure to learn of your safe return, and additional pleasure to notice the promptness with which the colored citizens of Boston welcomed you, with friend Rogers, on shore, and the reception they gave you at the Marlboro' Chapel. Thanks be to Providence, they knew their duty, and were ready and willing to perform it. It augurs well for the cause in which you have been engaged for the ten years past; and the proceedings of that evening at the Marlboro' was proof conclusive, that you had not been engaged in vain. Such a meeting, ten years ago, would have stirred, and I had almost said would have moved the foundations of the Old Bay State. Think of one of the finest and largest chapels in Boston being filled to overflowing with much of the learning, wisdom, piety and philanthropy of the city, to receive Wm. Lloyd Garrison and Nathl. P. Rogers, distinguished for their fearless advocacy of the colored man's rights—and, above all, colored ladies and gentlemen sitting promiscuously with this body. Think of it, mobocrats of Philadelphia! Look in upon that meeting, aristocrats of New-Haven! Pass judgment, negro-haters of Bath and Hallowell! Reflect upon it, humanity-scourgers of New-York, who prided yourselves in compelling your superiors in every respect, save that of slavery-ridden and debased human nature, to fly the public house kept by Mr. Goss, as late as May, 1840! What will the priests, levites, attorney generals, senators and governors say to all this? What can they say, other than that upon the question of slavery, our country is to be turned 'right side up,' (with care,) if you please? What, but that fanaticism has become sober truth, incendiarism has

59 *Liberator*, Sept. 25, 1840.

become patriotism, recklessness has become solicitude for the country's weal, and last, but not least, amalgamation has become a right in the estimation of the wiseacres of 1835, 6, 7, 8 and 9, providing silence gives consent. So much for the march of truth. Another feather is soon to be placed in the cap of my native State, (Massachusetts,) the first to strike for the freedom of the country. May she be the first to banish from her soil and associations the corroding fetters of prejudice, which, if we may be allowed an opinion, from the experience of the past, the view of the present, and the prospects of the future, is soon to be the case.

Upon our young men, and young women, every thing (comparatively speaking) depends. Too long have many of this class been indifferent to this question. It is our cause, and if we are unwilling to promote it, we deserve proscription, and are not only deaf to the cries of the enslaved, but false to our trust. Too often have I been pained to see young men with growing families around them, almost from appearances ignorant of the efforts being made in their behalf. Shame on the colored father or mother, who can rest contented in their lot, or with the prospect staring them in the face, that their children and their children's children must be subjected to the condition through which our fathers passed, and which we daily experience!

It need not be, if we will it; otherwise, it cannot be. No nation can keep four millions of people in bondage to Slavery's Moloch, or its handmaid Prejudice, when they shall decree it otherwise. Then let us rally to the moral contest, and, being armed with the weapons of truth, soberness, industry and knowledge, we will present a Spartan front, through which no army, led on by Slavery's call, can penetrate, and, ere long, the American eagle shall bear on his back the olive-branch of freedom to every colored man, woman, and child throughout the American continent.

You will be glad to hear that it is my happiness, at this time, to be travelling with our mutual friend and coadjutor, GEORGE THOMPSON, who, I have every reason to believe, should he be spared, is destined to prove the successful advocate of suffering humanity in the *East* as well as in the *West* Indies. The growing interest in this country, upon the question of British India, is alike surprising and encouraging. I have accompanied Mr. Thompson as far north as Aberdeen, and he is every where hailed, and cheered, and honored. Every day fresh proofs of devotedness to the cause he has espoused come in to him from every quarter; and if he possessed a hundred tongues, every one of them would be employed. As the British learn the three-fold effects of East India emancipation—viz: the enfranchisement of the East Indian, the prosperity of the working-classes of Great Britain, and the unavoidable overthrow of American Slavery—the universal shout will ring through the land. And shall America say, England shall buy and manufacture her blood-stained and tear-saturated cotton? No! Shall America say, Great Britain shall not carry out the god-like work she has so nobly begun? No! Then let American slavery perish— as perish it must, and that speedily; for survive it cannot long. It may live, for a time, by feeding upon its kind; but you and I may yet live to see its overthrow. Four out of six British papers, upon an average, speak favorably of the movement. Georgia may offer her rewards for the abduction of American citizens; but more mines must be discovered through the tears, and bones, and blood, and ashes of murdered slaves, ere she can hope to purchase the head of Old England, or intimidate her sons, or deter them from their work of philanthropy. No nation or people possess a superior to DANIEL O'CONNELL as a political advocate, or GEORGE THOMPSON as a moral advocate. Wo be to the system they combine against, Glad as we would be to see our friend Thompson on our side of the Atlantic, I feel convinced from observation since I have been honored with his companionship while travelling and lecturing for the advancement of the cause of injured Africa, that he is doing more for the overthrow of American Slavery, than he could possibly do were he in our country at this time. I fear we do not duly appreciate the services Mr. Thompson has rendered, and is at this time rendering in behalf of the oppressed and proscribed of our land. The debt of gratitude due him on our part is great indeed. I feel no hesitancy in saying that GEORGE THOMPSON is surpassed by no man in England or Scotland, in his persevering, consistent and successful efforts, both publicly and privately, for the emancipation and elevation of our people; and the more I mingle with the friends, and society at large, the more I am convinced of the truth of the statements. The first monument of honor erected by colored Americans to any living man should bear an appropriate inscription, demonstrative of their regard and affections for him. Could they, with me, listen to his appeals to English hearts, and English humanity, and English philanthropy, all thoughts of extravagance on my part would vanish.

In my next, I shall say something respecting the woman question in the north of Scotland. My departure from Scotland is attended with difficulty, owing to the many pressing invitations from different sources to visit and lecture in company with Mr. Thompson; but we intend starting for England soon. The family of Mr. Thompson are in the enjoyment of good health. With the anxious hope that our cause is prospering, and desiring to be kindly and affectionately remembered to the friends in Boston, I remain,

Ever your attached friend,
In bonds for the oppressed,
C. LENOX REMOND.[62]

Dear Friend Garrison:

The following is an extract of a letter I received by the steamer Acadia from my esteemed friend C. L. Remond. If it contains any thing of interest, you are at liberty to publish it, though it was not written for the press.

Yours, for the slave,
THOMAS COLE.

'Edinburgh, Oct. 2, 1840.

My dear friend Cole:

My health is hardly what I could wish. Autumnal winds and rains do not well suit my constitution; but they are so unlike and so superior to the yearly winds and rains of prejudice in my own country, that I am not in the least inclined to murmur. So far from it, a wet jacket occasionally upon the road scarcely disturbs me, until I find myself suffering from a cold as a consequence.

England and Scotland, now, are every thing to me that they have been represented to be; and could I forget the poor slave and our proscribed associates at home, I should lose sight entirely of my own color—only when I chance to meet an American, who only dares look or show his teeth; for bite he must not in this country. Monarchical governments don't allow it. They leave such blackguard work for *republicans*.

On getting into one of the cars at Liverpool for Manchester, the other day, (I mean one of the first class cars,) who should I meet but one of the agents of the New-York and Providence steam-boat company. And why did he not request my removal? As the Scots say—Oh, ay—he knew better! He knew that to make such a request would have given him a seat upon the top of the cars; provided he preferred it to a seat inside with one having a skin not colored like his own.

I was glad to notice, by the last Liberator, your name as one of the committee to welcome home Wm. Lloyd Garrison and N. P. Rogers—the steel of anti-slavery. In reference to the meeting at the Marlboro' Chapel, and also the dinner at Chelsea, (sitting the remarks of friend Garrison and Rogers aside in regard to myself,) it afforded me no inconsiderable pleasure to learn that my course, which was followed from convictions of duty, at the Convention in London, was approved by my colored fellow-citizens in Boston. I feel myself flattered by the adoption of the resolutions regarding my feeble efforts in this country, to advance the cause of anti-slavery. I can only say, in return for their kind notice, I will not withhold those efforts, either at home or abroad, until brick-bats and rotten eggs shall fly about my head a thousand times more than they did in Hamden last autumn.

One thought more, and I have done. I notice by the anti-slavery papers, that the friends who differ with us on the woman question are determined, since their return to the United States, to make it appear, if possible, that, upon the decision of individuals on this question in England, hinges one's anti-slavery character. While this absurdly reflects discredit upon the English abolitionists, if true, it makes them occupy an unenviable position in believing it necessary to cross the Atlantic to have judgment passed upon the merits or demerits of the (to them troublesome) question—not a few of whom on this side of the water, put forth a hundred times more labor to gag the women, than was exerted for their admission and right of speech. So great are the fears of many who have crossed, as well as those who have not crossed, that they appear like haunted men, and make charges against myself and others, and take us to task, not for any crime we did commit, but which they fear we may commit. It is like hanging a man to save him the trouble of dying; or drowning woman, for fear she will become a witch. Happy as I should have been to see the ladies seated as delegates, I have not lost a night's sleep in consequence of their rejection; and I hope I am not far behind friend Garrison as a woman's rights man; at least, I don't mean to be. I would yield to them the same rights I claim for myself—and no man can do more. I see no cause for alarm, or occasion for uneasiness. If those from our country, who voted against their reception, are satisfied, be it so; but, for them, or for any other person to say, that I have not, *as one of Mr. Garrison's associates,* been greatly honored, and kindly and hospitably entertained, is stating that which is incorrect, and doing many friends great injustice, some of whom differ with me on the question which has given birth to modern abolition in Massachusetts. * * * *

Your much attached friend,

C. LENOX REMOND.[63]

Mr. Thomas Cole.

FRIEND GARRISON:

Prior to your departure from England, you were informed of the arrival of the gentleman whose name heads this communication. Of his movements in England up to his appearance in Glasgow, I am unable to speak; but, by the slip cut from one of many cards sent to different gentlemen in Glasgow, and which I have appended, (and as you may suppose,) I am put not a little upon the nettles.

MR. GURLEY,

Secretary of the American Colonization Society,

Will explain the views of that Institution as promotive of African civilization, and give an account of the present condition and prospects of the Colony of LIBERIA, in Western Africa, at the Royal Exchange, on Thursday next, at 3 o'clock, P. M.

You are very respectfully invited to attend.

Let the card be printed in the largest type, and a hundred extra Liberators struck off and charged to me, and forwarded to the nominally free people of color in every village, town, and city of our country; and let them forthwith call public meetings, and pass resolves, demonstrative of their views and feelings respecting the American Colonization Society; and let the same be forwarded to me, together with the work of my friends Wright and Cornish on the same subject, with all possible despatch. While I can find means to travel, and bread and water to live upon, and as God shall give me health, and strength, and speech, all shall be exerted to the best of my ability in counteracting such influence as the ac-

[63] *Liberator,* Oct. 30, 1840.

credited Secretary of the American negro-haters' scheme of cruelty and extirpation may exert in its favor. Let the people of color and our friends distinctly understand, that if I am promptly responded to, and sustained, there is little doubt of success in thwarting him, with their resolves and remonstrances. I ask but a fair chance, and no favors of Mr. Gurley, before a British audience. George Thompson lives, and is willing now, as ever, to enter the arena with the Rev. Mr. Gurley, and contest inch by inch the high-handed injustice done the colored population from the moment the Society came forth haggard and deformed, as it ever has been, from its secret session-room, some twenty years ago,—a bastard child; and it has never lost its first impressions, although it has appeared in a thousand garbs.

I am happy to state, upon unquestionable authority, that Mr. Gurley's meeting in Glasgow was a total failure, having some fifteen or twenty persons only present to hear his explanation, and account of the condition and prospects of Liberia. The name of the gentleman or Society seems to have explained the people away—if there was any explanation about it. Such a scheme would meet a similar reception in any other country, save the one from which he comes.

I also learn, upon the best authority, that Mr. Gurley intends revisiting London, and hopes to make a favorable impression. I hope to be there, and trust it may be favorable to his return to the land of slavery and prejudice.

Friend Thompson unites with me in much love to you and friends across the water. In haste, as usual,

I subscribe myself,

Ever affectionately yours for the suffering,

C. LENOX REMOND.[64]

NEWCASTLE-ON-TYNE,
March 7th, 1841.

MY VERY DEAR FRIEND:

I take advantage of the sailing of the next packet to forward a line or two, informing you that, in connexion with this sheet, I mail the London Chronicle, containing a report of meetings held by Messrs. Gurley and Cresson, from which you will learn that the fears entertained by me, at the time of the departure of yourself

64 *Liberator*, Nov. 13, 1840.

and friend N. P. Rogers, from this country, were not altogether groundless. That Mr. Gurley has placed his standard high, no one will deny; that he will attain to it, is quite another question.

On Sunday, 21st ultimo, I was informed by a friend in Newcastle, that Mr. Gurley was to have a fourth meeting in favor of his wicked scheme; and, although engaged to lecture in Sunderland, 15 or 20 miles distant on the following (Monday) evening, I resolved, if possible, to be in London on the evening of his meeting. At the time of appointment, I appeared before a very large and intelligent assembly, in the Flag Lane Chapel, Sunderland. After addressing the audience 30 minutes, I gave them to understand why I wished to be in London on the Wednesday evening following; and, in order to do so, must beg to be excused, which excuse was readily granted by the usual demonstration. By the kindness of my friend Wm. Richardson, whose horse and gig were in waiting at the chapel door, I succeeded in reaching the depot for the 8 o'clock train, which immediately set off, and, at 8 o'clock on Tuesday evening, by travelling night and day, I was landed safely at the house of our friend Mrs. Moore, Queen-street Place; but, strange to tell, Mr. Gurley had left town that day for the Isle of Wight, in company with a sick friend. His return being a matter of much uncertainty, in two or three days I retraced my steps to this place, which has been for five weeks my head quarters of operations. Prior to starting for London, I had spoken twenty-three evenings out of thirty on the several subjects of slavery, temperance, prejudice, and colonization. At this time, I stand engaged to give a course of lectures in Sunderland and Durham, and am disappointed in doing so, from loss of voice and strength; but being in the hands of many kind and hospitable friends, I hope soon to be about again. From causes of which you doubtless are aware, I have not, for the past three months, been able to be heard (through the mist of new organization) for the poor slave; but hope now, during the remainder of my stay, to act unhampered.

Mr. Collins and myself separated in Darlington some six weeks since. I believe he is about proceeding to Ireland soon, if not already gone. Nobly do our Irish friends contest for truth and justice. I expect to go over in a few weeks to Ireland, and, before going, I hope to see a recent Liberator, or Standard. Either would be a treat. If either has been sent me for the last two months, I have failed in its receipt.

What can the Rev. N. Colver mean by sending such letters across to this country? Does he mean to brand every man as a scoundrel, who differs from him in sentiment or opinion? And would he charge infidelity upon every one who attended the convention recently held in Boston? Surely, such letters would lead me directly to question the genuineness of his christianity, as well as the saneness of his mind, to say nothing of his spirit. To cap the climax of absurdities, a printed letter is going the rounds of this country, over the signature of Capt. Charles Stuart, respecting myself. The charge is, first, that I am delegated to this country to collect aid for the American Anti-Slavery Society; and, secondly, that I am of the Garrison party! From this it would appear, that what was great, and good, and noble, and christian, and philanthropic, and *anti-slavery*—in 1835, has become small, and evil, and mean, and infidel, and slavish, and pro-slavery—in 1841! Indeed, may we not exclaim, 'How have the mighty fallen!' Surely, such inconsistency will never proselyte me to new organization at home, much less abroad. If the house, (old organization) is built upon the sand, it will fall; if upon a foundation of rock, it will stand; and that, too, in defiance of all the missiles envy, malice, sectarianism, calumny, falsehood and persecution can hurl against it, by those who wield such weapons even with remarkable dexterity.

In view of the conflict which appears to be waxing hotter and hotter at home, I can only trust and pray that the colored people will be true to themselves; and the *Standard*, around which they should rally as one man, will appear to them as plain as if written with a sunbeam upon yonder sky, if they are looking to the signs of the times. A crisis is fast approaching, when decision will indeed be necessary, and action the most prompt in character unavoidable. If they cannot trust their best friends in fair weather, they surely will be wanting in the hour of danger and of storm. If our people had spoken as they should have done, at the time of holding the first convention in Philadelphia, a work would have been done worthy of them and the cause they love. There is yet time for its accomplishment. We need more radicalism among us, before we can speak as becomes a suffering, oppressed and persecuted people. We have been altogether too fearful of martyrdom—quite too indefinite in our views and sentiments—too slow in our movements. These failings, (I will not call them faults,) the oppressor and the persecutor, together with the negro-hating colonizationist, have taken advantage of. Let every case where legal rights are withheld, be legally investigated. Let every colored man, called upon to pay taxes to any institution in which he is deprived or denied its privileges and advantages, withhold his taxes, though it costs imprisonment or confiscation. Let our motto be—*No privileges, no pay.*

I had hoped to reach home in time to be present during the anniversaries in May. In this, I shall be disappointed, from causes beyond my control.

Wishing to be kindly remembered to your family, and to the friends who may enquire after me, and with wishes for your continued health, welfare, and success, believe me to remain, truly,

Your affectionate friend, in bonds for truth and the
oppressed,   C. LENOX REMOND.[65]

SALEM, March 5, 1842.
MY VERY DEAR FRIEND MR. GARRISON:

A line from me has been delayed in the hope of seeing you before this; and since my disappointment, it may not be uninteresting to yourself and others if I intimate that, agreeably to the kind invitation of our mutually esteemed friend, the Rev. Samuel J. May, I visited South Scituate on Tuesday, 22d ultimo, arriving about 3 o'clock in the afternoon. I went immediately to the meeting-house, where I found a large audience assembled, and the children of Mr. May's parish engaged in reciting anti-slavery pieces, with which, I was informed, they had, in a very short time, made themselves acquainted; and my only regret was, that there were not thousands present from a distance to witness for themselves the highly interesting occasion. Many of the pieces were new to me, and never in my life have I seen a juvenile association acquit themselves more creditably. Among the pieces recited, familiar to me, was our friend J. G. Whittier's stanzas, 'Our fellow countrymen in chains,' 'The Yankee Girl,' two or three very pertinent dialogues, the letter of Dr. Rushton to General Washington, &c. The services continued about three hours. At the close of the recitations, I was requested, by friend May, to offer a few remarks; and I frankly confessed the scene was so new in kind and character in our pro-slavery country, that I scarcely knew how to express myself. However, I could not withhold the expression of my thanks, in behalf of the enslaved, to their friend Mr. May, for interesting the children in the worthy cause of suffering millions—and to the parents and

65 *Liberator*, May 21, 1841.

friends, for the encouragement they had given by their presence. And what a burning shame it is, that many of the pieces on the subject of slavery and the slave-trade, contained in different school books, have been lost sight of, or been subject to the pruning knife of the slaveholding expurgatorial system! To make me believe that those men, or bodies of men, who have regulated the educational institutions of our country, have humanity in their hearts, is to make me believe a lie; and not less so, in making me believe those christian ministers who profess to love God in words, and hate their brother in works; and I ask, if school committees and school-masters,—if christian synods, conventions, ministers and Sabbath-school teachers had resolved and taught, preached and prayed for the proscribed and enslaved colored men, women and children, we should at this time find the rising generation shrinking from the mention of their name—repelling them from the lyceum and lecture room—scouting them from the museum and picture gallery—denying them admission to the white schools, seminaries and colleges—spurning them from the cabin on shipboard, and from artisanship and mechanism on land? I opine otherwise. 'Judicious mothers will always keep in mind, that they are the first book read, and the last put aside, in every child's library: every look, word, tone and gesture, nay, even dress, makes an impression.' [Abbot's Magazine.] And what is true of mothers, I believe also true of fathers, teachers and ministers. I therefore repeat the expression of my gratitude to our long tried friend May, for the excellent example he has set, while I cannot but exclaim, 'Shame on the cant and hypocrisy of those who can teach virtue, preach righteousness, and pray blessings for those only, with skins colored like their own.'

But I have already extended this letter beyond my intention when I commenced, and will only add, that, on the evening of the same day of the anti-slavery recitations, a simultaneous temperance meeting was held, and addressed by the Rev. Mr. May, the Rev. Mr. Williams of Providence, and myself. I also passed the following day very happily in friend May's family, and in the evening gave a lecture on slavery before a very respectable and attentive audience; and have promised to visit Plymouth County again, and spend a week or two for the furtherance of our high and holy enterprise.

Believe me, very sincerely,

Your obliged friend,

C. LENOX REMOND.[66]

[66] *Liberator*, March 11, 1842.

SALEM, Sept. 16, 1842.

To the West Newbury Anti-Slavery Society:

ESTEEMED FRIENDS—Many thanks for your favor, inviting my attendance at the meeting of the Essex County Anti-Slavery Society, to be holden in your town on Thursday of next week. And in no small degree do I regret my inability to comply, from prior engagements in New-Hampshire about the same time; although I have faith to believe my place will be well supplied by older and abler advocates. It is matter of rejoicing with me that the day has gone by, when the success or interest of our meetings depends upon the presence of particular individuals; and I trust the hour is fast approaching when every person, feeling sufficient interest to attend anti-slavery meetings, will also feel the disposition to become themselves the speakers, regardless of age, sex, or acquirements; I long to see the trader from the market, the shoemaker with his apron, the farmer with his homespun frock, the ploughman with his vest, the seafaring man with his jacket and trowsers, the truckman with his white overhaul, and the operative from the factory, with the mason, carpenter and smith from their benches and anvils, standing forward, eager with feeling, thought and voice, to be heard in behalf of a common origin and a common liberty. From such sources, eloquence emanates spontaneously. Men, women and children, who never spent the better half of their best days in learning to speak, cannot fail to interest. They speak from the heart, and the natural heart seldom, if ever, when left free, proves traitor to its God, Liberty, or the Truth. I once loved to hang upon the lips of a favorite minister, the popular orator, and the prized student; but my taste, like their eloquence, was empty, heartless, and selfish; and painful experience tells me, it is a trade with them. Education and usage, together with the applause of aristocrats and oppressors, has well nigh rid them of their natural hearts. Hence their want of humanity, their destitution of liberality, their lack of honesty and toleration in the sacred cause of emancipation.

I need scarcely intimate that I am heartily sick of hearing and reading of the benevolence and humanity of ministers, and the patriotism and republicanism of 4th of July orators. The one is a mockery, and God, in my opinion, will so view it. The other is an insult, and man shall so resent it.

It amuses me to be almost daily reminded of my misfortune in being associated with Garrison, Wright, Rogers, Foster, Collins,

Pillsbury, and the like, in their heresies and denunciations of the Church and clergy. If my deeply interested friends knew the contempt I feel for their gratuitous cantings, and hypocritical pretences, they would cease to trouble themselves.—My banner of unceasing moral hostility upon the policy, or institutions constituting the 'Bulwark of American slavery,' shall ever, God helping me, hang upon the outer wall—the anxiety of many of them to throw this awful responsibility upon the politics of the country to the contrary notwithstanding.

Let none of the good and true be turned from the right by the pious cry after 'Liberty Party.' This is not the first snare set by the poor slave's clerical friends to ensnare the unwary, and change the tide of truth and right from its proper channel. Wooden nutmegs, spurious coin, and black coat asseverations, will hardly answer the purpose now-a-days, unless they are willing to change them for the Joseph's coat of old-fashioned anti-slavery, such as became the soldiers of '31, '33, '34, and '35. The coats worn by the true and consistent anti-slavery ministers of those days reflected too many complexions to make the pulpit (in the opinion of their hearers) their 'appropriate sphere.' Judge Birney is proverbial for his dignified bearing, his intelligent and investigating mind, cool temperament, and second-thought decisions; and I confidently believe that, in compiling the important and highly useful pamphlet on the connexion of the American Church with the system of slavery, he retained his characteristic discretion and sound judgment, as well as knowing whereof he affirmed.

Finally, my friends, of whatever faith, if you believe there is a God, the common Parent of the human race, who delights in justice, mercy and freedom, carry forward, I beseech you, the work in which you are engaged; and be it yours to enjoy His approving smile—the love and gratitude of the perishing and proscribed! And let American religion and wrong, American religion and cruelty, American religion and slave-breeding, American religion and prostitution, American religion and piracy, American religion and murder, cold-blooded, and calculated by America's largest measure, shake hands.

I am, your obliged friend, in bonds for God, truth and the oppressed,

C. LENOX REMOND.[67]

[67] *Liberator*, Oct. 7, 1842.

WESTERN NEW-YORK,
BUFFALO, Aug. 12, 1843.

ESTEEMED FRIEND:

Presuming that my good friends and fellow-laborers, Messrs. White, Monroe, and Gay, have kept you informed of our principal movements, I take my pen more for the purpose of making good my promise than otherwise. Our appointments, you will perceive, have been tolerably punctually kept in this State, and with the exception of Albany, have all been much better attended and more interest awakened, than I anticipated, considering the means and measures used to prevent the people from coming out. I find many, apparently unhappy, and others affect to be shocked at the remarks reported to my account, on the Liberty party in New Bedford, not long since, by our worthy friend, E. Quincy, in the Liberator. The Albany Patriot and Liberty Press have opened their columns to anonymous communications, exercising the largest liberty of the press on me, upon the presumption the report is a correct one, since I have in no instance disclaimed it. Now I confess I am amused at the sensitiveness of the gentlemen on this subject, and who manifest large courage in their false statements, and more contemptible comments, but not enough courage to write over their true signatures, otherwise I should have noticed their 'Liberty party' highnesses at an earlier day. Though I did not use, without limitation, the language attributed to me by Mr. Quincy, yet as I don't know that I differ from the view very materially, I am willing the anonymous writers should make the most of the report, so far as the fate of Massachusetts is concerned; and I must go farther by adding that I differ some from our friends, in their idea that Liberty party in New-York differs so very widely from that of the same name in our State. For instance, I heard much of Lockport: in fact, my expectations ran high before my arrival, on the high-minded, liberal, free and thoroughgoing abolitionism of the Liberty party advocates of this village, and here, of all places, I expected we should be welcomed and presumed to be disinterested in our position, until proved guilty of holding and advancing doctrines irreconcileable with genuine anti-slavery, they being judges. But I was disappointed. [For particulars, see letter of Mr. Gay.]

Sydney H. Gay presented a very reasonable and simple resolution on the Church connexion with slavery, when a warm and somewhat protracted discussion ensued. Messrs. Bridgeman, Chace,

Southworth and Prudence, opposing very strenuously, and Messrs. Gay, Monroe, White, Pickard and myself, advocating, and here I must do Mr. Pickard the justice by saying his course was characterized by the same frank, honorable and truly liberal spirit manifested in his sojourn and attendance on meeting in Massachusetts during the last winter, and those friends who heard him during the Conventions and discussions on the Church and clergy, will be pleased to learn that he acquitted himself in Lockport in the 'trial hour' of truth struggling against error and sectarianism, in a manner not less worthy of his power, intelligence and eloquence. I regard him among the faithful few; and the poor slave is indebted to him for his unyielding advocacy of truth and principle. And I would not omit to mention our good and true friends Mr. Robbins, who presided over the meeting, together with Messrs. Mead, Kline, and Mott and family, the latter being the brother of our worthy friends, the Misses Mott, of Albany. My time will not permit me to add more than the intimation that our meetings resulted in much good, and in the advancement of free principles. The resolution alluded to, was lost by a vote of 27 to 18, being a signal victory over the expectations of our opponents.

Of the meetings being at this time holden by Douglass and myself, I will speak in my next. Frederick and myself intend remaining during the sitting of the Convention of the people of color, and shall then join our respective parties in Ohio with all possible despatch. Please to excuse this hurried and rambling communication —and begging to be affectionately remembered to the several members of your family, and the friends generally,

I remain, very truly,

Your obliged friend,

C. LENOX REMOND.[68]

BUFFALO, August 30th, 1843.

ESTEEMED FRIEND:

My last letter from this city acquainted you with my intention to remain a short time in company with Frederick Douglass for the purpose of giving a series of lectures, thereby occupying the intervening time prior to the sitting of the National Convention of the people of color, which purpose I am happy to say, we succeeded in, beyond our expectations, making a strong interest in our cause. And as a consequence hundreds were in daily attendance upon the deliberations of the Convention. And as a letter from a friend resident in this city, to the Liberator, will anticipate particulars on this subject, I will pass them by, adding the simple remark, that in no place since my return from Great Britain, have I labored with more satisfactory results, and cheering prospects. And this I doubt not will prove an adequate apology to our Ohio friends for our delay in reaching that State. What I have stated of Buffalo, I am warranted in stating is equally true of Rochester. The fact is, that most of the strongest men among the Western people of color were present; and they being extremely prejudiced from report more than anything against Eastern abolition, we had a grand opportunity of disabusing their minds before the public and the Convention; indeed it was a crisis, and one I felt called upon to meet, by every consideration. Frederick and myself have spoken to large and increasing audiences, more than twice a day for the last three weeks; of the good done, others must testify. On Sabbath morning last, I addressed a very large and highly respectable assembly in the green in Rochester, then rode in company with a small party of friends to Mendon, and with Frederick spoke to many in front of the Friends' meeting-house, which was closed against us; then passed on to another part of the same town, and addressed one of the most crowded audiences I ever saw, in the Christian meeting-house; and I think an excellent impression was made.

I sorely lament the misfortune of friend Garrison's family. And when you write him, you will confer a favor by making my affectionate remembrances to him and his dear family and friends; repeating the request of the same to the friends generally, in which Frederick cordially unites. Frederick and myself start for Oakland, on Friday morning next, should nothing unforseen occur to disappoint.

Believe me to remain,

Very truly, your obliged friend,

C. LENOX REMOND.[69]

SALEM, March 20, 1844.

To the Members and Friends of the
Massachusetts A. S. Society.

DEAR FRIENDS:

Agreeably to the request of your Board of Managers, I take advantage of this, my earliest opportunity, to state that much suc-

[69] *Liberator*, Sept. 23, 1843.

cess has attended our Conventions through Plymouth and Barnstable counties, if large gatherings, warm hearts, hospitable homes,
and much excitement, are indicative of success; similar manifestations being true of every place where appointments were made,
Cohasset, South Dennis, and Barnstable, being excepted. The
heterodoxy of J. M. Spear, the infidelity of S. S. Foster, the odium
of Garrisonism, and the impudence of C. Lenox Remond, seem to
have preceded us in almost every place; but, with few exceptions,
I think, we succeeded in dispelling very many of the prejudices
entertained by individuals unacquainted with our hopes, purposes,
and objects; and on no occasion have we failed to state, unequivocally, that it was no part of our object to promote any particular
sect, or to establish a political party, but to press the grand, leading movement, viz. the 'immediate, unconditional abolition of
American slavery,' as the right of the slave, and the duty of the
master.

It may not be amiss to mention, in passing, that the arrangements for the Convention in Cohasset were given in charge of an
officer under John Tyler; and as one of the objects of the meeting
would have been to show the disgraceful position John Tyler, his
cabinet, adherents, and apologists, occupy to our country and the
world, we could hardly expect much assistance or sympathy from
him. However, by the kind invitation of our good friend Job
Bailey, we passed on to the village of North Scituate, and held an
excellent meeting in the school-house, on the same evening. On
the following day, we held a Convention in order at Scituate Harbor, in the Methodist meeting-house, and were not a little encouraged by the presence of eight or ten friends from Hingham. In
the evening, there was a large attendance, and on the second morning, we were considerably amused on learning in the course of the
discussions, that the house had been granted on the supposition that
the Convention was under the care and guidance of Liberty party
advocates, and not old organization; hence, some premised they
'caught a Tartar.' The meeting was a good one.

In East Abington, we found ourselves shut out from the Orthodox meeting-house, formerly open to anti-slavery; and were obliged
to crowd into a small Hall as well as we could, a large portion of
the audience sitting on shoe-boxes. Neither of us was sparing in
our rebukes upon those taking the back track movement, of shutting
the meeting-house doors in our faces, at this late hour of anti-

slavery controversy. The meeting was by no means the less spirited, and much wholesome excitement prevailed throughout the village at the time of our departure. The next day (Sunday,) there being no appointment, Mr. Foster addressed the good people of Hanson in the afternoon, and of Hanover in the evening. In the morning, I lectured in Hanson, and in the evening of the same day, in South Abington; my audience being estimated at some five or six hundred persons. I trust some truths were spoken, calculated to awaken additional investigation, and produce additional interest.

The appointment being altered by the advice of friends from East to North Bridgewater, we continued our meetings at the latter place two days, with gratifying effect. We put up at the tavern, kept by Edward Bennett, Esq., who attended the meetings from the beginning; and although considerably prejudiced against us from reports, and especially so towards S. S. Foster, he confessed, after giving us a fair hearing, (to use his own words,) that he was convicted and converted; and we esteem him a valuable acquisition to our righteous enterprise. We were hospitably entertained; every kindness was shown us; and at the close of the meetings, we were conveyed by Mr. Bennett to Abington, where the hall was crowded to excess each evening, many converts were made, and others confirmed in the true faith of old fashioned anti-slavery. In a word, taking into account the state of feeling previously existing there, it was by all pronounced a truly cheering meeting.

Our next Convention, at Pembroke, was also a good one. Although the people, as a general thing, residing in the immediate neighborhood, were extremely indifferent, many came from a distance, bringing with them lots of nice cakes, pies, puddings, apples, &c., and water being cheap and plenty, and a sort of thing which a bigoted, tyrannizing and selfish American gospel-dispensing clergy cannot conveniently monopolize, we partook freely of it, and every thing passed finely off. I would not, however, omit to mention, that the Rev. Mr. Allen, the Episcopalian minister of the parish, entertains a sort of holy horror of everything appertaining to the cause of the poor and oppressed; so much so, as we were told, that our very presence obliged him to take to his bed from its ill effects, which he retained until our departure,—and how much longer is matter of conjecture.

The Rev. Messrs. Hewitt and Whiting, of Abington and Hanson, were present, and took part in the debates, giving both influence and interest to the meeting. What a contrast!

On Friday and Saturday of the same week, our Convention was holden in Duxbury. Gershom Weston, Esq., was chosen chairman of the meeting. The objects of the same being stated in a clear manner, by Mr. Spear, and the ordinary preliminaries completed, Mr. Foster took the stand, and in one of his characteristic speeches of about an hour, it being at once free, bold and startling, gave the audience some little foretaste of what might be expected from succeeding sessions. For instance, among the measures for the completion of the unparalleled work in which we were engaged, he unequivocally demanded the dissolution of the union between Freedom and Slavery—charging the continuance of the world-desecrating system upon the North. A very lively debate ensued. Messrs. Weston, Stetson, Whittemore, Joycelin and Soule, of Duxbury, N. Whiting of Marshfield, S. S. Foster, L. Ford, J. M. Spear, and myself participated. A generous contribution in aid of the Hundred Conventions, was made; and the proceeds of the female contributions promised the Massachusetts A. S. Fair, for December next, I trust will give us an earnest of their regard and sympathy for the cause.

It has rarely been my lot to attend a series of meetings of more sterling interest than those of Duxbury; and the kindness, goodness and hospitality of Capt. Bradford's family will not be forgotten by us soon.

On Sabbath evening following, Mr. Foster and myself addressed a crowded assembly in the town house at Kingston, wherein our good friend J. B. Bartlett resides; and although a carpenter by profession, is worth an acre of a certain class of pulpit occupants in our country, who seem to have elevated themselves for the purpose of pouncing upon the weak, dumb, and enslaved of our guilty country, with destructive power.

On Monday morning, we passed on to Plymouth. Here, also, we were obliged to hold our Convention in the town hall, as the only place our friends could procure in the birth-spot of modern, social, civil, and religious freedom. The day was extremely unpropitious, and the travelling unusually bad, from the large quantity of snow fallen that morning; but we were agreeably surprised on seeing so many present. Bourne Spooner was chosen President, and Joseph Allen and William Thomas, Esqrs. Vice-Presidents. An invitation being given to all present to take part in the deliberations, L. Ford of Abington, who has not only accompanied us the most of our journeyings, but has cheerfully carried us from place to place, commenced the discussion by one of his usually frank addresses, in depression of the pro-slavery position of the American church and clergy. There being a number of the clergy present, they took exception to his remarks, and controversy soon became the order of the day. The Rev. Mr. Tomlinson distinguished himself as a discriminating and shrewd reasoner—the Rev. Mr. Mann as knowing but little on the subject, and less of the actual connexion of the American church with the infernal system of slavery— the Rev. Mr. Pearsons appeared, to but little advantage, and was less honest and courteous; and I regret to say, the Rev. Mr. Briggs, from whom much was expected by both foes and friends, appeared worse than either, reminding one of the old man and his ass in the fable—in trying to suit all, he pleased none, and disappointed himself; and I have no doubt blasted his anti-slavery character in the estimation of many of his true friends and admirers. Much excitement prevailed during the meetings, and at times there were strong indications of disturbance and outbreak, which were overruled by the timely interference of influential persons present. Suffice it to say, I have been assured that great good has resulted from the meeting to our holy cause; and many strong and ardent wishes have been expressed, that Mr. Foster and myself would return to Plymouth, and follow up the work. So, it seems, truth is prevailing, and hope reviving; and being armed with the truth, 'one shall chase a thousand, and two put ten thousand to flight;' whereby many shall learn in their wisdom, that to place more importance upon manner than matter, will prove a disastrous game to those who engage in it.

In conclusion, it is but justice that I express our indebtedness to Messrs. Spooner and sons, Thomas, Moulton, Allen, Rev. Mr. Lord, Harlow, and Stevens, for their prompt co-operation, sympathy and decision in the trial-hour of our cause.

Of our meeting in Barnstable county, I will speak in my next; meanwhile,

I remain truly yours for truth and the oppressed,
C. LENOX REMOND.[71]

SALEM, Nov. 13, 1844.

DEAR FRIEND:

I notice in the Boston Morning Chronicle of last week, and in the Emancipator and Weekly Chronicle of this morning, several

[71] *Liberator*, March 29, 1844.

communications, purporting to be reports of meetings recently held in New-Bedford and Salem, and involving, in a prejudicial sense, the course pursued by my friends Douglass, Phillips and Buffum, and myself:—the first, signed by Wm. R. Pitman and Elihu Grant—the second, over the signature of P.—the third, over the signature of Viator—and the fourth, I presume to be editorial.

Permit me to say, through the medium of your paper, to those friends likely to be abused by the foul slanders, that each and every statement, representation, charge and insinuation, contained in the reports of the proceedings, are alike mean and unmanly—destitute of an approach to truth, the color of justice, the semblance of moral honesty, or the shade of moral courage—and pronounce the authors, whoever they may be, as wilful detractors and fabricators, or unpardonably ignorant of the doings of the meetings they have presumed to reflect upon. If the former, they prove, upon the face of such knavish traducings, their Liberty party ship to be in a sinking condition, to require such desperate means to keep her afloat on the sea of public sentiment. If the latter, they ought ever after this to hold their peace. And without adding more, if my unequivocal denial of the truthfulness of the reports or communications shall be questioned, I pledge myself, not upon the honor of a Liberty party demagogue, but of a man, to hold them to the proof, upon names and characters not one of their maligning number shall dare to impeach.

Ever faithfully yours, for the Truth and Right,
CHAS. LENOX REMOND.[72]

PHILADELPHIA, April 5, 1845.

DEAR FRIEND PHILLIPS:

I have deferred writing until the present time, presuming some account of the movements of friend Foster and myself would be given to the 'Pennsylvania Freeman,' or the 'National Anti-Slavery Standard;' and apprehending Stephen will yet do so at his earliest opportunity, I do not intend writing particulars.

Since arriving in this State, I have spent some time in Bucks and Montgomery counties, a portion of it in company with Stephen, and the remainder holding meetings and lecturing myself, and in most places mobs and rumors of mobs have been the order of the day; but receiving personal injury only in a single instance, I will pass them without comment.

[72] *Liberator*, Nov. 22, 1844.

I held an excellent meeting at New Hope, and think a good impression was made upon the large and respectable audience present. At most places I have visited, I have found a few choice friends, intelligent, feeling, efficient, and determined to labor while the day lasts; in fact, I believe our good friends, the Lintons, Johnsons, Smiths, Irvings, Janneys, Beans, Parrises, Magills and Bowmans shall yet redeem their respective counties from their pro-slavery tendencies. The task to many may appear dark and doubtful, but those choice spirits are fully equal to the undertaking.

I have held a number of meetings in Philadelphia, principally among our colored friends, and am encouraged to believe there is an increasing interest among them, and that they would soon become generally co-operative and efficient again, could they be induced to subordinate their sectarian and political non-essentials to the great principles of free thought, free speech, and individual action—would they give Humanity a place over mere sect and party; and above all, would they resolve to enter no place where Anti-Slavery may not have free access, and kneel before no altar too sacred for the enunciation of the whole truth, and advocacy of the entire law.

I have also held public discussions, in a number of instances, on the merits of moral suasion and Liberty party, as instrumentalities for the overthrow of slavery; and I deeply regret to find among the young men of color of this city favoring the political side, the same want of honesty, magnanimity and fairness, so frequently characterising politicians every where, and often, without alluding to principles, denouncing, in unmeasured terms, the American A. S. Society, and asserting that Mr. Garrison and his coadjutors have caused the people of color to be mobbed from Dan to Beersheba; and I am sorry to say, no man has figured so largely in these unwarrantable attacks, unscrupulous assertions, and unmerited denunciations, as Frederick A. Hinton, who, at the lecture given on Monday evening last, in Rev. Mr. Collins' church, rose against the expressed wishes of the audience, and for the third time attacked the members of the American Society, distinctly stating that '*Garrison, for instance, advocated the abominable doctrine of men taking women for wives, and when tired of them, casting them off as they did their old shoes,*' &c. The principal portion of his remarks I was willing to have taken for what they were worth, taking into consideration the source from which they emanated; but the accusation made as stated in the foregoing, was more than I could quietly sit under, without entering my solemn protest, and signifying to the large assembly my determination to hold him to his proof through the columns of some public journal;—and in the name of the poor slave, his righteous cause, and the Society of which Mr. Garrison is presiding officer, and myself a humble representative, I call upon Mr. Hinton to give the public his proof of the charge, or retract as publicly. I shall decline saying more at present, giving Mr. Hinton time to exonerate himself, or stand condemned to the public and the world as one guilty of wilful detraction and slander.

Make such use of this hastily scrawled letter as you think ———— ———— ———— my kind remembrances to friends,

> Believe me to remain
> Faithfully yours,
> CHARLES LENOX REMOND.[73]

SALEM, June 9, 1845.

MY DEAR FRIEND GARRISON:

Ever since my right hand and arm were injured by my being violently thrown from a carriage in Ohio, I have found it both difficult and painful to write; and I would not trouble you with the publication of this imperfect communication, did I not feel it binding upon me, as a duty I owe to the enslaved, to those with whom I have acted in concert for many years, and to the cause at large, to bear my faithful testimony against the proceedings of Messrs. Rogers, French and Chandler of Concord, Folsom of Dover, Smith of Nashua, Clapp and Hutchinson of Lynn, at the recent meeting of the New-Hampshire A. S. Society;—and I have taken my pen more in grief than anger, in publicly appearing to witness against one who has been so dear to me as N. P. Rogers. I have long been aware that it cost white persons much to be my faithful and steadfast friends; and I have not only endeavored to appreciate their friendship, but my attachment has been proportionate.

It is well known that the meeting, as usual, was called in good faith, with the view and purpose of transacting its legitimate business, discussing any questions proposed, and finally to investigate the difficulties which have resulted in another unhappy division, attributable, I regret to say, to Messrs. Rogers, French, and their

73 *Liberator*, April 18, 1845.

adherents. No impartial observer will deny their aiding and abetting policy with the noisy, insulting, and confusion-making portion of those present. It should go abroad that the meeting was disturbed, bawled down, gagged, and brow-beaten by the friends of Mr. Rogers, and not by pro-slavery persons. The conduct of those who feel no sympathy with our cause was decorous and honorable, and especially creditable to the town of Concord. 'Keep this before the people.'

Two years since, I went to Concord, to attend a meeting of the same Society, by invitation, and my expenses were paid by New-Hampshire friends, through J. R. French. Similar scenes transpired then as now; but over them no particular individual had any control. Not so with the last meeting. Every motion and expression of Mr. Rogers was understood, and advantage taken of it by the friends of 'The Herald of Freedom.' For the first time, I rose on the afternoon of the second day, desiring to be heard in behalf of the unhappy bondmen. Permission was denied me by the ready tools of Mr. Rogers, clamoring for free speech and no organization. We asked to be allowed to transact the business of the Society for the ensuing year, and Mr. Rogers scoffed at the idea of doing business in Society capacity. Every entreaty was made, and appeal offered, but in vain. We did not go into New-Hampshire experiment-hunting, and Messrs. Rogers, Folsom and French knew it. The meeting was not called to witness the buffoonery of Mr. Smith, and they were aware of it; neither did that large number assemble to listen to J. B. Chandler's eccentricities, well mixed with Tomfoolery, for Mr. Rogers was apprised that most persons presumed Mr. Chandler in Ohio, if he had any whereabouts at all; yet still, strange to say, at this stage of the meeting, when many were leaving for their country homes, and the Society on the eve of adjournment, Mr. Rogers asked *us* to be patient. Grosser insult—as if the error lay in our patience, and all was honorable and fair and just and decorous and true anti-slavery on the part of the miserable rabble supporting him, and insulting and blackguarding us. Patience indeed! It had ceased to be a virtue with better men than I claim to be. Let Mr. Rogers counsel me to patience when kicked and spit upon by drunken rowdies along the wharves of New-York city, or when scourged in Philadelphia streets, or when pursued by slave-hunting ruffians, armed with dirks, pistols, and rusty muskets, as I have witnessed them in Indiana, or when the straight-jacket and iron weights are preparing for me on the banks of the Penobscot. But don't tantalize me by exhortations to patience, when abused by pretended anti-slavery men, by persons who have become tired of abolition drudgery. It is their fault, not ours, that they did not calculate upon crossing the moral Alps for the glorious cause; and that in winter weather as trying and destructive to our moral nature as it was trying and destructive to the physical natures of Napoleon and his army. We have deceived nobody; they have deceived themselves in supposing that at the expiration of fourteen years even, a beautiful climate, lovely landscapes, McAdamised roads, and peace and plenty, would greet them. Hard fare and rough usage await the faithful and brave, to the end of the struggle.

Ever truly yours,
For justice, truth and freedom,
C. LENOX REMOND.[74]

XI. WILLIAM C. NELL

The letters of William C. Nell, the first Negro to take seriously the writing of the history of the Negro race, are more than interesting. We are unfortunate in not having a large number of them, but those accessible illuminate certain aspects of the history of that time and enable the reader to appreciate the worth of this man.

ROCHESTER, (N. Y.,) Jan. 23, 1848.

ESTEEMED FRIEND GARRISON:

Mr. Douglass and myself accepted an invitation to this anniversary celebration of Franklin's birthday; and accordingly, at the appointed hour, we wended our way to the Irving house, accompanied by Mr. John Dick and another friend. The company had assembled, and were marching into the hall to the inspiring music of Adams's Bugle Band. We arrived just in time to unite with the procession. I had myself received a slight intimation that some objection had been manifested by a few, to the participation of Mr. Douglass and myself. This, however, gave me but little uneasiness, believing that come what would, the result would prove no detriment to the cause of freedom.

[74] *Liberator*, June 13, 1845.

Mr. Douglass had no cause to apprehend opposition until we had delivered our ticket at the diningroom door; when the host laid an embargo on our further ingress, declaring that we could not be admitted. It was in vain that we protested against his insult, and asserted our claim to equal treatment with others. We were called *intruders*, and told, that 'it was a violation of the rules of society for colored people to associate with whites,' and were threatened ejectment by the police. By this time, our presence at the door, the lookers on in the entry, and the passing of words between parties, had attracted the attention of the company just seated. We retired to a drawing-room, where the pro-slavery point was contended for by the host, who declared that several gentlemen had expressed a determination not to allow us a seat with them. We were about entering the hall to test the question in *propria personæ*, intending that decision to supersede what the host had proffered us.. Several of the company had now gathered, some of whom expressed regret at our treatment. It was now proposed to submit the question. JAMES KIRK, Jr., chairman of the committee of arrangements, briefly defined his position, and in a commendable manner advocated our rights. ALEXANDER MANN, Esq., editor of the Rochester American, and one of the Vice-Presidents, nobly came to the rescue, his remarks being loudly applauded —and when the question was called for by the chairman, almost the entire company responded *Aye*. The negative was represented by some six or eight, who must indeed have felt rebuked by this overwhelming vote. The host, who had, but a few moments before, manifested so bitter and hostile spirit towards us, now communicated the intelligence that 'there was a clean vote in our favor.' You may be sure that, after having been the victims of so much controversy, on entering the hall, we were 'the observed of all observers.' It was a painful as well as triumphant hour for Mr. Douglass and myself, for reasons which abolitionists hardly know how to appreciate. None but the *colored man*, the immediate recipient of American pro-slavery hate, can fully testify to the emotions excited by such a development. I care not to dwell upon it. Let me here state, however, that on being seated, the host offered a string of apologies for his conduct. Comment is unnecessary. After due attention to the work spread before them, preparations were made for the 'feast of reason and the flow of soul.' Wit and sentiment, music and poetry, each lent a charm to enliven

the scene. During the volunteer remarks, Mr. Douglass was called
for, and briefly proposed his sentiment. Shortly after, Alexander
Mann, Esq. announced to the company that he had a sentiment to
offer, which he hoped and believed would be responded to by every
gentleman present. 'Sir,' said he, 'on occasions of this kind, we
should cheerfully lay aside all personal or political prejudices.'
After speaking in this vein for a short time in a handsome and
liberal manner, the best calculated to allay any unpleasant feeling,
and preparing the minds of all, he tendered the following sentiment:—

Frederick Douglass—We recognize in the genius and cultivation of this orator and philanthropist, good augury of the elevation of his race.

Mr. Douglass, on rising, was warmly greeted. He confessed
himself much embarrassed by the coincident circumstances of his
present position; but would not control his gratitude, elicited by
the sentiment just offered, and so heartily responded to by the
company. He alluded to the treatment received by him while in
England, where *merit*, and not *color*, was the passport to the highest circles; but that his feelings of present satisfaction were of another character from any previously enjoyed. He adverted to his
connexion with the Press in Rochester, to the uniformly kind notice
extended to him by the gentlemen connected therewith, as also from
the citizens generally, contrasting it with the abusive and pro-
slavery expression of the New-York Sunday Despatch, New-York
Express, Bennett's Herald, and the Democratic Review, &c.—which
he was proud to acknowledge this evening's tribute as an offset.
Its recollection would be sufficient to alleviate the bitterness of
much past experience, and fortify him with strength for the future.
He wished to add, that whatever he had said or done in relation to
slavery, he conscientiously felt it demanded by love to his country,
and his oppressed and outraged brethren at the South and the
North. His speech was received with evident attention, and with
loud demonstrations of applause.

Philemon Canfield, Esq., who presided, testified his hearty satisfaction with the liberal spirit of the company, by rebuking by their
vote the wicked prejudice against color. Mr. C. 'is an old Hartford publisher, who, though advanced in years, is still devoted to
his profession in Rochester.' The anti-slavery war, waged for the
last eighteen years, has indeed been prolific in these exhibitions,

and as remarkable for the succession of victories, always the reward of the faithful and persevering. To compare the present with the past—those dark hours when your bugle blast was first sounded among the hills and valleys of New England—we can hardly believe the evidence daily presented of the onward progress of those mighty principles then proclaimed to the American nation. The treatment of the colored man in this country is a legitimate illustration of 'hating those whom we have injured,' and brings to my recollection that chapter in Waverley where Fergus Mac Ivar replies to his friend, when being led to execution—'You see the compliment they pay to our Highland strength and courage. Here we have lain until our limbs are cramped into palsey, and now they send six soldiers with loaded muskets to prevent our taking the castle by storm.' The analogy is found in the omnipotent and omnipresent influence of American pro-slavery in crushing every noble and praiseworthy aspiration of the persecuted colored man. As in nature, the smiles of summer are made sweeter by the frowns of winter, the calm of ocean is made more placid by the tempest that has preceded it; so in this moral battle, these incidental skirmishes will contribute to render the hour of victory indeed a blissful realization.

So sure as night precedes day—war ends in peace, and winter wakes spring—just so sure will the persevering efforts of Freedom's army be crowned with victory's perennial laurels.

Yours, to the end of the struggle,

WILLIAM C. NELL.[91]

ROCHESTER, (N. Y.) Feb. 19, 1852.

ESTEEMED FRIEND GARRISON:

Inspired by reading, in the *Liberator*, the narrative of the Ladies' Bazaar and the Annual Meeting of the Massachusetts Anti-Slavery Society, each so glorious in results, and so vivifying to me in reminiscences, I have at length obeyed the spirit prompting me to pen you a few lines, by way of most grateful remembrance. I believe Henry Martyn once recorded his conviction, that he who travelled far from home in pursuit of health, travels on a fool's errand. How applicable this may be in the present case, deponent is unable to say. Though not having regained my usual health, the feeling is sometimes mine, that I may yet see the opening buds and sunny skies of coming spring.

[91] *Liberator*, Feb. 11, 1848.

A glance at the popular lectures delivered in any locality, and the influences generated by them, to some minds present a significant item in a general summing up of character. The citizens of Rochester have this season listened (on the Athenæum and other rostrums) to several able lectures on miscellaneous subjects. The role commenced by a lecture from Henry Ward Beecher, who, for a manly vindication of the higher law, was applauded by the mass, and complimented by the Hunker press with what they intended for censure. He was succeeded by J. T. Headley, author of 'Napoleon and his Marshals.' On announcing his subject—Personal Freedom—the audience manifested both hopes and fears; some supposing that, from the premises laid down, sentiments would legitimately follow, which, if not radical, might at least have a direct reference, even by way of conclusion, to the millions of *persons* in this country, so signally deprived of *freedom*. Others, smarting from Mr. Beecher's denunciations of the Fugitive Slave Law, instinctively anticipated a little more of *that* 'same sort.' But both classes were disappointed, the lecture being made up in sketching the recent revolutions in Europe, while, in regard to freedom in the United States, a most memorable letting alone was exhibited.

Among other performances, of more or less acceptance, may be mentioned, the Historical Lectures of Rev. John Lord, and a characteristic poem by John G. Saxe; but, without disparagement of any, it may truly be said, that none have been better appreciated than the efforts of Ralph Waldo Emerson, John Pierpont, and Theodore Parker, enhancing the distinguished reputation long enjoyed by this trio of the Old Bay State literati. Your readers are conversant, through various mediums, with their matter and manner; yet I am disposed to mention what was specially true in this instance of the two latter. They did not sacrifice Humanity to the Muses, but alluded to slavery whenever its application would enforce a moral or confirm a fact. Samuel J. May, of Syracuse, in his recent pulpit ministrations in this city, was also, as you are of course prepared to hear, faithful to the slave, whose cause he has so long, so triumphantly vindicated. The words so fitly spoken by these champions of truth, and the attentive ear given by the people, when emancipated from their would-be leaders, have only served to deepen the regret occasioned by the non-appearance here of New England's gifted orator and Humanity's eloquent advocate, Wendell Phillips, to facilitate whose lecturing visit a combination of ways and means was hopefully put forth, but, most unfortunately, without success.

A most gratifying fact to me is the love and veneration cherished in many circles here for the name and fame of George Thompson, who, though beset by a rampant pro-slavery press, achieved a victory differing in some details, but none the less brilliant than those of Boston and Springfield. At a recent exhibition of a Young Ladies' Seminary, an essay was read on the Transatlantic Missions of Lafayette and George Thompson, eulogizing both in the loftiest strain for their services in the cause of freedom, which was but a just tribute awarded to each. Many, however, thought the former would have lost nothing, if the latter's claims to immortal honor had been more prominently dwelt upon; for while Lafayette's errand to this country was to assist a three-penny-tax-ridden people, George Thompson's sacrifices and efforts were consecrated, and in the face of fearful odds, to the advocacy of a race whose entire selves are held subordinate to a tyranny unparalleled in the world's annals. Let full justice, then, be awarded to Lafayette for the aid rendered these colonies in their revolutionary struggles; but to the strong hand and bold heart of George Thompson, whose life has been a battle-field—whose matchless eloquence and fearless manhood have been so potent in setting races free from bondage—to him will impartial history decree the chaplet of imperishable renown.

Sallie Holly held a large audience in close attention at Corinthian Hall, one evening last week, by her admirable lecture on American Slavery. Many who revered the late Myron Holly felt induced to hear his daughter in this, her first public address in her native city, though evidently not from their regard for anti-slavery truth, or faith in the propriety of woman's rights; but those who heard her without being deeply impressed, must be in a most unenviable state of mental and moral darkness. Her familiarity with the subject, her fund of argument and illustrative facts, and her fervency of appeal, constitute her a most valuable auxiliary to advance the anti-slavery cause. Impressed with this truth, my mind reverted to your early and constant advocacy of woman's equality. The seeds sown by you at a time when the public was indifferent have germinated, and now promise an abundant harvest. The fact of woman's equal participation in the lecture room, in the halls of science, and other departments hitherto monopolized by man, has become an every day occurrence. In the perilous years of '33–'35, a colored woman—Mrs. Maria W. Stewart—fired with a holy zeal to speak her sentiments on the improvement of colored Americans, encountered an opposition even from her Boston circle of friends, that would have damped the ardor of most women. But your words of encouragement cheered her onwards, and her public lectures awakened an interest acknowledged and felt to this day. The world cannot rob you of the great satisfaction of having been mainly instrumental in securing an audience for the oppressed on account of sex or complexion.

The Fugitive Slave Law has made its ravages in Rochester; but without those exciting scenes enacted in Boston and elsewhere, there have been occasions when both the foes and friends of freedom were marshalling their forces. The first foe saving the Union, the others rescuing a brother man from human bloodhounds. But the proximity of this city to Canada has ensured a ready flight in the fugitive's emergency. Several who had resided here for years, sustaining good business positions, have been compelled to abandon home and loved associations, for fear of being dragged back to bondage. Fugitives are constantly passing through here, giving no rest to their feet nor slumber to their eyelids, until the protecting ægis of Queen Victoria makes them welcome freemen on Canada's shore. A party of fifteen thus rid themselves of republican slavery on Thanksgiving day—to them truly a day consecrated with sincere thanksgiving to the God of freedom.

Some very interesting facts might be given relative to these American Kossuths—those who have filled various stations, in the mechanic's work shop and slaveholder's dwelling, and have slaked their thirst for knowledge under towering difficulties, and at last seized the golden moment to unrivet the chain, and, through complex trials, reach a haven where they can realize that

————————'No sea
Swells like the bosom of a man set free.'

Some who were present at the Syracuse and Christiana battle-grounds, where either their hands embodied, tongues wagged, or eyes looked treason to slavery, are now enjoying, in a monarch's domain, the liberty denied them in the American republic. The colored citizens have systematically aided their hunted brethren, and have just held a donation festival, exclusively for the benefit of the fugitive.

I am yet a sojourner with Isaac and Amy Post, whose names are synonymous with truth and zeal in Humanity's cause, whose active sympathies are indeed a panacea to the invalid of body or mind.

With unbounded regard, I remain,
Faithfully yours,
WILLIAM C. NELL.[92]

ESTEEMED FRIEND GARRISON:

During the past few weeks of a temporary sojourn in my native city, I have been somewhat an observer of those events, which, though in many respects but local, are nevertheless connected with the elevation of colored Americans generally; and as such, their record may, I trust, secure an insertion in the *Liberator*.

A series of public meetings has been held, under the auspices of colored citizens ranking with the Free Soil party. These gatherings have been characterized by great enthusiasm, and a willing ear for any citizen or stranger present whose voice could aid, directly or indirectly, the cause of human freedom. Though in the main intended as political meetings, yet every phase of an oppressed people's enlargement had its orator, and fervid, heart-stirring eloquence in the application of home truths, caustic denunciations of known delinquence, and warm approval bestowed upon the faithful, severally struck those chords, which, vibrating among the audience, have not yet ceased to bring forth abundant fruits.

Among the resolutions defining their position in the Presidential and State elections, the following served as a nucleus:—

Resolved, That as the Whig and so-called Democratic parties of this country are endeavoring to crush, debase and dehumanize us as a people, any man among us voting for their respective candidates, virtually recognizes the righteousness of their principles, and shall be held up to public reprobation as a traitor, a hissing and a by word, a pest and a nuisance, the off-scouring of the earth.

Resolved, That the candidates of the Free Democracy need no eulogy—they stand out in bold relief, as the representatives of principles which command the admiration and support of every lover of Truth, Justice and Humanity. Our hands, our hearts and our votes are theirs.

In discussing the first resolution, much sensitiveness was manifested by a few voters who were still wedded to the two great pro-

[92] *Liberator*, March 5, 1852.

slavery parties. (Thank God, there were but a few so recreant to their highest duty!) The blended powers of argument and sarcasm were levelled at these men, who seemed to think it their duty to espouse the cause by which they eat and drink.

The second resolution concentrated the remarks of many speakers, and when the names of prominent liberty candidates were mentioned, they were received with prolonged and deafening applause. Aside from the associations surrounding them as candidates, there were remembrances of specific acts by certain individuals, which became signals for renewed plaudits. JOHN P. HALE was cheered as the eloquent and gifted advocate for the defence in the trials of the alleged Shadrach rescuers; CHARLES SUMNER for his elaborate and learned argument before the Supreme bench of Massachusetts, contending for equal school rights of colored children. The old war-horse, JOSHUA R. GIDDINGS, for his bold defiance of the slave domination in Congress, was gratefully remembered, as were many others.

The disaffection of the colored citizens of New Bedford towards HORACE MANN, on account of some remarks of his construed by them as favoring our expatriation to Africa, did not materially detract from his quota of applause; for though there were those who feared such an inference *could* be drawn from his letter to the colored citizens of Ohio, yet the mass had too much confidence in his profession and practice to believe him guilty of that sin justly regarded by colored Americans as unpardonable. Opposition to the American Colonization Society is and ever should be a most vital element in the creed of colored Americans; and we cannot too jealously watch the sources from whence those influences emanate, corrupting public sentiment—though in the exercise of this duty, we may sometimes fail to discriminate between fidelity to our cause, and prematurely charging upon individuals a positive dereliction from truth and duty. Our vigilant friends at New Bedford have at least this merit, that their failing (if one) leaned to Freedom's side.

Regarding the Free Soil party as an offshoot from the old pioneer anti-slavery tree, the meeting unanimously adopted a resolution of unwavering confidence in the efforts of WILLIAM LLOYD GARRISON, and of sincere gratitude to him and his noble coadjutors, invoking their continued warfare upon American slavery.

Lewis Hayden said he was happy to notice several clergymen

present, whose co-operation in this department of anti-slavery labor was in strong contrast with the conduct of the main body of their ministerial brethren among the dominant class. He regretted that truth demanded the confession, that even among colored clergymen were to be found those who sustain ecclesiastical relations wholly inconsistent with their position as aspiring leaders of an oppressed people.

Robert Morris, Esq., cautioned the people against the proposed plans of the American Colonization Society and the Ebony Line of steamers. He also spoke of the operations of the Fugitive Slave Law, alluding to recent decisions *pro* and *con*, and occasionally indulged in some graphic sketches of the Shadrach rescue.

Robert Johnson expressed his concurrence in the prayer offered at the opening meeting, that every colored man would be sure to pay his taxes, and not forego the opportunity, as he had done for some years after being eligible; but he now rejoiced in the right of a citizen, and would always exercise it. The Free Democratic party, he believed, would exert a powerful influence for the slave's emancipation. Correcting himself, he recalled the appellation. Our brethren at the South should not be called *slaves*, but *prisoners of war*.

Rev. J. C. Beman, of Connecticut, congratulated his brethren of the old Bay State that they could enjoy the elective franchise—a right denied seven thousand citizens of his native State, the land of blue laws and 'steady habits.' He narrated the fact that his father, when presented with his manumission papers, was asked what name he had selected. He replied, that he had always loathed slavery and wanted to be a man; hence he adopted the name of *Be-man*. He (the speaker) had inherited from that father a burning desire for the elevation of his oppressed countrymen here, on American soil, and was unalterably hostile to the American Colonization Society.

Rev. J. B. Smith, of Rhode Island, recounted some incidents of his early life, which he said he held in undying remembrance. He alluded especially to the persevering efforts of his father and uncle to burst the chains of slavery. His father took him by the hand, and on leading him from a master's domain, made him swear that he would never be a slave. They were pursued by an armed posse with bloodhounds, and in attempting to ford a river rather than surrender his liberty, his life was sacrificed by a rifle shot from his merciless pursuers. That scene was even now vividly before him. He believed that resistance to tyrants was obedience to God, and hence, to his mind, the only drawback to the matchless Uncle Tom of Mrs. Stowe was his virtue of submission to tyranny—an exhibition of grace which he (the speaker) did not covet.

William J. Watkins eloquently enforced the duty of every colored voter to sustain the Free Soil party, when the most strenuous exertions of pro-slavery men were lavishly contributed to its defeat. It was recreancy in any colored man to be lukewarm during the contest. It had always been his pride to do battle for the right—a duty he learned from William Lloyd Garrison, who, on his liberation from a Baltimore prison, where he had been confined for his devotion to the anti-slavery cause, met him (the speaker), then a boy five years old, at his father's house, and told him to be always an abolitionist. In the light of that instruction he had ever endeavored to walk, and hoped to be faithful to the end.

Rev. James E. Crawford, of Nantucket, said he appreciated the importance of remembering the slave at the ballot-box, and cited some instances in his anti-slavery experience where it had been signally efficacious. He would not, however, regard politics as an end, but merely as a means for securing a certain good. He would have them ever keep in mind, that moral power was a more exalted and positive lever for promoting the anti-slavery or any other good cause. He expressed, in substance, the sentiment of Mrs. Child, that he who gives his mind to politics sails on a stormy sea, with a giddy pilot. He informed the audience that he dated his conversion to anti-slavery from October 21st, 1835, when, landing from shipboard, and walking up State street, Boston, he suddenly encountered that mob of 'gentlemen of property and standing,' who, with a rope around Mr. Garrison's neck, were bent upon his destruction. On learning that it was for words and deeds in behalf of the enslaved colored man, his heart and soul at that moment became fully committed to the cause for which our noble advocate was so near sacrificing his life.

Wm. C. Nell remarked, that in behalf of 428,000 nominally free colored Americans, and nearly four millions of chattel slaves in these United States, he could not but commend those who exercised the elective franchise in favor of liberty. Remembering that in Pennsylvania that right had been stolen from her 52,000 colored citizens, and that in several States, falsely termed free, it was restricted to property qualification, and in others absolutely denied, he rejoiced that to day it was our untrammeled right, in the old Bay State, and that its influences were felt not only in commingling with other citizens at the polls, but in every sphere of society.

But there were other ways of advancing the anti-slavery cause than at the ballot-box; and he concurred with other speakers in reference to the women, who he regretted were yet denied their right to vote, but their means of appeal to husbands, fathers and brothers, intelligently directed, were various and all-powerful. The emancipation of 800,000 slaves in the British West Indies was mostly attributable to the women's petition, two miles and a quarter long, which, as declared by members of Parliament, could no longer be resisted.

Among our white fellow-citizens participating, Dr. James W. Stone and Hon. Anson Burlingame were most prominent. The latter created much enthusiasm by his eloquent effort. He thought that the heroic, courageous and romantic escape of William and Ellen Craft from slavery had not its analogy in history; and that their refusal to retreat from the city, when hunted by the hounds of power, that others might be inspired by their example, was worthy of everlasting praise. He expressed the hope that when Thomas Sims should again fly for freedom, thousands of others might find it with him. After submitting an instructive narrative of the power wielded by the slave oligarchy over the tame and subservient North, he besought the colored citizens to remember that they too were a power on earth here in Massachusetts.

The first opportunity of hearing Rev. J. W. Loguen, of Syracuse, occurred at the conclusion of these meetings, and it was a treat which will long be remembered. His recital of the Jerry escape, and the reciprocal expressions between him and some of the *lookers-on* at the Shadrach rescue, elicited responsive cheers which made the welkin ring, and constituted a scene which slaveholding Commissioners would have groaned in spirit to witness.

Boston has indeed figured rather conspicuously in the history of fugitive slave cases. August 4th, 1836, two slaves of John B. Morris, of Baltimore, were spirited from the Supreme Court in Boston—mainly through the prowess of a few colored women; the memory of which deed is sacredly cherished and transmitted to posterity. Sheriff Sumner—the honored father of Charles Sumner, whose impulses for freedom are a choice inheritance—was severely censured because he did not prevent their escape; an undertaking which those who were present knew he could not accomplish if he would, and believed he would not if he could. The stirring events connected with the Latimer war, the hunting of William and Ellen Craft, the escape of Shadrach from the lion's den, and the unparalleled excitement of Thomas Sims's arrest, are each so many eloquent themes of appeal for renewed exertions in freedom's cause.

Charles Lenox Remond followed, in one of his felicitous speeches, during which—though careful to note the improving signs of the times—he felt called upon to enumerate various short-comings on the part of residents in Boston, the capital of the old Bay State, who, considering that fact, did not occupy so high an anti-slavery position as the emergency loudly demanded.

Other voices helped to augment the interest of these meetings, but the foregoing must suffice.

The position of the colored citizens of Boston is in many features a peculiar one; for while with truth it can be said that they enjoy certain facilities denied to their brethren in nearly all other sister cities, yet the extremes of equality and proscription meet in their case, as indicated by the pro-slavery School Committee Board. While in every other city and town in the State, colored children have free access to the district schools, here they are debarred that right. To such an extent have the feelings of a large majority been outraged in this matter, that Boston is fast losing many of her intelligent, worthy, aspiring citizens, who are becoming tax payers in adjoining localities, for the sole advantage of equal school rights. These rights are fully appreciated, and with a result which the annual report of the Cambridgeport School Committee of last year testifies to as follows:—

'In the Broadway Primary School, a singular fact was noticed; namely, the mixture of four different races amongst the pupils—the Anglo-Saxon, Teutonic, Celtic and African. But by the influence of the teachers and of habit, there exists perfect good feeling among them, and there is no apparent consciousness of a difference of race or condition.'

Two independent schools are now supported by parents in the city, rather than send their children to the Smith School, upheld as it is against their long-continued protest. How much longer such a state of things will exist, who can tell?

But though *this* incubus yet bears upon the progress of society, there are many visible signs of improvement in other departments. A few evenings since, it was my privilege to meet a company where happened to be present one young man upon whom had been conferred the degree of Master of Arts, he having passed through a course of theology, and being now engaged in reading law, with a prospect of an early admission to the bar of one of the Western States. In conversation with him were two young physicians, one just graduated from Dartmouth College, the other a student at Bowdoin, having perfected his medical education by three years' attendance at the hospitals in Paris. These gratifying features are multiplying much faster than many believe. In various cities and towns may now be found those Home Circles, where mental and moral worth, genius and refinement lend their charms, in giving to the world assurance that, despite accidental differences of complexion, here you behold a man, there a woman, competent to fill any station in civilized society.

It was my intention to have alluded to the vocal and instrumental concerts of the Excelsior Glee Club, and to the elocutionary and musical juvenile exhibitions, under the management of Miss Washington; also, to the interest manifested in a recent course of physiological lectures, volunteered by Dr. Archibald Miles; but enough has been detailed to show that the colored citizens of Boston are improving in some degree, though not so fast as their most sanguine friends could desire.

With increased faith in the 'good time coming,' I remain,

Faithfully yours,

WM. C. NELL.[93]

Boston, December, 1852.

FREDERICK DOUGLASS AND HIS PAPER.

Esteemed Friend Garrison:

Frederick Douglass, at Framingham, August 2d, remarked, 'that he held his columns free to any one who should think injustice had been done to any party.' Having myself been the victim of his injustice, in his paper of August 12th, I solicited a hearing therein, which has been denied me—August 19th—thus:— 'The editor does not feel called upon to give his columns to the circulation of his [my] speeches or letters.' Will you promote the

[93] *Liberator*, Dec. 10, 1852.

cause of truth and free discussion by inserting in THE LIBERATOR
the following rejected communication?   W. C. N.
    Boston, August 19th, 1853.

————

BOSTON, August 13, 1853.

MR. DOUGLASS:

In your paper of Aug. 12th, you have grossly misrepresented
my sayings and doings at the meeting recently held in Boston.   I,
therefore, ask you to publish the following communication.

In the first place, I must express to you the surprise manifested
here in view of the language of your editorial; for, at the meeting,
you acquitted me of any dishonorable or personal motive in the
presentation I felt called upon to make relative to your course, and,
moreover, promised you would do all in your power to promote
harmony and allay controversy; but the first development to your
readers is applying to me the epithet, 'contemptible tool.'

You put words into my mouth which I never used.   I did not
say, 'I am the injured party here; I am on trial.'   What I did say
was, 'I am the persecuted party'—persecuted, I meant, by yourself
and Mr. Morris.   I made no allusion to being 'on trial,' there being
no occasion for it.   I have no fears of any trial before a Boston
audience.

As to your holding me up as a practical enemy of the colored
people, my pen smiles at the idea.   When are you going to commence the task of proving your assertion?

I heed not your inuendoes nor your comments; I can wait the
decision of an impartial community.   But your readers should
know what I said and did on that occasion, hence I submit my remarks, as offered.

REMARKS ON THE FIRST EVENING.

MR. CHAIRMAN,—Concurring, as I am happy to do, in the general train of remark which we have just heard from Mr. Douglass,
I the more deeply regret his omission of another topic, which others
beside myself anticipated his making some allusion to.   But as
neither himself nor any other person has done so, the duty seems
to devolve upon me.

It is, of course, known to most of those present, that the time
has been when Mr. Douglass sustained very friendly relations toward Mr. Garrison and the pioneer Society.   It is also well known

that now that relation is changed, and within a few months past, his spirit seems more than ever alienated, and in his paper he has made use of language which to many, and certainly to me—when considering his former identity of interests with them—seems un-kind, ungenerous and ungrateful. I say this more in sorrow than in anger; but as I have long and intimately known Mr. Douglass—been associated with him in the publication of his paper—familiar with him and the old Society in their day of harmony and coöpera-tion—and, moreover, as I have, to persons present and elsewhere, in speaking of his paper, cheerfully commended, though not afraid to blame—it occurs to me that I am no less his friend than before, because I ask him to explain his new position. There are those here who desire it, and the words that he may offer may correct us if in error, and render his paper the more acceptable.

I have not risen to defend Mr. Garrison and his coadjutors; for, thank God! from me, and in this place, they need no defence. I have not risen to offend Mr. Douglass and his friends; to any thing of that kind, I am opposed by my whole moral, mental and physical constitution. But here, in the city where Mr. Garrison and the Pioneer Society are known and loved, it is fitting that an opportunity should be tendered for explanation.

SECOND EVENING.

MR. CHAIRMAN,—I disclaim any wish or desire to curtail the list of subscribers for Mr. Douglass's paper. I would not blot from the moral firmament one anti-slavery star. The colored people of Boston, like those of other places, are very delinquent in supporting anti-slavery papers, for even the pioneer sheet, THE LIBERATOR, has not from them a tithe of the patronage to which it is preëminently entitled. Let them all remain, to shed light on the slave's path to freedom. It is only because I would have Frederick Douglass's Paper emit a more friendly light, that I stand before you this evening.

Among the articles in Mr. Douglass's paper which I submit in justification of my statement, is that published by him May 27th, headed 'Infidelity,' followed with some of Mr. Garrison's com-ments, in THE LIBERATOR of June 10th.

This censure of the old Society, in consequence of the oft-ex-ploded charges of infidelity against some of its agents, brings to my mind that most eloquent passage in the anti-slavery lectures of

Mr. Douglass, a few years since:—'Commend me to that infidelity which takes off chains, rather than to the Christianity which puts them on.'

Mr. Douglass, on one occasion, dealt very unhandsomely with George Thompson; but as I have reason to believe he regretted the course he took and the language he used on that occasion, I will waive the reading of his remarks, and the comments of Mr. Thompson's friends in England. But it seems appropriate that I should present, in this connection, what I then expressed in letters to my friends, and what I always feel when he utters an unkind word toward any of his old friends:—

'My abiding feeling is one of sincere regret that George Thompson should have been attacked by a colored man, at least such an one historically as Frederick Douglass. He should have pondered *long* and *well*, before allowing his pen to indite or tongue to utter any thing disparagingly of George Thompson.

If there had been a crime committed, and a necessity for its exposure, the matter would present a wholly different aspect; as it is, I think an indecent haste was exhibited in the performance of a very ungrateful act.'

In Mr. D's paper of July 22, he calls upon Geo. W. Putnam of Lynn, who has recently become disaffected towards the Mass. Anti-Slavery Society, in a manner invoking a renewal of his warfare against them.

But I care not to enlarge, or go into details. My object is not controversy, but simply a presentation of facts, for all parties interested.

Mr. Douglass remarked, that two or three more such speeches as were delivered here by Mr. Foss would heal the wound, (which, after all, was not a very deep one,) between him and his old friends. Happy indeed would I be, Mr. Chairman, if my words on this occasion would be accepted in that light. Let us compare notes by the way-side—let Mr. D. cease his direct and indirect hostility toward his old friends, speak well of or laud to the skies any individuals or parties he may feel disposed to, discuss and argue with them, show his to be a more excellent way than theirs— all this is well and proper; but in doing this, let him not detract from and drag others down; for he and they, though honestly differing as to ways and means, can both work in a general way for the downfall of our common enemy, slavery.

WILLIAM C. NELL.[94]

94 *Liberator*, Sept. 2, 1853.

Mr. Editor:—Rev. Theodore Parker administered, in a recent Sunday discourse, a well-deserved rebuke of the spirit of caste, which in the Puritan city is exhibited towards that portion of God's heritage whose skins are colored unlike the majority; and for an illustration, referred to the concerts of Monsieur Jullien, at Music Hall, from one of which respectable colored persons had been excluded.

It is gratifying, however, to be enabled to say, that this statement, though sadly true at first, has a sequel redeeming in its features, and which would have been cheerfully presented by the speaker, had he been apprized of the facts. They are briefly these:—

A correspondence ensued between the rejected party and Mons. Jullien, who promptly replied, through his gentlemanly agent, Wm. F. Brough, Esq., 'that the exclusion of persons and the proscriptive clause in the advertisement, were both unauthorized by them, and promised that the latter should be at once withdrawn, and the parties and their friends should have the same facilities as other ticket holders.'

Suffice it to say, these agreements were fulfilled to the satisfaction of all concerned, and afterwards, through the series, there were no skin-scanning sub-officials to insult and proscribe such as availed themselves of an equal chance for revelling in the world-renowned music of Mons. Jullien's orchestra.

To a very great extent, the enlightened public sentiment of Boston has rendered obsolete the exclusion of colored persons from places of public resort, (all honor to the Germanians for their course in this respect,) and therefore many might naturally wonder why the example of the Howard Athenæum management should be imitated by door-keepers elsewhere. The solution of this problem may be found in the fact that the colored children of Boston are yet prohibited attending school in their respective wards, but, through summer's heat and winter's cold, must wend their way to the Smith school in Ward Six, subjecting them and their parents to manifold inconveniences, (not to mention the subversion of their rights as citizens,) the only class in the community thus outraged, and which furnishes a pretext for those pro-slavery abettors, who act on the presumption that, as colored children are the victims of proscription in Boston, aggressions may be committed upon colored men and women with impunity.

A desire to tender the *amende honorable* to Mons. Jullien and Wm. F. Brough, Esq., has prompted this communication; and the belief that you, Mr. Editor, cherish the hope that Boston may soon conquer her prejudices against an injured and patient race, warrants its being forwarded to the *Commonwealth* for publication. I remain faithfully yours,

WILLIAM C. NELL.[95]

BOSTON, Nov., 1853.

SOUTHFIELD, Oakland Co., Mich.,
Sept. 6th, 1858.

DEAR FRIEND GARRISON:

The papers have already, I presume, informed you somewhat of the recent kidnapping case, and the consequent excitement in Cincinnati. I happened to be in Detroit, where the betrayer and his two victims (all colored men) resided, and when the news reached there, you can easily imagine the effect produced upon the colored men and women, many of whom were acquainted with all the parties.

Miss Frances E. Watkins already had a meeting announced for Thursday evening, Sept. 2d, in the Croghan Street Baptist Church, but the arrival of Rev. Henry H. Garnet, fresh from Cincinnati, prompted an attempt to secure the City Hall for a large gathering of the citizens to protest against kidnapping in Detroit; but the Buchanan Democratic Convention being held there, was of itself sufficient to put a veto upon any hope of ingress for an anti-Fugitive-Slave Law demonstration.

The Colored Methodist Conference adjourned its evening session, and thus augmented the numbers which crowded the meeting. The exercises commenced at an early hour by Mr. Garnet's reading the appropriate hymn of Mr. Follen, commencing, 'What mean ye that ye bruise and bind?' This was sung with thrilling effect; after which a fervent prayer was offered by Rev. J. P. Campbell, in which every reference to the traitor, his deserved punishment, his victims and their sad fate, elicited heart-moving responses from various parts of the house.

Rev. Mr. Davis, Chairman, then introduced Rev. H. H. Garnet, who in a graphic and eloquent manner detailed the history of the kidnapping case, tracing Brodie's connection with it under written

95 *Liberator*, Dec. 16, 1853.

instructions from the slaveholders, until the imprisonment of the two captives in the jail at Covington, Ky. They had accepted Brodie's pledge to assist their return to the South, with a view to secure the liberation of some of their relatives from slavery. Instead of this blissful realization of their hopes, they were delivered into the hands of their self-styled owners, and by the very man in whom they had most implicitly trusted, receiving each one hundred lashes, and ordered to be sold further South, expressly to cut off all future chance of escape to the North. Mr. Garnet exhibited a pair of manacles, such as were worn by them on their way to jail, and a bull whip, as used in their severe flogging.

The young men of Cincinnati, on learning the facts, with that 'eternal vigilance' which is 'the price of liberty,' succeeded in getting possession of the traitor, and instituted measures for his trial. This occupied two hours, during most of which time Mr. Garnet was present, and it was mainly owing to his intercession that Brodie was not torn limb from limb. He escaped with life, after the infliction of three hundred blows with a paddle—one blow for each dollar of blood money which he had received for doing the infamous work of these Kentucky hunters of men. Two white men, in sympathy with the right, though pretending otherwise to him, acted as police men, and removed him from immediate danger of being killed. He breathed vengeance upon the colored people, threatened to expose the operations of the Underground Railroad, &c. &c.; but when a committee of colored men started for the purpose of hurrying him from Cincinnati, it was found that his gold had bribed the white men, who were endeavoring to screen him from further molestation. But the colored men were determined, and his whereabouts was made known. Brodie delivered himself into the hands of the authorities, who put him in jail to save his life.

It has since turned out that the slaveholding influences united for his defence. State warrants have been issued for the arrest of several colored men charged with participating in his trial and punishment; and the day I left Detroit, some of them had arrived there, to avoid that liability.

But to return to the meeting. Miss Watkins, in the course of one of her very best outbursts of eloquent indignation, charged the treachery of this colored man upon the United States Government, which is the arch traitor to liberty, as shown by the Fugitive Slave Law and the Dred Scott decision. A discussion ensued on the pertinent question, submitted by Mr. Garnet, What shall be done with the traitor on his arrival in Detroit? A resolution embodying their detestation of the man was passed, and at a late hour, the meeting adjourned.

One of these betrayed men has left a wife in Detroit, and a babe born since his departure. A committee of ladies have called to administer to her wants, and to do what in them lies to save her from the clutches of the kidnapper.

Yours, for the speedy downfall of slavery,
WILLIAM C. NELL.[96]

The following letter shows the keen conception of the significance of history, characteristic of this intelligent man, a classmate of Alexander Crummell and James McCune Smith, a worker in the Underground Railroad system, and an ardent abolitionist closely connected with Charles Sumner. To William C. Nell, the first Negro historian of consequence, he gives some interesting facts.

NEWPORT, March 3, 1860.

W. C. NELL, ESQ.:

DEAR SIR—I acknowledge the receipt of your invitation to attend the Attucks celebration at Boston, on the 5th inst. I have been cherishing the hope that I could be present; but I find it impossible. I would be with you, because it is an occasion of which I feel proud; proud, because it is to commemorate one, and a prominent one, of a number of incidents, in which colored Americans have played parts for liberty, which will cause their names to live. I might allude to many; I will mention Margaret Garner, who, when hotly pursued by ruthless slave-hunters, killed her little ones; calling upon her mother to assist her in sending their pure spirits to God, to make them really free, and not continue to breathe, and be slaves. Then the noble, nameless black hero of Tennessee; the slave who received seven hundred lashes, and died, refusing to disclose who his associates were, that were plotting for freedom. Then Leary, Copeland and Green, who risked and lost all, save immortal names, for liberty; and that liberty to be enjoyed by others.

As for the colored hero who is the subject of your celebration, I will leave him to the able array of speakers announced to speak; they will speak of him as his bright merits deserve.

[96] *Liberator*, Sept. 11, 1858.

I will allude to an idea, in connection with Crispus Attucks, which I would be proud to hear Wendell Phillips discourse upon. It is well known that, up to the 5th of March, 1770, there was a hesitancy and a dread felt by the Colonies' best friends, shared by Adams and others equally true to their interest, who hoped for concessions on the part of the mother country; this, though then deemed almost impossible, was nevertheless cherished. But the blow struck by Attucks; his bold defiance of all England; his intrepid leading on the populace, and the encounter—was the decisive blow that led to Independence. Had it not been *then* struck, there might have been delays; and delays, and some concessions following, resulting in a resolve to remain subjects of the mother country. And is it not possible that we might, in that event, now, like Canada, sustain such a relation to England? Then may we not say, that, but for the blow struck at the right time by a black man, the United States, with all that it of right and justice boasts, might not have been an independent republic?

May the moral blows now being struck for freedom by our friends, be as effectual in their consequences as were the blows struck by our forefathers, in so far as they struck off English shackles!

Yours, for the freedom for which Attucks died,

GEO. T. DOWNING.

IX.   WILLIAM WELLS BROWN

William Wells Brown, a fugitive slave educated in the North, became a prominent factor in the antislavery movement. He lectured throughout most of the free States in this country, and, along with others, presented the cause to the liberal classes of Europe. Appreciating the value of the written record, he produced several historical works presenting the leading facts of Negro history. He also wrote to antislavery men and agencies a number of letters, some of which are presented below because of their value in studying the history of this country immediately preceding the Civil War.

DEAR FRIEND GAY:—I left Cadiz this morning at four o'clock, on my way for Mount Pleasant. Passing through Georgetown at about five o'clock, I found the citizens standing upon the corners of the streets, talking as though something had occurred during the night. Upon inquiry, I learned that about ten o'clock at night, five or six men went to the house of a colored man by the name of John Wilkinson, broke open the door, knocked down the man and his wife, and beat them severely, and seized their boy, aged fourteen years, and carried him off into Slavery. After the father of the boy had recovered himself, he raised the alarm, and with the aid of some of the neighbors, put out in pursuit of the kidnappers, and followed them to the river; but they were too late. The villains crossed the river, and passed into Virginia. I visited the afflicted family this morning. When I entered the house, I found the mother seated with her face buried in her hands, weeping for the loss of her child. The mother was much bruised, and the floor was covered in several places with blood. I had been in the house but a short time, when the father returned from the chase of the kidnappers. When he entered the house, and told the wife that their child was lost forever, the mother wrung her hands and screamed out, "Oh, my boy! oh, my boy! I want to see my child!" and raved as though she was a maniac. I was compelled to turn aside and weep for the first time since I came into the State. I would that every Northern apologist for Slavery, could have been present to have beheld that scene. I hope to God that it may never be my lot to behold another such. One of the villains was recognized, but it was by a colored man, and the colored people have not the right of their oath in this State. This villain will go unwhipped of Justice. What have the North to do with Slavery? Ever yours, for the slave.   WM. W. BROWN.[75]

MOUNT PLEASANT, Sept. 27th, 1844.

S. H. GAY,—*Dear Friend:*—I presume that it is not generally known that we are doing anything for the slaves' cause in Western New-York. We are not asleep. We are at present engaged in holding a series of Conventions; the persons attending these meetings are J. C. Hathaway, G. B. Stebbins, J. B. Sanderson, G. M. Cooper, and myself. We held a Convention at Farmington, pursuant to notice. It was a grand meeting,—one long to be remembered. The friends of the slave from a distance were in attendance—friends that had not seen each other for months. They met, all laboring for

[75] *National Anti-Slavery Standard*, Nov. 7, 1844.

down-trodden humanity, and each congratulating the other. The main question was Disunion. It was discussed freely for two days. Third party men were there and tried to prop up, or keep us from tearing down the Union, or in other words, to keep us from showing the pro-slavery features of the Constitution; but it was no go. Among the able speeches made, there was one from our esteemed friend, Joseph C. Hathaway, which, by the way, was one that would have done honor to the head and heart of any man in the nation. His powers, as a public speaker, are not known, but ere long, they will be known and appreciated. At the close of the Convention, the call for the annual meeting was announced, and a wish was generally expressed by those present, that some of the esteemed friends might be prevailed on to come out and attend the annual meeting. Should it be announced that William Lloyd Garrison, Wendell Phillips, or some others of those devoted friends of the cause, would be present, our annual meeting would do double service in the cause of humanity. The main question which will occupy the attention at that meeting, will be the Disunion question, and the aid of such men will be needed. No man in the nation would call together a larger audience in this section, than Wendell Phillips, Esq. The cries of three millions of our countrymen and women are coming to us upon every breeze that comes from the South. The groans of Jonathan Walker, Charles T. Torrey, Burr, Work, and Thompson, are mingled with those of the slaves. Our own citizens cannot have the privilege of free locomotion; they cannot go to the South, and declare that all men are created equal, and are endowed by their Creator with certain inalienable rights, and apply it to American Slavery, without being thrown into prison, and compelled to drag out years in chains. Their groans should cause every citizen of the North to cry out, NO UNION WITH SLAVEHOLDERS.

Yours, for the cause,
W. W. BROWN.[76]

WILLIAMSON, Jan. 13th, 1845.

WARSAW, (N. Y.) Oct. 24, 1846.

FRIEND GAY:—I never write for the public eye, only when I am compelled. The progress of the cause in Western New-York, or at least in this vicinity, demands that something should be said, and, as I am alone, I must give you some account of the progress of the cause.

[76] *National Anti-Slavery Standard*, Jan. 30, 1845.

You are aware that I am in Wyoming county, though I came into
the county a few days later than I should have done, having been
detained by an accident. Two noble-hearted friends of the slave,
John W. Paney, and Rodolphus W. Hewitt, of Weathersfield, took
their wives in their wagons, and travelled over thirty miles to meet
and welcome me into the county.

Though the weather, for the most of the time, has been unfavorable, my meetings have been large. At Castile, I talked two evenings, and on the second evening I gave them the remedy (disunion) ; and, for ought that I could see or hear, it was well received.
I left, in this place, a number of copies of the "Constitution, a pro-
slavery compact," "disunion," and gave the Standard a large circulation, as you will see. The citizens of Castile are willing to give
our cause a fair investigation, and that, you know, is more than the
people generally are willing to do. Perry is called the Anti-Slavery
town in this county, but I found Castile far in advance of it.

On the 21st instant, I held a meeting at Warsaw. This place is
the county-seat for Wyoming county, and these county-seats are
hard places; they are a kind of a little city for the surrounding
country. Lawyers, doctors, priests, and rogues, are to be found in
those places. Though the county court was in session in this place,
and in session the evening I held my meeting, we had a good audience, and at the close of the meeting the Hon. Seth M. Gates, made
a move, and it was seconded by a Democrat, "Resolved, That Equal
Suffrage be extended to coloured citizens," and it was unanimously
carried. The next morning I received an invitation from Judge
Skinner, the first Judge of the county, to lecture in the Court-House
the next evening, saying that he would adjourn the court, and give
me up the Court-House, and come and hear me. I, of course, accepted the invitation, and on Friday evening I lectured in the
Court-House to a very large audience. Judges, lawyers, doctors,
priests, &c. all being present. Gen. Thayer was called to the chair.
He is a member of the democratic party, and a distinguished lawyer. The meeting, I think, had a good effect. This adjourning the
county court to hear a nigger, shows some progress in Anti-Slavery.
This Mexican war has opened the eyes of the people; they begin to
look at the American Union in its true light. The period has, indeed, arrived, the crisis has come, when the wise, the virtuous, the
patriotic, and the philanthropic of the United States, and the world,
must examine into this Americanism, this slaveholding, woman-

whipping, baby-stealing Republicanism. And when the people have examined it, as the members of the American Anti-Slavery Society have done, they will adopt our motto, and raise the cry of "No Union with slaveholders!" The cause is indeed progressing in Western New-York. How could it do otherwise under the management of Joseph C. Hathaway as general agent? He is just the man for the cause, and the cause is just the thing for him. His long and arduous efforts in the temperance cause, in this State, as well as his Anti-Slavery efforts, has gained for him a reputation and the respect and esteem of the people. Charles Lenox Remond, with his soul-stirring eloquence, has given an impetus to our cause in Western New-York. His labours here are appreciated by those who hear him. The people out here begin to see that the American Union is cemented together with the blood, the bones, and sinews of three millions of our countrymen; and they begin to hate the Union, and look upon the Constitution of the United States not only as slaveholding, but as a "Covenant with death and an agreement with hell," to keep our countrymen in chains.

Yours, truly,
W. W. BROWN.[77]

Meetings in Western New-York.

WATERLOO, February, 1, 1847.

MY DEAR GAY:—I must give you some account of my meetings for the last two or three weeks. After the annual meeting at Rochester, I visited Steuben county, and spent some six or eight days in holding meetings in Avoca, Clisbee's, Mud Creek, and Corning, returning to Bath from most of the meetings, and putting up with our friends, Elias Leonard and Henrietta Jane Platt. Their house is humanity's home for Steuben county. All the meetings were well attended. At Corning the meetings were exceedingly large. I held three in the Presbyterian church. My last appointment in the county was at Hammondsport, a village at the head of Crooked Lake. The coloured choir at Bath, composed of eight or ten persons, accompanied me to Hammondsport, a distance of eight miles, on a cold evening, over a very bad road. We arrived at Hammondsport, but the notice of the meeting had not reached there; so we were disappointed in having a meeting. But, a few friends as-

sembled at the house of our friend, Joseph Shaut, and there the
choir sung some of their melodious and soul-stirring pieces, and at
nine o'clock we started for Bath. It is but justice to say, that this
choir, composed of coloured persons, is the best in Bath, and said to
be the best in Steuben county. My next appointment was at Penn
Yan, the county seat for Yates county. This place is the residence
of Henry Bradley, a gentleman who figured very conspicuously
during the last election as candidate for Governor. I arrived at
Penn Yan at half-past six o'clock in the evening, just in time to fulfill my appointment. This being Saturday evening, the meeting
was small, it being also held in a small room. The next day, Sabbath, I attended meeting in the forenoon and afternoon in the Congregational church; understanding it to be an Anti-Slavery church.
The minister's subject on both occasions was on the "declension of
the Church," a very appropriate subject in my opinion at least, for
that church. That church being represented to me as Anti-Slavery,
I expected to have obtained it for the evening meeting. A good
friend, Myron Hamlin, made exertion to get it, but the pro-slavery
spirit within could not allow a fugitive slave to plead for his down-
trodden countrymen in their house. After refusing to let me lecture in their house, the minister, Mr. Hawley, gave notice that on
the next evening they would hold their monthly concert to pray for
the slave!

I thought to myself, that if Jesus had been upon the earth, and
in that house, he would have said to them as he did to the Scribes
and Pharisees, of old, "Wo unto you, Scribes and Pharisees, hypocrites; for ye devour widows houses, and for a pretense make long
prayers, therefore ye shall receive the greater damnation." And
again, "Ye shall know them by their fruits." This church had
gained quite an Anti-Slavery reputation in former years, under the
preaching of the Rev. Mr. Minernone, of Syracuse. But I will say,
that the Congregational church of Penn Yan, Yates county, N. Y.
of which Henry Bradley is a prominent member, is as bigoted,
sectarian, pro-slavery a church, as there is in the State of New-York.
And yet this high priest of sectarianism has been stumping it
through the State during the past fall, calling upon the Whigs and
Democrats to leave their pro-slavery political parties and join him:
while he remains in a church that shuts its doors against God's poor.
I speak of Mr. Bradley because he was nominated by the Liberty
party, and recommended by them to the Abolitionists of New-York

as the slave's friend. Mr. Bradley happened into a meeting that my friend, Giles B. Stebbins and myself were holding at Farmington last winter, and when it come to my turn to speak, I very cordially extended an invitation to Mr. Bradley, who came forward and occupied the balance of the evening. But when I met him in his own village, and in his own church, he passed me by like the priest and Levite of old. A friend remarked that Mr. Bradley was the leader of the Abolitionists in their village. As an American slave, then, I said, ''save me from my friends.'' The next day, Monday, I left Penn Yan for Geneva, thence to Canoga, where I had a good meeting.

J. C. Hathaway, C. L. Remond, and myself, held a convention at Seneca Falls, which I think had a good effect. We go from here to West Winfield, Herkimer county, where our friends are to hold a fair on the 10th and 11th of February.

There was a mistake in the time for holding the Waterloo Fair, but the mistake was not yours. The Waterloo, as will be seen by the Standard, is to be held February 25th. I write this in the hospitable mansion of the McClintocks. They are working faithfully for the Waterloo Fair. You shall hear from us from West Winfield.

Yours for the slave,
WM. W. BROWN.[78]

DEAR FRIEND GARRISON:

I have not forgotten the promise that I made you, before leaving America, to give you a letter occasionally for the Liberator. You have doubtless learned, ere this, that the steamer in which I came over made the shortest passage ever known. This, I need not inform you, added much to the pleasure of the voyage. Among the unusually large number of passengers on board were four or five slaveholders, and among these was a Judge Chinn, a Louisiana slaveholder, who had been appointed by our democratic government as Consul to Naples, and who was on his way out to occupy his post. The steamer had scarcely left the shore, before it was rumored that an American slave was on board, and that he was going out as a delegate to the Peace Congress at Paris. The latter part of the rumor gave additional interest to it, and soon there was no little anxiety manifested on the part of the passengers to know something of the history of the fugitive. My Narrative,—a few copies of

[78] *National Anti-Slavery Standard*, Feb. 11, 1847.

which I had with me,—was sought after, and extensively read, the reading of which produced considerable sensation among the passengers, especially the slaveholding and pro-slavery portion of them. This Judge Chinn had with him a free colored man as servant, and I was somewhat anxious to know what kind of protection he was to receive in travelling in this country, for you will recollect that I made application to the Hon. John M. Clayton, before leaving America, for a passport, which was refused me. So, upon inquiring of this servant, he showed me his passport, which proved to be nothing less than a regular passport from the hand of the Secretary of State. True, it was not from Mr. Clayton, but it was from his immediate predecessor, Mr. Buchanan. This proves conclusively, that if a colored person wishes the protection of the U. S. government in going into any foreign country, he must not think of going in any other capacity than that of a boot-black. Wherever the colored man goes, he must carry with him the badge of slavery to receive the protection of the Americans. The act of the government, in denying to its colored citizens the same protection that it extends to the whites, is more cowardly and mean, if possible, than any act committed for years. But it is entirely in keeping with American republicanism. I am glad to see that the English press generally has denounced this act of high-handed injustice and oppression.

After a pleasing passage of only nine days and twenty-two hours, we arrived at Liverpool. I remained there only long enough to take a view of the place, and then proceeded to Dublin, where I met with a warm reception from the Webbs, the Haughtons, and many other friends of the cause. I have become acquainted with none, since my arrival in this country, to whom I am more attached, than the hospitable family of Richard D. Webb. I remained in Dublin twenty days, but the friends of the slave there would not permit me to leave without adding to their many private manifestations of kindness that of a public welcome, an account of which you must gather from the newspapers.

On the 19th of August, I left Dublin, in company with R. D. Webb, for Paris, to attend the Peace Congress. So much has been said and written about the Congress, that I suppose any thing from me, at this late hour, would be considered stale, to say the least; but I will, however, venture to mention a circumstance or two, that may not have reached you through any other channel. As you are aware, the Congress met on Wednesday, the 23d, at 12 o'clock, and, strange to say, among the first that I saw on entering the hall, were three slaveholders, who came over in the same steamer with me, one of whom was Judge Chinn; but whether they were members of the Congress or not, I am unable to say. At any rate, they were supplied with the same card of admission that members were. However, they did not show any symptoms of colorphobia so natural to the American taste. A circumstance occurred at the close of the first session, which shows how easily Americans can lay aside their prejudices when they reach this country. While I was in conversation with Richard Codden, Esq., member of the British Parliament, and Victor Hugo, the President of the Congress, I observed a man standing near us, whom I recognized as one of the passengers in the same steamer with me from America, and who during the voyage was not at all backward in expressing his belief in the inferiority of the 'niggers,' and who would not deign to speak to me during the whole passage. At the close of the conversation, and as I was leaving the parties with whom I had been talking, this man advanced towards me with his hat in one hand and the other extended out, and addressed me with, 'How do you do, Mr. Brown? I hope I find you well, Sir.' 'Why, Sir, you have the advantage of me—I do not know you.' 'Why, Sir,' said he, 'don't you know me? I was a fellow-passenger with you from America. I wish you would introduce me to Mr. Cobden.' I felt so indignant at the downright impudence of the fellow, that I left him without making any reply. The change from an American to an European atmosphere makes a wonderful change in the minds of Americans. The man who would not have shaken hands with me in the city of New York or Boston, with a pair of tongs ten feet long, comes to me in the metropolis of France, and claims that we were 'fellow-passengers from America.' M. de Tocqueville, Minister of Foreign Affairs, gave a splendid Soiree to the members of the Congress. I perceived no difference whatever in the attention paid to those of a fairer complexion than that paid to me. I could but contrast the feeling that pervaded that assembly of men and women from all parts of the globe, to the low, mean and contemptible prejudices so common in the U. S. Here were representatives and Ministers Plenipotentiary from all governments, including the United States. Messrs. Walsh and Rush were there, and you know that they are proverbial for their pro-slavery feeling. The whites and blacks were all together, and

I did not hear the word 'nigger' once. If there was any difference paid to one more than to another, that difference was certainly paid to myself, not on account of my complexion, but on account of my identity with the oppressed million in America. On being presented to Madame de Tocqueville, I was received with the same courtesy that characterized the reception of others; but as soon as it was mentioned to the distinguished lady that I was an American slave, all conventionalities were laid aside by a cordial shake of the hand, that gave me double assurance that I was not only safe from the slave-hunter in Paris, but that I was a welcome guest in the saloon of the French Minister of Foreign Affairs. While there, I could but think of the bitter cold night in the winter of 1840, when I was compelled to walk the deck of the steamer Swallow on the Hudson river, on account of my complexion. I could but think of my being excluded from the saloon of the steamer Huntress, on the passage from Portland to Bath, in the State of Maine, but a few days before I left America, by which exclusion I was compelled to fast twelve hours.

The Peace Congress, though entirely different from our New England Conventions, was nevertheless a pleasant meeting, and was made doubly so to me by the appearance, at every session, of that noble band of abolitionists, the Chapmans and Westons. It was really pleasant to see six of them in the Congress at one time. I felt myself fortunate in being known as an abolitionist in America, if for no other purpose than that of sharing their society in France. At the close of the Congress, I paid them a visit at their summer residence at Versailles, and often while there, fancied myself in Boston. But a walk to the window, or the appearance of a French visitor, reminded me that I was in Versailles, and not Boston—in France, and not America. After remaining in France ten days, the most of which time I spent in visiting the monuments and public buildings for which Paris is so noted, I returned to London; where, for the first time, I had the pleasure of seeing that world-renowned philanthropist, George Thompson, Esq. I did not have to wait till he had read the letter of introduction that you were kind enough to furnish me with, before he knew who I was. He had read of the farewell meeting given to me by my colored friends in Boston, together with the announcement in the Liberator that I had left for England, and colored men are so scarce here, that as soon as I entered his room, he arose, and smilingly approaching me said—'I presume this is William W. Brown'; and answering him affirmatively, he gave me a hearty shake of the hand, and bade me welcome to the soil of old England. His first inquiry was about yourself and family, and then about the progress of the anti-slavery cause in America. Mr. Thompson has rendered me signal service since my arrival in this country. You will see by the papers that I am overwhelmed with welcome meetings. I have just attended a very large meeting in the London Tavern, to consider the proposition of the government of Austria for a loan to enable her to pay off the vast debt caused by the late war with the Hungarians. I had been furnished with a ticket for the 'reserved seats' before I went to the meeting; but on entering the hall, instead of being shown to the reserved seats, I was conducted to the platform, and soon found myself surrounded by such men as Lord Dudley Coutts Stewart, M. P., Richard Cobden, Esq., M. P., J. Williams, Esq., M. P., &c. &c. If such a meeting had been held in New York or Philadelphia, I could only have gained access to it by appearing there with a pitcher of water or some stationary in my hands for the use of the meeting, and as soon as that had been deposited on the platform, I would have been saluted with the familiar American phrase, 'I say, nigger, it's time for you to be off.' Here the man is measured by his moral worth, and not by the color of the skin or the curl of the hair.

I forgot to mention to you, that the Rev. Wm. Allen, D. D., of Northampton, made a speech at the breakfast given to the American delegates at Versailles, and in his speech he apologized for our slaveholding government, declaring that it had nothing to do with slavery. His speech, instead of gaining applause for him, brought down the condemnation of nearly the whole audience upon his own head. It is too late in the nineteenth century for men coming from America to attempt to whitewash her slaveholding institution. I am more than ever convinced, that some sterling abolitionist should be in this country at all times, if for no other purpose, to watch American Doctors of Divinity, who may happen to be here.

Yours for the slave,
WM. WELLS BROWN.

LONDON, October 12, 1849.[79]

The following letter from William Wells Brown is significant in that it shows how the abolition movement progressed in Great Britain by virtue of the stimulus which Americans visiting that country gave the cause.

[79] *Liberator*, Nov. 2, 1849.

DEAR MR. GARRISON:

I forward to you, by this day's mail, the papers containing accounts of the great meeting held in Exeter Hall last night. No meeting during this anniversary has caused so much talk and excitement as this gathering. No time could possibly have been more appropriate for such a meeting than the present. Uncle Tom's Cabin has come down upon the dark abodes of slavery like a morning's sunlight, unfolding to view its enormities in a manner which has fastened all eyes upon the 'peculiar institution,' and awakening sympathy in hearts that never before felt for the slave. Had Exeter Hall been capable of holding fifty thousand instead of five thousand, it would no doubt have been filled to its utmost capacity. For more than a week before the meeting came off, the tickets were all disposed of, and it was understood that hundreds were applying every day. With those who may be classed as Mrs. Stowe's converts, that lady was the centre of attraction for them; while the elder abolitionists came for the sake of the cause. I entered the great Hall an hour before the time, and found the building filled, there scarcely being standing room, except on the platform, which was in charge of the officials, to keep places for those who had tickets to that part of the house. At half-past six, the Earl of Shaftesbury appeared upon the platform, followed by the Committee and speakers, amid the most deafening applause. The Noble Earl, who has many more nobler qualities than that of a mere nobleman, made the opening speech, and, as you will see, a good one. While his lordship was speaking, Her Grace, the Duchess of Sutherland, came in, and took her seat in the balcony on the right of the platform, and an half hour after, a greater lady (the authoress of Uncle Tom) made her appearance, and took her seat by the side of the Duchess. At this stage of the meeting, there was a degree of excitement in the room that can better be imagined than described. The waving of hats and handkerchiefs, the clapping of hands, the stamping of feet, and the screaming and fainting of ladies, went on as if it had been in the programme, while the thieves were at work helping themselves out of the abundance of the pockets of those who were most crowded. A few arrests by the police soon taught the latter that there was no room there for pickpockets. Order was once more restored, and the speaking went on. Many good things were said by the different speakers, who were mostly residents of the metropolis. Professor Stowe, as you might expect, was looked upon as the lion of the speakers; but his speech disappointed all, except those of us who knew enough of American divines not to anticipate much from them on the subject of slavery. For my own part, I was not disappointed, for I have long since despaired of anything being done by clergymen; and the Professor's speech at Glasgow, and subsequent addresses, had prepared me to look for but little from him. He evidently wishes for no agitation on the subject, and said it would do no good as long as England purchased America's cotton. I look upon this cotton question as nothing more than to divert the public from the main subject itself. Mr. Stowe is not very young, yet he is only a child in the anti-slavery movement. He is now lisping his A, B, C, and if his wife succeeds in making him a good scholar, she will find it no easy thing.

The best speech of the evening was made by our countryman, Samuel R. Ward. Mr. Ward did himself great credit, and exposed the hypocrisy of the American pro-slavery churches in a way that caused Professor Stowe to turn more than once upon his seat. I have but little faith in the American clergy—either colored or white; but I believe Ward to be not only one of the most honest, but an uncompromising and faithful advocate of his countrymen. He is certainly the best colored minister that has yet visited this country.

I recognized in the audience several of our American friends. Among them was Mrs. Follen, Miss Cabot, J. Miller M'Kim, Miss Pugh, Professor Wm. G. Allen and lady, and Wm. and Ellen Craft. Upon the whole, the anti-slavery cause is in a more healthy state than it ever was before, and from all appearance much good will be done by the present excitement. The fact that no American clergyman has dared to appear at any of the anniversary meetings without professing anti-slavery principles, and that one at least (Rev. Mr. Prime) was denied a seat as a delegate at one of these meetings, shows the feeling already created in Great Britain; and I hope it will soon be understood in America, that no man will be welcomed here, unless he is an out-and-out abolitionist; and then the days of the slave's deliverance will be close at hand.

Yours, very sincerely,

WM. WELLS BROWN.

22 Cecil Street, Strand, London, May 17th, 1853.[30]

[30] *Liberator*, June 3, 1853.

LONDON, Aug. 29, 1854.

DEAR MR. GARRISON:

Having failed in getting a passage in the next Boston steamer, owing to the berths being all occupied, I have taken passage in the steamship 'City of Manchester,' which leaves Liverpool on the 6th of September, and unless some accident occurs, I shall arrive at Philadelphia on or about the 20th of the month. After an absence of more than five years from the United States, I look with a degree of interest to the time when I shall again have the privilege of shaking hands with those noble spirits whose faces I have so often seen in public meetings, and whose voices have so often welcomed me in private. But, oh! the change that must have taken place during these five years! When I look round me here, and see so many who were children when I came, and who are now grown up, and many who were enjoying health that are now in their graves, it causes me to feel that, on my return to America, I shall look in vain for numbers of faces that I have so often seen, and hands that I have so frequently pressed. Although I have travelled more than twenty thousand miles, through the British empire, and delivered more than a thousand lectures, besides attending public meetings, the time seems short. I have been more than once in nearly every town in the kingdom, and have made the acquaintance of some of the finest spirits of the age; and it is with a palpitating heart that I look forward to the day when I must bid farewell to a country that seems like home, and a people whose hospitality I have so long enjoyed. Whether my visit has been of any service to the cause of my enslaved countrymen or not, others must determine. At any rate, it has been of great service to me in enabling me to give my daughters an education, that I could not have given them in the United States, and affording me an opportunity of forming a more just idea of the governments and people of Europe than I could otherwise have done.

I leave my daughters here for a time; the youngest to continue her studies in France, the eldest as a teacher in England. In quitting Great Britain, I am glad, however, to leave behind me so able a representative as PARKER PILLSBURY. There never was a time when the people of this country were more eager to hear of the wrongs of the American slave than at the present time; and should Mr. Pillsbury's health permit, I am sure he will accomplish much for the cause.

I regret that ill health has for some months deprived the cause of the services of JOHN B. ESTLIN, Esq. Of all philanthropists whom I have met in this land, I know of none more devoted, or who would make greater sacrifices for the slave, than Mr. Estlin. I need not say, that in all his good works, he has a valuable coadjutor in his amiable and accomplished daughter. Theirs is indeed a life of usefulness. But when I see you, I can tell you more of them and their sacrifices, than I have time now to put on paper.

With the hope that I shall in a few days take you by the hand, I must conclude with   Yours, very truly,

W. WELLS BROWN.[81]

Referring to William Wells Brown, May 23, 1854, the *Liberator* said:

The friends of Mr. BROWN in England have kindly contributed the amount necessary to secure his ransom from bondage, so that he can return to his native land without being subjected to the terrible liability of being seized as a fugitive, and scourged to death on a Southern plantation. In a letter to Mr. NELL, he intimates that he may arrive in Boston in June or July. At whatever period he may come, he will find many to give him a most friendly greeting. Our cause never needed his presence and his labors so much as at the present crisis.

The following letter from his daughter JOSEPHINE, addressed to Mr. MAY, we have solicited for publication, as it exhibits the world-wide difference between England and America, (to the eternal shame of the latter,) in the treatment of the colored race. We print it without the alteration of a single word. Its chirography is uncommonly legible and graceful. Only think of the youthful daughter of an American fugitive slave at the head of a school, as teacher, of more than one hundred white young English ladies! Let the fact be published far and wide.

EAST PLUMSTEAD SCHOOL, PLUMSTEAD,
WOOLWICH, April 27th, 1854.

MY DEAR MR. MAY:

I am much obliged to you for the copy of 'A Sabbath Scene,' that you were kind enough to send me, and which my father has

[81] *Liberator*, Sept. 22, 1854.

just forwarded. There is no countryman of mine, whose poems I read with more pleasure than Whittier's, for he always writes something for the slave, and to the purpose.

I read very attentively the anti-slavery papers which come to my father, and often think I should like to be in my native land again. Yet the treatment I receive from the people here is so different from what I experienced in the United States, that I have great admiration for the English. While we resided in Buffalo, I did not go to school, owing to the fact that colored children were not permitted to be educated with the whites, and my father would not send me to the colored school, because it would have been, to some extent, giving sanction to the proscriptive prejudice. And even after coming into Massachusetts, where we were allowed to receive instruction in the same school with white children, we had to occupy a seat set apart for us, and therefore often suffered much annoyance from the other children, owing to prejudice. But here we have found it totally different.

On our arrival in this country, we spent the first year in France, in a boarding-school, where there were some forty other young ladies, and never once heard our color alluded to in disrespectful terms. We afterwards returned to London, and entered a school where more than two hundred young ladies were being educated; and here, too, we were always treated with the greatest kindness and respect. As we were trained in the last mentioned school for teachers, we were somewhat afraid that our color would be a barrier against our getting employment as teachers; but in this were happily disappointed. My sister is mistress of a school at Berden, in Essex, about forty miles from London. I have a school here with more than one hundred pupils, and an assistant two years older than myself. My pupils are some of them sixteen years of age, while I am not yet fifteen. I need not say to you, that both my assistant and pupils are all white. Should I return to America, it is scarcely probable that I could get a school of white pupils, and this makes me wish to remain here, for I am fond of teaching.

If my father and sister were with me, I am sure they would join in kind regards to you.

Believe me to remain,

Yours, very respectfully,

JOSEPHINE BROWN.

Wm. Wells Brown writes to Frederick Douglass, from London, under date of September 1st, that he had recently had interviews with West India Agents and Proprietors, who are not only willing but desirous to secure the emigration of colored citizens to Trinidad and Jamaica.   He says:—

Knowing that there were many proprietors and agents dissatisfied with the abolition of slavery in the West Indies, and that a species of slavery had been carried on under the name of emigration, I frankly told these men upon what conditions I thought our people would go to the West Indies.

But as to going there to be bound or fettered in any way, I assured him that no fugitive slave would ever consent to. And although I was assured that the utmost freedom would be enjoyed by all who might consent to go, I understand that a secret move is on foot in London to induce our unsuspecting people in Canada to go to the West Indies, and that agents are already in Canada for that purpose. The Rev. Josiah Henson is said to be one of these.

As my letter in the *Times* first brought this subject before the people, and fearing that some might be entrapped by this new movement, I take the earliest opportunity of warning all colored men to be on their guard, how they enter into agreements, no matter with whom, white or colored, to go to the West India Islands, least they find themselves again wearing the chains of slavery.

A movement that is concocted in secret, and that, too, by men, many of whom would place the chains upon the limbs of the emancipated people of the West Indies to-morrow, if they could, and which is kept from the knowledge of the abolitionists of this country, should find no countenance with our oppressed people. He who has made his escape from the cotton, sugar and rice fields of the Southern States is ready to finish his life among the cold hills of Canada, and, if needs be, to subsist upon the coarsest of food; but he is not willing to enter into a second bondage.

Then I would say again, Beware lest you are entrapped by the enemy !   Yours, for our people,

W. W. BROWN.[82]

SIR: Had not your many changes and rechanges prepared me to be astonished at nothing that you might say, or do, I would

[82] *Liberator*, Oct. 20, 1854.

have been somewhat surprised at the attack made upon me by you, in your paper of the 2d of March. You commence by saying "we do regret that he should feel called upon to show his faithfulness to the American Anti-Slavery Society by covering us with dishonour." Let me say to you, Frederick Douglass, that my difference with you has nothing whatever to do with the American Anti-Slavery Society, and no one knows that better than yourself. And I regard such an insinuation as fit only to come from one whose feelings are entirely lost to all sense of shame. My charge against you is, that, just before I left the United States for England, you wrote a *private* letter to a distinguished Abolitionist in Great Britain, injurious to me, and intended to forestall my movements there. In a note which I forwarded to you, to your address at Rochester, on the 20th of January last, I gave you to understand that I had been made aware of your having acted in that underhand manner. The following is a part of the note I sent you more than a month ago. "During my sojourn in England, and several months after my arrival there, and while spending a few days with a friend of yours, the post brought me a letter, which had been remailed in London, and it proved to be from you, dated at New Bedford. After I had finished reading the letter, your friend seemed anxious to learn its contents. I handed it to her, with the request that she would read it; your friend appeared much astonished at the kindness expressed by you to me, and exclaimed, 'Douglass has done you a great injustice,' and immediately revealed to me the contents of a letter which she had received from you, some months before, and which was written a short time previous to my departure from America. I need not say that the very unfavourable position in which your letter placed me before your friend, secured for me a cold reception at her hands. I need not name the lady; you know to whom I refer, unless you wrote to more than one." Your attack upon me, in your paper of the 2d inst., in which you ask for "facts," when my note containing the above had been in your possession more than a month, shows too well your wish to make a sneaking fling at me, instead of seeking for "facts," and acting the part of an honourable man. Why did you not give my note a place in your paper, and make such comments as you thought best? No, that would not have suited you. But, anxious to heap insult upon injury, you resort to the mode most congenial to your feelings and sense of justice. Had I not thought it due to the public to state the above "facts," I would have treated your scurillous paragraph with that silence and contempt that all such articles so justly deserve.   However, no future insinuation of yours, no matter how false or unjust, shall provoke from me a reply.

WILLIAM WELLS BROWN.[83]

Correspondence of The Anti-Slavery Standard.

SALEM, Ohio, March 19th.

MESSRS. EDITORS: After a fatiguing journey of three days, I find myself in the town of Salem, somewhat noted for being the centre of radical anti-slavery in the Buckeye State.   I left Springfield on the morning of the 10th inst., and came very near getting my neck broken before I had arrived at Albany.   When within ten miles of Pittsfield, the train run off the track, smashing and otherwise damaging several of the cars, but without injuring any of the passengers.   The jolting of the car in which I was seated, until the classic Dante that I was reading was fairly shaken out of my hand, was the first intimation I had of the approaching catastrophe.   The next moment, my head was unceremoniously introduced to the top of the car—which, but for its hardness and its being insured, would have been seriously damaged.   As our car plunged head first into the snow-bank, an indescribable scene occurred.   A tall man, and of otherwise large dimensions, was thrown forward and succeeded in breaking to pieces four seats, before he found himself on all fours.   Eight or ten other persons were emptied out of their seats, while the stove was upset.   When it was ascertained that all was over, a rush was made for the doors, by those who were not too frightened to run, or could regain their self-possession.   But those who attempted to escape found that the doors could not be opened.   At this juncture, a scene of rather an amusing character took place.   A Frenchman, who spoke very bad English, in trying to get out by one of the windows, became fastened, so that he could neither get in nor out.   The tall man that had broken down so many seats, in his exploring expedition, instead of getting up, cried out, "Let's have a word of prayer," and immediately commenced repeating the Lord's Prayer.   As I was trying to set the stove right, I heard the cry, "water, water—a lady had fainted," and saw a number of persons crowding to a seat occupied by the only lady in our car. As the doors could not be moved, neither water nor snow could be procured; and, there being no other women present, of course camphor bottles were scarce. However, an admirable substitute was introduced by the big Scotchman, who, by this time, had finished his prayers. Seeing that neither water, camphor or anything else could be obtained, the Highlander took from his pocket his box of snuff, and at once put a pinch to the lady's nose, which, by the bye, had the desired effect. A moment more, and the lady, with open eyes, exclaimed, "Don't crush my new bonnet." As the engine had not run off the track, it started for Pittsfield for a new set of cars. The day was one of the coldest we have had this winter. The windows of the cars were covered with frost, while the pelting snow was driving in through the ventilators. The trees, with their branches covered with snow and ice, looked like so many chandeliers hung in the forest, and the reflection of the sun upon them, and the snow-birds twittering in their tops, gave them a splendid appearance. The return of the engine with other cars relieved us from our unpleasant position, and enabled us to reach Albany a few hours after the time. Our friends gave me a large and attentive audience at Albany. The next night I spent at Buffalo, where I met some old and attached friends, who would only allow me to go through without a meeting upon condition that I should give them more than one lecture on my return in May. I was met at Cleveland by William H. Day, one of the most promising and intelligent coloured young men in the West, and one who, at some future day, will fill an important position among his oppressed race. You will, no doubt, remember that Mr. Day was editor of the *Aliened American,* published at Cleveland. Last winter, he was, by a vote of the Legislature of the State, excluded from it as a reporter. He is now the Librarian of the Cleveland Association. Mr. Day is about twenty-five years of age, has a fine forehead, expressive eyes, and a mouth beautifully cut, and indicative of decision and energy. Having gone through a regular course of studies at Oberlin, he has a polished education, and is qualified to fill, with credit to himself, the highest place to which he may be called.

Wm. H. Day is one of the few coloured men of this country who are capable of appreciating the anti-slavery cause. Indeed, the movement is too vast to be comprehended by the majority of whites, with all their education. In Ohio, Spring has fairly set in.

Yesterday was a dreary, wet and uncomfortable day, with melting snow and high wind. I cannot give a better idea of the state of the roads here than to assure you that, while I write, a horse with an empty cart is sticking in the mud before my door. But remember I am in a town.

Yours, very truly, W. W. B.[84]

NEW RICHMOND, Ohio, April 10, 1855.

AFTER lecturing, in most instances to large audiences, in a number of towns between New Lisbon and Massillon, I came on to Cincinnati, by way of Crestline and Dayton, over a new and rather ricketty railroad, which made me feel that although my head was insured, it was not entirely out of danger. The long journey was made pleasant by the fine weather and the sun pouring its effulgent beams of warmth and radiance over the fertile country through which we passed. When I inform you that it was at Cincinnati that I escaped from my old master, twenty-one years ago, you will believe me when I tell you that no language which I am master of can adequately describe the strange feelings with which I entered the Queen City of the West. How different the scene now! Twenty-one years ago, Cincinnati had only a population of about 35,000 or 40,000, now it numbers nearly 200,000 souls; then, many of its streets run through swamps and low lands; now, they are beautifully paved and will compare, in point of splendour, with some of our Eastern cities. In company with our friend W. W. Watson, I took a walk to the wharf, to view, once more, the spot where my old master's steamer lay when I leaped on shore, with an empty pocket but a full heart. A few buildings, still standing, enabled me to point out the identical place. The long string of steamers lying, apparently, as I saw them, when, with a throbbing heart and trembling limbs, I started for the land of *freedom*, carried me back to the days when I was a victim to the hydra-headed system that pollutes our moral atmosphere and stigmatizes the national. The lowness of the river brought me more to the Kentucky side, and the mean looking buildings in Covington, and its deserted streets, told too well the want of enterprise which slavery has entailed upon its inhabitants. In the afternoon of the same day, I strolled through the back part of the city, to see if I could recognise the place which was a marshy wood-land when I escaped, and in

[84] *National Anti-Slavery Standard*, March 31, 1855.

which I hid on the memorable day, until night-fall; but the swamp
had disappeared, and where trees then stood, now are to be seen
the beautiful brick dwellings with their green painted window-
blinds. When I escaped, there was no Underground Railroad.
The North Star was, in many instances, the only friend that the
weary and foot-sore fugitive found on his pilgrimage to his new
home amongst strangers, and, consequently, the means of getting
away from slavery was not as easy then as now. During my first
day at Cincinnati, the Rosetta slave-case was before the Court, and,
although I did not see the girl, I saw her claimant, the Rev. H. M.
Dennison, and the distinguished lawyers engaged in the suit on
both sides. I was pleased with the appearance as well as the speech
of ex-Senator Chase. Mr. Chase's successor (George Pugh, Esq.)
was Dennison's counsel, and the Reverend slaveholder could not
have secured a more devoted tool to the Slave Power than this
newly-elected Senator from the State of Ohio. Mr. Pugh is of
small stature, with a thin face and a receding forehead; hair, dark
brown; nose, long; and eyes rather deeply set. He is a good lawyer, an eloquent speaker, but said to be a most unprincipled man.
What a fall Ohio took when she elected this man to take the place
of S. P. Chase. I met the Donaldsons, Blackwells and a few others
of the slave's devoted friends there, and with whom I was much
pleased. It was not intended for me to speak at Cincinnati until
the Convention. But our coloured friends would not let me off, so
I lectured in the Baker street Baptist church, Bishop Paine in the
chair. The following day, Monday, I came to New Richmond, on
board the steamboat Bostona, and lost my dinner, or rather failed
to get it, because I would not eat with the *servants*. However, I
enjoyed the trip, although hungry. One can scarcely pass through
a more picturesque part of the country than when on a steamer
gliding up or down the Ohio river. The beautiful valleys have
been made to bloom, new arteries of commerce are filling up every
avenue made vacant by the disappearance of the injured red men
cf the forest. Splendid mansions now sit where the Indian once
roamed. The glorious scenery on both sides of the river, the soft
and lovely valleys through which the waters of the Ohio linger, with
a thousand coquettish wanderings, as if unwilling to leave, and
upon whose bosom is here and there a splendid steamer with its
steam and smoke curling towards the clouds, gives the whole an
indescribable appearance.

A large meeting welcomed me to New Richmond, from which place I visited Laurel, Filicity and Bethel. You will remember that the latter town was the birth-place and residence of Thomas Morris, who first "bearded the lion in his den" at Washington, in his reply to Henry Clay. Mr. Morris lies buried in a sweet spot about a quarter of a mile from the town, where a beautiful monument, with a fitting inscription, points out his grave, and where, like watchful sentinels, the lofty trees stand around.

I have just had the pleasure of shaking the hand of another passenger by the Underground Railroad. He was a young man of fine appearance, and had with him an only child of eight months. The poor man's wife had been given to her young mistress, who was just married, and the young lady wanting the waiting-maid without the "incumbrance," as they say in Britain, the child and disconsolate husband were left behind; and the injured man was told to select another wife. However, he thought the surest way to guard against such another outrage, was to escape. But the determination not to leave his child behind, shows a degree of attachment that cannot be surpassed by the most refined and educated whites. His trembling voice, and eyes filled with the deepest emotion, while he related the story of his wrongs, was an index to a heart filled with the keenest grief. We cannot conceive of deeper, deadlier wrongs than these. There is but little doubt that this poor fugitive, ere this, is safe on the other side of Jordan. The antislavery feeling here, so near the slave territory, seems to be more favourable to Free Soil than Free Men. From the window where I am seated, I see the slave toiling on the Kentucky side of Mason and Dixon's Line. Nature could scarcely throw together more picturesque scenery than that which surrounds Frandon, the home of the Donaldsons, from which this is written. Situated in this lovely valley, with the murmuring Ohio running at the foot of the garden, I see the rafts and flat-bottomed boats floating down the river, with the children playing and *"roosters"* crowing on the tops. From present appearance, the coming Convention at Cincinnati, on the 25th, 26th and 27th of this month, will be well attended. The late slave-case has, no doubt, created a feeling in the Queen City of the West that will give additional interest to the cause at the approaching meeting.

Yours very truly,   W. W. B.[85]

[85] *National Anti-Slavery Standard*, April 21, 1855.

DEAR MR. GARRISON:

I have been in the State of Maine three weeks, having visited Portland, Bath, and some other towns in their immediate vicinities. In Portland, on Sunday, the 15th inst., we had a good audience at 3 o'clock, and the City Hall crowded to excess in the evening, and on both occasions, the people gave good attention. Just as I took my seat on the platform in the evening, a rather tall, slim, wiry-walking, empty-headed, thin-faced, cunning-looking colored man, came to me, and introduced himself as 'John Randolph, son of John Randolph of Roanoke,' and inquired if I did not want him to introduce me to the meeting. Having, however, become pretty well acquainted with the audience by the afternoon lecture, and not altogether liking the son of the Virginia statesman, I declined the honor of his favor. Nothing daunted, Mr. Randolph took his seat by my side, and remained there during the lecture. Being requested by the committee to stop for a moment or two, to give them an opportunity to take up a collection, I did so, near the close. Mr. Randolph now made himself especially handy in receiving the contribution boxes, and emptying their contents into his own hat, and then busied himself in looking over the funds. I went on and finished up the meeting without interruption, except the clinking of the money. At the close of the evening, and as we were about leaving the Hall, Mr. R. handed me the money, already tied up in his white handkerchief,—which, by the by, was exceedingly highly scented with musk, rose water, or something else, which made it very uncomfortable for me to keep near me. On arriving at Mr. Foster's and opening the handkerchief, we found that John Randolph the younger had picked out the bills and large silver coin, and left us only the three cent pieces and the coppers. A more daring, barefaced theft was never committed than by this impudent scamp, whom I have heard of in nearly every town I have visited, as having been round getting subscriptions to a book he intends publishing, to contain an account of the life of his father. Of course, no such book will ever be forthcoming, and those who give him their money will be victimized by this impostor. Randolph calls himself a doctor, and attempts to lecture on Phrenology. A few days before I was in Portland, he attended the meetings held by Sojourner Truth, and made himself very officious with the collections on these occasions, by which she was the loser.   I need not say that 'who steals my purse steals trash,' but he who steals from poor Sojourner Truth is even worse than a common thief.

From Portland, I went to Buxton, and to Bath.   At the latter place, we had meetings morning, afternoon and evening.   I believe it was the first attempt to hold meetings in the hours of service on Sunday, yet each of the sessions was well attended, and especially in the evening, when the City Hall was very full.

At Bangor, I lectured on Sunday evening, the 29th, and again addressed the citizens on the First of August.   On both of these occasions, the City Hall was filled.   Tracts were distributed at all the meetings, and the people seemed to take a special interest in the series.   I was not a little surprised at the advanced state of public opinion on the subject of slavery in Maine.   The prejudice against *condition*, which prevails in most other States, is scarcely noticeable here.   I stopped days at the Bangor House, in Bangor, and received the accommodation that was given to those of a whiter hue.   Indeed, I could not have been better treated in any hotel in England.   This I always regard as a test, as far as the public is concerned.

There is to be a hotly contested election in this State next month.   A great effort will be made to get the State to endorse the present pro-slavery, or rather, slaveholding, administration; but I think Maine will repudiate, at the ballot-box, President Pierce and his slaveholding coadjutors.   I listened to an able and eloquent speech, last evening, from Hon. Mr. Washburn, M. C. from this State.   He has bolted from the old Whig party, and is now doing all in his power to destroy it.   With any thing like half the labor that has been given to the cause in Massachusetts, by our Society, I feel sure Maine would be the first anti-slavery State in the Union.   This is not because the people are better, but because they are further from the South, and have not so much dealing with slaveholders, as in Massachusetts.   The people here appear to be more attached to freedom than to the Constitution or the Union.   I have held some dozen or more meetings in the State, many of them on week day evenings, yet they were well attended.   The churches in Maine open their doors more readily, and religion does not fit so tightly to the people, as in some other States.   Unless the return of my daughters should call me out of the State, I shall spend the remainder of the month here.

Yours, very truly,

WM. WELLS BROWN.[86]

August 6th.

DEAR MR. GARRISON:

The Convention held at Collins Centre, Erie county, N. Y., on Saturday and Sunday, October 3 and 4, was the most numerously attended of any of the meetings yet held by us. Being within thirty miles of Buffalo, the pro-slavery influence of Millard Fillmore and the Silver-Greys, under the name of Native Americanism, shows itself there without disguise. The Convention came together at ten o'clock, and was addressed by Mr. POWELL and Miss ANTHONY, but no organization was effected until the afternoon, when GEORGE F. RING, Esq., of Collins Centre, was chosen President, and Mr. GEORGE WING Secretary. No resolutions were presented, but the principles of the American Anti-Slavery Society, and the subjects which were to be discussed, were fairly laid before the Convention, and the ball set in motion.

After remarks by Miss ANTHONY and Mr. POWELL, Mr. H. A. HEATH, a Republican Methodist, formerly a Houston Know-Nothing, made a short speech upon patriotism in general and the Union in particular, in which the heroism of the dead fathers and the sacredness of the Constitution were eulogized to the utmost capacity of the young speaker. He was, however, answered in a manner that taught him he was only a novice in anti-slavery matters, and hushed him during the remainder of the meetings.

In the evening, the house was crowded in every part, and the meeting lasted till ten o'clock. But the most interesting sessions and the largest audiences were reserved for Sunday, when farmers and others came in from a distance of twenty miles. The sheds and grounds around the church were filled with wagons and other vehicles, and the whole produced such an unusual appearance in that quiet neighborhood, that it called forth the remark from a pious sister, 'This looks like *camp-meetin' times.*'

The political parties, the Union and the Church, were held up

[86] *Liberator,* Aug. 17, 1855.

before the vast assembly in all their hideous deformities. Our Methodist brethren seemed somewhat annoyed by the picture of their denomination, as painted by Mr. POWELL and Miss ANTHONY; however, they stood the fire far better than I expected.

Three meetings were held during the day, each session several hours in length; yet the people appeared but little disposed to leave when the Convention was brought to a close, at 10 o'clock at night. Mr. POWELL, Mr. DAVID BAKER, of Washington co., N. Y., Miss ANTHONY and myself occupied most of the time. No one ventured to take sides for either of the political parties or the pro-slavery religious societies. A Mr. Hodge-Podge, the deputy post-master at Collins Centre, a rabid Know-Nothing, and one who his nearest neighbors say had a claim to the name of 'know-nothing' long before such a party came into existence, insultingly inquired what the Garrison Abolitionists could do by their 'blatting.' Mr. POWELL replied, and settled the Buchanan official, so that he did not open his mouth again. Mr. HEATH, the patriot of the first day, excused himself from speaking, upon the ground that he was not equal to the combat with such practised speakers, and that he did not wish to discuss politics on the Sabbath. But it was evident to the audience, that it was the truth we uttered that the Methodist brother was afraid of, and not the eloquence of the speakers.

The Collins Convention was indeed an interesting and important meeting, and already its influence is felt for good.

Mr. POWELL goes to Jamestown, Miss ANTHONY to I don't know where, and I to Buffalo. We all, however, are to meet at Girard, Pa., next week, where we are to attend another Convention.

Yours, for the right,

WM. WELLS BROWN.[87]

DEAR MR. GARRISON:

After attending the New York State Fair at Buffalo, on the 9th instant, and lecturing in the Rev. Dr. Prime's church, on Sunday evening the 11th, I visited Cataraugus county, and held meetings at Bagdad and Cataraugus, where I had large audiences. From the latter place I made my way to Girard, a village in one of the extreme counties in Western Pennsylvania, where Miss Anthony, Mr. Powell and myself were to attend a Convention. For want of

[87] *The Liberator*, Oct. 23, 1857.

interest in Girard, our friends changed the arrangements, and advertised us to lecture in separate places, which, upon the whole, worked well, for we found crowded houses and willing listeners in all of the gatherings. The strictest attention was paid to the most radical doctrines upon the Government and the Church. Although settled several years, this seems a comparatively new country, the log cabins of the early settlers still being occupied. To a New Englander, this part of our 'glorious Union' appears very strange. The people are generally kind and hospitable, but wonderfully green. But the oddest feature in our meetings is the swarms of little ones. O, the children! I never beheld so many babies in so short a time, since the commencement of my anti-slavery labors. At one meeting last week, I counted *twenty-seven* babies in their mothers' arms or in their laps. And such music I never before heard. Take an untuned piano, a cornstalk fiddle, a Swiss hurdy-gurdy, and a Scotchman with his bag-pipes, put them all in one room, and set them agoing, and you will have but a faint idea of the juvenile concert we had that evening. I waited till a late hour before commencing the meeting, with the hope that the little ones would stop; but I waited in vain. After being reminded by the dusty clock on the wall that it was ten minutes past seven, I counted five babies, whose open mouths were sending forth delicious music, and then commenced my lecture. I raised my voice to the highest note, and the little ones and I had it, 'which and tother,' for some time. At last, I was about giving it up as a bad job, when an elderly gentleman near me said, 'Keep on, sir, the babies will get tired by and bye, and will go to sleep.' This encouraged me, and I continued with renewed vigor; and sure enough, a half an hour more, and I realized the advice of the old man; for, as the clock struck 8, I found the babies all asleep, and I master of the field. It is astonishing how little the people out here are disturbed by the noise of the children; but I presume they have become used to it.

Mr. Isaac Brooks, one of the most devoted friends of freedom in this section, met us at Lockport, and took Mr. Powell and Miss Anthony to Linesville, some twenty-five miles, while I remained and lectured a second time. We could not have wished for a more enthusiastic or better attended meeting than we had at Linesville. The place of meeting was a double school-house, with the partition opened, and the two rooms thrown into one. The Baptist church, the only religious building in the town, was shut against us. The

Convention commenced on Saturday morning, and continued till Sunday night at half past 10, and was addressed by Miss Anthony, Mr. Powell and Myself. Unfortunately for the cause, Mr. Powell was indisposed, having taken a severe cold, which threatens to be serious. Nevertheless, he did good service, and the Convention was one of the best of the series. The Church, the Republican party and the Union claimed most of our attention. The Republicans in Pennsylvania are less anti-slavery than in any of the places I have yet visited. Mr. Wilmot, in a speech made at Erie just before the election, said—'The Democrats call us an abolition party, but I hurl the foul slander back into their teeth.' We find but little difficulty in most places about getting up meetings. The better portion of politicians of the Republican or Free Soil stamp attend our Conventions, and some help in getting up meetings. While I write, two or three Republicans are in the adjoining room, arranging for future lectures in other towns.

At Linesville, we found another large crop of children. The scene on Sunday beggars description. The house where we held the meeting was jammed in every part, except a small space in the centre of the room, where there were no seats. On their mothers' laps lay a dozen or two babies, while five or six who were old enough to run alone were let loose on the unseated spot on the floor. The latter were supplied with various articles to keep them quiet. One had its father's cane; a second a tin horn; a third its mother's bonnet; and a fourth its father's jacknife. One little boy, seven or eight years old, was lying on the floor, nibbling at his younger brother's toes, while the latter lay in its mother's arms, nibbling at something more substantial. One bright-eyed boy was chasing a dog about the floor; while another, with two caps on his head, was sailing about to the amusement of the other little ones. In different sections of the room were children standing on the tops of the desks, or hanging around their fathers' or mothers' necks. At this juncture, the house looked as if Barnum's baby show had adjourned to our meeting. Miss Anthony seemed very much amused at a little woman in a pink bloomer, seated on the front bench, with her feet, not long enough to reach the floor, hanging down, while a child a few weeks old, in her arms, nibbled away at its *dinner*.

O, the noise! I will not attempt to describe it. Suffice it to say, that some babies were crowing, some crying, and some snoring, while mothers were resorting to all sorts of means to keep their babies quiet. One was throwing her child up, and catching it; another patting her foot, and another singing 'bi-lo-baby.' You may guess how difficult it was to be heard in such an assembly. My head aches now, from the great exertion that I made to be heard above the noise of the children. And poor Powell, I pitied him, from the bottom of my heart, for he had not strength to speak to a still audience, to say nothing of such a noisy one as this; and while he was speaking, as if to make the scene more ridiculous, a tall, brawny man walked in, and, the benches being full, seated himself on the stove, which he thought had no fire in it,—but he soon found it too *peppery* for comfort. Just then, a child tumbled from the top of one of the desks, and Mr. Powell made his bow and retired. But they give us rice pudding out here for breakfast, and that gives me strength to meet the babies.

We are to hold meetings at Albion, Lockport, Coneautville, and one other place, the name of which I have forgotten, and then we go to Painesville. The people here are all alive for the Cleveland Convention, and we anticipate a large gathering and a glorious time.

Yours, truly,

W. W. BROWN.[88]

Linesville, Oct. 20, 1857.

DEAR MR. GARRISON:

Previous to attending the Painesville Convention, I lectured at Conneautville, Wellsburgh and Lockport. At the first-mentioned place, the meeting was held in the Baptist church, and I was followed the next evening by Mr. Powell and Miss Anthony, who intended to speak two evenings, if a place could be found in which to hold the meetings. But their faithfulness to the slave caused the church officials to *suspend* after the first night. At Wellsburgh, I had a very large and enthusiastic audience, and the meeting lasted till a late hour. Miss A. and I spoke at Lockport, where she made one of the most impressive speeches I ever listened to, which raised her high in the estimation of that little 'one horse village.' The Painesville Convention was well attended throughout, and left a good impression in the place. The illness of Mr. Powell, however, threw a damper over the feelings of his travelling companions, and his being compelled to return home fills us with apprehension and fear for his future health. We must hope for the best. He is too self-sacrificing and too eloquent an advocate of the slave to leave the field so young. To know him, is to love and admire him. Now that he has left us and gone home, I can speak of him the more freely. It was never my lot to travel with a more devoted or a more companionable person.

We left Painesville at half-past 2, but were late in reaching our places of meetings. Miss Anthony left us at Mentor, where she found a warm welcome at Mr. Clapp's, and had a full house. I went on to Kirtland, the place where Joe Smith and his followers started a colony twenty-four years ago. The Temple built by them still stands. It is made of rough stone, two stories high, and the roof pierced with five windows on either side, and looks very much like Faneuil Hall, and is about the size of that venerable pile. I stopped with Mr. Martindale, an old and unsophisticated farmer, who was glad to extend to me the hospitalities of his home. The meeting was held in the Baptist church, and, owing to the shortness of the notice, was small, but we were cordially invited to return.

On our way to Cleveland, our horse lost a shoe from one of his hind feet, which impeded our progress, and we did not reach the city till after 12 o'clock, when Dr. Brooke took charge of his aged friend, and relieved me of a not very interesting looking racer. Seeing in the *Bugle* an advertisement that the Bennet House was the best place for delegates to stop at, I went there—was told I could be accommodated, registered my name, and feeling a little hungry, prepared for dinner. When 'dinner' was sounded, I joined our anti-slavery friends, and started for the dining room; but, to the surprise of our party, I was met at the door and told that I must wait, and eat at the second table. To this proposition I said, 'No.' Some of our party, in their hurry for dinner, and being in the crowd, and not aware that I was excluded, took seats at the table, and partook of the viands. But Mr. Powell, Miss Anthony, Mr. Foss and Mrs. Colman, knew too much of the negro hate in the country to leave me until they saw me safely seated at the table. Therefore, when I was turned out, they followed me. As we left the dining-room, I heard a strong voice say—'If you turn my friend Mr. Brown from your table, you are a scoundrel.' I was not near enough to see who it was that uttered that sentence, but I should not wonder if he who thus gave vent to his justly indignant feelings was somewhat related to Andrew T. Foss. We soon assembled in the sittingroom for consultation, and had scarcely taken our seats, when the landlord (for the proprietor himself was from home) entered, and endeavored to still the troubled waters. He proposed to sit a *side table* for our party, let us take our meals in our rooms, or any thing except my going to the table. But he found us true to principle, and he called to his aid a friend of the proprietor. The conference lasted an hour, and finished with the landlord asking my pardon, throwing off all justification, and allowing me to take my seat at the first table. For the accomplishment of this, too much praise cannot be given to Miss Anthony, Mrs. Colman, Mr. Foss and Mr. Powell, especially the last, whose judgment is always good, and whose moral courage is of the stamp of Luther. I remained three days, and was never better treated than while at the Bennet House.

I have only a word to say about the Convention, and that is, to express a regret that the Committee should have thought fit to postpone the Northern Disunion Convention. That act threw a wet blanket over the meeting that we held, which kept us cool during all the sittings. However, the meeting was not without its good results.

Yours, truly,

WM. WELLS BROWN.[89]

DEAR MR. GARRISON:

I spent four or five days in Cleveland after the adjournment of the Convention, and discovered the almost only redeeming feature about that priest-ridden city. That redeeming feature is the intelligence, industry and respectability of the colored citizens. Though not large, the colored population of Cleveland surpass in thrift the same number in any other place in the North. Indeed, they will compare most favorably with an equal number of whites in any portion of Ohio. Most of them are from the South, where they were free, but were driven out by the tyrannical and oppressive laws of slavery, which they were unwilling longer to endure. Some of them are in good circumstances, and are engaged in business, employing their own capital. Messrs. Oliver & Henderson have a large and well-stocked store on Erie street, and appear to be liberally patronized by their white fellow-citizens. They are from Richmond, Va., and reside in their own dwellings. Mr. Oliver, though a resident of a slave State, managed to educate his children, and to bring them up with far more credit than most whites of the South. His two daughters are highly cultivated, and would grace any drawing-room in the land. The youngest is a sweet singer, and performs beautifully on the guitar. They feel deeply interested in the Anti-Slavery cause, and need only to become better acquainted with our movement to embrace it most cheerfully. Mr. Morris is from North Carolina. He is a merchant tailor, and has a fine run of custom. He is an educated man, and Mrs. Morris would do honor to any society in which she might appear. Mr. Parker keeps a provision store, and resides in a fine brick house, owned by himself. He is employed on the Mississippi river, and leaves the management of the store to Mrs. Parker, who possesses what Fowler calls 'goaheadativeness' to a far greater extent than most women. She would be a fortune to any business man. Mr. Swing and Mr. Stanley are tin manufacturers, and each has an establishment of his own. Mr. Marshall keeps a grocery, and another man, whose name I did not learn, has a blacksmith shop, and is doing well. Miss Allston, an accomplished young lady, is a teacher of music, being very proficient on the guitar and piano. Miss Stanley is a teacher in one of the day schools, and her education places her in the front rank of her profession.

There are many other colored persons in Cleveland who are doing well, and whose elevated positions will contribute much to the cause of the slave.—Amongst these are Mr. Vosburgh and Mr. Leech. The former rents out houses to his white neighbors, and the latter is a physician. Mr. Vosburgh deserves great credit for his industry.

The colored citizens of Cleveland took decidedly more interest in the late Convention than the whites; and the respectability and high tone of morals that characterize them have opened the doors of the public schools to their children. This fact alone speaks volumes for the colored citizens there. There are nearly seven million dollars' worth of property owned by this proscribed people in Ohio. Some of their farms are the finest I have seen. Colored mechanics are numerous here, and I write this letter under the hospitable roof of a black man who owns forty acres of land, and the grist-mill that stands upon it. Still, this man is shut out from the polls on election day, and his children kept out of school by law, while Ohio has been governed the last two years by a Republican State administration. Shame upon the party! for, like the Democrats, they believe that colored men 'have no rights that white men are bound to respect.' There is much negro hate, or what is called 'prejudice,' here, against all who have a drop of African blood coursing in their veins, and they need line upon line and precept upon precept.

A few evenings since, I met with a quaint old couple, who raised my mirthfulness to its highest pitch. The old man talked about little, except Andrew Jackson, and the wife thought that the greatest man that ever lived was Lorenzo Dow. All the sayings of General Jackson were rehearsed by the former, with the tobacco juice flying in every direction. The old lady thought, that 'if we only had such preaching now-a-days as Lorenzo Dow used to give us, slavery would soon die.' She feared that I had not religion enough, and got out Dow's life and sermons. As an offset, I took out a copy of THE LIBERATOR, and showed her a paragraph in a Southern paper, giving an account of the burning of a slave in Alabama. She read it, and seemed much moved. I told her that my religion was to help do away with the curse of American slavery. She drew up her face in an indescribable shape, and said, 'Well, it is too bad to burn people in that way. If the blacks commit murder, they ought to hang them *decently, and in a Christian-like manner,* and not act like barbarians.' I left the good people the next morning, knowing more about Gen. Jackson and Lorenzo Dow than I had thought it within the possibility of man or woman to teach me.

Having accepted an invitation to lecture again at Kirtland, I returned to that place on Thursday, the 15th, and spoke in the Baptist church to a large audience. I lectured in the same place the following evening, to an increased assembly.

At Euclid, I stirred up a hornet's nest among the Democrats, by saying that the present Administration was only a tool of the Slave Power. A supporter of James Buchanan produced the *Day Book* as an anti-slavery paper, and claimed that his party always intended to keep slavery out of Kansas. Finding that reason could have no influence upon such a man, I turned his whole course into ridicule, and the audience laughed him out of the hall. There is an old adage, that 'you must scorch a Muscovite to make him feel.' So it is with an inveterate supporter of the 'peculiar institution.'

A Convention was advertised to be held at Windsor on Saturday and Sunday, the 7th and 8th inst., where I was to meet Mr. Howland and Mrs. Colman; but the meetings were nearly washed away by a five days' storm. My almost iron frame yielded to the fatigues of a twenty-seven miles' ride over a rough road, through a drenching rain, that took us eight hours to accomplish the journey, and I was compelled to give the meeting up to my friends,—with the exception, however, of the morning, when I spoke half an hour or more.

I am now with a new company. Mr. Howland takes the place of Mr. Powell, who returns home on account of ill health, and Mrs. Colman fills the post made vacant by the absence of Miss Anthony, whose labors are needed in Eastern New York.

From Windsor, I visited Bloomfield, where I found that the reading of my drama a year ago in an adjoining county had created an impression in my favor, and I was hospitably entertained in the princely mansion of Charles Brown, Esq., who obtained, at his own expense, the Disciple Church for my second lecture, the first having been held in the vestry of the Presbyterian church. I could not have wished for better audiences or more patient listeners than I had at Bloomfield.

Upon the whole, I think our work goes on prosperously out here. In country places, the people come many miles on horseback and in wagons to attend the Conventions and meetings; and though they differ from us, they give good attention to what is said.

Next week, I shall be back in the edge of Pennsylvania, where I expect the *little ones* will welcome me with shouts of applause, in their way. But Dr. Johnson once said, 'Catch a Scotchman when he's young, and you may make something of him.' So I think, if we take the little people here, we may train them up in the way they should go. My great trouble now, however, is, mud. In many places, the roads are almost impassable.

Faithfully, yours,
WM. WELLS BROWN.[90]

Green, (Ohio,) Nov. 12, 1857.

[90] *Liberator*, Nov. 20, 1857.

XII. FREDERICK DOUGLASS

Frederick Douglass was without doubt the most brilliant Negro writer of his day. He expressed himself through books, letters, reports, and editorials. As the complete file of his newspaper, which he edited for a number of years, is not extant, we are compelled to rely upon his biography and letters to present his career in all of its ramifications. Unfortunately, near the outbreak of the Civil War, Douglass differed so widely from some of the anti-slavery workers that not very much of his correspondence was published in their organs. His autobiography, however, is fulsome, and his letters appearing below offer further opportunity for the study of this man and the period in which he lived.

LYNN, November 8th, 1842.

DEAR FRIEND GARRISON:

The date of this letter finds me quite unwell. I have for a week past been laboring, in company with bro. Charles Remond, in New-Bedford, with special reference to the case of our outraged brother, George Latimer, and speaking almost day and night, in public and in private; and for the reward of our labor, I have the best evidence that a great good has been done. It is said by many residents, that New-Bedford has never been so favorably aroused to her anti-slavery responsibility as at present. Our meetings were characterized by that deep and solemn feeling which the importance of the cause, when properly set forth, is always calculated to awaken. On Sunday, we held three meetings in the new town hall, at the usual meeting hours, morning, afternoon, and evening. In the morning, we had quite a large meeting, at the opening of which, I occupied about an hour, on the question as to whether a man is better than a sheep. Mr. Dean then made a few remarks, and after him, Mr. Clapp, of Nantucket, arose and gave his testimony to the truth, as it is in anti-slavery. The meeting then adjourned, to meet again in the afternoon. I said that we held our meetings at the regular meeting hours. Truth requires me to make our afternoon meeting an exception to this remark. For long before the drawling, lazy church bells commenced sounding their deathly notes, mighty crowds were making their way to the town hall. They needed no bells to remind them of their duty to bleeding humanity. They were not going to meeting to hear as to the best mode of performing water baptism; they were not going to meeting to have their prayers handsomely said for them, or to say them, merely, themselves; but to pray, not in word, but in deed and in truth; they were not going thither to be worshipped, but to worship, in spirit and in truth; they were not going to sacrifice, but to have mercy; they did not go there to find God; they had found him already. Such I think I may safely say of a large portion of the vast assembly that met in the afternoon. As I gazed upon them, my soul leaped for joy; and, but for the thought that the time might be better employed, I could have shouted aloud.—After a short space, allotted to secret or public prayer, bro. J. B. Sanderson arose and requested the attention of the audience to the reading of a few passages of scripture, selected by yourself in the editorial of last week. They did give their attention, and as he read the solemn and soul-stirring denunciations of Jehovah, by the mouth of his prophets and apostles, against oppressors, the deep stillness that pervaded that magnificent hall was a brilliant demonstration, that the audience felt that what was read was but the reiteration of words which had fallen from the great Judge of the universe. After reading, he proceeded to make some remarks on the general question of human rights. These, too, seemed to sink deep into the hearts of the gathered multitude. Not a word was lost; it was good seed, sown in good ground, by a careful hand; it must, it will bring forth fruit.

After him, rose bro. Remond, who addressed the meeting in his usual happy and deeply affecting style. When he had concluded his remarks, the meeting adjourned to meet again at an early hour in the evening. During the interval, our old friends and the slaves' friends, John Butler, Thomas Jones, Noah White, and others, were engaged in carrying benches from liberty hall to the town hall, that all who came might be accommodated with seats. They were determined to do something for humanity, though by so doing, they should be ranked with sabbath-breakers. Christianity prays for more of just such sabbath-breakers as these, and may God grant by an overwhelming revival of anti-slavery truth, to convert and send forth more just such.

The meeting met according to adjournment, at an early hour. The splendid hall was brilliantly lighted, and crowded with an earnest, listening audience, and notwithstanding the efforts of our friends before named to have them seated, a large number had to stand during the meeting, which lasted about three hours; where the standing part of the audience were, at the commencement of the meeting, there they were at the conclusion of it; no moving about with them; any place was good enough, so they could but hear. From the eminence which I occupied, I could see the entire audience; and from its appearance, I should conclude that prejudice against color was not there, at any rate, it was not to be seen by me; we were all on a level, every one took a seat just where they chose; there were neither men's side, nor women's side; white pew, nor black pew; but all seats were free, and all sides free. When the meeting was fully gathered, I had something to say, and was followed by bro. Sanderson and Remond. When they had concluded their remarks, I again took the stand, and called the attention of the meeting to the case of bro. George Latimer, which proved the finishing stroke of my present public speaking. On taking my seat, I was seized with a violent pain in my breast, which continued till morning, and with occasional raising of blood; this past off in about two hours, after which, weakness of breast, a cough, and shortness of breath ensued, so that now such is the state of my lungs, that I am unfit for public speaking, for the present. My condition goes harder with me, much harder than it would at ordinary times. These are certainly extraordinary times; times that demand the efforts of the humblest of our most humble advocates of our perishing and dying fellow-countrymen. Those that can but whisper freedom, should be doing even that, though they can only be heard from one side of their short fire place to the other. It is a struggle of life and death with us just now. No sword that can be used, be it never so rusty, should lay idle in its scabbard. Slavery, our enemy, has landed in our very midst, and commenced its bloody work. Just look at it; here is George Latimer a man—a brother—a husband—a father, stamped with the likeness of the eternal God, and redeemed by the blood of Jesus Christ, out-lawed, hunted down like a wild beast, and ferociously dragged through the streets of Boston, and incarcerated within the walls of Leverett-st. jail. And all this is done in Boston—liberty-loving, slavery-hating Boston—intellectual, moral, and religious Boston. And why was this—what crime had George Latimer committed? He had committed the crime of availing himself of his natural rights, in defence of which the founders of this very Boston enveloped her in midnight darkness, with the smoke proceeding from their thundering artillery. What a horrible state of things is here presented. Boston has become the hunting-ground of merciless men-hunters, and man-stealers. Henceforth we need not portray to the imagination of northern people, the flying slave making his way through thick and dark woods of the South, with white fanged blood-hounds yelping on his blood-stained track; but refer to the streets of Boston, made dark and dense by crowds of professed christians. Take a look at James B. Gray's new pack, turned loose on the track of poor Latimer. I see the blood-thirsty animals, smelling at every corner, part with each other, and meet again; they seem to be consulting as to the best mode of coming upon their victim. Now they look sad, discouraged;—tired, they drag along, as if they were ashamed of their business, and about to give up the chase; but presently they get a sight of their prey, their eyes brighten, they become more courageous, they approach their victim unlike the common hound. They come upon him softly, wagging their tails, pretending friendship, and do not pounce upon him, until they have secured him beyond possible escape. Such is the character of James B. Gray's new pack of two-legged blood-hounds that hunted down George Latimer, and dragged him away to the Leverett-street slave prison but a few days since. We need not point to the sugar fields of Louisiana, or to the rice swamps of Alabama, for the bloody deeds of this soul-crushing system, but to the city of the pilgrims. In future, we need not uncap the bloody cells of the horrible slave prisons of Norfolk, Richmond, Mobile, and New-Orleans, and depict the wretched and furlorn condition of their miserable inmates, whose groans rend the air, pierce heaven, and disturb the Almighty; listen no longer at the snappings of the bloody slavedrivers' lash. Withdraw your attention, for a moment, from the agonizing cries coming from hearts bursting with the keenest anguish at the South, gaze no longer upon the base, cold-blooded, heartless slave-dealer of the South, who lays his iron clutch upon the hearts of husband and wife, and, with one mighty effort, tears the bleeding ligaments apart which before constituted the twain one flesh. I say, turn your attention from all this cruelty

abroad, look now at home—follow me to your courts of justice—
mark him who sits upon the bench. He may, or he may not—God
grant he may not—tear George Latimer from a beloved wife and
tender infant. But let us take a walk to the prison in which George
Latimer is confined, inquire for the turn-key; let him open the large
iron-barred door that leads you to the inner prison. You need go
no further. Hark! listen! hear the groans and cries of George
Latimer, mingling with which may be heard the cry—my wife, my
child—and all is still again.

A moment of reflection ensues—I am to be taken back to Norfolk—must be torn from a wife and tender babe, with the threat
from Mr. Gray that I am to be murdered, though not in the ordinary way—not to have my head severed from my shoulders, not to
be hanged—not to have my heart pierced through with a dagger—
not to have my brains blown out. No, no, all these are too good
for me. No: I am to be killed by inches. I know not how; perhaps by cat-hauling until my back is torn all to pieces, my flesh is
to be cut with the rugged lash, and I faint; warm brine must now
be poured into my bleeding wounds, and through this process I
must pass, until death shall end my sufferings. Good God! save
me from a fate so horrible. Hark! hear him roll in his chains; 'I
can die, I had rather, than go back. O, my wife! O, my child!'
You have heard enough. What man, what Christian can look upon
this bloody state of things without his soul swelling big with indignation on the guilty perpetrators of it, and without resolving to
cast in his influence with those who are collecting the elements
which are to come down in ten-fold thunder, and dash this state of
things into atoms?

Men, husbands and fathers of Massachusetts—put yourselves in
the place of George Latimer; feel his pain and anxiety of mind;
give vent to the groans that are breaking through his fever-parched
lips, from a heart emersed in the deepest agony and suffering;
rattle his chains; let his prospects be yours, for the space of a few
moments. Remember George Latimer in bonds as bound with him;
keep in view the golden rule—'All things whatsoever ye would that
men should do unto you, do ye even so to them.' 'In as much as
ye did it unto the least of these my brethren ye have done it unto
me.'

Now make up your minds to what your duty is to George Latimer, and when you have made your minds up, prepare to do it and

take the consequences, and I have no fears of George Latimer going back. I can sympathize with George Latimer, having myself been cast into a miserable jail, on suspicion of my intending to do what he is said to have done, viz. appropriating my own body to my use.

My heart is full, and had I my voice, I should be doing all that I am capable of, for Latimer's redemption. I can do but little in any department; but if one department is more the place for me than another, that one is before the people.

I can't write to much advantage, having never had a day's schooling in my life, nor have I ever ventured to give publicity to any of my scribbling before; nor would I now, but for my peculiar circumstances.

Your grateful friend,
FREDERICK DOUGLASS.[98]

PHILADELPHIA, Aug. 17th, 1844.

FRIEND GARRISON:

In the Liberator of yesterday, I find a communication from Providence, over the signature of L. D. Y. giving a very interesting account of the celebration of British West India emancipation, held in Providence on the 2d of August. It was intimated in the letter, that my absence on the occasion caused some disappointment to our friends in that place, as I was to have been their chief speaker, and that notice had been given to that effect. Deeply regretting the disappointment, I feel it due to them, as well as to myself, to explain, through the Liberator, the reasons for my non-attendance; and that my task may not be too heavy, let me at once throw off a little of the responsibility placed upon me by L. D. Y. I did not understand that I was to be the chief speaker on that occasion. So far from it, I supposed that there were two other gentlemen, who would precede me.

About two weeks before the contemplated celebration, I received from the committee of arrangements a letter, requesting me to attend, in company with Rev. Mr. Pennington of Hartford, and Rev. Mr. Lewis of Providence. I received the impression from this letter, that the services of these gentlemen had already been engaged, whilst mine were yet to be engaged. I certainly did not dream of being the chief speaker. To the letter I returned a very

[98] *Liberator*, Nov. 18, 1842.

hasty answer, promising my attendance. Here the matter rested, until the week before the celebration, when, upon looking into a New-York paper, I saw that Mr. Pennington, instead of being at Providence on the 1st, was to be at New-York. Meanwhile, there was *no notice given in any of the anti-slavery papers*, of the contemplated celebration in Providence. This threw me into doubt as to whether the celebration would go on, as all the other celebrations were thus notified. I, however, was still resolved to go to Providence on the first, according to promise, and left home over night, that I might be in time in the morning to take the earliest train of cars from Boston to Providence. But, finding the morning exceedingly stormy, I deemed it useless to go. So much for the 1st of August. Now to the 2nd. On this day, I met Mr. Davis from Providence, who informed me that your celebration took place on the 1st; so I concluded it was useless to go on the 2nd.

This statement may not entirely clear me from the charge of neglect of duty. I think, however, that my friends in Providence will see it in mitigating circumstances enough to exonerate me from the charge of any intentional neglect.

Yours, for truth and justice,[99]

FREDERICK DOUGLASS.[100]

VICTORIA HOTEL, Belfast,
January 1st, 1846.

MY DEAR FRIEND GARRISON:

I am now about to take leave of the Emerald Isle, for Glasgow, Scotland. I have been here a little more than four months. Up to this time, I have given no direct expression of the views, feelings and opinions which I have formed, respecting the character and condition of the people of this land. I have refrained thus purposely. I wish to speak advisedly, and in order to do this, I have waited till I trust experience has brought my opinions to an intelligent maturity. I have been thus careful, not because I think what I may say will have much effect in shaping the opinions of the world, but because whatever of influence I may possess, whether little or much, I wish it to go in the right direction, and according

---

[99] *Liberator*, Aug. 30, 1844.

[100] In this connection one should read also another copy of Douglass's letter written at Belfast January 1, 1846. This letter was published in the *Journal of Negro History*, VIII, 102–107.

to truth. I hardly need say that, in speaking of Ireland, I shall be influenced by no prejudices in favor of America. I think my circumstances all forbid that. I have no end to serve, no creed to uphold, no government to defend; and as to nation, I belong to none. I have no protection at home, or resting-place abroad. The land of my birth welcomes me to her shores only as a slave, and spurns with contempt the idea of treating me differently. So that I am an outcast from the society of my childhood, and an outlaw in the land of my birth. 'I am a stranger with thee, and a so-journer as all my fathers were.' That men should be patriotic is to me perfectly natural; and as a philosophical fact, I am able to give it an *intellectual* recognition. But no further can I go. If ever I had any patriotism, or any capacity for the feeling, it was whipt out of me long since by the lash of the American soul-drivers.

In thinking of America, I sometimes find myself admiring her bright blue sky—her grand old woods—her fertile fields—her beau-tiful rivers—her mighty lakes, and star-crowned mountains. But my rapture is soon checked, my joy is soon turned to mourning. When I remember that all is cursed with the infernal spirit of slaveholding, robbery and wrong,—when I remember that with the waters of her noblest rivers, the tears of my brethren are borne to the ocean, disregarded and forgotten, and that her most fertile fields drink daily of the warm blood of my outraged sisters, I am filled with unutterable loathing, and led to reproach myself that any thing could fall from my lips in praise of such a land. Amer-ica will not allow her children to love her. She seems bent on compelling those who would be her warmest friends, to be her worst enemies. May God give her repentance before it is too late, is the ardent prayer of my heart. I will continue to pray, labor and wait, believing that she cannot always be insensible to the dictates of justice, or deaf to the voice of humanity.

My opportunities for learning the character and condition of the people of this land have been very great. I have travelled almost from the hill of 'Howth' to the Giant's Causeway, and from the Giant's Causeway to Cape Clear. During these travels, I have met with much in the character and condition of the people to approve, and much to condemn—much that has thrilled me with pleasure—and very much that has filled me with pain. I will not, in this letter, attempt to give any description of those scenes which have given me pain. This I will do hereafter. I have enough, and more than your subscribers will be disposed to read at one time, of the bright side of the picture. I can truly say, I have spent some of the happiest moments of my life since landing in this country. I seem to have undergone a transformation. I live a new life. The warm and generous co-operation extended to me by the friends of my despised race—the prompt and liberal manner with which the press has rendered me its aid—the glorious enthusiasm with which thousands have flocked to hear the cruel wrongs of my down-trodden and long-enslaved fellow-countrymen portrayed—the deep sympathy for the slave, and the strong abhorrence of the slave-holder, everywhere evinced—the cordiality with which members and ministers of various religious bodies, and of various shades of religious opinion, have embraced me, and lent me their aid—the kind hospitality constantly proffered to me by persons of the highest rank in society—the spirit of freedom that seems to animate all with whom I come in contact—and the entire absence of every thing that looked like prejudice against me, on account of the color of my skin—contrasted so strongly with my long and bitter experience in the United States, that I look with wonder and amazement on the transition. In the Southern part of the United States, I was a slave, thought of and spoken of as property. In the language of the LAW, *'held, taken, reputed and adjudged to be a chattel in the hands of my owners and possessors, and their executors, administrators, and assigns, to all intents, constructions, and purposes whatsoever.'*—Brev. Digest, 224. In the Northern States, a fugitive slave, liable to be hunted at any moment like a felon, and to be hurled into the terrible jaws of slavery—doomed by an inveterate prejudice against color to insult and outrage on every hand, (Massachusetts out of the question)—denied the privileges and courtesies common to others in the use of the most humble means of conveyance—shut out from the cabins on steamboats—refused admission to respectable hotels—caricatured, scorned, scoffed, mocked and maltreated with impunity by any one, (no matter how black his heart,) so he has a white skin. But now behold the change! Eleven days and a half gone, and I have crossed three thousand miles of the perilous deep. Instead of a democratic government, I am under a monarchical government. Instead of the bright blue sky of America, I am covered with the soft grey fog of the Emerald Isle. I breathe, and lo! the chattel becomes a man. I gaze around in vain for one who will question my equal humanity, claim me as his slave, or offer me an insult. I employ a cab—I am seated beside white people—I reach the hotel—I enter the same door—I am shown into the same parlor—I dine at the same table—and no one is offended. No delicate nose grows deformed in my presence. I find no difficulty here in obtaining admission into any place of worship, instruction or amusement, on equal terms with people as white as any I ever saw in the United States. I meet nothing to remind me of my complexion. I find myself regarded and treated at every turn with the kindness and deference paid to white people. When I go to church, I am met by no upturned nose and scornful lip to tell me, 'We don't allow niggers in here'!

I remember, about two years ago, there was in Boston, near the southwest corner of Boston Common, a menagerie. I had long desired to see such a collection as I understood were being exhibited there. Never having had an opportunity while a slave, I resolved to seize this, my first, since my escape. I went, and as I approached the entrance to gain admission, I was met and told by the doorkeeper, in a harsh and contemptuous tone, 'We don't allow niggers in here.' I also remember attending a revival meeting in the Rev. Henry Jackson's meeting-house, at New-Bedford, and going up the broad aisle to find a seat. I was met by a good deacon, who told me, in a pious tone, 'We don't allow niggers in here'! Soon after my arrival in New-Bedford from the South, I had a strong desire to attend the Lyceum, but was told, 'They don't allow niggers in here'! While passing from New York to Boston on the steamer Massachusetts, on the night of 9th Dec. 1843, when chilled almost through with the cold, I went into the cabin to get a little warm. I was soon touched upon the shoulder, and told, 'We don't allow niggers in here'! On arriving in Boston from an anti-slavery tour, hungry and tired, I went into an eating-house near my friend Mr. Campbell's, to get some refreshments. I was met by a lad in a white apron, 'We don't allow niggers in here'! A week or two before leaving the United States, I had a meeting appointed at Weymouth, the home of that glorious band of true abolitionists, the Weston family, and others. On attempting to take a seat in the Omnibus to that place, I was told by the driver, (and I never shall forget his fiendish hate,) 'I don't allow niggers in here'! Thank heaven for the respite I now enjoy! I had been in Dublin but a few days, when a gentleman of great respectability kindly offered to conduct me through all the public buildings of that beautiful city; and a little afterwards, I found myself dining with the Lord Mayor of Dublin. What a pity there was not some American democratic Christian at the door of his splendid mansion, to bark out at my approach, *'They don't allow niggers in here'!* The truth is, the people here know nothing of the republican negro hate prevalent in our glorious land. They measure and esteem men according to their moral and intellectual worth, and not according to the color of their skin. Whatever may be said of the aristocracies here, there is none based on the color of a man's skin. This species of aristocracy belongs pre-eminently to 'the land of the free, and the home of the brave.' I have never found it abroad, in any but Americans. It sticks to them wherever they go. They find it almost as hard to get rid of it as to get rid of their skins.

The second day after my arrival at Liverpool, in company with my friend Buffum, and several other friends, I went to Eaton Hall, the residence of the Marquis of Westminster, one of the most splendid buildings in England. On approaching the door, I found several of our American passengers, who came out with us in the Cambria, waiting at the door for admission, as but one party was allowed in the house at a time. We all had to wait till the company within came out. And of all the faces, expressive of chagrin, those of the Americans were pre-eminent. They looked as sour as vinegar, and bitter as gall, when they found I was to be admitted on equal terms with themselves. When the door was opened, I walked in, on an equal footing with my white fellow-citizens, and from all I could see, I had as much attention paid me by the servants that showed us through the house, as any with a paler skin. As I walked through the building, the statuary did not fall down, the pictures did not leap from their places, the doors did not refuse to open, and the servants did not say, *'We don't allow niggers in here'!*

A happy new year to you, and all the friends of freedom.

Excuse this imperfect scrawl, and believe me to be ever and always yours, FREDERICK DOUGLASS.[100]

DUBLIN, Sept. 16, 1845.

MY DEAR FRIEND GARRISON:

You will see that James and myself are still in old Ireland. Our stay is protracted in consequence of the publication here of

[100] *Liberator*, Jan. 30, 1845.

my narrative. I need hardly say we are happy, when I tell you
our home is the house of Mr. R. D. Webb,—the very impersonation
of old-fashioned, thorough-going anti-slavery; and that we are constantly cheered by the society of Mr. James Haughton, than whom,
there is not to be found a truer, or more devoted, vigilant, working,
persevering abolitionist on this side the Atlantic. We have also
been aided, cheered and strengthened by the noble and generous-
hearted James and Thomas Webb, in each of whose houses we have
been made perfectly at home.

Our hearts were all made glad by the arrival of the ever welcome Liberator and Standard, yesterday—although they bore the
sad intelligence of the fate of Cassius M. Clay's press. I can now
remember no occurrence of mobocratic violence against the anti-
slavery cause which sent such a chill over my hopes, for the moment, as the one in question. I regarded the establishment of his
press in Lexington, Kentucky, as one of the most hopeful and soul-
cheering signs of the times,—a star shining in darkness, beaming
hope to the almost despairing bondman, and bidding him to suffer
on, as the day of his deliverance is certain. But, alas! the mob has
triumphed, and the star apparently gone out.

The enemy came upon Cassius at an unfortunate hour. Availing themselves of his sickness, they have succeeded against him.
Yet the cause shall not suffer; the star, whose feeble light had
become painful, shall yet become a sun, whose brilliant rays shall
scorch, blister and burn, till slavery shall be utterly consumed. I
was almost sorry to be from home, when the voice of the feeblest
might be of value in concentrating public indignation against so
horrible an outrage upon the freedom of the press.

We shall, however, make the most of it in this land:—the damning deed shall ring throughout these kingdoms. The base, cruel,
cowardly and infernal character of that organized band of plunderers, shall be as fully revealed as I am capable of doing it. What
a brilliant illustration of republican love of freedom! How the
monarchs and aristocrats of the old world will tremble at the rapid
march of republican freedom! How they will hide their eyes for
very shame, when they think of their own tyranny, in comparison
with the free and noble institutions of America,—where freedom
of the press means freedom to advocate slavery, and where liberty
regulated by law means slavery protected by an armed band of
bloody assassins! But, thank Heaven! 'Oppression shall not always reign.'

Our success here is even greater than I had anticipated. We have held four glorious anti-slavery meetings—two in the Royal Exchange, and two in the Friends' meeting-house—all crowded to overflowing. Only think of our holding a meeting in the *meeting-house* of the Society of Friends! When at home, they would almost bolt us out of their yards. 'Circumstances alter cases.' If the Lynn Friends' meeting-house could be, by some process, placed on this side the Atlantic, its spacious walls would probably at once welcome an anti-slavery meeting; but, as things now stand, it must be closed to humanity—lest Friends get into the mixture!

I am to lecture to-morrow evening at the Music Hall. It will hold three thousand persons, and is let for about fifty dollars a night. But its generous proprietor, Mr. Classon, has kindly agreed to let me have it free of charge.

I have attended several temperance meetings, and given several temperance addresses. Friend Haughton, Buffum and myself spoke to-day on temperance, in the very prison in which O'Connell was put. I went out last Sunday to Bootertown, and saw Father Mathew administer the pledge to about one thousand. 'The cause is rolling on.'

One of the most pleasing features of my visit, thus far, has been a total absence of all manifestations of prejudice against me, on account of my color. The change of circumstances, in this, is particularly striking. I go on stage coaches, omnibuses, steamboats, into the first cabins, and in the first public houses, without seeing the slightest manifestation of that hateful and vulgar feeling against me. I find myself not treated as a *color*, but as a *man*—not as a thing, but as a child of the common Father of us all.

> In great haste,
> Ever yours,
> FREDERICK DOUGLASS.[101]

> Dublin, (Great Brunswick Street,)
> September 29th, 1845.

My Dear Friend Garrison:

I promised, on leaving America, to keep you informed of my proceedings whilst I remained abroad. I sometimes fear I shall be compelled to break my promise, if by keeping it is meant writing letters to you fit for publication. You know one of my objects in

[101] *Liberator*, Oct. 10, 1845.

coming here was to get a little repose, that I might return home refreshed and strengthened, ready and able to join you vigorously in the prosecution of our holy cause. But, really, if the labor of the last two weeks be a fair sample of what awaits me, I have certainly sought repose in the wrong place. I have work enough here, on the spot, to occupy every inch of my time, and every particle of my strength, were I to stay in this city a whole six months. The cause of temperance alone would afford work enough to occupy every inch of my time. I have invitation after invitation to address temperance meetings, which I am compelled to decline. How different here, from my treatment at home! In this country, I am welcomed to the temperance platform, side by side with white speakers, and am received as kindly and warmly as though my skin were white.

I have but just returned from a great Repeal meeting, held at Conciliation Hall. It was a very large meeting—much larger than usual, I was told, on account of the presence of Mr. O'Connell, who has just returned from his residence at Derrynane, where he has been spending the summer, recruiting for an energetic agitation of repeal during the present autumn. On approaching the door, or gateway leading to the Hall, and observing the denseness of the crowd, I almost despaired of getting in; but, having by the kindness of James Haughton, Esq. obtained a note of introduction to the Secretary of the Repeal Association, and being encouraged to persevere by the evident disposition of the friendly crowd to let me pass,—many of whom seemed to be holding in their breath, and thus contracting their dimensions, to allow me passage way,—I pressed forward, and with much difficulty succeeded in reaching the interior. The meeting had been in progress for some time before I got in. When I entered, one after another was announcing the Repeal rent for the week. The audience appeared to be in deep sympathy with the Repeal movement, and the announcement of every considerable contribution was followed by a hearty round of applause, and sometimes a vote of thanks was taken for the donors. At the close of this business, Mr. O'Connell rose and delivered a speech of about an hour and a quarter long. It was a great speech, skilfully delivered, powerful in its logic, majestic in its rhetoric, biting in its sarcasm, melting in its pathos, and burning in its rebukes. Upon the subject of slavery in general, and American slavery in particular, Mr. O'Connell grew warm and energetic, defending his course on this subject. He said, with an earnestness which I shall never forget, 'I have been assailed for attacking the American institution, as it is called,—negro slavery. I am not ashamed of that attack. I do not shrink from it. I am the advocate of civil and religious liberty, all over the globe, and wherever tyranny exists, I am the foe of the tyrant; wherever oppression shows itself, I am the foe of the oppressor; wherever slavery rears its head, I am the enemy of the system, or the institution, call it by what name you will. I am the friend of liberty in every clime, class and color. My sympathy with distress is not confined within the narrow bounds of my own green island. No—it extends itself to every corner of the earth. My heart walks abroad, and wherever the miserable are to be succored, or the slave to be set free, there my spirit is at home, and I delight to dwell.'

Mr. O'Connell was in his happiest mood while delivering this speech. The fire of freedom was burning in his mighty heart. He had but to open his mouth, to put us in possession of 'thoughts that breathe, and words that burn.' I have heard many speakers within the last four years—speakers of the first order; but I confess, I have never heard one, by whom I was more completely captivated than by Mr. O'Connell. I used to wonder how such monster meetings as those of Repeal could be held peaceably. It is now no matter of astonishment at all. It seems to me that the voice of O'Connell is enough to calm the most violent passion, even though it were already manifesting itself in a mob. There is a sweet persuasiveness in it, beyond any voice I ever heard. His power over an audience is perfect.

When he had taken his seat, a number withdrew from the Hall, and, taking advantage of the space left vacant thereby, I got quite near the platform, for no higher object than that of obtaining a favorable view of the Liberator. But almost as soon as I did so, friend Buffum had by some means (I know not what) obtained an introduction to Mr. John O'Connell, son of Daniel O'Connell, and nothing would do but I must be introduced also—an honor for which I was quite unprepared, and one from which I naturally shrunk. But Buffum; in real Yankee style, had resolved (to use a Yankee term) to 'put me through' at all hazards. On being introduced to Mr. O'Connell, an opportunity was afforded me to speak; and although I scarce knew what to say, I managed to say something, which was quite well received.

The Hutchinson family have been here a week or more, and have attended two of my lectures on slavery; and here, as at home, did much by their soul-stirring songs to render the meetings interesting.

My Narrative is just published, and I have sold one hundred copies in this city. Our work goes on nobly. James and myself leave here for Wexford on Monday next. We shall probably hold two meetings there, and from thence go to Waterford, and then to Cork, where we shall spend a week or ten days. I have also engagements in Belfast, which will detain me in Ireland all of one month longer.

Much love to my anti-slavery friends.

Ever one with you, through good and evil report,

FREDERICK DOUGLASS.[102]

DUBLIN, Sept. 1, 1845.

DEAR FRIEND GARRISON:

Thanks to a kind Providence, I am now safe in old Ireland, in the beautiful city of Dublin, surrounded by the kind family, and seated at the table of our mutual friend, JAMES H. WEBB, brother of the well-known RICHARD D. WEBB. I landed at Liverpool on Thursday morning, 28th August, and took lodgings at the Union hotel, Clayton Squire, in company with friend Buffum and our warm-hearted singers, the Hutchinson family. Here we all continued until Saturday evening, the 30th instant, when friend Buffum and myself (with no little reluctance) separated from them, and took ship for this place, and on our arrival here, were kindly invited by James, in the temporary absence of Richard D. Webb and family, to make his house our home.

There are a number of things about which I should like to write, aside from those immediately connected with our cause; but of this I must deny myself,—at least under present circumstances. Sentimental letter-writing must give way, when its claims are urged against facts necessary to the advancement of our cause, and the destruction of slavery. I know it will gladden your heart to hear, that from the moment we first lost sight of the American shore, till we landed at Liverpool, our gallant steam-ship was the theatre of an almost constant discussion of the subject of slavery—commencing cool, but growing hotter every moment as it advanced. It was

[102] *Liberator*, Oct. 24, 1845.

a great time for anti-slavery, and a hard time for slavery;—the one delighting in the sunshine of free discussion, and the other horror-stricken at its God-like approach. The discussion was general. If suppressed in the saloon, it broke out in the steerage; and if it ceased in the steerage, it was renewed in the saloon; and if suppressed in both, it broke out with redoubled energy, high upon the saloon deck, in the open, refreshing, free ocean air. I was happy. Every thing went on nobly. The truth was being told, and having its legitimate effect upon the hearts of those who heard it. At last, the evening previous to our arrival at Liverpool, the slaveholders, convinced that reason, morality, common honesty, humanity, and Christianity, were all against them, and that argument was no longer any means of defence, or at least but a poor means, abandoned their post in debate, and resorted to their old and natural mode of defending their morality by brute force.

Yes, they actually got up a MOB—a real American, republican, democratic, Christian mob,—and that, too, on the deck of a British steamer, and in sight of the beautiful high lands of Dungarvan! I declare, it is enough to make a slave ashamed of the country that enslaved him, to think of it. Without the slightest pretensions to patriotism, as the phrase goes, the conduct of the mobocratic Americans on board the Cambria almost made me ashamed to say I *had run away* from such a country. It was decidedly the most daring and disgraceful, as well as wicked exhibition of depravity, I ever witnessed, North or South; and the actors in it showed themselves to be as hard in heart, as venomous in spirit, and as bloody in design, as the infuriated men who bathed their hands in the warm blood of the noble Lovejoy.

The facts connected with, and the circumstances leading to, this most disgraceful transaction, I will now give, with some minuteness, though I may border, at times, a little on the ludicrous.

In the first place, our passengers were made up of nearly all sorts of people, from different countries, of the most opposite modes of thinking on all subjects. We had nearly all sorts of parties in morals, religion, and politics, as well as trades, callings, and professions. The doctor and the lawyer, the soldier and the sailor, were there. The scheming Connecticut wooden clock-maker, the large, surly, New-York lion-tamer, the solemn Roman Catholic bishop, and the Orthodox Quaker were there. A minister of the Free Church of Scotland, and a minister of the Church of England—the established Christian and the wandering Jew, the Whig and the Democrat, the white and the black—were there. There was the dark-visaged Spaniard, and the light-visaged Englishman—the man from Montreal, and the man from Mexico. There were slaveholders from Cuba, and slaveholders from Georgia. We had anti-slavery singing and pro-slavery grumbling; and at the same time that Governor Hammond's Letters were being read, my Narrative was being circulated.

In the midst of the debate going on, there sprang up quite a desire, on the part of a number on board, to have me lecture to them on slavery. I was first requested to do so by one of the passengers, who had become quite interested. I, of course, declined, well knowing that that was a privilege which the captain alone had a right to give, and intimated as much to the friend who invited me. I told him I should not feel at liberty to lecture, unless the captain should personally invite me to speak. Things went on as usual till between five and six o'clock in the afternoon of Wednesday, when I received an invitation from the captain to deliver an address upon the saloon deck. I signified my willingness to do so, and he at once ordered the bell to be rung and the meeting cried. This was the signal for a general excitement. Some swore I should not speak, and others said I should. Bloody threats were being made against me, if I attempted it. At the hour appointed, I went upon the saloon deck, where I was expected to speak. There was much noise going on among the passengers, evidently intended to make it impossible for me to proceed. At length, our Hutchinson friends broke forth in one of their unrivalled songs, which, like the angel of old, closed the lions' mouths, so that, for a time, silence prevailed. The captain, taking advantage of this silence, now introduced me, and expressed the hope that the audience would hear me with attention. I then commenced speaking; and, after expressing my gratitude to a kind Providence that had brought us safely across the sea, I proceeded to portray the condition of my brethren in bonds. I had not uttered five words, when a Mr. Hazzard, from Connecticut, called out, in a loud voice, 'That's a lie!' I went on, taking no notice of him, though he was murmuring nearly all the while, backed up by a man from New-Jersey. I continued till I said something which seemed to cut to the quick, when out bawled Hazzard, 'That's a lie!' and appeared anxious to strike me. I then said to the audience that I would explain to them the reason of Hazzard's conduct. The colored man, in our country, was treated as a being without rights. 'That's a lie!' said Hazzard. I then told the audience that as almost every thing I said was pronounced lies, I would endeavor to substantiate them by reading a few extracts from slave laws. The slavocrats, finding they were now to be fully exposed, rushed up about me, with hands clenched, and swore I should not speak. They were ashamed to have American laws read before an English audience. Silence was restored by the interference of the captain, who took a noble stand in regard to my speaking. He said he had tried to please all of his passengers—and a part of them had expressed to him a desire to hear me lecture to them, and in obedience to their wishes he had invited me to speak; and those who did not wish to hear, might go to some other part of the ship. He then turned, and requested me to proceed. I again commenced, but was again interrupted—more violently than before. One slaveholder from Cuba shook his fist in my face, and said, 'O, I wish I had you in Cuba!' 'Ah!' said another, 'I wish I had him in Savannah! We would use him up!' Said another, 'I will be one of a number to throw him overboard!'

We were now fully divided into two distinct parties—those in favor of my speaking, and those against me. A noble-spirited Irish gentleman assured the man who proposed to throw me overboard, that two could play at that game, and that, in the end, he might be thrown overboard himself. The clamor went on, waxing hotter and hotter, till it was quite impossible for me to proceed. I was stopped, but the cause went on. Anti-slavery was uppermost, and the mob was never of more service to the cause against which it was directed. The clamor went on long after I ceased speaking, and was only silenced by the captain, who told the mobocrats if they did not cease their clamor, he would have them put in irons; and he actually sent for the irons, and doubtless would have made use of them, had not the rioters become orderly.

Such is but a faint outline of an AMERICAN MOB ON BOARD OF A BRITISH STEAM PACKET.

Yours, to the end of the race,

FREDERICK DOUGLASS.[103]

103 *Liberator*, Sept. 26, 1845.

Great Brunswick Street,
Dublin, Dec. 1st, 1845.

Dear Sir:

Allow me to thank you for your noble and timely defence of my conduct on board the British steamship Cambria, during her passage, 27th Aug., from Boston, U. S. to Liverpool, England; and also to thank you for the friendly manner with which you regard and treat every movement tending to improve and elevate my long enslaved and deeply injured race.

In attempting to speak on board the Cambria, I acted in accordance with a sense of duty, and with no desire to wound or injure the feelings of any one on board. My object was to enlighten such of our passengers as wished to be enlightened, and to remove the objections to emancipation and false impressions concerning slavery, which I had heard urged during our passage.

Nor should I have done this, but that our popular and gentlemanly commander, as well as a most respectable number of our passengers, gave me a pressing invitation to do so. It is clear that slavery in our country can only be abolished by creating a public opinion favorable to its abolition, and this can only be done by enlightening the public mind—by exposing the character of slavery, and enforcing the great principles of Justice and Humanity against it. To do this with what ability I may possess, is plainly my duty. To shrink from doing so, on any fitting occasion, from a mere fear of giving offence to those implicated in the wickedness, would be to betray the sacred trust committed to me, and to act the part of a coward.

The question to be answered is: Had the passengers, through the Captain, a right to ask me to give them my views of slavery? To ask the question is to answer it. They had as much right to ask me my views on that subject, as those on any other subject. To deny that they had such right, would be to deny that they had the right to exchange views at all. If they had the right to ask, I had a right to answer, and to answer so as to be understood by those who wished to hear. But then, it will be said, the subject of slavery is not open to discussion. Who say so? The very men who are continually speaking and writing in its favor. But who has a right to say what subject shall or shall not be discussed on board of a British steamer? Certainly not the slaveholders of South Carolina, nor their slaveholding abettors in New-York or elsewhere.

If any one has such a right, the ship's commander has. Now, all I did on the occasion in question, was in perfect agreement with the wishes of the Captain and a large number of our most respectable passengers.

The English papers have had much to say respecting the affair, and of course have in all cases taken a view favorable to myself. I say of course, not because I regard English journalists more disposed to pursue an honorable course in general than those of America; but because they are all committed against negro slavery within their own dominions and elsewhere; and in this, whatever may be said of them in other respects, they hold a decided advantage over those of America.

The whole conduct of the Americans who took part in the mob on board the Cambria, was in keeping with the base and cowardly spirit that animated the mob in Lexington, Kentucky, which murderously undertook to extinguish the light of Cassius M. Clay's noble paper, because his denunciations of slavery were offensive to their slaveholding ears. Not being able to defend their 'peculiar institution' with words, they meanly—and I may add foolishly—resort to blows, vainly thinking thus to cover up their infamy. When will they learn that all such attempts only defeat the end which they are intended to promote, as it only calls attention to an institution which can pass without condemnation, only as it passes without observation. The selfishness of the slaveholder and the horrible practices of slavery must ever excite in the true heart the deepest indignation and most absolute disgust.

'To be hated, it needs but to be seen.'

Again accept my thanks, and believe me to be most gratefully,
Yours,

FREDERICK DOUGLASS.

MR. THURLOW WEED.[105]

TO WILLIAM LLOYD GARRISON.

CORK, Oct. 28, 1845.

DEAR FRIEND:

I am here, well and hearty, and I trust doing something for the promotion of our holy cause. I have already had several meetings

[105] *Liberator,* Jan. 16, 1846.

in this city, all of which have been very well attended by highly intelligent and influential people. The abolitionists here are of the true stamp. They look with the deepest interest on all movements for the abolition of slavery in America. When slavery was abolished in the West India Islands, it was proposed to disband their organization, but they nobly resolved never to disband, while the foul blot and bloody stain of slavery disgraced any portion of the globe. And although they have existed in an organized form for many years longer than any of our organizations in America, I find them as warm-hearted, active and energetic, as though they had just commenced operations. For much of the interest manifested toward the Massachusetts A. S. Bazaar by the ladies of this city, the cause is indebted to Charles Lenox Remond. His labors here were abundant, and very effective. He is spoken of here in terms of high approbation; and his name is held in affectionate remembrance by many whose hearts were warmed into life on this question by his soul-stirring eloquence.

My reception here has been truly flattering. Immediately after my arrival, a public breakfast was given to receive myself and friend Buffum—of the details of which, you are already informed. Since then, I have had every kindness shown me that the most ambitious could desire. I am hailed here as a temperance man as well as an abolitionist. My first speech here, as well as in Dublin, was on the temperance question. I have spoken on temperance several times since. On the 21st instant, Father Mathew, the living saviour of Ireland from the curse of intemperance, gave a splendid Soiree, as a token of his sympathy and regard for friend Buffum and myself. There were two hundred and fifty persons present. It was decidedly the brightest and happiest company, I think, I ever saw, any where. Every one seemed to be enjoying himself in the fullest manner. It was enough to delight any heart not totally bereft of feeling, to look upon such a company of happy faces. Among them all, I saw no one that seemed to be shocked or disturbed at my dark presence. No one seemed to feel himself contaminated by contact with me. I think it would be difficult to get the same number of persons together in any of our New-England cities, without some democratic nose growing deformed at my approach. *But then you know white people in America are whiter, purer, and better than the people here. This accounts for it!* Besides, we are the freest nation on the globe, as well as the most

enlightened, and can therefore afford to insult and outrage the
colored man with impunity. This is one of the peculiar privileges
of our peculiar institution. On the morning after the Soiree,
Father Mathew invited us to breakfast with him at his own house—
an honor quite unexpected, and one for which I felt myself unprepared. I however accepted his kind invitation, and went. I found
him living in a very humble dwelling, and in an obscure street. As
I approached, he came out of his house, and took me about thirty
yards from his door, and with uplifted hands, in a manner altogether peculiar to himself, and with a face beaming with benevolent
expression, he exclaimed—'Welcome! welcome! my dear Sir, to my
humble abode;' at the same time taking me cordially by the hand,
conducted me through a rough, uncarpeted passage to a green door
leading to an uncarpeted stairway, on ascending one flight of which
I found myself abruptly ushered into what appeared to be both
drawing and dining room. There was no carpet on the floor, and
very little furniture of any kind in the room; an old-fashioned side-
board, a few chairs, three or four pictures hung carelessly around
the walls, comprised nearly the whole furniture of the room. The
breakfast table was set when I went in. A large urn stood in the
middle, surrounded by cups, saucers, plates, knives and forks,
spoons, &c. &c., all of a very plain order—rather too plain, I
thought, for so great a man. His greatness, however, was not dependent on outward show; nor was it obscured from me by his
plainness. It showed that he could be great without the ordinary
attractions with which men of his rank and means are generally
anxious to surround themselves. Upon entering the room, Father
M. introduced me to Mr. Wm. O'Conner, an invited guest, a gentleman of property and standing, and though not a teetotaller, yet an
ardent admirer of Father Mathew. As an evidence of his devoted
attachment, honor and esteem, Mr. O'Conner has erected a splendid
tower on his own land, about four miles from Cork, in a very conspicuous place, having a commanding view of the harbor of Cork,
and a view of the beautiful hills for miles around. The presence
of this gentleman at the breakfast afforded me an excellent opportunity of witnessing Father Mathew's faithfulness to his friends.
I found him entirely uncompromising. This gentleman complained
a little of his severity towards the distillers of Cork, who had large
amounts invested in distilleries, and who could not be expected to
give their business up to their ruin. To which Father Mathew

replied in the natural way, that such men had no right to prosper by the ruin of others. He said he was once met by a very rich distiller, who asked him rather imploringly how he could so deliberately plot the ruin of so many good and unoffending people, who had their all invested in distilleries? In reply, Father Mathew then told with good spirit the following excellent anecdote: 'A very fat old duck went out early one morning in pursuit of worms, and after being out all day, she succeeded in filling her crop, and on her return home at night, with her crop full of worms, she had the misfortune to be met by a fox, who at once proposed to take her life, to satisfy his hunger. The old duck appealed, argued, implored, and remonstrated. She said to the fox—You cannot be so wicked and hard-hearted as to take the life of a harmless duck, merely to satisfy your hunger. She exhorted him against the commission of so great a sin, and begged him not to stain his soul with innocent blood. When the fox could stand her cant no longer, he said—'Out upon you, madam, with all your fine feathers; you are a pretty thing, indeed, to lecture me about taking life to satisfy my hunger—is not your own crop now full of worms! You destroy more lives in one day, to satisfy your hunger, than I do in a whole month!' Father Mathew has a fund of anecdotes, which he tells in the happiest manner, always to the point, and with most excellent effect. His whole soul appeared to be wrapped up in the temperance cause. The aim of his life appears to be to spread the blessings of temperance over the whole world. To accomplish this, he spares no pains. His time, strength and money are all freely given to the cause; and his success is truly wonderful. When he is at home, his house is literally surrounded with persons, many of whom have come miles to take the pledge. He seldom takes a meal without being interrupted by some one to take the pledge. He was called away twice while I was there, to dismiss a number who had come to take the pledge. This he did with great delight.

Cork contains one hundred thousand inhabitants. One half of this number have taken the pledge of Father Mathew. The change already wrought in the condition of the whole people of Ireland is almost, through his labors, miraculous; and the cause is still advancing. *Five millions, four hundred eighty-seven thousand, three hundred and ninety-five souls* have received the pledge from him— 'and still they come.' So entirely charmed by the goodness of this truly good man was I, that I besought him to administer the pledge to me. He complied with promptness, and gave me a beautiful silver pledge. I now reckon myself with delight the fifth of the last five of Father Mathew's 5,487,495 temperance children.

The papers here leave me little to say about my anti-slavery proceedings. They very readily report my movements.

Friend Buffum left me on the 21st October, to attend the great Anti-Corn-Law Bazaar, now holding at Manchester. We shall meet again in the course of a few weeks in Belfast.

My love to your dear family, and the true that surround you. Ever and always

Yours for freedom,

FREDERICK DOUGLASS.[104]

MONTROSE, (Scotland,) Feb. 26, 1846.

MY DEAR FRIEND GARRISON:

In my letter to you from Belfast, I intimated my intention to say something more about Ireland; and although I feel like fulfilling my promise, the Liberator comes to me so laden with foreign correspondence, that I feel some hesitancy about increasing it. I shall, however, send you this, and if it is worth a place in your columns, I need not tell you to publish it. It is the glory of the Liberator, that in it the oppressed of every class, color and clime, may have their wrongs fully set forth, and their rights boldly vindicated. Your brave assertion of its character in your last defence of free discussion, has inspired me with a fresh love for the Liberator. Though established for the overthrow of the accursed slave system, it is not insensible to other evils that afflict and blast the happiness of mankind. So, also, though I am more closely connected and identified with one class of outraged, oppressed and enslaved people, I cannot allow myself to be insensible to the wrongs and sufferings of any part of the great family of man. I am not only an American slave, but a man, and as such, am bound to use my powers for the welfare of the whole human brotherhood. I am not going through this land with my eyes shut, ears stopped, or heart steeled. I am seeking to see, hear and feel, all that may be seen, heard and felt; and neither the attentions I am receiving here, nor the connexion I hold to my brethren in bonds, shall prevent my disclosing the results of my observation. I believe that

[104] *Liberator,* Nov. 28, 1845.

the sooner the wrongs of the whole human family are made known, the sooner those wrongs will be reached. I had heard much of the misery and wretchedness of the Irish people, previous to leaving the United States, and was prepared to witness much on my arrival in Ireland. But I must confess, my experience has convinced me that the half has not been told. I supposed that much that I heard from the American press on this subject was mere exaggeration, resorted to for the base purpose of impeaching the characters of British philanthropists, and throwing a mantle over the dark and infernal character of American slavery and slaveholders. My opinion has undergone no change in regard to the latter part of my supposition, for I believe a large class of writers in America, as well as in this land, are influenced by no higher motive than that of covering up our national sins, to please popular taste, and satisfy popular prejudice; and thus many have harped upon the wrongs of Irishmen, while in truth they care no more about Irishmen, or the wrongs of Irishmen, than they care about the whipped, gagged, and thumb-screwed slave. They would as willingly sell on the auction-block an Irishman, if it were popular to do so, as an African. For heart, such men have adamant—for consciences, they have public opinion. They are a stench in the nostrils of upright men, and a curse to the country in which they live. The limits of a single letter are insufficient to allow any thing like a faithful description of those painful exhibitions of human misery, which meet the eye of a stranger almost at every step. I spent nearly six weeks in Dublin, and the scenes I there witnessed were such as to make me 'blush, and hang my head to think myself a man.' I speak truly when I say, I dreaded to go out of the house. The streets were almost literally alive with beggars, displaying the greatest wretchedness—some of them mere stumps of men, without feet, without legs, without hands, without arms—and others still more horribly deformed, with crooked limbs, down upon their hands and knees, their feet lapped around each other, and laid upon their backs, pressing their way through the muddy streets and merciless crowd, casting sad looks to the right and left, in the hope of catching the eye of a passing stranger—the citizens generally having set their faces against giving to beggars. I have had more than a dozen around me at one time, men, women and children, all telling a tale of woe which would move any but a heart of iron. Women, barefooted and bareheaded, and only covered by rags which seemed to be held together by the very dirt and filth with which they were covered—many of these had infants in their arms, whose emaciated forms, sunken eyes and pallid cheeks, told too plainly that they had nursed till they had nursed in vain. In such a group you may hear all forms of appeal, entreaty, and expostulation. A half a dozen voices have broken upon my ear at once:—'Will your honor please to give me a penny to buy some bread?' 'May the Lord bless you, give the poor old woman a little sixpence.' 'For the love of God, leave us a few pennies—we will divide them amongst us.' 'Oh! my poor child, it must starve, for God's sake give me a penny. More power to you! I know your honor will leave the poor creature something. Ah, do! ah, do! and I will pray for you as long as I live.' For a time I gave way to my feelings, but reason reminded me that such a course must only add another to the already long list of beggars, and I was often compelled to pass, as if I heeded not and felt not. I fear it had a hardening effect upon my heart, as I found it much easier to pass without giving to the last beggar, than the first. The spectacle that affected me most, and made the most vivid impression on my mind, of the extreme poverty and wretchedness of the poor of Dublin, was the frequency with which I met little children in the street at a late hour of the night, covered with filthy rags, and seated upon cold stone steps, or in corners, leaning against brick walls, fast asleep, with none to look upon them, none to care for them. If they have parents, they have become vicious, and have abandoned them. Poor creatures! they are left without help, to find their way through a frowning world—a world that seems to regard them as intruders, and to be punished as such. God help the poor! An infidel might ask, in view of these facts, with confusing effect—Where is your religion that takes care for the poor— for the widow and fatherless—where are its votaries—what are they doing? The answer to this would be, if properly given, wasting their energies in useless debate on hollow creeds and points of doctrine, which, when settled, neither make one hair white nor black. In conversation with some who were such rigid adherents to their faith that they would scarce be seen in company with those who differed from them in any point of their creed, I have heard them quote the text in palliation of their neglect, 'The poor shall not cease out of the land'! During my stay in Dublin, I took occasion to visit the huts of the poor in its vicinity—and of all places to

witness human misery, ignorance, degradation, filth and wretchedness, an Irish hut is pre-eminent. It seems to be constructed to
promote the very reverse of every thing like domestic comfort. If
I were to describe one, it would appear about as follows: Four mud
walls about six feet high, occupying a space of ground about ten
feet square, covered or thatched with straw—a mud chimney at
one end, reaching about a foot above the roof—without apartments
or divisions of any kind—without floor, without windows, and
sometimes without a chimney—a piece of pine board laid on the
top of a box or an old chest—a pile of straw covered with dirty
garments, which it would puzzle any one to determine the original
part of any one of them—a picture representing the crucifixion of
Christ, pasted on the most conspicuous place on the wall—a few
broken dishes stuck up in a corner—an iron pot, or the half of an
iron pot, in one corner of the chimney—a little peat in the fire-
place, aggravating one occasionally with a glimpse of fire, but sending out very little heat—a man and his wife and five children, and
a pig. In front of the door-way, and within a step of it, is a hole
three or four feet deep, and ten or twelve feet in circumference;
into this hole all the filth and dirt of the hut are put, for careful
preservation. This is frequently covered with a green scum, which
at times stands in bubbles, as decomposition goes on. Here you
have an Irish hut or cabin, such as millions of the people of Ireland
live in. And some live in worse than these. Men and women, married and single, old and young, lie down together, in much the same
degradation as the American slaves. I see much here to remind
me of my former condition, and I confess I should be ashamed to
lift up my voice against American slavery, but that I know the
cause of humanity is one the world over. He who really and truly
feels for the American slave, cannot steel his heart to the woes of
others; and he who thinks himself an abolitionist, yet cannot enter
into the wrongs of others, has yet to find a true foundation for his
anti-slavery faith. But, to the subject.

The immediate, and it may be the main cause of the extreme
poverty and beggary in Ireland, is intemperance. This may be
seen in the fact that most beggars drink whiskey. The third day
after landing in Dublin, I met a man in one of the most public
streets, with a white cloth on the upper part of his face. He was
feeling his way with a cane in one hand, and the other hand was
extended, soliciting aid. His feeble step and singular appearance

led me to inquire into his history. I was informed that he had
been a very intemperate man, and that on one occasion he was
drunk, and lying in the streets. While in this state of insensibility,
a hog with its fangs tore off his nose, and a part of his face! I
looked under the cloth, and saw the horrible spectacle of a living
man with the face of a skeleton. Drunkenness is still rife in Ireland. The temperance cause has done much—is doing much—but
there is much more to do, and, as yet, comparatively few to do it.
A great part of the Roman Catholic clergy do nothing about it,
while the Protestants may be said to hate the cause. I have been
frequently advised to have nothing to do with it, as it would only
injure the anti-slavery cause. It was most consoling to me to find
that those persons who were most interested in the anti-slavery
cause in the United States, were the same that distinguished themselves as the truest and warmest advocates of temperance and every
other righteous reform at home. It was a pleasure to walk through
the crowd with gentlemen such as the Webbs, Allens and Haughtons, and find them recognized by the multitude as the friends of
the poor. My sheet is full.

Always yours,

FREDERICK DOUGLASS.[106]

GLASGOW, April 16, 1846.

WM. LLOYD GARRISON:

MY DEAR FRIEND—I have given up the field of public letter-
writing to my friend Buffum, who will tell you how we are getting
on; but I cannot refrain from sending you a line, as a mere private
correspondent. My health is good, my spirit is bright, and I am
enjoying myself as well as one can be expected, when separated
from home by three thousand miles of deep blue ocean. I long to
be at home—'home, sweet, sweet home! Be it ever so humble, there
is no place like home.' Nor is it merely to enjoy the pleasure of
family and friends, that I wish to be at home: it is to be in the field,
at work, preaching to the best of my ability salvation from slavery,
to a nation fast hastening to destruction. I know it will be hard
to endure the kicks and cuffs of the pro-slavery multitude, to which
I shall be subjected; but then, I glory in the battle, as well as in
the victory.

I have been frequently counselled to leave America altogether,

[106] *Liberator*, March 27, 1846.

and make Britain my home. But this I cannot do, unless it shall be absolutely necessary for my personal freedom. I doubt not that my old master is in a state of mind quite favorable to an attempt at re-capture. Not that he wishes to make money by selling me, or by holding me himself, but to feed his revenge. I know he feels keenly my exposures, and nothing would afford him more pleasure than to have me in his power. He has suffered severe goadings, or he would not have broken the silence of seven years, to exculpate himself from the charges I have brought against him, by telling a positive lie. He says he can put his hand upon the Bible, and, with a clear conscience, swear he never struck me, or told any one else to do so! The same conscientious man could put his hand into my pocket, and rob me of my hard earnings; and, with a clear conscience, swear he had a right not only to my earnings, but to my body, soul and spirit! We may, in this case, reverse the old adage—'He that will lie, will steal'—and make it, 'He that will steal, will lie'—especially when, by lying, he may hope to throw a veil over his stealing. This positive denial, on his part, rather staggered me at the first. I had no idea the gentleman would tell a right down untruth. He has certainly forgotten when a lamp was lost from the carriage, without my knowledge, that he came to the stable with the cart-whip, and with its heavy lash beat me over the head and shoulders, to make me tell how it was lost, until his brother Edward, who was at St. Michael's, on a visit at the time, came forward, and besought him to desist; and that he beat me until he wearied himself. My memory, in such matters, is better than his. One would think, from his readiness to swear that he never struck me, that he held it to be wrong to do so. He does not deny that he used to tie up 'a cousin of mine, and lash her, and in justification of his bloody conduct quote, 'He that knoweth his master's will, and doeth it not, shall be beaten with many stripes.' He finds fault with me for not mentioning his promising to set me free at 25. I did not tell many things which I might have told. Had I told of that promise, I should have also told that he had never set one of his slaves free; and I had no reason to believe he would treat me with any more justice and humanity, than any other one of his slaves. But enough.

Scotland is in a blaze of anti-slavery agitation.—The Free Church and Slavery are the all-engrossing topics. It is the same old question of Christian union with slaveholders—old with us, but new with most people here. The discussion is followed by the same result as in America, when it was first mooted in the New-England Convention. There is such a sameness in the arguments, pro and con, that if you could be landed on this side of the Atlantic, without your knowledge, you would scarcely distinguish between our meetings here, and our meetings at home. The Free Church is in a terrible stew. Its leaders thought to get the slaveholders' money and bring it home, and escape censure. They had no idea that they would be followed and exposed. Its members are leaving it, like rats escaping from a sinking ship. There is a strong determination to have the slave money sent back, and the union broken up. In this feeling all religious denominations participate. Let slavery be hemmed in on every side by the moral and religious sentiments of mankind, and its death is certain.

I am always yours,

FREDERICK DOUGLASS.[107]

LONDON, May 23, 1846.

WM. LLOYD GARRISON :—

DEAR FRIEND—I take up my pen to give you a hasty sketch of a five days' visit to this great city. I arrived here from Edinburgh, on the 18th instant, and proceeded immediately to 5 Whitehead's Grove, the house of your early and devoted friend, GEORGE THOMPSON, from whom I had received a most cordial letter, inviting me to make his house my home, during my stay in London. The main object of my visit was to attend the annual meeting of the British and Foreign Anti-Slavery Society—to do which, I had received a pressing invitation from the Committee of that Society. The meeting was held on the day of my arrival in Freemason's Hall, great Queen street. The chair was taken by Sir Edward North Buxton, Bart.

Having heard much of the meetings of this Society, I was surprised and disappointed by the fewness of those assembled. There were not more present, on this occasion, than what we usually have at our business meetings of the American A. S. Society. The thinness of the meeting was accounted for by the secretary, Mr. Scoble, on the ground that there were several very important philanthropic meetings in progress at the same hour—meetings in which the friends of emancipation were deeply interested, and to which many

107 *Liberator*, May 15, 1846.

had gone, who otherwise would have been present at the anti-slavery meeting.

I will not trouble you with any minute account of this meeting, as you will find a pretty accurate sketch of its proceedings in a London paper, which I have already mailed for you. There was one pleasing feature, to which I will refer, and that was, the readiness with which the meeting responded to the sentiment of 'non-christian fellowship with slaveholders,' and the zeal, spirit and unanimity with which it joined in our uncompromising demand upon the Free Church of Scotland, to 'SEND BACK THE MONEY.' This was the more gratifying, in view of the manner in which this subject has been treated by some of the local auxiliary societies, which have stood aloof from the subject, and refused in any way to co-operate with us, because, as they allege, we are of the 'Garrison party' in America. This ground has been distinctly taken by the Edinburgh Anti-Slavery Committee. Instead of seconding our efforts, (whether intentionally, or otherwise,) they have played into the hands of the enemy, and have been quoted over and over again, by the Free Church press, against us. In assuming this position towards us, and the cause in which we are immediately engaged, they cannot but feel sensibly rebuked by the present example of the Parent Society; for that Society not only invited Mr. Thompson and myself to speak, but to speak on this very subject; and no parts of our speeches were more warmly received, or more enthusiastically cheered, than our several animadversions on the conduct of the Free Church of Scotland,—which Church now stands before this country and the world as the most prominent defender of the Christianity of man-stealers.

At the close of the meeting, Mr. Joseph Sturge came forward, and said that, in consequence of the fewness of the number who had had an opportunity of hearing me, he would do what he could to get me a meeting at the end of the week, when he was certain that a much larger meeting than the present could be obtained, if I would consent to address it. I agreed, and the meeting was held last night in Finsbury Chapel, one of the largest chapels in London. I shall also send you a newspaper report of this meeting. Meanwhile, I must say, it was one of the most effective and satisfactory meetings which I have attended since landing on these shores. You will observe, that the resolutions adopted by the meeting assert a broader and nobler platform, than that upon which our

Broad-street friends have for some time past acted. They have, as you are aware, taken sides with the New Organization and Liberty party, while they have decried and disparaged the efforts of yourself, and those who are earnestly laboring with you. The fact is, they have known very little of our efforts since 1840. Mr. Scoble, the Secretary, informs me that he has been left to gather information of our movements as best he could—that, while he has never, in a single instance, omitted to send you his Annual Report, he has in no instance received ours; so that he has been compelled to silence respecting us, for the want of information necessary to an intelligent opinion of our movement. I assured him that I thought our Reports had been sent, but that they had been miscarried, or that some accident had befallen them, as I could conceive of no reason for withholding them, or neglecting to send them; especially as I knew it to be a first principle with our Society, in the fullest manner to exchange opinions with every class of abolitionists, whether they be for or against the views held by us. But to the meeting.

In adopting the resolution, moved by Dr. Campbell, a new and better way is marked out. It asserts, as it should do, the duty and prerogative of British abolitionists to be, that of co-operating with, and encouraging, fellow-laborers in the United States of every anti-slavery creed. Let this resolution be universally adopted, and scrupulously adhered to, and there will be a happy termination to the bitter jarrings which have, during the last six years, marred and defaced the beauty and excellence of our noble work. Of course, this resolution does not pledge the British and Foreign A. S. Society to the principle contained in it, as it was only adopted at a public meeting; still, I believe the ground taken is one, upon which nine-tenths of all the abolitionists in this country are anxious to stand. They are, as they ought to be, unwilling to be understood as being unfriendly to any class or creed of anti-slavery men in the United States.

This has been a week of great activity with me. I have attended a meeting every day since I came into the city. On Monday, as I have before observed, I attended the anniversary of the British and Foreign Anti-Slavery Society. On Tuesday, I received an invitation, and spoke at a large and excellent meeting of the Peace Society. On Wednesday, I was invited to speak at a meeting of the *complete* Suffrage Association, called thus in contradistinction from the Chartist party, and differing from that party, in that it repudiates the use of physical force as a means of attaining its object. I am persuaded that, after the complete triumph of the Anti-Corn Law movement, the next great reform will be that of complete suffrage. The agitation which this must occasion will be louder, deeper and stronger than that attending the Anti-Corn Law movement. It comprehends dearer interests than those involved in the repeal of the Corn Laws. It is quite easy to see, that, in the triumph of complete suffrage in this country, aristocratic rule must end—class legislation must cease—the law of primogeniture and entail, the game laws, &c. will be utterly swept from the statute book. When people and not property shall govern, people will cease to be subordinate to property.

In the triumph of this movement may be read the destruction of the time-hallowed alliance of Church and State. The opposition to the gross injustice of compelling a man to support a form of worship, in which he not only feels no interest, but which he really hates, is great and increasing. The brilliant success of the Anti-Corn Law League has convinced the people of their power. The demand for the separation of Church and State, which is now but whispered, must sooner or later be heard in tones of thunder. The battle will be hot, but the right must triumph. God grant that they may make a better use of their political freedom, than the working people of the United States have hitherto done!—For, instead of taking sides with the oppressed, they have acted the unnatural and execrable part of the vilest oppressors. They stand forth in the front ranks of tyranny, and, with words of freedom on their deceitful lips, have given victory to a party, the chief pride, boast and glory of which is that of having blasted one of the fairest portions of our common earth with slavery. It is but just to the friends of political freedom here to say, that they regard the hypocritical pretenders to democratic freedom in America with absolute contempt, and ineffable disgust. The time was, when America was known abroad as the land of the free, but that time is past. No intelligent and honest man, whose love of liberty does not depend on the color of a man's skin, ever thinks of America in connection with freedom, but with abhorrence. Slavery gives character to the American people. It dictates their laws, gives tone to their literature, and shapes their religion. It stands up in their midst, the only sovereign power in the land. The friends of freedom here look upon America as one of the greatest obstacles in the way of political freedom, as she is now the great fact, illustrating the alleged truth, that the tyrant many are even more tyrannical than the tyrant few.

On Thursday, I accepted an invitation to attend and speak at the anniversary meeting of the National Temperance Society, held in the far-famed Exeter Hall. It was a splendid meeting. A resolution was adopted, proposing a World's Convention to be held in London, some time during the month of August. It was supported by Mr. Joseph Sturge and myself. I mention this, simply to call attention to a noble testimony borne by Mr. Sturge against slaveholders—a testimony which must have the best effect, just now. Mr. Sturge is a thorough temperance man, and gives largely in support of the cause. While speaking of the proposed Convention, and of the possibility of slaveholders being admitted into it as members, he declared that, if slaveholders were admitted, he would not sit in the Convention, or aid it in any way whatever. He had contemplated giving the Society £50; but he must find some other benevolent object upon which to bestow that sum, if slaveholders were admitted into the Convention. Subsequently, Mr. Alexander, a friend of temperance, and a member of the Society of Friends, has taken the same ground. These sentiments were loudly applauded by the meeting. The feeling of 'NO UNION WITH SLAVEHOLDERS' is becoming more and more general in London, and throughout this country. American slaveholders must prepare, not only to be excluded from the communion of British Christians, but peremptorily driven from the platform of every philanthropic association. Let them be hemmed in on every side. Let them be placed beyond the pale of respectability, and, standing out separated, alone in their infamy, let the storm gather over them, and its hottest bolts descend. Our justification is ample:—*the slaveholder is a man-stealer.*

I ought to have said, while speaking of the anti-slavery meeting at Finsbury Chapel, that Dr. Campbell suggested that, in as much as it would be of some importance to the anti-slavery cause to have me remain in this country longer than I could be induced to remain, absent from my family, measures be at once taken, by which a sufficient amount could be realized to enable me to bring my family to this country. This suggestion being seconded by my friend Mr. Thompson, in a very few minutes between £80 and £90 were contributed for the purpose. This result was entirely unexpected to me. I had not even mentioned my desire for any such thing to the meeting. I had said, however, to Mr. Thompson, and also to Mr. Sturge, that I could not remain absent from my family more than one year, and that I must go home in August, unless I should decide to bring my family to this country; and this may have led to the suggestion by Dr. Campbell.

I have just received a letter from Mr. Sturge, the chairman of the meeting at which the money was raised, saying he will cause to be forwarded to any person whom I may mention as my friend in the United States, five hundred dollars, to be appropriated to the removal of my family to this country. So I rest in the hope of soon being joined by my family in a land where they will not be constantly harassed by the apprehension, that some foul imp of a slaveholder may lay his infernal clutch upon me, and tear me from their midst. Master Hugh must bear the loss of my service *one* year longer, and it may be, I shall remain absent *two* years. Please send him a paper, containing this announcement, and exhort him to patience. It may serve to ease, if not cure, his anxious mind. He must feel my absence keenly, and must suffer greatly; for of all pain, I believe that of suspense is the most severe. By the way, one of the charges I have preferred against master Thomas Auld, and one which he seems the most angry about, respects his meanness; and the fact illustrative of this trait brought forward in my Narrative, is that he once owned a young woman, a cousin of mine, whose right hand had been so burnt as to make it useless to her through life—and finding this young woman of little or no value to him, he very *generously* gave her to his sister Sarah. Seized, I suppose, with a similar fit of benevolence, he has transferred his legal right of property in my body and soul, to his less fortunate brother Hugh. And master Hugh (for so I suppose I must call him,) seems to be very proud of the gift, and means to play the part of a hungry blood-hound in catching me. Possess your soul in patience, *dear* master Hugh, and regale yourself on the golden dreams afforded by the prospect—'*First catch your rabbit,*' &c. &c.

But I am wandering. My visit to this city has been exceedingly gratifying, on account of the freedom I have enjoyed in visiting such places of instruction and amusement as those from which I have been carefully excluded by the inveterate prejudice against color in the United States. Botanic and Zoological gardens, Museums and Panoramas, Halls of Statuary and Galleries of Paintings, are as free to the black as the white man in London. There is no distinction on account of color. The white man gains nothing by being white, and the black man loses nothing by being black. 'A man's a man for a' that.' I went on Tuesday morning, in company with Mr. and Mrs. Thompson, to see Cremore Garden, a place of recreation and amusement—a most beautiful and picturesque spot, delightfully situated on the bank of the Thames, at the west end of the city. I was admitted without a whisper of objection on the part of the proprietor or spectators. Every one looked as though they thought I had as much right there as themselves, and not the slightest dislike was manifested toward me on account of my negro origin, unless a gentleman from Boston, who was in the Garden while I was there, be an exception—and I will not say that he was. He had just brought to the Garden a panorama of Boston, rolled up in a long case, which was so heavy as to require eight men to carry it. Soon after its arrival, the proprietor told me what it was. I then said I knew Boston, and should be glad to see a panorama of it, but was informed it would not be presented for exhibition for two or three weeks, as the place was not quite ready for it. My American friend, whom I took to be the artist, on learning that I knew Boston, at once made toward me, without the slightest ceremony or circumlocution ordinarily resorted to by gentlemen when approaching a stranger, and bolting up to me, he asked, in much the same tone which a white man employs when addressing a slave by the way-side—'Well, boy, who do you belong to?'—'Do you know Boston?' 'Yes, Sir.' 'Well, if you know Boston, you know it is the handsomest city in the world!' This left me without a doubt as to the Yankee origin of my friend, and I felt quite at home in his presence. He eloquently descanted on the beauties of Boston, quoting various authorities as proof of his position, that Boston is the most beautiful city in the world. I replied, that Boston is a very handsome city, but I thought not the handsomest in the world—and proceeded to speak of Edinburgh. But a very few moments convinced me, that my patriotic friend had no ear for the praise of any other city than Boston; so we separated. We, however, met again in the course of half an hour, when his tone was quite altered, and his manner quite changed. We had a very pleasant interview. He asked if my name was Douglass, and being answered in the affirmative, expressed pleasure at seeing me, and said he had frequently heard of me since he came to this country.

There is one remarkable peculiarity in all the Americans with whom I have had the pleasure to meet on this side of the Atlantic, and that is, their adaptability to circumstances! Persons, who would feel themselves disgraced by being seen conversing with me in Boston, find no difficulty in being seated at the same table with me in London!

On Wednesday, I went to see the 'assembled wisdom' of this great nation—Parliament. Through the kindness of my friend George Thompson, I gained admission to the Speaker's Gallery, which is quite a privilege. Here I found myself beside the Rev. Mr. Kirk, of Boston, who seemed in no way shocked at being seated on the same bench with a negro, but rather pleased with having met me. I was fortunate in the choice of the time of going, for I could not have selected three hours when I could have heard a greater number of distinguished members. A bill was before the House, for restricting the hours of factory labor. Sir James Graham, Sir John Hobhouse, Lord George Bentinck, son of the Duke of Portland, Mr. Gisbourne, Mr. Wakely, Mr. Farrend, Mr. John Bright, Mr. Crawford, Mr. Brotherton, Sir Robert Peel, Lord John Russell, and several other members, addressed the House on the subject. When the vote was to be taken, the galleries were cleared, so that the spectator is not allowed to see who votes for or against a measure. I was much pleased with the respectful manner with which members spoke of each other. Never having enjoyed the privilege of witnessing the legislative proceedings of our great nation, I cannot say in what respect they differ, or in what respect the one is to be preferred to the other. All I know is, if I should presume to go into Washington as I have into London, and enter Congress as I have done the House of Parliament, the ardent defenders of democratic liberty would at once put me into prison, on suspicion of having been 'created contrary to the Declaration of American Independence.' On failing to prove a negative, I should be sold into slavery, to pay my jail fees! 'Hail, Columbia, happy land!' Under these circumstances, my republican friends must not think strange, when I say I would rather be in London than Washington. Liberty in Hyde Park is better than democracy in a slave prison—monarchical freedom is better than republican slavery—things are better than names. I prefer the substance to the shadow.

Since I came to this city, I have had the honor to be made a member of the Free Trade Club, composed in part of some of the most distinguished and influential gentlemen in the kingdom. But I must not speak of this, lest I should rouse the ire of the New-York Express, or provoke the fiery indignation of Bennett's Herald.

I have enjoyed a fine opportunity of becoming acquainted with Mr. George Thompson. I have been with him in private and in public—at home and abroad—when in the heat of intense excitement, and when mantled with the most tranquil repose—and in all circumstances, I have found him equal to the highest estimate I had formed of the man. He is the first great orator of whom I had formed a very high opinion, on the first hearing of whom I did not feel a degree of disappointment. He is far above any opinion I had formed of him. I have found him to be, emphatically, the man of every meeting which I have attended since I came to London. The announcement of his name is attended with demonstrations of applause, such as are seldom called forth by the mention of any other name.

Mr. Thompson is now deeply engaged in exposing the corrupt and despotic rule of the East India Company, and his labors in that department are equal to all his time and strength. Yet, such is his devotion to the cause of the American slave, that he is resolved to devote one or two weeks more to the agitation now going on in Scotland, against Christian fellowship with slaveholders, to induce the Free Church to send back the blood-stained money. As usual, you see him battling for the right.

But I must close this already too lengthy letter, or I would say more of this friend of God and man. Long may he live to plead the cause of our common humanity—to open his mouth for the dumb—to demand liberty for the heart-broken captive, unconditional emancipation for the whip-scared slave, succor for the afflicted, mercy for the suffering, and justice for the oppressed!

Yours to the end,

FREDERICK DOUGLASS.[108]

GLASGOW, (Scotland,) April 15, 1846.

MR. GREELEY:

MY DEAR SIR—I never wrote nor attempted to write a letter for any other than a strictly anti-slavery press; but being greatly encouraged by your magnanimity, as shown in copying my letter

---

[108] *Liberator*, June 26, 1846.

written from Belfast, Ireland, to the Liberator at Boston, I venture
to send you a few lines, direct from my pen.

I know not how to thank you for the deep and lively interest
you have been pleased to take in the cause of my long neglected
race, or in what language to express the gratification I feel in witnessing your unwillingness to lend your aid to 'break a bruised
reed,' by adding your weight to the already insupportable burden
to crush, the feeble though virtuous efforts of one who is laboring
for the emancipation of a people, who, for two long centuries, have
endured, with the utmost patience, a bondage, one hour of which,
in the graphic language of the immortal Jefferson, is worse than
ages of that which your fathers rose in rebellion to oppose.

It is such indications on the part of the press—which, happily,
are multiplying throughout all the land—that kindle up within me
an ardent hope that the curse of slavery will not much longer be
permitted to make its iron foot-prints in the lacerated hearts of my
sable brethren, or to spread its foul mantle of moral blight, mildew
and infamy, over the otherwise noble character of the American
people.

I am very sorry to see that some of your immediate neighbors
are very much displeased with you, for this act of kindness to myself, and the cause of which I am an humble advocate; and that an
attempt has been made, on the part of some of them, by misrepre-
senting my sayings, motives and objects in this country, to stir up
against me the already too bitter antipathy of the American people.
I am called, by way of reproach, a runaway slave. As if it were
a crime—an unpardonable crime—for a man to take his inalienable rights! If I had not run away, but settled down in the degrading arms of slavery, and made no effort to gain my freedom,
it is quite probable that the learned gentlemen, who now brand me
with being a miserable runaway slave, would have adduced the
fact in proof of the negro's adaptation to slavery, and his utter unfitness for freedom! *There's no pleasing some people.* But why
should Mr. James Brooks feel so much annoyed by the attention
shown me in this country, and so anxious to excite against me the
hatred and jealousy of the American people? I can very readily
understand why a slaveholder—a trader in slaves—one who has all
his property in human flesh, blinded by ignorance as to his own
best interest, and under the dominion of violent passions engen-
dered by the possession of discretionary and irresponsible power

over the bodies and souls of his victims—accustomed to the inhuman sight of men and women sold at auction in company with horses, sheep and swine, and in every way treated more like brutes than human beings—should repine at my success, and, in his blindness, seek to throw every discouragement and obstacle in the way of the slave's emancipation. But why a New-York editor, born and reared in the State of Maine, far removed from the contaminated and pestilential atmosphere of slavery, should pursue such a course, is not so apparent. I will not, however, stop here to ascertain the cause, but deal with fact; and I cannot better do this than by giving your readers a simple and undisguised statement of the motives and objects of my visit to this country. I feel it but just to myself to do so, since I have been denounced by the New-York Express as a 'glibtongued scoundrel,' and gravely charged, in its own elegant and dignified language, with 'running a muck in greedy-eared Britain against America, its people, its institutions, and even against its peace.'

Of the low and vulgar epithets, coupled with the false and somewhat malicious charges, very little need be said. I am used to them. Their force is lost upon me, in the frequency of their application. I was reared where they were in the most common use. They form a large and very important portion of the vocabulary of characters known in the South as plantation 'negro drivers.' A slaveholding gentleman would scorn to use them. He leaves them to find their way into the world of sound, through the polluted lips of his hired 'negro driver'—a being for whom the haughty slaveholder feels incomparably more contempt than he feels toward his slave. And for the best of all reasons—he knows the slave to be degraded, because he cannot help himself; but a white 'negro driver' is degraded, because of original, ingrained meanness. If I agree with the slaveholders in nothing else, I can say I agree with them in all their burning contempt for a 'negro driver,' whether born North or South. Such epithets will have no prejudicial effect against me on the mind of the class of American people, whose good opinion I sincerely desire to cultivate and deserve. And it is to these I would address this brief word of explanation.

The object, then, of my visit to this country is simply to give such an exposition of the degrading influence of slavery upon the master and his abettors as well as upon the slave—to excite such an intelligent interest on the subject of American slavery—as may re-act upon that country, and tend to shame her out of her adhesion to a system which all must confess to be at variance with justice, repugnant to Christianity, and at war with her own free institu-tions. 'The head and front of my offending hath this extent, no more.' I am one of those who think the best friend of a nation is he who most faithfully rebukes her for her sins—and he her worst enemy, who, under the specious and popular garb of patriotism, seeks to excuse, palliate, and defend them. America has much more to fear from such than all the rebukes of the abolitionists at home or abroad.

I am nevertheless aware, that the wisdom of exposing the sins of one nation in the ear of another, has been seriously questioned by good and clear-sighted people, both on this and on your side of the Atlantic. And the thought is not without its weight upon my own mind. I am satisfied that there are many evils which can be best removed by confining our efforts to the immediate locality where such evils exist. This, however, is by no means the case with the system of slavery. It is such a giant sin—such a mon-strous aggregation of iniquity, so hardening to the human heart, so destructive to the moral sense, and so well calculated to beget a character in every one around it favorable to its own continuance, that I feel not only at liberty, but abundantly justified in appeal-ing to the whole world to aid in its removal. Slavery exists in the United States because it is reputable, and it is reputable in the United States because it is not *dis*reputable out of the United States as it ought to be, and it is not so disreputable out of the United States as it ought to be because its character is not so well known as it ought to be. Believing this most firmly, and being a lover of Freedom, a hater of Slavery, one who has felt the bloody whip and worn the galling chain—sincerely and earnestly longing for the de-liverance of my sable brethren from their awful bondage, I am bound to expose its character, whenever and wherever an oppor-tunity is afforded me. I would attract to it the attention of the world. I would fix upon it the piercing eye of insulted Liberty. I would arraign it at the bar of Eternal Justice, and summon the Universe to witness against it. I would concentrate against it the moral and religious sentiment of Christian people of every 'class, color and clime.' I would have the guilty slaveholder see his con-demnation written on every human face, and hear it proclaimed in every human voice, till, overwhelmed with shame and confusion, he resolved to cease his wicked course, undo the heavy burden, and let the oppressed go free.

The people in this country who take the deepest interest in the removal of Slavery from America, and the spread of Liberty throughout the world, are the same who oppose the bloody spirit of war, and are earnestly laboring to spread the blessings of peace all over the globe. I have ever found the abolitionists of this country, the warmest friends of America and American institutions. I have frequently seen in their houses, and sometimes occupying the most conspicuous places in their parlors, the American Declaration of Independence.

An aged anti-slavery gentleman in Dublin, with whom I had the honor several times to dine during my stay in that city, has the Declaration of Independence and a number of the portraits of the distinguished founders of the American Republic. He bought them many years ago, in token of his admiration of the men and their principles. But, said he, after speaking of the sentiments of the Declaration—looking up as it hung in a costly frame—I am often tempted to turn its face to the wall, it is such a palpable contradiction of the spirit and practices of the American people at this time. This instrument was once the watchword of Freedom in this land, and the American people were regarded as the best friends and truest representatives of that sacred cause. But they are not so regarded now. They have allowed the crowned heads of Europe to outstrip them. While Great Britain has emancipated all her slaves, and is laboring to extend the blessings of Liberty wherever her power is felt, it seems, in the language of John Quincy Adams, that the preservation, propagation and perpetuation of slavery is the vital and animating spirit of the American Government. Even Hayti, the black Republic, is not to be spared; the spirit of Freedom, which a sanguinary and ambitious despot could not crush or extinguish, is to be exterminated by the free American Republic, because that spirit is dangerous to slavery. While the people of this country see such facts and indications, as well as the great fact that three millions of people are held in the most abject bondage, deprived of all their God-given rights—denied by law and public opinion to learn to read the sacred Scriptures, by a people professing the largest liberty and devotion to the religion of Jesus Christ—while they see this monstrous anomaly, they must look elsewhere for a paragon of civil and religious freedom. Sir, I am earnestly and anxiously laboring to wipe off this foul blot from the otherwise fair fame of the American people, that they may accomplish in behalf of human freedom that which their exalted position among the nations of the earth amply fits them to do. Would they but arise in their moral majesty and might—repent and purify themselves from this foul crime—break the galling fetters, and restore the long lost rights to the sable bondmen in their midst—they would encircle her name with a wreath of imperishable glory. Her light would indeed break forth as the morning—its brilliant beams would flash across the Atlantic, and illuminate the Eastern world.

I am, dear sir, very gratefully yours,

FREDERICK DOUGLASS.[109]

To the Editor of the 'Protestant Journal.'

MR. EDITOR: My attention has just been called to an attack upon myself in your paper of the 18th July, which seems deserving a word of reply. This attack is contained in an article from an American newspaper, the *Boston Traveller*. Were I in the United States, I should deem a reply to an assault coming through that journal entirely uncalled for. I should regard its bitterest abuse as compliment rather than a condemnation. I know the paper, and am fully justified in declaring it to be notorious for its slaveholding malignity, and reckless disregard of truth in everything affecting the question of slavery in the United States. In the article before me I am pretty strongly accused of allowing the chairman of a meeting recently held in Finsbury Chapel, London, to state of me that which I knew to be false. The statement referred to is in the following words: 'Our friend Douglass has been obliged to escape from America, leaving his wife and four children there, for fear of being seized by his late owner, who is vowing vengeance. He is, therefore, an exile from that country, because there is not an inch upon which he can with safety set his feet.' The writer of the assault upon me says this statement 'was not corrected by Douglass.' I admit it was not, and for the best of all reasons—it was essentially true, and needed no correction. The writer professes to have lived in the same village with me for several years, and that the above is the first intimation he has ever seen or heard that I had any occasion to seek concealment or expatriation to avoid being again reduced to bondage. All I have to say to this is, that the writer's ignorance is through no fault of mine. I have repeatedly given as one of the reasons for leaving the United States, a fear, that in consequence of publishing a narrative of my experience in slavery, and exposing the conduct of my owner, he might, to gratify his revengeful disposition, attempt to reduce me to slavery. My object was to be out of the way during the excitement and exasperation which I had good reason to apprehend would follow the publication of my narrative. The wisdom of this course has been fully confirmed by what has transpired since I left the United States. My former owner, Mr. Thomas Auld, has transferred his legal right to my body to his brother Hugh, who has publicly declared that, cost what it may, as sure as I set my feet upon American soil, so sure I shall again be reduced to slavery. The laws of the land, and the Constitution of the United States, give him full power to arrest me anywhere in that country. There. is not a State in the whole American Union, from Texas to Maine, in which I am not overshadowed with this terrible liability; and this my assailant very well knows, if he be not totally ignorant of the Constitution of the country. I think he has two purposes to serve in making the attack, and both are equally mean; one was to place me in an unfavorable light before the British public, in making me out a deceiver, and the other was to cover up the disgraceful fact, that in the United States, the land of boasted liberty and light, there is not a single inch of ground upon which a runaway slave may stand in safety. The writer speaks of my allegations against the American Board. He does not say what they are, but he says they have been nailed to the counter here (meaning in the United States.) I have never made a charge against that body which I am not prepared to prove. I have charged them with neglecting to give the Bible to the slave, and of taking the price of human blood, with which to send the gospel to the heathen. They admit it, and justify themselves by the conduct of the Free Church of Scotland. The writer says—'But our American readers will be amused at the course which things are taking, in reference to this high priest of anti-ministry, anti-churchism, and anti-Sabbathism.' If the writer means by this, that I have unmasked the slaveholding and woman-whipping churches and clergy of America, I plead guilty to the charge. The writer exclaims, with apparent extacy, 'He is lost to his country forever; for one of the speakers said that they would support him handsomely during life in England.' Not quite so fast, young man. No inducement could be offered strong enough to make me quit my hold upon America as my home. Whether a slave or a freeman, America is my home, and there I mean to spend and be spent in the cause of my outraged fellow-countrymen.

Yours, &c.,

FREDERICK DOUGLASS.[110]

Victoria Hotel, Belfast, July 23, 1846.

LONDON, August 18, 1846.

To the Lynn Anti-Slavery Sewing Circle:

MY DEAR FRIENDS—Owing to some cause at present unknown to me, but which you may understand and be able to explain, your kind letter of 16th June, did not reach me until the 3d of August. I mention this to account for what might otherwise be deemed culpable neglect. Now, what shall I say? for such are my circumstances that I can do little more than apologize for writing you a poor letter. Weighed down, oppressed, and almost overcome, by constant effort—by engagements, public and private, growing out of immediate contact with deeply interested friends here—I find it very difficult to gain a moment of calm repose, during which to commune with dear friends on your side the Atlantic: you will readily understand this, when you remember that the fact of my being a fugitive slave is new here. My peculiar position, without any personal attractions, subjects me to many calls and questions from which other lectures would be comparatively free. Thus engaged, and thus interested, you will readily see that what I write must be very imperfect. But, my dear friends, perfect or imperfect, with or without time, I have resolved to send you a line, responsive in spirit, if not in point of composition, to your warm and sympathetic letter. I thank you for it. I assure you that I speak nothing more than the truth when I say I felt gratified, cheered, and honoured, by that token of friendly interest, esteem, and affection. I felt proud in finding myself approvingly remembered by so many sterling friends, in and out of your choice circle, who placed their

[110] *Liberator*, Aug. 28, 1846.

names under that friendly epistle. Next to the approbation of heaven and one's own conscience, stands that of clear-sighted and sincere friends; and while it is quite easy to conceive of content-ment; with the former, it is difficult to conceive of happiness with-out the latter. A strong man may be able to stand without the proper sympathy; but I know of none so strong but who could be made stronger by it.

But I must not write you an essay on the excellence of human sympathy, but speak to you of the great cause which binds our hearts sympathetically together, the deliverance from thraldom of three millions of our long-neglected and deeply-abused race. I wish I could say something to cheer and strengthen you in this cause. I wish I were able to penetrate the future, and assure you of a speedy triumph of our cause; but this is not for me. I can only say, work on; your cause is good; work on; duty is yours—consequences the Almighty's.

I confess I feel sad, and sick at heart, by the present posture of political affairs in the United States. The spirit of Slavery reigns triumphant throughout all the land. Every step in the onward march of political events is marked with blood—innocent blood; shed, too, in the cause of Slavery. The war with Mexico rages; the green earth is drenched with warm blood, oozing out from hu-man hearts; the air is darkened with smoke; the heavens are shaken by the terrible roar of the cannon; the groans and cries of the wounded and dying disturb the ear of God. Yet how few in that land care one farthing for it, or will move one inch to arrest and remove the cause of this horrible state of things? I am sad; I am sick; the whole land is cursed, if not given over to destruction. Massachusetts, the brightest of every other State, is now but the tool of Texas. Texas may be said to give laws to the whole Union. She leads the way in plunder and murder; and Massachusetts, with all New England, follow in the crusade like hungry sharks in the bloody wake of a Brazilian slaveship. What a spectacle for men and angels!—Gov. Briggs issuing his order to send the sons of those who fell in the cause of freedom on Bunker Hill, to fight the battle of Slavery in Mexico! Gov. Briggs, the teetotaller! Gov. Briggs, the Baptist! issuing his order to raise troops in Massachu-setts, to establish with fire and sword the man-blasting and soul-damning system of Slavery! Who would have thought it? And yet it was to be expected. The deed was done long ago. The foundation of this frowning monument of infamy was laid when the States were first declared the *United States*. This is but another link around your necks of the galling chain which your fathers placed about the heels of my race. It is the legitimate fruit of compromise—of attempting a union of Freedom with Slavery. All was lost in that sad moment. The American Anti-Slavery Society has the right on this question. Her ground is the true one. I believe that the salvation of the country depends, under God, upon the effort of that society. The Union must be dissolved, or New England is lost and swallowed up by the slave-power of the country. Work on, dear friends, work on! walk by faith, and not by sight. Come good, or come evil—prosperity or adversity—work on! See that all which can be done by patriotic and humane women for the salvation of millions groaning in chains, is done; and whoever else may approve, you shall have the approbation of a good conscience, and the tear of grateful hearts, for your reward.

You speak of your remaining together, though unorganized. I am of course glad to hear of your prosperity, though I cannot say as much of your being *unorganized*. While it is not for me to direct you, who have laboured so long and so well in this cause, how you shall help me and my race, generally, yet you must allow me to say, that my conviction of the utility and importance of organization is strengthened by every day's experience. I find that friend H. Clapp has seen the utter absurdity of carrying forward a moral enterprise without an organization. He has changed his views, or he should not have acted as a delegate, and held the office of secretary, in the temperance World's Convention, held here last week. This he did where free speech was not tolerated, and where men spoke—only by and with the consent of the chairman. Nor was this objected to by Mr. Clapp. Is organization a curse in New England, and a blessing in Old England? Consistency thou art a jewel.

One word more. You remind me of the poor, in this country. I thank you for it. We have poverty here, but no Slavery; we have crime here, but no Slavery; we have suffering here, but no Slavery, and in all this, England has a decided advantage over America. Still, my dear friends, I am by no means unmindful of the poor; and you may rely upon me as one who will never desert the cause of the poor, no matter whether black or white.

May kind heaven smile upon your righteous efforts, and

strengthen your hearts for every duty, is the sincere wish of your
grateful and devoted friend.

FREDERICK DOUGLASS.[111]

REPLY OF FREDERICK DOUGLASS TO DR. COX.

Salisbury Road, EDINBURGH, Oct. 30, 1846.

SAMUEL HANSON COX, D. D.:

SIR—I have two objects in addressing you at this time. The
first is, to deny certain charges, and to correct certain injurious
statements, recently made by yourself, respecting my conduct at a
meeting of the 'World's Temperance Convention,' held in Covent
Garden Theatre, London, in the month of August last. My second
object will be to review so much of your course as relates to the
Anti-Slavery question, during your recent tour through Great
Britain and a part of Ireland. There are times when it would
evince a ridiculous sensibility to the good or evil opinions of men,
and when it would be a wasteful expenditure of thought, time and
strength, for one in my circumstances to reply to attacks made by
those who hate me, more bitterly than the cause of which I am an
humble advocate. While all this is quite true, it is equally true,
that there are times when it is quite proper to make such replies;
and especially so, when to defend one's self is to defend great and
vital principles, the vindication of which is essential to the triumph
of righteousness throughout the world.

Sir, I deem it neither arrogant nor presumptuous to assume to
represent three millions of my brethren, who are, while I am penning these words, in chains and slavery on the American soil, the
boasted land of liberty and light. I have been one with them in
their sorrow and suffering—one with them in their ignorance and
degradation—one with them under a burning sun and the slave-
driver's bloody lash—and am at this moment freed from those horrible inflictions, only because the laws of England are commensu-
rate with freedom, and do not permit the American man-stealer,
whose Christianity you endorse, to lay his foul clutch upon me,
while upon British soil. Being thus so completely identified with
the slaves, I may assume that an attack upon me is an attack upon
them—and especially so, when the attack is obviously made, as in
the present instance, with a view to injure me in the advocacy of

[111] *National Anti-Slavery Standard*, Oct. 15, 1846.

their cause. I am resolved that their cause shall not suffer through any misrepresentations of my conduct, which evil-minded men, in high or low places, may resort to, while I have the ability to set myself right before the public. As much as I hate American slavery, and as much as I abominate the infernal spirit which in that land seems to pervade both Church and State, there are bright spots there which I love, and a large and greatly increasing population, whose good opinion I highly value, and which I am determined never to forfeit, while it can be maintained consistently with truth and justice.

Sir, in replying to you, and in singling out the conduct of one of your age, reputation and learning, for public animadversion, I should, in most cases, deem an apology necessary—I should approach such an one with great delicacy and guardedness of language. But, in this instance, I feel entirely relieved from all such necessity. The obligations of courtesy, which I should be otherwise forward to discharge to persons of your age and standing, I am absolved from by your obviously bitter and malignant attack. I come, therefore, without any further hesitancy to the subject.

In a letter from London to the New-York Evangelist, describing the great meeting at Covent Garden Theatre, you say:

'They all advocated the same cause, showed a glorious unity of thought and feeling, and the effect was constantly raised—the moral scene was superb and glorious—when Frederick Douglass, the colored abolition agitator and ultraist, came to the platform, and so spoke *a la mode*, as to ruin the influence, almost, of all that preceded! He lugged in Anti-slavery or abolition, no doubt prompted to it by some of the politic ones, who can use him to do what they would not themselves adventure to do in person. He is supposed to have been well paid for the abomination.

What a perversion, an abuse, an iniquity against the law of reciprocal righteousness, to call thousands together to get them, some certain ones, to seem conspicuous and devoted for one sole and grand object, and then, all at once, with obliquity, open an avalanche on them for some imputed evil or monstrosity, for which, whatever be the wound or injury inflicted, they were both too fatigued and too hurried with surprise, and too straitened for time to be properly prepared. I say it is a trick of meanness! It is abominable!

On this occasion Mr. Douglass allowed himself to denounce America and all its temperance societies together, and a grinding community of the enemies of his people; said evil, with no alloy of good, concerning the whole of us; was perfectly indiscriminate in his severities, talked of the American delegates, and to them, as if he had been our schoolmaster, and we his docile and devoted pupils; and launched his revengeful missiles at our country, without one palliative, and as if not a Christian or a true anti-slavery man lived in the whole of the United States. The fact is, the man has been petted, and flattered, and used, and paid by certain abolitionists not unknown to us, of the *ne plus ultra* stamp, till he forgets himself; and though he may gratify his own impulses and those of old Adam in others, yet sure I am that all this is just the way to ruin his influence, to defeat his object, and to do mischief, not good, to the very cause he professes to love. With the single exception of one cold-hearted parricide, whose character I abhor, and whom I will not name, and who has, I fear, no feeling of true patriotism or piety within him, all the delegates from our country were together wounded and indignant. No wonder at it! I write freely. It was not done in a corner. It was inspired, I believe, from beneath, and not from above. It was adapted to re-kindle, on both sides of the Atlantic, the flames of national exasperation and war. And this is the game which Mr. Frederick Douglass and his silly patrons are playing in England and in Scotland, and wherever they can find 'some mischief still for idle hands to do'! I came here his sympathizing friend—I am so no more, as I more know him.

My own opinion is increasingly that this abominable spirit must be exorcised out of England and America, before any substantial good can be effected for the cause of the slave. It is adapted only to make bad worse, and to inflame the passions of indignant millions to an incurable resentment. None but an ignoramus or a mad man could think that this way was that of the inspired apostles of the Son of God. It may gratify the feelings of a self-deceived and malignant few, but it will do no good in any direction—least of all to the poor slave! It is short-sighted, impulsive, partisan, reckless, and tending only to sanguinary ends. None of this, with men of sense and principle.

We all wanted to reply, but it was too late; the whole theatre seemed taken with the spirit of the Ephesian uproar; they were furious and boisterous in the extreme; and Mr. Kirk could hardly obtain a moment, though many were desirous in his behalf, to say a few words, as he did, very calm and properly, that the cause of Temperance was not at all responsible for slavery, and had no connexion with it. There were some sly agencies behind the scenes —we know!

Now, the motive for representing, in this connexion, 'the effect constantly raised,' the 'moral scene sublime and glorious,' is very apparent. It is obviously not so much to do justice to the scene, as to magnify my assumed offence. You have drawn an exceedingly beautiful picture, that you might represent me as marring and defacing its beauty, in the hope thereby to kindle against me the fury of its admirers.

'Frederick Douglass, the colored abolitionist and ultraist, came to the platform.' Well, Sir, what if I did come to the platform? How did I come to it? Did I come with, or without, the consent of the meeting? Had your love of truth equalled your desire to cover me with odium, you would have said that, after loud and repeated calls from the audience, and a very pressing invitation from the chairman, 'Frederick Douglass came to the platform.'

But, Sir, this would not have served your purpose—that being to make me out an intruder, one without the wedding garment, fit to be cast out among the unbidden and unprepared. This might do very well in America, where for a negro to stand upon a temperance platform, on terms of perfect equality with white persons, it would be regarded as an insolent assumption, not to be borne with; but, Sir, it is scarcely necessary to say, that it will not serve your purpose in England. It is now pretty well known throughout the world, that color is no crime in England, and it is becoming almost equally known, that color is treated as a crime in America. *'Frederick Douglass, the colored abolition agitator and ultraist, came to the platform!'* Shocking! How could democratic Americans sit calmly by, and behold such a flagrant violation of one of the most cherished American customs—this most unnatural amalgamation! Was it not an aggravating and intolerable insult, to allow a negro to stand upon a platform, on terms of perfect equality with pure white American *gentlemen!* Monarchical England should be taught better manners; she should know that democratic America has the sole prerogative of deciding what shall be the social and civil position of the colored race. But, sarcasm aside, Sir, you claim to be a Christian, a philanthropist, and an abolitionist. Were you truly entitled to any one of these names, you would have been delighted at seeing one of Afric's despised children cordially received, and warmly welcomed to a world's temperance platform, and in every way treated as a man and a brother. But the truth probably is, that you felt both yourself and your country severely rebuked by my presence there; and, besides this, it was undoubtedly painful to you to be placed on the same platform, on a level with a negro, a fugitive slave. I do not assert this positively—it may not be quite true. But if it be true, I sincerely pity your littleness of soul.

You sneeringly call me an *'abolition agitator and ultraist.'* Sir, I regard this as a compliment, though you intend it as a condemnation. My only fear is, that I am unworthy of those epithets. To be an abolition agitator is simply to be one who dares to think for himself—who goes beyond the mass of mankind in promoting the cause of righteousness—who honestly and earnestly speaks out his soul's conviction, regardless of the smiles or frowns of men— leaving the pure flame of truth to burn up whatever hay, wood and stubble it may find in its way. To be such an one is the deepest

and sincerest wish of my heart. It is a part of my daily prayer
to God, that he will raise up and send forth more to unmask a pro-
slavery church, and to rebuke a man-stealing ministry—to rock the
land with agitation, and give America no peace till she repent, and
be thoroughly purged of this monstrous iniquity. While Heaven
lends me health and strength, and intellectual ability, I shall devote
myself to this agitation; and I believe that, by so acting, I shall
secure the smiles of an approving God, and the grateful approbation of my down-trodden and long abused fellow-countrymen.
With these on my side, of course I ought not to be disturbed by
your displeasure; nor am I disturbed. I speak now in vindication
of my cause, caring very little for your good or ill opinion.

You say I spoke 'so as to ruin the influence of all that had preceded'! My speech, then, must have been very powerful; for I had
been preceded by yourself, and some ten or twelve others, all powerful advocates of the Temperance cause, some of them the most so
of any I ever heard. But I half fear my speech was not so powerful as you seem to imagine. It is barely possible that you have
fallen into a mistake, quite common to persons of your turn of
mind,—that of confounding your own pride with the cause which
you may happen to plead. I think you will upon reflection confess, that I have now hit upon a happy solution of the difficulty.
As I look back to that occasion, I remember certain facts, which
seem to confirm me in this view of the case. You had eulogized
in no measured or qualified terms, America and American Temperance Societies; and in this, your co-delegates were not a whit
behind you. Is it not possible that the applause, following each
brilliant climax of your fulsome panegyric, made you feel the moral
effect raised, and the scene superb and glorious? I am not un-
aware of the effect of such demonstrations: it is very intoxicating,
very inflating. Now, Sir, I should be very sorry, and would make
any amends within my power, if I supposed I had really committed, the 'abomination' of which you accuse me. The Temperance cause is dear to me. I love it for myself, and for the
black man, as well as for the white man. I have labored, both in
England and America, to promote the cause, and am ready still to
labor; and I should grieve to think of any act of mine, which would
inflict the slightest injury upon the cause. But I am satisfied that
no such injury was inflicted. No, Sir, it was not the poor bloated
drunkard, who was 'ruined' by my speech, but your own bloated

pride, as I shall presently show—as I mean to take up your letter in the order in which it is written, and reply to each part of it.

You say I lugged in anti-slavery, or abolition. Of course, you meant by this to produce the impression, that I introduced the subject illegitimately. If such were your intention, it is an impression utterly at variance with the truth. I said nothing, on the occasion referred to, which in fairness can be construed into an outrage upon propriety, or something foreign to the temperance platform—and especially a 'world's Temperance platform.' The meeting at Covent Garden was not a *white* temperance meeting, such as are held in the United States, but a 'world's temperance meeting,' embracing the black as well as the white part of the creation—practically carrying out the scriptural declaration, that 'God has made of one blood, all nations of men, to dwell on all the face of the earth.' It was a meeting for promoting temperance throughout the world. All nations had a right to be represented there; and each speaker had a right to make known to that body, the peculiar difficulties which lay in the way of the temperance reformation, in his own particular locality. In that Convention, and upon that platform, I was the recognized representative of the colored population of the United States; and to their cause I was bound to be faithful. It would have been quite easy for me to have made a speech upon the general question of temperance, carefully excluding all reference to my enslaved, neglected and persecuted brethren in America, and thereby secured your applause;—but to have pursued such a course, would have been selling my birthright for a mess of pottage,—would have been to play the part of Judas, a part which even you profess to loathe and detest. Sir, let me explain the motive which animated me, in speaking as I did at Covent Garden Theatre. As I stood upon that platform, and surveyed the deep depression of the colored people of America, and the treatment uniformly adopted, by white temperance societies, towards them—the impediments and absolute barriers thrown in the way of their moral and social improvement, by American slavery, and by an inveterate prejudice against them, on account of their color—and beheld them in rags and wretchedness, in fetters and chains, left to be devoured by intemperance and kindred vices—and slavery like a very demon, standing directly in the way of their reformation, as with a drawn sword, ready to smite down any who might approach for their deliverance—and found myself in a position where I could rebuke this evil spirit, where my words would be borne to the shores of America, upon the enthusiastic shouts of congregated thousands—I deemed it my duty to embrace the opportunity. In the language of John Knox, 'I was in the place where I was demanded of conscience to speak the truth—and the truth I *did* speak—impugn it who so list.' But, in so doing, I spoke perfectly in order, and in such a manner as no one, having a sincere interest in the cause of Temperance, could take offence at—as I shall show by reporting, in another part of this letter my speech as delivered on that occasion.

'He was, no doubt, prompted to do it by some of the politic ones, who can use him to do what they themselves would not adventure to do in person.' The right or wrong of obeying the promptings of another depends upon the character of the thing to be done. If the thing be right, I should do it, no matter by whom prompted; if wrong, I should refrain from it, no matter by whom commanded. In the present instance, I was prompted by no one— I acted entirely upon my own responsibility. If, therefore, blame is to fall anywhere, it should fall upon me.

'He is supposed to have been well paid for the abomination.' This, Sir, is a cowardly way of stating your own conjecture. I should be pleased to have you tell me, what harm there is in being well paid! Is not the laborer worthy of his hire? Do you preach without pay? Were you not paid by those who sent you to represent them in the World's Temperance Convention? There is not the slightest doubt that you were paid—and *well paid*. The only difference between us, in the matter of pay, is simply this—you were paid, and I was not. I can with a clear conscience affirm, that, so far from having been well paid, as you supposed, I never received a single farthing for my attendance—or for any word which I uttered on the occasion referred to—while you were in all probability well supported, 'well paid,' for all you did during your attendance. My visit to London was at my own cost. I mention this, not because I blame you for taking pay, or because I regard as specially meritorious my attending the meeting without pay; for I should probably have taken pay as readily as you did, had it been offered; but it was not offered, and therefore I got none.

You stigmatize my speech as an 'abomination'; but you take good care to suppress every word of the speech itself. There can be but one motive for this, and that motive obviously is, because there was nothing in the speech which, standing alone, would inspire others with the bitter malignity against me, which unhappily rankles in your own bosom.

And is slavery only an *imputed* evil? Now, suppose I had lugged in Anti-Slavery, (which I deny,)—you profess to be an abolitionist. You, therefore, ought to have been the last man in the world to have found fault with me, on that account. Your great love of liberty, and sympathy for the down-trodden slave, ought to have led you to 'pardon something to the spirit of Liberty,' especially in one who had the scars of the slave-driver's whip on his back, and who, at this moment, has four sisters and one brother in slavery. But, Sir, you are not an abolitionist, and you only assumed to be one during your recent tour in this country, that you might *sham* your way through this land, and the more effectually stab and blast the character of the real friends of emancipation. Who ever heard of a true abolitionist speaking of slavery as an 'imputed evil,' or complaining of being 'wounded and injured' by an allusion to it—and that, too, because that allusion was in opposition to the infernal system? You took no offence when the Rev. Mr. Kirk assumed the Christian name and character for slaveholders in the World's Temperance Convention. You were not 'wounded or injured,'—it was not a 'perversion, an abuse, an iniquity against the law of reciprocal righteousness.' You have no indignation to pour out upon him. Oh, no! But when a *fugitive slave* merely alluded to slavery as obstructing the moral and social improvement of my race, you were 'wounded and injured,' and rendered indignant! This, sir, tells the whole story of your abolitionism, and stamps your pretensions to abolition as brazen hypocrisy or self-deception.

You were 'too fatigued, too hurried by surprise, too straitened for time.' Why, Sir, you were in 'an unhappy predicament.' What would you have done, had you not been 'too fatigued, too hurried by surprise, too straitened for time,' and unprepared? Would you have denied a single statement in my address? I am persuaded you would not; and had you dared to do so, I could at once have given evidence in support of my statements, that would have put you to silence or to shame. My statements were in perfect accordance with historical facts—facts of so recent date, that they are fresh in the memory of every intelligent American. You knew I spoke truly of the strength of American prejudice against the colored people. No man knows the truth on this subject better than yourself. I am, therefore, filled with amazement that you should seem to deny, instead of confirming my statements.

Much more might be said on this point; but having already extended this letter to a much greater length than I had intended, I shall simply conclude by a reference to your remark respecting your professed sympathy and friendship for me, previous to the meeting at Covent Garden. If your friendship and sympathy be of so mutable a character as must be inferred from your sudden abandonment of them, I may expect that yet another change will return to me the lost treasure. At all events, I do not deem it of sufficient value to purchase it at so high a price as that of the abandonment of the cause of my colored brethren, which appears to be the condition you impose upon its continuance.

Very faithfully,
FREDERICK DOUGLASS.

Now, Sir, to show the public how much reliance ought to be placed on your statements, and what estimate they should form of your love of truth and Christian candor, I will give the substance of my speech at Covent Garden Theatre, and the circumstances attending and growing out of its delivery. As 'the thing was not done in a corner,' I can with safety appeal to the FIVE THOUSAND that heard the speech, for the substantial correctness of my report of it. It was as follows:—

Mr. Chairman—Ladies and Gentlemen—I am not a delegate to this Convention. Those who would have been most likely to elect me as a delegate, could not, because they are to-night held in the most abject slavery in the United States. Sir, I regret that I cannot fully unite with the American delegates, in their patriotic eulogies of America, and American Temperance Societies. I cannot do so, for this good reason—there are, at this moment, three millions of the American population, by slavery and prejudice, placed entirely beyond the pale of American Temperance Societies. The three million slaves are completely excluded by slavery—and four hundred thousand free colored people are almost as completely excluded by an inveterate prejudice against them, on account of their color. (Cries of shame! shame!)

I do not say these things to wound the feelings of the American delegates. I simply mention them in their presence, and before this audience, that, seeing how you regard this hatred and neglect of the Colored people, they may be induced, on their return home, to enlarge the field of their Temperance operations, and embrace within the scope of their influence, my long neglected race—(great cheering and some confusion on the platform.) Sir, to give you some idea of the difficulties and obstacles in the way of the Temperance reformation of the colored population in the United States, allow me to state a few facts. About the year 1840, a few intelligent, sober and benevolent colored gentlemen in Philadelphia, being acquainted with the appalling ravages of intemperance among a numerous class of colored people in that city, and finding themselves neglected and excluded from white societies, organized societies among themselves—appointed committees—sent out agents— built temperance halls, and were earnestly and successfully rescuing many from the fangs of intemperance.

The cause went nobly on till the 1st of August, 1842, the day when England gave liberty to eight hundred thousand souls in the West Indies. The colored Temperance Societies selected this day to march in procession through the city, in the hope that such a demonstration would have the effect of bringing others into their ranks. They formed their procession, unfurled their teetotal banners, and proceeded to the accomplishment of their purpose. It was a delightful sight. But, Sir, they had not proceeded down two streets, before they were brutally assailed by a ruthless mob— their banner was torn down, and trampled in the dust—their ranks broken up, their persons beaten, and pelted with stones and brickbats. One of their churches was burned to the ground, and their best temperance hall was utterly demolished. (Shame! shame! shame! from the audience—great confusion and cries of 'sit down' from the American delegates on the platform.)

In the midst of this commotion, the chairman tapped me on the shoulder, and whispering, informed me that the fifteen minutes allotted to each speaker had expired; whereupon the vast audience simultaneously shouted, 'Don't interrupt!—don't dictate! go on! go on! Douglass! Douglass!!' This continued several minutes; after which, I proceeded as follows:—

'Kind friends, I beg to assure you that the chairman has not, in the slightest degree, sought to alter any sentiment which I am anxious to express on the present occasion. He was simply reminding me, that the time allotted for me to speak had expired. I do not wish to occupy one moment more than is allotted to other speakers. Thanking you for your kind indulgence, I will take my seat.'

Proceeding to do so, again there were loud cries of 'go on! go on!' with which I complied, for a few moments, but without saying any thing more that particularly related to the colored people of America.

When I sat down, the Rev. Mr. Kirk, of Boston, rose, and said—'Frederick Douglass has unintentionally misrepresented the Temperance Societies of America. I am afraid that his remarks have produced the impression on the public mind, that the Temperance Societies support slavery—('No! no! no! no!!' shouted the audience.) If that be not the impression produced, I have nothing more to say.'

Now, Dr. Cox, this a fair, unvarnished story of what took place at Covent Garden Theatre, on the 7th of August, 1846. For the truth of it, I appeal to all the Temperance papers in the land, and the 'Journal of the American Union,' published at New-York, Oct. 1, 1846. With this statement, I might safely submit the whole question to both the American and British public; but I wish not merely to correct your misrepresentations, and expose your falsehoods, but to show that you are animated by a fierce, bitter and untruthful spirit toward the whole anti-slavery movement.

And for this purpose, I shall now proceed to copy and comment upon extracts from your letter to the New-York Evangelist. In that letter, you exclaim, respecting the foregoing speech, delivered by me, every word of which you take pains to omit: 'What a perversion, an abuse, an iniquity against the law of reciprocal righteousness, to call thousands together, and get them, some certain ones, to seem conspicuous and devoted for one sole and grand object, and then, all at once, with obliquity, open an avalanche on them for some imputed evil or monstrosity, for which, whatever be the wound or the injury inflicted, they were both too fatigued and too hurried with surprise, and too straitened for time, to be properly prepared. I say it is a trick of meanness! It is abominable!'

As to the 'perversion,' 'abuse,' 'iniquity against the law of reciprocal righteousness,' 'obliquity,' 'a trick of meanness,' 'abominable,'—not one word is necessary to show their inappropriateness, as applied to myself, and the speech in question, or to make more glaringly apparent the green and poisonous venom with which your mouth, if not your heart, is filled. You represent me as opening 'an avalanche upon you for some *imputed* evil or monstrosity.'[112]

MY DEAR FRIEND:

A severe illness of two weeks' duration, from which I have now but partially recovered, has prevented me from replying to, and

[112] *Liberator*, Nov. 27, 1846.

explaining certain representations and charges, which have recently found their way into the public press, seriously affecting my moral character.

Many reasons might be urged in favor of treating this mean and scandalous fabrication with silent contempt. The character which I have maintained for six years, open to the most searching investigation—the disguising nature of the imputations, and obvious motive for making them—and the well-known impurity and filthiness of the quarter from which they emanated—might afford some justification for pursuing a course of absolute silence; leaving the public to form what judgment they pleased of the truth or falsity, the justice or injustice of the attack upon me.

There is, however, something so direct, so impudent, and so apparently consistent in this malicious assault, that I feel that duty to the cause with which I am connected, to myself, and to the noble band of friends who have ever thrown around me the broad shield of their protection, requires at my hand a full, free and open explanation of the ground of the assault; and as complete a vindication of myself as the real facts in the case will permit me to make.

My first impulse, on being informed of this bold attempt to destroy my influence, and ruin me forever, was in favor of bringing the slanderers before some legal tribunal of the country. But upon reflection, I felt that such a course would be unwise, perplexing, and fruitless. This was not, however, because I lacked confidence in the law or its administrators, but from a knowledge of the loathsome creatures who stand forth as my accusers. The unscrupulous wretches who could string together such a list of lies, are not to be expected to have any very sacred regard for an oath. As a lawyer once said—'When a case originates in Pandemonium, we are to expect none but demons for witnesses.' If, however, it shall be found necessary to bring the matter before a legal tribunal, I shall not hesitate to adopt the necessary means to bring both the perpetrators and the circulators of this foul slander, where they may have an opportunity of making good their charges, if they can. Meanwhile, I will take up their articles, all filthy as they are, and examine every material sentence in them.

The first notice of my passage from Albany to New-York, I found in a paper called 'The Switch,' and purporting to be published in Albany. But on inquiry where it was printed, by whom edited and published, I found that those whereabouts are prudently kept unknown. The editor is unknown, and it is the policy of the managers to keep unknown, that they may lie and slander with impunity. In any other country making pretension to civilization, such a nuisance would be speedily ferreted out, and abated. But, alas for the freest nation on the globe! liberty is too often made to license all conceivable brutality, and to give impunity to the vilest slanderers. The article in the 'Switch' begins as follows:

NIGGERS AND NASTINESS.

'The offence is rank—it smells to Heaven.'

A depraved portion of the people, and of the press, have for some time past been gratifying their morbid tastes in lionizing a disgusting, impertinent negro, who styles himself Frederick Douglass. The feelings of the decent portion of the community have, times without number, been outraged by having this 'soot head' thrust into their midst. It is a needless task for us to recapitulate the instances of this 'wool head's' sauciness.

Comment on this is only necessary to fix attention upon the *animus* of the writer. It is a fit introduction to what follows. Mark! 'depraved portion of the people and press'—'disgusting and impertinent negro'—'soot head'—'wool head's sauciness,' &c. These hail from the lowest of the American mould. Those who kindly regard me in this country are the purest and best in the world; they are in truth, the salt of the earth, the lights of the world; and therein is a motive for assaulting me.

My 'impertinence and sauciness' have ever consisted in presuming to be, and behaving as a man—in paying no more deference to a white man, than to a black man of equal moral and intellectual worth—in bowing to no skin-deep superiority, but rendering honor only where honor is due. I am said to be 'disgusting.' How, when, where, and to whom? Not as a coach-driver, dressed in tinselled livery, driving some delicate white ladies through Albany, or Broadway, New York. Not as a footman, on some gilded carriage. Not as a waiter in some fashionable hotel. Not as a servant, a barber, a cook, or a steward. No! I am never disgusting to the most refined white Americans, in any of these capacities! Even a white lady—a *white American lady*—might be seen near me, in these capacities, without exciting vulgar abuse and filthy insinuations. But when does white complacency, in this matter, cease, and ineffable disgust commence, in the bosoms of our alabastar fellow-countrymen? Just when the colored man's inequality is dropped, and his equality is assumed. The negro then becomes horribly disgusting! I am not insensible to this feeling of disgust. There are constant occasions for calling it forth. I was never more disgusted in my life than when in Albany, low, filthy, tobacco-chewing, slobbering white blackguards presumed to insult me on account of the color of my skin. This, I think, is something at which we may properly be disgusted.

One word more about disgust. There is a strange diversity in its manifestation, indicating how completely a pure taste may be perverted. Some animals, for instance—and man among the number—display the strangest perversity of taste. The buzzard and the condor are utterly disgusted with sound meat, and prefer to flesh their talons in carrion. These birds go around, like the editor of the 'Switch,' dealing largely in the most disgusting and putrid flesh! A dog afflicted with hydrophobia, is utterly disgusted with the sight and scent of pure cold water; and a white man afflicted with colorphobia will invariably manifest signs of disgust at the sight of a respectable colored man. 'Colorphobia' and buzzards—mad dogs and condors—'think of these things!'

I will now pass to the next extract. Speaking of me, he says—

'Last week he was here, and was gallanted to the Assembly Chamber by a female of this city, who so far forgot what was due to the community and to the delicacy of her sex, as to introduce this offensive creature into the Ladies' Gallery, where she left him. Mr. Stoutenburgh, the gentlemanly and attentive officer having charge of that department, on discovering him, immediately told him that a place was especially designated for colored persons, and pointed it out to him, but Sambo refused to go, on which Mr. S. was compelled to eject him forcibly. The lady soon after returned, and asked Mr. S. where her 'friend and companion' had gone, on which Mr. S. informed her that he had turned him out, and directed him to the place appropriated to such as he. The female subsequently found her 'friend and companion,' and they left the Capitol 'cheek by jowl.'

It is perfectly true, that I was in Albany at the time here mentioned; and quite true, that I was accompanied to the Assembly Chamber by a lady—*a white lady*, (very criminal!)—and, naturally enough, she took me to that part of the House to which, as a lady, she felt herself entitled to go. It is not true, that when Mr. Stoutenburgh discovered me, he told me that a place was especially

designated for colored persons. He did point me to the gentleman's gallery, and there was no hesitancy, on my part, in going to
it; and nothing imperious in his manner in pointing it out to me.
Not an unfriendly word passed between us. The whole story of
my being 'forcibly ejected' is a deliberate lie, to serve a purpose.
I went into the gentlemen's gallery, and enjoyed a sight of the assembled wisdom of the great state of New-York, as I have frequently enjoyed a similar sight of the assembled wisdom of Great
Britain. After having been permitted freely to enter Parliament—
both Lords and Commons—and witness their deliberations, in company with white persons, it was not to be expected that I should be
afraid to enter an Assembly Chamber, where that living embodiment of 'Subterranean' filth and fury, Mike Walsh, is recognized
as an *honorable* member.

Having now glanced at the lighter shades, I come at once to the
darker and more important aspects of the subject. The 'Switch'
says—

'Shortly after this, these 'friends and companions' went to
New-York in company. On the morning of their arrival, Captain
Cruttenden observed that a negro came down from the state rooms
with a white woman, and was indignant on learning that the pair
had occupied state rooms which communicated with each other by a
door, and cautioned his assistant against permitting the like occurrence. On a return trip of the Hendrick Hudson, a few days afterwards, the same oddly matched companions were again on board,
and the woman sent the chambermaid to the captain's office for two
state rooms, the keys of which the chambermaid delivered to her.
The female, on inspection, told the chambermaid that the rooms
were not what she wanted—that they must have a door leading
into each other. The person in charge of the office, without hesitation, changed their location, and gave the same rooms which these
friends and companions had occupied the night before. Capt.
Cruttenden discovered it in the morning, and on their coming
down told the nigger never to *darken* the saloon of any boat commanded by him again, and ordered him ashore. The fellow's wool
bristled somewhat, and his companion colored slightly, and they
departed in company.'

I will now state the circumstances of this transaction, in my
own way, and shall admit all that I know to be true, and deny all
that I know to be false in the above statement. On Monday, May
10th, I was in company with my wife, at Albany, where I went to
see my daughter, whom I had not seen for nearly two years. Hav-

ing been announced to speak the next morning at the anniversary
meeting of the American Anti-Slavery Society in New-York, and
suffering under severe cold and hoarseness, and well knowing the
brutal manner in which colored persons are uniformly treated in
steamers on the Hudson river—compelled sometimes to stroll the
decks nearly all night, before they can get a place to lie down, and
that place frequently unfit for a dog's accommodation—and being
unwilling to risk my health to any such chances, I availed myself
of the kindness of my friend alluded to, who secured for me a
state room on board of the Hendrick Hudson; and also secured the
adjoining one for herself. On going into mine, in the evening, I
found, as above stated, that the two rooms communicated with each
other by a door. But a thought of its propriety or impropriety
never crossed my mind; and, at that time, I did not know but that
every state room on board communicated in a similar manner. Myself and friend conversed together during the evening, when she
went to her state room, and I remained in mine. I neither saw
nor heard my friend till next morning, when we landed at New-
York. I then went to her state-room door to assist her with her
baggage; and after walking about a full half hour in the presence
of the Captain, while the crowd was pressing on shore, we left the
steamer together, without the slightest sign of disapprobation that
I could see from any quarter. On my return from New-York, my
friend secured similar state rooms, and we occupied them, without
the least interruption from the Captain, or any officer, servant or
passenger on board. When we left the steamer in the morning,
the Captain did utter some filthy remarks, calling me a 'nigger,'
&c., and telling me never to take a state room on board his steamer
again. I made no reply, but went off about my business, well knowing that my color was the cause of his brutality, and that, had I
been a white man, I might have occupied the state rooms a dozen
times over, without calling forth any foul imputations from himself, or any one else. As to what is alleged to have been said by
my friend to the chambermaid, it may or may not be true; and,
true or false, it is a small matter. We needed neither bolts, bars,
nor locks, to keep us in the path of virtue and rectitude. The
'Switch' closes its article as follows, which shows that, vile and
profligate as it is, it is a shade less atrocious than the 'Subterranean':

'We wish it distinctly understood, that we cast no imputations on the character of the white woman, who thus gads about the country with a negro, but she certainly manifests a depravity of taste, that should induce her friends to look sharply after her—and as for this thunder-cloud, he should be kicked into his *proper place, and kept there.*

We shall resume this subject next week.'

Having disposed of the 'Switch,' I come to that loathsome dabbler in 'Subterranean' pollution, Mike Walsh. The depravity of the man is marvellous. My work with him will be necessarily short; for his statement is made up from the 'Switch,' and improved upon to suit his own impure fancy.

My answer to it is, that, aside from the simple fact that myself and friend occupied adjoining and communicating state rooms—and the fact that the Captain was indignant that I, a *colored* person, should do so—this whole story, from beginning to end, in gross and scope, in letter and spirit, in principle and inference, is a foul, deliberate, unmixed, and malicious fabrication. The whole narration, in all its details, particulars and specifications—so far as they relate to my conduct—is a series of the most daringly wicked falsehoods; and none, but one over whom the sway of the devil is complete, could have invented and penned them.

Ever yours in the cause of purity and liberty,

FREDERICK DOUGLASS.[113]

Lynn, June 7th, 1847.

THE RANSOM.

LETTER TO FREDERICK DOUGLASS, WITH HIS REPLY.

DONCASTER, Dec. 12th, 1846.

DEAR FREDERICK:

This is the first letter of advice I ever wrote to you—it is the last. I like to bear the responsibility of my own existence. I like to see others bear theirs. I say what I am about to say, because I think it is my right and duty to say it; at the same time, not wishing to interfere with your right to follow my advice, or not, as you shall see fit. That Certificate of your freedom, that *Bill of Sale* of your body and soul, from that *villain,* Auld, who dared to claim you as a chattel, and set a price on you as such, and to demand and take a price for you as such, I wish you would not touch it. I can-

113 *Liberator,* June 11, 1847.

not bear to think of you as being a party to such a transaction, even by silence. If *others* will take that paper, and keep it as an evidence of your freedom, you cannot prevent them; but I wish you would see it to be your duty, publicly to disown the deed, and never to recognize that *hateful Bill!*—nor to refer to it, as of any authority to establish the fact that you are a *Freeman,* and not a *Slave*—a *Man,* and not a *Chattel.*

The moment you entered a non-slave State, your position ceased to be *Frederick Douglass,* versus *Thomas Auld,* and became *Frederick Douglass,* versus the *United States.* From that hour, you became the antagonist of that Republic.

As a nation, that confederacy, professing to be based upon the principle, that God made you free, and gave you an inalienable right to liberty, claims a right of property in your body and soul—to turn you into a chattel, a slave, again, at any moment. That claim you denied; the authority and power of the whole nation you spurned and defied, when, by running away, you spurned that miserable wretch, who held you as a slave. It was no longer a contest between you and that praying, psalm-singing slave-breeder, but a struggle between you and 17,000,000 of liberty-loving Republicans. By their laws and constitution, you are not a *freeman,* but a *slave;* you are not a *man,* but a *chattel.* You planted your foot upon their laws and constitution, and asserted your freedom and your manhood. You arraigned your antagonist—the slave-breeding Republic—before the tribunal of mankind, and of God. You have stated your case, and pleaded your cause, as none other could state and plead it. Your position, as the slave of that Republic, as the marketable commodity, the dehumanized, outraged *man* of a powerful nation, whose claim and power over you, you have dared to despise, invests you with influence among all to whom your appeal is made, and gathers around you their deep-felt, absorbing, and efficient sympathy. Your appeal to mankind is not against the grovelling thief, Thomas Auld, but against the more daring, more impudent and potent thief—the Republic of the United States of America. You will lose the advantages of this truly manly, and, to my view, sublime position; you will be shorn of your strength—you will sink in your own estimation, if you accept that detestable certificate of your freedom, that blasphemous forgery, that accursed Bill of Sale of your body and soul; or, even by silence, acknowledge its validity. So I think. I cannot think of the transaction without vexation. I would see you free—you *are* free—you always *were* free, and the man is a villain who claims you as a slave, and should be treated as such; and the nation is a blasphemous hypocrite, that claims power over you as a chattel. I would see your right to freedom, and to a standing on the platform of humanity, openly acknowledged by every human being—not on the testimony of a bit of paper, signed and sealed by an acknowledged thief, but by the declaration of a penitent nation, prostrate at your feet, in tears, suing to you and to God for forgiveness, for the outrages committed against God and man, in your person.

That slave-breeding nation has dared to claim you, and 3,000,000 of your fellow-men, as chattels—slaves—to be bought and sold; and has pledged all its power to crush you down, and to keep you from rising from ignorance to knowledge—from degradation to respectability—from misery to happiness—from slavery to freedom—from a *Chattel* to a *Man*. As an advocate for yourself, and your 3,000,-000 brethren, you have joined issue with it—and, in the name of God and humanity, you will conquer! The nation must and shall be humbled before its victims,—not by a blasphemous bill of sale, alias Certificate of freedom, for which £150 are paid, but by renouncing its claim, blotting out its slavery-sustaining constitution, acknowledge itself conquered, and seek forgiveness of the victims of its injustice and tyranny. The plea, that this is the same as a ransom paid for a capture of some Algerine pirate, or Bedouin Arab, is naught. You have already, by your own energy, escaped the grasp of the pirate Auld. He has no more power over you. The spell of his influence over you is forever broken. Why go to him? Why ask the sacrilegious villain to set a price upon your body and soul? Why give him his price? The mean, brutal slaveholder—daring to price your freedom, your soul, in dollars and cents, and with cool, consummate impudence, and villany unsurpassed, saying, 'I'll be satisfied with 750 dollars—I'll give up my right of property in your person, and acknowledge you to be a freeman, and not a slave—a *man*, and not a *beast*—for £150.' 'Satisfied,' forsooth! You cancelled his villanous claims, when you turned your back upon him, and walked away. But the nation claims you as a slave. It does! Let it dare to assert that claim, and attempt your re-enslavement! It is worth running some risk, for the sake of the conflict, and the certain result.

Your wife and children are there, it is true, and you must return to them; but the greater will be your power to grapple with the monster; the shorter and more glorious will be the conflict; the more sure and complete the victory, if you go as the antagonist of a nation that claims you as a slave, as a chattel, a man turned into an article of merchandise. You would be armed with an irresistible power, when, as a self-emancipated captive, you arraigned that piratical Republic before the world. You would be sheltered and sustained by the sympathies of millions. The advantages of your present position should not be sacrificed to a desire for greater security.

But I will go no further. You will think that what I have said has more of indignation than of reason in it. It may be so. Feeling is often a safer and a wiser guide than logic. Of all guilty men, the American slaveholder is the most guilty, and the meanest, the most impudent, most despicable, and most inexcusable in his guilt; except, it may be, those, who, in the non-slave States, and in Scotland and England, stand sponsors for his social respectability and personal Christianity, and who thus associate our Redeemer in loving fellowship with men who are the living embodiment of the sum of all villany.

Before concluding, I wish to add, that, in what I have said, I would not arraign the motives of those who have, as they believe, sought to befriend you in this matter. I believe Anna Richardson, and all who have taken part in this transaction, have been actuated by the purest motives of kindness to you and your family, and by a desire, through the purchase of your freedom, to benefit the American slaves. But they have erred in judgment, as it appears to me. Forgive this, if it needs forgiveness. I delight to see you loved and honored by all, and to see you made an instrument, by the God of the oppressed, of humbling in the dust, that gigantic liar and hypocrite, the American Republic, that stands with the Bible and Declaration of Independence in its hands, and its heel planted on the necks of 3,000,000 of slaves.

Thine sincerely,

H. C. WRIGHT.

FREDERICK DOUGLASS'S REPLY.

22, St. Ann's Square, Manchester, 22d Dec., 1846.

HENRY C. WRIGHT:

DEAR FRIEND:—Your letter of the 12th December reached me at this place, yesterday. Please accept my heartfelt thanks for it. I am sorry that you deemed it necessary to assure me, that it would be the last letter of advice you would ever write me. It looked as if you were about to cast me off for ever! I do not, however, think you meant to convey any such meaning; and if you did, I am sure you will see cause to change your mind, and to receive me again into the fold of those, whom it should ever be your pleasure to advise and instruct.

The subject of your letter is one of deep importance, and upon which, I have thought and felt much; and, being the party of all others most deeply concerned, it is natural to suppose I have an opinion, and ought to be able to give it on all fitting occasions. I deem this a fitting occasion, and shall act accordingly.

You have given me your opinion: I am glad you have done so. You have given it to me direct, in your own emphatic way. You never speak insipidly, smoothly, or mincingly; you have strictly adhered to your custom, in the letter before me. I now take great pleasure in giving you my opinion, as plainly and unreservedly as you have given yours, and I trust with equal good feeling and purity of motive. I take it, that nearly all that can be said against my position is contained in your letter; for if any man in the wide world would be likely to find valid objections to such a transaction as the one under consideration, I regard you as that man. I must, however, tell you, that I have read your letter over, and over again, and have sought in vain to find anything like what I can regard a valid reason *against the purchase of my body, or against my receiving the manumission papers, if they are ever presented to me.*

Let me, in the first place, state the facts and circumstances of the transaction which you so strongly condemn. It is your right to do so, and God forbid that I should ever cherish the slightest desire to restrain you in the exercise of that right. I say to you at once, and in all the fulness of sincerity, speak out; speak freely; keep nothing back; let me know your whole mind. 'Hew to the line, though the chips fly in my face.' Tell me, and tell me plainly, when you think I am deviating from the strict line of duty and principle; and when I become unwilling to hear, I shall have attained a character which I now despise, and from which I would hope to be preserved.   But to the facts.

I am in England, my family are in the United States.   My sphere of usefulness is in the United States; my public and domestic duties are there; and there it seems my duty to go.   But I am *legally* the property of Thomas Auld, and if I go to the United States, (no matter to what part, for there is no City of Refuge there, no spot sacred to freedom there,) Thomas Auld, *aided by the American Government*, can seize, bind and fetter, and drag me from my family, feed his cruel revenge upon me, and doom me to unending slavery.   In view of this simple statement of facts, a few friends, desirous of seeing me released from the terrible liability, and to relieve my wife and children from the painful trepidation, consequent upon the liability, and to place me on an equal footing of safety with all other anti-slavery lecturers in the United States, and to enhance my usefulness by enlarging the field of my labors in the United States, have nobly and generously paid Hugh Auld, the agent of Thomas Auld, £150—in consideration of which, Hugh Auld (acting as his agent) and the Government of the United States agree, that I shall be free from all further liability.

These, dear friend, are the facts of the whole transaction.   The principle here acted on by my friends, and that upon which I shall act in receiving the manumission papers, I deem quite defensible.

First, *as to those who acted as my friends, and their actions.* The actuating motive was, to secure me from a liability full of horrible forebodings to myself and family.   With this object, I will do you the justice to say, I believe you fully unite, although some parts of your letters would seem to justify a different belief.

Then, as to the measure adopted to secure this result.   Does it violate a fundamental principle, or does it not?   This is the question, and to my mind the only question of importance, involved in the discussion.   I believe that, on our part, no just or holy principle has been violated.

Before entering upon the argument in support of this view, I will take the liberty (and I know you will pardon it) to say, I think you should have pointed out some principle violated in the transaction, before you proceeded to exhort me to repentance.   You have given me any amount of indignation against 'Auld' and the United States, in all which I cordially unite, and felt refreshed by reading; but it has no bearing whatever upon the conduct of myself, or friends, in the matter under consideration. It does not prove that I have done wrong, nor does it demonstrate what is right, or the proper course to be pursued. Now that the matter has reached its present point, before entering upon the argument, let me say one other word; it is this—I do not think you have acted quite consistently with your character for promptness, in delaying your advice till the transaction was completed. You knew of the movement at its conception, and have known it through its progress, and have never, to my knowledge, uttered one syllable against it, in conversation or letter, till now that the deed is done. I regret this, not because I think your earlier advice would have altered the result, but because it would have left me more free than I can now be, since the thing is done. Of course, you will not think hard of my alluding to this circumstance. Now, then, to the main question.

The principle which you appear to regard as violated by the transaction in question, may be stated as follows:—*Every man has a natural and inalienable right to himself.* The inference from this is, '*that man cannot hold property in man*'—*and as man cannot hold property in man, neither can Hugh Auld nor the United States have any right of property in me—and having no right of property in me, they have no right to sell me—and, having no right to sell me, no one has a right to buy me.* I think I have now stated the principle, and the inference from the principle, distinctly and fairly. Now, the question upon which the whole controversy turns is, simply, this: does the transaction, which you condemn, really violate this principle? I own that, to a superficial observer, it would seem to do so. But I think I am prepared to show, that, so far from being a violation of that principle, it is truly a noble vindication of it. Before going further, let me state here, briefly, what sort of a purchase would have been a violation of this principle, which, in common with yourself, I reverence, and am anxious to preserve inviolate.

1st. It would have been a violation of that principle, had those who purchased me done so, *to make me a slave, instead of a freeman.* And,

2ndly. It would have been a violation of that principle, had those who purchased me done so with a view to compensate the slaveholder, for what he and they regarded as his rightful property.

In neither of these ways was my purchase effected. My liberation was, in their estimation, of more value than £150; the happiness and repose of my family were, in their judgment, more than paltry gold. The £150 was paid to the remorseless plunderer, not because he had any just claim to it, but to induce him to give up his legal claim to something which they deemed of more value than money. It was not to compensate the slaveholder, but to release me from his power; not to establish my *natural right* to freedom, but to release me from all legal liabilities to slavery. And all this, you and I, and the slaveholders, and all who know anything of the transaction, very well understand. The very letter to Hugh Auld, proposing terms of purchase, informed him that those who gave, *denied his right to it.* The error of those, who condemn this transaction, consists in their confounding the crime of buying men *into slavery*, with the meritorious act of buying men out of slavery, and the purchase of legal freedom with abstract right and natural freedom. They say, 'If you BUY, you recognize the right to sell. If you receive, you recognize the right of the giver to give.' And this has a show of truth, as well as of logic. But a few plain cases will show its entire fallacy.

There is now, in this country, a heavy duty on corn. The government of this country has imposed it; and though I regard it a most unjust and wicked imposition, no man of common sense will charge me with endorsing or recognizing the right of this government to impose this duty, simply because, to prevent myself and family from starving, I buy and eat this corn.

Take another case:—I have had dealings with a man. I have owed him one hundred dollars, and have paid it; I have lost the receipt. He comes upon me the second time for the money. I know, and he knows, he has no right to it; but he is a villain, and has me in his power. The law is with him, and against me. I must pay or be dragged to jail. I choose to pay the bill a second time. To say I sanctioned his right to rob me, because I preferred to pay rather than go to jail, is to utter an absurdity, to which no sane man would give heed. And yet the principle of action, in each of these cases, is the same. The man might indeed say, the claim is unjust—and declare, I will rot in jail, before I will pay it. But this would not, certainly, be demanded by any principle of truth, justice, or humanity; and however much we might be disposed to respect his daring, but little deference could be paid to his wisdom. The fact is, we act upon this principle every day of our lives, and we have an undoubted right to do so. When I came to this country from the United States, I came in the *second* cabin. And why? Not because my natural right to come in the *first* cabin was not as good as that of any other man, but because a wicked and cruel prejudice decided, that the second cabin was the place for me. By coming over in the second, did I sanction or justify this wicked proscription? Not at all. It was the best I could do. I acted from necessity.

One other case, and I have done with this view of the subject. I think you will agree with me, that the case I am now about to put is pertinent, though you may not readily pardon me for making yourself the agent of my illustration. The case respects the passport system on the Continent of Europe. That system you utterly condemn. You look upon it as an unjust and wicked interference, a bold and infamous violation of the *natural* and *sacred* right of locomotion. You hold, (and so do I,) that the image of our common God ought to be a passport all over the habitable world. But bloody and tyrannical governments have ordained otherwise; they usurp authority over you, and decide for you, on what conditions you shall travel. They say, you shall have a passport, or you shall be put in prison. Now, the question is, have they a right to prescribe any such terms? and do you, by complying with these terms, sanction their interference? I think you will answer, no; submission to injustice, and sanction of injustice, are different things; and he is a poor reasoner who confounds the two, and makes them one and the same thing. Now, then, for the parallel, and the application of the passport system to my own case.

I wish to go to the United States. I have a natural right to go there, and be free. My natural right is as good as that of Hugh Auld, or James K. Polk; but that plundering government says, I shall not return to the United States in safety—it says, I must allow Hugh Auld to rob me, or my friends, of £150, or be hurled into the infernal jaws of slavery. I must have a 'bit of paper, signed and sealed,' or my liberty must be taken from me, and I must be torn from my family and friends. The government of Austria said to you, 'Dare to come upon my soil, without a passport, declaring you to be an American citizen, (which you say you are not,) you shall at once be arrested, and thrown into prison.'

What said you to that Government? Did you say that the threat was a villanous one, and an infamous invasion of your right of loco-motion? Did you say, 'I will come upon your soil; I will go where I please! I dare and defy your government!' Did you say, 'I will spurn your passports; I would not stain my hand, and degrade myself, by touching your miserable parchment. You have no right to give it, and I have no right to take it. I trample your laws, and will put your constitutions under my feet! I will not recognize them!' Was this your course? No! dear friend, it was not. Your practice was wiser than your theory. You took the passport, sub-mitted to be examined while travelling, and availed yourself of all the advantages of your 'passport'—or, in other words, escaped all the evils which you ought to have done, without it, and would have done, but for the tyrannical usurpation in Europe.

I will not dwell longer upon this view of the subject; and I dismiss it, feeling quite satisfied of the entire correctness of the reasoning, and the principle attempted to be maintained. As to the expediency of the measures, different opinions may well pre-vail; but in regard to the principle, I feel it difficult to conceive of two opinions. I am free to say, that, had I possessed one hun-dred and fifty pounds, I would have seen Hugh Auld *kicking*, be-fore I would have given it to him. I would have waited till the emergency came, and only given up the money when nothing else would do. But my friends thought it best to provide against the contingency; they acted on their own responsibility, and I am not disturbed about the result. But, having acted on a true principle, I *do not feel free to disavow their proceedings.*

In conclusion, let me say, I anticipate no such change in my position as you predict. I shall be Frederick Douglass still, and once a slave still. I shall neither be made to forget nor cease to feel the wrongs of my enslaved fellow-countrymen. My knowledge of slavery will be the same, and my hatred of it will be the same. By the way, I have never made my own person and suffering the theme of public discourse, but have always based my appeal upon the wrongs of the three millions now in chains; and these shall still be the burthen of my speeches. You intimate that I may reject the papers, and allow them to remain in the hands of those friends who have effected the purchase, and thus avail myself of the security afforded by them, without sharing any part of the responsibility of the transaction. My objection to this is one of honor. I do not think it would be very honorable on my part, to remain silent during the whole transaction, and giving it more than my silent approval; and then, when the thing is completed, and I am safe, attempt to play the *hero*, by throwing off all responsibility in the matter. It might be said, and said with great propriety, 'Mr. Douglass, your indignation is very good, and has but one fault, and that is, *it comes too late!*' It would be a show of bravery when the danger is over. From every view I have been able to take of the subject, I am persuaded to receive the papers, if presented,—not, however, as a proof of my right to be free, for *that is self-evident*, but as a proof that my friends have been legally robbed of £150, in order to secure that which is the birth-right of every man. And I will hold up those papers before the world, in proof of the plundering character of the American government. It shall be the brand of infamy, stamping the nation, in whose name the deed was done, as a great aggregation of hypocrites, thieves and liars,—and their condemnation is just. They declare that all men are created equal, and have a natural and inalienable right to liberty, while they rob me of £150, as a condition of my enjoying this natural and inalienable right. It will be their condemnation, in their own hand-writing, and may be held up to the world as a means of humbling that haughty republic into repentance.

I agree with you, that the contest which I have to wage is against the government of the United States. But the representative of that government is the slaveholder, *Thomas Auld*. He is commander-in-chief of the army and navy. The whole civil and naval force of the nation are at his disposal. He may command all these to his assistance, and bring them all to bear upon me, until I am made entirely subject to his will, or submit to be robbed myself, or allow my friends to be robbed, of seven hundred and fifty dollars. And rather than be subject to his will, I have submitted to be robbed, or allowed my friends to be robbed, of the seven hundred and fifty dollars.   Sincerely yours,

FREDERICK DOUGLASS.[114]

LYNN, April 21, 1847.

MY DEAR FRIEND:

I hasten to inform you of my safe arrival at home. I left Liverpool per steamship Cambria, at 12 o'clock on Sunday, April

[114] *Liberator*, Jan. 29, 1847.

4th, and reached Halifax on Sunday evening, the 18th, and here on Tuesday afternoon, about 6,—thus performing the voyage in sixteen days and six hours.

My passage was not the most agreeable; for, aside from the head winds, a rough sea, and the innumerable perils of the deep, I had the cruel, and almost omnipotent and omnipresent spirit of American slavery with which to contend.

After an interesting tour of twenty months through the British isles,—during which, I made use of all the various means of conveyance, by land and sea, from town to town, and city to city, my feelings as a man, and my rights as a passenger, sacredly regarded, and never being able to detect the slightest dislike to me on account of my color,—I bid farewell to monarchical England, and look toward democratic America; and while yet three thousand miles away from her shores, at the first step, I am smitten with the pestilential breath of her slave system! I came home a proscribed man; and this, solely to propitiate American pro-slavery hate. The American public demanded my exclusion from the saloon of the steamship, and the company owning the steamer had not the virtue to resist the demand. The dominion of slavery is no longer confined under the star-spangled banner, but extends itself, and bears sway, even under that of Great Britain. But, without farther preface, I will at once put you in possession of the facts in the case.

On the 4th of last March, in company with my friend Mr. George Moxhay, of the Hall of Commerce, London, I called upon the agent of the Cunard line of steamers, for the purpose of securing a berth in one of the Company's vessels, to sail for the United States on the 4th of April. I was informed by the agent, that there was but one berth unsold, and that was berth 72, in the Cambria. This berth I took, and paid for—paying first class price. I then asked the agent, whether there would be any difficulty in my enjoying any of the rights and privileges on board the ship, granted to white passengers. 'Certainly not,' was the reply. On hearing this, I left the office.

Reposing on the honor and the integrity of the Company, and never dreaming of the possibility of a contingency to deprive me of my berth, I made myself perfectly easy till the afternoon of the 3d April, the day previous to our contemplated departure from Liverpool to Boston. I then went on board with my baggage; and here, to my surprise, disappointment and mortification, I learned that my berth was given to another—that on account of the color of my skin, it had been decided that I should not have the berth for which I had paid, and to which I was justly entitled! Confused and confounded by this intelligence, I went to the office of the agent in Liverpool, for an explanation of what I had heard on board the steamer, which was now lying in the Mersey, about two miles from the shore. The agent, Mr. McIver, with the harshness of an American slaveholder, told me that the agent from whom I had purchased my ticket, had no right to sell it to me. I replied that I knew nothing more of the authority of the agent to sell tickets, than what I learned from the public press. He was there advertised as the authorized agent of the Company, and persons wishing to secure passage in the Company's ships were requested to call upon him. I had as much right to regard Mr. Foord as the agent in London, as to regard Mr. McIver the agent in Liverpool. They were both the advertised agents of the Company. But here was not the difficulty, as I afterwards compelled him to confess. This was a deceitful stratagem, (I will say nothing of its meanness,) to deprive me of my berth, without openly incurring the responsibility of trampling upon, and robbing a traveller of his rights, on account of the color of his skin.

The agent said, that great dissatisfaction had been given to the *American* travelling public, by my having been permitted on the quarter deck, when crossing the Atlantic in the summer of 1845, and that much ill-feeling had been created against the line in America by what I said against American slavery during the voyage; and that while he would not undertake to defend American prejudice, he must, nevertheless, prevent the recurrence of any such event again; and that, if I went home in the ship, I must go in an apartment wholly separate from the white passengers; but that I should have every accommodation in the way of attention, and apartments enjoyed by other passengers. Subject to this restriction, I must never enter the saloon,—the part of the ship the most commodious, and where other passengers took their meals. I must eat alone—sleep alone—*be alone.* These were my limits on board the British steamship Cambria. By this regulation, I was not only deprived of the privilege of eating in the saloon, but also shut out from religious worship. We had two Sundays during the voyage, and in conformity to the religious ideas of the Company, as well as of the British public, had regular religious services performed on board. They called upon *'our Father,'* the Creator of the heavens and the earth—the God who has made of one blood all nations, *the black as well as the white*—to bless them—while they cursed and excluded me on account of the color of my skin. This, I thought, was American slaveholding religion, *under British colors,* and I felt myself no great loser by being excluded from its benefits.

Aside from this proscription, I was as well provided for as any other passenger. Indeed, my apartments were much to be preferred to any which I saw on board. I was treated with the utmost politeness by every officer on board, and received every attention from the servants during the whole voyage. It may be asked, then, why do I yet complain? The answer is, that my position was one of coercion, when it ought to have been that of option. The difference is as wide as that of freedom and slavery; and the man who cannot see the one, cannot see the other.

In haste, yours, sincerely,

FREDERICK DOUGLASS.[115]

AUSTINBURGH, (Ohio) August 20, 1847.

MY DEAR FRIEND—I can send you but the barest outline of our Western tour thus far. Friend Garrison and myself, are moving from place to place, with such rapidity, and the places of meeting are at such "magnificent distances" from each other, that we have little or no time left us to report progress. To make our tour useful, we are compelled to devote ourselves unreservedly to the work of enlisting by private, as well as public effort, the hearts of those with whom we are brought in contact. Our private society is sought for with as much honestness and avidity, as are our public addresses. Mr. Garrison is the honoured centre of every circle into whose midst we are brought. His conversational powers are inexhaustible; he seems as fresh at midnight as at midday. Our friends eagerly flock around to hear his words of strength and cheer, while our enemies as eagerly draw around to catch him in his words. The former go away delighted with the man, while the latter skulk away, disappointed and chagrined, that they have

[115] *Liberator,* April 30, 1847.

found so little at which to be offended. Mr. Garrison's visit must do much to disabuse the public mind in this region, and to produce a mighty reaction in favour of radical Eastern Abolitionism. The Liberty party, and pro-slavery papers, have overshot themselves in regard to him.—They have so maligned, and slandered him, and have so distorted, perverted, and misrepresented his views, that they have created the most intense curiosity among the people to see and hear him, and having associated his person with the representations of his mind, that his bare presence, without the utterance of a word, is all sufficient to create an impression most favourable to him, and at once to dispel the dread, and gloomy apprehensions created concerning him. When he opens his mouth, and pours forth his truthful voice, the dark and foul spirit of slander falls before him, like Dagon before the ark.—People come expecting to see a fierce, proud, ambitious, and bitter looking man, a gloomy spirit, altogether dissatisfied with himself, and all the world around him; a stranger to peace, a man of war, if not of blood; completely wrapped up within the narrow limits of a single idea, perfectly above everything interesting to other men, an infidel, atheist, and madman, rejoicing over the triumphs of evil, and inflexibly bent upon the destruction of everything good. Such is the man which the pious, and pro-slavery papers of our land have taught the honest "Buckeyes" to look for in the person of William Lloyd Garrison, and in seeing him, they readily perceive how great has been the deception practiced upon them, and very naturally many of them are filled with indignation, and loathing, for their mean and dastardly deceivers. Thus the cause goes gloriously on, and thus is the wisdom of the crafty confounded, and the counsels of the ungodly brought to naught. Good is thus brought out of evil, and the wrath of man made to praise God.

On Wednesday, and Thursday, 11th and 12th August, we held five very interesting meetings in Pittsburg. The day meetings were held in the open air, and were very well attended. The evening meetings were held in Temperance Hall, a large room, but by no means sufficient to hold the numbers that pressed to hear.—The door-ways, and windows, and yard of the Hall, were crowded, while many were compelled to leave, without gaining admission to these. Hundreds remained on the outside of the building from an early hour till eleven o'clock at night. What a commentary on the religion of Pittsburg it is, that every church in the place was closed against us. All were too holy in which to plead the cause of our own common humanity. The great Christian cause of the age, like early Christianity itself, is too much despised by the world, to be admitted into the house of God. When saving men in our land, shall have become as popular as killing men now is in Mexico, we shall not only have churches open to our use, but, perhaps, be voted into religious societies as honorary members. In that day, the philanthropic Garrison may possibly be regarded as religious as the pious man-butcher, Zachary Taylor.

On Friday morning, 13th, we took the steamboat Beaver, from Pittsburg to New Brighton—the home of our kind friend, Milo A. Townsend, and our Anti-Slavery poetess, Grace Greenwood. A number of our friends accompanied us from Pittsburg to that place, a goodly number of whom were coloured persons. It is usual to dine on this boat between Pittsburg and Beaver, but on this occasion, strange to tell, no dinner was furnished, for the very American reason, that a goodly number of persons on board were coloured, and it was deemed probable that some of them might presume to dine, and would thus give offence to the white skinned aristocracy. So like the American delegates to the Evangelical Alliance, we concluded to preserve the peace by "going without our dinners."

We held two meetings at New Brighton, afternoon and evening, and here, too, the churches were closed against us, and we were compelled to take an upper room in a flour store. Thus making good the proposition, that humanity is received more cordially in the street than in the church. Our meetings at New Brighton were the last we held in Pennsylvania.

On Saturday, 14th instant, we took a boat on the Beaver and Warren Canal for Youngstown, Ohio, where Messrs. Foster and Walker were advertised to hold a meeting on the 14th, and 15th. On this boat, we received very kind and polite attention, and were allowed to take our meals with the other passengers. The trip from New Brighton to Youngstown, is exceedingly pleasant at this season of the year. The scenery on parts of the Beaver, is quite equal in beauty, if not in grandeur, to the Hudson. The hills on either side are lofty, precipitous, and covered with tall and finely proportioned trees. Verdant fields occasionally intersect the lofty and cragged hills, and form a beautiful variety of scene; now gratifying the eye, and at once leading it on to the discovery of new, and still more interesting points of beauty.

We reached Youngstown on Sunday morning, 15th instant, and were hospitably received by Mr. Andrews, the gentlemanly proprietor of the Youngstown Hotel. This gentleman kindly entertained us free of charge. The meetings in this place, like those held elsewhere on our Western tour, were held in the open air. Seats were arranged, and a platform erected in a beautiful grove, near the village. A good deacon of one of the churches whose doors were shut against us in this place, threatened us with prosecution, if we dared to arrange any seats on the ground during the Sabbath day. The threat, however, had no other effect than to summon a number of friends to the grove early in the morning, to arrange as many seats as might be necessary to accommodate the multitude. The meeting was large and spirited. The churches were all nearly vacated, and a large portion of their congregations came to worship in God's great temple, and to show their love for the All Good by doing good to His children.

Yours, sincerely,
FREDERICK DOUGLASS.[116]

MY DEAR SIR—I am at home again; and, in compliance with your earnest request, avail myself of this, my first opportunity, to send you an article for your gallant little sheet. I have to thank you for the file you sent me on board the 'Hendrick Hudson.' I have given each number a hasty perusal, and have quite satisfied myself that you are on the right ground—of the right spirit—and that you possess the energy of head and of heart to make your paper a powerful instrument in defending, improving, and elevating our brethren in the (so called) free States, as well as hastening the downfall of the fierce and blood-thirsty *evangelical* tyrants in the slave States. Blow away on your 'Ram's Horn'! Its wild, rough, uncultivated notes may grate harshly on the ear of refined and cultivated *chimers;* but sure I am that its voice will be pleasurable to the slave, and terrible to the slaveholder. Let us have a full, clear, shrill, unmistakeable sound. 'No compromise—no concealment'—no lagging for those who tarry—no *'slurs'* for popular favor—no lowering your tone for the sake of harmony. The harmony of this country is discord with the ALMIGHTY. To be in harmony with God is to be in open discord and conflict with the powers of Church and State in this country. Both are drunk on the warm blood of our brethren. 'Blow on—blow on,' and may the God of the oppressed give effect to your blowing.

Through the kindness of a friend, I have before me the 'New-York Sun' of 13th May. It contains a weak, puerile, and characteristic attack upon me, on account of my speech in the Tabernacle, before the American Anti-Slavery Society on the 11th instant. The article in question affords me a text from which I could preach you a long sermon; but I will neither trespass on your space, nor weary the patience of your readers, by treating the article in that way. I do not call attention to it, because I am anxious to defend myself from its malevolent contents, but to congratulate you upon the favorable change in the public mind which it indicates, and to enjoy a little (I trust innocent) sport at the expense of the editor.

We have been laughed at and ridiculed so much, that I am glad, once in a while, to be able to turn the tables on our white brethren. The editor informs his readers, that his object in writing the article is, to protest against 'the unmitigated abuse heaped upon our country by the colored man Douglass.' Now, who will doubt the patriotism of a man who will venture so much on behalf of his country? The Sun is truly a patriot. 'The colored *man* Douglass.' Well done! Not '*nigger*' Douglass—not *black*, but *colored* —not *monkey*, but *man*—the *colored* MAN *Douglass*. This, dear sir, is a decided improvement on the old mode of speaking of us. In the brilliant light of the Sun, I am no longer a *monkey*, but a MAN ——and, henceforth, I may claim to be treated as a man by the 'Sun.' In order to prepare the patient for the pill, and to prove his title to be regarded an unmixed American, he gilds the most bloody and detestable tyranny all over with the most holy and beautiful sentiments of liberty. Hear him—'*Freedom of speech in this country should receive the greatest* LATITUDE.' This sounds well; but is it not a strange text, from which to preach a sermon in favor of putting down freedom of speech by *mob violence?* 'If men do not speak freely of our institutions, how are we to discover their errors or reform their abuses, should any exist?' A pertinent question, truly, and worthy of the thought and study of the profound and philosophical editor of the 'Sun.' But now see a nobler illustration of the story of the 'cow and the milk pail'— blowing hot and blowing cold, and blowing neither hot nor cold. The editor says—'*There is, however, a limit to this very freedom of speech. We cannot be permitted to go into a gentleman's house,*

accept his hospitality, yet ABUSE *his fare, and we have no right to
abuse a country under whose government, we are safely residing
and securely protected.'*

Here we have it, all reasoned out as plain as logic can make it—
the limit of freedom of speech accurately defined. But allow me to
throw a little light upon the Sun's logic—if I can do so without
entirely spoiling his *simile*. Poor thing, it would be a pity to hurt
that. Does it not strike you as being first rate? To my mind, it is
the best thing in the whole piece, and lacks only one thing—(but
this probably makes no difference with the 'Sun'—it may be its
chief merit,) and that is, *likeness*—it lacks likeness. A gentleman's house and the government of this country are wholly dis-
similar. Let me suggest to him—without meaning any disrespect
to you, that a cook shop (a thing which I am surprised he should
ever forget) bears a far greater resemblance to the government of
this country, than that of a gentleman's house and hospitality.
Let cook shop represent Country—'Bill of Fare'—'Bill of Rights;'
and the 'Chief Cook'—Commander-in-Chief.—(I fancy I hear the
editor say, this looks better.) Enters editor of the 'Sun' with a
keen appetite. He reads the bill of fare. It contains the names
of many palatable dishes. He asks the cook for soup, he gets 'dish
water.' For salmon, he gets a serpent; for beef, he gets bull-frogs;
for ducks, he gets dogs; for salt, he gets sand; for pepper, he gets
powder; and for vinegar, he gets gall;—in fact, he gets for you
the very opposite of everything for which you ask, and which from
the bill of fare, and loudmouthed professions, you had a right to
expect. This is just the treatment which the colored people receive in this country at the hand of this government. Its Bill of
Rights is to practise towards us a bill of wrongs. Its self-evident
truths are self-evident lies. Its majestic liberty, malignant tyranny. The foundation of this government—the great Constitution
itself—is nothing more than a compromise with man-stealers, and
a cunningly devised complication of falsehoods, calculated to deceive foreign Nations into a belief that this is a free country; at
the same time that it pledges the whole Civil, Naval and Military
power of the Nation to keep three millions of people in the most
abject slavery. He says I abuse a country under whose government I am safely residing, and securely protected. I am neither
safely residing, nor securely protected in this country. I am living
under a government which authorized Hugh Auld to rob me of

seven hundred and fifty dollars, and told me if I did not submit, if I resisted this robber, I should be put to death. This is the protection given to me, and every other colored man from the South, and no one knows this better than the Editor of the New York Sun. And this piece of robbery, the 'Sun' calls the *rights* of the Master, and says that the English people recognised those rights by giving me money with which to purchase my freedom. The 'Sun' complains that I defend the right of invoking England for the overthrow of American Slavery. Why not receive aid from England to overthrow American Slavery, as well as for Americans to send bread to England to feed the hungry? Answer me that! What would the 'Sun' have said, if the British press had denounced this country for sending a ship-load of grain into Ireland, and denied the right of the American people to sympathize, and succor the afflicted and famine-stricken millions of that unhappy land? What would it have said? Why, it and the whole American Press would have poured forth one flood of unmixed censure and scathing rebuke. England would have been denounced; the British public would have been branded as murderers. And if England had forbidden Captain Forbes to land his cargo, it might have been regarded just cause for war. And yet the interference in the one case is as justifiable as in the other. My Dear Sir, I have already extended this letter to a much greater length than I at first intended, and will now stop by wishing you every success in your noble enterprize.

Ever yours in our righteous cause,

FREDERICK DOUGLASS.[117]

Lynn, Mass. May 18, '47.

My Dear Gay:—I regret that my first letter for the Standard should be such an one as I am now about to write, and that I have to record facts which may create anxiety among the Anti-Slavery friends in the East, on account of the safety of friend Garrison, and myself. We were last night confronted by a most brutal and disgraceful mob—the first fruits of our Western tour, a sort of foretaste of what may await us further West. To the everlasting shame, and infamy of the people of Harrisburg, I record the fact that they are at this moment under the dominion of mob law; that the freedom of speech and the right of peaceably assembling is

[117] *Liberator,* June 4, 1847.

cloven down; and that the officers appointed to preserve order and
to protect the rights and privileges of the people, have basely, by
their indifference, consented to this sacrifice to the Moloch of
Slavery. Let this infernal act of devotion to tyranny be published
and republished at home and abroad, in the New and in the Old
World, that all may learn the true character of American freedom,
and our republican love of law and order. But to the facts.

A meeting was convened in the court house of this town last
night, to hear addresses on Slavery by Mr. Garrison and myself.
At the time appointed Mr. Garrison was present, and commenced
the meeting by a calm statement of facts respecting the character
of Slavery and the slave power, showing in how many ways it was
a matter deeply affecting the rights and interests of the Northern
people. He spoke with little or no interruption for the space of
an hour, and then introduced me to the audience. I spoke only for
a few moments when through the windows was poured a volley of
unmerchantable eggs, scattering the contents on the desk in which
I stood, and upon the wall behind me, and filling the room with
the most disgusting and stifling stench. The audience appeared
alarmed, but disposed to stay, though greatly at the expense of
their olfactory nerves. I, thinking I could stand it as well as my
audience, proceeded with my speech, but in a very few moments
we were interrupted and startled by the explosion of a pack of
crackers, which kept up a noise for about a minute similar to the
discharge of pistols, and being on the ladies' side, created much
excitement and alarm. When this subsided, I again proceeded,
but was at once interrupted again by another volley of addled
eggs, which again scented the house with Slavery's choice incense.
Cayenne pepper and Scotch snuff were freely used, and produced
their natural results among the audience. I proceeded again and
was again interrupted by another grand influx of rotten eggs.
One struck friend Garrison on the back, sprinkling its *essence* all
over his honoured head. At this point a general tumult ensued,
the people in the house became much disturbed and alarmed, and
there was a press toward the doorway, which was completely
wedged with people. The mob was now howling with fiendish
rage. I could occasionally hear amid the tumult, fierce and bloody
cries, "*throw out the nigger*, THROW OUT THE NIGGER." Here
friend Garrison rose, with that calm and tranquil dignity, altogether peculiar to himself, and said—(speaking for himself and

me.) Our mission to Harrisburg is ended. If there be not sufficient love of liberty, and self respect in this place, to protect the
right of assembling, and the freedom of speech, he would not degrade himself by attempting to speak under such circumstances
and he would therefore recall the appointment for Sunday night,
and go where he could be heard. The wise ones knew the meaning
of his speech. They saw that the character of the·town was about
to be consigned to deserved infamy and one of their number, a
thin, delicate looking man rose, much excited. It was Mr. Petrigen,
a private Secretary of the Governor of the State. He said that he
for one, wished to hear Messrs. Garrison and Douglass speak, but
he must defend the character of the people of Harrisburg from
the charge of mobocracy, brought against them by Mr. Garrison.
Nobody was to blame, as nobody could prevent the mob. It consisted of blackguards; the people of Harrisburg had nothing to do
with it, nor could they prevent it, and he hoped that that gentleman (alluding to Mr. Garrison) would not go away and slander
the people by making them responsible for the mob. He would
repeat it, the people had nothing to do with it, and they could not
prevent it. Now all this was saying to the mob—go on, mob on,
there is no power anywhere to prevent you. This infamous incite-
ment to the mob, was nobly rebuked by a gentleman of great respectability of the name of Rawen. He said, he rose to defend
Harrisburg from the charge of incapacity to quell a mob, and protect the right of speech. They could do it, and if they did not do
so, it was because they did not choose to do so. He asked Mr.
Petrigen where was the police? If they had not the power to
disperse a few blackguards and boys? Mr. Garrison again rose
and said, his remarks were entirely hypothetical, and if a meeting
could be conducted with order and propriety he was quite willing
to remain and hold another meeting agreeable to public notice.
In the midst of this discussion there was thrown in another volley
of rotten eggs, and cries of "throw out the nigger, throw out the
nigger," was repeated about the doors and windows of the house.
It was now impossible to proceed with the meeting, and there being
no attempt on the part of anybody to disperse the mob, Mr. Garrison announced the close of the meeting. The audience however
remained for some time. Very few seemed willing to venture out;
the doorway continued crowded and for a long time it was difficult
to pass out at all. The stones now began to fly, a pile of which

had been brought near the door; causing much trepidation for my safety. At this time a white lady kindly offered to walk with me and protect me, from the mob, I felt it best to decline her very disinterested offer, as I had good reason to believe that such an arrangement would exasperate the mob, and only enhance my danger. I finally took the arm of a coloured gentleman, Mr. Wolk, and several coloured friends filling up the rear, we walked out. As soon as I reached the steps I was discovered by the cowardly mob, who from their holes of darkness uttered infernal yells crying out "there he goes, there he goes," and at the same time throwing stones, and brick-bats at me—one went humming by my head and another striking me on the back, but without doing me serious injury. "Give it to him, give it to him," they cried, "let the d—d nigger have it." Two friends behind me received heavy blows, one of them was quite stunned and bruised, but they stood around me and received the blows intended for me. I very soon succeeded in disengaging myself from the crowd and by turning a corner I succeeded in very soon eluding my pursuers, and thus saved myself. All credit is due to a few coloured friends who seemed willing and glad to be ramparts for me and to receive all the blows intended for me. Mr. Garrison was not discovered by the mob. My coming out first drew off the mob from the door before he came out. I am happy to find he received no blows except the eggs, the stench of which was bad enough. Comment here, is unnecessary, the atrocious character of the proceedings is sufficiently palpable, and Harrisburg one day will be ashamed of it.

Friend Garrison and myself leave here to-morrow morning for Pittsburg, where we hope to meet with a more cordial welcome. In great haste, very sincerely yours,

FREDERICK DOUGLASS.[118]

LYNN, July 18, 1847.

MY DEAR FRIEND.:

I have observed in the Liberator, of the two past weeks, with considerable surprise and much regret, that the conclusion to which I have come, with respect to publishing, *at present,* an anti-slavery newspaper, has very unwisely and unnecessarily been made the occasion of attack upon yourself, and of most unkind, uncharitable

118 *The National Anti-Slavery Standard,* Aug. 19, 1847.

and unjust imputations on the motives of leading friends of the cause in Boston. The parties engaged in this work of mischief imagine me hemmed in on every side—overpowered—and my will completely subjected to the Boston Board—and direct their efforts for my deliverance from thraldom, without stopping to inquire as to the correctness of their conjectures. This is absolutely grievous; and I feel it due to yourself and friends, and all concerned, to say at once, distinctly and publicly, that, in this matter, I have acted independently, and wholly on my own responsibility.

Yours, sincerely,

FREDERICK DOUGLASS.

Wm. Lloyd Garrison.

☞ This letter of Mr. Douglass is a sufficient reply to the unjust insinuations and impertinent remarks which have been made in certain quarters, in regard to the relinquishment of his original design to establish a newspaper on his return home, as contemplated by him in England, and approved of by his numerous friends abroad; on the supposition, however, that the enterprise would be *sui generis*, as well as serviceable to the anti-slavery cause, in this country. Those professed friends, who are so determined that he shall alter the decision to which he has come, and who do not scruple to malign those whose judgment on this point is not in accordance with their own, pay him a very poor compliment, in representing him to be without independence of judgment or freedom of action, and under the control of a few individuals in Boston, actuated by narrow or mercenary views. If this is their opinion of his stability of character, how they can regard him as fit to be entrusted with the management of a press, that shall reflect credit upon himself, and be distinguished for its efficiency, is more than we can comprehend. From all such friends, he may reasonably pray to be saved, while he is abundantly able to take care of his enemies.

The *Chronotype* has basely insinuated, that Mr. Douglass has been persuaded to abandon his intention, lest his paper should 'injure the circulation of two anti-slavery papers, [meaning, unquestionably, the Anti-Slavery Standard and the Liberator,] conducted by white men.' What special good-will the editor of that paper cherishes toward genuine, unswerving abolitionism, the

American A. S. Society, or Mr. Douglass as the advocate and representative of that Society, we have yet to learn. Advice from such a quarter is to be regarded with lively suspicion, and as of very doubtful value, to say the least. We have no desire to renew an old controversy, which will ever constitute a most instructive chapter in the history of the anti-slavery movement; but when an individual, who did what he could to divide our ranks, and who seceded from us to assist in building up a hostile organization, and who from that hour to the present has manifested an alien spirit, comes forward in the garb of disinterested friendship to counsel Mr. Douglass not to regard either his own convictions, or the opinions of his long-tried and faithful friends, as to the best manner of aiding our cause, it is time for him to be reminded that his old transgressions are not forgotten, and that he is not exactly qualified to be listened to as an impartial witness in the case, especially by those whom he has betrayed. It is an old device of an enemy, to attempt to excite suspicions and jealousies among attached friends, with the hope of causing a breach between them.

The next person who exhibited symptoms of dissatisfaction with the decision of Mr. Douglass, was an anonymous correspondent of the Liberator, signing himself '*Libertas.*' If he is a special friend of Mr. D., or one who has long and actively labored in our ranks, we see no reason why he should keep in the dark, or proffer his advice under a fictitious signature. He, too, charitably took up the fling of the *Chronotype,* and intimated that a selfish fear lest the circulation of certain papers might be abridged, in case the journal by Mr. Douglass should be commenced, may have induced the advice that has been given to Mr. D.

The last who has expressed his dissent is one of our subscribers at Mansfield, whose communication on the subject we published last week with his name appended to it, and who has sent us another one, the publication of which is rendered unnecessary by the letter of Mr. Douglass. To the low imputation cast upon us and others, by the *Chronotype* and *Libertas,* we declined to make any reply. Why we did so, our Mansfield correspondent says he is unable to understand. Indeed! If he does not regard us as being influenced by selfish considerations, then he ought to know that conscious integrity and due self-respect alike forbid our giving any heed to a charge so grovelling and unfounded, proceeding from such sources, and elicited under such circumstances. If he supposes us actuated by such considerations, then we have nothing to offer to convince him that we are not of a despicable spirit.

As to the circulation of the Liberator, how to extend it, or how to prevent its being extremely limited, while under our control, we have never yet studied any policy about it.   Although we are now, and always have been since its commencement, dependant upon its subscription list for subsistence, with such aid as a friendly spirit has from time to time rendered *impromptu* to keep it from extinction, we have had in view but one purpose,—the free, untrammelled utterance of our thoughts, at whatever cost, and the faithful advocacy of the cause of the imbruted slave.   There is not another journal in the United States so widely unpopular, and so much denounced by the corrupt and tyrannical, as the Liberator; and yet we might, if we chose, greatly increase the number of its patrons, and make it an acceptable journal to the public, and elicit in its behalf general commendation,—*if* we would only be governed by policy instead of principle, and cease arraigning the people for their sins.

It should be recollected that those friends in England, who desired to give to Mr. Douglass a substantial token of their regard, were led to decide upon the presentation of a printing-press to him, solely at his own suggestion; and that he made the suggestion for the reasons he has already given to the public, through the medium of the Liberator.   Instead of dreaming that he should find, on his return home, no less than four newspapers published and edited by colored persons, he expected to find the field entirely unoccupied. With this impression, it is not surprising that the philanthropic contributors abroad should deem it an excellent project to place Douglass at the head of a newspaper, to convince those, who are still inclined to disparage the intellect of the colored race, that they are governed by an unreasonable prejudice.   Probably, they were generally ignorant of the fact, that, within the last fifteen years, several journals of this character, such as 'The Colored American' in New-York, and 'The Elevator' in Philadelphia, had been published; so that *the day has long since gone by* for the people of this country to be surprised at the appearance of a periodical, edited with ability by a man of color.

Our Mansfield correspondent says that not one of the four newspapers now published by colored men is located in New England; and hence he thinks there is ample scope for another to be conducted by Mr. Douglass. In his opinion, it would have an immense circulation; and though he seems inclined to believe it would speedily close the existence of the Liberator and Emancipator, (which papers, he says, 'have had their day, and can no longer arouse the mass of the community to action,') he is equally sanguine that it would as speedily put an end to slavery. Indeed, he gravely asks us, as though it were a certain event, whether we ought not to be willing to have the slave system smitten to the dust by this sumrinary process, rather than to insist on the preservation of the Standard and Liberator as of paramount importance! Our friend is highly imaginative, and he finds no difficulty whatever in securing for the contemplated journal unprecedented patronage, and in clothing Mr. Douglass with Jove-like power to destroy with his thunderbolts the demon slavery, by a single discharge.

Now, we have not been slow to perceive, nor backward to acknowledge, the genius and talent of our friend Douglass; and we have no doubt that, as the editor of a newspaper, he would be in a situation to bring credit to himself, and to exert a good influence. But we are not very sanguine as to the amount of patronage he would obtain, and permanently secure, for his journal. It is true, that his case is a somewhat peculiar one, and that circumstances have occurred to render him an object of special interest, both at home and abroad. But it is dangerous to build upon novelty, or popular curiosity. This is capricious, volatile, evanescent. We claim to have some practical acquaintance of twenty years with the difficulties and perplexities to be encountered by every one, no matter how brilliant his talents, who attempts to launch a reformatory journal on the sea of popular conflict. It would not be in the power of Gabriel himself to obtain much patronage or applause as an editor, if he were faithful to his trust, and utterly indifferent to the length of his subscription list.

It may be, that the Standard and Liberator would obtain a wider circulation, if they were conducted with more ability; but we suspect that no additional amount of genius or talent infused into their columns would essentially augment their income, so long as they continued to enunciate the same unpalatable truths, and maintain the same 'ultra' positions, that they now do. Now, a paper edited by Mr. Douglass would be scarcely less objectionable to the public, in its advocacy of the anti-slavery cause, than the Standard or Liberator. Who, then, would be eager to give it their support?

The Whigs? But it would sternly reprobate the course pursued by them as a party. The Democrats? But they would find in its columns, the most scorching reproofs of their bastard democracy. The adherents of the Liberty party? But it would reprobate that party as an obstacle to the spread of genuine abolitionism. The personal friends of Mr. Douglass, and those who go for 'ultra' reform? Doubtless, to them, chiefly, would he be compelled to look for encouragement; nor would he look in vain. But, with the many heavy burdens already imposed upon them by the exigencies of the times, their support would be necessarily partial, and, it is to be apprehended, inadequate. It is absurd to suppose that his attacks upon Church and State, and his denunciations of the American Constitution and Union, and his castigations of the existing political parties, would be tolerated, nay, approved, on account of the color of his skin, any more than those of the editor of the Standard or the Liberator.

Will it be said, that the friends in England would ensure success to the enterprise by their subscriptions? We do not underrate their willingness to extend their assistance in this manner; but, if they should give the press and printing materials, it would hardly be just, and certainly would not be in accordance with their expectations, to tell them that they must also furnish a large portion of the subscribers. The truth is, much as very many persons in England desire to receive American papers in which they feel a special interest, with the present high rates of postage they are generally debarred from gratifying their wishes. Had it not been for this excessive tax, we might have easily procured many subscribers for the Liberator during our mission abroad. It would operate against a paper published by Mr. Douglass, if not to the same extent, at least so far as to make the number of permanent subscribers comparatively small.

It may be said that the free colored population of the North could easily sustain such a paper, without any co-operation on the part of their white friends. Yes, they could, if they would! But what are the probabilities in this case?

In the first place, all past experiments have failed through their apathy, or lack of union, or want of a just appreciation of the value of a press consecrated to the assertion of their rights. This is not conclusive, but admonitory.

In the second place, four papers are now struggling for existence among them; and, for the time being, what patronage they can give has been solicited for these, and to some extent secured.

In the third place, Mr. Douglass has no special influence over them; nor would the doctrines he would feel compelled to enunciate be any more palatable to them, than those which they are unable to understand or to practice, as set forth in other anti-slavery periodicals. The fact of his complexional identity with them would scarce have the weight of a feather in the scale; for the color of a man's skin is with them a matter of trifling importance, and very justly too!

In the fourth place, the anti-slavery struggle has almost wholly transcended them as a distinct class, and thus demonstrated the sublime fact, that it is not a struggle in behalf of the black man, but of MAN as such. Many of them are politicians, like the whites —Whigs, Democrats, Liberty men, &c. &c. Ask them to sacrifice their party predilections, to disfranchise themselves under this government for conscience sake, to practically endorse the doctrine of 'no union with slaveholders,' in order that the props which sustain the huge system of slavery may be cast down, and they are as reluctant to do so as the white electors. A still larger number of them are connected with pro-slavery churches, either directly or indirectly, but most inconsistently and injuriously. Enforce upon them the duty of separation, 'come-outism,' and they cling as tenaciously to their church relationship as the whites. As a body, they are much priest-ridden; and those who ride them will have no motive to induce them to subscribe for any paper that will advocate their religious freedom and independence.

In the last place, whatever patronage they might be prompted to extend to a paper edited by Mr. Douglass, would be of very uncertain duration. They now find so many to advocate their cause, they feel no particular interest in any periodical. Certainly, by all the remembrances of 'auld lang syne,' if there were any paper, one might suppose, that they would continue to cherish and support, it would be the Liberator—the paper which has stood foremost in their behalf, and never compromised their cause to the breadth of a hair—the paper which has confessedly shaken slavery to its foundation, frustrated the plot of African colonization, and rallied around their standard a strong and invincible host. But how stands the account? We state the fact, not by way of complaint, but simply of illustration. For some time after the Liberator commenced, and while it was battling single-handed against the enemies of freedom, we had four hundred subscribers among the free colored population in the city of New York, and as large a number in Philadelphia. Now they do not take a dozen copies in either city. If this striking disparity is not very creditable to them —and we are constrained to say that we hardly think it is—still, there are many reasons (some of them very good ones) why they have ceased to feel that lively interest in us personally, and in the Liberator, that they once manifested. Among these, prominently, is the multiplication of anti-slavery advocates and presses. Hence, we argue, that to add one more press to the number, even though it is to be conducted by our gifted friend Douglass, would not, in all probability, be very likely to secure much support from them.

It was a knowledge of facts like these, that led us carefully to weigh the proposition for establishing a newspaper, at the present time, by Frederick Douglass; and that brought us to the conclusion, that it would be wise in him to defer the risk and the drudgery of such a task, and to give himself unreservedly to the great and successful work of addressing the multitudes who are every where eager to hear his eloquent and triumphant appeals.

We have had too much experience in the printing business, and in editing a newspaper, not to know how difficult it is for any man, destitute of capital, to place a new journal upon a solid foundation, even if its object be not to conflict with the religion and politics of the times for being in league with tyranny. Thousands have made the attempt, sanguine of success, but the result has been disastrous. The land is full of the wrecks of such experiments. But an 'ultra' reformatory journal is the last to receive a living patronage, however ably conducted. Besides, it is not every one who has talents, even if they are of a high order, who can successfully edit a newspaper. Of those who attempt to fill the editorial station, a large majority prove themselves to have mistaken their vocation. We have known men eminent for scholarship and literary ability, who were unable to make an interesting journal, for lack of experience, judgment and *tact*. It can be affirmed of no one, positively, in advance, that he will make a capital editor. The result may be successful, or signally abortive. We have no doubt that Mr. Douglass would display much editorial ability, but the experiment remains to be made. Of one thing, we and his friends are certain: as a lecturer, his power over a public assembly is very great, and it is manifestly his gift to address the people *en masse*. With such powers of oratory, and so few lecturers in the field where so many are needed, it seems to us as clear as the noon-day sun, that it would be no gain, but rather a loss, to the anti-slavery cause, to have him withdrawn to any considerable extent from the work of popular agitation, by assuming the cares, drudgery and perplexities of a publishing life. It is quite impracticable to combine the editor with the lecturer, without either causing the paper to be more or less neglected, or the sphere of lecturing to be seriously circumscribed.[119]

AUSTINBURG, September, 1847.

The infernal system of Slavery is receiving a powerful shock in the West. The enthusiasm of our friends is unequalled. I am informed, on all sides, that the meetings now being held, are such as were never held before. The whole Western Reserve is now in a healthy state of Anti-Slavery agitation. The theme is on every lip, and is spreading far and wide. We are having a real Anti-Slavery revival. The most astonishing crowds flock to hear, and, I trust, to believe. Opposition to our holy cause seems stunned. Scarce a head is seen above the multitude to oppose the triumphant success of our glorious enterprise. The power of Church and State are shaken. The pro-slavery priesthood look woful as they behold their glory departing. The people are fired with a noble indignation against a slaveholding Church, and filled with unutterable loathing of a slave-trading religion. The real character of our Government is being exposed. The flimsy arguments with which our Liberty party friends have attempted to make out a case of Anti-Slavery for the Constitution are blown into fragments.—The present administration is justly regarded as a combination of land-pirates and free-booters. Our *gallant* army in Mexico is looked upon as a band of legalized murderers and plunderers. Our psalm-singing, praying, pro-slavery priesthood are stamped with hypocrisy; and all their pretensions to a love for God, while they hate and neglect their fellow-man, is branded as impudent blasphemy. The fire is lighted,—let it rise—let it spread. Let the winds of an approving Heaven fan it, and, guided by the hand that stays the thunder-bolt, and directs the storm, its holy flames shall burn up, and utterly consume the last vestige of tyranny in our land. The

[119] *Liberator*, July 23, 1847.

West is decidedly the best Anti-Slavery field in the country.—The people are more disposed to hear—less confined and narrowed in their views, and less circumscribed in their action by sectarian trammels, than are the people of the East. I seriously believe, had we the means to follow up the agitation already commenced in this State for six months, twelve months would not pass, ere every black law which now disgraces the statute-books of Ohio would be repealed, and the free coloured people stand on as good a footing as that enjoyed by the coloured people of Massachusetts. The field here is truly ripe for the harvest, and my spirit is only cast down when I remember how few there are to labour in this part of our vineyard. With money and right-minded men we could place Ohio in advance of Massachusetts in twelve months. The people of this vast State are now ready to hear, believe, and act, but how can they hear without a preacher? We have now five lecturing agents in this field, besides Messrs. Foster, Garrison and myself; we are all labouring ardently, but we are few when you consider the vastness of the field and the readiness to hear on the subject.

I meant ere this to have sent you a hasty sketch of the character and proceedings of the Anniversary Meeting of the Western Anti-Slavery Society, but have been so hurried and driven by appointments, and so completely occupied with immediate and indispensable duties, as to make attention to this impossible. I have attended many Anti-Slavery meetings in the East, and in the West, but this exceeded, by far, any which I ever attended. It will long be remembered as one of the most interesting gatherings ever summoned at the bugle call of liberty. The presence of friends Garrison and Foster did much to give a zest and glory to the occasion, but added to these we had our cause pleaded by the magic eloquence of Music. The charms of liberty were set forth in song by the "Cowles family" of Austinburg, and greatly was the cause enhanced by their efforts. I shall never forget the impression made upon the audience by the first song. Four thousand persons stood charmed, and overcome by the melting melody of our friends; there was scarcely a dry eye among the vast audience, and all hearts seemed melted into one. The meeting was held three days, and was full of interest to the last. The first day was rather unpropitious, the weather being uncomfortably cold and cloudy, but the second and third were fine, clear, bright, warm, and beautiful. The heavens above and the earth below smiled naturally and lov-

ingly upon our philanthropic gathering, and added their beauty
and splendour to the scene, making the whole "superb and glorious." The meeting was held in what is extensively known in this
region as the great "Oberlin Tent." Some idea of its greatness
may be learned by the fact that it will hold five thousand persons.
This portable "Fanuil Hall" was spread out in an open field near
the main road through Lyme, and for three days was the scene of
more human life than has been witnessed in these regions since the
days of "hard Cider and Coonskins." Besides the thousands who
crowded to hear on the subject of Slavery, there were hundreds
who came from curiosity to see the crowd, and many for purposes
of gain. Those who came for gain had their booths, and tents, and
covered wagons, pitched all around us. There was a constant auc-
tioneering going on without, while our meetings were going on
within. In this respect our meeting resembled more the great political gatherings of the day than our usual Anti-Slavery meetings,
except that our meeting was more orderly than they. It was pleasant to see our cause *look* popular for once. Too much praise cannot
be bestowed upon the Anti-Slavery friends in New Lyme. Their
industry, and hospitality were abundant and soul-cheering. You
will be pleased to know that the women of the place took an active
and intelligent interest in the meeting, and in the cause. When in
the West four years ago, the lack of interest on the part of the
women was, (you will remember,) the most painful part of our
experience. I have observed that where an interest is taken in this
subject there is more intellectual life and vigour among women,
and much more happiness. Anti-Slavery is doing much here for
the elevation and improvement of woman. The political Anti-
Slavery meetings, are generally regarded as meetings with which
women have nothing to do, and they can do little or nothing toward
quickening their energies or expanding their intellects. On this
occasion the *women* held Anti-Slavery fairs, and though little was
realized, it was not for want of persevering effort. There was one
mistake on their part which caused a failure, but it was a mistake
on the side of liberty. They admitted all persons free of charge;
and curiosity being on tiptoe, the room was so crowded with spectators that no room was left for buyers. Not one half of the useful
and beautiful articles brought together were sold. They intend
holding another in a few days at Ravenna, where I presume they
will profit by their experience at New Lyme. The leading lady of

this Bazaar movement, is well entitled to be called the Mrs. Chapman of the West. I think she will eventually be quite as successful. She is young in the cause but thoroughly devoted to it. She became deeply interested in the movement by the noble efforts of that faithful, eloquent, and intrepid advocate of the fettered bondman, Abby Kelley Foster. To this friend of God and man, the praise belongs of giving to the West, and to the cause, another Maria Weston Chapman.

Since the anniversary, we have held large meetings at Painsville, Munson, Twinsburg, Oberlin, Richfield, and Medina. All the meetings have been well attended, but those of Munson, and Richfield may be called monster meetings, numbering from three to six thousand. At all of these meetings, aside from the Anti-Slavery speeches, and the good resulting from them, a great deal of practical work has been done. No opportunity is missed to get in our publications, a great many useful books are sold, and subscribers to our papers obtained. We have done but little yet for the Standard or Liberator, as our efforts have been mainly directed to the support of the Bugle. We go to Massillon to-morrow.[120]

CLEVELAND, (O.) September 17, 1847.

MY DEAR FRIEND:—Mr. Garrison and myself are still pursuing our Western course, and steadily persevering (though much worn with our labours) in the fulfilment of our appointments, which are only like angels visits in that they are "far between." Our industrious and devoted friend, the general agent, in making our appointments thus far, has studied more the wants of the cause than the weakness of our frames. We have an appointment for every day, and some of these are thirty and forty miles apart. I know that these distances will appear quite paltry to our Eastern friends, in the land of railroads and steamboats. But as the Rev. Bishop Meade says, in his celebrated sermon, on reconciling slaves to *evangelical floggings*, "if you consider it right you must needs think otherwise of it." We are carried by horses, fed with corn instead of fire—bone instead of iron. And you know, as said a certain rather windy orator, when a locomotive passed the house in which he was holding forth, and completely drowned his voice, *"wind must yield to the superiority of steam."* We have any number of railroads, but they are quite similar to those you passed over four

[120] *The National Anti-Slavery Standard*, Sept. 9, 1847.

years ago, during the ever memorable "One Hundred Conventions." The mention of these conventions will be sufficient to initiate you into some of the hardships of our journey.

The enthusiasm of our friends, out here, is glorious.—They cannot wait for our arrival into their towns, but come twenty, thirty, and even forty miles, with their own teams, to meet us. They generally commence their kind communications to us by giving us some idea of the great importance of their locality, and of the importance of being promptly on the ground, and occupying every available moment in the propagation of our principles and measures; and when we are about to leave we are sympathetically informed, sometimes by the same persons, that we are fast wearing ourselves out, and that we ought to stay a day or two longer, omitting some appointment ahead, and thus secure time for necessary rest. These speeches, though somewhat inconsistent, are the natural outpourings of kind hearts. Thus far, we have resisted this sort of eloquence, and fulfilled all our appointments. Since the meetings at Medina and Richfield, of both which I believe you have been informed, we have held four meetings at Massillon and four at Leesburgh. Our meetings in these places were not so large as those held in other parts of this State, yet they would appear large in any part of New-York or New England.

This State is very justly called the giant of the West. Everything connected with it is on the most gigantic scale. She is a giant in population, in energy, and in improvement. She possesses, too, those moral elements of greatness which might easily make her the pioneer State, in resisting, successfully, the aggressions of Slavery on the North, and leading the way to the redemption of millions in the South. Her contiguity to a slave State gives her many advantages over States more removed from Slavery. Ohio may, if she will, abolish Slavery in Kentucky, and Western Virginia. At present her hands are tied,—the fetters of Slavery are on her giant limbs,—she is corrupted by Slavery. The moral pestilence that walketh in darkness along her southern border, has spread blight and mildew over her legislation. Her statute-book is polluted,—she is disgraced by her villainous black laws. Let her repeal those infernal laws—blot them forever from her statute-book, and thus cease to afford impunity to every white ruffian who may desire to insult, or plunder, who may desire to rob, or commit other outrages on her coloured population, and her power to do good would become apparent, and her moral greatness would be equal to her numerical and political strength. Till this is done, she is not in a position to exert much moral influence on the South. Before she can ask freedom for the coloured man of Kentucky, she must do justice to the black man of Ohio.

You are aware that what are called the black laws of this State, disallow and prohibit the testimony of coloured persons against white persons in courts of law. By this diabolical arrangement, law, as a means of protecting the property and persons of the weak, becomes meaningless, since it gives a "Thug" commission to any and every white villain, and permits them to insult, cheat, and plunder coloured persons with the utmost impunity. A score of facts might be mentioned of cases where persons having the fortune to have a white skin, have, in the presence of coloured persons, taken away their property without remuneration, and the guilty persons could not be brought to condign punishment, because their victims were black.

These shameful laws are not the natural expression of the moral sentiment of Ohio, but the servile work of pandering politicians, who, to conciliate the favour of slaveholders, and win their way into political power, have enacted these infernal laws. Let the people of Ohio demand their instant repeal, and the complete enfranchisement of her coloured people, and their gallant State would speedily become the paragon of all the free States, securing the gratitude and love of her coloured citizens, and wiping out a most foul imputation from the character of her white citizens. She might then well boast that *justice* within her borders, like its author in Heaven, is without respect to persons. I may mention that our friends here have it in contemplation to get up an agitation this winter, against those laws, which it is hoped will end in their repeal. Should they succeed, a staggering blow will be given to Slavery in Kentucky. The slaveholders will begin to feel that the North is fast combining against them, and must soon make their calling a bye-word and a hissing throughout all the land. Should Ohio take the step, Indiana may follow; this done and Kentucky is forsaken. The work must be done soon, or the moral effect will be lost; for the time is coming, when it will be but small work to repeal such laws, even in the slave States. The power to do good, if not soon embraced, must soon be taken from the North.

Since the above was written, we have held meetings at Salem,

New Lisbon, Ravenna, Warren, and Cleveland. Our meeting at
Salem was a great one—in some respects the greatest of the series.
It was held two days, commencing Saturday morning, and con-
tinuing till late Sunday afternoon, deepening in interest to the last.
In addition to the lofty appeals and powerful eloquence of Messrs.
Garrison and Foster, we had with us, James and Lucretia Mott.
I have never seen Mrs. Mott under more favourable circumstances.
It was admirable to see her rise up in all her elegance and dignity
of womanhood—her earnest but tranquil countenance, overshadowed and animated with the inspiration of sincere benevolence—at
once arresting attention, dispelling prejudice, and commanding the
entire respect of the assembled thousands. A slight pause, and all
eyes are fixed, and all ears turned—a deep stillness pervades the
audience, and her silvery voice, without effort or vehemence, is distinctly heard, even far beyond the vast multitude. Her truthful
words came down upon the audience like great drops of summer
rain upon parched ground. Mrs. Mott attended the meetings at
Warren, Ravenna, and New Lisbon, and greatly added to the interest of the meetings in all these places. She parted with us at
Ravenna, and pursued her course toward Indiana, where she is
intending to hold religious meetings. Our meetings in this place
have been well attended, and exceedingly spirited, and nothing occurred (as we somewhat feared from intimations thrown out in the
Plaindealer) to mar the harmony and beauty of the occasion.

We shall leave here this morning for Buffalo, N. Y. where our
next meeting is to be held. But one hasty word before we leave,
with respect to western hospitality. Our tour thus far has been
made very agreeable and happy by the noble generosity, and the
kind and affable deportment of all with whom we have come in
contact. There is nothing mean, narrow, or churlish about a true
Buckeye—find him where or how you will, rich or poor, in a
miserable log cabin, or a magnificent mansion, he is the same open,
free, and truly generous man. Agreeing with or differing from
you, of the same religious faith and politics, or differing from you
in both, it makes no difference. Once make him feel you are an
honest man and you are welcomed with all the fullness of genuine
hospitality, to his heart and his home.

> "I ask not for his lineage
> I ask not for his birth
> If the stream be pure what matters it,
> The source from which it burst."

Since we have been in this State, we have been as warmly welcomed and as cordially received at the homes of Liberty party men, as by Old Organizationists; and so may I say of Whigs, and sometimes Democrats. And in no case was there unfaithfulness or shunning to declare the whole truth, with reference to each and all these parties.   F. D.[121]

From the *North Star*.

TO H. G. WARNER, ESQ., (EDITOR OF THE ROCHESTER COURIER.)

Sir:—My reasons—I will not say my apology, for addressing to you this letter, will become evident, by perusing the following brief statement of facts.

About the middle of August of the present year—deeply desiring to give my daughter, a child between nine and ten years old, the advantages of a good school—and learning that 'Seward Seminary' of this city was an institution of that character—I applied to its principal, Miss Tracy, for the admission of my daughter into that Seminary. The principal—after making suitable enquiries into the child's mental qualifications, and informing me of the price of tuition per term, agreed to receive the child into the school at the commencement of the September term. Here we parted. I went home, rejoicing that my child was about to enjoy advantages for improving her mind, and fitting her for a useful and honorable life. I supposed that the principal would be as good as her word—and was more disposed to this belief when I learned that she was an abolitionist—a woman of religious principles and integrity—and would be faithful in the performance of her promises, as she had been prompt in making them. In all this I have been grievously—if not shamefully disappointed.

While absent from home, on a visit to Cleveland, with a view to advance the cause of education and freedom among my despised fellow countrymen—with whom I am in all respects identified, the September term of the 'Seward Seminary' commenced, and my daughter was promptly sent to that school. But instead of receiving her into the school according to agreement—and as in honor the principal was bound to do, she was merely thrust into a room separate from all other scholars, and in this prison-like solitary confinement received the occasional visits of a teacher appointed to

[121] *National Anti-Slavery Standard*, Sept. 23, 1847.

instruct her. On my return home, I found her still going to school, and not knowing the character of the treatment extended to her, I asked with a light heart, as I took her to my side, well my daughter, how do you get on at the Seminary? She answered with tears in her eyes, '*I get along pretty well, but father, Miss Tracy does not allow me to go into the room with the other scholars because I am colored.*' Stung to the heart's core by this grievous statement, and suppressing my feelings as well as I could, I went immediately to the Seminary to remonstrate with the principal against the cruelty and injustice of treating my child as a criminal on account of her color—subjecting her to solitary confinement because guilty of a skin not colored like her own. In answer to all that I could say against such treatment, I was answered by the principal, that since she promised to receive the child into school, she had consulted with the trustees, (a body of persons I believe unknown to the public,) and that they were opposed to the child's admission to the school—that she thought at first of disregarding their opposition, but when she remembered how much they had done for her in sustaining the institution, she did not feel at liberty to do so; but she thought if I allowed her to remain and be taught separately for a term or more, that the prejudice might be overcome, and the child admitted into the school with the other young ladies and misses. At a loss to know what to do for the best interest of the child, I consulted with Mrs. Douglass and others, and the result of the consultation was, to take my child from the Seminary, as allowing her to remain there in such circumstances, could only serve to degrade her in her own eyes, and those of the other scholars attending the school. Before, however, carrying out my determination to withdraw the child from the Seminary, Miss Tracy, the principal, submitted the question of the child's reception to each scholar individually, and I am sorry to say, in a manner well calculated to rouse their prejudices against her. She told them if there was one objection to receiving her, she should be excluded; and said if any of them felt that she had a prejudice, and that that prejudice needed to be strengthened, that they might have time to whisper among themselves, in order to increase and strengthen that prejudice. To one young lady who voted to receive the child, she said, as if in astonishment; 'did you mean to vote so? Are you *accustomed* to black persons?' The young lady stood silent; the question was so extraordinary, and withal so ambiguous, that she knew not what answer to make to it. Despite, however, of the unwomanly conduct of the principal, (who, whatever may be her religious faith, has not yet learned the simplest principle of Christianity—do to others as ye would that others should do unto you)—thanks to the uncorruptible virtue of childhood and youth, in the fulness of their affectionate hearts, they welcomed my child among them, to share with them the blessings and privileges of the school; and when asked where she should sit if admitted, several young ladies shouted 'By me, by me, by me.' After this manifestation of sentiment on the part of the scholars, one would have supposed that all opposition on the part of the principal would have ceased; but this was not the case. The child's admission was subjected to a severer test. Each scholar was then told by the principal, that the question must be submitted to their parents, that if one parent objected, the child would not be received into the school. The next morning, my child went to school as usual, but returned with her books and other materials, saying that one person objected, and that she was therefore excluded from the Seminary.

Now, sir, these are the whole facts, with one important exception, and that fact is, that you are the person, the only person of all the parents sending young ladies and misses to that Seminary, who was hardened and mean enough to take the responsibility of excluding that child from school. I say, to you exclusively belongs the honor or infamy, of attempting to degrade an innocent child by excluding her from the benefit of attending a respectable school.

If this were a private affair, only affecting myself and family, I should possibly allow it to pass without attracting public attention to it; but such is not the case. It is a deliberate attempt to degrade and injure a large class of persons, whose rights and feelings have been the common sport of yourself, and such persons as yourself, for ages, and I think it unwise to allow you to do so with impunity. Thank God, oppressed and plundered as we are and have been, we are not without help. We have a press, open and free, and have ample means by which we are able to proclaim our wrongs as a people, and your own infamy, and that proclamation shall be as complete as the means in my power can make it. There is a sufficient amount of liberality in the public mind of Rochester to see that justice is done to all parties, and upon that liberality I rely. The young ladies of the school who saw the child, and had the best means of determining whether her presence in the schoolroom would be offensive or degrading to them, have decided in favor of admitting her, without a dissenting vote. Out of all the parents to whom the question of her admission was submitted, not one, excepting yourself, objected. You are in a minority of *one*. You may not remain so; there are perhaps others, whom you may corrupt, and make as much like yourself in the blindness of prejudice, as any ordinarily wicked person can be.

But you are still in a minority, and if I mistake not, you will be in a *despised minority*. You have already done serious injury to Seward Seminary. Three young ladies left the school immediately after the exclusion of my daughter, and I have heard of three more, who had intended to go, but who have now declined going to that institution, because it has given its sanction to that anti-democratic, and ungodly caste. I am also glad to inform you that you have not succeeded as you hoped to do, in depriving my child of the means of a decent education, or the privilege of going to an excellent school. She had not been excluded from Seward Seminary five hours, before she was welcomed into another quite as respectable, and *equally* Christian to the one from which she was excluded. She now sits in a school among children as pure, and as white as you or yours, and no one is offended. Now I should like to know how much better are you than me, and how much better your children than mine? We are both worms of the dust, and our children are like us. We differ in color, it is true, (and not much in that respect,) but who is to decide which color is most pleasing to God, or most honorable among men? But I do not wish to waste words or argument on one whom I take to be as destitute of honorable feeling, as he has shown himself full of pride and prejudice.

FREDERICK DOUGLASS.[122]

ROCHESTER, June 7, 1851.

GENTLEMEN:

I am deeply sensible of the honor you have done me, by inviting me to join you, in the token of respect to George Thompson you propose to give in Boston, on the eve of his departure from the United States to his native land. To participate, how humbly soever, in such a demonstration, would afford me sincere pleasure. But I cannot be present, and I much regret that I cannot.

[122] *Liberator*, Oct. 6, 1848.

In common with all the sable sons of America, I owe George Thompson a mighty debt of gratitude, respect and love. His labors in behalf of my afflicted, enslaved and plundered people have been productive of good, to an extent which eternity alone can fully disclose. My heart grows warm at the mention of his name. That name is associated in my mind with the names of the noblest benefactors of suffering man. There were two courses plainly set before George Thompson, when he landed on the shores of this republic, in the autumn of 1850. He was a free man. He was not compelled to adopt any given course. There are men, many of them, who seem doomed, by virtue of their very organization, to a limited and contracted sphere of action. In them the ability to wish is present, but the ability to do is absent. George Thompson belongs not to this class. Long before he came to this country, his philanthropy, zeal, industry, and splendid genius, rendered him before the whole civilized world a light of surprising brightness—a gem greatly to be coveted—a prize worth securing.

Wealth, honor and ease invited him to their sumptuous entertainments, only asking as a condition that he should array himself in the smooth garments of worldly prudence. Had he complied, instead of being assailed, maligned, calumniated, mobbed and threatened with assassination, as he has been, he would have been welcomed, applauded, caressed, and hailed every where as a distinguished guest from one end of this Union to the other. His early anti-slavery sentiments would have been charitably forgiven—as those of Theobold Mathew and Daniel Webster have been—and his course might have been one series of brilliant demonstrations. But George Thompson had a heart—he saw the poor, weak, emaciated bondmen in chains—his heart was touched by the mournful wail; wealth, luxury and ease lost their gilded charms; he turned his back upon the scorner, and his face to the despised, and generously gave himself to toil. With the disinterested spirit of the Israelitish deliverer, he preferred to suffer affliction with the people of God, to enjoying the pleasures of sin for a season.

Honor him who is an honor to humanity. He is a man of many millions. We do not often meet his like—a miracle of true courage—daunted by no danger—disheartened by no opposition—a moral hero, not less than an intellectual giant, whom all the reproaches of a mighty nation have been unable to silence or subdue.

God bless George Thompson! and methinks I hear from every slave dungeon in the land a responsive Amen.

I am, gentlemen, with many regrets that I cannot be with you,
Very truly yours,
FREDERICK DOUGLASS.[123]

To Messrs. S. E. Sewall, Wendell Phillips, Theodore Parker, *Committee.*

XIII. SLAVERY AND THE CHURCH

The whites and blacks promoting the anti-slavery cause did not fail to expose the church as the bulwark of slavery. Doing this, of course, they incurred the ill will of the potentates who branded such abolitionists as infidels, just as any one of our day would be dubbed, should he countenance the thought that an oppressor of the Negro is not a righteous man. These Negro writers, however, kept up the attack as the letters below indicate.

FROM SAMUEL R. WARD, BOSTON

BOSTON, April 3, 1850.

Gentlemen: I was not at home when your letter of the 20th ult. came to my office. It was forwarded to me by my clerk, but by some delay in the mails for which I cannot account, it did not reach me till day before yesterday. Since that time, I have been more than ordinarily occupied with professional engagements: wherefore, I pray you to pardon the non-answering of your very kind invitation sooner.

It would give me great pleasure to meet the friends of Freedom and of Zion in Cincinnati on the 17th inst. I know that your call will of necessity attract a great many of the truest hearts in your own State and all the free States, and not a few of the citizens of the slave States. To meet such men, and to be profitted by their wise and learned counsels, would be to me, would my engagements allow it, a gratification such as I seldom enjoy.

My opinion in respect to ''the present position of our American Israel, and on the proper course to be pursued to deliver the churches from the terrible stain which slavery inflicts upon their character," are the opinions of too humble and obscure an individual to be of any weight in your Convention. But such as they are, you are welcome to them.

My view of the case, may be peculiar to myself, but I regard the churches, the orthodox churches of our country, as having departed from God and the Bible, on the subject of Slavery, and as a consequence they have yielded up the truth on other great vital subjects.

No one sin is more frequently nor more strongly prohibited and rebuked in the Sacred Volume, than the sin of oppression. Of no sin does the Old Testament make more marked demands that the Ancient Israel of God should repent, than of the sin of oppression. And from the first preaching of our Lord and Master, to the last forgiving words that fell from his dying lips, He ever laid down principles, as fundamental to His system of religion, which in their very nature are the directest opposites to the oppression of man, and are also the clearest enunciations of the inviolability of human rights. There is, to my mind, no one point in which the Scriptures of the Old and the New Testaments more perfectly harmonize than in this. Of course, I treat, and hold as bordering upon heresy of a damnable character, those monstrous assumptions which declare the Bible to favor Slavery. I regard this doctrine as one of the saddest evidences of our relapse from the "truth as it is in Jesus." When St. Paul, who knew all about it, says that "the heir differeth nothing from a servant," it makes no odds what translation be given to *doulas*, it is certain that, according to the Jewish laws and customs, the heir and the servant were in the same civil and social condition. To say otherwise, is to contradict the plainest teachings of the Divine Word. So, when the Apostle tells us, that "the law was made for men-stealers," and places men-stealers among the worst and most abominable of all wicked men, it is very near to downright infidelity to say either that the Bible sanctions or that it does *not directly* condemn and interdict Slavery. In too many directions around us, these horrible positions are taken, while in too many others, the Word of the Lord against oppression is made less controlling and authoritative, than the demands of sectarianism. So, it seems to my humble vision, our American churches have indulged an "evil heart of unbelief in departing from the living God."

The neglecting the cause of the poor and needy, who have

Jehovah for their especial Guardian, cannot be done without involving with it other transgressions of a most alarming, because of
a most aggravating character. So to do, is to act most unlike God,
most unlike Him, who being "the express image of the Father's
glory," "went about doing good," and who demands of us, that
we should in this, as well as in every thing else, follow Him. If,
however, it is in our heart to neglect, overlook, disregard, much
more to oppose, this part of His life and teaching; if, unlike Him,
we can suffer the sick and the imprisoned, or any other class of the
unfortunate and suffering, to appeal to us in vain for sympathy,
prayer, effort for their relief, then is our religion *fundamentally*
corrupt, as much so as was that of ancient Scribes and Pharisees,
and its corruption flows from the source whence *that* originated.
"Pure religion, and undefiled before God and the Father, is this:
to visit the fatherless and the widows in their affliction, and to keep
himself unspotted from the world." Now, the neglecting of the
"fatherless and the widows in their affliction," is the opposite to
"pure and undefiled religion," and it is without the power of
"keeping himself unspotted from the world." I grieve to say it,
but the truth must be plainly spoken, such seems to be the state of
the church in the present day. She has refused to be what the
Corinthian church was, a laborer together with God on this great
subject, and as there is no medium ground betwixt the two; that
very refusing makes her the co-worker of Satan. "He that is *not*
for me, *is* against me, and he that *gathereth not* with me scattereth
abroad," saith He who will judge us all in the final day, by that
simplest and most searching of all criteria, "Inasmuch as ye did
it or did it not to *these least,*" the hungry, thirsty, naked, sick and
imprisoned.

It is not strange, then, that sectarianism, respect of persons,
pride, and avarice, should be more dominant in the church, than
are their opposites. These are but the legitimate fruits of our
neglect of the "two great commandments" upon which "hang all
the law and prophets;" commandments, obedience to which is indispensable to the inheriting of eternal life, as the Savior taught.

"The course to be pursued to deliver the churches from the
terrible stain which slavery has inflicted upon them," is to seek to
bring them back again to God. It pleased God "to save by the
foolishness of preaching." This must be the means to reclaim
"our American Israel." Salvation is in no other name than the

name of Jesus. He, and He only, is the Savior of His people from
their sins. Let the truth home to their hearts, plainly, kindly,
perseveringly, "whether they shall hear or forbear to hear," and
trust "Him who giveth the early and the latter rain," for the results. Speak out, in your resolutions and your address, against
the crying abominations of that institution, "truth," as Isaiah did,
as Jesus did, and God's pledge is, that the "word shall not return
to Him void."

I cannot but hope and pray, that great and good results will
flow from your Convention. God is always pleased with our efforts
to draw nearer to Him, and to reclaim our wandering brethren.
May His smiles attend you, and His Spirit guide you.

In Christian bonds, your obedient servant,

SAM. R. WARD.[124]

FROM LEWIS WOODSON, PITTSBURGH, PA.

PITTSBURGH, April 15, 1850.

Gentlemen: Your note of the 15th ult., inviting me to attend
the Christian Anti Slavery Convention, in Cincinnati, on the 17th
inst., came duly to hand, and it would give me much pleasure to
comply with your invitation, but circumstances will not admit of it.

The object of your Convention is a good one, and the time at
which it is to be held most opportune.

That slavery should exist in the Church, is a most intolerable
abuse. No two institutions could be more unlike each other than
Slavery and Christianity. View them in any light we may, they
are a perfect contrast. There is not a virtue, not a grace in Christianity, whose opposite may not be found in Slavery. How, then,
can they be made to maintain a consonant and co-equal existence?
The thing is self-evidently absurd.

A Christianity without humanity, without benevolence, without
mercy, without justice, is no Christianity at all. It is a libel upon
the character of true Christianity and the examples and teachings
of its Divine Author. His life was spent in doing good to the
bodies, as well as the souls of men; in rendering them *happy on
earth,* as well as preparing them for heaven. * * * The great
Author of Christianity never intended that slavery * * * should

[124] *Minutes of the Christian Anti-Slavery Convention, April 17–20, 1850,*
66–68.

become a part and parcel of it. The example which he set, the precepts which he uttered, the GREAT PRINCIPLES which he laid down, show that this was not his intention. On the contrary, if they were reduced to practice and fully carried out, they would extirpate slavery from the earth.

The removal of slavery from the Church, is the appropriate work of Christian men. Infidels cannot do it. Their meddling with the vices of the Church, has a tendency to make her cling to them.

The time of the Convention, as I have said, is most opportune. The nation is agitated. Light is called for, and it is the duty of the Church to give it. God has made his Church the light of the world,—the salt of the earth. It is the source of knowledge on all questions of morals and piety; and when men would know what they should believe and practice in reference to their present and eternal happiness, they should enquire of the Church. In the Church is deposited that moral salt which is to save the world from moral putrefaction; but if this salt lose its savor, how then can the world be saved?

It is a principle in natural things, that the value and efficacy of every article is in proportion to its purity. Hence, the purer the Church is, the more valuable and efficacious she will be in promoting the happiness and salvation of the world.

The purification of the Church I have long desired to see; for I know that the day in which it is cast out of the Church, is the day of its destruction.

That God may preside over the deliberations of your Convention, and conduct to the best of conclusions, is my most humble and devout prayer.

LEWIS WOODSON.[125]

XIV. EMIGRATION TO CENTRAL AMERICA

One of the ways in which the free Negroes expressed their opposition to African colonization was by presenting a counter proposal to the effect that such emigrants should be settled in the tropics of America. The various countries to which their attention was directed were Texas, Trinidad,

[125] *Minutes of the Christian Anti-Slavery Convention, April 17–20, 1850,* 77.

Haiti, and other points in the West Indies. The following letters addressed to F. P. Blair, as a result of his speech bearing on the emancipation and colonization of the Negroes, present this point of view.

FROM REV. JAMES T. HOLLY, OF NEW HAVEN, CONN., RECTOR OF ST. LUKE'S

Hon. Sir: As the communication I voluntarily intruded upon your attention in relation to your recent speech in favor of colonizing the free blacks in Central America has been so kindly received by you, I am encouraged to pursue the subject, especially since you have given me the liberty to do so.

I have already called your attention to the fact that the subject has actively occupied the attention of this class of persons themselves since 1854, when an organization was formed among them, to promote their own emigration to the West Indies, Central and South America. I now wish to speak of the extent of this organization, its sympathizers, and the steps that have been taken to attain its end.

You have doubtless noticed, by the copy of the published proceedings of its organic Convention which I transmitted to you, that delegates from the British Province of Canada and eleven States of this Union (three of them being slave States) assembled in that Convention. And in the official organization of the National Board as a Central Executive Committee, corresponding members among the free colored people of no less than five slaveholding States were attached to that Board.

But even the organization in its extent is but a feeble expression of the growing feelings of discontent at their anomalous condition in this country, now rife among the free blacks, both North and South. Many are not identified with this movement, because they look upon the effort to remove and colonize themselves as wholly impracticable without the helping hand of men of power, influence, and wealth, among the whites of this country. And despairing now to obtain this influence in favor of their removal to the intertropical regions of this continent whilst the African colonization scheme preoccupied the attention of the American people, they have looked upon this organization of their own people as a fond Utopia, to be dreamed of, but never to be realized. Hence they have been too hopeless of accomplishing their heart's desire to join publicly in this movement hitherto.

But now that your speech in Congress opens a new era in their hopes, and they thereby witness the dawn of a brighter day for the successful accomplishment of their hopes, I can assure you that thousands can be readily enrolled as emigrants to the intertropical regions of our continent with the slightest effort. I speak now from a familiar and somewhat extended acquaintance and intercourse with them, with especial reference to this subject, during the past five years, by travelling and sojourning among them in the New England, Middle, and Northwestern States and Canada—having at the same time met and conversed with free colored men from almost every slave State in our Union.

I am confident that with proper inducements to be held out before them in regard to security for liberty, property, and prospects for well doing, I could muster two hundred emigrant families, or about one thousand free colored persons, annually, for the next five years, of the very best class for colonial settlement and industry, from various parts of the United States and Canada, who will gladly embark for homes in our American tropics. At the end of this period, it would need no especial efforts to promote the emigration, because it would regulate itself thereafter. Five thousand pioneers by this time having already settled themselves in Central America, having commenced to do well in their new homes, would spread the glad tidings among friends and relations remaining behind them in the United States, and the intelligence flying from family to family like an electric spark, a spontaneous emigration, double that of the first, will follow in the second five years, and this number will be trebled or quadrupled in the succeeding decade.

The feelings of the free blacks in relation to African colonization are no criterion by which to judge of the success of American intertropical emigration. The blacks have the most inveterate prejudice against being separated from the New World, that has been the field of their labors and sufferings for the past three centuries. It is a little hard even to leave the very spot on which they chanced to be born, for they are a very domestic race, and strong in their local attachments. Nevertheless, they can and will easily reconcile themselves to the irresistible fate of local separation from the whites of this country, when they can locate on the same continent, within a few days sail of the scenes of their nativity, and situated, as they would be, in the grand American thoroughfare between our Atlantic and Pacific States. This constant intercourse they would enjoy with white Americans, by means of travel through the tropics between the two ocean shores of our country, would make the blacks feel as if they had not lost their homes with us; and, therefore, would render them contented and happy in their lot. This can never be the case in African colonization, since by this scheme they are not only expatriated from their country, but also exiled from our Western World. Hence, I believe, I have data from personal knowledge, which will fully justify the expectation, that with proper efforts, more emigrants of this class will be removed to Central America in ten years than has been removed to Liberia during the forty years efforts of the colonization scheme. As a further insight to you of the depth and extent of this movement among the free blacks themselves, I send you a copy of the proceedings of a Convention held by the colored people of the United States and Canada as early as 1853, in which the subject of emigration to the West Indies, Central and South America, was broached. And I also transmit another pamphlet, published early in 1854, containing a newspaper controversy between three of the ablest negro writers in the country, on the subject of this self-same emigration. This controversy was preliminary to the assembling of their organic Convention in the same year.

This movement, although almost entirely confined among the blacks, so far, yet it can boast some interested sympathizers among the whites, to whose attention it has been presented, and who only await a more tangible and influential organization, and a more definite knowledge of what is to be done, in order to lend it a helping hand. Among others, I may mention C. W. Elliot, Esq., author of a History of New England, and F. L. Olmsted, Esq., author of a recent work entitled *Our Seaboard Slave States*. Numerous others can be easily interested, when the subject has been put in working shape by those who have the practical ability to do it. Having now spoken of the extent of this movement among the free blacks themselves, and also referred to a few sympathizers it has already invoked in an unostentatious manner among the whites, I now turn to speak of the practical efforts this organization has put forth in pursuance of its objects.

In one year after its organic Convention, a commissioner was appointed by the National Board or Central Committee of the same, to proceed to Hayti on a mission to Faustin First, for the purpose of making and receiving propositions on the subject of encouraging colored Americans to emigrate to that island, by holding a conference thereon with the Haytien Government. This commissioner went to Port-au-Prince during the summer of 1855 to prosecute his mission, and returned and reported its results at the biennial session of this Board of Emigration, held in Cleveland, Ohio, August 26, 27, 1856. The commissioner was cordially received by the Haytien Government, and his propositions kindly entertained and considered; but in consequence of the domestic complications arising out of the internal feuds, and the civil war then brewing between Hayti and Dominica, the Government of the Emperor Faustin was not prepared to accede to or advance any propositions on the subject of this emigration, any further than the announcement of the fact that it would be happy to welcome all such emigrants whenever they might be pleased to come to Hayti.

The propositions submitted by the commissioner were substantially as follows:

1. The Haytien Government was desired to offer encouragements to emigrants of color coming to Hayti, to establish themselves in the mountains and valleys of that island, to cultivate with their own hands private homesteads to be donated to them by the Government.

2. The Haytien Government to guaranty to these emigrants the enjoyment and equal civil and political rights with the natives of the country, and liberty of conscience in religious worship.

3. None of the emigrants or their children to do military duty until seven years after their arrival in Hayti; ministers of the gospel, physicians, lawyers, and school teachers, to be always exempt from that duty.

4. The Government to aid in the erection of manufacturing establishments, sugar refineries, grist and saw mills, for such emigrants as might be competent to conduct such works. The advances of the Government in this respect to be reimbursed out of the future profits of these works.

5. The Government to exempt from duty all materials, tools, furniture, &c., brought or imported by emigrants in the island for the purpose of carrying on their labors.

6. The emigrants to become Haytien citizens, invested with all the privileges, prerogatives, and immunities of the same, after one year's residence, on taking the oath of allegiance.

7. The Haytien Government to appoint a commissioner to reside in the United States and co-operate with the National Board or Central Committee of the Emigration Society in the general supervision of the embarkation of the emigrants from the United States.

8. On condition that the Haytien Government would fulfil the above requirements, the National Board would guaranty a select emigration of two hundred families or one thousand persons per annum for five years, and one thousand families or five thousand persons in addition thereto, if these governmental inducements should be continued two years longer. After seven years duration, the scheme to be abandoned, and left to regulate itself as a voluntary and spontaneous individual emigration thereafter.

These propositions were left open for the subsequent consideration and action of the Haytien Government. But as the Government has not since responded any further on this subject, the prospect of a movement in that direction remains *in statu quo.* But whilst darkness seems to be still brooding over the one, yet on the other hand new prospects seem to be dawning in the direction of Central America, by the bold and unequivocal position you have been pleased to assume voluntarily, in the Congress of the United States. It is fit that the subject should be agitated there by such an able advocate as you have proved yourself to be, in order that it may go forth with a telling effect upon the whole country. But opportune agitation in Congress in this manner is all that I believe can be done for years to come, with our Government, on the subject. The practical details of the movement must now be laid and carried out in its incipiency, by a company or an association of private individuals, of influence, character, and standing, throughout the whole country, but who shall at the same time be backed, animated, and cheered, by able supporters and defenders in Congress. This association ought to be formed as early as possible, and when formed, it ought to patronize and encourage the organization that the colored people have affected among themselves for this purpose. An intelligent and able commissioner ought to be dispatched in behalf of this association, to enter into stipulations with the Central American Government in regard to these contemplated emigrants. And this commissioner might be accompanied by some intelligent colored man, to be named by their Board or Central Committee, in whom they might repose the utmost confidence, when he brought back a report of the condition, prospects, and advantages, of that country.

Arrangements thus made for emigration, and a pioneer list of emigrants enrolled, consisting of agricultural laborers, mechanics, teachers, and professional men, then this association, composed of distinguished individuals, will invoke philanthropic contributions of money, mechanics' tools, and agricultural implements, to fit out and facilitate the removal of such of this number of emigrants as might need aid in these respects.

Thus prepared, the first expedition will sail, consisting of fifty families, or two hundred and fifty persons, and every three months thereafter, for the ensuing five years, let the same number be quietly transported. At the end of this period, I will guaranty the most skeptical and prejudiced will be converted to the scheme, and our Government will at last feel the necessity of making it a national movement, by throwing in some way her protecting aegis over this rapidly-accumulating portion of her own depleted population, that will then promise to be so advantageous to her in every respect, commercially and politically, in their newly-acquired homes in our highway to the Pacific. . . .

With this hope, I remain your obedient servant,

JAMES THEODORE HOLLY,[126]
Corresponding Secretary.

NEW HAVEN, January 30, 1858.

LETTER FROM J. M. WHITFIELD, EDITOR OF THE AFRICAN-AMERICAN REPOSITORY, (A COLORED MAN).

BUFFALO, NEW YORK, Feb. 1, 1858.

Dear Sir: Having read a portion of your late speech in Congress in favor of colonizing free blacks in Central or South America, I have taken the liberty of addressing you, feeling, as one of that race, and an advocate of the same policy, a vital interest in its success.

In August, 1854, a Convention was held at Cleveland of those colored men in favor of emigration to the West India islands, Central and South America. That Convention organized a Board of Emigration, which appointed a commissioner (Rev. J. T. Holly,

---

[126] *An Address delivered before the Mercantile Library Association of Boston, Massachusetts,* 34 to 37.

now rector of St. Luke's church, New Haven) to go to Hayti, and confer with the Haytien Government upon this subject.

That Government expressed itself ready to offer the most liberal inducements to emigrants, and to grant them every assistance in its power. It was also intended to send a commissioner to the British islands, New Granada, and the Central American States, but for lack of pecuniary means were unable to do so. And here, allow me to say, is one of the curses of our condition in this country: we are all so miserably poor that we are unable to help each other, and so scattered that it is impossible to have union of action even where there is perfect unanimity of sentiment; so that while there are hundreds—yes, thousands—of enterprising and industrious colored men, ready and anxious to embark immediately in any feasible movement of emigration to either of the places named, the means to commence such a movement properly are not attainable among them. . . .

The Colonization Society removes to Africa a few hundreds yearly, at an expense which, if judiciously applied according to the practical principles developed by Mr. Thayer in his organized system of Kansas emigration, would plant twice as many *thousands* in Central America, with everything requisite for their rapid progress; and the true interest of both the white and black races seems to require such a policy.

The fact is, the Saxon and negro are the only positive races on this continent, and the two are destined to absorb into themselves all the others; and, like two positive poles, they repel each other; and if the one is destined to occupy all the temperate regions of this hemisphere, it is equally certain that the other will predominate within the tropics. The Slavery propagandists unwittingly admit the same, when they declare negro labor to be indispensable in those regions. The question which suggests itself to the intelligent mind is, shall things be permitted and encouraged to reach their natural developments, which no combination of circumstances can prevent, (however much it may retard it,) by the peaceful influence of free labor? or shall the Slavery propagandists be allowed to interfere and check for a time the march of civilization, when the ultimate result must be to usher in, through war and anarchy, the very same state of things, which might have been much sooner and easier reached by peaceful and legitimate means, to the great benefit of the whole civilized world? You have answered the question in a manner which indicates the far-seeing statesman as well as the noble-hearted philanthropist, and I sincerely hope that a majority of Congress may be induced to adopt the same just and liberal policy.

Respectfully, yours,

J. M. WHITFIELD.[127]

LETTER FROM M. R. DELANY, (A BLACK MAN).

CHATHAM, C. W., Feb. 24, 1858.

Sir: I take the liberty of sending you, which I beg you will at your earliest leisure peruse, a paper written and reported by myself to a Convention of colored people at the place indicated, which was then accepted in the form of a report emanating from a committee.

I beg, sir, that you will give it your earliest attention, and favor me with your opinion thereon, knowing that as an enlightened statesman you will readily account for anything that may be too pointed or tart.

I have not as yet had the gratification of seeing your speech, but have been strongly requested by Messrs. Holly and Whitfield, of New Haven and Buffalo, to communicate with you on the subject. I was at the time I wrote the report a resident of Pittsburgh, Pa.

See report on the Political Destiny of the Colored Race on the American Continent, page 33.

I have the honor to be, sir, your most obedient servant,

M. R. DELANY.[128]

LETTER FROM ALFRED V. THOMPSON (A BLACK MAN).

CINCINNATI, OHIO, *June* 5, 1858.

Sir: I have read your speech two or three times on the colonizing of colored people in South America, and am much interested in it, and must say I am highly pleased with the plan. I have showed it to several, and they are much pleased with the document, and have worn out the speech, and hope you will send us three copies.

It is just the plan for us disfranchised Americans. I am nat-

---

[127] *An Address delivered before the Mercantile Library Association of Boston, Massachusetts,* 37–38.

[128] *Ibid.,* 34.

urally of an enterprising disposition, and have never found any cause to so elate me since I espoused emigration in 1842, when we left for Liberia with the view that we as a people could not attain to any honorable position in this country, nationally speaking. I was much pleased with our condition in Africa, from the fact that I saw no superior on account of color. (The Government was a Republic something like this. I don't like the British Government, though I prefer it to our condition in this.) Our reason for leaving Liberia, after living there for eighteen months, was on account of bad health, and through the advice and persuasion of Dr. J. W. Lugenbeel, our attendant family physician, who said if we remained we should certainly die; therefore, we left for Jamaica. Out of the company of emigrants that left America for Africa, numbering two hundred and twenty-five, at the expiration of eighteen months there was not living more than eighty-five or one hundred. We lost two children in the undertaking; my wife and myself suffered immensely. After we left for Jamaica, we stopped for three months at Sierra Leone, Africa. We lived in Kingston for three years, and in other parts of the island. Lived in Boston, New York, and Philadelphia, for two years, having remained out of the United States several years, and having travelled considerable at my own expense, I might say I have some experience in emigration. But, notwithstanding all this loss of time and deprivation, I have acquired a small property and a nice little business. But, with the proper assistance, I am willing to try it again, though my wife says she will never leave the land of her forefathers. There is a great demand on me from the colored population for information in regard to this project, and I hope you will send me the necessary documents to post myself. You mention in your speech several documents that would be of immense advantage in defending my position. I wish to know how and by what means the necessary aid and protection is to be given, and if in your opinion the Government will give any assistance. We have had three meetings on this subject, and thought of forming ourselves into a joint stock company, and issue $100 bonds and aid ourselves as much as possible, and to beg from individuals, State Governments, sell bonds, &c., &c. Please inform me where I can obtain a constitution and by-laws of the Massachusetts Emigrant Aid Society. I learned my trade with Mr. Andrew Johnson, of Tennessee, Ex-Governor, now member of the Senate, who can give any infor-

mation in regard to me. He will recollect the boy he used to call
Alfred. You will do me a great favor to answer this soon.

I am, with much respect, your most obedient servant,

ALFRED VANACTER THOMPSON.[129]

LETTER FROM J. D. HARRIS, (A BLACK MAN).

CLEVELAND, OHIO, Dec. 10, 1858.

Dear Sir: Having full faith in the principle of your able speech
delivered in Congress Jan. 14, 1858, in which you urge the necessity of acquiring territory outside of the United States for the
settlement of the freed colored people, I take the liberty of addressing you this letter.

I assure you that the thinking portion of the colored people
appreciate your efforts in that direction; for while it is evident that
the white and black races cannot exist in this country on terms of
equality, it is equally certain the latter will not long be content
with anything less.

Against the Government, its laws, and its customs, they are fast
beginning to rebel; and even while I write, in consequence of a late
fugitive slave case, this spirit is spreading to a marvellous extent.

The Government drives us to Canada, where we are indeed free,
but where it is plain we cannot become a very great people. We
want more room, where it is not quite so cold—we want to be
identified with the ruling power of a nation; and unless this be
obtained, Canada must be looked to as a strong military post for
future use, in the very vitals of America.

But you will not forgive me for addressing you (if at all) in a
tone so pointed, and I therefore cease, humbly beseeching you will
bring the subject again before Congress; and when you have so
far progressed as to need an agent among our people, whether it be
to spread such information as will awaken them to their true interests, or to carry out some plan or expedition that may be devised,
begging to be remembered as one who deeply feels the present
embarassing condition of his race, and who is willing to sacrifice
his time, his comfort, and his life, in order to create for them a
higher and more ennobling position.

I have the honor to be, &c.,

J. D. HARRIS.[130]

129 *An Address delivered before the Mercantile Library Association of
Boston, Massachusetts, January 26, 1859, 33.*

130 *Ibid.,* 34.

XV. The Martyrdom of John Brown

There must be some historic value in learning what the Negroes thought of John Brown, the martyr, who died that they might be free. Reading the comments of others, one would think that he was universally condemned, for we seldom hear a good word spoken in behalf of John Brown today. A professor of history at Harvard University confessed that he hates the very memory of John Brown to the extent that whenever he passes his statue in the home of a friend he feels like kicking it in the back. A Columbia University professor of history classifies John Brown as a highwayman and a cutthroat. These comments show how prejudiced and biased are the leading "historians" who are shaping the thought of the youth of tomorrow with respect to our dramatic makers of history. As these prominent writers are not yet sufficiently enlightened to appreciate John Brown's martyrdom any more than the contemporaries of his race in 1859, it may be well to learn from the following letters what the Negroes said of John Brown when he was passing through the ordeal.

FROM FREDERICK DOUGLASS.

CANADA WEST, Oct. 31, 1859.

MR. EDITOR: I notice that the telegraph makes Mr. Cook (one of the unfortunate insurgents at Harper's Ferry, and now in the hands of the thing calling itself the Government of Virginia, but which in fact is but an organized conspiracy by one party of the people against the other and weaker,) denounce me as a coward—and to assert that I promised to be present at the Harper's Ferry Insurrection. This is certainly a very grave impeachment, whether viewed in its bearings upon friends or upon foes, and you will not think it strange that I should take a somewhat serious notice of it. Having no acquaintance whatever with Mr. Cook, and never having exchanged a word with him about the Harper's Ferry insurrection, I am induced to doubt that he could have used the language concerning me which the wires attribute to him. The lightning, when speaking for itself, is among the most direct, reliable and truthful of things; but when speaking for the terror-stricken slaveholders at Harper's Ferry, it has been made the swiftest of liars. Under their nimble and trembling fingers, it magnified seventeen men into seven hundred—and has since filled the columns of the New York *Herald* for days with interminable contradictions. But, assuming that it has told only the simple truth, as to the sayings of Mr. Cook in this instance, I have this answer to make to my accuser: Mr. Cook may be perfectly right in denouncing me as a coward. I have not one word to say in defence or vindication of my character for courage. I have always been more distinguished for running than fighting—and, tried by the Harper's Ferry insurrection test, I am most miserably deficient in courage—even more so than Cook, when he deserted his old brave captain, and fled to the mountains. To this extent Mr. Cook is entirely right, and will meet no contradiction from me or from anybody else. But wholly, grievously, and most unaccountably wrong is Mr. Cook, when he asserts that I promised to be present in person at the Harper's Ferry insurrection. Of whatever other imprudence and indiscretion I may have been guilty, I have never made a promise so rash and wild as this. The taking of Harper's Ferry was a measure never encouraged by my word or by my vote, at any time or place; my wisdom or my cowardice has not only kept me from Harper's Ferry, but has equally kept me from making any promise to go there. I desire to be quite emphatic here—for of all guilty men, he is the guiltiest who lures his fellow-men to an undertaking of this sort, under promise of assistance, which he afterwards fails to render. I therefore declare that there is no man living, and no man dead, who if living, could truthfully say that I ever promised him or anybody else, either conditionally or otherwise, that I would be present in person at the Harper's Ferry insurrection. My field of labor for the abolition of slavery has not extended to an attack upon the United States arsenal. In the teeth of the documents already published, and of those which hereafter may be published, I affirm no man connected with that insurrection, from its noble and heroic leader down, can connect my name with a single broken promise of any sort whatever. So much I deem it proper to say negatively.

The time for a full statement of what I know, and of *all* I know, of this desperate but sublimely disinterested effort to emancipate the slaves of Maryland and Virginia, from their cruel taskmasters, has not yet come, and may never come. In the denial which I have now made, my motive is more a respectful consideration for the opinions of the slave's friends, than from my fear of being made an accomplice in the general *conspiracy* against Slavery. I am ever ready to write, speak, publish, organize, combine, and even to conspire against Slavery, when there is a reasonable hope for success. Men who live by robbing their fellow-men of their labor and liberty, have forfeited their right to know anything of the thoughts, feelings, or purposes of those whom they rob and plunder. They have by the single act of slaveholding voluntarily placed themselves beyond the laws of justice and honor, and have become only fitted for companionship with thieves and pirates—the common enemies of God and of all mankind. While it shall be considered right to protect oneself against thieves, burglars, robbers and assassins, and to slay a wild beast in the act of devouring his human prey, it can never be wrong for the imbruted and whip-scarred slaves, or their friends, to hunt, harass and even strike down the traffickers in human flesh. If anybody is disposed to think less of me on account of this sentiment; or because I may have had a knowledge of what was about to occur, and did not assume the base and detestable character of an informer, he is a man whose good or bad opinion of me may be equally repugnant and despicable. Entertaining this sentiment, I may be asked, why I did not join John Brown—the noble old hero whose one right hand has shaken the foundation of the American Union, and whose ghost will haunt the bed-chambers of all the born and unborn slaveholders of Virginia through all their generations, filling them with alarm and consternation! My answer to this has already been given, at least, impliedly given: 'The tools to those that can use them.' Let every man work for the abolition of Slavery in his own way. I would help all, and hinder none. My position in regard to the Harper's Ferry insurrection may be easily inferred from these remarks, and I shall be glad if those papers which have spoken of me in connection with it would find room for this brief statement.

I have no apology for keeping out of the way of those gentlemanly United States Marshals, who are said to have paid Rochester a somewhat protracted visit lately, with a view to an interview with me. A government recognizing the validity of the *Dred Scott* decision, at such a time as this, is not likely to have any very charitable feelings towards me; and if I am to meet its representatives, I prefer to do so, at least, upon equal terms. If I have committed any offence against Society, I have done so on the soil of the State of New York, and I should be perfectly willing *there* to be arraigned before an impartial jury; but I have quite insuperable objections to being caught by the hands of Mr. Buchanan, and '*bagged*' by Gov. Wise. For this appears to be the arrangement. Buchanan does the fighting and hunting, and Wise '*bags*' the game.

Some reflections may be made upon my leaving on a tour to England, just at this time. I have only to say, that my going to that country has been rather delayed than hastened by the insurrection at Harper's Ferry. All knew that I had intended to leave here in the first week of November.

FREDERICK DOUGLASS.[181]

FROM COLORED CITIZENS OF CHICAGO TO JOHN BROWN.

CHICAGO, November 17.

Dear Friend: We certainly have great reasons, as well as intense desires, to assure you that we deeply sympathize with you and your beloved family. Not only do we sympathize in tears and prayers with *you* and *them*, but we *will* do so in a more tangible form, by contributing material aid to help those of your family of whom you have spoken to our mutual friend, Mrs. L. Maria Child. How could we be so ungrateful as to do less for one who has suffered, bled, and now ready to die for the cause! "Greater love can no man have, than to lay down his life for the poor, despised, and lowly."

Your friends,

H. O. W., and others.[182]

FROM A WOMAN OF THE RACE HE DIED FOR.

KENDALVILLE, INDIANA, Nov. 25.

Dear Friend: Although the hands of Slavery throw a barrier between you and me, and it may not be my privilege to see you in your prison-house, Virginia has no bolts or bars through which I dread to send you my sympathy. In the name of the young girl sold from the warm clasp of a mother's arms to the clutches of a libertine or a profligate,—in the name of the slave mother, her heart rocked to and fro by the agony of her mournful separations,—

---

[181] *Liberator*, Nov. 11, 1859.
[182] James Redpath, *Echoes of Harper's Ferry*, 391.

I thank you, that you have been brave enough to reach out your hands to the crushed and blighted of my race. You have rocked the bloody Bastile; and I hope that from your sad fate great good may arise to the cause of freedom. Already from your prison has come a shout of triumph against the giant sin of our country. The hemlock is distilled with victory when it is pressed to the lips of Socrates. The Cross becomes a glorious ensign when Calvary's page-browed sufferer yields up his life upon it. And, if Universal Freedom is ever to be the dominant power of the land, your bodies may be only her first stepping stones to dominion. I would prefer to see Slavery go down peaceably by men breaking off their sins by righteousness and their iniquities by showing justice and mercy to the poor; but we cannot tell what the future may bring forth. God writes national judgments upon national sins; and what may be slumbering in the storehouse of divine justice we do not know. We may earnestly hope that your fate will not be a vain lesson, that it will intensify our hatred of Slavery and love of freedom, and that your martyr grave will be a sacred altar upon which men will record their vows of undying hatred to that system which tramples on man and bids defiance to God. I have written to your dear wife, and sent her a few dollars, and I pledge myself to you that I will continue to assist her. May the ever-blessed God shield you and your fellow-prisoners in the darkest hour. Send my sympathy to your fellow-prisoners; tell them to be of good courage; to seek a refuge in the Eternal God, and lean upon His everlasting arms for a sure support. If any of them, like you, have a wife or children that I can help, let them send me word.

Yours in the cause of freedom,

F. E. W.[133]

FROM THE COLORED WOMEN OF BROOKLYN.

BROOKLYN, Nov. 26.

In behalf of the colored women of Brooklyn. Dear Sir: We, a portion of the American people, would fain offer you our sincere and heartfelt sympathies in the cause you have so nobly espoused, and that you so firmly adhere to. We truly appreciate your most noble and humane effort, and recognize in you a Saviour commissioned to redeem us, the American people, from the great National Sin of Slavery; and though you have apparently failed in the

[133] James Redpath, *Echoes of Harper's Ferry*, 418.

object of your desires, yet the influence that we believe it will eventually exert, will accomplish all your intentions. We consider you a model of true patriotism, and one whom our common country will yet regard as the greatest it has produced, because you have sacrificed all for its sake. We rejoice in the consciousness of your perfect resignation. We shall ever hold you dear in our remembrance, and shall infuse the same feelings in our posterity. We have always entertained a love for the country which gave us birth, despite the wrongs inflicted upon us, and have always been hopeful that the future would augur better things. We feel now that your glorious act for the cause of humanity has afforded us an unexpected realization of some of our seemingly vain hopes. And now, in view of the coming crisis which is to terminate all your labors of love for this life, our mortal natures fail to sustain us under the trying affliction; but when we view it from our religious standpoint, we feel that earth is not worthy of you, and that your spirit yearneth for a higher and holier existence. Therefore we willingly give you up, and submit to His will "who doeth all things well."

Yours with warm regard,

M. S. J. T.[134]

[134] James Redpath, *Echoes of Harper's Ferry*, 419.

LETTERS LARGELY PERSONAL OR PRIVATE

Most of these letters differ from others of this series in that they were not written for publication. Some of those addressed to the American Colonization Society and most of those to the anti-slavery workers and agencies were the results of efforts to be heard. Among these below are found a few communications of this kind but they serve here to illuminate others which they accompany. The thought herein expressed, therefore, is not always that of some one with a problem to solve. The aim of most of this correspondence is to inform friends of the situation in which the writers found themselves, to thank them for favors, and to implore their assistance in the future. These letters as a rule, moreover, were not written by the enterprising Negroes who expressed themselves on the issues affecting the race. Most of these persons, especially the fugitives, belonged to the lower walks of life.

CAESAR BROWN TO MRS. SOPHIA BROWN [1]

NASSAU N P May 30th 1800

MRS. SOPHIA BROWN
Dear Mistress,

By the death of my laste mistress, which I regret most sincerely, I find myself left your slave, notwithstanding the constant assurances of Mr. Brown my former Master & his wife to the contrary, who really did promise to make me free at their death. All the slaves myself included are to be sold here or sent to you, they have all been apraised at a proper valuation, except me, on whom the have fixed the immoderate price of 500 Dollars. My only motive for intruding this letter on you, is to beg that you will consider my Master's promise which you know to be true, you likewise know with what real fidelity I have served him and his wife, and you must be convinced of my attachment to my young Master & you, indeed I am convinced that you will render me every service in your power & endeavor to make my situation somewhat more independent than it has been hitherto. If it is your

---

[1] Mrs. Sophia Brown was addressed at Perth Amboy, New Jersey.

wish to have me in New York I will with pleasure go there and serve you forever, but if on the contrary it is your intention I should be sold with the rest of the slaves, I beg you so far to indulge me as to lower the price at which I am valued and I will try to purchase my own freedom, with the assistance of some friends in this place. Master Patrick Brown has promised to advance me a little money towards procuring my emancipation if you chuse to part with me. It is My dear Madam my wish to purchase my freedom and I hope you will have the goodness to consent to it and to moderate the present sum at which I am apraised. I must pray you to consent to write me your determination—please to enclose your letter to Martin P Brown.

> I have the Honor
> to be,
> Dear Madam,
> Your Faithful Slave,
> CAESAR BROWN [2]

Mr. Eugene Portlette Southall, Assistant Principal of the Booker T. Washington High School, of Norfolk, Virginia, has given the Association for the Study of Negro Life and History some valuable papers of his family, among which are the following letters throwing light on the migration of Negroes from France to the West Indies and thence to this country. In his letter concerning these papers Mr. Southall says:

"My great-grandfather William Portlett was a native of France. He migrated to one of the French West Indian Islands. He left the island during a native insurrection and came by ship to Norfolk.[3] His wife was Marie Louise Courton. A son, William Portlett, my grandfather, was born about 1806. In 1830 he married a slave, Dianah Mallory. To this union eight children were born as follows: William, Eugene, Virginia, Victoria, Marie Louise, Midah, Baptiste and Eliza (my mother).

"From one of the old family acquaintances I learned an

---

[2] This letter was obtained from the manuscript collection of the New York Historical Society.

[3] The particular disturbance in the West Indies was the insurrection in Hayti led by Toussaint Louverture and Dessalines. Refugees from these islands settled in this country in the neighborhood of Baltimore, Norfolk, Charleston, and New Orleans.

interesting narrative about my grandmother's people which may be of interest to you: My grandmother Dianah Mallory Portlett was of Indian descent. Her mother Diza Mallory was stolen from her Indian parents at Yorktown by slave-traders and sold as a slave in the Norfolk slave market. I have no documentary proof of this, but I have heard the old people relate this many times. A granddaughter and name-sake of Diza Mallory still survives.

"This account is corroborated by our family Bible, by personal interviews with the few surviving acquaintances of my grandparents and by some recently found letters and deeds to property acquired by my grandfather."

CHEVREGNY 28 Aourt 1817
MON AMIR

En reponce a la tienne daté du deux juin par laquelle tu nous mande que tu'es en Bonne Sante Ainsi que la Chere epouse cela nous nous fait plaisir ainsi que toute la famille et nous Souhaitons la continu-ation quand a nous toujour bien Viellemens accablés de maux ne pouvant plus faire usage de mes menbre, C'est ce que m' a determiné a ambandonné notre petit avoir a nos enfans par traite de nouriture le n'est pas quil ya a faire bonne chere mais ne pouvant plus le faire valoir jai été obligé di venir, mes enfans me donnent par mois chacun quatre francs, et on Vend en ce moment un pain de dix livres le franc juge de ma triste existence je reste toujours dans ma Maison en Bas et Veronique habite le haut Cest une consolation pour nous, Cher Ami Voyant ma triste Situation si tu pouvait nous aider en peu tu gagnerais le Ciel pour assister un pere et une mere dans leurs grand Age et necessité je ten prie au nom de tout Ce quil y a de plus Sacré si tu és pour nous faire quelque choses de nous le faire le plus tot qui'l te sera possible.   Car plus tard il ne Sarait peut étre plus tems Dieu dispose de nous a Sa volonté fait du bien a tes pauvre pere et mere et Dieu ten recompencera,

ton Beau frere la bove est mort alarmée et ta filleule est morte Ainsi Nicote est remariée a un Nomme Sudoyer Carrieur a Mont Bavin, tu me demande les noms des Maris de tes trois jeune Soeur, le marie d' Angelique Louis le Clerc a Chevregny, le mari de francoise Louis henry Maurice A Nouvion et celui de Veronique Louis Maurice tous deux frere, il sont bien reconnaissant de ce que tu pense a eux ils te remercient ainsi que ta chere epouse et vous font bien leur complimen tes autre Soeur et Beau frere te font aussi bien des Complimens, ton oncle de Mons entaonnoir est mort ainsi que sa femme et ton Cousin est Marié a Mons entaonnoir. Je lui ait fait part de ta lettre il te font bien des complimens tout ce que Je te peut apprendre pour nouvelle que la Misère dans Ce pais est a Son Comble ta pauvre Mere se joine a moi pour vous embrasser tous deux du meilleur des Coeur je te le reitere si tu peut nous faire du bien fais le le plus tot possible Car plus tard tu ne trouverai rien a Dieu embrasse ta Chere epouse pour nous pour Comble de Malheur le pais a été réduit de la Grele le 12 de Ce mois il y en avait qui pesait jus qua 25 once.

Lecrivain te Souhaite une Bonne Sante ton

AMIS BOLLEAU

P.S. tu nous fera plaisir de nous dire le hombre de ta famille.

CHEVREGNY 6 Aout 1818

Nous avons recu cher amis votre lettre daté du 4 Juin dernier par laquelle tu me mande que tu te porte bien cela nous fait un sensible plaisir ainsi que de Savoir que ta chere epouse est aun en Bonne Santé Je temprie Nous tembrassons moi et ma femme ta chere mere mais surtout enbrasse ton aimable et chere epouse pour nous Notre plus grand malheur ce sera de la jamais pouvoir Connaitre il est étonnant cher ami que vous nayez pas recu ma lettre de la reponce à la votre pour vous acuser la reception de largent que vous avez eu la bonte de me faire passer par monsieur Couteau votre consul—Cependant j ai recu votre lettre et largent au premier Janvier et aussitot je me suis empressé de vous écrire pour vous remercier du grand Bienfait que vous mavez fait et je ne sais a quoi attribuer le retard cependant j ai fait affranchir la lettre jusqu'au dernier port de France cela ma couté 21 Sous mais n'importe Jespere que celle-ci aura un mellieur Succées

Oui chers enfans que je considere comme deux Dieu a cet epoque Jetais (ou nous etions) presque sans pain et sans pois et remplis de Misere et de Chimere toujours Songeant avous J'etais pret a prendre la Basase et a aller de porte en porte mon plus grand malheur cest de ne pouvoir pas marcher librement ny ta pauvre mere. Nous faisions de de prieres et de Voeux pour vous lors que Dieu les a exaucés Sur le Champ. Oui mon chere enfant la mane a tombé en ce moment pour nous comme quand Dieu la fit tomber pour les Ysraélites mes autres pauvres enfans netant pas a leur aises ne pouvait me donner leur part de la pauvre petite penssion et jetais Sans Secours. Depuis ce tems nous sommes en peu plus a notre aise en nous menageeant bien doucement Vu que le pain n'est plus si chere il vaut apresent 2 f 60 la livre Quel remerciment ne vous devons nous pas me cheres enfans a lage de 73 ans chacun que nous avons et 51 ans de mariage on est plus guerre en force pour pouvoir en gagner avec Ses Bras, Je ne Sait quel langage tenir pour vous faire sentir notre tendresse paternelle et maternelle notre occupations est de prier Dieu pour tous Nos Amis en particulier pour nos Bienfaiteurs qui Sont vous mes chers enfans, Cest pourquoi nous le prions quil vous conserve la Santé que vous ayez paix et union dans votre menage et qu'à la fin il vous accorde ainsi qua vous l'heureuse eternité voila nos voeux Nous esperons cette Année une Ample recolte enblée, grande recolte en vin et en pomme on en a jamais tant vû tout les pommiers qui tu a plante ils en rompent ils sont de toute Beauté jespere que cette année on ne mangera point tant de pommes de terre que celle que nous quittons je te dirai que voila trois moi quil na pas tombé deau ici malgré cela les choses vont bien monsieur le Cure Desnoyers est encore bien portant alage de quatre vingt Sept Ans   toute les Soeurs et leurs mari leurs enfans se portent bien ils sont bien Content du bien que vous mavez fait et que vous promettez de me faire ils vous embrassent et vous font bien des complimens, Veronique et (tes soeurs) en particuliers Sont toujours avec nous et nous sommes tres content deux ils vous prient aussi de recevoir leurs amitiés.

Je finis chers enfans la larme aloeil ainsi que votre chere mere en vous embrassant mil et mil fois du plus profond du Coeur en vous Souhaintant une Bonne Santé et vous prie de vous souvenir denous votre pere Medard portellettee

Lecrivain vous souhaite une bonne Sante votre amis Botteau.

CHEVREGNY le 3 Octobre 1821

On vieut, Mon cher fils, de me remettre la lettre du trois Aout dernier les temoignages d'attachement qu'elle contient m'ont sensiblement affecté. Cepourquoi je me empresse de repondre au plus brief afin de recevoir encore une seconde lettre avant que de paroître devant Notre grand Souverain.

je suis charmé d'avoir recu cette lettre parce que je m'annuyoit beaucoup de ne plus en recevoir et attendu que je suis près de ma Carriere, Je craignis que Dieu ne m'otte de ce monde avant d'etre Satisfait à mes desirs; du prèsent je quitte volontier d'ici bas pour

rejoindre le très-haut: Cependant que la volonte de dieu soit faite.
Arrivé bientot a ma quatre vingtième année; je ne suis pas, comme
tu le penses bien sans besoin at sans infirmité; c'est pourquoi je me
soumetre a tes bonnes intentions.   Je suis bien aise d'apprendre qu'
après avoir ete exposé a perdre un bras, tu sois bien rétabli Tes
freres, tes soeurs et leurs enfans il se portent bien tous, ont ete
sensibles a ton bon souvenir, et ils me prient de t'embrasser pour
eux et de t'assurer de leur amitié.

La recolte en· vin est nulle cette année ce qui diminue de beaucoup les ressources et l'aisance dans toutes la familles.

Tu m'obligera donc si tu peu de m'envoyer quelqu' argent,
comme tu (as eu) l'intention, pour rendre ma situation et celle de ta
chere mere moins penible.

Il ne faut par que je te recommande de presser cette envoye, tu
penses bien qu'étant arrivé deux viellards a un âge trés avancés, tes
Secours différés pourraient venir trop tard.
ta Chere mère et moi nous t'embrassons de toute notre coeur, aimsi
que ta chere Epouse Notre fille.

Et suis pour la vie Medard portellett ton tendre pere Je suis
chargé de la part de Mr. Allard qui est le Maire de Notre commune.
Et   Notre cousin Nicolas Peyois, qui est Aussi notre adjoint,
de te temoigner leur amitié il le font bien leurs compliments
Nota.   Pour parvenir à la prochaine fois que tu m'écrira une lettre
je te prie de mettre l'addresse, aimsi conçu
        à Monsieur Etienne Allard Maire de la commune de Chev-
regny, pour remettre à Medard Portelette.
De même aussi pour les jondre, à la même addresse; parceque Se
Sera le plus certain en cas si nous etions quitté de ce monde.

FROM JOHN MILLER TO HIS WIFE[4]

PHILADELPHIA   June 9th 1833
    MY DEAR WIFE
I have took the first opportunity that I had to write these few lines
to you, because I felt very ancious to hear from you and shall still
feel ancious untill I do hear from you, not only to hear from you but
I must see you.   I am ancious to know how you felt on your
journey down, and how you reachd mothers from Wilmington.

[4] John Miller was the grandfather of Miss Esther C. Porter, of the Berean
Training School, Philadelphia.   His wife was then visiting her mother at Newport,
Delaware.

that is if you have reachd yet. But I do trust that you did get safe down and are enjoying yourself. Please to give my best respects to one and all. Now I shall await untill I hear from you, but please not to make it to very long before you write to me for I am very ancious to hear from you. I shall not waite many days that is if I am spaird and am well enough I shall come down as soon as I can. please to let me hear from you as soon as you can. my throat and breast with my cold is something better but not much. My dear wife I hope you will take great care of yourself do not climb over yonder fence to often do not roam through yonder woods to often do not walk over yonder feilds to often but take care of yourself and remember what I told you before you left home. and in the mean time I remain yours and you mine as long as life remains

Your affectionate husband

JOHN MILLER JR

FROM MARY STOKES TO JOHN MILLER [5]

PHILADELPHIA 6 mo 22, 1846

To ANNE MILLER

        Once more my Aunt E W Cope requests me to write to thee on behalf of thy little daughter Philena Miller—I should suppose thee would ever remember the dieing request of thy worthy husband John Miller—at that awful time he requested my Aunt E. W. Cope to take his children and take care of them—which she has done faithfully—Elizabeth is growing to be a fine girl at my Brother John Stokes's, Caroline has a very good home and they both seem very happy—Now she does request thee will let Philena return to town with Mary Kinkaid who will be the bearer of this letter—Aunt has an opportunity of placing her at a good school, where she will learn to read and sew and improve in everything—If thee should live to be old these three daughters may be a great comfort to thee—Now do not let anything prevent thy sending the child by Mary Kincaid as there is just room for her in the school now—Aunt will send clothes for her to wear to town, and after she comes she will get her more—I shall always be glad to hear she is doing well and remain Thy Friend Mary Stokes   Mary Kincaid has brought a piece of calico for the dress.

[5] Mary Stokes was a Philadelphia Quakeress. She is here writing John Miller's wife after his death. Miss Stokes was concerned with the education of his youngest daughter.

    This letter and the one following were taken from the collection of manuscripts of the Association for the Study of Negro Life and History.

J. J. ROBERTS TO SARAH H. COLSON [6]

MONROVIA, LIBERIA
January 1st, 1836.

VERY DEAR MADAM:

It is feelings of deep regret that I under-
take the painful duty to inform you of the dissolution of our partner
and your beloved Husband William N. Colson.

The particulars of his death you will no doubt hear from your
brother Mr. Elebeck who expects to return to the U. States in a
few days or weeks at most if opportunity offers.

There can be no doubt Mr. Colson came to his death by his own
imprudence; he was quite harty (hardy) during the passage and
his health continued good until his arrival at Monrovia with the
exception of slight fever at Sierra Leone at which place he was very
imprudent in exposing himself to night air and much exercise by
preaching, of which I worried and advised him but all to no purpose;
he persisted in his course but upon the whole I think that did not
affect him very materially.

[6] James M. Colson, a free Negro of Petersburg, was married to Fannie Meade
some time after 1850. To this union there was born the following nine children
arranged according to age:

    Melvina Colson-West.
    James M. Colson, Jr.
    Fannie M. Colson-Roundtree.
    Hattie J. Colson-Freeman, 200 Central Ave., Orange, N. J.
    Charles S. Colson, Williamsport, Penn.
    Henry H. Colson, Suffolk, Virginia.
    Ella G. Colson-Jackson, 123 New Street, Petersburg, Virginia.
    Mary Colson-Woody, 200 Central Ave., Orange, N. J.
    Grace Colson-Jeffrey, 221 W. 141st Street, N. Y. City.

James M. Colson, Jr., was graduated from Dartmouth College in 1881 with
distinction. He later became a professor in the Virginia Normal and Collegiate
Institute not long after 1890. Still later he became the principal of the Dinwiddie
Normal School, Dinwiddie, Virginia. He died in 1912. (The members of the
family who are now living appear with the addresses given above.) Mrs. Ella
Colson Jackson of Petersburg has in her possession four letters centering around the
forbears of the present generation. William N. Colson was the father of James
M. Colson, Sr., grandfather of the nine children listed above. William N. Colson
was one of the first adventurers to Liberia. He was intimately associated with
the first president of Liberia, J. J. Roberts. In the following letter Roberts is
writing from Monrovia to Mrs. Sarah H. Colson of Petersburg telling her of the
death of her husband—Willian N. Colson.

[7] I am told that J. J. Roberts, president of Liberia, was a native of Petersburg.
This letter arrived in New York June 14th, 1836. His handwriting is very good.

These letters of the Colson Family were obtained by Prof. L. P. Jackson,
of the Virginia Normal and Industrial Institute, Petersburg, Virginia.

The fifteenth day after his arrival here he was attacked with the fever and passed the ninth day, after which we think there is little danger, in the seasoning, on the tenth he was up and quite smart and considered out of danger, and so pronounced by the Phisition (physician) but sad to relate his love for writing proved fatal, the vessel was ready to sail the next day, and in violation of all persuasion he insisted and wrote eight or nine letters and those two very lengthy as you know is his custom for the U. States.

These exertions have proved fatal to too many, a Wright, an Anderson, a Laird and many others have fallen by such imprudence.

The next day there could be traced in his gestures signs of delerium; the next day worse, and the third day he was quite a mad man & so continued until his death which occured on Thursday afternoon ½ Past O clock November 1st 1835, during this whole time he complained of no pain only in the head; all medical aid that could be obtained in the (   ) was had, Drs. Skinner, McDowell, & Davis done all in their power for his relief.

But enough of this sad tale; with Mr. Williams, I can certainly assure you as I was with him much of the time he had every attention possible, after his death he was decently intered, and followed to the grave by a large concourse of friends that cincerely mourned your loss and that of the community.

I know that you are a woman of too much discretion to need any consolation from one so incapable; would to God I could say something in this your time of trouble but this I will say you must remember to be, the Lord gave and the Lord hath taken away; he works in a mysterious way his wonders to perform; though seems hard at this time, but God does all things well for them that love and fear him; you can not tell for what cause He has thought proper to remove him from this world of bustle and confusion for his part he is gone to the realms above, he is gone to Abrahams bosom, and expects to meet you there where parting will be no more.   Do not think had he remained in America he would not have died, God is the ruler of the Universe and protects as well in the wiles of Africa, as in the fields of America.   I say do not accuse providence in this, I say again God does all things for the best.

God has promised to be the widows husband and the Orphants (orphans) Father may it so be in your case is the prayer of your particular friend,

                                                    J. J. ROBERTS.

Mrs. Sarah H. Colson
      Petersburg, Va,
            U. S.

N. H. ELEBECK TO SARAH N. COLSON

STATEN ISLAND
June 15th, 1836.

DEAR SISTER;

This will inform I have arrived at New York in good health after a passage of forty seven days on board of Big Luna from Monrovia Africa from hence she sailed on the 27th of April with 47 Tons Cainwood, 8 Puncheons Palm Oil and 500 lbs Ivory on Board; Produce belonging to Roberts, Colson, & Co., consigned to Messrs Grant & Stone consignees of the firm, who are Merchants of Philadelphia.

The Brig certainly will deliver her cargo in New York, whether Grant & Stone have Agents in this place to attend to this Shipment, I am not prepared to say, the Brig is now curranteened (quarantined) but tomorrow her time will expire when she will come up to the city.

Though I have no authority to transact business in your stead, yet circumstances inspires me to attend to the weighinf of the above articles on their discharge, then with all possible dispatch I make my way Southward.

N.B.   All Mr. Colsons papers & clothing I have with me and perceive that you have a (the) power of attorney he left in your hands.   There is a small due bill of Roberts among the Papers in Colsons name & also the Invoice of the Tobacco Co which was purchased in Petersburg of Ben Jones & Co., which Invoice is not entered in our Invoice Book but contents distinguishes themselves in our day Book whether the shipment is paid for out of Mr. Colsons private funds or not I am not prepared to say, be that as it may.

There is a consignment of goods belonging to Thomas Bell merchant of New York & former consignee of Roberts, Colson & Co., the amount of which as Brot. up on our Ledger is $1200. Owing to the shipment of Roberts, Colson & Co., being kept by him undoubtedly the whole amount of his shipment was reserved and not remitted for the safety of the House.   Consequently the loss on Mr. Bells account do not exceede $350 an amount not large enough to be felt by the concern.

Roberts may come to this country shortly as he has instructed Grant & Stone to reserve the Amt. of proceeds until they hear from him.   Roberts & Williams Bills with the concern amt to more than $3000.   The amt. of Mr. Colsons bills with mine $350 this includes

my board & washing.   In much haste as it is now past two o'clock.
I still Remain

Your Brother   N. H. ELEBECK

To Mrs. Sarah H. Colson
        Petersburg, Va.[8]

This last letter is also from Elebeck to his sister in Petersburg.

PHILADELPHIA, July 19th, 1836.

DEAR SISTER;

I received yours this moment bearing date 16th
Inst as it is now 8 o'clock P.M., and the mail closes for the South at
nine, I have little time to spare, this will inform you my health is
none of the best but thank the Lord I am enabled to attend to
business.   Capt. Ables poor fellow died the week before I arrived
in this city in the Hospital, I did not enquire particularly of Mr.
Grant what Capt. sailed in the Caroline, in my next I send you word
not having time enough to make that enquiry by this mail.   There
are no vessel that will sail from this Point for the Coast of Africa
with the exception of the Vessel from New York Mr. Daily alludes
to.

Most respectfully in much haste

Your Brother
N. H. ELEBECK

To Mrs. Sarah H. Colson

N.B. direct your letters no. 182
South six street care of Charles Short
        I expect to leave this city for New York tomorrow morning
at 6 o'clock A.M. and return Sunday evening God being willing Mr.
Daileys Brother having left this city two days ago for New York I
am afraid the vessel will sail before I see him, the Letters you have
intending Daileys to carry out as answers to Roberts.   You will
direct them to New York no. 155 Vanderhorse or direct them to me
"C Shorts" as I will ascertain the street and send them on.
        To Sarah H. Colson.

[8] This letter of June 15th, 1836, throws some light on the previous one.   It is
written by N. H. Elebeck to his widowed sister Mrs. Sarah H. Colson.   Her
husband is the character Roberts tells about in the other letter.   As this letter
shows, Colson and Roberts had a mercantile enterprise in partnership in Liberia.

WILLIAM J. WALKER TO HIS SON [9]

FREDERICKSBURG February 2, 1850

DEAR JOHN

With pen in hand I seate myself to write you in ancer to your very kind letter which came to hand on the first of this present month—It found us well thank God—and we are in hope's when these lines reaches you They will find you injoyin all the blessings of a kind and benevolent Redeemer—Dear John you stated in yours that it was the secont letter you had writen—well it is the secont one we have received—and this is the secont one I have written in ancer to yours your grand Mother Departed this life on the 20th of November and Harry Hulet Dide Just about one month before your grand Mother and Brother A Daniel Dide on the 22 of January 1850 and one of the largest possession I ever saw in this place turn out on such a cation boath societys turned out with their bages which seen was monefull But pretty—I think I have gaven you all the News of Interest there fore I will turn my thoughts to sumthin elce—I will make none your request to the Brethren Askin of them to pray for you and Dear John dont you forget to approach a throne of grace often and I pray God that you may grow in grace and in the knolege of the truth as is in our lord and Saviour Jesus Christ and read you Bible at every Idle moment you will find It a grate strenght in your Christian Warfare in this world yes and in the world to come I pray God that you and Brother Brook may be preserved unto the secont comming of our lord and Saviour—Jesus Christ—Ever Be foun washing in the blood of the lamb I will see Mr. J Chew and ask of him when Mr. Minor's Brother will leave and will have your Shirts Ready if God be willing—Dear John I have one more thing to say Before I close and it is this of all the pretty Spanish girls you have seen I do hope you will not Come Clare Back home to pick up nothing let your old song Be true get you a wife from old Virginia old Virginia Shore—John for the sake of your happyness here after take the advice which I gave I am now about to close and my last wish is that you may hold out faithfull to the end—old fredericksburg is in the same place.   let me here from you often farewell if we never meet on erth I hop to mee you in heaven where parting is noe more   Davy H sends his love to you your Mother and Sister all join In love to you I Close good by John good by   Yours untell

Death   WILLIAM J. WALKER

---

[9] At this time this young man John was away with the navy.

The letter is found in the collection of manuscripts of the Association for the Study of Negro Life and History.

JOHN MOSHELL TO HIS MASTER

Mr. Garey as i understand you have Bought me i am willing to go
and live with you as my master—and if you have no employment
for me i am willing to be hired out to the distilling business as i
have followed it many years in this sitty i have a famyly in this
plasse and would be glad you would take me out of this place for
keeping me hear at expences to you and no servis to me from
Your negrow
JOHN MOSHELL

NEW YORK NEW GAIL

FROM ADAM PLUMMER AND HIS RELATIVES [10]

MT. HEBRON July 2nd
1856

DEAR PLUMMER

I am sorry that I have not been able to write
to you before.   I was very much troubled to hear of your sickness,
but I hope you are well now.   I was very much pleased to hear
from you by William, and have been looking for you every Saturday
since.   I will be very glad to see you this Saturday, and I cannot
think that we are parted for life.   I am very much in want of your
assistance and if you cannot come yourself please send me some
money by William when he comes up if you can.   Please send me
word by William how my two children are if you do not come
yourself.   Master has promised to be your protector if you can
possibly come.   Please find out how mother and all my sisters and
brothers are and let me know.   Please ask Sally for my parasol and
bring it to me.   Saunders woke up Saturday night and asked if
papy had come.   The children went nearly to Elysville to meet you.
I together with all the children send you our love
Your loving Wife   EMILY PLUMMER
P. S.   Please awnser my letter as soon possible.[11]

---

[10] Adam Plummer, of Riverdale, Maryland, had a wife Emily Plummer
living at Hyattsville, Maryland.   These were the parents of Nellie Arnold
Plummer, who served for many years as a teacher in the District of Columbia.
This was evidently written by some white person of the home.   Emily
Plummer the wife of Adam Plummer could not write, but he could.

[11] These letters are found in the collection of manuscripts of the Association
for the Study of Negro Life and History.

January 3th 1858

MY DEAR WIFE I take this oppertunity of write you a few lines in answer and to inform you. my comeing over the Road on wensday. the Leicett man would not give me any Leichet nor Speake for me to the conducter for seat in the cars. So I Got on without Libitys. and he said it aut to be the Case nomore. So I got home at Thre oClock p.m marander is well today and Love to you and all her bothers and sisters and she is go to Mr Thylman Hillary at Three Sister this year while sorrows Encampass me round, and Endless disTresses i see astonsihed. i cry can a mortal be found. That surrounded with Troubles Like me. few hours of peace i Enjoy. and They are Succeeded by pain, if a momont of praising my God I Emgay, I have hours again to Complain oh. when shall my sorrows subside. or when shall My sufferings cease. I am not so well today   I turn you thanks I have a Coff and Chool I am your
Husban
ADAM FPLUMMER at Riversdale
near Bladensbug
Emily plummer

Monday March the 8   1858   and a snowy day

MY DEAR WIFE I take this oppertuinty of writeing you a few lins in answer, and I to inquire how you and your Childrens are. and geting a Long at Distime and I had not the pleasure of Hireing form you sence I came Away last Chrismast. i sopose you have a wish to Heire form your Childrens and not form me. I wrote you a letter on first January and I have not Reseveed any answer yet and Besides thus the man who keep the ticket office at Camden; Station. He would not Reeveit as a guide for me thos I get on the cars. but I not to be the Casse nomore DC. And Miss Marandia Plummer is left three sister on the 7 febuary She is now in Georgetown with Mr. Clark the methadiese Priceher. he and Thylman Scott Came up to see His father and mother on the 14 day feb in his return home he went though Bladensboug he taken by Mr wallLace to Elaxanderia that night and wos put in Levi Herdle pen; and on Saturday his father go to see his son and take some Close for him but whn come there his son was gon for new or Leans so his father Return home with sorrowfull heart   he and Mr Hillerry send for me verry W.b. pertilar. for he say that it be better for now and Therafter.   I suppose he mant to sold my son but i have not seen him yet.   While sorrows encampass me Round and Endless Distresses I see astonished I cry can a mortal be found thats surrounded with troubles like me few Hours of peace I enjoy and they are succeeded by pain. If a moment of praising my God I enjoy I have Hours again to complain this of him you offen Speak of and consolation given and of Him you sweetly siad that our Hearts are broken.

This is for Emily Plummer

I am your affectuonate Husban ADAM F

PLUMMER at Riversdale near Bladensbourg

April 3th 1859

MY DEAR WIFE i take this opertunity to answer your letter. and the same day in the moning I wish that I could see you in my haerte and in a few minnutes after a littel boy came runing to me at my House with a Letter coldse Dait March 31 and I reseve it with open Hands and Joyfull Heart, and it Read thus. I am not well myself and the Childrens have ben sick colds you are mistaken that I do not wish to here form you and the Childrens, for i have some things for you and your Childrens last Chrismus it is not my with wish that i cannot here form you or see but I am not satisfied in my mind with your care for three years or more I wish that I came to see you as wish or is before in time pas. but I think it is verry serve on me and Hard that I cannot come to see forms to go with at time I Exspect to came up in April 23 If i can to see you and your Chilldrens

form three sister

your Son Elias plummer is well about a week for I go to see him Miss Marandia plummer is the same form George Town D C Green St No 135

my Bother Henry plummer form Goodwood came up to my house Last sunday and saying that the all is well there they all give thir love to you and your Chilldreans with greates care of my self is not well for I havethe Dierar verry bad I have it for a mounth for it makes me verry week and feblee

Mach 21   form yarrow and the Death of Dr penn

Lawyer Stephen is the truss theete

I am your uncomfitable Husband sitll

and   ADAM PLUMMER form Rivers Dale 'seity, Md.

GEORGETOWN December 2nd
1859

DEAR FATHER

I will write to you the second time and I hope
you will grant my request. I hope to see you shortly. I sent
Mother a letter last night and told her I had not heard from you
yet. I was afraid that you were sick or that you had not got my
letter. I suppose that old Mr. John Brown has kept you in the
house. I would have been down on Saturday last but as some of
the family were sick i could not get off, so I will wait a while longer.
I went out in the city Sunday to try to hear from you, Grandmother told me that she saw you at market on Saturday. Aunt
Rachel has not answered my letter yet. Have you heard from them
lately. Please inquire for my brother and let me know how he is.
Mother say'es the children are crazy to see me. Sandies has
gathered some chesnut'es for me. I write you this note to let
you know that I have not forgotten you. I want a good slip of
that grape vine I want it for a lady. Dont you eat all the Cellery
up before I come down. Please save me some eggs. I have no
news to write. Now I must close. From
> your beloved daughter
> SARAH MARANDA PLUMMER

P.S. Give my love
to all enquireing friends.
> S. M. Pummer

May 11 1860

MY DEAR WIFE I take
this opportuneity of writing you a few lins a gane in answer
as I have not herd form you. seance I seen you. I wrote to you
in febuary. in the care of Mrs. Sarah I Nicholson and I have not
heard form you yet I have a letter form Miss Marandare form
Georgetown in May 2th she say all is well. She a bundle for me
but do not expect to go to see her untell June 01th for I have a
wish to come up to see you all on the 26th of May. your Mother
came to Riversdale on 5th of April and she was well and in good
health and she stay three days and then Return home she came to
visit her sick sister: Lucy Scott but she is better now the Dr say
she have the Gravels. the Death tarleton Brown Apirl 21th I
seen henry Brooks on 22 at tarleton Bevring he say that all is
well at home. till sondis and Margarat to loock for me. for I come
in to see them. I am your verry Respecfully
> husban ADAM PLUMMER

wodloun   September 7
1860
my Deare husband

i have not receaved a leter from you saince you went home
wither you rote or no i dont now i supose you heard of merandys
trubles plese rite and let me heare from you as for my self i am
very porly the chrildon are all well let me know how my boy is
marandy says mother is coming up the last of this month plese
rite as sune as you recive this

from yur wife
EMLY PLUMER
the childon all send thare love to you and
wont to se you.

September 18 1860
MY DEARE

HUSBAND i recived you bind leter and was very much oblige to you
for what you sent me the fridy night after i rote to you i was
confined with too babys one was a boy and the other a girl every
body that se them says they are the fines chrilden thay every sar
when mother came and scene them she was delited i am as well as
can bee expected the chrilden ar all well and join me in love to
you from your wife

EMLY PLUMER

Direct your letter to M Plummer Care
Hanson Kelly New Orleans La

NEW ORLEANS LA May 24th 1861
DEAR MOTHER.

I take my pen and hand to write you
a few lines, I am well to day and hope my letter will find you the
same; I have been a long time from gorgetown, I suppose you have
had so many letters to read that you would not care about hearing
from me.

I write with much grief to say that I was in Alexandria two months,
and could not hear from any of you; Jackson ogle went to Washington every three weeks to see his wife, he saw my grandmother
and of course she knew where I was, I hope you will not think hard
of my scolding for that's not half I laid up for you.

I do not blame you because you could not come to see me, I think
it very hard that father did not come to see me as he was nearer

than you were, though I may hear from you, yet I may never expect
to see you again; you will please write to Grandma give my love
to her, and tell her I am sorry I didnot come to see her when I
went to show mu aunt where she lived,
And tell her I hope she will continue to have redemption through
God I have been very low spirited since I left you all, but I will
try to do the best I can I hope that you will not forget that I am
still alive; I send my love to you and to all my inquiring friends,
Remember me to my brother, And tell him I hope he has not
forgotten to write to me as he promised to do I write you much
grief and my heart is full of sorrow, and I can do no better and I
hope you will not Grieve after me, but in the good Providence of
God I hope we willmeet to part no more; though you will be sorry
to hear I am so far yet you will be glad to hear that I met with my
aunt Sarah and she was very glad to see me yet she did not know
me until I made myself known unto her. She has been stopping
at StCharles hotel I do not know whether she has left there or not.
she said when I wrote to give her love to sister and all the children
I hope you will have a pleasant time over my letter give my best
respects to Mrs. Thompson and the children.

I suppose you will answer my letter
as soon as you can   I remain as ever your
because I want to   affec daughter S. M PLUMMER
hear from you as bad as you do from me.

FROM WM. EDEN TO ANTHONY WESTON [12]

OAKLAND, March 29th 56

DEAR SIR

I write to inform you that Mr Lowndes is under
the impression that the large fan is not able to clear itself and
that he thought you was going to put a fan with the large one and
divide the feed. Mr Anderson told him it is the best fan he ever
seen and that the whole machinery performs better than any on the
river. Mr Lowndes then said harry told him that the fan had too
much to do. That when they feed heavy she cant wind at all and
he will never have a mill till another fan be put to take half the
feed. Mr Anderson says he lies. That the only time the fan wont

[12] Anthony Weston was the grandfather of Whitfield McKinlay, a well-known
real estate dealer now in Washington, D. C. Weston was a builder of rice
mills as this letter indicates. He was a contractor of some importance.
The letter is found in the collection of manuscripts of the Association for
the Study of Negro Life and History.

wind clean is when the wind is against the fan but as soon as they get the straw sheds she will wind clean always This is only a conversation. You must not mention it. I would like you to come up early as possible it will be to both our advantage. we are well I hope this will find all well

Yours,

WM EDEN

Joseph C. Bustill, the main figure in the correspondence here, was an abolitionist and an agent of the Underground Railroad. He was a prominent member of the Bustill Family, the sketch of which appeared in Volume X, Number 4 of the *Journal of Negro History*.

FROM JOSEPH C. BUSTILL

HARRISBURG, April 28, '56.

FRIEND STILL:—Your last came to hand in due season, and I am happy to hear of the safe arrival of those gents.   *   *

I have before me the Power of Attorney of Mr. John S. Fiery, son of Mr. Henry Fiery, of Washington county, Md., the owner of those three men, two women and three children, who arrived in your town on the 24th or 25th of March. He graciously condescends to liberate the oldest in a year, and the remainder in proportional time, if they will come back; or to sell them their time for $1300. He is sick of the job, and is ready to make any conditions. Now, if you personally can get word to them and get them to send him a letter, in my charge, informing him of their whereabouts and prospects, I think it will be the best answer I can make him. He will return here in a week or two, to know what can be done. He offers $500 to see them.

Or if you can send me word where they are, I will endeavor to write to them for his special satisfaction; or if you cannot do either, send me your latest information, for I intend to make him spend a few more dollars, and if possible get a little sicker of this bad job. Do try and send him a few bitter pills for his weak nerves and disturbed mind.

Yours in great haste,   JOS. C. BUSTILL.[13]

---

[13] William Still, *Underground Railroad*, 323.

HARRISBURG, May 26, '56.

FRIEND STILL:—I embrace the opportunity presented by the visit of our friend, John F. Williams, to drop you a few lines in relation to our future operations.

The Lightning Train was put on the Road on last Monday, and as the traveling season has commenced and this is the Southern route for Niagara Falls, I have concluded not to send by way of Auburn, except in cases of great danger; but hereafter we will use the Lightning Train, which leaves here at 1½ and arrives in your city at 5 o'clock in the morning, and I will telegraph about 5½ o'clock in the afternoon, so it may reach you before you close. These four are the only ones that have come since my last. The woman has been here some time waiting for her child and her beau, which she expects here about the first of June. If possible, please keep a knowledge of her whereabouts, to enable me to inform him if he comes.   *   *   *   *   *   *   *   *   *

I have nothing more to send you, except that John Fiery has visited us again and much to his chagrin received the information of their being in Canada.

Yours as ever,   JOS. C. BUSTILL.[14]

APRIL 15th, 1857.

SIR—We arrived here safely. Mr. Syrus and his lady is well situated. They have a place for the year round 15 dollars per month. We are all well and hope that you are all the same. Now I wish to know whether you would please to send me some money to go after those people. Send it here if you please.

Yours truly,   OTHO TAYLOR.

WILLIAM STILL.

N. B. HARRIS TO JOSEPH C. BUSTILL

OBERLIN OHIO July 30th / 62

MR. JOS. C BUSTILL   *Dear Sir*

Will you please inform me for the benefit of many of my Regement who are inquiring if you are expecting to Go to Hayti this fall. if so about what time are you expecting to start?

I have a good regement who are now makeing active perperation to sail on the 20 of Oct. Destined for Port-de Poix which place I think can not but be in a few years the Greatest American Settle-

ment in Hayti. Alow me also to State to you that the friend of
Hayti in that noble country were expecting great thing of Your
State regement and I trust will not finely be disapointed.

I have the honor of Remaining Your Resp.

N. B. HARRIS

Oberlin. O.

To Cor. Jos. C. Bustill
Harrisburg, Pa.[15]

JACOB A. WHITE TO JOSEPH C. BUSTILL

PHILADELPHIA, August 19, 1862.

DEAR BUS.,

Your interesting favor of the 11th came duly to hand
and was perused with much pleasure. From your description of
"matters and things" in Saratoga, I have concluded that you are in
the midst of "stirring" times. I hope the "liveliness" of the season
will not interfere with the writing of your proposed description of
Saratoga Springs and Union Hall. On Thursday the 7th we (father,
Mart, Ize, Young Cy, Miller & I) went to Snow Hill and made a
finish. The lines were all correctly fixed and the stones set. There
is a dispute about one stone, but father insisted on his survey and
set the stone, leaving it for the dissatisfied party to order a new
survey or adjust the matter in any other way he saw fit. On Thursday the 28th we propose to go to Little Ease, somewhere in Jersey,
I don't Know where. I wish you were here to go along. Dave is
home again but whether he will go or not I cannot say. There is
nothing of especial interest transpiring among us just now. The
President's address to the colored people of the District is being
discussed in political Anglo-African circles, and a diversity of
opinion, of course, exists. We all await with anxiety the action
of the Committee. The organization of Gov. Sprague's Negro
Brigade is creating some stir. It is said that his Rhode Island
Regiment is now full and that a regiment is now getting up in
New York. It is also understood that certain officials are in
Philada. endeavoring to make up a regiment here. Enlistments in
our city for a Rhode Island Brigade is discouraged by the right-
thinking for evident reasons. I have just heard that a meeting

[15] The remaining letters of the Bustill Family were taken from the manuscripts
of the Association for the Study of Negro Life and History. These letters were
obtained from Mrs. Anne Bustill Smith, a relative of Joseph C. Bustill. She is
a resident of Chicago.

was held last night, at which two Committees were appointed—
One for the purpose of conferring with Gov. Curtin on matters
connected with the Negro & the War; and the other for the purpose
of enrolling the names of all the colored persons in the State who are
liable to do military duty.   By a letter received by Mrs. Bustill
from Mrs. Williams in Harrisburg, we learn that there are very
troublous times there.   Numbers of soldiers are at large in the city
and their prejudice against *"the peculiar people"* is evidenced by
the Kicks and cuffs they administer to our poor sable brethren.
It is dangerous for colored people to walk the street after night.
The house of a colored man has been burned to the ground, and a
deplorable state of affairs is said to exist.   Rumors of the *making
up of the proscribed* in various parts of our city are prevalent and I
have concluded that it is wise policy for Jacob to move around
cautiously & go home early.   It is generally understood that, on
the part of the "Greeks", resistance will be made to the draft.
These people don't see exactly why it is that the *Negurs* can't go to
the War, while the Irish women are incensed when they think that
they are to be deprived of the companionship of their husbands
while no such sad catastrophe is liable to befall the *Nagur* women.
Times are indeed getting troublous and, if, to escape the "impending
crisis", we are compelled to seek refuge among the palms of Hayti,
it will at least be a gratification to our colonization friends here
as well as to our brothers in Jeffrard's dominions.   But I must wind
up.   Remember me to Messrs. Shadd, Stephens and my other
Saratogian Friends and write soon.   Mrs. Bustill wants to know
about your gold pen.   She can't find it.   I wish, if you have time,
you would get me a holder like yours in New York.

Yrs. C (JACOB A. WHITE JR., his cousin)

PHIL March 20th 63

FAITH

    How are You and family, this leaves us very well taking all
things in consideration.   I have the Book ready for Amelia.   Fred
Douglass was here for three days and lectured twice the last one
was on the Crisis in Bethel Church to a mixed multitude and made
an appeal for recruits for the 54 Massachusetts Reg. but only got
five.   The work goes on very privately and nearly 300 have left this
city and the interior of the State 30 left yesterday morning.
This is the Spirit of you Ancestors in regard to Colored Reg.   There
is a motion on foot to establish a Colored Semetary Committee of

the Ladie's. Notices have been sent to all the churches at the
instance of a married daughter of Judge Grier, which meets the
approval of many. I think that the feelings and sentiments of the
whites are changing very rapidly in favor of your people for my part
I pray daily for them. *Ahem*
Bass sends his regards to you and says he has written. My wife
respects to you both, and a kiss for the Baby I suppose you have
heard of poor Glen Goodrich he has been sentenced to 5 years in
the Eastern Penitentiary for Rape on a common prostitute. (if
you have not heard I will write particulars) Arrangement are being
made to open a regular rendezvous at 6th Ave and Lombard for the
Coons. Great efforts are being made in the Legislature of this
State to prevent the imigration of Negroes to this State but so far
but little success have attended them and in every instance the
petitions have been offered by low Scunally fellows who can only
exist in the mire and filth of their own pollution and in one instance
a man was kept by a Mongrel wench and owes his existence and
comforts to her debased degraded mode of living and notwithstanding he is the father of several ill begotten base borns. he is continully
crying out against the impudence of the Negroes and Mulattoes
and that they cannot live in this country. The Democrats are are
outright secesh and declare boldly for Jeff Davis and put all the
blame of the war upon the Negroes and Abolitionist. and deny that
the first blow was struck at Fort Sumpter but say that John Brown
struck it at Harpers Ferry at the instigation of Abolitionist hence
the war, and so we go.

HOPE

90

LOMARD ST

PHIL June 11th 63

FAITH,

How are you and yours, this leaves my family and self
well—the Madam looks forward to the next month with expectations and dreads of no ordinary character and I to feel much interest
but as I place my trust in him, who declares "they that put their
trust in Me shall never be confounded" I hope—A few days ago
I was enroled for the draft which will take place in about a month.
Many of the Colored people are alarmed and others declare if they
have to go they will enlist in the Mass. Reg. as there is no provision
made by this State for the families of Colored Soldiers.

Public sentiment has undergone a great change in the past month or two, and more especially since the brilliant exploites of the several Colored Regements. it is the Subject of conversation of every crowd—but the infernal copper-heads are incensed and will not publish the true statements, let them wallow in the mire and filth of their own pollution until damnation ends their career. How are matters with you, Give my regards to Your Wife Child and Miss Williams—My wife sends her love to you all. I have a busy season and if I collect one half I will do well. I think however the prospects are good. It is now ½ past 7 and cloudy and I cant see to write more. I am sorry I kept you out of the Book so long If you want the Bee or any other receipt it will afford me great pleasure to send it or them Bess is well

Yours truly
HOPE

PHIL Sept 8th 63

HOPE

My Dear Fellow

       It has been a long time since I wrote you (except the last) which I explained. My hand is well and I can weild the pen readily as ever. Yours of the 30 came to hand finding us well. My wife and son came on finely, John and Clarisa are pleased beyond expression. I was much amused a few days ago with their argument as follows. J. " the Baby [16] is more my brother than yours.—C. " No he aint he is more mine,—J. " I know better your name is Guy and my name is Wilson so is the Baby's—at this C gave in and came into the Office for my decision which gave general satisfaction. The Baby is a Bounser and evinces all the grace and Christian Character of his Father Mrs. W°. regards to yourself, Wife Child and Amelia. Bass came home on Saturday and says he will write you in a few days. Recruiting is dull at present but Camp Penn is being filled with conscripts up to this time there are seven full companies. I have been offered several good Positions from Asst Surg down to Hospital Steward all of which I have declined, but my choice would be the latter as it is less exposing and does not require so much manual or pedestrian labor. As I am under the impression that Jacob keeps you posted in the News

---

[16] The baby referred to was the only son, Maurice Hall Wilson. He was later graduated at the Institute for Colored Youths and served the law firm of Benjamin F. Teller and Brother as scribe for several years.

I will not duplicate. According to all accounts poor J Harding is
in a very critical way I trust he is conscious of his condition and
that as he sinks temporally he may rise spiritually to exist in bliss.
Lizzie Steward (Mrs Offer) was buried yesterday, having died in
the triumphs of faith after much intense suffering from a cancer and
affection. There is a great commotion in the 19th Ward to day.
It appears the Reading R R Co have been missing their coal for
some time until on Sunday evening Four cars of 4 tons each were
left on the track and by the next day all was (gone). a watch was
set which resulted in the capture of about 50 persons Male and
Female principaly Germans who make a regular business of it.
I come across the paper and here it is read.

"How are the Irish out your way they were awful here a few weeks
ago but have cooled off considerably and you rarely hear nigger.
Camp Wm Penn and *I* have had a great influence on the public
and have brought and still bringing them to their sober senses.
Jake is a substitute Broker I think the firm is White, Catto & Co
One Colored man from Harrisburg named Woolfe has made some
$500 from the business and is still making Money but some of
them burn the poor substitutes awfully.

Yours

FAITH

J. C. WHITE TO JOSEPH C. BUSTILL

OFFICE OF PENNA. STATE E. R. LEAGUE,
717 LOMBARD STREET,
PHILADA., July 19, 1865.

MR. JOS. C. BUSTILL,

Sir,

At a meeting of the Phila. Members of the
State League held last evening, you were duly appointed Chairman
of a Committee of 3 for the purpose of holding meetings in furtherance of the objects of the League in the 6th District.

Your colleagues are Messrs. N. W. Depee & Jas. R. Gordon.

You will please confer with Mr. Wm. D. Forten,
Chairman of the Committee on Business for Meetings.

Yours for Equal Rights

J. C. WHITE JR.
Secretary.

OFFICE OF PENNA. STATE E. R. LEAGUE,
717 LOMBARD STREET,
PHILADA., July 19, 1865.

MR. JOS. C. BUSTILL,
    Sir,

        At a meeting of the Philada. Members of the
State League held last evening, You were duly appointed Chairman
of a Committee of 5 for the purpose of establishing Leagues wherever
they may be necessary throughout the city.
    Your colleagues are Messrs.
        J. M. C. Crummill of 3rd District
        J. C. White, Jr.   " 3rd   "
        J. W. Purnell   " 5th   "
        R. M. Adger   " 6th   "
    Yours for Equal Rights

                    J. C. WHITE JR.
                        Secretary.

FROM A SLAVE, RICHARD HACKLEY, TO JOHN A. BROADUS, HIS MASTER [17]

UNIVERSITY OF VIRGINIA,
November 5, 1860

MY DEAR MASTER:

            As I feel like writing a few lines, and to show you
that I think of you very often, I take the present opportunity of
doing so.   I am quite well now, thank the Lord, and we are all so
far as I know, and I hope when these lines reach you that you and
yours may be quite well.   I heard from Mr. St. Clair's yesterday—
all well.
    My dear Master, I hear much of the coming election.   I hope
that Mr. Lincoln or no such man may ever take his seat in the
presidential chair.   I do most sincerely hope that the Union may
be preserved.   I hear through the white gentlemen here that South
Carolina will leave the Union in case he is elected.   I do hope she
won't leave, as that would cause much disturbance and perhaps
fighting.   Why can't the Union stand like it is now?   Well do I
recollect when I drove a wagon in the old wars, carrying things for

---

[17] This letter was obtained from the wife of Prof. S. C. Mitchell, of the
University of Richmond.   She is the daughter of the gentleman addressed.

the army; but I hope we shall have no more wars, but let peace be in all the land.

I have been wanting to go up to see my wife, but have not been able, but will do so soon, I hope. Next year I should like to live nearer her. With my best respects to you and Mistress, I am as ever, your devoted servant,

RICHARD HACKLEY.

JOURDON ANDERSON TO COLONEL P. H. ANDERSON, [18] HIS FORMER MASTER

DAYTON, OHIO, August 7, 1865.

To MY OLD MASTER, COLONEL P. H. ANDERSON, Big Spring, Tennessee.

Sir: I got your letter, and was glad to find that you had not forgotten Jourdon, and that you wanted me to come back and live with you again, promising to do better for me than anybody else can. I have often felt uneasy about you. I thought the Yankees would have hung you long before this, for harboring Rebs they found at your house. I suppose they never heard about your going to Colonel Martin's to kill the Union soldier that was left by his company in their stable. Although you shot at me twice before I left you, I did not want to hear of your being hurt, and am glad you are still living. It would do me good to go back to the dear old home again, and see Miss Mary and Miss Martha and Allen, Esther, Green, and Lee. Give my love to them all, and tell them I hope we will meet in the better world, if not in this. I would have gone back to see you all when I was working in the Nashville Hospital, but one of the neighbors told me that Henry intended to shoot me if he ever got a chance.

I want to know particularly what the good chance is you propose to give me. I am doing tolerably well here. I get twenty-five dollars a month, with victuals and clothing; have a comfortable home for Mandy,—the folks call her Mrs. Anderson,—and the children—Milly, Jane, and Grundy—go to school and are learning well. The teacher says Grundy has a head for a preacher. They go to Sunday school, and Mandy and me attend church regularly. We are kindly treated. Sometimes we overhear others saying, "Them

[18] Jourdon Anderson, the writer, was a freedman addressing his former master.

colored people were slaves" down in Tennessee. The children feel hurt when they hear such remarks; but I tell them it was no disgrace in Tennessee to belong to Colonel Anderson. Many darkeys would have been proud, as I used to be, to call you master. Now if you will write and say what wages you will give me, I will be better able to decide whether it would be to my advantage to move back again.

As to my freedom, which you say I can have, there is nothing to be gained on that score, as I got my free papers in 1864 from the Provost-Marshal-General of the Department of Nashville. Mandy says she would be afraid to go back without some proof that you were disposed to treat us justly and kindly; and we have concluded to test your sincerity by asking you to send us our wages for the time we served you. This will make us forget and forgive old scores, and rely on your justice and friendship in the future. I served you faithfully for thirty-two years, and Mandy twenty years. At twenty-five dollars a month for me, and two dollars a week for Mandy, our earnings would amount to eleven thousand six hundred and eighty dollars. Add to this the interest for the time our wages have been kept back, and deduct what you paid for our clothing, and three doctor's visits to me, and pulling a tooth for Mandy, and the balance will show what we are in justice entitled to. Please send the money by Adam's Express, in care of V. Winters, Esq., Dayton, Ohio. If you fail to pay us for faithful labors in the past, we can have little faith in your promises in the future. We trust the good Maker has opened your eyes to the wrongs which you and your fathers have done to me and my fathers, in making us toil for you for generations without recompense. Here I draw my wages every Saturday night; but in Tennessee there was never any pay-day for the negroes any more than for the horses and cows. Surely there will be a day of reckoning for those who defraud the laborer of his hire.

In answering this letter, please state if there would be any safety for my Milly and Jane, who are now grown up, and both good-looking girls. You know how it was with poor Matilda and Catherine. I would rather stay here and starve—and die, if it come to that—than have my girls brought to shame by the violence and wickedness of their young masters. You will also please state if there has been any schools opened for the colored children in your neighborhood. The great desire of my life now is to give my children an education, and have them form virtuous habits.

Say howdy to George Carter, and thank him for taking the pistol from you when you were shooting at me.

From your old servant,

JOURDON ANDERSON.[19]

Love letters written by Negroes before the Civil War are both interesting and valuable. The Editor has not as yet collected a large number, but the following are sufficient to show the importance of such documents:

FROM C. A. STEWART

WASHINGTON CITY, Dec 25,th 1850

MY DEAR JOSEPHINE,

it is with much pleasure, that I now assume this present opportunity of addressing you this letter, hoping it may find you and your mother quite well and injoying the blessings of kind providence, may I inform you that these lines leaves me and my family quite will, and likewise all of the young Ladies, I wish you a Merry Christmas, and christmas Gift. I have just gott home from the first word, I am quite happy to inform you that I have spent quite a joyful Christman with the young Ladies—but the one which was needful was youself, and my sweet girl think this not flattery. and above all, receive this as comeing from a true and devoted lover, but my Dear you have had sufficient proof of this fact, therefore isnt worth while for me to make any farther declarations to you. I have delivered your letters to the girls, and they were well. I havenot seen Miss Charlotte Beans as yet, for she wasnot in. when I called upon her. I seen Miss Henrietta Nichols, today and taken tea with her this Evening. togeather with Miss Brooks. and Miss Martin these ladies I suppose are strangers to you. I called on Miss Jones and Miss Mary Ann Chapman, this eveing and they were quite well, I have had some kisses to day from the ladies, as christman Gifts. but I have not had one from you, and when shall I be Able for to get another sweet kiss from those lovely lips of yours, I wish you would come down to Washington. for I think it would be better for your health. I have seen Mr. Isaac King- he came in to see me last Eveing he is well but the madam isnt well at present, and I havenot seen her he sends his love to you. My old friend Mr. ISaac Morton taken dinner with me

[19] Maria Child, *The Freedmen'sBook*, 265–267.

today—he is well, and sends his respects to you and your mother, I had Miss Brooks and Miss Martin to dine with also, and several other friends, Miss Elina Syfacx has gott married to A Mr. Reves of Virginia I arrived her to late for the wedding, but I have some of the wedding cake—and I send you a piece of it—so when you see this cake, think of me, and your wedding day—there is a great many young Ladies here. but a very few young Gentlemen. I am happy to to inform you that my cold has gott something better. the people talk a great deal about you and me, but I donot care what they say. but you are my chosen one. I hop you will Ever be constant to me, and I will be true to you. but my dear I fear nothing, for I know you will be true to me, as I am to you, please gave my love to your Mother and most of all for youself. I hop you have spent a Merry Christmas. I shold like to have been with you but I at present am deprived this privilege. Give my Respects to Miss Moring, and kiss her for me, as she is a warm friend of yours.

I must come to a close by wishing you a merry merry christmas and a happy New Year

May God Bless you my sweet girl, and preserve you from danger. until we meet again and oh may our meeting be soon.

I am most Sincerely
Your Most Devoted Lover &c
· C. A. STEWART

Please Answer this directly
To Miss Josephine Jameson
Philadelphia, Pa.

The following are letters of Lewis H. Douglass to H. Amelia Loguen whom he later married. He was a son of Frederick Douglass, and she the daughter of Bishop J. W. Loguen, a distinguished churchman who became a bishop of the African Methodist Episcopal Zion Church.

SYRACUSE April 10th/62

MY DEAR LEWIS:

Pardon my negligence in allowing so many weeks to pass away without writing and accept this tardy letter. Your note of Apr. 8, has acted as a reminder, and I with pleasure write.

Since I last wrote to you I have lost by death a dear aunt whose name was Mary Wills and her home was with my grandfather in Rusti Chautauque Co. N. Y. The Dr. called her disease Billious

Fever, She died on the 10th of March. Father and Mother attended her funeral, leaving me to keep house and care for aunt Tinnie and little Tinnie who were both sick. I flatter myself that I did remarkably well "considering".

Spring has brought with it as usual, the ever dreaded, yearly school examinations, *dreaded* because they are so *very tedious.* Monday I thought of nothing but Chloride of Sodium, Nitrate of Silver detection of arsenic, uses of Zinc etc etc; Tuesday, Parlez-vous français? Comment-vous appelez-vous? and Je me porte tres bien, yesterday oh! terrible thought Plane Trigonometry; do you wonder then that last night I dreamed of being in France? After of trying to show that Chemistry is one of the most useful and interesting studies imaginable and lastly I was alone in some queer place trying to accertain the height of a "fort on a distant hill inaccessable on account of an intervening swamp". O! how refreshing on awaking this morning to know that all *such* is for a time past and that vacation is close at hand.

Quite a contrast in the reception of Wendall Phillips in Washington and the manner in which he was treated in Cincinnati, how filled up this world is with mean unprincipled men, will they ever be reformed?

Prof. Porter is in town and his little lady is at some water cure East.

Please let me know when your sister Rosa returns and I will write to her.

Give my love to your mother and believe me
Yours truly
H. AMELIA LOGUEN.

ROCHESTER, June 14/62.

MY OWN DEAR AMELIA: How can I express the pleasure it affords me to receive a letter written by the hand of her I love? To me that pleasure is inexpressible and I can not attempt to find words that will in any way give an idea of that pleasure, fearful that I may find myself netted by an inextricable net of conglomerated nonsense. I may say that your letter of the 12th brought you more fully before my sight if possible, and in that way added an increased pleasantness to my thoughts and dreams of you.

Men and women talk of Love, can any one describe it? Can any one give the reason why one person loves another to the exclusion of every one else, that is why one man loves a lady more than

he does another and *vice versa* when ladies and gentlemen are so
nearly alike. I know many ladies, who are amiable kind, talented
and refined, all that a man could wish, and yet I cannot love them
or do not love them as I love you, and they may be like you, but to
me they are different, now who can tell wherein is the difference.
It cannot be antipathy on my part for they are all I could desire,
reasonably, thus I am led to think that love is an unreasonable
passion, that persons who love each other do so through the exercise
of some other power than reason. For the life of me I cannot tell
the reason that I love you. I may give a reason but it is impossible
to give one that would not apply to many girls. So I say reason or
no reason, some undefinable force attracts me to you, and I have no
means of resisting it and would not if I had.

As the sun rises in the mornings and brightens into freshness,
beauty and grandeur, hills, meadows, and forests that have been
clouded in gloom by the black and awful midnight; so day after day
freshens and brightens that respect esteem and love I bear you.
Not like the hills, meadows and forests disappearing from the sight
in an impenetrable gloom of intense darkness by night but as a
city appears to an early riser who ascends a hill that overlooks it,
and sees it standing encircled and imprisoned by a misty vapor, just
transparent enough to enable you to look beyond and see it standing
in its majesty, is my love for you in my dreams by night. As it is
getting late I must retire. There I liked to have forgotten that *my*
mother earnestly desired to have *your* mother come and make her
a visit in August or earlier if convenient. Believe me my dear
Amelia that I remain always

Affectionately
LEW.

SYRACUSE, August 6, 1862

MY DEAR AMELIA. "Some one" called to-day after a pleasant
visit to the land of his birth. "Some one" is very happy to know
that another some one is enjoying herself. I will write when I
get home.

Yours affectionately
"SOME ONE"

ROCHESTER, Aug. 18, 1862.

MY OWN DEAR AMELIA: Your letter of the 16th inst. reached me
to-day finding me enjoying good health. I am glad that you

thought my last was interesting for I assure you without the slightest affectation that it appeared to me as a very miserable apology for a letter.

I have been and still am at a loss to express in words the deep feeling of mingled love and gratitude with which I was inspired by reading that kind letter of yours of the 27th July, breathing words from a heart filled with a confidence which a pure unalloyed affection can only inspire.

What but an honest and true love would prompt a lady situated as you my dear are, to forsake father, mother, sisters and brothers dear and take up with such an individual as I am whom you scarcely know, and who may be the vilest wretch on earth. No, but your love of me, tells me that I am not a vile wretch, for you my dear are too noble minded and good to desire to join yourself to such. But my dear Amelia I can say I thank you for that letter, and were I not a man I might shed tears of gratitude.

Syracuse people as well as other people will talk. I did not know that it was as generally known that I was in Syracuse as you tell me but it don't make any difference to me whether it was or not, I enjoyed myself with brother Gerrit as I see you know. Yes dear, Gerrit showed me around town, and among the things he showed me, was a lesson in economy, I may say a highly important lesson, being no less than a very cheap way of keeping one's *understanding* polished so that he might go through the world a shining light. The process was simple, so simple that even the smallest child might use it with perfect ease, one thing however I noticed connected with the teaching was that the teacher Mr. G. S. L. took great pains not to use the wonderfully cheap process and had I followed in *his* footsteps I am quite positive I never would have learned the lesson. I have only one objection to the process, that is it is spread on too thick and the polish clings with the tenacity of a tooth ache, and vulgar people not much acquainted with chemistry might take it for *mud*.

Your dear and to me precious countenance was missing at your home that day, but the kindness of your (our) mother and brother Gerrit went far to make all pleasant. Gerrit is a trump and if he ever comes to Rochester tell him I shall see him through.

I am in no writing mood as you will plainly see, so I must bid you good night and pleasant dreams to you, let them not be however of "picaninnies".

Ever Affectionately
LEW.

Remember me to Sate.   What will Blowgia say when she sees my
writing in your album.   LHD

                              MORRIS ISLAND. S. C. July 20
MY DEAR AMELIA: I have been in two fights, and am unhurt.   I
am about to go in another I believe to-night.   Our men fought well
on both occasions.   The last was desperate we charged that terrible
battery on Morris Island known as Fort Wagoner, and were repulsed
with a loss of 3 killed and wounded.   I escaped unhurt from amidst
that perfect hail of shot and shell.   It was terrible.   I need not
particularize the papers will give a better than I have time to give.
My thoughts are with you often, you are as dear as ever, be good
enough to remember it as I no doubt you will.   As I said before we
are on the eve of another fight and I am very busy and have just
snatched a moment to write you.   I must necessarily be brief.
Should I fall in the next fight killed or wounded I hope to fall with
my face to the foe.
    If I survive I shall write you a long letter.   DeForrest of your
city is wounded George Washington is missing, Jacob Carter is
missing, Chas Reason wounded Chas Whiting, Chas Creamer all
wounded.   The above are in hospital.
    This regiment has established its reputation as a fighting regi-
ment not a man flinched, though it was a trying time.   Men fell
all around me.   A shell would explode and clear a space of twenty
feet, our men would close up again, but it was no use we had to
retreat, which was a very hazardous undertaking.   How I got out
of that fight alive I cannot tell, but I am here.   My Dear girl I
hope again to see you.   I must bid you farewell should I be killed.
Remember if I die I die in a good cause.   I wish we had a hundred
thousand colored troops we would put an end to this war.   Good
Bye to all Your own loving   Write soon   LEWIS

    The most numerous of all letters of Negroes hitherto
accessible are those of fugitives written to their friends after
the flight to free soil.   Most of these letters appear in books
written by antislavery workers and in their manuscript collections.   Southerners might have preserved some of them had
they been received in that quarter, but few were addressed
to that section because they might have been used as evidence
to convict their friends.   Those in which the fugitives seemed
to express themselves unconsciously are given below.

LETTERS OF THOMAS H. JONES

WILMINGTON, N. C., July 11, 1849.

MY DEAR WIFE.—I write these few lines to inform you that I am well, and hope they may find you and the children well, and all the friends. My dear wife, I long to see you and the children one time more in this world. I hope to see you all soon. Don't get out of heart, for I will come as soon as I can. I hope it will not be long, for God will be my helper, and I feel he will help me. My dear wife, you must pray for me that God may help me. Tell John he must be a good boy till I see him. I must not forget sister Chavis. She must pray for me, that God may help me come out. Tell her I say that she must be faithful to God; and I hope, dear wife, you will be faithful to God. Tell sister Chavis that Henry will be out soon, and he wants her to keep a good heart and he will send money out to her. Tell her he says she must write to him as soon as she can, for he will not stay long behind her. As soon as he gets his money he will come. I hope to see you all very soon. Tell my Brethering to pray for me, that God may help me get there safe, and make my way clear before me. Help me by your prayers, that God may be with me. Tell brother Robert H. Cousins that he must pray for me; for I long to meet him one time more in this world. Sister Tucker and husband give their love to you and sister Chavis, and say that you must pray for them. Dear wife, you may look for me soon. But what way I will come, I can't tell you now. You may look for me in three weeks from now. You must try and do the best you can till I come. You know how it is with me, and how I have to come. Tell the Church to pray for me, for I hope to reach that land if I live, and I want the prayers of all God's children. I can't say any more at this time; but I remain, your dear husband, till death,

THOMAS JONES.

WILMINGTON, N. C., July 17, 1849.

MY DEAR WIFE.—I write to tell you I am well, and I hope these few lines will find you and the children well. I long to see you all one time more. Do pray for me, that God may help me to get to you all. Do ask sister to pray the Lord to help me. I will trust in God, for I know that He is my friend, and He will help me. My dear wife, tell my children I say they must be good till I see them once more. Do give my love to brother R. H. Cousins, and tell him I hope to meet him in two or three weeks from now. Then I can tell him all I want to say to him. Tell sister Chavis I say, do not come back to this place till I come. Her husband says he wants her to stay, and he will come on soon. My dear wife, I want you to do the best you can till I come. I will come as soon as I can. You and sister Chavis must live together, for you went together, and you must try to stay together. Do give my love to sister Johnson and husband, and all of my friends. Ask them all to pray for me, that God may be with me in all that I do to meet you all one time more. My dear wife, you know how I told you, you must mind how you write your letters. You must not forget to write as if you did not like New York, and that you will come home soon. You know what I told you to do, and now you must not forget it when you write. I will send you some money in my next letter. I have not sold my houses yet, and if I can't sell, I will leave them all, and come to you and the children. I will trust in that God who can help the poor. My dear, don't forget what I told you to do when you write. You know how I have to do. Be careful how you write. I hope to be with you soon, by the help of God. But, above all things, ask all to pray for me, that God may open the way for me to come safe. I hope to be with you soon, by the help of the Lord. Tell them if I never come, to go on, and may God help them to go forth to glorious war. Tell them to see on the mountain top the standard of God. Tell them to follow their Captain, and be led to certain victory. Tell them I can but sing with my latest breath, happy, if I may to the last speak His name, preach Him to all, and cry, in death, "Behold the Lamb." Go on, my dear wife, and trust in God for all things.

I remain your husband,
THOMAS JONES.

WILMINGTON, N. C., July 25, 1849.

MY DEAR WIFE.—Do tell my children they must be good children till I come to them; and you, my dear wife, must do the best you can; for I don't know how I will come, but I will do the best I can for you. I hope God will help me, for if He don't, I don't know what I will do. My dear wife, I have not sold my houses yet, but I will do the best I can. If I had money I would leave all I have and come, for I know the Lord will help me. It is for want of money that I can't come. But I hope, my dear wife, the Lord will help me out. Tell brother Cousins I hope he and all the people of God will pray for me; and you, my dear wife, must not forget to pray for me. Ask brother Cousins, if he pleases, to put my children to some school. Dear wife, you know the white people will read your letters to me; do mind how you write. No one but God knows my heart. Do pray for me.

I remain your husband till death,
THOMAS JONES.

P. S.—My dear wife, I received your letter the 24th of July, and was truly glad to hear you arrived safe in New York. Please tell brother Cousins I will write to him in a few days, and I will send you some money. My dear wife, do mind how you write. You must not forget I am in a slave place, and I can't buy myself for the money. You know how it is, and you must tell brother Cousins. I have not sold yet, but if I can't sell, I will come some how, by the help of the Lord. John Holmes is still in my way. I want you to write a letter, and say in it, that you will be home in two months, so I can let them read it, for they think I will run away and come to you. So do mind how you write, for the Lord's sake.

THOMAS JONES.

WILMINGTON, N. C., Aug. 4, 1849.

MY DEAR SISTER.—I hope to see you in a few days, and all my friends. I hope, dear sister, you will not forget to pray for me, for by the help of God, I will see you in a few days. Your husband is coming on soon, but I will be on before him. I would have been on before now, but I could not get my money. I have had a hard time to get money to leave with. I am sorry to hear that you think we can't get a living where you are. My dear sister, a smart man can get a living anywhere in the world, if he try. Don't think we can't live out there, for I know God will help us. You know God has promised a living to all His children. Don't forget that God is ever present, for we must trust Him till death. Don't get out of heart, for I know we can live out there, if any one can. You may look for me before your husband. Don't leave New York before I come, for you know what I told you before you left Wilmington. If you come back to this place before I get off, it will make it bad for me. You know what the white people here are. Please don't come yet.   I am, your brother in the Lord, till death,

THOMAS JONES.

P. S.—I sent the letter you wrote to Mr. John Ranks. I thought you will wait for a letter from your husband, and I hope you will be better satisfied in your mind that we can get a living out there. Your husband has wrote to you last week; I hope you have got the letter. Oh, that you may trust in God every day, for I know God is your friend, and you must pray night and day that He may help you. I long to see you one time more in this world. We went into the new Church on the 9th day of this month. God was with us on that day, and we had a good time. Though my time with them is short, I hope God will be with them, and may we all meet in the kingdom at last. So pray for me, my dear sister, Aunt Narvey has been dead nearly four weeks. She died happy in the Lord, and is gone home to rest. I hope we may meet in the kingdom at last. Good night, my dear sister.

THOMAS JONES.

WILMINGTON, August 7, 1849.

MY DEAR WIFE.—I long to see you once more in this world, and hope it will not be very long before I am with you. I am trying, my dear wife, to do all I can to get to you. But I hope you will not forget to mind how you write to me. If you should not mind how you write, you will do me great harm. You know I told you to write that you would be home in two months, or three months at the longest. But in two months I told them you would be home. Now, my dear, you must mind, and don't forget, for you know how it is here; a man can't say that his soul is his own; that is, a colored man. So do mind how you write to me. Tell sister Chavis I say she must write to me; and I hope soon I will write my last letter. I will let you know in my next letter how all things are with me. Dear wife, don't get out of heart, for God is my friend. The will of God is my sure defence, nor earth nor hell can pluck me thence, for God hath spoken the word. My dear wife, in reply to your kind letter, received the second day of this month, I have wrote these few lines. I hope you will pray for me. Your dear husband,

THOMAS JONES.

P. S.—To brother Cousins.—My dear brother, I hope you will not think hard of me for not writing to you, for you know how it is with me out here. God knows that I would write to you at any time, if it was not for some things. You know the white people don't like for us to write to New York. Now, let me ask your prayers, and the prayers of the Church, and God's children, that I may see you all soon. I know that God is my friend, for He doth my burden bear. Though I am but dust and ashes, I bless God, and often feel the power of God. Oh, my brother, pray for me, who loves you all, for I have found of late much comfort in the word of God's love. When I come where you are, in the work of the Lord, and I hope the time will soon come when the gospel will be preached to the whole world of mankind. Then go on, dear brother, and do all you can for the Lord. I hope the Lord will help me to get where you are at work soon. Nothing more, but I remain, your brother in the Lord,

THOMAS JONES.

BROOKLYN, Aug. 10, 1849.

MY DEAR HUSBAND.—I got your kind letter of the 23d July, and rejoiced to hear that you was well. I have been very sick myself, and so has Alexander; but, thanks to the Lord, these lines leave me and the children right well. I hope in God they will find you and my son and my mother, and all enquiring friends, enjoying the same blessings. My dear, you requested me and Mrs. Chavis to stay together, but she has taken other people's advice beside mine and Mr. Cousin's, and has gone away. She started from home before we knew a word of it. She left me on the eighth of this month. Do give my love to Betsey Webb and to her husband. Tell her I am sorry she has not come on before now. I am waiting to see her before I start for home. My dear husband, you know you ought to send me some money to pay my board. You know I don't love to leave in this way with my children. It is true that brother Cousins has not said anything to me about it. You keep writing that you are going to send it in your next letter; you know I like to act independent, and I wish you to help me do so now, if you please. Do give my compliments to Aunt Moore, and tell her the children all send their love to her. They send their love to you, and say they want to kiss you mighty bad. The children send their love to brother Edward. I long to see you, husband. No more at present, but remain your loving wife till death,

RYNAR JONES.

WILMINGTON, N. C., Aug. 12, 1849.

MY DEAR WIFE,—I received your paper of the 10th to-day. I am glad to hear that you are well, and the children and friends. I have written to brother Cousins, and told him to tell you that I had not sold out yet. But I hope to sell in a few days, and then I will send you some money. My dear wife, you know that I will do all I can for you and for my children, and that with all my heart. Do try and wait on me a few days, and I hope you will see me and the money too. I am trying to do all I can to sell out, but you know how it is here, and so does brother Cousins. I will do all I know, for I think of you, my dear wife, and the children, day and night. If I can get my money, I will see you soon, by the help of God and my good friend, and that is a woman; she is waiting for me to come every day. My dear wife, all I want is money and your prayers, and the prayers of my friends. I know that God will help me out of my trouble; I know that God is my friend, and I will trust to Him. You wrote to me that Mrs. Chavis left New York. She has not got home yet. I hope, dear wife, that you have done all your part for her. Do give my love to brother Cousins; ask him to pray for me, and all God's people to pray for me, a poor slave at this time. My dear wife, since I wrote last I have seen much of the goodness of the Lord. Pray for me, that I may see more, and that I may trust in Him. My dear wife, I want you should pray for me, night and day, till you see me. For, by the help of God, I will see you all soon. I think now it will be but a few days. Do give my love to my children, and tell them that I want to kiss them all. Good night, my dear, I must go to bed. It is one o'clock at night, and I have a pain in my head at this time. Do tell brother Cousins that I say he must look out for me, on John street, in a few days. Nothing more, but I remain your husband till death,

THOMAS JONES.

Brooklyn, August 23, 1849.

My Dear Husband.—It is with the affectionate feeling of a wife I received your letter of the 19th inst. It found me and the children well, and we were glad to hear that you was well. But we feel very sorry you have not sold out yet; I was in hopes you would have sold by the time you promised, before I got home. Your letter found Mr. Cousins and his wife very sick. Mr. C. has not been out of the house going on two weeks. He was taken by this sickness, so common, which carries so many people off, but, by the help of God and good attendance, he is much on the mend, and his wife also. You ask how much I pay for board. It is three dollars a week for myself and children. In all the letters you have written to me, you don't say a word of mother or Edward. It makes me feel bad not to hear from them. Husband, I have not paid Mr. Cousins any board, and am waiting for you to send me some money. I will pray for you hourly, publicly and privately, and beseech the Almighty God, till I see you again. I shall trust in God; He will do all things for the best.

> I am yours till death do us part.
>
> RYNAR JONES.

WILMINGTON, N. C., Aug. 30, 1849.

MY DEAR WIFE,—I have been quite sick for three weeks, but, thank God, I am better at this time, and hope these few lines will find you and the children all well. I hope, my dear wife, that you have not got out of heart looking for me; you know how it is here; I did think I would have got my money here before this time. But I can't get it, and I will leave all and come to you as soon as I can. So don't get out of heart, my dear wife; I have a hard trial here; do pray for me, that the Lord may help me to see you all soon. I think of you day and night, and my dear children; kiss them for me; I hope to kiss them soon. Edward is sold to Owen Holmes; but I think Mr. Josh. Wright will get him from H. I have done all I could for Edward. Don't think of coming back here, for I will come to you or die. But I want you should write one more letter to me, and say you will be home in a month. Mr. Dawson will be in New York next week, and you will see him; mind how you talk before him, for you know how it is, though he is a friend to me. Now, you must mind what I tell you, my dear wife, for if you don't you will make it hard for me. Now, my dear wife, you must not come back here for your brother and sister; they talk too much; but mind what I say to you, for you know I will do all I can for you; you must not think that you will not get any money, for you shall have it soon. Don't get out of heart, my dear wife; I hope I shall see you soon. Nothing more, but I remain your husband till death.

> THOMAS JONES.[20]

[20] *The Experience of Thomas H. Jones*, 36–46.

PETER VAN WAGENEN [21] TO HIS MOTHER

'My Dear and Beloved Mother:

'I take this opportunity to write to you and inform you that I am well, and in hopes for to find you the same. I am got on board the same unlucky ship Done, of Nantucket. I am sorry for to say, that I have been punished once severely, by shoving my head in the fire for other folks. We have had bad luck, but in hopes to have better. We have about 230 on board, but in hopes, if don't have good luck, that my parents will receive me with thanks. I would like to know how my sisters are. Does my cousins live in New York yet? Have you got my letter? If not, inquire to Mr. Peirce Whiting's. I wish you would write me an answer as soon as possible. I am your only son, that is so far from your home, in the wide, briny ocean. I have seen more of the world than ever I expected, and if I ever should return home safe, I will tell you all my troubles and hardships. Mother, I hope you do not forget me, your dear and only son. I should like to know how Sophia, and Betsey, and Hannah, come on. I hope you all will forgive me for all that I have done.　　　　　　　　　　　　　　　　Your son,

'PETER VAN WAGENEN.'

'My Dear Mother:

'I take this opportunity to write to you, and inform you that I have been well and in good health. I have wrote you a letter before, but have received no answer from you, and was very anxious to see you. I hope to see you in a short time. I have had very hard luck, but are in hopes to have better in time to come. I should like if my sisters are well, and all the people round the neighborhood. I expect to be home in twenty-two months or thereabouts. I have seen Samuel Laterett. Beware! There has happened very bad news to tell you, that Peter Jackson is dead. He died within two days' sail of Otaheite, one of the Society Islands. The Peter Jackson that used to live at Laterett's; he died on board the ship Done, of Nantucket, Captain Miller, in the latitude 15 53, and longitude 148 30 W. I have no more to say at present, but write as soon as possible.

'Your only son,
'PETER VAN WAGENEN.'

[21] Peter Van Wagenen was one of the characters mentioned in the life of Sojourner Truth, with family ties broken by circumstances. See *Narrative of Sojourner Truth, a Northern Slave*, 77–79.

'DEAR MOTHER:

'I take this opportunity to write to you and inform you that I am well and in good health, and in hopes to find you in the same. This is the fifth letter I have wrote you, and have received no answer, and it makes me very uneasy. So pray write as quick as you can, and tell how all the people is about the neighborhood. We are out from home twenty-three months, and in hopes to be home in fifteen months. I have not much to say; but tell me if you have been up home since I left or not. I want to know what sort of a time is at home. We had very bad luck when we first came out, but since we have had very good; so I am in hopes to do well yet; but if I don't do well, you need not expect me home these five years. So write as quick as you can, wont you? So, now I am going to put an end to my writing, at present. Notice—when this you see, remember me, and place me in your mind.

> Get me to my home, that's in the far-distant west,
> To the scenes of my childhood, that I like thebest;
> There the tall cedars grow, and the bright waters flow,
> Where my parents will greet me, white man, let me go!

> Let me go to the spot where the cateract plays,
> Where oft I have sported in my boyish days;
> And there is my poor mother, whose heart ever flows,
> At the sight of her poor child, to her let me go, let me go!

'Your only son,
'PETER VAN WAGENEN.'

FROM AN AFRICAN BOY NAMED KA-LE [22]

WESTVILLE Sept

MR TAPPAN I going write you letter I want tell you some thing I bless you because I love you I want pray for you every night and every morning and evening and I want love you too much I will write letter for my thing for you from that time Jesus began to preach and to say repent for the kingdom of heaven is at hand my friend I write this paper for you because I love you too much I pray for you Lords pray Our father who art in heaven hallowed be friend Mr Tappan I bless you because I love you and I love write you letter my friend I want love all teachers who teach me and all my people good things about Jesus Christ and God and heaven

---

[22] Ka-le was about eleven years of age. He had been a slave in Cuba. See *The American and Foreign Anti-Slavery Reporter*, July, 1840, p. 13.

and every things I bless them that teach me good I pray for them I want write some thy name thy kingdom come thy will be done in earth as it is in heaven give us this day our daily bread And forgive us our debts as and we forgive our debtors and lead us not into temptation but deliver us from evil for thine is the kingdom and the power and the glory for everg Amen O God keep all my teachers and all my friend and all my enemy that No love me all I love them I try to write letter of paper for Mr Tappan and Jesus said unto him foxes have holes and birds of the air have nests but the son of man hath not where to lay his head and Jesus said unto him No man having put his hand to the plough and looking back is fit for the kingdom of God

my name KALE I
send your letter by James Birney

There is some historic value in the following letter of Henry Bibb's former master and his reply:

W. H. GATEWOOD TO HENRY BIBB

Bedford, Trimble County, Ky.

Mr. H. Bibb.

Dear Sir:—After my respects to you and yours &c., I received a small book which you sent to me that I peroseed and found it was sent by H. Bibb I am a stranger in Detroit and know no man there without it is Walton H. Bibb if this be the man please write to me and tell me all about that place and the people I will tell you the news here as well as I can your mother is still living here and she is well the people are generally well in this country times are dull and produce low give my compliments to King, Jack, and all my friends in that cuntry I read that book you sent me and think it will do very well—George is sold, I do not know anything about him I have nothing more at present, but remain yours &c

W. H. GATEWOOD.

February 9th, 1844.

P.S. You will please to answer this letter.

HENRY BIBB TO W. H. GATEWOOD

"Dear Sir:—I am happy to inform you that you are not mistaken in the man whom you sold as property, and received pay for as such. But I thank God that I am not property now, but am regarded as a man like yourself, and although I live far north, I am enjoying a comfortable living by my own industry. If you should ever chance to be traveling this way, and will call on me, I will use you better than you did me while you held me as a slave. Think not that I have any malice against you, for the cruel treatment which you inflicted on me while I was in your power. As it was the custom of your country, to treat your fellow men as you did me and my little family, I can freely forgive you.

I wish to be remembered in love to my aged mother, and friends; please tell her that if we should never meet again in this life, my prayer shall be to God that we may meet in Heaven, where parting shall be no more.

"You wish to be remembered to King and Jack. I am pleased, sir, to inform you that they are both here, well, and doing well. They are both living in Canada West. They are now the owners of better farms than the men are who once owned them.

You may perhaps think hard of us for running away from slavery, but as to myself, I have but one apology to make for it, which is this: I have only to regret that I did not start at an earlier period. I might have been free long before I was. But you had it in your power to have kept me there much longer than you did. I think it is very probable that I should have been a toiling slave on your plantation today, if you had treated me differently.

To be compelled to stand by and see you whip and slash my wife without mercy, when I could afford her no protection, not even by offering myself to suffer the lash in her place, was more than I felt it to be the duty of a slave husband to endure, while the way was open to Canada. My infant child was also frequently flogged by Mrs. Gatewood, for crying, until its skin was bruised literally purple. This kind of treatment was what drove me from home and family, to seek a better home for them. But I am willing to forget the past. I should be pleased to hear from you again, on the reception of this, and should also be very happy to correspond with you often, if it should be agreeable to yourself. I subscribe myself a friend to the oppressed, and Liberty forever. HENRY BIBB.

WILLIAM GATEWOOD.
Detroit, March 23d, 1844.[23]

[23] *Narrative of the Life and Adventures of Henry Bibb, an American Slave,* 175–178.

FROM J. W. C. PENNINGTON

29 6th AVENUE, NEW YORK, May 24th, 1854.

MY DEAR MR. STILL:—Your kind letter of the 22d inst has come to hand and I have to thank you for your offices of benevolence to my bone and my flesh, I have had the pleasure of doing a little for your brother Peter, but I do not think it an offset. My burden has been great about these brethren. I hope they have started on to me. Many thanks, my good friend. Yours Truly.

J. W. C. PENNINGTON.[24]

WM. STILL TO B. McKIERNON

PHILADELPHIA, Aug. 16th, 1851.

To B. McKIERNON, ESQ.: *Sir*—I have received your letter from South Florence, Ala., under date of the 6th inst. To say that it took me by surprise, as well as afforded me pleasure for which I feel to be very much indebted to you, is no more than true. In regard to your informants of myself—Mr. Thornton, of Ala., and Mr. Samuel Lewis, of Cincinnati—to them both I am a stranger. However, I am the brother of Peter, referred to, and with the fact of his having a wife and three children in your service I am also familiar. This brother, Peter, I have only had the pleasure of knowing for the brief space of one year and thirteen days, although he is now past forty and I twenty-nine years of age. Time will not allow me at present, or I should give you a detailed account of how Peter became a slave, the forty long years which intervened between the time he was kidnapped, when a boy, being only six years of age, and his arrival in this city, from Alabama, one year and fourteen days ago, when he was re-united to his mother, five brothers and three sisters.

None but a father's heart can fathom the anguish and sorrows felt by Peter during the many vicissitudes through which he has passed. He looked back to his boyhood and saw himself snatched from the tender embraces of his parents and home to be made a slave for life.

During all his prime days he was in the faithful and constant service of those who had no just claim upon him. In the meanwhile he married a wife, who bore him eleven children, the greater part of whom were emancipated from the troubles of life by death, and three only survived. To them and his wife he was devoted. In-

[24] William Still, *Underground Railroad*, 173.

deed I have never seen attachment between parents and children, or husband and wife, more enitre than was manifested in the case of Peter.

Through these many years of servitude, Peter was sold and resold, from one State to another, from one owner to another, till he reached the forty-ninth year of his age, when, in a good Providence, through the kindness of a friend and the sweat of his brow, he regained the God-given blessings of Liberty. He eagerly sought his parents and home with all possible speed and pains, when, to his heart's joy, he found his relatives.

Your present humble correspondent is the youngest of Peter's brothers, and the first one of the family he saw after arriving in this part of the country. I think you could not fail to be interested in hearing how we became known to each other, and the proof of our being brothers, etc., all of which I should be most glad to relate, but time will not permit me to do so. The news of this wonderful occurrence, of Peter finding his kindred, was published quite extensively, shortly afterwards, in various newspapers, in this quarter, which may account for the fact of "Miller's" knowledge of the whereabouts of the "fugitives." Let me say, it is my firm conviction that no one had any hand in persuading "Miller" to go down from Cincinnati, or any other place after the family. As glad as I should be, and as much as I would do for the liberation of Peter's family (now no longer young), and his three "likely" children, in whom he prides himself—how much, if you are a father, you can imagine; yet I would not, and could not, think of persuading any friend to peril his life, as would be the case, in an errand of that kind.

As regards the price fixed upon by you for the family, I must say I do not think it possible to raise half that amount, though Peter authorized me to say he would give you twenty-five hundred for them. Probably he is not as well aware as I am, how difficult it is to raise so large a sum of money from the public. The applications for such objects are so frequent among us in the North, and have always been so liberally met, that it is no wonder if many get tired of being called upon. To be sure some of us brothers own some property, but no great amount; certainly not enough to enable us to bear so great a burden. Mother owns a small farm in New Jersey, on which she has lived for nearly forty years, from which she derives her support in her old age. This small farm contains between forty and fifty acres, and is the fruit of my father's toil. Two of my brothers own small places also, but they have young families, and consequently consume nearly as much as they make, with the exception of adding some improvements to their places.

For my own part, I am employed as a clerk for a living, but my salary is quite too limited to enable me to contribute any great amount towards so large a sum as is demanded. Thus you see how we are situated financially. We have plenty of friends, but little money. Now, sir, allow me to make an appeal to your humanity, although we are aware of your power to hold as property those poor slaves, mother, daughter and two sons,—that in no part of the United States could they escape and be secure from your claim —nevertheless, would your understanding, your heart, or your conscience reprove you, should you restore to them, without price, that dear freedom, which is theirs by right of nature, or would you not feel a satisfaction in so doing which all the wealth of the world could not equal? At all events, could you not so reduce the price as to place it in the power of Peter's relatives and friends to raise the means for their purchase? At first, I doubt not, but that you will think my appeal very unreasonable; but, sir, serious reflection will decide, whether the money demanded by you, after all, will be of as great a benefit to you, as the satisfaction you would find in bestowing so great a favor upon those whose entire happiness in this life depends mainly upon your decision in the matter. If the entire family cannot be purchased or freed, what can Vina and her daughter be purchased for? Hoping, sir, to hear from you, at your earliest convenience, I subscribe myself,

Your obedient servant,
WM. STILL.

To B. McKiernon, Esq.[25]

FROM JOHN H. HILL

Hamilton, Sept. 15th, 1856.

Dear Friend Still:—I write to inform you that Miss Mary Wever arrived safe in this city. You may imagine the happiness manifested on the part of the two lovers, Mr. H. and Miss W. I think they will be married as soon as they can get ready. I presume Mrs. Hill will commence to make up the articles to-morrow. Kind Sir, as all of us is concerned about the welfare of our enslaved brethren at the South, particularly our friends, we appeal to your sym-

---

[25] This letter and those following it were taken from the collection of manuscripts of William Still, most of which were published in his *Underground Railroad*.

pathy to do whatever is in your power to save poor Willis Johnson from the hands of his cruel master. It is not for me to tell you of his case, because Miss Wever has related the matter fully to you. All I wish to say is this, I wish you to write to my uncle, at Petersburg, by our friend, the Capt. Tell my uncle to go to Richmond and ask my mother whereabouts this man is. The best for him is to make his way to Petersburg; that is, if you can get the Capt. to bring him. He have not much money. But I hope the friends of humanity will not withhold their aid on the account of money. However we will raise all the money that is wanting to pay for his safe delivery. You will please communicate this to the friends as soon as possible.

Yours truly,   JOHN H. HILL.

FROM HAM & EGGS, SLAVE

PETERSBURG, VA., Oct. 17th, 1860.

MR. W. STILL:—*Dear Sir*—I am happy to think, that the time has come when we no doubt can open our correspondence with one another again. Also I am in hopes, that these few lines may find you and family well and in the enjoyment of good health, as it leaves me and family the same. I want you to know, that I feel as much determined to work in this glorious cause, as ever I did in all of my life, and I have some very good hams on hand that I would like very much for you to have. I have nothing of interest to write about just now, only that the politics of the day is in a high rage, and I don't know of the result, therefore, I want you to be one of those wide-a-wakes as is mentioned from your section of country now-a-days, &c. Also, if you wish to write to me, Mr. J. Brown will inform you how to direct a letter to me.

No more at present, until I hear from you; but I want you to be a wide-a-wake.

Yours in haste,   HAM & EGGS.

FROM SHERIDAN FORD, IN DISTRESS

BOSTON, MASS., Feb. 15th, 1855.
No. 2, Change Avenue.

MY DEAR FRIEND:—Allow me to take the liberty of addressing you and at the same time appearing troublesomes you all friend. but subject is so very important that i can not but ask not in my name but in the name of the Lord and humanity to do something

for my Poor Wife and children who lays in Norfolk Jail and have
Been there for three month i Would open myself in that frank and
hones manner. Which should convince you of my cencerity of
Purpoest don't shut your ears to the cry's of the Widow and the
orphant & i can but ask in the name of humanity and God for he
knows the heart of all men. Please ask the friends humanity to do
something for her and her two lettle ones i cant do any thing Place
as i am for i have to lay low Please lay this before the churches
of Philadelphaise beg them in name of the Lord to do something for
him i love my freedom and if it would do her and her two children
any good i mean to change with her but cant be done for she is Jail
and you most no she suffer for the jail in the South are not like yours
for any thing is good enough for negros the Slave hunters Says & may
God interpose in behalf of the demonstrative Race of Africa Whom
i claim desendent i am sorry to say that friendship is only a name
here but i truss it is not so in Philada i would not have taken this
liberty had i not considered you a friend for you treaty as such
Please do all you can and Please ask the Anti Slavery friends to do
all they can and God will Reward them for it i am shure for the
earth is the Lords and the fullness there of as this note leaves me
not very well but hope when it comes to hand it may find you and
family enjoying all the Pleasure life Please answer this and Pardon
me if the necessary sum can be required i will find out from my
brotherinlaw i am with respéctful consideration

SHERIDAN W. FORD.

Yesterday is the fust time i have heard from home Sence i left
and i have not got any thing yet i have a tear yet for my fellow man
and it is in my eyes now for God knows it is tha truth i sue for your
Pity and all and may God open their hearts to Pity a poor Woman
and two children. The Sum is i believe 14 hundred Dollars Please
write to day for me and see if the cant do something for humanity.

FROM JOS. C. BUSTILL

HARRISBURG, March 24, '56.

FRIEND STILL:—I suppose ere this you have seen those five
large and three small packages I sent by way of Reading, consisting
of three men and women and children. They arrived here this
morning at 8½ o'clock and left twenty minutes past three. You
will please send me any information likely to prove interesting in
relation to them.

Lately we have formed a Society here, called the Fugitive Aid Society. This is our first case, and I hope it will prove entirely successful.

When you write, please inform me what signs or symbols you make use of in your despatches, and any other information in relation to operations of the Underground Rail Road.

Our reason for sending by the Reading Road, was to gain time; it is expected the owners will be in town this afternoon, and by this Road we gained five hours' time, which is a matter of much importance, and we may have occasion to use it sometimes in future. In great haste,   Yours with great respect,

JOS. C. BUSTILL.

FROM A SLAVE SECRETED IN RICHMOND

RICHMOND, VA., Oct. 18th, 1860.

To MR. WILLIAM STILL:—*Dear Sir*—Please do me the favor as to write to my uncle a few lines in regard to the bundle that is for John H. Hill, who lives in Hamilton, C. W. Sir, if this should reach you, be assured that it comes from the same poor individual that you have heard of before; the person who was so unlucky, and deceived also. If you write, address your letter John M. Hill, care of Box No. 250. I am speaking of a person who lives in P.va. I hope, sir, you will understand this is from a poor individual.

FROM JOHN THOMPSON

MR. STILL:—You will oblige me much Iff you will Direct this Letter to Vergenia for me to my Mother & iff it well sute you Beg her in my Letter to Direct hers to you & you Can send it to me iff it sute your Convenience I am one of your Chattle.

JOHN THOMPSON,
Syracuse, Jeny 6th.

Direction—Matilda Tate Care of Dudley M Pattee Worrenton Farkiear County Verginia.

FROM JOHN THOMPSON TO HIS MOTHER

MY DEAR MOTHER:—I have imbrace an opportunity of writing you these few lines (hoping) that they may fine you as they Leave me quite well I will now inform you how I am geting I am now a free man Living By the sweet of my own Brow not serving a nother man & giving him all I Earn But what I make is mine and iff one Plase do not sute me I am at Liberty to Leave and go some where elce & can ashore you I think highly of Freedom and would not exchange it for nothing that is offered me for it I am waiting in a Hotel   I suppose you Remember when I was in Jail I told you the time would Be Better and you see that the time has come when I Leave you my heart was so full & yours But I new their was a Better Day a head, & I have Live to see it   I hird when I was on the Underground R. Road that the Hounds was on my Track but it was no go I new I was too far out of their Reach where they would never smell my track when I Leave you I was carred to Richmond & sold & From their I was taken to North Carolina & sold & I Ran a way & went Back to Virginna   Between Richmond & home & their I was caught & Put in Jail & their I Remain till the oner come for me then I was taken & carred Back to Richmond then I was sold to the man who I now Leave he is nothing But a But of a Feller   Remember me to your Husband & all in quirin Friends & say to Miss Rosa that I am as Free as she is & more happier I no I am getting $12 per month for what Little work I am Doing   I hope to here from you a gain   I your Son & ever By

JOHN THOMPSON.

FROM WILLIAM JONES

Mr. Still:—I take this opportunity of writing a few lines to you hoping that tha may find you in good health and femaly. i am well at present and doing well at present i am now in a store and getting sixteen dollars a month at the present.   i feel very much o blige to you and your family for your kindnes to me while i was with you i have got a long without any trub le a tal.   i am now in albany City.   give my lov to mrs and mr miller and tel them i am very much a blige to them for there kind ns. give my lov to my Brother nore Jones tel him i should like to here from him very much and he must write.   tel him to give my love to all of my perticular frends and tel them i should like to see them very much. tel him that he must come to see me for i want to see him for sum thing very perticler.   please ansure this letter as soon as posabul and excuse me for not writting sooner as i dont write myself.   no more at the present.   WILLIAM JONES.

derect to one hundred 125 lydus. stt

BALTIMO APRIL 16, 1859.

W. STILL:—Dear brother i have taken the opportunity of writing you these few lines to inform you that i am well an hoping these few lines may find you enjoying the same good blessing please to write me word at what time was it when isreal went to Jerico i am very anxious to hear for thare is a mighty host will pass over and you and i my brother will sing hally luja i shall notify you when the great catastrophe shal take place   No more at the present but remain your brother   N. L. J.

FROM JAMES MERCER

TORONTO, MARCH 17th, 1854.

MY DEAR FRIEND STILL:—I take this method of informing you that I am well, and when this comes to hand it may find you and your family enjoying good health. Sir, my particular for writing is that I wish to hear from you, and to hear all the news from down South. I wish to know if all things are working Right for the Rest of my Brotheran whom in bondage. I will also Say that I am very much please with Toronto, So also the friends that came over with. It is true that we have not been Employed as yet; but we are in hopes of be'en so in a few days. We happen here in good time jest about time the people in this country are going work. I am in good health and good Spirits, and feeles Rejoiced in the Lord for my liberty. I Received cople of paper from you to-day. I wish you see James Morris whom or Abram George the first and second on the Ship Penn., give my respects to them, and ask James if he will call at Henry W. Quarles on May street oppisit the Jews synagogue and call for Marena Mercer, give my love to her ask her of all the times about Richmond, tell her to Send me all the news. Tell Mr. Morris that there will be no danger in going to that place. You will also tell M. to make himself known to her as she may know who sent him. And I wish to get a letter from you.

JAMES M. MERCER.

FROM JOHN H. HILL

MY FRIEND, I would like to hear from you, I have been looking for a letter from you for Several days as the last was very interesting to me, please to write Right away.

Yours most Respectfully, JOHN H. HILL.

FROM WILLIAM HENRY GILLIAM

St. Catharines, C. W., May 15th, 1854.

My Dear Friend:—I receaved yours, Dated the 10th and the papers on the 13th, I also saw the pice that was in Miss Shadd's paper About me. I think Tolar is right About my being in A free State, I am and think A great del of it. Also I have no compassion on the penniless widow lady, I have Served her 25 yers 2 months, I think that is long Enough for me to live A Slave. Dear Sir, I am very sorry to hear of the Accadent that happened to our Friend Mr. Meakins, I have read the letter to all that lives in St. Catharines, that came from old Virginia, and then I Sented to Toronto to Mercer & Clayton to see, and to Farman to read fur themselves. Sir, you must write to me soon and let me know how Meakins gets on with his tryal, and you must pray for him, I have told all here to do the same for him. May God bless and protect him from prison, I have heard A great del of old Richmond and Norfolk. Dear Sir, if you see Mr. or Mrs. Gilbert Give my love to them and tell them to write to me, also give my respect to your Family and A part for yourself, love from the friends to you Soloman Brown, H. Atkins, Was. Johnson, Mrs Brooks, Mr. Dykes. Mr. Smith is better at presant. And do not forget to write the News of Meakin's tryal. I cannot say any more at this time; but remain yours and A true Friend ontell Death.

W. H. GILLIAM, the widow's Mite.

St. Catharine, Canada, June 8th, 1854.

Mr. Still, Dear friend:—I received a letter from the poor old widow, Mrs. L. E. White, and she says I may come back if I choose and she will do a good part by me. Yes, yes I am choosing the western side of the South for my home. She is smart, but cannot bung my eye, so she shall have to die in the poor house at last, so she says, and Mercer and myself will be the cause of it. That is all right. I am getting even with her now for I was in the poor house for twenty-five years and have just got out. And she said she knew I was coming away six weeks before I started, so you may know my chance was slim. But Mr. John Wright said I came off like a gentleman and he did not blame me for coming for I was a great boy. Yes I here him enough he is all gas. I am in Canada, and they cannot help themselves.

About that subject I will not say anything more. You must write to me as soon as you can let me here the news and how the Family is and yourself. Let me know how the times is with the U. G. R. R. Co. Is it doing good business? Mr. Dykes sends his respects to you. Give mine to your family.

Your true friend,

W. H. GILLIAM.

FROM JOHN CLAYTON

TORONTO, March 6th, 1854.

DEAR MR. STILL:—I take this method of informing you that I am well both in health and mind You may rest assured that I fells myself a free man and do not fell as I did when I was in Virginia thanks be to God I have no master into Canada but I am my own man. I arrived safe into Canada on friday last. I must request of you to write a few lines to my wife and jest state to her that her friend arrived safe into this glorious land of liberty and I am well and she will make very short her time in Virginia. tell her that I likes here very well and hopes to like it better when I gets to work I don't meane for you to write the same words that are written above but I wish you give her a clear understanding where I am and Shall Remain here untel She comes or I hears from her.

Nothing more at present but remains yours most respectfully,

JOHN CLAYTON.

You will please to direct the to Petersburg Luenena Johns or Clayton John is best.

FROM MARY D. ARMSTEAD

NEW BEDFORD, August 26, 1855.

MR. STILL:—I avail my self to write you thes few lines hopeing they may find you and your family well as they leaves me very well and all the family well except my father he seams to be improveing with his shoulder he has been able to work a little I received the papers I was highly delighted to receive them I was very glad to hear from you in the wheler case I was very glad to hear that the persons ware safe I was very sory to hear that mr Williamson was put in prison but I know if the praying part of the people will pray for him and if he will put his trust in the lord he will bring him out more than conquer please remember my Dear old farther and sisters and brothers to your family kiss the children for me I hear that the yellow fever is very bad down south now if the underground railroad could have free course the emergrant would cross the river of gordan rapidly I hope it may continue to run and I hope the wheels of the car may be greesed with more substantial greese so they may run over swiftly I would have wrote before but circumstances would not permit me Miss Sanders and all the friends desired to be remembered to you and your family I shall be pleased to hear from the underground rail road often

Yours respectfully,
MARY D. ARMSTEAD.

FROM ISAAC FORMAN

Toronto, Feb. 20th, 1854.

Mr. William Still:—*Sir*—Your kind letter arrived safe at hand on the 18th, and I was very happy to receive it. I now feel that I should return you some thanks for your kindness. Dear sir I do pray from the bottom of my heart, that the high heavens may bless you for your kindness; give my love to Mr. Bagnel and Mr. Minkins, ask them if they have heard anything from my brother, tell Mr. Bagnel to give my love to my sister-in-law and mother and all the family. I am now living at Russell's Hotel; it is the first situation I have had since I have been here and I like it very well. Sir you would oblige me by letting me know if Mr. Minkins has seen my wife; you will please let me know as soon as possible. I wonder if Mr. Minkins has thought of any way that he can get my wife away. I should like to know in a few days. Your well wisher,　　　　　　　　　　　　　ISAAC FORMAN.

Toronto, May 7, 1854.

Mr. W. Still:—*Dear Sir*—I take this opportunity of writing you these few lines and hope when they reach you they will find you well. I would have written you before, but I was waiting to hear from my friend, Mr. Brown. I judge his business has been of importance as the occasion why he has not written before. Dear sir, nothing would have prevented me from writing, in a case of this kind, except death.

My soul is vexed, my troubles are inexpressible. I often feel as if I were willing to die. I must see my wife in short, if not, I will die. What would I not give no tongue can utter. Just to gaze on her sweet lips one moment I would be willing to die the next. I am determined to see her some time or other. The thought of being a slave again is miserable. I hope heaven will smile upon me again, before I am one again. I will leave Canada again shortly, but I don't name the place that I go, it may be in the bottom of the ocean. If I had known as much before I left, as I do now, I would never have left until I could have found means to have brought her with me. You have never suffered from being absent from a wife, as I have. I consider that to be nearly superior to death, and hope you will do all you can for me, and inquire from your friends if nothing can be done for me. Please write to me immediately on receipt of this, and say something that will cheer up my drooping spirits. You will oblige me by seeing Mr. Brown and ask him if he would oblige me by going to Richmond and see my wife, and see what arrangements he could make with her, and I would be willing to pay all his expenses there and back. Please to see both Mr. Bagnel and Mr. Minkins, and ask them if they have seen my wife. I am determined to see her, if I die the next moment. I can say I was once happy, but never will be again, until I see her; because what is freedom to me, when I know that my wife is in slavery? Those persons that you shipped a few weeks ago, remained at St. Catherine, instead of coming over to Toronto. I sent you two letters last week and I hope you will please attend to them. The post-office is shut, so I enclose the money to pay the post, and please write me in haste.

I remain evermore your obedient servant,

I. FORMAN.

FROM WILLIAM BRINKLY

CAMDEN, DEL., March 23d, 1857.

DEAR SIR;—I tak my pen in hand to write you, to inform you what we have had to go throw for the last two weaks. Thir wir six men and two woman was betraid on the tenth of this month, thea had them in prison but thea got out was conveyed by a black man, he told them he wood bring them to my hows, as he wos told, he had ben ther Befor, he has com with Harrett, a woman that stops at my hous when she pases tow and throw yau. You don't no me I supos, the Rev. Thomas H. Kennard dos, or Peter Lowis. He Road Camden Circuit, this man led them in dover prisin and left them with a whit man; but tha tour out the winders and jump out, so cum back to camden. We put them throug, we hav to carry them 19 mils and cum back the sam night wich maks 38 mils. It is tou much for our littel horses. We must do the bes we can, ther is much Bisness dun on this Road. We hav to go throw dover and smerny, the two wors places this sid of mary land lin. If you have herd or sean them ples let me no. I will Com to Phila be for long and then I will call and se you. There is much to do her. Ples to wright, I Remain your frend, WILLIAM BRINKLY.

Remember me to Thom. Kennard.

FROM EMMA BROWN

TORONTO, March 14th, 1855.

DEAR MR. STILL:—I take this opportunity of addressing you with these few lines to inform you that I arrived here to day, and hope that this may find yourself and Mrs. Still well, as this leaves me at the present. I will also say to you, that I had no difficulty in getting along. the two young men that was with me left me at Suspension Bridge. they went another way.

I cannot say much about the place as I have ben here but a short time but so far as I have seen I like very well. you will give my Respect to your lady, & Mr & Mrs Brown. If you have not written to Petersburg you will please to write as soon as can I have nothing More to Write at present but yours Respectfully

EMMA BROWN (old name MARY EPPS).

FROM JOSEPH ROBINSON

SAINT CATHARINE, April 16, 1855.

MR. WILLIAM STILL, DEAR SIR:—Your letter of date April 7th I have just got, it had been opened before it came to me. I have not received any other letter from you and can get no account of them in the Post Office in this place, I am well and have got a good situation in this city and intend staying here. I should be very glad to hear from you as soon as convenient and also from all of my friends near you. My Brother is also at work with me and doing well.

There is nothing here that would interest you in the way of news. There is a Masonic Lodge of our people and two churches and societys here and some other institutions for our benefit. Be kind enough to send a few lines to the Lady spoken of for that mocking bird and much oblige me. Write me soon and believe me your obedient Servt

Love & respects to Lady and daughter

JOSEPH ROBINSON.

FROM NAT AMBIE

AUBURN, June 10th, 1858.

MR. WILLIAM STILL:—Sir, will you be so Kind as to write a letter to affey White in straw berry alley in Baltimore city on the point Say to her at nat Ambey that I wish to Know from her the Last Letar that Joseph Ambie and Henry Ambie two Brothers and Ann Warfield a couisin of them two boys I state above I would like to hear from my mother sichy Ambie you will Please write to my mother and tell her that I am well and doing well and state to her that I perform my Relissius dutys and I would like to hear from her and want to know if she is performing her Relissius dutys yet and send me word from all her children I left behind say to affey White that I wish her to write me a Letter in Hast my wife is well and doing well and my nephew is doing well Please tell affey White when she writes to me to Let me know where Joseph and Henry Ambie is

Mr. Still Please Look on your Book and you will find my name on your Book They was eleven of us children and all when we came through and I feal interrested about my Brothers I have never heard from them since I Left home you will Please Be Kind annough to attend to this Letter When you send the answer to this Letter you will Please send it to P. R. Freeman Auburn City Cayuga County New York

Yours Truly   NAT AMBIE.

FROM JOHN SCOTT

MONTREAL, September 1st 1859.

DEAR SIR:—It is with extreme pleasure that I set down to inclose you a few lines to let you know that I am well & I hope when these few lines come to hand they may find you & your family in good health and prosperity I left your house Nov. 3d, 1857, for Canada I Received a letter here from James Carter in Peters burg, saying that my wife would leave there about the 28th or the first September and that he would send her on by way of Philadelphia to you to send on to Montreal if she come on you be please to send her on and as there is so many boats coming here all times a day I may not know what time she will. So you be please to give her this direction, she can get a cab and go to the Donegana Hotel and Edmund Turner is there he will take you where I lives and if he is not there cabman take you to Mr Taylors on Durham St. nearly opposite to the Methodist Church. Nothing more at present but Remain your well wisher   JOHN SCOTT.

FROM ISRAEL WHITNEY

HAMILTON, Oct. 16, 1858.

WILLIAM STILL—*My Dear Friend:*—I saw Carter and his friend a few days ago, and they told me, that you was well. On the seventh of October my wife came to Hamilton. Mr. A. Hurberd, who came from Virginia with me, is going to get married the 20th of November, next. I wish you would write to me how many of my friends you have seen since October, 1857. Montgomery Green keeps a barber shop in Cayuga, in the State of New York. I have not heard of Oscar Ball but once since I came here, and then he was well and doing well. George Carroll is in Hamilton. The times are very dull at present, and have been ever since I came here. Please write soon. Nothing more at present, only I still remain in Hamilton, C. W.   ISRAEL WHITNEY.

FROM WILLIAM COOPER

SYRACUSE, June 9th, 1858.

MR. STILL:—*Dear Sir:*—One of your Underground R. R. Passenger Drop you these few Lines to let you see that he have not forgoten you one who have Done so much for him well sir I am still in Syracuse, well in regard to what I am Doing for a Living I no you would like to hear, I am in the Painting Business, and have as much at that as I can do, and enough to Last me all the Summer, I had a knolledge of Painting Before I Left the South, the Hotell where I was working Last winter the Proprietor fail & shot up in the Spring and I Loose evry thing that I was working for all Last winter. I have Ritten a Letter to my Friend P. Christianson some time a goo & have never Received an Answer, I hope this wont Be the case with this one, I have an idea sir, next winter iff I can this summer make Enough to Pay Expenses, to goo to that school at McGrowville & spend my winter their. I am going sir to try to Prepair myself for a Lectuer, I am going sir By the Help of god to try and Do something for the Caus to help my Poor Breathern that are suffering under the yoke. Do give my Respect to Mrs Stills & Perticular to Miss Julia Kelly, I supose she is still with you yet, I am in great hast you must excuse my short letter. I hope these few Lines may fine you as they Leave me quite well. It will afford me much Pleasure to hear from you.

yours Truly,   WILLIAM COOPER.
John Thompson is still here and Doing well.

FROM EDMUND TURNER

HAMILTON, CANADA WEST Mar. 1, 1858.

MR. STILL, DEAR SIR:—I have taken the oppertunity to enform you yur letter came to hand 27th I ware glad to hear from you and yer famly i hope this letter May fine you and the famly Well i am Well my self My Brother join me in Love to you and all the frend. I ware sorry to hear of the death of Mrs freaman. We all must die sune or Late this a date we all must pay we must Perpar for the time she ware a nise lady dear sir the all is well and san thar love to you Emerline have Ben sick But is better at this time. I saw the hills the war well and san thar Love to you. I war sory to hear that My brother war sol i am glad that i did come away when i did god works all the things for the Best he is young he may get a long in the wole May god Bless hem ef you have any News from Petersburg Va Plas Rite me a word when you anser this Letter and ef any person came form home Letter Me know. Please sen me one of your Paper that had the under grands R wrod give My Love to Mr Careter and his family I am Seving with a barber at this time he have promust to give me the trad ef i can lane it he is much of a gentman. Mr Still sir i have writing a letter to Mr Brown of Petersburg Va Pleas reed it and ef you think it right Plas sen it by the Mail or by hand you wall see how i have writen it the will know how sent it by the way this writing ef the ancer it you can sen it to Me i have tol them direc to yor care for Ed. t. Smith Philadelphia i hope it may be right i promorst to rite to hear Please rite to me sune and let me know ef you do sen it on write wit you did with that ma a bught the cappet Bage do not fergit to rite tal John he mite rite to Me. I am doing as well is i can at this time but i get no wagges But my Bord but is satfid at that thes hard time and glad that i am Hear and in good helth. Northing More at this time

yor truly   EDMUND TURNER.

A WARNING TO SLAVE–HOLDERS SENT WITH THE FOREGOING LETTER

Well may the Southern slaveholder say, that holding their Fellow men in Bondage is no (sin, because it is their delight as the Egyptians, so do they; but nevertheless God in his own good time will bring them out by a mighty hand, as it is recorded in the sacred oracles of truth, that Ethiopia shall soon stretch out her hands to God, speaking in the positive (shall). And my prayer is to you, oh, slaveholder, in the name of that God who in the beginning said, Let there be light, and there was light. Let my People go that they may serve me; thereby good may come unto thee and to thy children's children. Slave-holder have you seriously thought upon the condition yourselves, family and slaves; have you read where Christ has enjoined upon all his creatures to read his word, thereby that they may have no excuse when coming before his judgment seat? But you say he shall not read his word, consequently his sin will be upon your head. I think every man has as much as he can do to answer for his own sins. And now my dear slave-holder, who with you are bound and fast hastening to judgment? As one that loves your soul repent ye, therefore, and be converted, that your sins may be blotted out when the time of refreshing shall come from the presence of the Lord.

In the language of the poet:

> Stop, poor sinner, stop and think,
>   Before you further go;
> Think upon the brink of death
>   Of everlasting woe.
> Say, have you an arm like God,
>   That you his will oppose?
> Fear you not that iron rod
>   With which he breaks his foes?

Is the prayer of one that loves your souls.

EDMUND TURNER.

N. B. The signature bears the name of one who knows and felt the sting of Slavery; but now, thanks be to God, I am now where the poisonous breath taints not our air, but every one is sitting under his own vine and fig tree, where none dare to make him ashamed or afraid.   EDMUND TURNER, formerly of Petersburg, Va.

HAMILTON, June 22d, 1858, C. W.

To MR. WM. STILL, DEAR SIR:—A favorable opportunity affords the pleasure of acknowledging the receipt of letters and papers; certainly in this region they were highly appreciated, and I hope the time may come that your kindness will be reciprocated we are al well at present, but times continue dull. I also deeply regret the excitement recently on the account of those slaves, you will favor me by keeping me posted upon the subject. Those words written to slaveholder is the thought of one who had sufferd, and now I thought it a duty incumbent upon me to cry aloud and spare not, &c., by sending these few lines where the slaveholder may hear. You will still further oblige your humble servant also, to correct any inaccuracy. My respects to you and your family and all inquiring friends.

Your friend and well wisher,   EDMUND TURNER.

FROM JEFFERSON PIPKINS

Sept. 28, 1856.

To WM. STILL. SIR:—I take the liberty of writing to you a few lines concerning my children, for I am very anxious to get them and I wish you to please try what you can do for me. Their names are Charles and Patrick and are living with Mrs. Joseph G. Wray Murphysborough Hartford county, North Carolina; Emma lives with a Lawyer Baker in Gatesville North Carolina and Susan lives in Portsmouth Virginia and is stopping with Dr. Collins sister a Mrs. Nash you can find her out by enquiring for Dr. Collins at the ferry boat at Portsmouth, and Rose a coloured woman at the Crawford House can tell where she is. And I trust you will try what you think will be the best way. And you will do me a great favour. Yours Respectfully,   JEFFERSON PIPKINS.

P. S. I am living at Yorkville near Toronto Canada West. My wife sends her best respects to Mrs. Still.

FROM JAME MASEY

ST. CATHARINES, C. W., April 24, 1857.

DEAR WIFE—I take this opertunity to inform you that I have Arive in St. Catharines this Eving, After Jorney of too weeks, and now find mysilf on free ground and wish that you was here with me But you are not here, when we parted I did not know that I should come away so soon as I did, But for that of causin you pain I left as I did, I hope that you will try to come. But if you cannot, write to me as soon as you can and tell me all that you can But dont be Desscuredged I was sory to leave you, and I could not help it for you know that I promest see you to sister, But I was persuaded By Another man go part with it grived mutch, you must not think that I did not care for you. I cannot tell how I come, for I was some times on the earth and some times under the earth Do not Bee afraid to come But start and keep trying, if you are afrid fitch your tow sister with you for compeny and I will take care of you and treat you like a lady so long as you live. The talk of cold in this place is all a humbug, it is wormer here than it was there when I left, your father and mother has allways treated me like their own child I have no fault to find in them. I sent my Respects to them Both and I hope that they will remember me in Prayer, if you make a start come to Philidelpa tell father and mother that I am safe and hope that they will not morn after me I shall ever Remember them. No more at present But yours in Body and mind, and if we no meet on Earth I hope that we shall meet in heven. Your husbern. Good night.

JAME MASEY.

FROM HENRY TRUSTY

St. Catharines, C. W. June 21, 1857.

Dear Sir.—I take this opportunity to inform you that I am well at present, and hope that these few lines may find you injoying the same Blessing, I have Been for some time now, But have not written to you Before, But you must Excuse me. I want you to give my Respects to all my inquiring friends and to my wife, I should have let you know But I was afraid and all three of my little children too, P. H. Trusty if he was mine Wm. T. Trusty and to Alexander I have been A man agge But was assurd nuthin, H. Trusty, a hard grand citt. I should lic know how times is, Henry Turner if you get this keep it and read it to yourself and not let any one else But yourself, tell ann Henry, Samuel Henry, Jacob Bryant, Wm Claton, Mr James at Almira Receved at Mr Jones house the Best I could I have Been healthy since I arrived here. My Best Respect to all and my thanks for past favours. No more at present But Remain youre obedented Servent &c.

HENRY TRUSTY.

Please send me an answer as son as you get this, and oblige yours,

MR TRUSTY.

FROM C. W. THOMPSON

Detroit, Sept. 17, 1862.

Dear Brother in Christ:—It affords me the greatest pleasure imaginable in the time I shall occupy in penning these few lines to you and your dear loving wife; not because I can write them to you myself, but for the love and regard I have for you, for I never can forget a man who will show kindness to his neighbor when in distress. I remember when I was in distress and out of doors, you took me in, I was hungry, and you fed me, for these things God will reward you, dear brother. I am getting along as well as I can expect. Since I have been out here, I have endeavored to make every day tell for itself, and I can say, no doubt, what a great many men cannot say, that I have made good use of all the time that God has given me, and not one week has been spent in idleness. Brother William, I expect to visit you some time next summer to sit and have a talk with you and Mrs. Still. I hope to see that time, if it is God's will. You will remember me, with my wife, to Mrs. Still. Give my best respects to all inquiring friends, and believe me to be yours forever. Well wishes both soul and body. Please write to me sometimes.   C. W. THOMPSON.

FROM RICHARD EDONS

KINGSTON, July 20, 1857.

MR. WILLIAM STILL—*Dear Friend:*—I take the opertunity of wrighting a few lines to let you no that we air all in good health hoping thos few lines may find you and your family engoying the same blessing. We arived in King all saft Canada West Abram Galway gos to work this morning at $1 75 per day and John pediford is at work for mr george mink and i will opne a shop for my self in a few days   My wif will send a daugretipe to your cair whitch you will pleas to send on to me Richard Edons to the cair of George Mink Kingston C W   Yours with Respect,

RICHARD EDONS.

FROM MANUAL T. WHITE

SYRACUSE, July 29, 1857.

MY DEAR FRIEND, MR. STILL:—I got safe through to Syracuse, and found the house of our friend, Mr. J. W. Loguen. Many thanks to you for your kindness to me. I wish to say to you, dear sir, that I expect my clothes will be sent to Dr. Landa, and I wish, if you please, get them and send them to the care of Mr. Loguen, at Syracuse, for me. He will be in possession of my whereabouts and will send them to me. Remember me to Mr. Landa and Miss Millen Jespan, and much to you and your family.

Truly Yours,   MANUAL T. WHITE.

FROM J. W. LOGUEN

SYRACUSE, Oct. 5, 1856.

DEAR FRIEND STILL:—I write to you for Mrs. Susan Bell, who was at your city some time in September last. She is from Washington city. She left her dear little children behind (two children). She is stopping in our city, and wants to hear from her children very much indeed. She wishes to know if you have heard from Mr. Biglow, of Washington city. She will remain here until she can hear from you. She feels very anxious about her children, I will assure you. I should have written before this, but I have been from home much of the time since she came to our city. She wants to know if Mr. Biglow has heard anything about her husband. If you have not written to Mr. Biglow, she wishes you would. She sends her love to you and your dear family. She says that you were all kind to her, and she does not forget it. You will direct your letter to me, dear brother, and I will see that she gets it.

Miss F. E. Watkins left our house yesterday for Ithaca, and other places in that part of the State. Frederick Douglass, Wm. J. Watkins and others were with us last week; Gerritt Smith with others. Miss Watkins is doing great good in our part of the State. We think much indeed of her. She is such a good and glorious speaker, that we are all charmed with her. We have had thirty-one fugitives in the last twenty-seven days; but you, no doubt, have had many more than that. I hope the good Lord may bless you and spare you long to do good to the hunted and outraged among our brethren.

Yours truly,   J. W. LOGUEN,
Agent of the Underground Rail Road.

FROM SAMUEL W. JOHNSON

My Dear Wife I now embrace this golden opportunity of writing a few Lines to inform you that I am well at present engoying good health and hope that these few lines may find you well also My dearest wife I have Left you and now I am in a foreign land about fourteen hundred miles from you but though my wife my thoughts are upon you all the time My dearest Frances I hope you will remember me now gust as same as you did when I were there with you because my mind are with you night and day the Love that I bear for you in my breast is greater than I thought it was if I had thought I had so much Love for you I dont think I ever could Left

being I have escape I and has fled into a land of freedom I can but
stop and look over my past Life and say what a fool I was for
staying in bondage as Long My dear wife I dont want you to get
married before you send me some letters because I never shall get
married until I see you again My mind dont deceive and it appears
to me as if I shall see you again at my time of writing this letter I
am desitute of money I have not got in no business yet but when I
do get into business I shall write you and also remember you Tell
my Mother and Brother and all enquiring friends that I am now
safe in free state I cant tell where I am at present but Direct your
Letters to Mr. William Still in Philadelphia and I will get them
Answer this as soon as you can if you please for if you write the
same day you receive it it will take a fortnight to reach me No
more to relate at present but still remain your affectionate husband
Mr. Still please defore this piece out if you please

SAMUEL WASHINGTON JOHNSON.

ST. CATHARINE, UPPER CANADA WEST.

MR. WILLIAM STILL:—I am now in safety I arrived at home
safe on the 11th inst at 12 o'clock M. So I hope that you will now
take it upon yourself to inform me something of that letter I left
at your house that night when I left there and write me word how
you are and how is your wife I wish you may excuse this letter for
I am so full that I cannot express my mind at all I am only got
$1.50 and I feel as if I had an independent fortune but I dont want
you to think that I am going to be idle because I am on free ground
and I shall always work though I am not got nothing to do at present
Direct your letter to the post office as soon as possible.

SAMUEL W. JOHNSON.

FROM ELIJAH HILTON

TORONTO, Canada West, July 28.

Dear friend in due respect to your humanity and nobility I now
take my pen in hand to inform you of my health I am enjoying a
reasonable proportion of health at this time and hope when these
few lines come to hand they may find you and family the same dear
Sir I am in Toronto and are working at my ole branch of business
with meny of my friends I want you to send those to toronto to
Mr Tueharts on Edward St what I have been talking about is my
Clothes I came from Richmond Va and expect my things to come to

you So when they come to you then you will send them to Jesse Tuehart Edward St no 43.

I must close by saying I have no more at present I still remain your brother,

ELIJAH HILTON.

FROM WILLIAM BROWN

NEW BEDFORD, August 22d, 1855.

DEAR SIR:—I send you this to inform you that I expect my wife to come that way. If she should, you will direct her to me. When I came through your city last Fall, you took my name in your office, which was then given you, Michael Vaughn; since then my name is William Brown, No. 130 Kempton street. Please give my wife and child's name to Dr. Lundy, and tell him to attend to it for me. Her name is Esther, and the child's name Louisa.

Truly yours, WILLIAM BROWN.

FROM FLARECE P. GAULT

BOSTON, March 22, 1858.

MY DEAR SIR—I received your photograph by Mr Cooper and it afforded me much pleasure to do so i hope that these few lines may find you and your family well as it leaves me and little Dicky at present i have no interesting news to tell you more than there is a great revival of religion through the land i all most forgoten to thank you for your kindness and our little Dick he is very wild and goes to school and it is my desire and prayer for him to grow up a useful man i wish you would try to gain some information from Norfolk and write me word how the times are there for i am afraid to write i wish yoo would see the Doctor for me and ask him if he could carefully find out any way that we could steal little Johny for i think to raise nine or ten hundred dollars for such a child is out-raigust just at this time i feel as if i would rather steal him than to buy him give my kinde regards to the Dr and his family tell Miss Margret and Mrs Landy that i would like to see them out here this summer again to have a nice time in Cambridge Miss Walker that spent the evening with me in Cambridge sens much love to yoo and Mrs. Landy give my kindes regards to Mrs Still and children and receive a portion for yoo self i have no more to say at present but remain yoor respectfully.

FLARECE P. GAULT.

When you write direct yoo letters Mrs. Flarece P. Gault, No 62 Pinkney St.

FROM E. WEEMS

WASHINGTON, D. C., September 19th, 1857.

WM. STILL, ESQ., Philadelphia, Pa. SIR:—I have just sent for my son Augustus, in Alabama. I have sent eleven hundred dollars which pays for his body and some thirty dollars to pay his fare to Washington. I borrowed one hundred and eighty dollars to make out the eleven hundred dollars. I was not very successful in Syracuse. I collected only twelve dollars, and in Rochester only two dollars. I did not know that the season was so unpropitious. The wealthy had all gone to the springs. They must have returned by this time. I hope you will exert yourself and help me get a part of the money I owe, at least. I am obliged to pay it by the 12th of next month. I was unwell when I returned through Philadelphia, or I should have called. I had been from home five weeks.

My son Augustus is the last of the family in Slavery. I feel rejoiced that he is soon to be free and with me, and of course feel the greatest solicitude about raising the one hundred and eighty dollars I have borrowed of a kind friend, or who has borrowed it for me at bank. I hope and pray you will help me as far as possible. Tell Mr. Douglass to remember me, and if he can, to interest his friends for me.

You will recollect that five hundred dollars of our money was taken to buy the sister of Henry H. Garnett's wife. Had I been able to command this I should not be necessitated to ask the favors and indulgences I do.

I am expecting daily the return of Augustus, and may Heaven grant him a safe deliverance and smile propitiously upon you and all kind friends who have aided in his return to me.

Be pleased to remember me to friends, and accept yourself the blessing and prayers of your dear friend, EARRO WEEMS.

P. S. Direct your letter to E. L. Stevens, in Duff Green's Row, Capitol Hill, Washington, D. C.

E. W.

FROM J. H. HILL

Nine months I was trying to get away. I was secreted for a long time in a kitchen of a merchant near the corner of Franklyn and 7th streets, at Richmond, where I was well taken care of, by a lady friend of my mother. When I got Tired of staying in that place, I wrote myself a pass to pass myself to Petersburg, here I stopped with a very prominent Colored person, who was a friend to Freedom

stayed here until two white friends told other friends if I was in the
city to tell me to go at once, and stand not upon the order of going,
because they had hard a plot.   I wrot a pass, started for Richmond,
Reached Manchester, got off the Cars walked into Richmond, once
more got back into the same old Den, Stayed here from the 16th of
Aug. to 12th Sept.   On the 11th of Sept. 8 o'clock P. M. a message
came to me that there had been a State Room taken on the steamer
City of Richmond for my benefit, and I assured the party that it
would be occupied if God be willing.   Before 10 o'clock the next
morning, on the 12th, a beautiful Sept. day, I arose early, wrote my
pass for Norfolk left my old Den with a many a good bye, turned
out the back way to 7th St., thence to Main, down Main behind 4
night waich to old Rockett's and after about 20 minutes of delay I
succeed in Reaching the State Room.   My Conductor was very
much Excited, but I felt as Composed as I do at this moment, for I
had started from my Den that morning for Liberty or for Death
providing myself with a Brace of Pistels.

Yours truly J. H. HILL.

TORONTO, October 4th, 1853.

DEAR SIR:—I take this method of informing you that I am well,
and that I got to this city all safe and sound, though I did not get
here as soon as I expect.   I left your city on Saterday and I was on
the way untel the Friday following.   I got to New York the same
day that I left Philadelphia, but I had to stay there untel Monday
evening.   I left that place at six o'clock.   I got to Albany next
morning in time to take the half past six o'clock train for Rochester,
here I stay untel Wensday night.   The reason I stay there so long
Mr. Gibbs given me a letter to Mr Morris at Rochester.   I left that
place Wensday, but I only got five miles from that city that night.
I got to Lewiston on Thurday afternoon, but too late for the boat to
this city.   I left Lewiston on Friday at one o'clock, got to this city
at five.   Sir I found this to be a very handsome city.   I like it
better than any city I ever saw.   It are not as large as the city that
you live in, but it is very large place much more so than I expect to
find it.   I seen the gentleman that you given me letter to.   I
think him much of a gentleman.   I got into work on Monday.   The
man whom I am working for is name Myers; but I expect to go to
work for another man by name of Tinsly, who is a master workman
in this city.   He says that he will give me work next week and
everybody advises me to work for Mr. Tinsly as there more surity in
him.

Mr. Still, I have been looking and looking for my friends for several days, but have not seen nor heard of them. I hope and trust in the Lord Almighty that all things are well with them. My dear sir I could feel so much better sattisfied if I could hear from my wife. Since I reached this city I have talagraphed to friend Brown to send my thing to me, but I cannot hear a word from no one at all. I have written to Mr. Brown two or three times since I left the city. I trust that he has gotten my wife's letters, that is if she has written. Please direct your letters to me, near the corner Sarah and Edward street, until I give you further notice. You will tell friend B. how to direct his letters, as I forgotten it when I writt to him, and ask him if he has heard anything from Virginia. Please to let me hear from him without delay for my very soul is trubled about my friends whom I expected to of seen here before this hour. Whatever you do please to write. I shall look for you paper shortly.

Believe me sir to be your well wisher.

JOHN H. HILL.

TORONTO, October 30th, 1853.

MY DEAR FRIEND:—I now write to inform you that I have received my things all safe and sound, and also have shuck hand with the friend that you send on to this place one of them is stopping with me. His name is Chas. Stuert, he seemes to be a tolerable smart fellow. I Rec'd my letters. I have taken this friend to see Mr. Smith. However will give him a place to board untell he can get to work. I shall do every thing I can for them all that I see the gentleman wish you to see his wife and let her know that he arrived safe, and present his love to her and to all the friend. Mr. Still, I am under ten thousand obligation to you for your kindness when shall I ever repay? S. speek very highly of you. I will state to you what Custom house master said to me. He ask me when he Presented my efects are these your efects. I answered yes. He then ask me was I going to settle in Canada. I told him I was. He then ask me of my case. I told all about it. He said I am happy to see you and all that will come. He ask me how much I had to pay for my Paper. I told him half dollar. He then told me that I should have my money again. He a Rose from his seat and got my money. So my friend you can see the people and tell them all this is a land of liberty and believe they will find friends here. My best love to all.

My friend I must call upon you once more to do more kindness

for me that is to write to my wife as soon as you get this, and tell
her when she gets ready to come she will pack and consign her things
to you. You will give her some instruction, but not to your expenses but to her own.

When you write direct your letter to Phillip Ubank, Petersburg,
Va. My Box arrived here the 27th.

My dear sir I am in a hurry to take this friend to church, so I
must close by saying I am your humble servant in the cause of
liberty and humanity.   JOHN H. HILL.

So I ask you to send the fugitives to Canada. I don't know
much of this Province but I beleaves that there is Rome enough for
the colored and whites of the United States. We wants farmers
mechanic men of all qualification &c, if they are not made we will
make them, if we cannot make the old, we will make our children.

Now concerning the city toronto this city is Beautiful and
Prosperous Levele city. Great many wooden codages more than
what should be but I am in hopes there will be more of the Brick
and Stonn. But I am not done about your Republicanism. Our
masters have told us that there was no living in Canada for a Negro
but if it may Please your gentlemanship to publish these facts that
we are here able to earn our bread and money enough to make us
comftable. But I say give me freedom, and the United States may
have all her money and her Luxtures, yeas give Liberty or Death.
I'm in America, but not under Such a Government that I cannot
express myself, speak, think or write So as I am able, and if my
master had allowed me to have an education I would make them
American Slave-holders feel me, Yeas I would make them tremble
when I spoke, and when I take my Pen in hand their knees smote
together. My Dear Sir suppose I was an educated man. I could
write you something worth reading, but you know we poor fugitives
whom has just come over from the South are not able to write much
on no subject whatever, but I hope by the aid of my God I will try
to use my midnight lamp, untel I can have some influence upon the
American Slavery. If some one would say to me, that they would
give my wife bread untel I could be Educated I would stoop my
trade this day and take up my books.

But a crisis is approaching when assential requisite to the
American Slaveholders when blood Death or Liberty will be required
at their hands. I think our people have depened too long and too
much on false legislator let us now look for ourselves. It is true that

England however the Englishman is our best friend but we as men ought not to depened upon her Remonstrace with the Americans because she loves her commercial trade as any Nations do.   But I must say, while we look up and acknowledge the Power greatness and honor of old England, and believe that while we sit beneath the Silken folds of her flag of Perfect Liberty, we are secure, beyond the reach of the aggressions of the Blood hounds and free from the despotism that would wrap around our limbs by the damable Slaveholder.   Yet we would not like spoiled childeren depend upon her, but upon ourselves and as one means of strengthening ourselves, we should agitate the emigration to Canada.   I here send you a paragraph which I clipted from the weekly Glob.   I hope you will publish so that Mr. Williamson may know that men are not chattel here but reather they are men and if he wants his chattle let him come here after it or his thing.   I wants you to let the whole United States know we are satisfied here because I have seen more Pleasure since I came here then I saw in the U. S. the 24 years that I served my master.   Come Poor distress men women and come to Canada where colored men are free.   Oh how sweet the word do sound to me yeas when I contemplate of these things, my very flesh creaps my heart thrub when I think of my beloved friends whom I left in that cursid hole.   Oh my God what can I do for them or shall I do for them.   Lord help them.   Suffer them to be no longer depressed beneath the Bruat Creation but may they be looked upon as men made of the Bone and Blood as the Anglo-Americans.   May God in his mercy Give Liberty to all this world.   I must close as it am late hour at night.   I Remain your friend in the cause of Liberty and humanity,

JOHN H. HILL, a fugitive.

If you know any one who would give me an education write and let me know for I am in want of it very much.

Your with Respect,

J. H. H.

TORONTO, November 12th, 1853.

MY DEAR STILL:—Your letter of the 3th came to hand thursday and also three copes all of which I was glad to Received they have taken my attention all together Every Time I got them.   I also Rec'd. a letter from my friend Brown.   Mr. Brown stated to me that he had heard from my wife but he did not say what way he heard.   I am looking for my wife every day.   Yes I want her to come then I will be better sattisfied. My friend I am a free man and feeles alright about that matter. I am doing tolrable well in my line of business, and think I will do better after little. I hope you all will never stop any of our Brotheran that makes their Escep from the South but send them on to this Place where they can be free man and woman. We want them here and not in your State where they can be taken away at any hour. Nay but let him come here where he can Enjoy the Rights of a human being and not to be trodden under the feet of men like themselves. All the People that comes here does well. Thanks be to God that I came to this place. I would like very well to see you all but never do I expect to see you in the United States. I want you all to come to this land of Liberty where the bondman can be free. Come one come all come to this place, and I hope my dear friend you will send on here. I shall do for them as you all done for me when I came on here however I will do the best I can for them if they can they shall do if they will do, but some comes here that can't do well because they make no efford. I hope my friend you will teach them such lessons as Mrs. Moore Give me before I left your city. I hope she may live a hundred years longer and enjoy good health. May God bless her for the good cause which she are working in. Mr. Still you ask me to remember you to Nelson. I will do so when I see him, he are on the lake so is Stewart. I received a letter to-day for Stewart from your city which letter I will take to him when he comes to the city. He are not stoping with us at this time. I was very sorry a few days ago when I heard that a man was taken from your city.

Send them over here, then let him come here and take them away and I will try to have a finger in the Pie myself. You said that you had written to my wife ten thousand thanks for what you have done and what you are willing to do. My friend whenever you hear from my wife please write to me. Whenever she come to your city please give instruction how to travel. I wants her to come the faster way. I wish she was here now. I wish she could get a ticket through to this place. I have mail a paper for you to day.

We have had snow but not to last long. Let me hear from you. My Respect friend Brown. I will write more when I have the opportunity. Yours with Respect,

JOHN H. HILL.

P. S. My dear Sir. Last night after I had written the above, and had gone to bed, I heard a strange voice in the house, Saying to

Mr. Myers to come quickly to one of our colod Brotheran out of the street. We went and found a man a Carpenter laying on the side walk woltun in his Blood. Done by some unknown Person as yet but if they stay on the earth the law will deteck them. It is said that party of colord people done it, which party was seen to come out an infame house.

Mr. Myers have been down to see him and Brought the Sad news that the Poor fellow was dead. Mr. Scott for Henry Scott was the name, he was a fugitive from Virginia, he came here from Pittsburg Pa. Oh, when I went where he laid what a shock, it taken my Sleep altogether night. When I got to Sopt his Body was surrounded by the Policeman. The law has taken the woman in cusidy. I write and also send you a paper of the case when it comes out.   J. H. HILL.

ToRONTO, December 29th, 1853.

My DEAR FRIEND:—It affords me a good deel of Pleasure to say that my wife and the Children have arrived safe in this City. But my wife had very bad luck. She lost her money and the money that was belonging to the children, the whole amount was 35 dollars. She had to go to the Niagara falls and Telegraph to me come after her. She got to the falls on Sat'dy and I went after her on Monday. We saw each other once again after so long an Abstance, you may know what sort of metting it was, joyful times of corst. My wife are well Satisfied here, and she was well Pleased during her stay in your city. My Trip to the falls cost Ten Eighty Seven and half. The things that friend Brown Shiped to me by the Express costed $24¼. So you can see fiting out a house Niagara falls and the cost for bringing my things to this place, have got me out of money, but for all I am a free man.

The weather are very cold at Present, the snow continue to fall though not as deep here as it is in Boston. The people haves their own Amousements, the weather as it is now, they don't care for the snow nor ice, but they are going from Ten A. M. until Twelve P. M., the hous that we have open don't take well because we don't Sell Spirits, which we are trying to avoid if we can.

Mr. Still, I hold in my hand A letter from a friend of South, who calls me to promise that I made to him before I left. My dear Sir, this letter have made my heart Bleed, since I Received it, he also desires of me to remember him to his beloved Brethren and then to Pray for him and his dear friends who are in Slavery. I shall

Present his letter to the churches of this city. I forward to your care for Mrs. Moore, a few weeks ago. Mrs. Hill sends her love to your wife and yourself.

Please to write, I Sincerely hope that our friends from Petersburg have reached your city before this letter is dated. I must close by saying, that I Sir, remain humble and obedient Servant,

J. H. H.

TORONTO, March 8th, 1854.

MY DEAR FRIEND STILL:—We will once more truble you opon this great cause of freedom, as we know that you are a man, that are never fatuged in Such a glorious cause. Sir, what I wish to Say is this. Mr. Forman has Received a letter from his wife dated the 29th ult. She States to him that She was Ready at any time, and that Everything was Right with her, and she hoped that he would lose no time in sending for her for she was Ready and awaiting for him. Well friend Still, we learnt that Mr. Minkens could not bring her the account of her child. We are very sorry to hear Such News, however, you will please to read this letter with care, as we have learnt that Minkens Cannot do what we wishes to be done; we perpose another way. There is a white man that Sale from Richmond to Boston, that man are very Safe, he will bring F's wife with her child. So you will do us a favour will take it upon yourself to transcribe from this letter what we shall write. I. E. this there is a Colored gen. that workes on the basin in R—d this man's name is Esue Foster, he can tell Mrs. forman all about this Saleor. So you can place the letter in the hands of M. to take to forman's wife, She can read it for herself. She will find Foster at ladlum's warehouse on the Basin, and when you write call my name to him and he will trust it. this foster are a member of the old Baptist Church. When you have done all you can do let us know what you have done, if you hears anything of my uncle let me know.

TORONTO, March 18th, 1854.

MY DEAR STILL:—Yours of the 15th Reached on the 11th, found myself and family very well, and not to delay no time in replying to you, as there was an article in your letter which article Roused me very much when I read it; that was you praying to me to be cautious how I write down South. Be so kind as to tell me in your next letter whether you have at any time apprehended any danger in my letters however, in those bond southward; if there have been, allow me to beg ten thousand pardon before God and man, for I am not design to throw any obstacle in the way of those whom I left in South, but to aide them in every possible way. I have done as you Requested, that to warn the friends of the dager of writing South. I have told all you said in yours that Mr. Minkins would be in your city very soon, and you would see what you could do for me, do you mean or do speak in reference to my dear uncle. I am hopes that you will use every ifford to get him from the position in which he now stand. I know how he feels at this time, for I have felt the same when I was a runway. I was bereft of all participation with my family for nearly nine months, and now that poor fellow are place in same position. Oh God help I pray, what a pitty it is that I cannot do him no good, but I sincerely hope that you will not get fatigued at doing good in such cases, nay, I think other wises of you, however, I Say no more on this subject at present, but leave it for you to judge.

On the 13th inst. you made Some Remarks concerning friend Forman's wife, I am Satisfied that you will do all you can for her Release from Slavery, but as you said you feels for them, so do I, and Mr. Foreman comes to me very often to know if I have heard anything from you concerning his wife, they all comes to for the same.

God Save the Queen. All my letters Southward have passed through your hands with an exception of one.

JOHN H. HILL.

TORONTO Sept 14th 1854

MY DEAR FRIEND STILL:—this are the first oppertunity that I have had to write you since I Recd your letter of the 20th July. there have been sickness and Death in my family since your letter was Recd. our dear little Child have been taken from us one whom we loved so very Dear. but the almighty God knows what are best for us all.

Louis Henry Hill, was born in Petersburg Va May 7th 1852. and Died Toronto August 19th 1854 at five o'clock P. M.

Dear Still I could say much about the times and insidince that have taken place since the coming of that dear little angle jest spoken of. it was 12 months and 3 days from the time that I took departure of my wife and child to proceed to Richmond to awaite a conveyance up to the day of his death.

it was thursday the 13th that I lift Richmond. it was saturday

the 15th that I land to my great joy in the city of Phila. then I put
out for Canada.   I arrived in this city on Friday the 30th and to
my great satisfaction.   I found myself upon Briton's free land.   not
only free for the white man bot for all.

this day 12 months I was not out of the reach the slaveholders,
but this 14th day of Sept. I am as Free as your President Pearce.
only I have not been free so long   However the 30th of the month I
will have been free only 12 months.

It is true that I have to work very hard for comfort but I would
not exchange with ten thousand slave that are equel with their
masters.   I am Happy, Happy.

Give love to Mrs. Still.   My wife laments her child's death too
much.   wil you be so kind as to see Mr. Brown and ask him to write
to me, and if he have heard from Petersburg Va.   Yours truely

J. H. HILL.

TORONTO, Jan. 19th 1854.

MY DEAR STILL:—Your letter of the 16th came to hand just in
time for my perpose I perceivs by your statement that the money
have not been to Petersburg at all done just what was right and I
would of sent the money to you at first, but my dear friend I have
called upon you for so many times that I have been ashamed of
myself to call any more So you may perceive by the above written
my obligations to you, you said that you had written on to Petersburg, you have done Right which I believes is your general way of
doing your business.   the money are all right I only had to pay a 6d
on the Ten dollars.   this money was given to by a friend in the city
N. york, the friend was from Richmond Virginia (a white man) the
amount was fifteen dollars, I forward a letter to you yesterday which
letter I forgot to date.   my friend I wants to hear from virginia the
worst of all things.   you know that we expect some freneds on and
we cannot hear any thing from them which makes us uneasy for
fear that they have attempt to come away and been detected.   I
have ears open at all times, listen at all hours expecting to hear
from them   Please to see friend Brown and know from him if he has
heard anything from our friends, if he have not. tell him write and
inquiare into the matter why it is that they have not come over,
then let me hear from you all.

We are going to have a grand concert &c I mean the Abolisnous
Socity.   I will attend myself and also my wife if the Lord be willing
you will perceive in previotts letter that I mension something con-

cerning Mr Forman's wife if there be any chance whatever please to proceed, Mr Foreman sends his love to you Requested you to do all you can to get his wife away from Slavery.

Our best respects to your wife. You promised me that you would write somthing concerning our arrival in Canada but I suppose you have not had the time as yet, I would be very glad to read your opinion on that matter

I have notice several articles in the freeman one of the Canada weaklys concerning the Christiana prisoners respecting Castnor Hanway and also Mr. Rauffman. if I had one hundred dollars to day I would give them five each, however I hope that I may be able to subscribe something for their Relefe. in Regards to the letters have been written from Canada to the South the letters was not what they thought them to be and if the slaveholders know when they are doing well they had better keep their side for if they comes over this side of the lake I am under the impression they will not go back with somethin that their mother boned them with whether thiar slaves written for them or not. I know some one here that have written his master to come after him, but not because he expect to go with him home but because he wants to retaleate upon his persecutor, but I would be sorry for man that have written for his master expecting to return with him because the people here would kill them. Sir I cannot write enough to express myself so I must close by saying I Remain yours.   JOHN H. HILL.

TORONTO, January 7th, 1855.

MY DEAR FRIEND:—It is with much pleasure that I take this opportunity of addressing you with these few lines hoping when they reeches you they may find yourself and family enjoying good health as they leaves us at present.

And it is with much happiness that I can say to you that Mrs. Mercer arrived in this city on yesterday. Mr. Mercer was at my house late in the evening, and I told him that when he went home if hear anything from Virginia, that he must let me know as soon as possible. He told me that if he went home and found any news there he would come right back and inform me thereof. But little did he expect to find his dearest there. You may judge what a meeting there was with them, and may God grant that there may be some more meetings with our wives and friends. I had been looking for some one from the old sod for several days, but I was in good hopes that it would be my poor Uncle. But poor fellow he are yet groaning under the sufferings of a horrid sytam, Expecting every day to Receive his Doom. Oh, God, what shall I do, or what can I do for him? I have prayed for him more than 12 months, yet he is in that horrid condition. I can never hear anything Directly from him or any of my people.

Once more I appeal to your Humanity. Will you act for him, as if you was in slavery yourself, and I sincerely believe that he will come out of that condition? Mrs. M. have told me that she given some directions how he could be goten at, but friend Still, if this conductor should not be successfull this time, will you mind him of the Poor Slave again. I hope you will as Mrs. Mercer have told the friend what to do I cannot do more, therefore I must leve it to the Mercy of God and your Exertion.

The weather have been very mile Ever since the 23rd of Dec. I have thought considerable about our condition in this country Seeing that the weather was so very faverable to us. I was thinking a few days ago, that nature had giving us A country & adopted all things Sutable.

You will do me the kindness of telling me in your next whether or not the ten slaves have been Brought out from N. C.

I have not hard from Brown for Nine month he have done some very Bad letting me alone, for what cause I cannot tell. Give my Best Respect to Mr. B. when you see him. I wish very much to hear from himself and family. You will please to let me hear from you. My wife Joines me in love to yourself and family.

Yours most Respectfully,

JOHN H. HILL.

P. S. Every fugitive Regreated to hear of the Death of Mrs. Moore. I myself think that there are no other to take her Place.

yours   J. H. H.

HAMILTON, August 15th, 1856.

DEAR FRIEND:—I am very glad to hear that the Underground Rail Road is doing such good business, but tell me in your next letter if you have seen the heroic fellow that cut off the head of the Patrol in Maryland. We wants that fellow here, as John Bull has a great deal of fighting to do, and as there is a colored Captain in this city, I would seek to have that fellow Promoted, Provided he became a soldier.

Great respect,   JOHN H. HILL.

P. S.—Please forward the enclosed to Mr. McCray.

HAMILTON, Jan. 5th, 1857.

MR. STILL:—Our Pappers contains long details of insurrectionary movements among the slaves at the South and one paper adds that a great Nomber of Generals, Captains with other officers had being arrested. At this day four years ago I left Petersburg for Richmond to meet the man whom called himself my master, but he wanted money worser that day than I do this day, he took me to sell me, he could not have done a better thing for me for I intended to leave any how by the first convaiance. I hard some good Prayers put up for the suffers on last Sunday evening in the Baptist Church. Now friend still I beleve that Prayers affects great good, but I beleve that the fire and sword would affect more good in this case. Perhaps this is not your thoughts, but I must acknowledge this to be my Polacy. The world are being turned upside down, and I think we might as well take an active part in it as not. We must have something to do as other people, and I hope this moment among the Slaves are the beginning. I wants to see something go on while I live.

Yours truly,   JOHN H. HILL.

HAMILTON, June 5th, 1858.

DEAR FRIEND STILL:—I have just heard that our friend Capt. B. have being taken Prisoner in Virginia with slaves on board of his vessel. I hard this about an hour ago. the Person told me of this said he read it in the newspaper, if this be so it is awfull. You will be so kind as to send me some information. Send me one of the Virginia Papers. Poor fellow if they have got him, I am sorry, sorry to my heart. I have not heard from my Uncle for a long time if have heard or do hear anything from him at any time you will oblige me by writing. I wish you to inquire of Mr. Anderson's friends (if you know any of them), if they have heard anything from him since he was in your city. I have written to him twice since he was here according to his own directions, but never received an answer. I wants to hear from my mother very much, but cannot hear one word. You will present my best regards to the friend. Mrs. Hill is quite sick.

Yours truly,   J. H. HILL.

P. S.—I have not received the Anti-Slavery Standard for several weeks. Please forward any news relative to the Capt.

J. H. H.

FROM W. H. ACTKINS

ST. CATHARINES, August 4, 1854.

MY DEAR SIR:—It is with plesure that I now take my pen to inform you that I am well at present and I hope that these few lines may find you injoying good health, and will you plese to be so kind as to send a leter down home for me if you plese to my wife, the reason that I beg the favor of you I have written to you several times and never recieve no answer, she don't no whar I am at I would like her to no, if it is posible elizeran Actkins, and when you write will you plese to send me all the news, give my respect to all the fambley and allso to Mr lundey and his fambley and tell him plese to send me those books if you plese the first chance you can git. Mrs. Wood sends her love to Mr. Still answer this as soon as on hand, the boys all send their love to all, the reason why i sends for a answer write away i expect to live this and go up west nex mounth not to stay to git some land, i have no more at present, i remain your friend.

W. H. ACTKINS.

ST. CATHARINES, C. W., October 5th, 1854.

MR. WILLIAM STILL:—*Dear Friend:*—I take the liberty to address to you a few lines in behalf of my wife, who is still at Norfolk, Va. I have heard by my friend Richmond Bohm, who arrived lately, that she was in the hands of my friend Henry Lovey (the same who had me in hand at the time I started). I understood that she was about to make her start this month, and that she was only waiting for me to send her some means. I would like for you to communicate the substance of this letter to my wife, through my friend Henry Lovey, and for her to come on as soon as she can. I would like to have my wife write to me a few lines by the first opportunity. She could write to you in Philadelphia, 31 North Fifth street. I wish to send my love to you & your family & would like for you to answer this letter with the least possible delay in the care of Hiram Wilson.

Very respectfully yours,   W. H. ATKINS.

P. S. I would like for my friend Henry Lovey to send my wife right on to Philadelphia; not to stop for want of means, for I will forward means on to my friend Wm Still. My love to my father & mother, my friend Lovey & to all my inquiring friends. If you cannot find it convenient to write, please forward this by the Boat.

H. W. A.

FROM HARRIET EGLIN

SENNETT, June, 1856.

MR. WILLIAM STILL:—*Dear Sir:*—I am happy to tell you that Charlotte Gildes and myself have got along thus far safely. We have had no trouble and found friends all the way along, for which we feel very thankful to you and to all our friends on the road since we left. We reached Mr. Loguen's in Syracuse, on last Tuesday evening & on Wednesday two gentlemen from this community called and we went with them to work in their families. What I wish you would do is to be so kind as to send our clothes to this place if they should fall into your hands. We hope our uncle in Baltimore will get the letter Charlotte wrote to him last Sabbath, while we were at your house, concerning the clothes. Perhaps the best would be to send them to Syracuse to the *care of Mr. Loguen* and he will send them to us. This will more certainly ensure our getting them. If you hear anything that would be interesting to Charlotte or me from Baltimore, please direct a letter to us to this place, to the care of Revd. Chas. Anderson, Sennett, Cayuga Co., N. Y. Please give my love and Charlotte's to Mrs. Still and thank her for her kindness to us while at your house. Your affectionate friend,

HARRIET EGLIN.

SENNETT, July 31st, 1856.

MR. WM. STILL:—*My Dear Friend:*—I have just received your note of 29th inst. and allow me dear sir, to assure you that the only letter I have written, is the one you received, an answer to which you sent me. I never wrote to Baltimore, nor did any person write for me there, and it is with *indescribable grief*, that I hear what your letter communicates to me, of those who you say have gotten into difficulty on my account. My Cousin Charlotte who came with me, got into a good place in this vicinity, but she could not content herself to stay here but just *one week*—she then went to Canada—and she is the one who by writing (if any one), has brought this trouble upon those to whom you refer in Baltimore.

She has written me two letters from Canada, and by neither of them can I ascertain *where she lives*—her letters are mailed at Suspension Bridge, but she does not live there as her letters show. In the first she does not even sign her name. She has evidently employed some person to write, who is nearly as ignorant as herself. If I knew where to find her I would find out *what* she has written.

I don't know but she has told where I live, and may yet get me

and my friends here, in trouble too, as she has some in other places.
I don't wish to have you trouble yourself about my clothes, I am in
a place where I can get all the clothes I want or need. Will you
please write me when convenient and tell me what you hear about
those who I fear are suffering as the result of their kindness to me?
May God, in some way, grant them deliverance. Oh the misery,
the sorrow, which this cursed system of Slavery is constantly bringing upon millions in this land of boasted freedom!

Can you tell me where Sarah King is, who was at your house
when I was there? She was going to Canada to meet her husband.
Give my love to Mrs. Still & accept the same yourself. Your much
indebted & obliged friend,   HARRIET EGLIN.

SENNETT, October 28th, 1856.

DEAR MR. STILL:—I am happy to tell you that I am well and
happy. I still live with Rev. Mr. Anderson in this place, I am
learning to read and write. I do not like to trouble you too much,
but I would like to know if you have heard anything more about
my friends in Baltimore who got into trouble on our account. Do
be pleased to write me if you can give me any information about
them. I feel bad that they should suffer for me. I wish all my
brethren and sisters in bondage, were as well off as I am. The girl
that came with me is in Canada, near the Suspension Bridge. I
was glad to see Green Murdock, a colored young man, who stopped
at your house about six weeks ago, he knew my folks at the South.
He has got into a good place to work in this neighborhood. Give
my love to Mrs Still, and believe me your obliged friend,

HARRIET EGLIN.

P. S. I would like to know what became of Johnson,[26] the man
whose foot was smashed by jumping off the cars, he was at your
house when I was there.   H. E.

FROM W. BOURAL

TORONTO, March 28th, 1854.

SIR, MR. STILL—It does me pleasure to forward you this letter
hopeing when this comes to hand it may find your family well, as
they leaves me at present. I will also say that the friends are well.

[26] Johnson was an unfortunate young fugitive, who, while escaping, beheld his
master or pursuer in the cars, and jumped therefrom, crushing his feet shockingly
by the bold act.

Allow me to say to you that I arrived in this place on Friday last safe and sound, and feeles well under my safe arrival. Its true that I have not been employed as yet but I lives hopes to be at work very shortly. I likes this city very well, and I am in hopes that there a living here for me as much so as there for any one else. You will be please to write. I am bording at Mr. Phillip's Centre Street.

I have nothing more at present. Yours most respectfull.

W. BOURAL.

FROM DANIEL ROBINSON

NEW BEDFORD, Mass., March 22d, 1854.

DEAR SIR:—I am happy to inform you that I arrived in this place this morning well and cheerful. I am, sir, to you and others under more obligations for your kindly protection of me than I can in any way express at present. May the Lord preserve you unto eternal life. Remember my respects to Mr. Lundy and family. Should the boat lay up please let me know.

Yours respectfully,   DAVID ROBINSON.

Please forward to Dr. H. Lundy, after you have gotten through. With respects, &c.   D. R.

FROM PATTERSON SMITH

ST. CATHRINES Oct 29th.

MY DEAR FRIEND:—yours of the 15th came to hand and I was glad to hea from you and your dear family were well and the reason that I did not write sooner I expected get a letter from my brother in pennsylvania but I have not received any as yet when I wrote last I directed my letter to philip scott minister of the asbury church baltimore and that was the reason that I thought it strange I did not get an answer but I did not put my brother name to it I made arrangements before I left home with a family of smiths that I was to write to and the letter that I enclose in this I want you to direct it to D Philip scott in his care for mrs cassey Jackson Duke Jacksons wife and she will give to Priana smith or Sarah Jane Smith those are the persons I wish to write to I wish you to write on as quick as you can and let them know that there is a lady coming on by the name of mrs Holonsworth and she will call and see you and you will find her a very interesting and inteligent person one worthy of respect and esteem and a high reputation I must now bring my letter to a close no more at present but remain your humble servant

PATTERSON SMITH

In my letters I did not write to my friends how they shall write to me but in the letter that you write you will please to tell them how they shall write to me.

FROM GEORGE W. FREELAND

SINCATHANS, canada west.

Brother Still:—I im brace this opportunity of pening you a few lines to in form you that I am well at present & in hopes to find you & family well also I hope that god Will Bless you & and your family & if I never should meet you in this world I hope to meet you in glory Remember my love to Brother Brown & tell him that I am well & hearty tell him to writ Thomas word that I am well at present you must excuse me I will Rite when I return from the west.

GEORGE W. FREELAND.

Send your Letters in the name of John Anderson.

FROM SAMUEL GREEN

SALFORD, 22, 1857.

Dear Sir   I take my pen in hand to Request a faver of you if you can by any means without duin InJestus to your self or your Bisness to grant it as I Bleve you to be a man that would Sympathize in such a ones Condition as my self   I Reseved a letter that Stats to me that my Fater has ben Betraed in the act of helping sum frend to Canada and the law has Convicted and Sentanced him to the Stats prison for 10 yeares his White Frands ofered 2 thousen Dollers to Redem him but they would not short three thousen.   I am in Canada and it is a Dificult thing to get a letter to any of my Frands in Maryland so as to get prop per infermation abot it—if you can by any means get any in telligence from Baltimore City a bot this Event Plese do so and Rit word and all so all the inform mation that you think prop per as Regards the Evant and the best mathod to Redeme him and so Plese Rite soon as you can   You will oblige your sir Frand and Drect your letter to Salford P. office C. W.

SAMUEL GREEN.

FROM JOHN HALL

HAMILTON, March 25th, 1856.

MR. STILL:—Sir and Friend—I take the liberty of addressing you with these few lines hoping that you will attend to what I shall request of you.

I have written to Virginia and have not received an answer yet. I want to know if you can get any one of your city to go to Richmond for me. If you can, I will pay the expense of the whole. The person that I want the messenger to see is a white girl. I expect you know who I allude to, it is the girl that sent me away. If you can get any one to go, you will please write right away and tell me the cost, &c. I will forward the money and a letter. Please use your endeavors.   Yours Respectfully,   JOHN HALL.
Direct yours to Mr. Hill.

HAMILTON, Sept. 15th, 1856.

TO MR. STILL, DEAR SIR:—I take this opportunity of addressing these few lines to you hoping to find you in good health I am happy to inform you that Miss Weaver arrived here on Tuesday last, and I can assure you it was indeed a happy day. As for your part that you done I will not attempt to tell you how thankful I am, but I hope that you can imagine what my feelings are to you. I cannot find words sufficient to express my gratitude to you, I think the wedding will take place on Tuesday next, I have seen some of the bread from your house, and she says it is the best bread she has had since she has been in America. Sometimes she has impudence enough to tell me she would rather be where you are in Philadelphia than to be here with me. I hope this will be no admiration to you for no honest hearted person ever saw you that would not desire to be where you are, No flattery, but candidly speaking, you are worthy all the praise of any person who has ever been with you, I am now like a deserted Christian, but yet I have asked so much, and all has been done yet I must ask again, My love to Mrs. Still. Dear Mr. Still I now ask you please to exercise all your influence to get this young man Willis Johnson from Richmond for me It is the young man that Miss Weaver told you about, he is in Richmond I think he is at the corner of Fushien Street, & Grace in a house of one Mr. Rutherford, there is several Rutherford in the neighborhood, there is a church call'd the third Baptist Church, on the R. H. side going up Grace street, directly opposite the Baptist church at the corner, is Mrs. Meads Old School at one corner, and Mr. Rutherfords is at the other corner. He can be found out by seeing Fountain Tombs who belongs to Mr. Rutherford and if you should not see him, there is James Turner who lives at the Governors, Please to see Captain Bayliss and tell him to take these directions and go to John Hill, in Petersburgh, and he may find him. Tell Captain Bayliss that if he ever did me a friendly thing in his life which he did do one friendly act, if he will take this on himself, and if money should be lacking I will forward any money that he may require, I hope you will sympathize with the poor young fellow, and tell the captain to do all in his power to get him and the costs shall be paid. He lies now between death or victory, for I know the man he belongs to would just as soon kill him as not, if he catches him, I here enclose to you a letter for Mr. Wm. C. Mayo, and please to send it as directed. In this letter I have asked him to send a box to you for me, which you will please pay the fare of the express upon it, when you get it please to let me know, and I will send you the money to pay the expenses of the carriage clear through. Please to let Mr. Mayo know how to direct a box to you, and the best way to send it from Richmond to Philadelphia. You will greatly oblige me by so doing. In this letter I have enclosed a trifle for postage which you will please to keep on account of my letters I hope you wont think hard of me but I simply send it because I know you have done enough, and are now doing more, without imposing in the matter I have done it a great many more of our people who you have done so much fore. No more from your humble and oldest servant.

JOHN HALL, Norton's Hotel, Hamilton.

MONDAY, Sept. 29, 56.

SIR:—I take this opportunity of informing you that we are in excellent health, and hope you are the same, I wrote a letter to you about 2 weeks ago and have not yet had an answer to it I wish to inform you that the wedding took place on Tuesday last, and Mrs. Hall now sends her best love to you, I enclose a letter which I wish you to forward to Mr. Mayo, you will see in his letter what I have said to him and I wish you would furnish him with such directions as it requires for him to send them things to you. I have told him not to pay for them but to send them to you so when you get them write me word what the cost of them are, and I will send you the money for them. Mary desires you to give her love to Mrs. Still. If any letters come for me please to send to me at Nortons Hotel, Please to let me know if you had a letter from me about 12 days ago. You will please Direct the enclosed to Mr. W. C. Mayo, Richmond, Va. Let me know if you have heard anything of Willis Johnson Mr. & Mrs. Hill send their kind love to you, they are all well, no more at present from your affect.,

JOHN HALL Nortons Hotel.

HAMILTON, December 23d, 1856.

DEAR SIR:—I am happy to inform you that we are both enjoying good health and hope you are the same. I have been expecting a letter from you for some time but I suppose your business has prevented you from writing. I suppose you have not heard from any of my friends at Richmond. I have been longing to hear some news from that part, you may think "Out of sight and out of mind," but I can assure you, no matter how far I may be, or in what distant land, I shall never forget you, if I can never reach you by letters you may be sure I shall always think of you. I have found a great many friends in my life, but I must say you are the best one I ever met with, except one, you must know who that is, 'tis one who if I did not consider a friend, I could not consider any other person a friend, and that is Mrs. Hall. Please to let me know if the navigation between New York & Richmond is closed. Please to let me know whether it would be convenient to you to go to New York if it is please let me know what is the expense. Tell Mrs Still that my wife would be very happy to receive a letter from her at some moment when she is at leisure, for I know from what little I have seen of domestic affairs it keeps her pretty well employed, And I know she has not much time to write but if it were but two lines, she would be happy to receive it from her, my reason for wanting you to go to New York, there is a young man named Richard Myers and I should like for you to see him. He goes on board the Orono to Richmond and is a particular friend of mine and by seeing him I could get my clothes from Richmond, I expect to be out of employ in a few days, as the hotel is about to close on the 1st January and I hope you will write to me soon I want you to send me word how you and all the family are and all the news you can, you must excuse my short letter, as it is now near one o'clock and I must attend to business, but I have not written half what I intended to, as time is short, hoping to hear from you soon I remain yours sincerely,

JOHN HALL.

Mr. and Mrs. Hill desire their best respects to you and Mrs. Still.

FROM HENRY WASHINGTON

ST. CATHARINES, C. W. Nov. 12, 1855.

MR. WILLIAM STILL:—*Dear Sir:*—I have received a letter from Joseph G. Selden a friend in Norfolk, Va., informing me of the death of my wife, who deceased since I saw you here; he also informs me

that my clothing will be forwarded to you by Jupiter White, who
now has it in his charge. You will therefore do me a great favor, if
you will be so good as to forward them to me at this place St.
Catharines, C. W.

The accompanying letter is the one received from Mr. Selden
which I send you, that you may see that it is all right. You will
please give my respects to Mrs. Still and family.

Most respectfully yours,

HENRY WASHINGTON.

FROM JAMES H. FORMAN

NIAGARA FALLS, June 5th, 1856.

MR. STILL:—Sir—I take my pen in hand to write you theas few
lines to let you know that I am well at present and hope theas few
lines may find you the same. Sir my object in writing to you is that
I expect a young Lady by the name of Miss Mariah Moore, from
Norfolk, Virginia. She will leave Norfolk on the 13th of this month
in the Steamship Virginia for Philadelphia you will oblige me very
much by seeing her safely on the train of cars that leaves Philadelphia for the Suspension Bridge Niagara Falls pleas to tell the
Lady to telegraph to me what time she will leave Philadelphia so i
may know what time to meet her at the Suspension Bridge my
Brother Isaac Forman send his love also his family to you and your
family they are all well at present pleas to give my respects to Mr.
Harry Londay, also Miss Margaret Cunigan, no more at present.

I remain your friend,   JAMES H. FORMAN.

When you telegraph to me direct to the International Hotel,
Niagara Falls, N. Y.

NIAGARA FALLS, July 24th, 1856.

DEAR SIR:—I take this opportunity of writing these few lines to
you hoping that they may find you enjoying good health as these
few lines leave me at present. I thank you for your kindness. Miss
Moore arrived here on the 30th of June and I was down to the cars
to receive her. I thought I would have written to you before, but
I thought I would wait till I got married. I got married on the
22d of July in the English Church Canada about 11 o'clock my wife
sends all her love to you and your wife and all enquiring friends
please to kiss your two children for her and she says she is done
crying and I am glad to hear she enjoyed herself so well in Phila-

delphia give my respects to Miss Margaret Cuningham and I am
glad to hear her sister arrived my father sends his respects to you no
more at present but remain your friend,

JAMES H. FORMAN.

Direct your letter to the International Hotel, Niagara Falls.

FROM ROBERT JONES

HAMILTON, C. W., August 9th, 1856.

MR. WM. STILL:—*Dear Friend:*—I take this opportunity of
writing you these few lines to inform you of my health, which is
good at present, &c. * * * *

I was talking to you about going to Liberia, when I saw you last,
and did intend to start this fall, but I since looked at the condition
of the colored people in Canada. I thought I would try to do
something for their elevation as a nation, to place them in the
proper position to stand where they ought to stand. In order to do
this, I have undertaken to get up a military company amongst them.
They laughed at me to undertake such a thing; but I did not relax
my energies. I went and had an interview with Major J. T.
Gilepon, told him what my object was, he encouraged me to go on,
saying that he would do all he could for the accomplishment of my
object. He referred to *Sir Allan McNab, &c.* * * * * I took
with me Mr. J. H. Hill to see him—he told me that it should be
done, and required us to write a petition to the *Governor General*,
which has been done. * * * * The company is already
organized. Mr. Howard was elected Captain; J. H. Hill, 1st
Lieutenant; Hezekiah Hill, Ensign; Robert Jones, 1st Sergeant.
The company's name is, Queen Victoria's Rifle Guards. You may,
by this, see what I have been doing since I have been in Canada.
When we receive our appointments by the Government. I will
send by express, my daguerreotype in uniform.

My respects, &c. &c., ROBERT JONES.

FROM WILLIAM DONAR

NEW BEDFORD, Nov. 3, 1859.

DEAR SIR:—i embrace this opertunity to inform you that i
received your letter with pleasure, i am enjoying good health and
hope that these few lines will find you enjoying the same blessing.
i rejoise to hear from you i feel very much indetted to you for not
writing before but i have been so bissy that is the cause, i rejoise to

heare of the arrival of my wife, and hope she is not sick from the
roling of the sea and if she is not, pleas to send her on here Monday
with a six baral warlian and a rifall to gard her up to my residance i
thank you kindly for the good that you have don for me. Give my
respects to Mrs. Still, tell her i want to see her very bad and you also
i would come but i am afraid yet to venture, i received your letter
the second, but about the first of spring i hope to pay you a visit or
next summer. i am getting something to do every day. i will
write on her arrivall and tell you more. Mr. R. White sends his
love to you and your famerly and says that he is very much indetted
to you for his not writing and all so he desires to know wheather his
cloths has arived yet or not, and if they are please to express them
on to him or if at preasant by Mrs. Donar. Not any more at
preasent. i remain your affectionate brother,

WILLIAM DONAR.

FROM ELLEN SAUNDERS

NEW BEDFORD, Mass., October 16th, 1854.

MR. STILL:—Dear Sir—I now take my pen in my hand to inform
you of my health which is good at present all except a cold I have
got but I hope when these few lines reach you you may be enjoying
good health. I arrived in New Bedford Thursday morning safely
and what little I have seen of the city I like it very much my friends
were very glad to see me. I found my sister very well. Give my
love to Mrs. Still and also your dear little children. I am now out
at service. I do not think of going to Canada now. I think I
shall remain in this city this winter. Please tell Mrs. Still I have
not met any person who has treated me any kinder than she did
since I left. I consider you both to have been true friends to me.
I hope you will think me the same to you. I feel very thankful to
you indeed. It might been supposed, out of sight out of mind, but
it is not so. I never forget my friends. Give my love to Florence.
If you come to this city I would be very happy to see you. Kiss
your dear little children for me. Please to answer this as soon as
possible, so that I may know you received this. No more at
present. I still remain your friend,

ELLEN SAUNDERS.

FROM FRANCES HILLIARD

TORONTO, CANADA, U. C., October 15th, 1855.

MY DEAR MR. STILL:—Sir—I take the opportunity of writing you a few lines to inform you of my health. I am very well at present, and hope that when these few lines reach you they may find you enjoying the same blessing. Give my love to Mrs. Still and all the children, and also to Mr. Swan, and tell him that he must give you the money that he has, and you will please send it to me, as I have received a letter from my husband saying that I must come on to him as soon as I get the money from him. I cannot go to him until I get the money that Mr. Swan has in hand. Please tell Mr. Caustle that the clothes he spoke of my mother did not know anything about them. I left them with Hinson Brown and he promised to give them to Mr. Smith. Tell him to ask Mr. Smith to get them from Mr. Brown for me, and when I get settled I will send him word and he can send them to me. The letters that were sent to me I received them all. I wish you would send me word if Mr. Smith is on the boat yet—if he is please write me word in your next letter. Please send me the money as soon as you possibly can, for I am very anxious to see my husband. I send to you for I think you will do what you can for me. No more at present, but remain

Yours truly,   FRANCES HILLIARD.

Send me word if Mr. Caustle had given Mr. Smith the money that he promised to give him.

ST. CATHARINES, C. W., Aug. 20th, 1855.

To MR. WM. STILL, DEAR FRIEND:—It gives me pleasure to inform you that I have had the good fortune to reach this northern Canaan. I got here yesterday and am in good health and happy in the enjoyment of Freedom, but am very anxious to have my wife and child here with me.

I wish you to write to her immediately on receiving this and let her know where I am you will recollect her name Sarah Miles at Baltimore on the corner of Hamburg and Eutaw streets. Please encourage her in making a start and give her the necessary directions how to come. She will please to make the time as short as possible in getting through to Canada. Say to my wife that I wish her to write immediately to the friends that I told her to address as soon as she hears from me. Inform her that I now stop in St. Catharines near the Niagara Falls that I am not yet in business but expect to

get into business very soon—That I am in the enjoyment of good
health and hoping that this communication may find my affectionate
wife the same.   That I have been highly favored with friends
throughout my journey I wish my wife to write to me as soon as she
can and let me know how soon I may expect to see her on this side
of the Niagara River.   My wife had better call on Dr. Perkins and
perhaps he will let her have the money he had in charge for me but
that I failed of receiving when I left Baltimore.   Please direct the
letter for my wife to Mr. George Lister, in Hill street between
Howard and Sharp.   My compliments to all enquiring friends.
          Very respectfully yours,   SAMUEL MILES.
     P. S. Please send the thread along as a token and my wife will
understand that all is right.   S. M.

FROM ANTHONY AND ALBERT BROWN

HAMELTON, March 7th 1856.

MR. WM. STILL:—*Sir:*—I now take the opportunity of writting
you a few lins hoping to find yourself and famly well as thes lines
leves me at present, myself and brother, Anthony & Albert brown's
respects.   We have spent quite agreeable winter, we ware emploied
in the new hotel, name Anglo american, wheare we wintered and don
very well, we also met with our too frends ho came from home with
us, Jonas anderson and Izeas, now we are all· safe in hamilton, I
wish to cale you to youre prommos, if convenient to write to
Norfolk, Va., for me, and let my wife mary Elen Brown, no where I
am, and my brothers wife Elickzener Brown, as we have never
heard a word from them since we left, tel them that we found our
homes and situation in canady much better than we expected, tel
them not to think hard of us, we was boun to flee from the rath to
come, tel them we live in the hopes of meting them once more this
side of the grave, tel them if we never more see them, we hope to
meet them in the kingdom of heaven in pece, tel them to remember
my love to my cherch and brethren, tel them I find there is the same
prayer-hearing God heare as there is in old Va; tel them to remember our love to all the enquiring frends, I have written sevrel
times but have never reseived no answer, I find a gret meny of my
old accuaintens from Va., heare we are no ways lonesom, Mr. Still,
I have written to you once before, but reseve no answer.   Pleas let
us hear from you by any means.   Nothing more at present, but
remane youre frends,
          ANTHONY & ALBERT BROWN.

HAMILTON June 26th, 1856.

MR. WM. STILL:—*kine Sir:*—I am happy to say to you that I have jus reseved my letter dated 5 of the present month, but previeously had bin in form las night by Mr. J. H. Hall, he had jus reseved a letter from you stating that my wife was with you, oh my I was so glad it case me to shed tears.

Mr. Still, I cannot return you the thanks for the care of my wife, for I am so Glad that I dont now what to say, you will pleas start her for canaday. I am yet in hamilton, C. W, at the city hotel, my brother and Joseph anderson is at the angle american hotel, they send there respects to you and family my self also, and a greater part to my wife. I came by the way of syracruse remember me to Mrs. logins, tel her to writ back to my brothers wife if she is living and tel her to com on tel her to send Joseph Andersons love to his mother.

i now send her 10 Dollers and would send more but being out of employment some of winter it pulls me back, you will be so kine as to forward her on to me, and if life las I will satisfie you at some time, before long. Give my respects and brothers to Mr. John Dennes, tel him Mr. Hills famly is wel and send there love to them, I now bring my letter to a close, And am youre most humble Servant,   ANTHONY BROWN.

P. S. I had given out the notion of ever seeing my wife again, so I have not been attending the office, but am truly sorry I did not, you mention in yours of Mr. Henry lewey, he has left this city for Boston about 2 weeks ago, we have not herd from him yet.

A. BROWN.

FROM ALBERT METTER

STANFORD, June 1st, 1855, Niagara districk.

DEAR SIR:—I set down to inform you that I take the liberty to rite for a frend to inform you that he is injoying good health and hopes that this will finde you the same he got to this cuntry very well except that in Albany he was vary neig taking back to his oald home but escaped and when he came to the suspention bridg he was so glad that he run for freadums shore and when he arived it was the last of october and must look for sum wourk for the winter he choped wood until Feruary times are good but money is scarce he thinks a great deal of the girl he left behind him he thinks that there is non like her here non so hansom as his Rachel right and let him hear from you as soon as convaniant no more at presant but remain yours,   ALBERT METTER.

FROM JOHN ATKINSON

St. Catharines, Sept. 4th.

DEAR SIR:—I now embrace this favorable opportunity of writing you a few lines to inform you that I am quite well and arrived here safe, and I hope that these few lines may find you and your family the same. I hope you will intercede for my clothes and as soon as they come please to send them to me, and if you have not time, get Dr. Lundy to look out for them, and when they come be very careful in sending them. I wish you would copy off this letter and give it to the Steward, and tell him to give it to Henry Lewy and tell him to give it to my wife. Brother sends his love to you and all the family and he is overjoyed at seeing me arrive safe, he can hardly contain himself; also he wants to see his wife very much, and says when she comes he hopes you will send her on as soon as possible. Jerry Williams' love, together with all of us. I had a message for Mr. Lundy, but I forgot it when I was there. No more at present, but remain your ever grateful and sincere friend,

JOHN ATKINSON.

St. Catharines, C. W., Oct. 5th, 1854.

MR. WM. STILL:—Dear Sir—I have learned of my friend, Richmond Bohm, that my clothes were in Philadelphia. Will you have the kindness to see Dr. Lundy and if he has my clothes in charge, or knows about them, for him to send them on to me immediately, as I am in great need of them. I would like to have them put in a small box, and the overcoat I left at your house to be put in the box with them, to be sent to the care of my friend, Hiram Wilson. On receipt of this letter, I desire you to write a few lines to my wife, Mary Atkins, in the care of my friend, Henry Lowey, stating that I am well and hearty and hoping that she is the same. Please tell her to remember my love to her mother and her cousin, Emelin, and her husband, and Thomas Hunter; also to my father and mother. Please request her to write to me immediately, for her to be of good courage, that I love her better than ever. I would like her to come on as soon as she can, but for her to write and let me know when she is going to start. Affectionately Yours,

JOHN ATKINS.

W. H. ATKINSON, Fugitive, Oct., 1854.

FROM SEVERAL FUGITIVES

"TORONTO, C. W., Aug. 17th, 1856.

MR. STILL:—Dear Sir—These few lines may find you as they leave us, we are well at present and arrived safe in Toronto. Give our respects to Mrs. S.—— and daughter. Toronto is a very extensive place. We have plenty of pork, beef and mutton. There are five market houses and many churches. Female wages is 62½ cents per day, men's wages is $1 and york shilling. We are now boarding at Mr. George Blunt's, on Centre street, two doors from Elm, back of Lawyer's Hall, and when you write to us, direct your letter to the care of Mr. George Blunt, &c. (Signed), James Monroe Peter Heines, Henry James Morris, and Matthew Bodams."

FROM HENRY JAMES MORRIS

TORONTO, Canada West, upper, 18th day of the 9th mo., 1856.

MR. WILLIAM STILL:—Dear Sir—I hope these lines may find you and your family as they leave me give my respects to little Caroline and her mother.

Dear Sir, I have received two letters from my wife since I saw you, and the second was awful. I am sorry to say she says she has been treated awful since I left, and she told the lady she thought she was left free and she told her she was as much slave as ever she was that the state was not to be settled until her death and it would be a meracle if she and her child got it then and that her master left a great many relations and she diden no what they would do. Mr. Still dear sir I am very sorry to hear my wife and child are slaves if you please dear sir inform me what to do for my dear wife and child. She said she has been threatened to be put in jail three times since I left also she tells me that she is washing for the captain of a vesel that use to run to Petersburg but now he runs to Baltimore and he has promas to take her to Delaware or New York for 50 dollars and she had not the money, she sent to me and I sent her all I had which was 5 dollars dear sir can you inform me what to do with a case of this kind the captains name is Thomas.

My wife is name lucy an morris my child is name lot, if you please dear sir answer me as soon as you can posable.

HENRY JAMES MORRIS, Toronto C. W.

Henry James Morris in care of Wm. George Blunt, Centre st., 2 doors from Elam.

FROM REBECCA JONES

PARKER HOUSE, School street, Boston, Oct. 18th, '56.

MY DEAR SIR:—I can hardly express the pleasure I feel at the receipt of your kind letter; but allow me to thank you for the same.

And now I will tell you my reasons for going to California. Mrs. Tarrol, a cousin of my husband, has sent for me. She says I can do much better there than in Boston. And as I have my children's welfare to look to, I have concluded to go. Of course I shall be just as likely to hear from home *there* as *here*. Please tell Mr. Bagnale I shall expect one letter from him before I leave here.

I should like to hear from my brothers and sisters once more, and let me hear every particular. You never can know how anxious I am to hear from them; do please impress this upon their minds.

I have written two letters to Dr. Lundy and never received an answer. I heard Mrs. Lundy was dead, and thought that might possibly be the reason he had not replied to me. Please tell the Doctor I should take it as a great favor if he would write me a few lines.

I suppose you think I am going to live with my husband again. Let me assure you 'tis no such thing. My mind is as firm as ever. And believe me, in going away from Boston, I am going away from him, for I have heard he is living somewhere near. He has been making inquiries about me, but that can make no difference in my feelings to him. I hope that yourself, wife and family are all quite well. Please remember me to them all. Do me the favor to give my love to all inquiring friends. I should be most happy to have any letters of introduction you may think me worthy of, and I trust I shall ever remain   Yours faithfully,

REBECCA JONES.

P. S.—I do not know if I shall go this Fall, or in the Spring. It will depend upon the letter I receive from California, but whichever it may be, I shall be happy to hear from you very soon.

FROM DANIEL ROBERTSON

HAVANA, August 11, 1856, Schuylkill Co., N. Y.

MR. WM. STILL—Dear Sir:—I came from Virginia in March, and was at your office the last of March. My object in writing you, is to inquire what I can do, or what can be done to help my wife to escape from the same bondage that I was in. You will know by your books that I was from Petersburg, Va., and that is where my wife now is. I have received two or three letters from a lady in that place, and the last one says, that my wife's mistress is dead, and that she expects to be sold. I am very anxious to do what I can for her before it is too late, and beg of you to devise some means to get her away. Capt. the man that brought me away, knows the colored agent at Petersburg, and knows he will do all he can to forward my wife. The Capt. promised, that when I could raise one hundred dollars for him that he would deliver her in Philadelphia. Tell him that I can now raise the money, and will forward it to you at any day that he thinks that he can bring her. Please see the Captain and find when he will undertake it, and then let me know when to forward the money to you. I am at work for the Hon. Charles Cook, and can send the money any day. My wife's name is Harriet Robertson, and the agent at Petersburg knows her.

Please direct your answer, with all necessary directions, to N. Coryell, of this village, and he will see that all is right.

Very respectfully,   DANIEL ROBERTSON.

FROM THOMAS F. PAGE

BOSTON, Mass., Feb. 25th, 1857.

WILLIAM STILL, Esq.:—Dear Sir—I have not heard from you for some time. I take this opportunity of writing you a few lines to let you and all know that I am well at present and thank God for it. Dear Sir, I hear that the under ground railroad was in operation. I am glad to hear that. Give my best respects to your family and also to Dr. L., Mr. Warrick, Mr. Camp and familys, to Mr. Fisher, Mr. Taylor to all Friends names too numerous to mention. Please to let me know when the road arrived with another cargo. I want to come to see you all before long, if nothing happens and life lasts. Mrs. Gault requested me to learn of you if you ask Mr. Bagnal if he will see father and what he says about the children. Please to answer as soon as possible. No more at present from a friend,

THOMAS F. PAGE.

NIAGARA FALLS, N. Y., Oct. 6th, '58.

DEAR SIR:—I received your kind letter and I was very glad to hear from you and your family. This leaves me well, and I hope when this comes to hand it may find you the same. I have seen a large number of your U. G. R. R. friends in my travels through the Eastern as well as the Western States. Well there are a good many from my own city who I know—some I talk to on private matters and some I wont. Well around here there are so many—Tom, Dick and Harry—that you do not know who your friend is. So it don't hurt any one to be careful. Well, somehow or another, I do not like Canada, or the Provinces. I have been to St. John, N. B., Lower Province, or Lower Canada, also St. Catharines, C. W., and all around the Canada side, and I do not like it at all. The people seem to be so queer—though I suppose if I had of went to Canada when I first came North to live, I might like it by this time. I was home when Aunt had her Ambrotype taken for you. She often speaks of your kindness to her. There are a number of your friends wishes you well. My little brother is going to school in Boston. The lady, Mrs. Hillard, that my Aunt lives with, thinks a good deal of him. He is very smart and I think, if he lives, he may be of some account. Do you ever see my old friend, Capt. Fountain? Please to give my love to him, and tell him to come to Boston, as there are a number of his friends that would like to see him. My best respects to all friends. I must now bring my short epistle to a close, by saying I remain your friend truly,

THOMAS F. PAGE.

FROM CAROLINE GRAVES

TORONTO, Jan. 22, 1856.

DEAR SIR:—WILLIAM STILL—I have found my company they arrived here on monday eving I found them on tusday evening. Please to be so kind as to send them boxes we are here without close to ware we have some white frendes is goin to pay for them at this end of the road. The reason that we send this note we are afraid the outher one woudent go strait because it wasent derected wright. Please to send them by the express then thay wont be lost. Please to derect these boxes for Carline Graives in the car of mrs. Brittion. Please to send the bil of the boxes on with them. Mrs. Brittion, Lousig street near young street.

FROM JOHN KNIGHT

BOSTON, Oct. 22, 1850, 11 Oclk P. M.

Wm. Craft—Sir—I have to leave so Eirley in the moring that I cold not call according to promis, so if you want me to carry a letter home with me, you must bring it to the United States Hotel to morrow and leave it in box 44, or come your self to morro eavening after tea and bring it. let me no if you come your self by sending a note to box 44 U. S. Hotel so that I may know whether to wate after tea or not by the Bearer. If your wife wants to see me you cold bring her with you if you come your self.

JOHN KNIGHT.

P. S.   I shall leave for home eirley a Thursday moring. J. K.

FROM LEWIS COBB

TORONTO, April 25, 1857.

To MR. WM. STILL—Dear Sir:—I take this opportunity of addressing these few lines to inform you that I am well and hope that they may find you and your family enjoying the same good health. Please to give my love to you and your family. I had a very pleasant trip from your house that morning. Dear sir, you would oblige me much, if you have not sent that box to Mr. Robinson, to open it and take out the little yellow box that I tied up in the large one and send it on by express to me in Toronto. Lift up a few of the things and you will find it near the top. All the clothes that I have are in that box and I stand in need of them. You would oblige me much by so doing. I stopped at Mr. Jones' in Elmira, and was very well treated by him while there. I am now in Toronto and doing very well at present. I am very thankful to you and your family for the attention you paid to me while at your house. I wish you would see Mr. Ormsted and ask him if he has not some things for Mr. Anthony Loney, and if he has, please send them on with my things, as we are both living together at this time. Give my love to Mr. Anthony, also to Mr. Ormsted and family. Dear sir, we both would be very glad for you to attend to this, as we both do stand very much in need of them at this time. Dear sir, you will oblige me by giving my love to Miss Frances Watkins, and as she said she hoped to be out in the summer, I should like to see her. I have met with a gentleman here by the name of Mr. Truehart, and he sends his best love to you and your family. Mr. Truehart desires to know whether you received the letter he sent to you, and if so, answer it as soon as possible. Please answer this letter as soon as possible. I must now come to a close by saying that I remain your beloved friend,   LEWIS COBB.

The young man who was there that morning, Mr. Robinson, got married to that young lady.

TORONTO, June 2d, 1857.

To MR. WM. STILL—Dear Sir:—I received yours dated May 6th, and was extremely happy to hear from you. You may be surprised that I have not answered you before this, but it was on account of not knowing anything concerning the letter being in the post-office until I was told so by a friend. The box, of which I had been inquiring, I have received, and am infinitely obliged to you for sending it. Mr. and Mrs. Renson are living in Hamilton, C. W. They send their best love to you and your family. I am at present residing in Toronto, C. W. Mr. Anthony Loney has gone on to Boston, and is desirous of my coming on to him; and as I have many acquaintances there, I should like to know from you whether it would be advisable or not Give, if you please, my best love to your family and accept the same for yourself, and also to Mr. James Ormsted and family. Tell James Ormsted I would be glad if he would send me a pair of thick, heavy boots, for it rains and hails as often out here in the summer, as it does there in the winter. Tell him to send No. 9, and anything he thinks will do me good in this cold country. Please to give to Mr. James Ormsted to give to Mr. Robert Seldon, and tell him to give it to my father. Mr. and Mrs. Truehart send their love to you and your family. If the gentleman, Mr. R. S., is not running on the boat now, you can give directions to Ludwill Cobb, in care of Mr. R. Seldon, Richmond, Va. Tell Mr. Ormsted not to forget my boots and send them by express. No more at present, but remain yours very truly,

Please write soon.   LEWIS COBB.

FROM LEWIS BURRELL

TORONTO, C. W., Feb. 2, 1859.

MR. WM. STILL:

DEAR SIR:—It have bin two years since I war at your house, at that time I war on my way to cannadia, and I tould you that I had a wife and had to leave her behind, and you promiest me that you would healp me to gait hir if I ever heaird from hir, and I think my dear frend, that the time is come for me to strick the blow, will you healp me, according to your promis. I recived a letter from a frend in Washington last night and he says that my wife is in the city of Baltimore, and she will come away if she can find a frend to healp hir, so I thought I would writ to you as you are acquanted with foulks theare to howm you can trust with such matthas. I

could write to Mr Noah davis in Baltimore, who is well acquanted
with my wife, but I do not think that he is a trew frend, and I could
writ to Mr Samual Maden in the same city, but I am afread that a
letter coming from cannada might be dedteced, but if you will writ
to soume one that you know, and gait them to see Mr Samual
Maden he will give all the information that you want, as he is
acquanted with my wife, he is a preacher and belongs to the Baptis
church.   My wifes name is Winne Ann Berrell, and she is oned by
one Dr. Tams who is on a viset to Baltimore, now Mr Still will you
attend to this thing for me, fourthwith, if you will I will pay you
four your truble, if we can dow any thing it must be don now, as she
will leave theare in the spring, and if you will take the matter in
hand, you mous writ me on to reseption of this letter, whether you
will or not.   Yours truly,

                                         LEWIS BURRELL.

No. 49 Victoria St., Toronto, C. W.

FROM OSCAR D. BALL

                                         OSWEGO, Oct 25th, 1857.

   DEAR SIR:—I take this opportunity of writing you these few
lines to inform you that I am well and hope these few lines will find
you the same (and your family you must excuse me for not writing
to you before.   I would have written to you before this but I put
away the card you gave me and could not find it until a few days
sins.   I did not go to Canada for I got work in Oswego, but times
are very dull here at present.   I have been out of employ about five
weeks I would like to go to Australia.   Do you know of any
gentleman that is going there or any other place, except south that
wants a servant to go there with him to wait on him or do any other
work, I have a brother that wants to come north.   I received a
letter from him a few days ago.   Can you tell me of any plan that I
can fix to get him give my respects to Mrs. Still and all you family.
Please let me know if you hear of any berth of that kind.   Nothing
more at present I remain your obedient servant,

                                         OSCAR D. BALL

   But my name is now John Delaney.   Direct your letter to John
Delaney Oswego N. Y. care of R. Oliphant.

FROM JOHN DELANEY

OSWEGO, Nov. 21st, 1857.

MR. WILLIAM STILL, ESQ. DEAR SIR:—Your letter of the 19th came duly to hand I am glad to hear that the Underground Rail Road is doing so well I know those three well that you said come from alex I broke the ice and it seems as if they are going to keep the track open. but I had to stand and beg of those two that started with me to come and even give one of them money and then he did not want to come. I had a letter from my brother a few days ago, and he says if he lives and nothing happens to him he will make a start for the north and there is many others there that would start now but they are afraid of getting frost bitten, there was two left alex about five or six weeks ago. ther names are as follows Lawrence Thornton and Townsend Derrit. have they been to philadelphia from what I can learn they will leave alex in mourning next spring in the last letter I got from my brother he named a good many that wanted to come when he did and the are all sound men and can be trusted. he reads and writes his own letters. William Triplet and Thomas Harper passed through hear last summer from my old home which way did those three that you spoke of go times are very dull here at present and I can get nothing to do. but thank God have a good boarding house and will be sheltered from the weather this winter give my respects to your family Montgomery sends his also Nothing more at presant

Yours truly   JOHN DELANEY.

FROM JOHN B. WOODS

GLANDFORD, August 15th, 1858.

DEAR SIR:—I received your letter and was glad to hear that your wife and family was all well and I hope it will continue so. I am glad to inform you that this leaves me well. Also, Mr. Wm. Still, I want for you to send me your opinion respecting my circumstances. I have made up my mind to make an adventure after my family and I want to get an answer from you and then I shall know how to act and then I will send to you all particulars respecting my starting to come to your house. Mr. Still I should be glad to know whare Abraham Harris is, as I should be as glad to see him as well as any of my own brothers. His wife and my wife's mother is sisters. My wife belongs to Elson Burdel's estate. Abraham's wife belongs to Sam Adams. Mr. Still you must not think hard of me for writing you these few lines as I cannot rest until I release my dear family. I have not the least doubt but I can get through without the least trouble.

So no more at present from your humble servant,

JOHN B. WOODS.

FROM EDWARD LEWIS

SKANEATELES, Dec. 17, 1857.

DEAR SIR:—As I promised to let you hear from me as soon as I found a home, I will now fulfill my promise to you and say that I am alive and well and have found a stopping place for the winter.

When we arrived at Syracuse we found Mr. Loguen ready to receive us, and as times are rather hard in Canada he thought best for us not to go there, so he sent us about twenty miles west of Syracuse to Skaneateles, where George Upshur and myself soon found work. Henry Grimes is at work in Garden about eight miles from this place.

If you should chance to hear any of my friends inquiring for me, please direct them to Skaneateles, Onondaga county, N. Y.

If you can inform me of the whereabouts of Miss Alice Jones I shall be very much obliged to you, until I can pay you better. I forgot to ask you about her when I was at your house. She escaped about two years ago.

Please not to forget to inquire of my wife, Rachel Land, and if you should hear of her, let me know immediately. George Upshur and myself send our best respects to you and your family. Remember us to Mrs. Jackson and Miss Julia. I hope to meet you all again, if not on earth may we so live that we shall meet in that happy land where tears and partings are not known.

Let me hear from you soon. This from your friend and well wisher,

EDWARD LEWIS,
formerly, but now WILLIAM BRADY.

FROM GEORGE BALLARD

ST. CATHARINES, JULY 19th, 1858.

DEAR SIR:—With pleasure I now inform you that I am well, and hope this may find you and yours the same also. I hope kind sir you will please to see Mr. Paul Hammon, to know when he will try to get my Mother and Sister I wish him to send me word when he will go so I may meet him in Philadelphia.

And I will Endevor to meet him there With some money to assist him in getting them. Let me know when you start for them so I may be able to meet you there, please after this letter passes from you sir, give it to John Camper tell him to give it to his Mother, so that my Mother can get it, be careful and not let no white man get hold of it. I am now living with my cousin Leven Parker, near Saint Catharines, $10 a month. No more at present, from your friend,   GEORGE BALLARD.

ANONYMOUS

CAMDEN, June 13, 1858.

MR. STILL:—I writ to inform you that we stand in need of help if ever we wonted help it is in theas day, we have Bin trying to rais money to By a hors but there is so few here that we can trust our selves with for fear that they may serve us as tom otwell served them when he got them in dover Jail. But he is dun for ever, i wont to no if your friends can help us, we have a Road that more than 100 past over in 1857. it is one we made for them, 7 in march after the lions had them there is no better in the State, we are 7 miles from Delaware Bay. you may understand what i mean. I wrote last december to the anti Slavery Society for James Mot and others concerning of purchasing a horse for this Bisnes if your friends can help us the work must stil go on for ther is much frait pases over this Road, But ther has Ben but 3 conductors for sum time. you may no that there is but few men, sum talks all dos nothing, there is horses owned by Collard peopel but not for this purpose. We wont one for to go when called for, one of our best men was nigh Cut By keeping of them too long, By not having means to convay them tha must Be convad if they pass over this Road safe tha go through in 2 nights to Wilmington, for i went there with 28 in one gang last November, tha had to ride for when thea com to us we go 15 miles, it is hard Road to travel i had sum conversation with mr. Evens and wos down here on a visit. pleas try what you can do for us this is the place we need help, 12 mile i live from mason and Dixson Line. I wod have come but cant have time, as yet there has been some fuss about a boy ho lived near Camden, he has gone away, he ses me and my brother nose about it but he dont.

There is but 4 slaves near us, never spoke to one of them but wonce she never gos out pleas to tri and help, you can do much if you will it will be the means of saving ourselves and others. Ancer this letter.

Pleas to writ let me no if you can do anything for us. I still remain your friend.

FROM JOSEPH BALL

TORONTO, Nov. 7th, 1857.

DEAR MR. STILL:—As I must again send you a letter fealing myself oblidge to you for all you have done and your kindness. Dear Sir my wife will be on to Philadelphia on the 8th 7th, and I would you to look out for her and get her an ticket and send her to me Toronto. Her name are May Ball with five children. Please send her as soon as you can.

Yours very truly,   JOSEPH BALL.

Will you please to telegrape to me, No. 31 Dummer st.

FROM JOHN DADE

ST. CATHARINES, Canada.

MR. STILL, SIR:—I ar rivd on Friday evenen bot I had rite smart troble for my mony gave out at the bridge and I had to fot et to St. Catherin tho I went rite to worke at the willard house for 8 dolor month bargend for to stae all the wentor bot I havent eny clouse nor money please send my tronke if et has come. Derate et to St. Catharines to the willard house to John Dade and if et ant come plice rite for et soon as posable deract your letter to Rosenen Dade Washington send your deraction please tend to this rite a way for I haf made a good start I think that I can gate a longe en this plase. If my brother as well send him on for I haf a plase for him ef he ant well please dont send him for this as no plase for a sik possan. The way I got this plase I went to see a fran of myen from Washington. Dan al well and he gave me werke. Pleas ancer this as soon as you gat et you must excues this bad riting for my chance wars bot small to line this mouch,

JOHN H. DADE.

If you haf to send for my tronke to Washington send the name of John Trowharte. Sir please rite as soon as you gat this for et as enporten.   JOHN H. DADE.

FROM JACOB BLOCKSON

SAINT CATHARINES. Cannda West, Dec. 26th, 1858.

DEAR WIFE:—I now infom you I am in Canada and am well and
hope you are the same, and would wish you to be here next august,
you come to suspension bridge and from there to St. Catharines,
write and let me know.   I am doing well working for a Butcher this
winter, and will get good wages in the spring I now get $2,50 a week.

I Jacob Blockson, George Lewis, George Alligood and James
Alligood are all in St. Catharines, and met George Ross from Lewis
Wright's, Jim Blockson is in Canada West, and Jim Delany, Plun-
noth Connon.   I expect you my wife Lea Ann Blockson, my son
Alexander & Lewis and Ames will all be here and Isabella also, if
you cant bring all bring Alexander surely, write when you will come
and I will meet you in Albany.   Love to you all, from your loving
Husband,   JACOB BLOCKSON.
fare through $12,30 to here.

MR. STILL: SIR:—you will please Envelope this and send it to
John Sheppard Bridgeville P office in Sussex county Delaware, seal
it in black and oblige me, write to her to come to you.

FROM STEPNEY BROWN

CLIFTON HOUSE, NIAGARA FALLS, August the 27.

DEAR BROTHER:—It is with pleasure i take my pen in hand to
write a few lines to inform you that i am well hopeping these few
lines may fine you the same i am longing to hear from you and your
family i wish you would say to Julis Anderson that he must realy
excuse me for not writing but i am in hopes that he is doing well.
i have not heard no news from Virgina.   plese to send me all the
news say to Mrs. Hunt an you also forever pray for me knowing that
God is so good to us.   i have not seen brother John Dungy for 5
months, but we have corresponded together but he is doing well in
Brandford.   i am now at the falls an have been on here some time
an i shall with the help of the lord locate myself somewhere this
winter an go to school excuse me for not annser your letter sooner
knowing that i cannot write well you please to send me one of the
earliest papers send me word if any of our friends have been passing
through i know that you are very busy but ask your little daughter
if she will annser this letter for you i often feel that i cannot turn god
thanks enough for his blessings that he has bestoueth upon me.

Say to brother suel that he must not forget what god has consighn to his hand, to do that he must pray in his closet that god might teach him. say to mr. Anderson that i hope he have retrad an has seeked the lord an found him precious to his own soul for he must do it in this world for he cannot do it in the world to come. i often think about the morning that i left your house it was such a sad feeling but still i have a hope in crist do you think it is safe in boston my love to all i remain your brother,

STEPNEY BROWN.

BRANTFORD, March 3d, 1860.

MR. WILLIAM STILL, DEAR SIR:—I now take the pleasure of writing to you a few lines write soon hoping to find you enjoying perfect health, as I am the same.

My joy within is so great that I cannot find words to express it. When I met with my friend brother Dungy who stopped at your house on his way to Canada after having a long chase after me from Toronto to Hamilton he at last found me in the town of Brantford Canada West and ought we not to return Almighty God thanks for delivering us from the many dangers and trials that beset our path in this wicked world we live in.

I have long been wanting to write to you but I entirely forgot the number of your house Mr. Dungy luckily happened to have your directions with him.

Religion is good when we live right may God help you to pray often to him that he might receive you at the hour of your final departure. Yours most respectfully.

STEPNEY BROWN, per Jas. A. Walk.

P. S. Write as soon as possible for I wish very much to hear from you. I understand that Mrs, Hunt has been to Richmond, Va. be so kind as to ask her if she heard anything about that money. Give my love to all inquiring friends and to your family especially. I now thank God that I have not lost a day in sickness since I came to Canada.

Kiss the baby for me. I know you are busy but I hope you will have time to write a few lines to me to let me know how you and your family are getting on. No more at present, but I am yours very truly,   STEPNEY BROWN, per Jas. A. Walkinshaw.

BRANTFORD, Oct. 25, '60

DEAR SIR:—I take the pleasure of dropping you a few lines, I am yet residing in Brantford and I have been to work all this summer at the falls and I have got along remarkably well, surely God is good to those that put their trust in him I suppose you have been wondering what has become of me but I am in the lands of living and long to hear from you and your family.   I would have wrote sooner, but the times has been such in the states I have not but little news to send you and I'm going to school again this winter and will you be pleased to send me word what has become of Julius Anderson and the rest of my friends and tell him I would write to him if I knew where to direct the letter, please send me word whether any body has been along lately that knows me.   I know that you are busy but you must take time and answer this letter as I am anxious to hear from you, but nevertheless we must not forget our maker, so we cannot pray too much to our lord so I hope that mr. Anderson has found peace with God for me myself really appreciate that hope that I have in Christ, for I often find myself in my slumber with you and I hope we will meet some day.   Mr. Dungy sends his love to you I suppose you are aware that he is married, he is luckier than I am or I must get a little foothold before I do marry if I ever do.   I am in a very comfortable room all fixed for the winter and we have had one snow.   May the lord be with you and all you and all your household.   I remain forever your brother in Christ,
STEPNEY BROWN.

FROM CATHERINE BRICE

ALBANY, Jan. the 30, 1858.

MRS. WILLIAM STILL:—i sit don to rite you a fue lines in saying hav you herd of John Smith or Bengernin Pina i have cent letters to them but i hav know word from them John Smith was oned by Doker abe Street Bengermin oned by Mary hawkings i wish to kno if you kno am if you will let me know as swon as you get this.   My lov to Mis Still i am much oblige for those articales.   My love to mrs george and verry thankful to her Rosean Johnson oned by docter Street when you cend the letter rite it Cend it 63 Gran St in the car of andrue Conningham rite swon dela it not write my name Cathrin Brice.

Let me know swon as you can.

FROM J. W. DUNGY

BRANTFORD, March 3d, 1860.

MR. WM. STILL, DEAR SIR:—I have seated myself this evening to write you a few lines to inform you that I have got through my journey, and landed safely in Brantford, where I found my friend, Stepney Brown, and we expressed great joy at meeting each other, and had a great shaking of hands, and have not got done talking yet of the old times we had in Virginia.

I thank God I am enjoying vigorous health, and hope you all are well, as it is written in the first Psalm, "Blessed is the man that walketh not in the counsel of the ungodly, nor standeth in the way of sinners, nor sitteth in the seat of the scornful."

I wish you may think of me often and pray for me that I may grow a man, one of the followers of our meek and lowly Saviour. Give my love to Mrs. Still, and family, and the Rev. Mr. Gibbs, that was residing with you when I was there.

I must now inform you a little about Canada, at least as much of it as I have seen and heard. I arrived in the city of Hamilton, on the 15th February, 1860, at nine o'clock in the evening, and the weather was dreary and cold, and the cars laid over there until ten o'clock next day, and I went up into the city and saw a portion of it. I then started for Toronto, arrived there same day at 12 o'clock. There I met friends from Richmond, remained there several days; during the time we had a very extensive snow storm, and I took the opportunity of walking around the city looking at the elephants, and other great sights. I liked it very much; but upon hearing that my friend and brother Stepney Brown was in Brantford, I became disatisfied and left for Brantford on the 21st February, 1860. I have found it a very pleasant, and have been told it is the prettiest place in Canada.

It is built upon the Grand River, which is two hundred miles long, and empties into Lake Erie. It rises to a great height every spring, and great masses of ice come down, bringing bridges, saw-logs, trees, and fairly sweeps everything before it. The people who live upon the flats are in great danger of being drowned in their houses.

I got a situation immediately at the Kerby House, by the influence of my friend and brother, Stepney Brown, who I must say has been very kind to me, as also have the people of Brantford. The Kerby House is the largest hotel in the town about 250 rooms, and a stable at the back, with a gas-house of its own. No more at present, but remain,

Yours very respectfully,

JOHN WILLIAM DUNGY.

P. S. Write at your earliest convenience, and oblige your friend,

J. W. D.

BRANTFORD, April 20th.

MR. STILL, DEAR SIR:—I feel myself quite lonesome this evening, and not hearing from you lately I take this oppertunity to drop you a few lines. I have not much to say, brother Brown has left for the falls, and expects to return next winter. The weather is mild and warm at this time; the grass is putting up and begins to look like spring. I thank the Lord I am enjoying good health at this time. I hope this letter will find you and your family well, give my compliments to them all and Mr. Gibbs and the young lady that was at your house when I was there. Times has been hard this winter, but they are increasing for the better. I wrote to you a few days ago, I don't know whether you got my letter. I asked in my letter if Mr. Williams was on the pennsylvania, that runs from their to Richmond, Va. I should have written to him, but I did not know his number, I also named a friend of mine, Mr. Plumer if he arrives their pleas tu tell him to come to Brantford, where I am for there are good chances for business I think a great deal about my colored brethren in the South but I hope to be a benefit to them one of these days. We have quite a melancholy affair about one of our colored brothers who made his escape from the South those who took him up have gone back to obtain witness to convict him for murder. These witness is to be here on Monday 23 inst but the defendence of the law says they shant take him back unless they bring good witness and men of truth I will write you more about it after the trial comes of. I must say a little about myself. I want to devote myself to study if I can for the next twelve months. I expect to leave the Kirby House on the 5th of may. I have taken a barber shop which is a very good situation and one hand employed with me. I would be much oblige to you if you would give me some advice what to do. I sent you the morning herald yesterday which contained a accident which occurd on the G. trunk R. W. you will see in it that we don't have much politics here. The late destructive fire we had I thought it would have kept brantford back this summer but it is increasing slowly   I have nothing more to say at this time.   I hope the Lord may bless you all and take care of you in this world, and after time receive you in his everlasting kingdom through Jesus Christ our Lord.   Answer this as soon as convenient.   Good bye.   Yours respectfully

J. W. DUNGY.

BRANTFORD, C. W., JANUARY 11th, 61.

MR. WM. STILL, DEAR SIR:—I take this opportunity to drop you a few lines to let you hear from me.   I am well at this time, hoping this will find you the same.

I acknowledge my great neglectness of you with great regret that I have not answered your letter before this, I hope you will excuse me as I have succeeded in getting me a wife since I wrote to you last.

My mind has been much taken up in so doing for several months past.   Give my compliments to your wife and your family, and Mr. Gibbs, also hoping they are all well.   Tell Mrs. Still to pray for me that I may grow in grace and the knowledge of the truth as it is in Jesus.

I often think of you all.   I pray that the time may come when we will all be men in the United States.   We have read here of the great disturbance in the South.   My prayer is that this may be a deathblow to Slavery.   Do you ever have any Underground Rail Road passengers now?   Times have been very prosperous in Canada this year.

The commercial trade and traffic on the railways has been very dull for these few months back.   Business on the Buffalo and Lake Huron railway has been so dull that a great number of the hands have been discharged on account of the panic in the South.

Canada yet cries, Freedom! Freedom! Freedom!

I must now say a little about my friend and brother Stepney Brown, he lived about six months at the Niagara Falls and is now going to school here in Brantford, he sends his best respects to you all.   He and I often sit together at night after the labor of the day is over talking about our absent friends wishing we could see them once more.

Mr. Brown and myself have been wishing for one or two of your slavery standards and would be much obliged to you if you would send some of the latest.

Please let me hear from you as soon as possible. I must now bring my letter to a close and remain your affectionate friend,

J. W. DUNGY.

P. S. May the Lord be with you.		J. W. DUNGY.

Address your letter to John W. Dungy, Brantford, C. W.

FROM LOUISA F. JONES

BOSTON, May 15th, 1858.

DEAR FRIEND:—I have selected this oppotunity to write you a few lines, hopeing thay may find you and yours enjoying helth and happiness. I arrived hear on Thirsday last, and had a lettor of intoduction giving to me by one of the gentlemen at the Antoslavery office in New York, to Mr. Garrison in Boston, I found him and his lady both to bee very clever. I stopped with them the first day of my arrivel hear, since that Time I have been living with Mrs. Hilliard I have met with so menny of my acquaintances hear, that I all most immagion my self to bee in the old country. I have not been to Canaday yet, as you expected. I had the pleasure of seeing the lettor that you wrote to them on the subject. I suffored much on the road with head ake but since that time I have no reason to complain, please do not for git to send the degarritips in the Shaim-pain basket with Dr. Lundys, Mr. Lesley said he will send them by express. tell Julia kelly, that through mistake, I took one of her pocket handkerchift, that was laying on the table, but I shall keep it in remembranc of the onner. I must bring my lettor to a close as I have nothing more to say, and believe me to be your faithfull friend.			LOUISA F. JONES.

P. S.   Remember me to each and every member of your familly and all Enquiring Friends.

MISCELLANEOUS LETTERS

FROM L. A. SPALDING TO A. STEWARD AND OTHERS

DEAR FRIENDS:

I have received a letter from Israel Lewis, New York, requesting me to forward fifty dollars to the treasurer of the Wilberforce Colony, which I will do at the first convenience. I sent fifty dollars some time since, which I presume was received.

I have also received a letter from B. Lundy, who speaks very flatteringly of the Settlement; but gives me some information relating to Lewis, which will injure you, unless you act wisely.

Now I suggest for your consideration, whether it would not be best to keep perfectly quiet relative to him, until after he returns and settles with the directors. If he cannot then satisfy you, he will no doubt surrender up his documents and agency like a man, and leave you to appoint another.

By all means you must agree among yourselves, not suffering any difference of opinion to become public. Your enemies will seize upon this, and injure your prospects; besides, you gain nothing by it. Your friends too, could then say that you acted imprudently. I hope to have a good account of the settlement of your difficulties if any should exist.

Respectfully your Friend,
LYMAN A. SPALDING.[27]

Austin Steward & Benj. Paul.
Lockport, N. Y., 2d Mo., 4th, 1832.

FROM REV. S. E. CORNISH TO A. STEWARD

DEAR STEWARD:

I have this day received your letter, and God willing, I will be with you in the course of ten or twelve days. Please to keep your people together, until I come. I will see that they be not oppressed by that notorious Israel Lewis. I believe him to be

[27] Spalding and Lundy were white men cooperating with the Negroes who were trying to solve their problems in Canada.

625

one of the worst men living, whose deeds will yet come to light.
Do stay in the Colony and keep all things as they are until I come.

Yours, with high esteem,

SAMUEL E. CORNISH.

P.S.—I am glad that Mrs. Steward is in Rochester; your Colony
is by no means suited to her talents and refined mind. She never
could be happy there. My love to all the Colonists; I will do every
thing for them in my power.

S. E. C.

REPLY TO J. BUDD BY A. STEWARD

To THE REV. J. BUDD,

Sir:—We feel under renewed obligation to you,
for you friendly advice; but we have already sent out several
copies of our circular to different places, and probably some of them
have been printed before this time.

We have no object in view, but truth, justice,—the greatest
good of the Settlement, and of our brethren in general. Israel
Lewis has, however, collected large sums of money, for our relief,
of which we have not had the benefit. Nearly two years ago, he
was appointed agent for the Colony, to collect funds to build a
meeting-house, to endow schools, & c. In less than one year he
received more than two thousand dollars, which he squandered;
and we have neither meeting-house nor schools, nor ever will
have, so long as the money goes into the hands of Lewis. All that
we would have forgiven him gladly, if he would consent to be still
and not usurp the agency against the wishes of the people.

Sir, is it not expected that he would appear well; as you say,
that "the whole deportment and manner of Lewis, who has been in
this place, evidently have impressed the people in his favor,"—
while collecting money with the eye of the public upon him. But
follow him home into another kingdom, and there see the man in
his true character; stripped of his borrowed plumage,—and we will
guarantee that you would agree with us, in believing that he is an
arch hypocrite.

We should be sorry to prejudice the public against our Settlement, more especially when we are actuated by the purest motives,
—that of preventing the Christian public from being imposed upon,
by drawing large sums from them for us, as they suppose, when in
truth such sums never reach us at all.

Sir, we know that you are actuated by the purest motives, but you are deceived in the character of the man, (Lewis). When I was living in the States and only saw him there, collecting money for the poor, I thought him honest as you now do; but two or three year's residence in Wilberforce Colony, has abundantly satisfied me that his object is to get money, that he may live in a princely style, and not for the benefit of the poor as he pretends.

Such are the true facts in the case. We should be glad to have the name of James S. Seymour, Esq., added to the list, and any other prominent citizen you may think would help the cause.

In regard to the investigation at Albany, we do not see how the public are to arrive at the facts in the case from any statement Lewis may make; for all his statements that I have seen in print, are positively void of truth, in the most essential part, so that they are of little or no importance at all unless substantiated by other testimony.

The circular contains no testimony that has not been heretofore laid before the public. Mr. Benjamin Paul recently wrote a letter to the editors of "The Baptist Register," in which he stated that Lewis had fed and clothed the colonists like a father, which is not true; and so sensible was Paul of the fact, that when the letter reached here, together with the suprize it created wherever Lewis was known, that Paul cheerfully contradicted it, confessed that he was mistaken, and thus made it known to the public.

We certainly have no sectional feelings in the matter, though Lewis has labored hard to impress the public with a contrary belief; and he has even brought false charges of the basest kind against our most respectable citizens, all to draw the attention of the public from the true facts in the case.

It is a general time of health here in the Colony. The season is very favorable; our crops look well, and with the blessings of God we shall raise enough to supply our wants this year.

> Yours, with due respect,
> In behalf of the Colonists,
> A. STEWARD.

WILBERFORCE, June, 1833.

A. STEWARD TO G. BANKS AND OTHERS

MESSRS. BANKS, WILBER, BROCKENBERG & HARRIS:

I have received a communication through your corresponding secretary, Mr. James C. Brown, and I hasten to answer it.

The last communication I have received from Mr. N. Paul, was in December 1833, at which time he was vigorously prosecuting his mission, as will more fully appear by the annexed copy of said letter, which I cheerfully send you. His return is expected daily.

COPY OF N. PAUL'S LETTER

MY DEAR BROTHER STEWARD:

When I last addressed you, I informed you that I expected to leave this country before a return letter from you could be expected. I therefore stated, if I remember correctly, that you need not write.

I now find that I shall be detained much longer than I then calculated; and this detention is owing to the Slavery question. The friends of the cause, advised me to forego my object, until that question was settled; and then they would turn their attention to my cause, and render me what assistance they could.

All their united strength was needed now, while that question was pending. But thanks be to God, that is now settled. On the first day of August next, will be the proudest day that ever Britain knew; for from that time henceforth, there will not remain a single slave throughout His Majesty's dominions.

The friends of the cause are now turning their attention to Slavery in the United States, and are about to form a society for the abolition of Slavery throughout the world. They all think highly of our Settlement, and will give it their cordial support.

The leading abolitionists have given me letters of recommendation throughout the Kingdom, and have appointed one of their most effective men to travel with me,—his name is John Scoble, a very ready, intelligent, earnest, and an eloquent speaker. I think I can do more now in one month, than I could in three before the question was settled in regard to their own slaves.

You will at once see that although the people concluded my object to be an important one, yet, they generally thought that they ought to lend all their aid in removing the stain from their own land first. This stain is now effectually effaced, and my meetings are exceedingly crowded. I addressed an audience at Norwich of from three to four thousand persons, week before last, when about five hundred dollars was collected. So you see I am getting on. I start, the Lord willing, next week for Scotland, and shall spend the winter there and in the North of England. In the spring I shall return

and take passage for Canada.   I doubt not, that you are anxiously
looking for my return; yet, you cannot want to see me more than
I want to return; but I tell you now as I have told you before, that
I shall not return until I have done all that can be done by my labor.

Yours,
N. PAUL.

Sirs:

The above copy will give you all the recent information we
have received concerning the mission of our foreign agent.

Please accept my kindest regards, with my acknowledgements
of your distinguished consideration, while I remain,

Yours truly,
AUSTIN STEWARD.

WILBERFORCE, U. C.

FROM BISHOP ONDERDONK TO THE REV. PETER WILLIAMS [28]

COLLEGE PLACE, July 12, 1834.

REV. AND DEAR SIR:

I am sure I need not assure you of the sincere sympathy which I
feel for you and your people.   The inclosed * was prepared by me
to be read to them to-morrow, if they had been assembled.   Perhaps, however, you have pursued the most prudent course in
closing your church.

Let me advise you to resign, at one, your connexion, in every
department, with the Anti-Slavery Society, and to make public
your resignation.   I cannot now give you all my reasons.   Let me
see you as soon as you can.   I can better say than write all I think.
Make the within known in any way, and as extensively as you can.
"The raging of the sea, and the madness of the people," you know
are connected in Holy Writ, and the one might as well be attempted
to be stopped as the other.   My advice, therefore is, give up at
once.   Let it be seen that on whichsoever side right may be, St.
Philip's Church will be found on the Christian side of meekness,
order, and self-sacrifice to common good, and the peace of the
community.   You will be no losers by it, for the God of peace will
be to you also a God of all consolation.

[28] A Pastoral Letter from the Bishop to the parish of St. Philip's Church,
which, owing to the congregation not assembling on Sunday, has not yet been
communicated to them. *African Repository*, pages 185-186. (From *New York
Spectator*, July 15, 1834.)

Let me hear from you or see you soon. And believe me to be, with faithful prayer for you and yours, your affectionate brother in Christ.

BENJ. T. ONDERDONK.

REV. MR. WILLIAMS,
To THE CITIZENS OF NEW YORK:—

It has always been painful to me to appear before the public. It is especially painful to me to appear before them in the columns of a newspaper, at a time of great public excitement like the present; but when I received Holy orders, I promised "reverently to obey my Bishop, to follow with a glad mind his godly admonitions, and to submit myself to his godly judgment."

My Bishop, without giving his opinions on the subject of Abolition, has now advised me, in order that the Church under my care "may be found on the Christian side of meekness, order, and self-sacrifice to the community," to resign connexion with the Anti-Slavery Society, and to make public my resignation. There has been no instance hitherto, in which I have not sought his advice in matters of importance to the Church, and endeavored to follow it when given; and I have no wish that the present should be an exception.

But in doing this, I hope I shall not be considered as thrusting myself too much upon public attention, by adverting to some facts in relation to myself and the subject of the present excitement, in the hope that when they are calmly considered, a generous public will not censure me for the course I have pursued.

My father was born in Beekman street in this city, and was never, in all his life, further from it than Albany; nor have I ever been absent from it longer than three months, when I went to Hayti for the benefit of my brethren who had migrated there from this country. In the revolutionary war, my father was a decided advocate for American Independence, and his life was repeatedly jeopardized in its cause. Permit me to relate one instance, which shows that neither the British sword, nor British gold, could make him a traitor to his country. He was living in the state of Jersey, and Parson Chapman, a champion of American liberty, of great influence throughout that part of the country, was sought after by the British troops. My father immediately mounted a horse and rode round among his parishioners, to notify them of his danger, and to call them to help in removing him and his goods to a place of safety. He then carried him to a private place, and as he was returning a British officer rode up to him, and demanded in the most peremptory manner, "where is Parson Chapman?" "I cannot tell," was the reply. On that he drew his sword, and raising it over his head, said, "Tell me where he is, or I will instantly cut you down." Again he replied, "I cannot tell." Finding threats useless, the officer put up his sword and drew out a purse of gold, saying, "If you will tell me where he is, I will give you this." The reply still was, "I cannot tell." The officer cursed him and rode off.

This attachment to the country of his birth was strengthened and confirmed by the circumstances that the very day on which the British evacuated this city, was the day on which he obtained his freedom by purchase through the help of some republican friends of the Methodist Church, who loaned him money for that purpose, and to the last year of his life he always spoke of that day as one which gave double joy to his heart, by freeing him from domestic bondage and his native city from foreign enemies.

The hearing him talk of these and similar matters, when I was a child, filled my soul with an ardent love for the American government, and made me feel, as I said in my first public discourse, that it was my greatest glory to be an American.

A lively and growing interest for the prosperity of my country pervaded my whole sole and led to the belief, notwithstanding the peculiarly unhappy condition of my brethren in the United States, that by striving to become intelligent, useful and virtuous members of the community, the time would come when they would all have abundant reason to rejoice in the glorious Declaration of American Independence.

Reared with these feelings, though fond of retirement I felt a burning desire to be useful to my brethren and to my country; and when the last war between this country and Great Britain broke out, I felt happy to render the humble services of my pen, my tongue, and my hands, towards rearing fortifications to defend our shores against invasion. I entreated my brethren to help in the defence of the country, and went with them to the work; and no sacrifice has been considered too great by me, for the benefit of it or them.

These were among the feelings that led me into the ministry, and induced me to sacrifice all my worldly prospects, and live upon the scanty pittance which a colored minister must expect to receive for his labors, and to endure the numerous severe trials peculiar to his situation.

My friends who assisted me in entering into the ministry, know that if the Church with which I am connected as a Pastor, could have been established without my becoming its minister, I should have been this day enjoying the sweets of private life, and there has not been a day since I have entered upon the duties of my office, that I would not have cheerfully retired to earn my living in some humbler occupation, could I have done so consistently with my sense of duty.

By the transaction of last Friday evening, my church is now closed, and I have been compelled to leave my people. Whether I shall be permitted to return to them again, I cannot say, but whether or not, I have the satisfaction of feeling that I have laboured earnestly and sincerely for their temporal and spiritual benefit, and the promotion of the public good.

In regard to my opposition to the Colonization Society it has extended no farther than that Society has held out the idea, that a colored man, however he may strive to make himself intelligent, virtuous and useful, can never enjoy the privileges of a citizen of the United States, but must ever remain a degraded and oppressed being. I could not, and do not believe that the principles of the Declaration of Independence, and of the Gospel of Christ, have not power sufficient to raise him, at some future day, to that rank. I believe that such doctrines tend very much to discourage the efforts which are making for his improvement at home. But whenever any man of color, after having carefully considered the subject, has thought it best to emigrate to Africa, I have not opposed to him, but have felt it my duty to aid him, in all my power, on his way, and I have the satisfaction of being able to prove that the most prominent and most useful men in the Colony have been helped there by me.

I helped John B. Russwurm to go to Liberia, and as a token of gratitude for my aid in the case, he sent me his thermometer, which I have now hanging up in my house. I helped James M. Thompson, whom all speak of as a most excellent man, and a good scholar, to go there. He was a member of my church; and when he went there, I gave him letters of recommendation, and procured a number of books, to enable him to introduce the Episcopal service; and I offered lately to contribute my mite towards establishing the Episcopal Church there. I was the first person who advised James

R. Daily (Russwurm's partner) to go and establish himself in Liberia as a merchant. When Washington Davis was sent to this city, by Governor Ashmun, to study medicine, as a physician for the colony, I received him in my house, and boarded him a week, without charging the Society for it, though they offered to bear the expense.

When I found that strong prejudices were forming against me, because of my disapprobation of some of the Society's measures, and that my usefulness was thereby affected, I ceased to speak on the subject, except in the private circle of my friends, or when my opinions were asked privately by others; and in my short address to the Phenix Society, last spring, I carefully avoided the subject; and the only sentiment I uttered, referring to it, was this: "Who that witnesses an assembly like this, composed of persons of all colors, can doubt that people of all colors can live in the same country, without doing each other harm?"

It was my anxiety to promote the object of the Phenix Society, which is the improvement of the people of color in this city, in morals, literature, and the mechanic arts, that brought me to an acquaintance with the members of the Anti-Slavery Society. For several years, I had given considerable attention to the education of our people, and was much interested about our Public Schools.

I was anxious that some of our youth should have the opportunity of acquiring a liberal education, and felt that it was my duty to strive to rear up some well qualified colored ministers. I selected two lads of great promise, and made every possible effort to get them a collegiate education. But the Colleges were all closed against them. Anti-Slavery men generously offered to aid us in establishing a Manual Labor College, or High School, for ourselves, and to aid us in all the objects of the Phenix Society. I joined with them in this work heartily, and wished them all success, as I still do in their endeavors, by all means sanctioned by law, humanity and religion, to obtain freedom for my brethren, and to elevate them to the enjoyment of equal rights with the other citizens of the community; but I insisted that while they were laboring to restore us to our rights, it was exclusively our duty to labor to qualify our people for the enjoyment of those rights.

Hence when the Anti-Slavery Convention was held in Philadelphia, though strongly solicited, I refused to attend, and though I was then appointed a member of the Board of Managers, I never met with that Board but for a few moments at the close of their session, and then without uttering a word. I was also appointed, at the anniversary in May, a member of the executive Committee. But when asked if I would serve, I replied that I could not attend to it, and have never attended but on one occasion, when I went for the sole purpose of advising the Board to be careful not to take any measures that would have a tendency to encourage in our people a spirit of vanity, and I urged this advice by saying that by so doing, our people, and the cause of emancipation, would both be injured. This opinion I have, on all proper occasions expressed, and have endeavored to enforce by example; for, in all the Anti-Slavery Meetings held in the Chapel, I have always taken my seat in the gallery, excepting that on the day of the Anniversary I felt it to speak to one of the committee in the orchestra, or stage, and did not return. My brethren have rebuked me for this course, but I have not censured them for theirs. They did as they thought best, and I did as I thought best; but I have learned that it is a most difficult matter to avoid extremes on subjects of great public excitement, without being more censured than those who go to all lengths with either party.

Having given this simple and faithful statement of facts; I now, in conformity to the advice of my Bishop, publicly resign my station as a member of the Board of Managers of the Anti-Slavery Society, and of its executive committee, without, however, passing any opinion respecting the principles on which that society is founded.

I would have offered my resignation long before this, had I not thought that there might be occasions, when by having the privilege of addressing the Board, I might exercise a restraining influence upon measures calculated to advance our people faster than they were prepared to be advanced, and the public feeling would bear. But I am not disposed to blame the members of the Anti-Slavery Society for their measures. I consider them as good men, and good Christians, and true lovers of their country, and of all mankind. I thought they had not an opportunity of knowing my brethren, nor the state of public prejudice against them, as well as myself, and all I supposed that I could do was to aid them in this particular.

I hope that both they and the public generally will judge charitably of this hastily drawn communication.

                                   PETER WILLIAMS,[29]
                         Rector of St. Philip's Church, Centre St.

NEW YORK, July 14, 1834.

[29] *African Repository*, X, pp. 186–188.

WILLIAM C. NELL TO SAMUEL J. MAY

EN ROUTE FROM PHILADELPHIA TO BOSTON,
October 21, 1855.

RESPECTED FRIEND:

Being unavoidably absent from home during your commemoration of the second decade of the Boston or Garrison Mob, I reconciled myself mainly by the fact, that thereby I had the opportunity afforded me of visiting that victim of judicial despotism and slaveholding arbitration, PASSMORE WILLIAMSON.

Twenty years ago this day, WILLIAM LLOYD GARRISON, for promulgating the idea of immediate emancipation, was delivered from the murderous hands of a Boston mob, composed of "gentlemen of property and standing," into Leverett Street Jail; and at this hour, PASSMORE WILLIAMSON endures martyrdom in Moyamensing Prison for his application of immediate emancipation to Jane Johnson and her two boys from her self-styled owner, John H. Wheeler.

My reflections upon the two historical events of 1835 and 1855, induced my noting down the following reminiscences, hoping space may be found for them in your published report.

I well remember the emphatically cloudy day, October 21, 1835, and the various scenes and incidents which characterised it, shrouding with indelible disgrace and infamy my native city.

A friend of mine then boarded at a house in Boylston street, where, at the tea-table that evening, were assembled many Boston merchants. The Abolition Mob was the theme of conversation; and while a majority evinced their pro-slavery spirit by approving of what had occurred, two gentlemen warmly dissented,—one of whom, DAVID TILDEN, Esq., immediately became a subscriber to *The Liberator*, and so continued until his decease, a few years since.

A sister of the coachman who so adroitly eluded the mob, and landed Mr. Garrison safely at the jail, often alluded to the impression made by that hour upon her brother.

I have obtained the following facts from colored Anti-Slavery friends, whose feelings were deeply moved on the occasion.

JOHN T. HILTON accompanied DAVID H. ELA (a printer in Cornhill, since deceased) to the meeting. They found the stairs impassable, in consequence of the crowd, and an altercation ensued. Mr. Ela was struck a severe blow by a man who rebuked him for upholding Abolitionists and "niggers." He resisted, until the parties were separated by the crowd rushing to seize Garrison in

Wilson's Lane. The women came down the stairs amidst the hootings and insults of the mob. Two prominent men were engaged in tearing down the sign. Mr. Hilton heard a printer inform the mob where Garrison was secreted, in the rear of the building, where he (Mr. H.) went with the rest, to do what he could to rescue him, or, at all events, to be at his side. He saw Mr. Garrison dragged into State street, divested of coat and hat, and did not leave until Sheriff Parkman had him in the City Hall.

JOHN BOYER VASHON, of Pittsburg, Pa., was an eye-witness to the terrible scene, which was heart-rending beyond his ability ever afterwards to express, as, of all living men, JOHN B. VASHON loved WILLIAM LLOYD GARRISON most; and this feeling of affection continued, for aught that is known, to the day of his death. When the mob passed along Washington street, shouting and yelling like madmen, the apprehensions of Mr. Vashon became fearfully aroused. Presently there approached a group which appeared even more infuriated than the rest, and he beheld, in the midst of this furious throng, Garrison himself, led on like a beast to the slaughter. He had been on the field of battle, had faced the cannon's mouth, seen its lightnings flash and heard its thunders roar, but such a sight as this was more than the old citizen soldier could bear, without giving vent to a flood of tears. The next day, the old soldier, who had helped to preserve his country's liberty on the plighted faith of security to his own, but who had lived to witness freedom of speech and of the press stricken down by mob violence, and life itself in jeopardy, because that liberty was asked for him and his, with spirits crushed and faltering hopes, called to administer a word of consolation to the bold and courageous young advocate of immediate and universal emancipation. Mr. Garrison subsequently thus referred to this circumstance in his paper:—"On the day of that riot in Boston, he dined at my house, and the next morning called to see me in prison, bringing with him a new hat for me, in the place of one that was cut in pieces by the knives of men of property and standing."

Rev. JAMES E. CRAWFORD, now of Nantucket, boarded in Boston at the time of the mob, and, walking up State street, suddenly encountered the riotous multitude. On learning that Mr. Garrison was mobbed for words and deeds in behalf of the enslaved colored man, his heart and soul became fully dedicated to the cause of immediate emancipation.

At a meeting of colored citizens, held in Boston, August 27th, 1855, on the subject of Equal School Rights, WILLIAM H. LOGAN alluded to his receiving from Sheriff Parkman, soon after the mob, a pair of pantaloons, (or the remnants thereof,) which had been torn from Mr. Garrison during the struggle. Mr. G. being present at the meeting, remarked, that, until that moment, he had never known what became of them.

Imprisonment is a feature of martyrdom with which Abolitionists in the United States have become familiar, especially Mr. Garrison, who, at the bidding of slavery, was, in 1829, incarcerated in Baltimore. But these persecutions are to be accepted as jewels in their crown, as seals of their devotion to the cause of millions now in the prison-house of bondage.

For whose speedy emancipation, I remain,

Fraternally yours,

WILLIAM C. NELL.[30]

A. STEWARD TO W. C. NELL

DEAR SIR:

We are glad to acknowledge your favor of October last, and to hear of your safe arrival in England, your health and fair prospects.

Since my removal to Wilberforce, I have opened a school, which Mrs. Steward has engaged to teach for one year; while I shall probably devote my time to traveling through the States, for the benefit of the Colony, which is indeed poor, and in want of some assistance; and yet, not a dollar have we in the treasury to help them with.

Mr. Paul has not returned, though we are daily expecting him. Our friends in New York, still have confidence in his pledge to do right; and we are anxiously expecting its fulfilment.

Your wife, Mrs. Nell, and the children are well, and we are still doing all in our power for their comfort; but my means, in consequence of having been so much abroad the past season, are limited; by which you will see, my dear Sir, the necessity of remitting funds to me, that I may make your family more comfortable in all things, without distressing my own.

The settlers are well, and are looking with hopeful expectancy for you to do something handsome for them, in which I do hope they may not be disappointed. Lewis is still in New York. We have appointed another agent, named Scott, but who is doing nothing for the Colony now.

---

[30] *Proceedings of the Anti-slavery Meeting held in Stacy Hall, Boston, on the Twentieth Anniversary of the Mob of October 21, 1835*, pages 72–73.

May the blessing of God rest upon you, and your endeavors;
your good deportment put to silence your enemies; may they who
foresee that you will cheat the poor colored children, be sadly mistaken, and your good deeds finally enrol your name on the proud
list of philanthropists, headed by a Wilberforce and a Clarkson.

Yours, in great haste,
AUSTIN STEWARD.

WILBERFORCE, Dec., 1835.

When the proslavery forces became aggressive there was
much fear of kidnapping in the North as the following letter
indicates:

FROM DAVID RUGGLES

MR. EDITOR: I have hesitated to call the public attention to
the "outrage" alleged to have been committed on board the "Brig
Brilliante, on the night of the 24th inst.," to correct the false reports
in relation to that outrage and myself, until now; when I trust,
that the newspapers have ceased to abuse their mind in relation to it.

It is a duty which I owe to them and myself, to state the facts
in this, and in a subsequent outrage, so far as I am acquainted with
them; and to pronounce the charges against me in the matter of
"riot" or "outrage" or "assault" to be *malicious* and *false*.

I have never visited that vessel at any time, except in open day,
when humanity urged, and duty directed me. And the idea of
my boarding a slave ship at night "within the jurisdiction of the
United States," in the port of New York; to release by force her
captives from on board, when I have been acquainted with the fact
for the last three months that there is a conspiracy on foot to kidnap
and to sacrifice me upon the altar of slavery—need not be harbored
for one moment in the minds of the most prejudiced. I will state
a fact in another place, to show that the savage slave catchers who
came with their pistols, dirks, and clubs, and handcuffs, and a gag
to pounce upon me and drag me to the South, did not themselves
believe the charge.

That I aided in employing every legal and proper means in our
courts of law, to let the slave go free, I admit, and shall endeavor to
do so in every like suspicious case; but I sought not, I merit not the
praise of releasing them—I left that duty to be performed, that
laurel to be won by "the proper authorities," whose duty it is to
execute the laws of our country, which prohibits the "*bringing in,
or importing African slaves into the jurisdiction of the United States*

from any foreign place, kingdom or country, in any manner whatever."

After being instructed in the fact that "the proper authorities" are willing to submit to the *"bringing in,"* and even to the importers holding such slaves in our city prison, until it might suit their convenience to remove them on board the vessel, or (if he reserves his *intent to sell*) to the South—I held and still hold that that vessel ought to be libelled, and the case carried up to a higher tribunal; but since I am informed that the Portuguese who called at my office and stated the Brilliante belongs to the Governor or Mayor of Rio Jeneiro; that she is one of fifteen or twenty slavers which he employs in the slave trade; that he shipped to come to this port; she is to get an outfit to go to the coast of Africa for a cargo of slaves; and the one who informed me on a subsequent occasion, that the vessel returned from the coast with slaves a few weeks before they left Rio Janeiro; have not been seen on board the vessel for several days, I may not, in the absence of the proof to convict the captain and condemn the brig, proceed further; while at the same time I am satisfied that that vessel merits large suspicion.

It is said "that two of the slaves are liberated!" I have to regret that they are not all liberated by the law, as much as I regret the reputed occasion was furnished by the friends of the poor emaciated victims, that the pro-slavery party could raise the cry "Outrage!" "Negro riot!" and "Assault," to enlist the public sympathy in favor of De Souza, the oppressor, while he transports the oppressed to some southern slave market to be sold to the highest bidder! Money is scarce—men are the most valuable commodity that can be sent to the southern market;—they offer "Two Thousand Dollars a head *for able bodied slaves*" in *Florida*.

And according to the moral and political cancer, the Courier and Enquirer, of this morning, which professes to be acquainted with De Souza's financial affairs, and intimates that the lawyers have fleeced him very close—if this be true, it would, I think be unsafe to say that he has not taken the hint from the late decision in his own case, and *reserved* his *intent*, and sold them to the South.

But let us return to the *Savage Outrage*.—On Wednesday morning, 28th December, between one and two o'clock, several notorious slave-catchers made an attack upon the house in which I board, and attempted to force open the doors. I arose from my bed, and stepped to the door, and inquired, who's there? "Is Mr. Ruggles in?" "Yes." "I wish to see you, sir." "Who are you." "A friend—David, open the door." "What is your name?" "Why—

why, it is Nash: I have come to see you on business of importance."
"What's the matter?" "Nothing—I only wish to see you on some
private business." "This is rather an unseasonable hour Mr.
Nash, to settle private business; call in the morning at eight
o'clock." "Open this door or I will force it open." "It shall not
be opened to-night, sir, unless you tell your errand." "Then I will
get authority from High Constable Hays," [he retired, and soon
returned] "I have got authority from High Constable Hays to break
open this door! Come on boys." He forced open the door; he
and others of his clan made a rush up to my room like hungry dogs;
but finding that they had missed their victim, they commenced an
assault upon the defenceless landlady; menaced her with clubs,
pistols and dirks, that she might produce me. Mr. Joseph Michaels
appeared, as the mate of the "suspected slaver" Brilliante, had his
dagger raised to strike his sister, and bade him "*hold the blow*, or I
will strike you down!"

The assistance of the watch was called by them. Mr. M. was
seized, and the handcuffs that Nash brought for me placed upon
him, and he was dragged to the watch house, where I am informed
Nash took from his cap a half sheet of paper, which he said was the
writ that he had obtained from High Constable Hays to take me as a
slave.—After disposing of M. Michaels, he and his clan returned to
Lispenard street, in company with the watchman, and others who
were disinterested. Nash said, "had I have caught the fellow out
the door, we would have fixed him." "Yes," said the savage
Portuguese, brandishing his dirk, "if he would not go, I would soon
have put an end to his existence: he would never interfere with
Brazilians again."

"What did he do?" "Why," replied Nash, "he went down on
board the Brilliante and assaulted the captain."

"How do you know it was him!" Nash said, "If he did not do
it, some of the blacks did, and he is the ring leader among them."

Nash did not call to see me at 8 o'clock in the morning; at 12
o'clock, I proceeded to see him, or to make a statement of the facts
in the case before the Mayor.

As I entered the City Hall, I was pounced upon by Boudinot,
who dragged me to the Police Office. I desired him not to drag me
in that manner, and to show his authority to arrest me, because I
would walk to the office with him—He refused to do so, and jammed
me against one of the marble pillars—said he, "I was after you
last night!"

When I appeared before the magistrate, he said that he understood that I had been engaged in a riot on board the brig Brilliante on the night of the 24th ult. and that I must find bail to appear before the Sessions to answer to the charge. My friend stepped out for my bail. Boudinot immediately dragged me to the city prison, and gave the jailor a paper, who said, "I have no right to lock up, that is not a commitment." "Yes it is," said Boudinot, "shut the fellow up!"

In less than 20 minutes, they had me on the way to Bellevue Prison. They said, "we have got him now, he shall have no quarters, we will learn him to publish us as kidnappers!"

Now, whether these men did *intend* to take me from my bed and send me to the South with Waddy, the notorious southern slave catcher, who, I am informed, sailed for Savannah on Wednesday morning, or to "put an end to my existence," if I *resisted*, I cannot say in the absence of proof; I hope they did not. But from their conduct, and from the manner in which, I am informed, Boudinot, Nash, John Lyon, and Waddy carried off Peter John Lee, from Rye —and from what I have understood, (for some two or three months past) they intended to do with me, I must confess, considering all the circumstances in the case, that I do believe that this was a desperate effort to execute their threats by sending me to the South. Nash is not a police officer, therefore the magistrate could not allow him a warrant to apprehend any one. Boudinot did not enter the house; he doubtless expected that I would attempt to escape in the street, that he might take me with the warrant, which he informed a gentleman he obtained from Governor Marcy in 1832 or '33, by which he can arrest any colored person that Waddy may point out to him named "Jesse," "Abraham," "Peter," or "Silvia," and send him or her South, without taking such person before a magistrate, as they did Peter John Lee.

Now, I thank Heaven that I am still permitted to live, and take fresh courage in warning my endangered brethren against a gang of kidnappers, which continues to infest our city and the country, to kidnap men, women and children, and carry them to the South. While Boudinot holds a warrant, by which he says he has been sending colored people to the South, for the last three years, and with which he boasts that he can "arrest and send any black to the South"—no man, no woman, no child is safe.

Our houses may be broken open at night by northern or southern and Portuguese slave catchers; we may be assaulted and threatened with clubs, pistols or dirks, and handcuffed and gagged, and carried away to the South, while HUMANITY and JUSTICE continue to sleep!

Most affectionately and diligently yours, in the cause of Human Freedom,   DAVID RUGGLES.

New York, Jan. 4th, 1836.[31]

This letter shows the feeling of the fugitive with respect to his people whom he had left in bondage.

TO MY FATHER, MOTHER, BROTHERS, AND SISTERS [32]

DEARLY BELOVED IN BONDS,

About seventeen long years have now rolled away, since in the Providence of Almighty God, I left your embraces, and set out upon a daring adventure in search of freedom. Since that time, I have felt most severely the loss of the sun and moon and eleven stars from my social sky. Many, many a thick cloud of anguish has pressed my brow and sent deep down into my soul the bitter waters of sorrow in consequence. And you have doubtless had your troubles and anxious seasons also about your fugitive star.

I have learned that some of you have been sold, and again taken back by Colonel ——. How many of you are living and together, I cannot tell. My great grief is, lest you should have suffered this or some additional punishment on account of my *Exodus*.

I indulge the hope that it will afford you some consolation to know that your son and brother is yet alive. That God has dealt wonderfully and kindly with me in all my way. He has made me a Christian, and a Christian Minister, and thus I have drawn my support and comfort from that blessed Saviour, who came *to preach good tidings unto the meek, to bind up the broken hearted, to proclaim liberty to the captives, and the opening of the prison to them that are bound. To proclaim the acceptable year of the Lord and the day of vengeance of our God: to comfort all that mourn. To appoint unto them that mourn in Zion, to give unto them beauty for ashes, the oil of joy for mourning, the garment of praise for the spirit of heaviness, that they might be called trees of righteousness, the planting of the Lord that he might be glorified.*

[31] First Annual Report of the New York Committee of Vigilance for the year 1837, pp. 73–77.

[32] This letter was written in 1844.

If the course I took in leaving a condition which had become intolerable to me, has been made the occasion of making that condition worse to you in any way, I do most heartily regret such a change for the worse on your part. As I have no means, however, of knowing if such be the fact, so I have no means of making atonement, but by sincere prayer to Almighty God in your behalf, and also by taking this method of offering to you these consolations of the gospel to which I have just referred, and which I have found to be pre-eminently my own stay and support. My dear father and mother; I have very often wished, while administering the Holy Ordinance of Baptism to some scores of children brought forward by doting parents, that I could see you with yours among the number. And you, my brothers and sisters, while teaching hundreds of children and youths in schools over which I have been placed, what unspeakable delight I should have had in having you among the number; you may all judge of my feeling for these past years, when while preaching from Sabbath to Sabbath to congregations, I have not been so fortunate as even to see father, mother, brother, sister, uncle, aunt, nephew, niece, or cousin in my congregations. While visiting the sick, going to the house of mourning, and burying the dead, I have been a constant mourner for you. My sorrow has been that I know you are not in possession of those hallowed means of grace. I am thankful to you for those mild and gentle traits of character which you took such care to enforce upon me in my youthful days. As an evidence that I prize both you and them, I may say that at the age of thirty-seven, I find them as valuable as any lessons I have learned, nor am I ashamed to let it be known to the world, that I am the son of a bond man and a bond woman.

Let me urge upon you the fundamental truths of the Gospel of the Son of God. Let repentance towards God and faith in our Lord Jesus Christ have their perfect work in you, I beseech you. Do not be prejudiced against the gospel because it may be seemingly twisted into a support of slavery. The gospel rightly understood, taught, received, felt and practised, is anti-slavery as it is anti-sin. Just so far and so fast as the true spirit of the gospel obtains in the land, and especially in the lives of the oppressed, will the spirit of slavery sicken and become powerless like the serpent with his head pressed beneath the fresh leaves of the prickly ash of the forest.

There is not a solitary decree of the immaculate God that has been concerned in the ordination of slavery, nor does any possible development of his holy will sanctify it.

He has permitted us to be enslaved according to the invention of wicked men, instigated by the devil, with intention to bring good out of the evil, but He does not, He cannot approve of it. He has no need to approve of it, even on account of the good which He will bring out of it, for He could have brought about that very good in some other way.

God is never straitened; He is never at a loss for means to work. Could He not have made this a great and wealthy nation without making its riches to consist in our blood, bones, and souls? And could He not also have given the gospel to us without making us slaves?

My friends, let us then, in our afflictions, embrace and hold fast the gospel. The gospel is the fulness of God. We have the glorious and total weight of God's moral character in our side of the scale.

The wonderful purple stream which flowed for the healing of the nations, has a branch for us. Nay, is Christ divided? "The grace of God that bringeth salvation hath appeared to (for) all men, teaching us that denying ungodliness and worldly lust, we should live soberly, righteously, and godly in this present world, looking for that blessed hope and glorious appearing of the great God and our Saviour Jesus Christ, who gave himself for us that he might redeem us from all iniquity, and purify unto himself a peculiar people, zealous of good works."—Titus ii. 11–14.

But you say you have not the privilege of hearing this gospel of which I speak. I know it; and this is my great grief. But you shall have it; I will send it to you by my humble prayer; I can do it; I will beg our heavenly Father, and he will preach this gospel to you in his holy providence.

You, dear father and mother cannot have much longer to live in this troublesome and oppressive world; you cannot bear the yoke much longer. And as you approach another world, how desirable it is that you should have the prospect of a different destiny from what you have been called to endure in this world during a long life.

But it is the gospel that sets before you the hope of such a blessed rest as is spoken of in the word of God, Job iii. 17, 19. "There the wicked cease from troubling, and there the weary be at rest; there the prisoners rest together; they hear not the voice of the oppressors. The small and great are there; and the servant is free from his master."

Father, I know that thy eyes are dim with age and weary with weeping, but look, dear father, yet a little while toward that haven.

Look unto Jesus, "The author and finisher of thy faith," for the moment of thy happy deliverance is at hand.

Mother, dear mother, I know, I feel, mother, the pangs of thy bleeding heart, that thou hast endured, during so many years of vexation. Thy agonies are by a genuine son-like sympathy mine; I will, I must, I do share daily in those agonies of thine. But I sincerely hope that with me you bear your agonies to Christ who carries our sorrows.

O come then with me, my beloved family, of weary heart-broken and care-worn ones, to Jesus Christ, "casting all your care upon him, for he careth for you."—2 Peter v. 7.

With these words of earnest exhortation, joined with fervent prayer to God that He may smooth your rugged way, lighten your burden, and give a happy issue out of all your troubles, I must bid you adieu.

Your son and brother,
JAS. P.
Alias J. W. C. PENNINGTON.

TO COLONEL F—— T——, OF H——, WASHINGTON COUNTY, MD. 1844.

DEAR SIR,

It is now, as you are aware, about seventeen years since I left your house and service, at the age of twenty. Up to that time, I was, according to your rule and claim, your slave. Till the age of seven years, I was, of course, of little or no service to you. At that age, however, you hired me out, and for three years I earned my support; at the age of ten years, you took me to your place again, and in a short time after you put me to work at the blacksmith's trade, at which, together with the carpentering trade, &c., I served you peaceably until the day I left you with exception of the short time you had sold me to S—— H——, Esq., for seven hundred dollars. It is important for me to say to you, that I have no consciousness of having done you any wrong. I called you master when I was with you from the mere force of circumstances; but I never regarded you as my master. The nature which God gave me did not allow me to believe that you had any more right to me than I had to you, and that was just none at all. And from an early age, I had intentions to free myself from your claim. I never consulted any one about it; I had no advisers or instigators; I kept my own counsel entirely concealed in my own bosom. I never meditated any evil to your person or property, but I regarded you as my oppressor, and I deemed it my duty to get out of your hands by peaceable means.

I was always obedient to your commands. I laboured for you diligently at all times. I acted with fidelity in any matter which you entrusted me. As you sometimes saw fit to entrust me with considerable money, to buy tools or materials, not a cent was ever coveted or kept.

During the time I served you in the capacity of blacksmith, your materials were used economically, your work was done expeditiously, and in the very best style, a style second to no smith in your neighbourhood. In short, sir, you know well that my habits from early life were advantageous to you. Drinking, gambling, fighting, &c., were not my habits. On Sabbaths, holidays, &c., I was frequently at your service, when not even your body-servant was at home.

Times and times again, I have gone on Sunday afternoon to H——, six miles, after your letters and papers, when it was as much my privilege to be "*out of the way,*" as it was C——.

But what treatment did you see fit to return me for all this? You, in the most unfeeling manner, abused my father for no cause but speaking a word to you, as a man would speak to his fellow-man, for the sake simply of a better understanding.

You vexed my mother, and because she, as a tender mother would do, showed solicitude for the virtue of her daughters, you threatened her in an insulting brutal manner.

You abused my brother and sister without cause, and in like manner you did to myself; you surmised evil against me. You struck me with your walking-cane, called me insulting names, threatened me, swore at me, and became more and more wrathy in your conduct, and at the time I quitted your place, I had good reason to believe that you were meditating serious evil against me.

Since I have been out of your hands, I have been signally favoured of God, when I infer that in leaving you, I acted strictly in accordance with his holy will. I have a conscience void of offence towards God and towards all men, yourself not excepted. And I verily believe that I have performed a sacred duty to God and myself, and a kindness to you, in taking the blood of my soul peaceably off your soul. And now, dear sir, having spoken somewhat pointedly, I would, to convince you of my perfect good will towards you, in the most kind and respectful terms, remind you of your coming destiny. You are now over seventy years of age, pressing on to eternity with the weight of these seventy years upon you. Is this not enough without the blood of some half-score of souls?

You are aware that your right to property in man is now disputed by the civilized world. You are fully aware, also, that the question, whether the Bible sanctions slavery, has distinctly divided this nation in sentiment. On the side of Biblical Anti-slavery, we have many of the most learned, wise and holy men in the land. If the Bible affords no sanction to slavery, (and I claim that it cannot,) then it must be a sin of the deepest dye; and can you, sir, think to go to God in hope with a sin of such magnitude upon your soul?

But admitting that the question is yet doubtful, (which I do only for the sake of argument,) still, sir, you will have the critical hazard of this doubt pressing, in no very doubtful way, upon your declining years, as you descend the long and tedious hill of life.

Would it not seem to be exceedingly undesirable to close an eventful probation of seventy or eighty years and leave your reputation among posterity suspended upon so doubtful an issue? But what, my dear sir, is a reputation among posterity, who are but worms, compared with a destiny in the world of spirits? And it is in light of that destiny that I would now have you look at this subject. You and I, and all that you claim as your slaves, are in a state of probation; our great business is to serve God under His righteous moral government. Master and slave are the subjects of that government, bound by its immutable requirements, and liable to its sanctions in the next world, though enjoying its forbearance in this. You will pardon me then for pressing this point in earnest good faith. You should, at this stage, review your life without political bias, or adherence to long cherished prejudices, and remember that you are soon to meet those whom you have held, and do hold in slavery, at the awful bar of the impartial Judge of all who doeth right. Then what will become of your own doubtful claims? What will be done with those doubts that agitated your mind years ago; will you answer for threatening, swearing, and using the cowhide among your slaves?

What will become of those long groans and unsatisfied complaints of your slaves, for vexing them with insulting words, placing them in the power of dogish and abusive overseers, or under your stripling, misguided, hot-headed son, to drive and whip at pleasure, and for selling parts or whole families to Georgia? They will all meet you at that bar. Uncle James True, Charles Cooper, Aunt Jenny, and the native Africans; Jeremiah, London, and Donmore, have already gone a-head, and only wait your arrival—Sir, I shall meet you there. The account between us for the first twenty years of my life, will have a definite character upon which one or the other will be able to make out a case.

Upon such a review as this, sir, you will, I am quite sure, see the need of seriousness. I assure you that the thought of meeting you in eternity and before the dread tribunal of God, with a complaint in my mouth against you, is to me of most weighty and solemn character. And you will see that the circumstances from which this thought arises are of equal moment to yourself. Can the pride of leaving your children possessed of long slave states, or the policy of sustaining in the state the institution of slavery, justify you in overlooking a point of moment to your future happiness?

What excuse could you offer at the bar of God, favoured as you have been with the benefits of a refined education, and through a long life with the gospel of love, should you, when arraigned there, find that you have, all your life long, laboured under a great mistake in regard to slavery, and that in this mistake you had died, and only lifted up your eyes in the light of eternity to be corrected, when it was too late to be corrected in any other way.

I could wish to address you (being bred, born, and raised in your family) *as a father in Israel, or as an elder brother in Christ, but I cannot; mockery is a sin.* I can only say then, dear sir, farewell, till I meet you at the bar of God, where Jesus, who died for us, will judge between us. Now his blood can wash out our stain, break down the middle wall of partition, and reconcile us not only to God but to each other, then the word of his mouth, the sentence will set us at one. As for myself, I am quite ready to meet you face to face at the bar of God. I have done you no wrong; I have nothing to fear when we both fall into the hands of the just God.

I beseech you, dear sir, to look well and consider this matter soundly. In yonder world you can have no slaves—you can be no man's master—you can neither sell, buy, or whip, or drive. Are you then, by sustaining the relation of a slaveholder, forming a character to dwell with God in peace?

With kind regards,

I am, sir, yours respectfully,

J. W. C. PENNINGTON.[33]

[33] *The Fugitive Blacksmith*, 74–84.

This letter was taken from the paper mentioned herein and published with the following comment:

"We cut the above from the *N. Y. Evangelist*, an abolition paper, with no other views than to show how colored people get along in the free city of New York. Mr. Pennington is a man of color, formerly from this State, has received the honorary degree of Doctor of Divinity from some European Institution, and is a man of unquestioned ability. As he intimates, he is denied admission to public vehicles on account of his color, only. He says he rides with the white people side by side in European cities, but is only denied the privilege in New York. Why then settle in New York? He is not a native of that city, no ties of birth or early association retain him there. He says his predecessor in that ministerial charge was brought to an early grave by these very hardships which he has voluntarily offered to undergo. Then why accept the charge, and why complain after accepting? The fact is, the home for such men as Dr. Pennington, is not New York City, nor any city on the American Continent. Broad fertile Africa is the true home of the black man. It is enough for him to control the destiny of the most valuable quarter of the globe. He can never conquer this land or the prejudices, if he chooses so to call them, of its inhabitants."

MR. EDITOR:—You are aware that I am pastor of the Presbyterian church on the corner of Prince and Marion streets, in this city. My congregation extends from No. 1 Pearl street to 65th street, and from Hoboken to Brooklyn and Williamsburg; so that in the discharge of my pastoral duties, I am constantly called to different points, and from one extremity to the other of this immense field. And yet, sir, according to usage in this community, I cannot avail myself of the use of any of the lines of omnibuses, or any of the multiplying lines of railways in the city.

I will state two, out of many facts, to show how severely the thing works. On the morning of our last Thanksgiving day, I went to Newtown, L. I., and held service, with the intention of being back in season for the 3 o'clock service at my own church in Prince street. I returned to the city, making my time comfortably till I got to Grand street Ferry, on Williamsburg side, where missing by two steps the boat, I saw that time would fail me on this side unless I took an omnibus. I got over the ferry 20 minutes to 3 o'clock, just as a Grant street omnibus was starting, and which would pass Marion street, within two blocks of my church, in 15 minutes. I attempted to get in, but was rudely refused, and having to walk fully a mile and a quarter, I arrived long after the hour of public service, and in a very uncomfortable state, both physically and mentally, for my work.

At the early part of our recent warm season, a worthy female member of my church, who was a teacher in the Colored Orphan Asylum, on the Fifth Avenue near Fortieth street, died, and I was notified to attend her funeral. The funeral was appointed for one o'clock—I heard of it about twelve. I was in the lower part of the city visiting, at the time. I went at once to my residence, No. 50 Laurens street, changed, and started for the Asylum. Now, could I have had a 'bus, I could have got there in ample time for the services at 1 o'clock. On the block above my house is a carriage stand, where I stopped and attempted to negotiate for a hack, but $1.50 was the lowest cent I could get one for, to go the distance! So in painful excitement I walked the entire distance, under the burning sun of one of our hottest days, getting there after the hour and not fit for service.

Sir, these cases I could multiply, but it is not necessary. You have an illustration of the working of the usage, and of its most oppressive influence. And why is it that a man in the public service of one of the largest congregations in the city, has to submit to such a system of oppression? It is not because I smoke segars in the 'busses, as I see some white men do. It is not because I chew and spit tobacco in the 'busses, as some white men do. It is not because I carry a great pet dog with me, and say to every one "If you love me you love my dog"—not excepting finely dressed ladies in the 'busses. But it is simply and only because I am a black man, obediently carrying about on my person the same skin, with the same color, which the Almighty has seen fit to give me. In this matter of the color of a man, "he that reproacheth the Almighty, let him answer it." I do not.

But seriously, Mr. Editor, it is a hard case that a man should be compelled, in the public service, to walk ounce after ounce of his heart's best blood out of him every day, and not be allowed to avail himself of the public conveyances designed to save time, health and life. It is known to impartial witnesses that my predecessor, Rev.

Theo. S. Wright, though one of the most valued ministers that ever lived in this city, had his life shortened several years by this oppressive usage; and I feel that I am walking in his footsteps. Have I a right thus knowingly to dig for myself an untimely grave? Has the New York public a right to require at my hands this unreasonable amount of exposure?

I shall be told that the majority of the public will object to my riding in the 'busses. Is that true? Will the members of a Christian public object to me, a minister of Christ, using the facilities of a public conveyance, while about my Master's business? Besides, hundreds of the persons who now ride in our stages, are the same with whom I have rode in the 'busses at London, Liverpool, Glasgow, Edinburg, Brussels, Paris, &c. I only mention this, to show the inconsistency of this usage. I ask for simple justice at the hands of my countrymen.

J. W. PENNINGTON.[10]

WILLIAM W. FINDLAY TO THE COLORED PEOPLE OF INDIANA

"DEAR FRIENDS,—The writer being a colored man, it may be supposed that he desires the well-being of his race, not of a part of the colored race, but of the whole race of Africans, in this land and in Africa. Nor do I consider myself guilty of affection, when, I say, that I ardently desire their elevation, and am willing to contribute all I can to that end. It has long been an inquiry with me, how can our race be elevated? *How can colored men be made truly independent?* After much anxious and painful inquiry, I have concluded, that to be *truly* independent, we must enjoy rights and privileges *as broad* and *as liberal* as those enjoyed by the white citizen of the United States; in other words, have the right of electing our law-makers and our magistrates; and all the offices of state should be accessible to our color; and not only so, but we should be free to move in such circles of society as we may be entitled to by our moral worth, character, and talents; and likewise, free to form alliance with those classes of society. These, in my humble opinion, are the rights and privileges *we must possess* before we can be *independent.*

"But now let us inquire in candor, do we as a people enjoy such independence? Do colored men, in the most liberal of the northern states, enjoy such independence? You all know that they do not.

[10] *African Repository*, XXIX, 82–85.

The sad reverse is the case. And will the time soon come, in the history of American society, when the colored man will be permitted to enjoy such independence—independence, not only in civil things, but independence in all the more delicate matters of social equality? I must honestly confess, I think not. And further: I am bold to confess, that any thing short of the above-described independence will not satisfy me; nor should any thing short satisfy the man of an independent spirit.

"But such independence we can not obtain in the United States; therefore, I will seek it outside the United States. *I will seek it where I know I can find it*, and that is in the republic of Liberia, which is the only Christian republic where the colored man can find a quiet and secure home. Nor do I act dishonorably, in thus escaping from civil and social oppression; for I am only doing what thousands of the first and best settlers in the United States did; and I think it an honor to follow their example, in seeking liberty, though, like them, I be compelled to seek it in a wilderness. And the object of this appeal is, to invite you who love true independence, and are willing to endure some toil to obtain it, to go with us to that land of liberty, where we may likewise aid in the elevation and enlightenment of our whole race, *which duty is more obligatory on us* than upon the white race, many of whom are willing to *sacrifice* their lives and property in the work of converting Africa.

"Some of you may blame us for not staying in this land and contending for all the above rights of man. Our answer to all such complaints is this: we believe that civil slavery in this land will be abolished by divine Providence without the co-operation of the free colored man; he requires not our aid in this work—he can and will in his own way, sweep slavery from the civil institutions of America. But I honestly doubt whether it is the will or order of Providence to grant us perfect social equality *with the white race at this time*, nor am I disposed to strive or quarrel with them for this favor, but would follow the example of Abraham, who disliked the strife that had sprung up between him and Lot, and religiously proposed separation as a remedy for the quarrel, and a means of perpetuating peace; so we should separate from the white race, that we may be free and they enjoy peace; for, doubtless, God has given this land to them. Acting from the above religious and honorable views, we confidently expect that God will bless us in our movements.

"It is the design of the writer and some of his friends, to go out to Liberia about the month of October or November next, and it is desirable to have as many emigrants from Indiana as we can muster. Liberia holds out many attractions for the man of color, but the greatest is that of liberty and independence. Thousands have gone from this land to that, and all who have been industrious have done well; many of them are becoming wealthy, but what is best, *they are all free!* Come, let us go and cast our lot in with them and be free likewise. If any of you have been cherishing the spirit of independence, and long for such freedom as the free republic of Liberia offers, and if you desire a passage to that land, just let your wishes be known to the Agent of the American Colonization Society of this state. Address Rev. J. Mitchell, at Indianapolis, who will be pleased to book your name as an emigrant, and procure for you a passage out, and send you all the information you may want. No time should be lost. *Act now*—act for yourselves, your children, and your race. "WM. W. FINDLAY.[34]

"*Covington, Ia., April 6, 1849.*"

Rev. SAMUEL MAY, JR., *General Agent Mass. A. S. Society.*

FREDERICK DOUGLASS PROBABLY TO SAMUEL J. MAY

MY DEAR SIR,

Your letter came yesterday and I immediately ordered the number of my paper to your address for which you Sent. I hope you will get them Safely.

I hope your plan for agitating this State will succeed. I will pledge whatever of influence I possess in aid of such agitation. A series of such meetings as you propose could not fail to act benificially on our cause throughout the country.

The election of *Gerrit Smith*—What an era! But this grand event will be comparatively lost unless the agitation is kept up. With men and money we could carry the State for freedom in *1856*

I was sorry not to have seen more of you at the celebration—but in a crowd so large even a tall man might pass unobserved.

Very truly Yours,

FREDERICK DOUGLASS.[35]

FRED DOUGLASS

Nov. 10, 1852

[34] Charles Elliott's *Sinfulness of American Slavery*, Vol. II, pp. 45–48.

[35] This letter and the two following it were obtained from the manuscript collection of the New York Historical Society.

Mr. Douglass less than Twenty years ago was a slave, unable to read or write. Now he is one of the best writers and ablest speakers in our country.

REV. SAML. J. MAY

Following the principles laid down and practiced by Pestelozzi, Owen, and the father of General Armstrong, Douglass here antedates Booker T. Washington as a bold advocate of industrial education:

ROCHESTER, March 8, 1853

MY DEAR MRS. STOWE:

You kindly informed me, when at your house a fortnight ago, that you designed to do something which would permanently contribute to the improvement and elevation of the free coloured people in the United States. You especially expressed interest in such of this class as had become free by their own exertions, and desired most of all to be of service to them. In what manner and by what means you can assist this class most successfully, is the subject upon which you have done me the honour to ask my opinion. . . I assert then that *poverty, ignorance* and *degradation* are the combined evils; or in other words, these constitute the social disease of the free coloured people of the United States.

To deliver them from this triple malady, is to improve and elevate them, by which I mean, simply to put them on an equal footing with their white fellow countrymen in the sacred right to "*Life, Liberty*, and the pursuit of happiness." I am for no fancied or artificial elevation, but only ask fair play. How shall this be obtained? I answer, first, not by establishing for our use high schools and colleges. Such institutions are, in my judgment, beyond our immediate occasions and are not adapted to our present most pressing wants. High schools and colleges are excellent institutions, and will in due season be greatly subservient to our progress; but they are the result, as well as they are the demand of a point of progress, which we as a people have not yet attained. Accustomed as we have been, to the rougher and harder modes of living, and of gaining a livelihood, we cannot, and we ought not to hope that in a single leap from our low condition, we can reach that of *Minister, Lawyers, Doctors, Editors, Merchants*, etc. These will doubtless be attained by us; but this will only be, when we have patiently and laboriously, and I may add, successfully, mastered and passed through the intermediate gradations of agriculture and the mechanical arts. Besides, there are—and perhaps this is a better reason for my view of this case—numerous institutions of learning in this country, already thrown open to coloured youth. To my thinking, there are quite as many facilities now afforded to the coloured people, as they can spare the time from the sterner duties of life, to avail themselves of. In their present condition of poverty, they cannot spare their sons and daughters two or three years at boarding-schools or colleges, to say nothing of finding the means to sustain them while at such institutions. I take it, therefore, that we are well provided for in this respect; and that it may be fairly inferred from the fact, that the facilities for our education, so far as schools and colleges in the Free States are concerned, will increase quite in proportion with our future wants. Colleges have been open to coloured youth in this country during the last dozen years. Yet few comparatively, have acquired a classical education; and even this few have found themselves educated far above a living condition, there being no methods by which they could turn their learning to account. Several of this latter class have entered the ministry; but you need not be told that an educated people is needed to sustain an educated ministry. There must be a certain amount of cultivation among the people to sustain such a ministry. At present we have not that cultivation amongst us; and therefore, we value in the preacher, strong lungs, rather than high learning. I do not say, that educated ministers are not needed amongst us, far from it! I wish there were more of them! but to increase their number, is not the largest benefit you can bestow upon us.

We have two or three coloured lawyers in this country; and I rejoice in the fact; for it affords very gratifying evidence of our progress. Yet it must be confessed, that in point of success, our lawyers are as great failures as our ministers. White people will not employ them to the obvious embarrassment of their causes, and the blacks, taking their *cue* from the whites, have not sufficient confidence in their abilities to employ them. Hence educated coloured men, among the coloured people, are at a very great discount.

It would seem that education and emigration go together with us, for as soon as a man rises amongst us, capable, by his genius and learning, to do us great service, just so soon he finds that he can serve himself better by going elsewhere. In proof of this, I might instance the Russwurms, the Garnets, the Wards, the Crummells and others, all men of superior ability and attainments, and capable of removing mountains of prejudice against their race, by their simple presence in the country; but these gentlemen, finding themselves embarrassed here by the peculiar disadvantages to which I have referred, disadvantages in part growing out of their education, being repelled by ignorance on the one hand, and prejudice on the other, and having no taste to continue a contest against such odds, they have sought more congenial climes, where they can live more peaceable and quiet lives. I regret their election, but I cannot blame them; for with an equal amount of education and the hard lot which was theirs, I might follow their example. . . .

There is little reason to hope that any considerable number of the free coloured people will ever be induced to leave this country; even if such a thing were desirable. This black man—*un*like the Indian—loves civilization. He does not make very great progress in civilization himself but he likes to be in the midst of it, and prefers to share its most galling evils, to encountering barbarism. Then the love of the country, the dread of isolation, the lack of adventurous spirit, and the thought of seeming to desert their "brethren in bonds," are a powerful check upon all schemes of colonization, which look to the removal of the coloured people, without the slaves. The truth is, dear madam, we are *here*, and here we are likely to remain. Individuals emigrate—nations never. We have grown up with this republic, and I see nothing in her character, or even in the character of the American people as yet, which compels the belief that we must leave the United States. If then, we are to remain here, the question for the wise and good is precisely that you have submitted to me—namely: What can be done to improve the condition of the free people of colour in the United States?

The plan which I humbly submit in answer to this inquiry—and in the hope that it may find favour with you, and with the many friends of humanity who honour, love, and cooperate with you—is the establishment in Rochester, N. Y., or in some other part of the United States equally favourable to such an enterprise, of an INDUSTRIAL COLLEGE in which shall be taught several important branches of the mechanical arts. This college to be opened to coloured youth. I will pass over the details of such an institution as I propose. . . . Never having had a day's schooling in all my life I may not be expected to map out the details of a plan so comprehensive as that involved in the idea of a college. I repeat, then, I leave the organisation and administration to the superior wisdom of yourself and the friends who second your noble efforts.

The argument in favour of an Industrial College—a college to be conducted by the best men—and the best workmen which the mechanical arts can afford; a college where coloured youth can be instructed to use their hands, as well as their heads; where they can be put into possession of the means of getting a living whether their lot in after life may be cast among civilized or uncivilized men; whether they choose to stay here, or prefer to return to the land of their fathers—is briefly this: Prejudice against the free coloured people in the United States has shown itself nowhere so invincible as among mechanics. The farmer and the professional man cherish no feeling so bitter as that cherished by these. The latter would starve us out of the country entirely. At this moment I can more easily get my son into a lawyer's office to learn law than I can into a blacksmith's shop to blow the bellows and to wield the sledge-hammer. Denied the means of learning useful trades we are pressed into the narrowest limits to obtain a livelihood. In times past we have been the hewers of wood and the drawers of water for American society, and we once enjoyed a monopoly in menial enjoyments, but this is so no longer. Even these enjoyments are rapidly passing away out of our hands. The fact is—every day begins with the lesson, and ends with the lesson—that coloured men must learn trades; and must find new employment; new modes of usefulness to society, or that they must decay under the pressing wants to which their condition is rapidly bringing them.

We must become mechanics; we must build as well as live in houses; we must make as well as use furniture; we must construct bridges as well as pass over them, before we can properly live or be respected by our fellow men. We need mechanics as well as ministers. We need workers in iron, clay, and leather. We have orators, authors, and other professional men, but these reach only a certain class, and get respect for our race in certain select circles. To live here as we ought we must fasten ourselves to our country-men through their every day cardinal wants. We must not only be able to *black* boots, but to *make* them. At present we are un-known in the Northern States as mechanics. We give no proof of genius or skill at the county, State, or national fairs. We are unknown at any of the great exhibitions of the industry of our fellow-citizens, and being unknown we are unconsidered.

The fact that we make no show of our ability is held conclusive of our inability to make any, hence all the indifference and contempt with which incapacity is regarded, fall upon us, and that too, when we have had no means of disproving the infamous opinion of our natural inferiority. I have during the last dozen years denied before the Americans that we are an inferior race; but this has been done by arguments based upon admitted principles rather than by the presentation of facts. Now, firmly believing, as I do, that there are skill, invention, power, industry, and real mechanical genius, among the coloured people, which will bear favourable testimony for them, and which only need the means to develop them, I am decidedly in favour of the establishment of such a college as I have mentioned. The benefits of such an institution would not be confined to the Northern States, nor to the free coloured people. They would extend over the whole Union. The slave not less than the freeman would be benefited by such an institution. It must be confessed that the most powerful arguments now used by the Southern slaveholder, and the one most soothing to his conscience, is that derived from the low condition of the free coloured people of the North. I have long felt that too little attention has been given by our truest friends in this country to removing this stumbling block out of the way of the slave's liberation.

The most telling, the most killing refutation of slavery, is the presentation of an industrious, enterprising, thrifty, and intelligent free black population. Such a population I believe would rise in the Northern States under the fostering care of such a college as that supposed.

To show that we are capable of becoming mechanics I might adduce any amount of testimony; but dear madam, I need not ring the changes on such a proposition. There is no question in the mind of any prejudiced person that the negro is capable of making a good mechanic. Indeed, even those who cherish the bitterest feelings towards us have admitted that the apprehension that negroes might be employed in their stead, dictated the policy of excluding them from trades altogether. But I will not dwell upon this point as I fear I have already trespassed too long upon your precious time, and written more than I ought to expect you to read.

Allow me to say in conclusion, that I believe every intelligent coloured man in America will approve and rejoice at the establishment of some such institution as that now suggested. There are many respectable coloured men, fathers of large families, having

boys nearly grown up, whose minds are tossed by day and by night
with the anxious enquiry, "what shall I do with my boys?" Such
an institution would meet the wants of such persons. Then, too,
the establishment of such an institution would be in character with
the eminently practical philanthropy of your trans-Atlantic friends.
America could scarcely object to it as an attempt to agitate the
public mind on the subject of slavery, or to *dissolve the Union*. It
could not be tortured into a cause for hard words by the American
people, but the noble and good of all classes would see in the effort
an excellent motive, a benevolent object, temperately, wisely, and
practically manifested.

Wishing, you, dear madam, renewed health, a pleasant passage,
and safe return to your native land.

> I am most truly, your grateful friend,
> FREDERICK DOUGLASS.[35]

The following letter of Anthony Burns, extradited as a
fugitive slave, then in Boston, offers further opportunity for
the study of the man about whom there was so much contemporary comment:

ANTHONY BURNS TO THE BAPTIST CHURCH AT UNION, FAUQUIER CO., VIRGINIA

"In answer to my request by mail, under date July 13,
1855, for a letter of dismission in fellowship and of recommendation to another church, I have received a copy of the
Front Royal Gazette, dated Nov. 8, 1855, in which I find a
communication addressed to myself and signed by John
Clark, as pastor of your body, covering your official action
upon my request, as follows:

"THE CHURCH OF JESUS CHRIST, AT UNION, FAUQUIER CO., VIRGINIA.

"To all whom it may concern:

Whereas, Anthony Burns, a member of this church, has made
application to us, by a letter to our pastor, for a letter of dismission,
in fellowship, in order that he may unite with another church of the
same faith and order; and whereas, it has been satisfactorily

---

[35] John Lobb, *Life and Times of Frederick Douglass* (London, 1882), pp. 248–
252.

established before us, that the said Anthony Burns absconded from the service of his master, and refused to return voluntarily—thereby disobeying both the laws of God and man; although he subsequently obtained his freedom by purchase, yet we have now to consider him only as a *fugitive from labor* (as he was before his arrest and restoration to his master), have therefore

"*Resolved*, Unanimously, that he be excommunicated from the communion and fellowship of this church.

"Done by order of the church, in regular church meeting, this twentieth day of October, 1855.

                              "WM. W. WEST, *Clerk.*"

Thus you have excommunicated me, on the charge of "disobeying both the laws of God and men," "in absconding from the service of my master, and refusing to return voluntarily."

I admit that I left my master (so called), and refused to return; but I deny that in this I disobeyed either the law of God, or any real *law* of men.

Look at my case. I was stolen and made a slave as soon as I was born. No man had any right to steal me. That manstealer who stole me trampled on my dearest rights. He committed an outrage on the law of God; therefore his manstealing gave him no right in me, and laid me under no obligation to be his slave. God made me a *man*—not a *slave;* and gave me the same right to myself that he gave the man who stole me to himself. The great wrongs he has done me, in stealing me and making me a slave, in compelling me to work for him many years without wages, and in holding me as merchandize,—these wrongs could never put me under obligation to stay with him, or to return voluntarily, when once escaped.

You charge me that, in escaping, I disobeyed God's law. No, indeed! That law which God wrote on the table of my heart, inspiring the love of freedom, and impelling me to seek it at every hazard, I obeyed, and, by the good hand of my God upon me, I walked out of the house of bondage.

I disobeyed no law of God revealed in the Bible. I read in Paul (Cor. 7: 21), "But, if thou mayest be made free, use it rather." I read in Moses (Deut. 23: 15, 16), "Thou shalt not deliver unto his master the servant which is escaped from his master unto thee. He shall dwell with thee, even among you in that place which he shall choose in one of thy gates, where it liketh him best; thou shalt not oppress him." This implies my right to flee if I feel myself oppressed, and debars any man from delivering me again to my professed master.

I said I was stolen. God's Word declares, "He that stealeth a man and selleth him, or if he be found in his hand, he shall surely be put to death." (Ex. 21: 16.) Why did you not execute God's law on the man who stole me from my mother's arms? How is it that you trample down God's law against the *oppressor*, and wrest it to condemn me, the *innocent* and *oppressed?* Have you forgotten that the New Testament classes "mansteaalers" with "murderers of fathers" and "murderers of mothers," with "manslayers and whoremongers?" (1 Tim. 1: 9, 10.)

The advice you volunteered to send me, along with this sentence of excommunication, exhorts me, when I shall come to preach like Paul, to send every runaway home to his master, as he did Onesimus to Philemon. Yes, indeed I would, *if you would let me.* I should love to send them back *as he did*, "NOT NOW AS A SERVANT, but *above a servant:*—A BROTHER—a brother beloved—both in *the flesh* and in the Lord;" both a brother-man, and a brother-Christian. Such a relation would be delightful—to be put on a level, in position, with Paul himself. "If thou count me, therefore, a *partner*, receive him *as myself*." I would to God that every fugitive had the privilege of returning to such a condition—to the embrace of *such* a *Christianity*—"not now as a servant, but above a servant,"—a "partner,"—even as Paul himself was to Philemon!

You charge me with disobeying the *laws of men.* I utterly deny that those things which outrage all right are laws. To be real laws, they must be founded in equity.

You have thrust me out of your church fellowship. So be it. You can do no more. You cannot exclude me from heaven; you cannot hinder my daily fellowship with God.

You have used your liberty of speech freely in exhorting and rebuking me. You are aware that I too am now where I may think for myself, and can use great freedom of speech, too, if I please. I shall therefore be only returning the favor of your exhortation if I exhort you to study carefully the golden rule, which reads, "All things whatsoever ye would that men should do to you, do ye even so to them; for this is the law and the prophets." Would you like to be *stolen*, and then *sold?* and then worked without wages? and forbidden to read the Bible? and be torn from your wife and children? and then, if you were able to make yourself free, and should, as Paul said, *"use it rather,"* would you think it quite right to be cast out of the church for this? If it were done, so wickedly, would you be afraid God would indorse it? Suppose you were to put your soul in my soul's stead; how would *you* read the law of love?

ANTHONY BURNS.[37]

In the following correspondence Austin Steward, a leading Negro colonizer in Canada, harks back to the factional strife among the antislavery workers, but at the same time throws sufficient light on other matters to justify their insertion here.

A. STEWARD TO WM. L. GARRISON

MR. GARRISON,

Dear Sir:—In a recent examination of the business transactions between the Board of Managers of the Wilberforce Colony, and their agent Rev. N. Paul, I find a charge made by him, and allowed by the board, of the sum of two hundred dollars, which he paid to yourself. Finding no receipt or acknowledgement from you, I write to ask you to favor me with one, or an explanation of the facts in the case, either of which will greatly oblige me, as I design to make it public.

Truly yours, &c.,

A. STEWARD.

CANANDAIGUA, N. Y., May, 1856.[38]

MR. GARRISON'S REPLY TO A. STEWARD

DEAR SIR:

You state that Rev. N. Paul, as agent for the Wilberforce Settlement, U. C., in rendering his accounts on his return from England, charged the Board of Managers with the sum of two hundred dollars, paid by him to me while in England; that said sum was allowed by the board; adding that you do not recollect of my acknowledging or giving credit to the Settlement for it.

In reply, I can only assure you that there must be a mistake in regard to this item. I borrowed no money, nor had I any occasion

[37] C. E. Stevens, *Anthony Burns, A History,* 280–283.
[38] Austin Steward, *Twenty-two Years a Slave and Forty Years a Freeman,* 341–360. See also *The Journal of Negro History,* X, 365–375.

to ask a loan of my friend Paul, my expenses being defrayed by funds contributed by friends in this country; nor could I with propriety receive, nor he give me any part of the money contributed for the benefit of the Wilberforce Settlement; hence a loan or gift from him, could have been nothing more than a personal matter between ourselves. Moreover, had he at that time or any other, given me in good faith the sum named as belonging to the Settlement, (believing that as we were laboring together, for the interest of one common cause, the board would not hesitate to allow it,) he would certainly have demanded a receipt, which it would have pleased me to give, of course, that he might satisfy the board that their liberality had been disbursed according to their wishes, or his judgment. But receiving no money from your agent, will be a sufficient reason for not acknowledging it, or giving due credit to the Settlement.

I can account for this charge on his part, in no way, except that as he was with me a part of the time I was in London, and we traveled together a part of the time, during which, he ably and effectively assisted me in exposing that most iniquitous combination, "The American Colonization Society,"—he charged to me, (that is, to my mission) sundry items of expense which he undoubtedly believed justly incurred by his helping me to open the eyes of British philanthropists to the real design of that society; and I shall ever remember with gratitude, his heartiness and zeal in the cause and in my behalf. I owe much to the success that so signally crowned my mission, to his presence, testimony, and eloquent denunciation of the colonization scheme. I, however, received no money from him, and can but think that the above explanation was the occasion of his making the charge, and which I trust will leave on his memory, no intentional wrong.

WM. L. GARRISON

BOSTON, MASS., June 1856.[*]

[*] Garrison, of course, like many other white friends, gave the Negroes whatever advice and assistance he could.

INDEX

A

Abolitionists, Negro, 159–510
Actkins, N. H., letter of, 592
Adams, Enos, 181
Africa, 1–158, 221, 243
Africans, opinion of, 233
Alabama, colonization in, 63–74
Alexander, Mr., a friend of temperance, 418
Allen, William G., letters of, 282–290, 361
Allen, Macon B., letter of, 280–281
Allen, Joseph, 322
Allen, Bishop Richard, 224
Allen, Rev. Mr., 321
Allen, 323
Ambie, Nat, letter of, 569
American Colonization Society, letters to, 1–158
American Convention for Promoting the Abolition of Slavery, letter to, 236–237
Anderson, Francis S., letter of, 266–267
Anderson, Col. P. H., letter to, 537–539
Anderson, Jacob, letter from, 54–55
Anderson, Jourdon, letter from, 537–539
Andrews, Mr., 464
Anonymous letters, 220–244, 616–617
Anthony, Susan B., 374, 375, 376, 377, 379, 380, 383
Anticorn Law movement, 417
Antislavery workers and agencies, letters to, 159–510; the question of, 630–634, 635–637
Armstead, Mary D., letter of, 565–566
Artist, N. D., letters of, 97–106
Ashburton, Lord, 255
Ashburton treaty, 254
Association of Education and Industry, 250, 253
Atkinson, John, letter of, 606

Atkinson, W. H., letter of, 606
Attucks, Crispus, 349
Auld, Thomas, letters to, 202, 210, 419, 428, 449
Australia, mention of, for colonization, 244

B

Bailey, Job, 320
Bailey, Dr., 286
Baker, David, 375
Baker, E. W., letter of, 97
Ball, Joseph, letter of, 617
Ball, Oscar D., letter of, 613
Ballard, George, letter of, 615–616
Baltimore, George H., letters from, 48–50
Baltimore, letter from a Negro in, 152–153
Banks, G., letter to, 627–628
Banneker, Benjamin, letters and papers of, XXII–XXXII
Barlon, John, letter of, 151
Bartlett, J. B., 322
Beebe, Benjamin S., letters of, 127–131
Beecher, H. W., lecture by, 332
Bell, Phillip A., note, 193
Bell, Rebecca Fenwick, 257
Bell, William, 181, 185
Beman, Rev. J. C., 337
Bennett, Edward, 321
Benson, George W., 256
Bibb, Henry, letter to, 554; letter from, 554–555
Birney, Judge, 316
Bland, James M., letter from, 74
Blockson, Jacob, letter of, 618
Bodine, L., 257
Bolling, Peter B., letters from, 51–52
Borden, N. A., 257
Bostonian, a colored, letter from, 222
Boural, W., letter, 594–595
Bowen, Nathaniel, letter of, 154–155

Bradburn, George, 301
Bradley, Henry, 354, 355
Bremer, Fredrieka, 291
Brice, Catherine, letter of, 620
Bridgeman, 317
Briggs, Governor, 430
Briggs, Rev. Mr., 323
Brinkly, William, 567–568
Broadhus, John A., letter to, 536–537
Brooklyn, the colored women of, a letter from, to John Brown, 509–510
Brooklyn, a letter from a colored citizen in, 238
Brooks, Isaac, 376
Brooks, James, 423
Brown, Anthony and Albert, letter of, 605
Brown, Caesar, letter from, 511–512
Brown, Charles, 383
Brown, Emma, letter of, 568
Brown, James C., communications from, mentioned, 184
Brown, John, letters on, 505–510
Brown, Josephine, school of, 363–364
Brown, Sophia, letter to, 511–512
Brown, Stepney, letters of, 619–620
Brown, William Wells, letters of, 213–216, 349–383; mention of, 286
Buchanan, James, 382, 508
Budd, J., letter to, 626
Buffum, 324, 394, 398, 405, 408
Burleigh, letter addressed to, 178
Burlingame, Anson, 339
Burnham, W. H., letter from, 90
Burns, Anthony, letters of, 268–269, 659–662
Burr, 351
Burrell, Lewis, letter of, 612–613
Bustill, Joseph C., letters from, 529–530, 560–561; letters to, 531–536
Butcher, Jos., letter addressed to, 178
Butler, John, 385
Butler, Peter, letters from, 93–94, 189
Buxton, Sir Edward North, Bart, 414

C

Cabot, Miss, 285
California, proposed for colonization, 244
Camp, Abraham, 2–3

Campbell, J. P., 346
Campbell, Dr., 416, 418, 419
Campbell, Rev. Dr., 200, 201
Campbell's, Mr., 393
Canada, 179–191, 283, 504, 625–629, 637–638, 662–663
Canfield, Philemon, 330
Central America, emigration to, proposed, 494–504
Chace, 317
Chandler of Concord, 326
Chapman, Maria W., 195
Charleston, a free man of color from, 4–8
Chase, Ex-Senator, 370
Child, L. Maria, 508
Chinn, Judge, of Louisiana, 355
Christiana, the affair of, 263
Clapp, H., 431
Clapp, Mr., 384
Clark, J. Freeman, 286
Clark, Peter H., letter of, 132–133
Clarke, Geo. L., letter addressed to, 177
Clarkson, Thomas, 167
Clay, Cassius M., the press of, 395; paper of, 404
Clay, Henry, 302
Clayton, John, letter from, 565
Clayton, J. M., 356
Cleveland, Frederick Douglass in, 485; Negroes in, 380–382
Cobb, Lewis, letters of, 611–612
Cobden, Richard, 357, 359
Codding, Ichabod, 294
Coddington, William, 172
Cole, Thomas, letters of, 171–174, 295, 307
Collins, 311, 315
Collins, Rev. Mr., 325
Colman, Mrs., 379, 380
Colonization, 159–164, 230, 238–239, 244, 246, 283, 309, 494–505, 651–653
Colonization Society, the American, letters to, 1–158
Colonizationists, 159, 160, 161, 162, 163, 167, 227, 228, 238, 239, 240, 243, 244, 252, 309, 310, 336
"Colored American," a letter from, 241–244

"Colored Baltimorean, a," letter from, 238–241
"Colored Citizen of Brooklyn, a," a letter from, 238
"Colored Citizens of Chicago," a letter from, to John Brown, 508
"Colored Gentleman in Maryland," a letter from, 235–236
"Colored lady," a letter from, 230–232
Colson, Sarah H., letter to, 518–519, 520–521
Colver, Rev. N., 312
Committee of Thirteen, 291
Concord Latimer Convention, 254
Controversial correspondence, 179–202
Cook, an insurgent at Harper's Ferry, 505
Cook, John F., letter from, 53
Cooper, G. M., 350
Cooper, William, letter from, 570
Copeland, 348
Cornish, Samuel E., letter of, 625–626
Cox, Samuel Hanson, letter to, 432, 442
Craft, William and Ellen, letters of, 262–265; mention of, 339, 340
Crane, A. J., letter of, 97
Crawford, James E., 338
Cresson, Elliott, 168, 310
Crummell, Alexander, 348
Cuffee, Paul, 278
Cutler, J. B., letter of, 191–192
"C. D. T.," a Philadelphian, letter of, 161–163

D

Dade, John, letter of, 617
Dangerfield, Abraham, 181
Dartmouth College, 277, 341
Davis, Mr., 390
Davis, Rev. Mr., 346
Day, William H., 368
De Lamotta, C. L., letter of, 110–115
De Tocqueville, M., 357
Dean, Mr., 384
Delany, John, letter of, 614
Delany, Martin R., letters of, 292–293, 502
Dennison, H. M., 370
Deputie, Charles, letters of, 149–151
Dewey, Orville, reply of Dr. J. McCune Smith to, 270–280

Dick, John, 328
Dickerson, A. H., letter of, 123
Discrimination on account of color, 444–448; in education, 485–488
Donar, William, letter from, 601–602
Douglass, Frederick, letters concerning, 196–202, 341–344; letters of, 202–213, 384–490, 505–508, 653–659; mention of, 293, 318, 319, 365; purchase of, 448–458
Douglass, Lewis, letters of, 540–544
Douglass, R., 297
Douglass, Sara, 257
Dow, Lorenzo, 382
Downing, George T., letter of, 348–349
Dred Scott Decision, 507
Drew, James, a letter from, 13–14
Dublin, Frederick Douglass in, 409, 410
Dublin, Lord Mayor of, 394
Dungy, J. W., letters of, 621–624
Dunstan, letter from, 52
Dutton, Stephen, 184
Duval, Mr., 267

E

East India, 306
Eden, William, letter from, 528–529
Edons, Richard, letter from, 575
Educational efforts, 340, 341, 654–658
Elebeck, H. H., letter from, 520–521
Elgin, Harriett, letters of, 593–594
Elliott, C. W., cited, 497
Emancipation Act of New York, 271
Emerson, R. W., 332
Emigration to Central America, letters on, 494–504
England, Negro abolitionists in, 164, 165, 166, 168
Ennals, Sara, 257
Estlin, John B., 263, 285, 363
"Euthymus," a letter from, 232–234
Evans, Alfred, letter from, 53–54

F

Fair, A. S., 322
Farlan, Terry McHenry, 157–158
Fayetteville, N. C., trouble at, 229
Fenemur, Mariah, letter of, 109–110
Fillmore, Millard, 290
Findlay, W. W., letters of, 122, 651–653

Follen, Mrs., 285
Folsom of Dover, 326, 327
Ford, L., 322
Ford, Sheridan, letter from, 559–560
Forman, Isaac, letters of, 566–567
Forman, James H., letters from, 600–601
Forten, James, letter of, 174–175
Foss, Andrew T., 379, 380
Foster, S. S., 320, 321, 322, 323
Foster, 315, 463
Frazer River, mention of, for colonization, 244
Frederick Douglass's Paper, 195
Free Church, 415, 422, 428
Freeland, George W., letter of, 596
Free Trade Club, 421–422
French, J. R., of Concord, 326, 327
Fugitive Slave Bill, 247
Fugitive Slave Law, ravages of, 332, 334
Fugitive Slaves, letters of, to former owners, 202–220
Fugitives, letters from, 607, 544–624, 642–648, 659–662
Fuller, 304
"F. E. W.," 508–509

G

Galusha, 304
Garner, Margarett, 348
Garnet, H. H., letter of, 193–195; mention of, 346
Garrison, Wm. Lloyd, letters addressed to the paper of, 159–490
Gates, Seth M., 352
Gatewood, W. H., letter from, 554; letter to, 554–555
Gault, Flarece P., letter of, 578
Gay, S. H., 317, 318, 353
Giddings, Joshua R., 336
Gilliam, William Henry, letters of, 564–565
Glasgow, Frederick Douglass in, 412–414
Grant, Elihu, 324
Graves, Caroline, letter from, 610
Gray, James B., 387
Green, Samuel, letter from, 596
Green, 348

Greenwood, Grace, 463
Grosvenor, 304
Gurley, Rev. Mr., 310, 311

H

Hackley, Richard, letter from, 536–537
Hale, John P., a classmate, 3, 336
Hall, John, letter from, 596–599
"Ham and Eggs," letter from, 559
Hamlin, Myron, 354
Hammett, Rev. Mr., 239, 240, 241
Hammon, Jupiter, sketch of, VI; address of, to the Negroes of New York, VII–XVI
Hammond, Governor, letters of, 401
"Hannibal," a letter from, 227
Harlow, 323
Harper's Ferry, John Brown at, 505–510
Harris, Alexander, letter of, 109
Harris, J. D., a letter from, 504
Harris, Philip, 181, 189
Harris, Sion, letter from, 84
Harrisburg, mob at, 468–470
Hathaway, J. C., 350, 351, 353, 355
Haughton, James, 396, 397
Hayden, Lewis, 336
Hayti, proposed for colonization, 235, 494–505; mention of, 426
Hazard, Mr., of Connecticut, 401–402
Heath, H. A., 374, 375
Henson, Josiah, 365
Hewitt, Rodolphus W., 352
Hewitt, Rev. Mr., 321
Higgins, Mary, a letter from, 95–96
Hill, John H., letters of, 558–559, 563, 579–591
Hilliard, Frances, letter of, 603
Hilton, Elijah, letter of, 577–578
Hilton, J. T., 193
Hinton, Frederick A., 325, 326
Hodgkin, Dr., 168
Holbert, Lewis C., letters from, 47–48
Holly, J. Theodore, 125–127; a letter from, 495–500
Holly, Myron, 333
Holly, Sallie, 333
Hopper, Isaac T., 258
Hopper, John, 258
Howland, Mr., 383

Hudson, Erasmus D., 256
Hughes, Branch, letter from, 52
Hugo, Victor, 357
Hunt, Washington, 290
Hutchinson of Lynn, 326
Hutchinson family, 399
"H. O. W." and others, 508

I

Indian race, 273

J

Jackson, Andrew, 382
Jackson, Charles, 185
Jackson, Francis, letter to, 298
Jackson, Henry, meeting house of, 393
Jackson, Sherry J., letters from, 61-63
Jamieson, Josephine, letter to, 539-540
Jarvis, Dr., of Dorchester, 275
Jay, John, 258
Jays, 278
Jeffers, W., 297
Jinnings, Thomas, 257
Johnson, Andrew, 503
Johnson, Robert, 337
Johnson, Samuel W., 576-577
Jones, Bynar, letters of, 549, 550
Jones, John, a letter from, 9-10
Jones, John W., letter of, 155-156
Jones, Louisa F., letter of, 624
Jones, Rebecca, letter from, 608
Jones, Robert, letter from, 601
Jones, S. Wesley, letter from, 63-74
Jones, Thomas, 385
Jones, Thomas H., letters of, 545-551
Jones, Watkins, letter from, 95
Jones, William, letter from, 562
Jordan, J. B., letters of, 116-122
Joycelin, 322
Judson, Andrew T., letter to, 167-168;
    mention of, 169

K

"Kale," letter from, 553-554
Kansas, migration to, 501
Ketchum, Hiram, 258
Kidnapping, 638-642
Kirk, James, 329
Kirk, Rev. Mr., of Boston, 421, 439,
    442

Kline, 318
Knapp, 244
Knight, John, letter from, 610
Kossuth, L., references to visit and
    mission of, 288, 289, 290, 291, 292

L

Lafayette College, 277
Lafayette's errand, 333
Lane, James D., 258
Latimer, George, 384, 386, 387, 388, 389
Leary, 348
Lee, Daniel, 303
"Leo," a letter from, 223
Leonard, Elias, 353
Letters Largely Personal or Private, 511-
    624
*Letters to the American Colonization
    Society*, 1-158
*Letters to Antislavery Workers and
    Agencies*, 159-510
Lewis, Edward, letter of, 615
Lewis, Israel, 181, 184, 185, 186, 187,
    188, 189, 190
Lewis, Samuel J., letters from, 88-90
Lewis, Rev. Mr., 389
Liberator, quotations from, 159-510
Liberia, 1-158, 309, 503, 518-521
Liberty party, 462
Lind, Jenny, 291
Logue, Sara, letter from, 217-218
Loguen, H. Amelia, letters of, 540-544
Loguen, J. W., a letter to, 216-219;
    letters of, 267-268, 576; mention of,
    339
Longevity, 274, 275
Lord, John, 332
Lord, Rev. Mr., 323
Loveredge, P., 257
Lugenbeel, J. W., 503
Lundy, Benjamin, 186, 235
Lyon, Cecelia D., letter from, 50
"L. D. Y.," signature, 389

M

McDuffie, George, 194
McKim, J. Miller, 286, 361
"Man of Color, a," a letter from, 220-
    222, 225, 227
Manly protest, 177-178

Mann, Alexander, 329
Mann, Bureell W., letters from, 15–47
Mann, Horace, attack on theories of, 282–284; mention of, 336
Mann, Rev. Mr., 323
Marsh, E. M., 195
Marshall, Seth, 259
Martyrdom of John Brown, letters on, 505–510
Maryland, a letter from a colored gentleman in, 235–236; a slave trader in, 246
Masey, Jame, letter from, 573–574
Massachusetts Emigrant Aid Society, 503
Matthew, Father, 396, 405, 406, 407, 489
May, Samuel J., 332; letters to, 635–637, 653
May, Rev. Mr., 267, 314
Mead, 318
Mercer, James, letter from, 563
Metter, Albert, letter of, 605
Mexico, proposed for colonization, 235
Migration to Kansas, 501
Miles, Archibald, 341
Miles, Samuel, letter of, 603–604
Miller, John, letter from, 516–517; letter to, 517
Miscellaneous Letters, 625–663
Missionary Society, Mobile Colored, letter from, 157
Mitchell, Sam'l V., letter from, 94–95
Mitchell, Alderman, decision of, 178
Mob in action, 468
Mobile, colonization in, 124–125
Mobile Colored Missionary Society, letter from, 157
Mobley, Hardy, letters of, 145–146
Monroe, 317, 318
Moody, Samson Harris, a letter of, 236–237
Moore, Charles, letters of, 152
Moore, Mary, letter of, 108
Moore, Mrs., 311
Morris, Henry James, letter of, 607
Morris, John B., 339
Morris, Robert, caution of, 337
Morris, Thomas, 371
Moshell, John, letter from, 523

Mott, 318
Moulton, 323
Moxhay, George, 459
Murray, John, 301
Murrays, 278
Murry, Joseph, statement of, 190
"M. S. J. T.," 509

N

Nash, Alanson, 258
Negro Abolitionists in England, 287, 295, 296–297, 298, 299
"Negro in Baltimore, a," 152
"Negro in Savannah, a," 4
Nell, William C., 200, 201, 257, 338; letters of, 328–348, 635–637
New Orleans, colonization in, 116–122
New York, Emancipation Act of, 270; African Free School, 273; Negro population of, 279
"Niggers and Nastiness," 444
Northampton Association of Education and Industry, 250, 253, 255
North Carolina, Governor of, 236

O

Oberlin, 277
Ockham School, Wm. and Ellen Craft at, 262, 263, 264, 265
O'Conner, Wm., 406
O'Connell, Daniel, 176, 301, 302, 303, 306, 396, 397, 398
Ohio, 482, 483, 484
Olmsted, F. L., cited, 497
Onderdonk, Bishop, letter of, 629–630
Oneida Institute, 277
Opinions of a free man of color, 4–8

P

Packard, 318
Page, Thomas F., 609–610
Paney, John W., 352
Parker, Theodore, 332, 345
Parliament, visit of Frederick Douglass to, 421
Parthian Warfare, 280
Paul, Benjamin, 181, 186
Paul, Nathaniel, letters of, 163–170, 628–629; in controversy, 179, 180, 182, 183, 625–630, 637–638, 662–663

Payne, Alfred, letter from, 95–96
Peace Congress in Paris, 355, 356, 357, 358, 359
Pearson, Rev. Mr., 323
Pease, Elizabeth, 303
Pennington, J. W. C., 389, 390; letters of, 556, 642–651
Personal letters, 511–624
Peterson, John, 257
Peterson, Samuel, 189
Petrigen, Mr., private secretary, 469
Philadelphia, Negro Church in, 9–10
"Philadelphian, a colored," letters from, 224–225, 227–230
Phillips, Charles Estlin, 264
Phillips, W. P., 324, 332, 351
Pierpont, John, 332
Pillsbury, Parker, 316, 362
Pipkins, Jefferson, letter from, 573
Pittman, Wm. R., 324
Platt, Henrietta Jane, 353
Plummer, Adam, letters of, 523–528
Plummer, Emily, letters to, 523–528
Population, Negro, 270–280
Portlette, Medard, letters of, 512–516
Portlette, William, sketch of, 512
Post, Amy, 335
Post, Isaac, 335
Powell, William P., letter of, 246–247, 287
Powell, Mr., 374, 375, 376, 377, 378, 379, 383
Price, Capt. Enoch, 213
Prigg vs. *Pennsylvania*, 253
Private Correspondence, 511–624
Prudence, 318
Pugh, Miss Sarah, 286
Purchase of Frederick Douglass, 448–458
Purvis, Robert, letters of, 175–179, 195–196; mention of, 257
Purvis, Sara Forten, 257
Putnam, George W., of Lynn, 344

Q

Quincy, E., 317

R

"R," a letter from, 161
Randolph, John, son of, 372

Ray, C. B., 193, note
Reason, P., 257
Remond, Charles Lenox, letters of, 294–328; mention of, 200, 340, 353, 384, 386, 405
Remond, Miss, 178
Richardson, Eliza, 257
Richardson, James, 171
Richardson, James, Jr., 171
Richardson, Wm., 311
Richmond, Virginia, Negroes in, 15–47; attitude of white Churchmen of, toward slaves, 15–47
Rights, civil and social, 649–651
Robbins, 318
Roberts, J. J., letter from, 518–519
Robertson, Daniel, letter from, 608–609
Robertson, Ross, statement of, 191
Robinson, David, letter of, 595
Robinson, Joseph, letter of, 568
Rogers, N. P., 300, 301, 303, 304, 308, 311, 315, 326, 327
Ruggles, David, letters of, 250–260, 638–642
Rush, Christopher, 277
Rush, Stephen Christopher, 256
Rushton, Dr., 313
Russwurm, John B., 2; letters concerning, 160, 161–163

S

Sample, Geo., letter of, 153
Sanderson, J. B., 350, 385, 386
Saunders, Ellen, letter of, 602
Savannah, a letter from a Negro in, 4
Saxe, John G., 332
Saxton, Henry, letter of, 149
Schools, struggle of Negro to enter, in Boston, 340
Scoble, Mr., 414, 416
Scott, John, letter of, 569
Sedgwick, Theodore, 258
Segregation, 649–651
Seward Seminary, conditions at, 485–488
Sharpe, Rev. James, 187, 191
Sherman, Anthony, letters of, 147–149
Shropshire, Titus, letters from, 55–61
Slave trade, Texan, 273

Slavery and the Church, letters on, 490–494
Smith, Edwards, letter of, 107–108
Smith, Gerrit, 291
Smith, Rev. J. B., 337
Smith, James L., letter of, 260–262
Smith, Dr. James McCune, letters of, 270–280; mention of, 257, 348
Smith, Patterson, letter of, 595
Smith, Thomas G., letter from, 81–83
Smith of Nashua, 326
Soule, 322
South America, proposal to colonize, with Negroes of United States, 494–504
South Carolinian, a letter from a, 4–8
Southworth, 318
Spalding, Lyman A., letter of, 625
Spooner, Bourne, 322
Spooner and sons, 323
Spear, J. M., 320, 322
Springfield, Massachusetts, colonization in, 128–131; Negroes in, 129–131
Starkey, James R., letters from, 76–81
Stebbins, G. B., 350, 355
Stetson, 322
Stevens, 323
Steward, Austin, statements of, 180–181, 184–187, 188–189, 190–191; letter to, 625, 662–663; letters of, 625–629, 637–638, 662
Stewart, C. A., letter from, 539–540
Stewart, H. B., letter from, 84–88
Stewart, Lord Dudley Coutts, 359
Still, William, letters to, 556–624
Stokes, Elie W., letter of, 115
Stone, James W., 339
Storer, F., 186
Stowe, Professor, 360
Strother, Daniel, letters from, 91–93
Stuart, Capt. Charles, 312
Sturge, Joseph, 284, 287, 415, 418, 419
Sutherland, Her Grace Duchess of, 306
Sumner, Alphonso M., letter from, 75
Sumner, Charles, 336
"S. R. W.," 290–292

T

Talbot, A., 187, 188, 190–191
Tappan, Lewis, 255

Taylor, Otho, letter from, 530
Taylor, E. Duglas, letter of, 123–125
Taylor, Zachary, 463
Teage, H., letter of, 115–116
Temperance, 405, 406, 407, 436, 437, 438, 439, 462
Testimony of Freedmen, in letters of, 260–270
Texan slave trade, 273
Thomas, John, 291, 292
Thomas, William, 322
Thomas, 323
Thompson, A. C. C., 212
Thompson, A. V., a letter from, 502–504
Thompson, C. W., letter from, 574–575
Thompson, George, 284, 299, 301, 302, 303, 305, 306, 307, 310, 333, 351, 358, 359, 414, 488, 489
Thompson, John, letter from, 561–562
Thompson, Mr. and Mrs., 420, 421, 422
Thurston, Rev. David, 294
Tomlinson, Rev. Mr., 323
Tompkins, 278
Torrey, Charles T., 196, 351
Townsend, Milo A., 463
Trusty, Henry, letter from, 574
Truth, Sojourner, 372, 373
Tucker, Professor, work of, 275
Turner, Edmund, letter from, 571–573
Tyler, John, 320

U

Uncle Tom's Cabin, 264
Underwood, Henri, letter of, 96
Upper Canada, colony in, 179

V

Van Buren, Martin, defeat of, 173
Van Wagenen, Peter, letters of, 552–553
Vashon, J. B., letter of, 244–246
Virginia, legislature of, 236

W

Wake, R. F., 257
Walker, David, 222–224
Walker, Jonathan, 351

Walker, Mr., 463

Walker, William J., letter from, 522

Walker's Appeal, 222-224

Ward, S. R., letters of, 290-292, 490-493; mention of, 285, 286, 361

Washington, Augustus, letter of, 133-144

Washington, Henry, letter from, 599-600

Watkins, Frances E., 346, 347; a letter from, 508-509

Watkins, William J., 338

Watson, W. W., 369

Webb, James H., 395, 399

Webb, Richard D., 356, 395, 399

Webb, Thomas, 395

Webster, Daniel, 264, 299, 302, 489

Weems, E., letter from, 579

West, John W., letter of, 146-147

West Indies, colonists directed to, 494-504

Western Theological Seminary, 277

Weston, Anthony, letter to, 528-529

Weston, Gershom, 322

Weston family, 393

Wheatley, Phillis, letters of, XVI-XXI

Whipper, Wm., 257

White, J. C., letters from, 531-532, 535-536

White, Noah, 385

White, Manuel T., letter from, 575

White, 317, 318

White Slave, 264

Whitehead, John, 189

Whitfield, J. M., letter from, 500-502

Whiting, N., 321, 322

Whitlemore, 322

Whitney, Israel, letter from, 570

Whittier, J. G., quoted, 313

Wilberforce, William, 166, 170

Wilberforce, Canada, 179-181, 182, 183, 184, 188

Wilcox, 259

Williams, J., 359

Williams, Peter, letter of, 630-634

Williams, Rev. Mr., 314

Wilmot, David, 377

Wilson, Hiram, 254

Wilson, Isaah T., letter of, 106-107

Wine, Lisbon, statement of, 189-190

Wing, George, 374

Winn, James, letter of, 131-132

Wise, Governor, of Virginia, 508

Women, colored, of Brooklyn, a letter from, to John Brown, 509-510

Wood, Miss, 178

Woods, John B., letter of, 614-615

Woodson, Lewis, letter of, 493-494

Work, 351

Wright, H. C., letter of, to Frederick Douglass, 448-451; reply of Douglass to, 452-458

Wright, 315

Wyatt, Simon, 181

W. J. W., letter of, 247-250

Z

Zuel, John J., 257

A CATALOG OF SELECTED
DOVER BOOKS
IN ALL FIELDS OF INTEREST

A CATALOG OF SELECTED DOVER
BOOKS IN ALL FIELDS OF INTEREST

100 BEST-LOVED POEMS, Edited by Philip Smith. "The Passionate Shepherd to His Love," "Shall I compare thee to a summer's day?" "Death, be not proud," "The Raven," "The Road Not Taken," plus works by Blake, Wordsworth, Byron, Shelley, Keats, many others. 96pp. 5³⁄₁₆ x 8¼.   0-486-28553-7

100 SMALL HOUSES OF THE THIRTIES, Brown-Blodgett Company. Exterior photographs and floor plans for 100 charming structures. Illustrations of models accompanied by descriptions of interiors, color schemes, closet space, and other amenities. 200 illustrations. 112pp. 8⅜ x 11.   0-486-44131-8

1000 TURN-OF-THE-CENTURY HOUSES: With Illustrations and Floor Plans, Herbert C. Chivers. Reproduced from a rare edition, this showcase of homes ranges from cottages and bungalows to sprawling mansions. Each house is meticulously illustrated and accompanied by complete floor plans. 256pp. 9⅜ x 12¼.
      0-486-45596-3

101 GREAT AMERICAN POEMS, Edited by The American Poetry & Literacy Project. Rich treasury of verse from the 19th and 20th centuries includes works by Edgar Allan Poe, Robert Frost, Walt Whitman, Langston Hughes, Emily Dickinson, T. S. Eliot, other notables. 96pp. 5³⁄₁₆ x 8¼.   0-486-40158-8

101 GREAT SAMURAI PRINTS, Utagawa Kuniyoshi. Kuniyoshi was a master of the warrior woodblock print — and these 18th-century illustrations represent the pinnacle of his craft. Full-color portraits of renowned Japanese samurais pulse with movement, passion, and remarkably fine detail. 112pp. 8⅜ x 11.   0-486-46523-3

ABC OF BALLET, Janet Grosser. Clearly worded, abundantly illustrated little guide defines basic ballet-related terms: arabesque, battement, pas de chat, relevé, sissonne, many others. Pronunciation guide included. Excellent primer. 48pp. 4³⁄₁₆ x 5¾.
      0-486-40871-X

ACCESSORIES OF DRESS: An Illustrated Encyclopedia, Katherine Lester and Bess Viola Oerke. Illustrations of hats, veils, wigs, cravats, shawls, shoes, gloves, and other accessories enhance an engaging commentary that reveals the humor and charm of the many-sided story of accessorized apparel. 644 figures and 59 plates. 608pp. 6 ⅛ x 9¼.
      0-486-43378-1

ADVENTURES OF HUCKLEBERRY FINN, Mark Twain. Join Huck and Jim as their boyhood adventures along the Mississippi River lead them into a world of excitement, danger, and self-discovery. Humorous narrative, lyrical descriptions of the Mississippi valley, and memorable characters. 224pp. 5³⁄₁₆ x 8¼.   0-486-28061-6

ALICE STARMORE'S BOOK OF FAIR ISLE KNITTING, Alice Starmore. A noted designer from the region of Scotland's Fair Isle explores the history and techniques of this distinctive, stranded-color knitting style and provides copious illustrated instructions for 14 original knitwear designs. 208pp. 8⅜ x 10⅞.   0-486-47218-3

Browse over 9,000 books at www.doverpublications.com

ALICE'S ADVENTURES IN WONDERLAND, Lewis Carroll. Beloved classic about a little girl lost in a topsy-turvy land and her encounters with the White Rabbit, March Hare, Mad Hatter, Cheshire Cat, and other delightfully improbable characters. 42 illustrations by Sir John Tenniel. 96pp. 5³⁄₁₆ x 8¼. 0-486-27543-4

AMERICA'S LIGHTHOUSES: An Illustrated History, Francis Ross Holland. Profusely illustrated fact-filled survey of American lighthouses since 1716. Over 200 stations — East, Gulf, and West coasts, Great Lakes, Hawaii, Alaska, Puerto Rico, the Virgin Islands, and the Mississippi and St. Lawrence Rivers. 240pp. 8 x 10¾. 0-486-25576-X

AN ENCYCLOPEDIA OF THE VIOLIN, Alberto Bachmann. Translated by Frederick H. Martens. Introduction by Eugene Ysaye. First published in 1925, this renowned reference remains unsurpassed as a source of essential information, from construction and evolution to repertoire and technique. Includes a glossary and 73 illustrations. 496pp. 6⅛ x 9¼. 0-486-46618-3

ANIMALS: 1,419 Copyright-Free Illustrations of Mammals, Birds, Fish, Insects, etc., Selected by Jim Harter. Selected for its visual impact and ease of use, this outstanding collection of wood engravings presents over 1,000 species of animals in extremely lifelike poses. Includes mammals, birds, reptiles, amphibians, fish, insects, and other invertebrates. 284pp. 9 x 12. 0-486-23766-4

THE ANNALS, Tacitus. Translated by Alfred John Church and William Jackson Brodribb. This vital chronicle of Imperial Rome, written by the era's great historian, spans A.D. 14-68 and paints incisive psychological portraits of major figures, from Tiberius to Nero. 416pp. 5³⁄₁₆ x 8¼. 0-486-45236-0

ANTIGONE, Sophocles. Filled with passionate speeches and sensitive probing of moral and philosophical issues, this powerful and often-performed Greek drama reveals the grim fate that befalls the children of Oedipus. Footnotes. 64pp. 5³⁄₁₆ x 8 ¼. 0-486-27804-2

ART DECO DECORATIVE PATTERNS IN FULL COLOR, Christian Stoll. Reprinted from a rare 1910 portfolio, 160 sensuous and exotic images depict a breathtaking array of florals, geometrics, and abstracts — all elegant in their stark simplicity. 64pp. 8⅜ x 11. 0-486-44862-2

THE ARTHUR RACKHAM TREASURY: 86 Full-Color Illustrations, Arthur Rackham. Selected and Edited by Jeff A. Menges. A stunning treasury of 86 full-page plates span the famed English artist's career, from *Rip Van Winkle* (1905) to masterworks such as *Undine, A Midsummer Night's Dream,* and *Wind in the Willows* (1939). 96pp. 8⅜ x 11. 0-486-44685-9

THE AUTHENTIC GILBERT & SULLIVAN SONGBOOK, W. S. Gilbert and A. S. Sullivan. The most comprehensive collection available, this songbook includes selections from every one of Gilbert and Sullivan's light operas. Ninety-two numbers are presented uncut and unedited, and in their original keys. 410pp. 9 x 12. 0-486-23482-7

THE AWAKENING, Kate Chopin. First published in 1899, this controversial novel of a New Orleans wife's search for love outside a stifling marriage shocked readers. Today, it remains a first-rate narrative with superb characterization. New introductory Note. 128pp. 5³⁄₁₆ x 8¼. 0-486-27786-0

BASIC DRAWING, Louis Priscilla. Beginning with perspective, this commonsense manual progresses to the figure in movement, light and shade, anatomy, drapery, composition, trees and landscape, and outdoor sketching. Black-and-white illustrations throughout. 128pp. 8⅜ x 11. 0-486-45815-6

Browse over 9,000 books at www.doverpublications.com

THE BATTLES THAT CHANGED HISTORY, Fletcher Pratt. Historian profiles 16 crucial conflicts, ancient to modern, that changed the course of Western civilization. Gripping accounts of battles led by Alexander the Great, Joan of Arc, Ulysses S. Grant, other commanders. 27 maps. 352pp. 5⅜ x 8½.   0-486-41129-X

BEETHOVEN'S LETTERS, Ludwig van Beethoven. Edited by Dr. A. C. Kalischer. Features 457 letters to fellow musicians, friends, greats, patrons, and literary men. Reveals musical thoughts, quirks of personality, insights, and daily events. Includes 15 plates. 410pp. 5⅜ x 8½.   0-486-22769-3

BERNICE BOBS HER HAIR AND OTHER STORIES, F. Scott Fitzgerald. This brilliant anthology includes 6 of Fitzgerald's most popular stories: "The Diamond as Big as the Ritz," the title tale, "The Offshore Pirate," "The Ice Palace," "The Jelly Bean," and "May Day." 176pp. 5⅜ x 8½.   0-486-47049-0

BESLER'S BOOK OF FLOWERS AND PLANTS: 73 Full-Color Plates from Hortus Eystettensis, 1613, Basilius Besler. Here is a selection of magnificent plates from the *Hortus Eystettensis*, which vividly illustrated and identified the plants, flowers, and trees that thrived in the legendary German garden at Eichstätt. 80pp. 8⅜ x 11.
0-486-46005-3

THE BOOK OF KELLS, Edited by Blanche Cirker. Painstakingly reproduced from a rare facsimile edition, this volume contains full-page decorations, portraits, illustrations, plus a sampling of textual leaves with exquisite calligraphy and ornamentation. 32 full-color illustrations. 32pp. 9⅜ x 12¼.   0-486-24345-1

THE BOOK OF THE CROSSBOW: With an Additional Section on Catapults and Other Siege Engines, Ralph Payne-Gallwey. Fascinating study traces history and use of crossbow as military and sporting weapon, from Middle Ages to modern times. Also covers related weapons: balistas, catapults, Turkish bows, more. Over 240 illustrations. 400pp. 7¼ x 10⅛.   0-486-28720-3

THE BUNGALOW BOOK: Floor Plans and Photos of 112 Houses, 1910, Henry L. Wilson. Here are 112 of the most popular and economic blueprints of the early 20th century — plus an illustration or photograph of each completed house. A wonderful time capsule that still offers a wealth of valuable insights. 160pp. 8⅜ x 11.
0-486-45104-6

THE CALL OF THE WILD, Jack London. A classic novel of adventure, drawn from London's own experiences as a Klondike adventurer, relating the story of a heroic dog caught in the brutal life of the Alaska Gold Rush. Note. 64pp. 5³⁄₁₆ x 8¼.
0-486-26472-6

CANDIDE, Voltaire. Edited by Francois-Marie Arouet. One of the world's great satires since its first publication in 1759. Witty, caustic skewering of romance, science, philosophy, religion, government — nearly all human ideals and institutions. 112pp. 5³⁄₁₆ x 8¼.   0-486-26689-3

CELEBRATED IN THEIR TIME: Photographic Portraits from the George Grantham Bain Collection, Edited by Amy Pastan. With an Introduction by Michael Carlebach. Remarkable portrait gallery features 112 rare images of Albert Einstein, Charlie Chaplin, the Wright Brothers, Henry Ford, and other luminaries from the worlds of politics, art, entertainment, and industry. 128pp. 8⅜ x 11.   0-486-46754-6

CHARIOTS FOR APOLLO: The NASA History of Manned Lunar Spacecraft to 1969, Courtney G. Brooks, James M. Grimwood, and Loyd S. Swenson, Jr. This illustrated history by a trio of experts is the definitive reference on the Apollo spacecraft and lunar modules. It traces the vehicles' design, development, and operation in space. More than 100 photographs and illustrations. 576pp. 6¾ x 9¼. 0-486-46756-2

Browse over 9,000 books at www.doverpublications.com

A CHRISTMAS CAROL, Charles Dickens. This engrossing tale relates Ebenezer Scrooge's ghostly journeys through Christmases past, present, and future and his ultimate transformation from a harsh and grasping old miser to a charitable and compassionate human being. 80pp. 5‰ x 8¼. 0-486-26865-9

COMMON SENSE, Thomas Paine. First published in January of 1776, this highly influential landmark document clearly and persuasively argued for American separation from Great Britain and paved the way for the Declaration of Independence. 64pp. 5‰ x 8¼. 0-486-29602-4

THE COMPLETE SHORT STORIES OF OSCAR WILDE, Oscar Wilde. Complete texts of "The Happy Prince and Other Tales," "A House of Pomegranates," "Lord Arthur Savile's Crime and Other Stories," "Poems in Prose," and "The Portrait of Mr. W. H." 208pp. 5‰ x 8¼. 0-486-45216-6

COMPLETE SONNETS, William Shakespeare. Over 150 exquisite poems deal with love, friendship, the tyranny of time, beauty's evanescence, death, and other themes in language of remarkable power, precision, and beauty. Glossary of archaic terms. 80pp. 5‰ x 8¼. 0-486-26686-9

THE COUNT OF MONTE CRISTO: Abridged Edition, Alexandre Dumas. Falsely accused of treason, Edmond Dantès is imprisoned in the bleak Chateau d'If. After a hair-raising escape, he launches an elaborate plot to extract a bitter revenge against those who betrayed him. 448pp. 5‰ x 8¼. 0-486-45643-9

CRAFTSMAN BUNGALOWS: Designs from the Pacific Northwest, Yoho & Merritt. This reprint of a rare catalog, showcasing the charming simplicity and cozy style of Craftsman bungalows, is filled with photos of completed homes, plus floor plans and estimated costs. An indispensable resource for architects, historians, and illustrators. 112pp. 10 x 7. 0-486-46875-5

CRAFTSMAN BUNGALOWS: 59 Homes from "The Craftsman," Edited by Gustav Stickley. Best and most attractive designs from Arts and Crafts Movement publication — 1903–1916 — includes sketches, photographs of homes, floor plans, descriptive text. 128pp. 8¼ x 11. 0-486-25829-7

CRIME AND PUNISHMENT, Fyodor Dostoyevsky. Translated by Constance Garnett. Supreme masterpiece tells the story of Raskolnikov, a student tormented by his own thoughts after he murders an old woman. Overwhelmed by guilt and terror, he confesses and goes to prison. 480pp. 5‰ x 8¼. 0-486-41587-2

THE DECLARATION OF INDEPENDENCE AND OTHER GREAT DOCUMENTS OF AMERICAN HISTORY: 1775-1865, Edited by John Grafton. Thirteen compelling and influential documents: Henry's "Give Me Liberty or Give Me Death," Declaration of Independence, The Constitution, Washington's First Inaugural Address, The Monroe Doctrine, The Emancipation Proclamation, Gettysburg Address, more. 64pp. 5‰ x 8¼. 0-486-41124-9

THE DESERT AND THE SOWN: Travels in Palestine and Syria, Gertrude Bell. "The female Lawrence of Arabia," Gertrude Bell wrote captivating, perceptive accounts of her travels in the Middle East. This intriguing narrative, accompanied by 160 photos, traces her 1905 sojourn in Lebanon, Syria, and Palestine. 368pp. 5⅜ x 8½. 0-486-46876-3

A DOLL'S HOUSE, Henrik Ibsen. Ibsen's best-known play displays his genius for realistic prose drama. An expression of women's rights, the play climaxes when the central character, Nora, rejects a smothering marriage and life in "a doll's house." 80pp. 5‰ x 8¼. 0-486-27062-9

DOOMED SHIPS: Great Ocean Liner Disasters, William H. Miller, Jr. Nearly 200 photographs, many from private collections, highlight tales of some of the vessels whose pleasure cruises ended in catastrophe: the *Morro Castle, Normandie, Andrea Doria, Europa,* and many others. 128pp. 8⅞ x 11¾. 0-486-45366-9

THE DORÉ BIBLE ILLUSTRATIONS, Gustave Doré. Detailed plates from the Bible: the Creation scenes, Adam and Eve, horrifying visions of the Flood, the battle sequences with their monumental crowds, depictions of the life of Jesus, 241 plates in all. 241pp. 9 x 12. 0-486-23004-X

DRAWING DRAPERY FROM HEAD TO TOE, Cliff Young. Expert guidance on how to draw shirts, pants, skirts, gloves, hats, and coats on the human figure, including folds in relation to the body, pull and crush, action folds, creases, more. Over 200 drawings. 48pp. 8¼ x 11. 0-486-45591-2

DUBLINERS, James Joyce. A fine and accessible introduction to the work of one of the 20th century's most influential writers, this collection features 15 tales, including a masterpiece of the short-story genre, "The Dead." 160pp. 5³⁄₁₆ x 8¼. 0-486-26870-5

EASY-TO-MAKE POP-UPS, Joan Irvine. Illustrated by Barbara Reid. Dozens of wonderful ideas for three-dimensional paper fun — from holiday greeting cards with moving parts to a pop-up menagerie. Easy-to-follow, illustrated instructions for more than 30 projects. 299 black-and-white illustrations. 96pp. 8⅜ x 11. 0-486-44622-0

EASY-TO-MAKE STORYBOOK DOLLS: A "Novel" Approach to Cloth Dollmaking, Sherralyn St. Clair. Favorite fictional characters come alive in this unique beginner's dollmaking guide. Includes patterns for Pollyanna, Dorothy from *The Wonderful Wizard of Oz,* Mary of *The Secret Garden,* plus easy-to-follow instructions, 263 black-and-white illustrations, and an 8-page color insert. 112pp. 8¼ x 11. 0-486-47360-0

EINSTEIN'S ESSAYS IN SCIENCE, Albert Einstein. Speeches and essays in accessible, everyday language profile influential physicists such as Niels Bohr and Isaac Newton. They also explore areas of physics to which the author made major contributions. 128pp. 5 x 8. 0-486-47011-3

EL DORADO: Further Adventures of the Scarlet Pimpernel, Baroness Orczy. A popular sequel to *The Scarlet Pimpernel,* this suspenseful story recounts the Pimpernel's attempts to rescue the Dauphin from imprisonment during the French Revolution. An irresistible blend of intrigue, period detail, and vibrant characterizations. 352pp. 5³⁄₁₆ x 8¼. 0-486-44026-5

ELEGANT SMALL HOMES OF THE TWENTIES: 99 Designs from a Competition, Chicago Tribune. Nearly 100 designs for five- and six-room houses feature New England and Southern colonials, Normandy cottages, stately Italianate dwellings, and other fascinating snapshots of American domestic architecture of the 1920s. 112pp. 9 x 12. 0-486-46910-7

THE ELEMENTS OF STYLE: The Original Edition, William Strunk, Jr. This is the book that generations of writers have relied upon for timeless advice on grammar, diction, syntax, and other essentials. In concise terms, it identifies the principal requirements of proper style and common errors. 64pp. 5⅜ x 8½. 0-486-44798-7

THE ELUSIVE PIMPERNEL, Baroness Orczy. Robespierre's revolutionaries find their wicked schemes thwarted by the heroic Pimpernel — Sir Percival Blakeney. In this thrilling sequel, Chauvelin devises a plot to eliminate the Pimpernel and his wife. 272pp. 5³⁄₁₆ x 8¼. 0-486-45464-9

Browse over 9,000 books at www.doverpublications.com

AN ENCYCLOPEDIA OF BATTLES: Accounts of Over 1,560 Battles from 1479 B.C. to the Present, David Eggenberger. Essential details of every major battle in recorded history from the first battle of Megiddo in 1479 B.C. to Grenada in 1984. List of battle maps. 99 illustrations. 544pp. 6½ x 9¼. 0-486-24913-1

ENCYCLOPEDIA OF EMBROIDERY STITCHES, INCLUDING CREWEL, Marion Nichols. Precise explanations and instructions, clearly illustrated, on how to work chain, back, cross, knotted, woven stitches, and many more — 178 in all, including Cable Outline, Whipped Satin, and Eyelet Buttonhole. Over 1400 illustrations. 219pp. 8⅜ x 11¼. 0-486-22929-7

ENTER JEEVES: 15 Early Stories, P. G. Wodehouse. Splendid collection contains first 8 stories featuring Bertie Wooster, the deliciously dim aristocrat and Jeeves, his brainy, imperturbable manservant. Also, the complete Reggie Pepper (Bertie's prototype) series. 288pp. 5⅜ x 8½. 0-486-29717-9

ERIC SLOANE'S AMERICA: Paintings in Oil, Michael Wigley. With a Foreword by Mimi Sloane. Eric Sloane's evocative oils of America's landscape and material culture shimmer with immense historical and nostalgic appeal. This original hardcover collection gathers nearly a hundred of his finest paintings, with subjects ranging from New England to the American Southwest. 128pp. 10⅜ x 9. 0-486-46525-X

ETHAN FROME, Edith Wharton. Classic story of wasted lives, set against a bleak New England background. Superbly delineated characters in a hauntingly grim tale of thwarted love. Considered by many to be Wharton's masterpiece. 96pp. 5³⁄₁₆ x 8 ¼. 0-486-26690-7

THE EVERLASTING MAN, G. K. Chesterton. Chesterton's view of Christianity — as a blend of philosophy and mythology, satisfying intellect and spirit — applies to his brilliant book, which appeals to readers' heads as well as their hearts. 288pp. 5⅜ x 8½. 0-486-46036-3

THE FIELD AND FOREST HANDY BOOK, Daniel Beard. Written by a co-founder of the Boy Scouts, this appealing guide offers illustrated instructions for building kites, birdhouses, boats, igloos, and other fun projects, plus numerous helpful tips for campers. 448pp. 5³⁄₁₆ x 8¼. 0-486-46191-2

FINDING YOUR WAY WITHOUT MAP OR COMPASS, Harold Gatty. Useful, instructive manual shows would-be explorers, hikers, bikers, scouts, sailors, and survivalists how to find their way outdoors by observing animals, weather patterns, shifting sands, and other elements of nature. 288pp. 5⅜ x 8½. 0-486-40613-X

FIRST FRENCH READER: A Beginner's Dual-Language Book, Edited and Translated by Stanley Appelbaum. This anthology introduces 50 legendary writers — Voltaire, Balzac, Baudelaire, Proust, more — through passages from *The Red and the Black, Les Misérables, Madame Bovary,* and other classics. Original French text plus English translation on facing pages. 240pp. 5⅜ x 8½. 0-486-46178-5

FIRST GERMAN READER: A Beginner's Dual-Language Book, Edited by Harry Steinhauer. Specially chosen for their power to evoke German life and culture, these short, simple readings include poems, stories, essays, and anecdotes by Goethe, Hesse, Heine, Schiller, and others. 224pp. 5⅜ x 8½. 0-486-46179-3

FIRST SPANISH READER: A Beginner's Dual-Language Book, Angel Flores. Delightful stories, other material based on works of Don Juan Manuel, Luis Taboada, Ricardo Palma, other noted writers. Complete faithful English translations on facing pages. Exercises. 176pp. 5⅜ x 8½. 0-486-25810-6

Browse over 9,000 books at www.doverpublications.com

FIVE ACRES AND INDEPENDENCE, Maurice G. Kains. Great back-to-the-land classic explains basics of self-sufficient farming. The one book to get. 95 illustrations. 397pp. 5⅜ x 8½. 0-486-20974-1

FLAGG'S SMALL HOUSES: Their Economic Design and Construction, 1922, Ernest Flagg. Although most famous for his skyscrapers, Flagg was also a proponent of the well-designed single-family dwelling. His classic treatise features innovations that save space, materials, and cost. 526 illustrations. 160pp. 9⅜ x 12¼.
0-486-45197-6

FLATLAND: A Romance of Many Dimensions, Edwin A. Abbott. Classic of science (and mathematical) fiction — charmingly illustrated by the author — describes the adventures of A. Square, a resident of Flatland, in Spaceland (three dimensions), Lineland (one dimension), and Pointland (no dimensions). 96pp. 5³⁄₁₆ x 8¼.
0-486-27263-X

FRANKENSTEIN, Mary Shelley. The story of Victor Frankenstein's monstrous creation and the havoc it caused has enthralled generations of readers and inspired countless writers of horror and suspense. With the author's own 1831 introduction. 176pp. 5³⁄₁₆ x 8¼. 0-486-28211-2

THE GARGOYLE BOOK: 572 Examples from Gothic Architecture, Lester Burbank Bridaham. Dispelling the conventional wisdom that French Gothic architectural flourishes were born of despair or gloom, Bridaham reveals the whimsical nature of these creations and the ingenious artisans who made them. 572 illustrations. 224pp. 8⅜ x 11. 0-486-44754-5

THE GIFT OF THE MAGI AND OTHER SHORT STORIES, O. Henry. Sixteen captivating stories by one of America's most popular storytellers. Included are such classics as "The Gift of the Magi," "The Last Leaf," and "The Ransom of Red Chief." Publisher's Note. 96pp. 5³⁄₁₆ x 8¼. 0-486-27061-0

THE GOETHE TREASURY: Selected Prose and Poetry, Johann Wolfgang von Goethe. Edited, Selected, and with an Introduction by Thomas Mann. In addition to his lyric poetry, Goethe wrote travel sketches, autobiographical studies, essays, letters, and proverbs in rhyme and prose. This collection presents outstanding examples from each genre. 368pp. 5⅜ x 8½. 0-486-44780-4

GREAT EXPECTATIONS, Charles Dickens. Orphaned Pip is apprenticed to the dirty work of the forge but dreams of becoming a gentleman — and one day finds himself in possession of "great expectations." Dickens' finest novel. 400pp. 5³⁄₁₆ x 8¼.
0-486-41586-4

GREAT WRITERS ON THE ART OF FICTION: From Mark Twain to Joyce Carol Oates, Edited by James Daley. An indispensable source of advice and inspiration, this anthology features essays by Henry James, Kate Chopin, Willa Cather, Sinclair Lewis, Jack London, Raymond Chandler, Raymond Carver, Eudora Welty, and Kurt Vonnegut, Jr. 192pp. 5⅜ x 8½. 0-486-45128-3

HAMLET, William Shakespeare. The quintessential Shakespearean tragedy, whose highly charged confrontations and anguished soliloquies probe depths of human feeling rarely sounded in any art. Reprinted from an authoritative British edition complete with illuminating footnotes. 128pp. 5³⁄₁₆ x 8¼. 0-486-27278-8

THE HAUNTED HOUSE, Charles Dickens. A Yuletide gathering in an eerie country retreat provides the backdrop for Dickens and his friends — including Elizabeth Gaskell and Wilkie Collins — who take turns spinning supernatural yarns. 144pp. 5⅜ x 8½. 0-486-46309-5

HEART OF DARKNESS, Joseph Conrad. Dark allegory of a journey up the Congo River and the narrator's encounter with the mysterious Mr. Kurtz. Masterly blend of adventure, character study, psychological penetration. For many, Conrad's finest, most enigmatic story. 80pp. 5³⁄₁₆ x 8¼.　　　　　　0-486-26464-5

HENSON AT THE NORTH POLE, Matthew A. Henson. This thrilling memoir by the heroic African-American who was Peary's companion through two decades of Arctic exploration recounts a tale of danger, courage, and determination. "Fascinating and exciting." — *Commonweal*. 128pp. 5⅜ x 8½.　　　　　　0-486-45472-X

HISTORIC COSTUMES AND HOW TO MAKE THEM, Mary Fernald and E. Shenton. Practical, informative guidebook shows how to create everything from short tunics worn by Saxon men in the fifth century to a lady's bustle dress of the late 1800s. 81 illustrations. 176pp. 5⅜ x 8½.　　　　　　0-486-44906-8

THE HOUND OF THE BASKERVILLES, Arthur Conan Doyle. A deadly curse in the form of a legendary ferocious beast continues to claim its victims from the Baskerville family until Holmes and Watson intervene. Often called the best detective story ever written. 128pp. 5³⁄₁₆ x 8¼.　　　　　　0-486-28214-7

THE HOUSE BEHIND THE CEDARS, Charles W. Chesnutt. Originally published in 1900, this groundbreaking novel by a distinguished African-American author recounts the drama of a brother and sister who "pass for white" during the dangerous days of Reconstruction. 208pp. 5⅜ x 8½.　　　　　　0-486-46144-0

THE HUMAN FIGURE IN MOTION, Eadweard Muybridge. The 4,789 photographs in this definitive selection show the human figure — models almost all undraped — engaged in over 160 different types of action: running, climbing stairs, etc. 390pp. 7⅞ x 10⅝.　　　　　　0-486-20204-6

THE IMPORTANCE OF BEING EARNEST, Oscar Wilde. Wilde's witty and buoyant comedy of manners, filled with some of literature's most famous epigrams, reprinted from an authoritative British edition. Considered Wilde's most perfect work. 64pp. 5³⁄₁₆ x 8¼.　　　　　　0-486-26478-5

THE INFERNO, Dante Alighieri. Translated and with notes by Henry Wadsworth Longfellow. The first stop on Dante's famous journey from Hell to Purgatory to Paradise, this 14th-century allegorical poem blends vivid and shocking imagery with graceful lyricism. Translated by the beloved 19th-century poet, Henry Wadsworth Longfellow. 256pp. 5³⁄₁₆ x 8¼.　　　　　　0-486-44288-8

JANE EYRE, Charlotte Brontë. Written in 1847, *Jane Eyre* tells the tale of an orphan girl's progress from the custody of cruel relatives to an oppressive boarding school and its culmination in a troubled career as a governess. 448pp. 5³⁄₁₆ x 8¼.
　　　　　　0-486-42449-9

JAPANESE WOODBLOCK FLOWER PRINTS, Tanigami Kônan. Extraordinary collection of Japanese woodblock prints by a well-known artist features 120 plates in brilliant color. Realistic images from a rare edition include daffodils, tulips, and other familiar and unusual flowers. 128pp. 11 x 8¼.　　　　　　0-486-46442-3

JEWELRY MAKING AND DESIGN, Augustus F. Rose and Antonio Cirino. Professional secrets of jewelry making are revealed in a thorough, practical guide. Over 200 illustrations. 306pp. 5⅜ x 8½.　　　　　　0-486-21750-7

JULIUS CAESAR, William Shakespeare. Great tragedy based on Plutarch's account of the lives of Brutus, Julius Caesar and Mark Antony. Evil plotting, ringing oratory, high tragedy with Shakespeare's incomparable insight, dramatic power. Explanatory footnotes. 96pp. 5³⁄₁₆ x 8¼.　　　　　　0-486-26876-4

Browse over 9,000 books at www.doverpublications.com

THE JUNGLE, Upton Sinclair. 1906 bestseller shockingly reveals intolerable labor practices and working conditions in the Chicago stockyards as it tells the grim story of a Slavic family that emigrates to America full of optimism but soon faces despair. 320pp. 5³⁄₁₆ x 8¼. 0-486-41923-1

THE KINGDOM OF GOD IS WITHIN YOU, Leo Tolstoy. The soul-searching book that inspired Gandhi to embrace the concept of passive resistance, Tolstoy's 1894 polemic clearly outlines a radical, well-reasoned revision of traditional Christian thinking. 352pp. 5³⁄₁₆ x 8¼. 0-486-45138-0

THE LADY OR THE TIGER?: and Other Logic Puzzles, Raymond M. Smullyan. Created by a renowned puzzle master, these whimsically themed challenges involve paradoxes about probability, time, and change; metapuzzles; and self-referentiality. Nineteen chapters advance in difficulty from relatively simple to highly complex. 1982 edition. 240pp. 5⅜ x 8½. 0-486-47027-X

LEAVES OF GRASS: The Original 1855 Edition, Walt Whitman. Whitman's immortal collection includes some of the greatest poems of modern times, including his masterpiece, "Song of Myself." Shattering standard conventions, it stands as an unabashed celebration of body and nature. 128pp. 5³⁄₁₆ x 8¼. 0-486-45676-5

LES MISÉRABLES, Victor Hugo. Translated by Charles E. Wilbour. Abridged by James K. Robinson. A convict's heroic struggle for justice and redemption plays out against a fiery backdrop of the Napoleonic wars. This edition features the excellent original translation and a sensitive abridgment. 304pp. 6⅛ x 9¼.
0-486-45789-3

LILITH: A Romance, George MacDonald. In this novel by the father of fantasy literature, a man travels through time to meet Adam and Eve and to explore humanity's fall from grace and ultimate redemption. 240pp. 5⅜ x 8½.
0-486-46818-6

THE LOST LANGUAGE OF SYMBOLISM, Harold Bayley. This remarkable book reveals the hidden meaning behind familiar images and words, from the origins of Santa Claus to the fleur-de-lys, drawing from mythology, folklore, religious texts, and fairy tales. 1,418 illustrations. 784pp. 5⅜ x 8½. 0-486-44787-1

MACBETH, William Shakespeare. A Scottish nobleman murders the king in order to succeed to the throne. Tortured by his conscience and fearful of discovery, he becomes tangled in a web of treachery and deceit that ultimately spells his doom. 96pp. 5³⁄₁₆ x 8¼. 0-486-27802-6

MAKING AUTHENTIC CRAFTSMAN FURNITURE: Instructions and Plans for 62 Projects, Gustav Stickley. Make authentic reproductions of handsome, functional, durable furniture: tables, chairs, wall cabinets, desks, a hall tree, and more. Construction plans with drawings, schematics, dimensions, and lumber specs reprinted from 1900s *The Craftsman* magazine. 128pp. 8⅛ x 11. 0-486-25000-8

MATHEMATICS FOR THE NONMATHEMATICIAN, Morris Kline. Erudite and entertaining overview follows development of mathematics from ancient Greeks to present. Topics include logic and mathematics, the fundamental concept, differential calculus, probability theory, much more. Exercises and problems. 641pp. 5⅜ x 8½. 0-486-24823-2

MEMOIRS OF AN ARABIAN PRINCESS FROM ZANZIBAR, Emily Ruete. This 19th-century autobiography offers a rare inside look at the society surrounding a sultan's palace. A real-life princess in exile recalls her vanished world of harems, slave trading, and court intrigues. 288pp. 5⅜ x 8½. 0-486-47121-7

Browse over 9,000 books at www.doverpublications.com